Accessing Biodiversity and Sharing the Benefits: Lessons from Implementing the Convention on Biological Diversity

D1716781

With the support of:

Federal Ministry
for Economic Cooperation
and Development

Genetic Resources
Conservation Program
University of California
USA

Accessing Biodiversity and Sharing the Benefits: Lessons from Implementing the Convention on Biological Diversity

Edited by

Santiago Carrizosa, Stephen B. Brush, Brian D. Wright, and Patrick E. McGuire

IUCN Environmental Policy and Law Paper No. 54

IUCN Environmental Law Programme

IUCN – The World Conservation Union
2004

Published by: IUCN, Gland, Switzerland and Cambridge, UK, in collaboration with BMZ, Germany and GRCP, University of California, Davis CA USA

K
3488
A9
2004

Citation: Carrizosa, Santiago, Stephen B. Brush, Brian D. Wright, and Patrick E. McGuire (eds.) 2004. *Accessing Biodiversity and Sharing the Benefits: Lessons from Implementation of the Convention on Biological Diversity*. IUCN, Gland, Switzerland and Cambridge, UK. xiv+316 pp.

ISBN: 2-8317-0816-8

Cover design by: IUCN Environmental Law Centre

Cover photo: Strawberry anemone (*Corynactis californica*) in Pacific coastal waters at Monterey Bay, California/*Photo by* Santiago Carrizosa

Layout by: Patrick E. McGuire, GRCP

Produced by: IUCN Environmental Law Centre

Printed by: medienHaus Plump GmbH, 53619 Rheinbreitbach, Germany

Available from: IUCN Publications Services Unit
219c Huntingdon Road, Cambridge CB3 0DL, United Kingdom
Tel: +44 1223 277894
Fax: +44 1223 277175
E-mail: books@iucn.org
www.iucn.org/bookstore

A catalogue of IUCN publications is also available.

The text of this book is printed on paper made from low chlorine pulp.

Table of Contents

Foreword

Modern developments in biotechnology and the continuing expansion of global trade have allowed society to gain greater access to, and to derive benefits from, the world's biological and genetic diversity. Eleven years ago the Convention on Biological Diversity (CBD) entered into force, with a goal of ensuring that in the process of obtaining and sharing such benefits, society would promote the conservation and sustainable use of the world's biological diversity. Since then countries have been attempting to incorporate the CBD objectives into national legislation, with varying success from country to country. Several Pacific Rim nations were pioneers in the development of access and benefit-sharing (ABS) laws and policies and faced a wide variety of technical and legal difficulties in designing and implementing novel access rules and regulations.

As countries struggle with creating ABS regimes and implementing them, they find a dearth of information about the process and the experience of others. The purpose of this book is to start to address this vacuum, by providing a comparative analysis of national ABS legislation and policies in the 41 Pacific Rim countries that signed the CBD. The ABS Project of the Environmental Law Center at the World Conservation Union (IUCN-ELC) and the University of California Genetic Resources Conservation Program (UC GRCP) are pleased to present the results of a three-year process of cooperation, consultation, and analysis that involved more than 60 ABS experts from all the Pacific Rim countries that signed the CBD. This is the broadest survey of the status of national ABS policy and legislation conducted to date. Clearly the aim of this fruitful partnership and process is not to present a consensus document. It is, however, an important publication with valuable insights that will contribute not only to the development and refinement of national ABS policies, but also to the consideration of any future international regime on ABS.

This publication would not have been possible without the generous support of the University of California Pacific Rim Research Program, the ABS Project (IUCN-ELC), the German Ministry for Economic Cooperation and Development (BMZ), and UC GRCP. It is being published by IUCN due to the recognition by Tomme Young (Senior Legal Officer with IUCN-ELC, ABS Project) of the value of having this knowledge reach as broad an international audience as possible. The initiative and the product itself can be attributed to Santiago Carrizosa (UC GRCP) who conceived it, obtained funding for it, identified and solicited quality responses and text from the more than 60 participating experts, and then carried out a masterful comparative analysis of the results.

We are grateful to all of the experts who contributed to the publication, which reflects their own professional views and not necessarily those of the supporting organizations.

Patrick McGuire, Director, UC GRCP
John Scanlon, Director, IUCN-ELC

Acknowledgements

This volume is a testimony to the dynamic and changing nature of ABS laws and policies in the 41 Pacific Rim countries that signed the Convention on Biological Diversity. The multiple findings, insights, and perspectives presented in this report are a snapshot in time that was initiated in late 2001 and culminated in mid-2004. This process of collaboration and consultation would not have been possible without the support of two grants from the University of California Pacific Rim Research Program and financial support from the Environmental Law Center (ELC) of the World Conservation Union (IUCN). We owe a particular debt of gratitude to Tomme Young (ABS Project and IUCN-ELC) and Florence Mou (University of California Pacific Rim Research Program) whose support to our research made possible the publication of our findings. The compilation and understanding of the intricacies of ABS laws and policies was possible thanks to the insights and expertise of over 60 academics, scientists, and policy makers from the Pacific Rim region who are listed in Appendices 2 and 3 of this publication. A special thanks goes to Jorge Cabrera, Carolina Lasén, and Manuel Ruiz who read draft chapters patiently and thoroughly and provided helpful and insightful comments that improved their quality.

During 2002 and 2003 preliminary results of our research were discussed at five international workshops and seminars that addressed ABS issues and we benefited from the comments of many participants. Three of these events were held in the United States of America, one in Chile and the other one in Indonesia. Inevitably, we are unable to acknowledge the names of all the persons that provided input at these events and for this we are regretful. Some of the participants that provided useful comments are Paz J. Benavidez, Susan Bragdon, Will Burns, Geoff Burton, Jorge Cabrera-Medaglia, Fernando Casas, Kimberlee Chambers, Leif Christoffersen, Matthew Cohen, Adi Damania, Morgane Danielou, Jade Donavanik, David Duthie, O'Kean Ehmes, José Carlos Fernández-Ugalde, Luis Flores, Marco Gonzales, Anne Haira, Jil Harkin, Dominique Hervé, Leonard P. Hirsch, Timothy J. Hodges, Vainuupo Jungblut, Stephen King, Laura Lewis, Mohamed bin Osman, María Isabel Manzur, Tetiro Mate, James Miller, Vera Monshetseva, Karina Nabors, Doug Neumann, Valerie Normand, Coral Pasisi, Amanda Penn, Jeanine Pfeiffer, Sally Petherbridge, Anne Perrault, Silvia Rodríguez, Joshua Rosenthal, Manuel Ruiz, Preston Scott, Breana Smith, Sourioudong Sundara, Brendan Tobin, Eric Van Dusen, Joe Vogel, B. Satyawan Wardhana, Dayuan Xue, and Tomme Young.

Our efforts to understand the complexities of access and benefit-sharing policies were greatly aided by many colleagues and friends who contributed ideas, experience, and encouragement to this project. In particular we are grateful to Kelly Banister, Doug Calhoun, Tagaloa Cooper, Kate Davis, Holly Doremus, Maria Elisa Febres, Elisabeth Gaibor, Lyle Glowka, Douveri Henao, Chaweewan Hutacharern, Javier Guillermo Hernandez, Sarah Laird, Jorge Larson-Guerra, Antonio LaViña, Christian Lopéz-Silva, Clark Peteru, Calvin Qualset, Mary Riley, Kerry ten Kate, Claudia Sobrevila, and Cedric Schuster.

Santiago Carrizosa
Stephen B. Brush
Brian D. Wright
Patrick E. McGuire

List of Abbreviations and Acronyms

ABS .... Access and benefit sharing

AG .... Attorney-General's Chambers (Malaysia)

AHWG .... Ad Hoc Open-Ended Working Group

AIMS................ Australian Institute of Marine Science

ANAM .... National Authority for the Environment (Panama)

ANZECC.......... Australian and New Zealand Environment and Conservation Council

APPTMI .... Act on Protection and Promotion of Traditional Medicinal Intelligence (Thailand)

ARA .... Academic Research Agreement (Philippines)

ASEAN .... Association of Southeast Asian Nations

ASOEN .... Senior Officials on Environment (Philippines)

ASOMPS .... Asian Symposium on Medicinal Plants, Species and Other Natural Products (Philippines)

ATCC .... American Type Culture Collection (USA)

BFAR .... Bureau of Fisheries and Aquatic Resources (Philippines)

BTG................. British Technology Group (Costa Rica)

CABSSBR .... Conditions for Access to and Benefit Sharing of Samoa's Biodiversity Resources

CALM .... Department of Conservation and Land Management (Australia)

CBD................. Convention on Biological Diversity

CITES .... Convention on International Trade in Endangered Species of Wild Fauna and Flora

COABIO .... Advisory Commission on Biodiversity (Costa Rica)

COMPITCH..... Council of Indigenous and Traditional Medicine Men and Parteros (Mexico)

CONABIO .... National Commission for the Knowledge and Use of Biodiversity (Mexico)

CONAGEBIO National Commission for the Management of Biodiversity (Costa Rica)

CONADI .... National Corporation on Indigenous Development (Chile)

CONAF .... National Forestry Corporation (Chile)

CONAMA .... National Commission of the Environment (Chile)

CONICYT........ National Commission on Scientific and Technological Research (Chile)

COP .... Conference of the Parties

CRA .... Commercial Research Agreement (Philippines)

CRADA........... Cooperative Research and Development Agreement (USA)

CSIRO............. Commonwealth Scientific and Industrial Research Organization (Australia)

CSWG............. Commonwealth-State Working Group (Australia)

DA .... Department of Agriculture (Philippines)

DAFF .... Department of Agriculture, Fisheries and Forestry (Australia)

DAO .... DENR Administrative Order (Philippines)

DENR.............. Department of Environment and Natural Resources (Philippines)

DLSE............... Department of Lands, Surveys and Environment (Samoa)

DNP................. Departamento Nacional de Planeacion (Colombia)

DNWP............. Department of National Parks, Wildlife, and Plant Conservation (Thailand)

DOA .... Department of Agriculture (Malaysia)

DOF................. Department of Fisheries (Malaysia)

DOST .... Department of Science and Technology (Philippines)

ECOSUR.......... El Colegio de la Frontera Sur (Mexico)

EEEPGA .... Ecological Equilibrium and Environmental Protection General Act (Mexico)

EIA................... Environmental Impact Assessment

EO 247............. Executive Order 247 (The Philippines)

EPA .... Queensland Environment Protection Agency (Australia)

EPBCA............ Environment Protection and Biodiversity Conservation Act (Australia)

EPBCAR .... Environment Protection and Biodiversity Conservation Amendment Regulations (Australia)

EPU .... Economic Planning Unit (Malaysia)

ETC................. Action Group on Erosion, Technology and Concentration

FAO................. United Nations Food and Agriculture Organization

FCCC .... United Nations Framework Convention on Climate Change

FECON .... Federation for the Conservation of the Environment (Costa Rica)

FIELD .... Foundation for International Environmental Law and Development

FPIC ....Free prior informed consent (Philippines)

FRIM ....Forest Research Institute Malaysia

FTTA.................Federal Technology Transfer Act (USA)

GAP.................General Access Procedure (Costa Rica)

GATT................General Agreement on Tariffs and Trade

GEF...................Global Environment Facility

GLE.................General Law of the Environment No 41 (Panama)

GLENR .... General Law of the Environment and Natural Resources No. 217 (Nicaragua)

GMAC.............. Genetic Modification Advisory Committee (Malaysia)

GMO .... Genetically modified organism

GR .... Genetic resources

IACBGR........... Inter-Agency Committee on Biological and Genetic Resources (Philippines)

ICBG .... International Cooperative Biodiversity Group

ICC...................Indigenous Cultural Community (Philippines)

IDB ....Inter-American Development Bank

IFA .... Institute of Fishing and Aquaculture (Costa Rica)

IIE .... Queensland Information and Innovation Economy (Australia)

INBio............... National Biodiversity Institute (Costa Rica)

INDECOPI....... National Institute for the Defense and Protection of Traditional Knowledge (Peru)

INIA .... National Institute for Agriculture Research (Chile)

IP ....Indigenous peoples

IPA ....Intellectual Property Australia

IPA ....Industrial Property Act (Mexico)

IPAF ....Integrated Protected Areas Fund (Philippines)

IPC ....Intellectual Property Code of the Philippines

IPRs..................Intellectual property rights

IPRA ....Indigenous Peoples' Rights Act (Philippines)

IRRDB ....International Rubber Research and Development Board (Malaysia)

ISIS ....Institute of Strategic and International Studies (Malaysia)

ITPGRFA ....International Treaty on Plant Genetic Resources for Food and Agriculture (FAO)

IUCN ....The World Conservation Union

JICA ....Japan International Cooperation Agency

LAUBGR..........Law for Access and Use of Biological and Genetic Resources (Mexico)

LB ....Law of Biodiversity (Costa Rica)

LC ....Letter of Collection

LI.....................Letter of Intent

LWC.................Law of Wildlife Conservation (Costa Rica)

MARDI ....Malaysian Agricultural Research and Development Institute

MARENA ....Ministry for the Environment and Natural Resources (Nicaragua)

MINAE.............Ministry of the Environment and Energy (Costa Rica)

MIRENEM.......Ministry of Natural Resources, Energy, and Mines (Costa Rica)

MNS.................Malaysian Nature Society

MOA ....Memorandum of Agreement (Philippines)

MOE.................Ministry of Environment (Colombia)

MOSTE............Ministry of Science, Technology, and the Environment (Malaysia)

MOU ....Memorandum of Understanding

MTA ....Material Transfer Agreement

NASYCA ....National System of Conservation Areas (Costa Rica)

NBAP ....National Biodiversity Action Plan

NBP..................National Biodiversity Policy (Colombia)

NBS..................National Biodiversity Strategy

NBSAP.............National Biodiversity Strategy and Action Plan

NCA ....National Competent Authority (Colombia)

NCBD ....National Committee on Biological Diversity (Malaysia)

NCI ....National Cancer Institute (USA)

NEPA ....National Environmental Policy Act (USA)

NGO ....Nongovernmental organization

NIH ....National Institutes of Health (USA)

NIPAS ....National Integrated Protected Areas System (Philippines)

NPS ....National Park Service (USA)

NRCT...............National Research Council (Thailand)

NUMHP ....Nigerian Union of Medical Herbal Practitioners

ODEPA.............Agricultural Studies and Policies Office (Chile)

OMIECH..........Organization of Indigenous Healers of the State of Chiapas (Mexico)

PACSD ....Palawan Council for Sustainable Development (Philippines)

PAMB...............Protected Area Management Board (Philippines)

PAWB...............The Protected Areas and Wildlife Bureau (Philippines)

PCSD ....Philippine Council for Sustainable Development

PFE...................Permanent Forest Estate (Malaysia)

PIC ....Prior informed consent

PLM ....Pamantasan ng Lungsod ng Maynila (Philippines)

PROFEPA ....Federal Attorney for the Protection of the Environment (Mexico)

PVPA................Plant Variety Protection Act

QLD ....State of Queensland (Australia)

RFD ....Royal Forest Department (Thailand)

RFSRCFA ....Regulation on Forestry Studying and Research Conducting within Forested Areas (Thailand)

RITM................Research Institute for Tropical Medicine (Philippines)

RPRS ....Research Proposal Reviewing Subcommittee (Thailand)

RSDA ....Rural Sustainable Development Act (Mexico)

SAG..................Agriculture and Livestock Service (Chile)

SEMARNAT ....Secretariat of Environment and Natural Resources (Mexico)

SERNAPESCA Fishing Undersecretariat, the National Fishing Board (Chile)

SEPA ....Environmental Protection Administration (China)

SFDGA ....Sustainable Forestry Development General Act (Mexico)

SPC ....South Pacific Commission

SPDA ....Peruvian Society for Environmental Law

SPREP..............South Pacific Regional Environment Program

TAMA ....Traditional Alternative Medicine Act (Philippines)

TGRC...............C.M. Rick Tomato Genetics Resource Center (USA)

TK .... Traditional knowledge
TO .... Technical office (Costa Rica)
TPVPA .... Thai Plant Variety Protection Act
TRIPS .... Agreement on Trade-Related Aspects of
                      Intellectual Property Rights
TS .... Technical secretariat (Philippines)
UKM .... Universiti Kebangsaan Malaysia
UNAM .... National Autonomous University of Mexico
UNEP .... United Nations Environment Programme
UNU/IAS .... United Nations University/Institute of
                      Advanced Studies
UP .... University of the Philippines
UPM .... Universiti Putra Malaysia
UPOV .... International Union for the Protection of New
                      Varieties of Plants
USA .... United States of America
USPTO .... United States Patent and Trademark Office
UZACHI .... Zapotec and Chinantec Communities Union
                      (Mexico)
VSD .... Veterinary Services Department (Malaysia)
WGA .... Wildlife General Act (Mexico)
WIPO .... World Intellectual Property Organization
WRI .... World Resources Institute (USA)
WSSD .... World Summit on Sustainable Development
WTO .... World Trade Organization
WWF .... World Wildlife Fund
WWF-SPP .... World Wildlife Fund-South Pacific Program

Introduction

Santiago Carrizosa

Today, genetic resources are no longer the common heritage of humankind and they cannot be treated as freely accessible commodities. The 1992 United Nations Convention on Biological Diversity (CBD)[1] and the 2001 FAO International Treaty on Plant Genetic Resources for Food and Agriculture (ITPGRFA) (see Box 1) recognized the sovereign rights of countries to control the use of their genetic resources. These two agreements also stressed that the authority to determine access to genetic resources rests with national governments and is subject to national policies. The objectives of the CBD are the conservation of biological diversity, its sustainable use, and the fair and equitable sharing of benefits derived from the use of genetic resources. Similarly, the objectives of the ITPGRFA are the conservation, sustainable use, and equitable sharing of the benefits derived from plant genetic resources for food and agriculture. This Treaty also stressed that these objectives shall be accomplished by "linking this Treaty to the Food and Agriculture Organization of the United Nations and to the Convention on Biological Diversity" (FAO 2001).

The CBD, sometimes also called the "biotrade convention", encouraged member countries to facilitate access to genetic resources and take measures to ensure the fair and equitable sharing of benefits derived from the use of these resources. The CBD emphasized that access to genetic resources should be on mutually agreed terms and subject to prior informed consent of the resource provider. Since the CBD came into force, bilateral agreements have been the main vehicle to facilitate access under the few national access and benefit-sharing (ABS) policies that were developed to include the objectives and principles of the CBD. On the other hand, under the ITPGRFA, ABS goals will be achieved through a multilateral system of exchange of genetic resources. This access system is limited to plant genetic resources for food and agriculture; access to genetic resources for chemical, pharmaceutical, nonfood, and nonagricultural uses would still be negotiated bilaterally in accordance with national ABS policies and the CBD. Initially, the exchange of germplasm of the food and forage crops listed in the ITPGRFA Annex, and subject to modification, will be regulated by this multilateral system (FAO 2001).

In April 2002, the sixth Conference of the Parties to the CBD adopted the 2001 Bonn Guidelines on Access to Genetic Resources and Fair and Equitable Sharing of the Benefits Arising out of their Utilization (hereafter, Bonn Guidelines on ABS). These guidelines apply to all genetic resources covered by the CBD, with the exception of those covered by the ITPGRFA. The guidelines are voluntary, flexible, and were designed mainly to facilitate the development process of national ABS policies and contracts. The guidelines outline the roles and responsibilities of users and providers or genetic resources and encourage stakeholders to use a bilateral approach to facilitate ABS goals. The guidelines describe key issues that include: a) involvement of relevant stakeholders and capacity building; b) steps in the ABS process; c) elements of a prior-informed-consent system; d) monetary and nonmonetary benefits; e) incentives; f) national monitoring and reporting; and g) accountability. In late 2002, the Plan of Implementation that came out of the Johannesburg World Summit on Sustainable Development (WSSD) recommended a) the promotion of the wide implementation of and continued work on the 2001 Bonn Guidelines on ABS as an input for countries developing ABS policies and b) the negotiation of the development of an international regime to promote the fair and equitable sharing of benefits derived from the use of genetic resources. In March 2003, at the Open-Ended Inter-Sessional Meeting on the Multi-Year Program of Work for the Conference of the Parties to the CBD, delegates decided to broaden the mandate of the plan of implementation and included into the international regime the "access" component in addition to benefit sharing. However, there was disagreement about the legal nature of this regime. Many developing countries called for a legally binding regime, but the United States of America (USA) stressed that in Johannesburg the WSSD deliberately left out the term "legally binding" from the plan of implementation. No agreement was reached at the meeting. In December 2003, this and other issues about the international regime were debated further at the second meeting of the Ad Hoc Open-Ended Working Group (AHWG) on ABS. Delegates failed to reach consensus and the debate continued at the seventh meeting of the Conference of the Parties (COP 7) to the CBD in February 2004. At COP 7, delegates did not resolve major issues such as the binding nature of the international regime on ABS. However, they reached consensus on the terms of reference for the international regime and mandated the AWHG on ABS to develop and negotiate the international regime on ABS based on the terms of reference. Members of the working group will elaborate and negotiate the nature, scope, and elements of the international regime. Before COP 8, the AWHG on ABS will hold two sessions, one in Thailand and one in Spain. The ABS regime will address strategies for the protection of traditional knowledge. Therefore, the AWHG on ABS together with the Ad Hoc Open-Ended Inter-Sessional Working Group on Article 8(j) of the CBD will examine *sui generis* systems, databases, registers, intellectual property

---

Box 1. Overview of the International Treaty on Plant Genetic Resources for Food and Agriculture (ITPGRFA)

Manuel Ruiz

The ITPGRFA is a binding legal agreement adopted by the United Nations Food and Agriculture Organization (FAO) Conference on 3 November 2001. Despite the fact that the USA and Japan abstained from approving the treaty, there were no votes against it. The USA, however, signed the treaty in November 2002. Forty countries (the minimum required for its entry into force) ratified, approved, accepted, or acceded to the ITPGRFA and it entered into force on 29 June 2004.

Background

The ITPGRFA is the result of a long and complex process initiated in 1983 when the *International Undertaking on Plant Genetic Resources*, a nonbinding legal instrument, was approved by FAO Resolution 8/83. The Undertaking reflected the concerns of countries regarding access to and use of plant genetic resources, the role of intellectual property, especially patents and plant breeders' rights as applied to biological materials, the relation between sovereignty and the principle of "common heritage of mankind" and small farmers' contribution to the conservation of plant genetic resources (later reflected in the adoption by the Undertaking of the "Farmers' Rights" concept). Tensions and frictions were evident among biodiversity-rich countries in the South and industrialized and technologically advanced but biodiversity-poor countries in the North.

In 1992, at the United Nations Conference on Environment and Development (UNCED), the Convention on Biological Diversity (CBD) established a set of new binding principles and rules applicable to access to genetic resources in general. Agenda 21 (another outcome of UNCED) specifically called for the FAO to both strengthen the Undertaking and harmonize it with the CBD. In November 1993, FAO's Resolution 7/93 recognized the need to review the Undertaking as applied to plant genetic resources for food and agriculture in particular and develop a binding treaty in conformity with the CBD rules. In 1993 the process of revising the Undertaking was begun within the FAO and the Commission on Genetic Resources for Food and Agriculture adopted a revised Undertaking in July 2001 (http://www.fao.org/ag/cgrfa/IU.htm). This then became the ITPGRFA when adopted by consensus at the FAO headquarters in Rome in November 2001.

Objective and scope

The ITPGRFA objectives are "the conservation and sustainable use of plant genetic resources for food and agriculture and the fair and equitable sharing of the benefits arising out of their use, in harmony with the Convention on Biological Diversity, for sustainable development and food security" (Article 1.1). Although its initial general provisions (on conservation and sustainable use in general) apply to all plant genetic resources for food and agriculture, it is its access and benefit sharing (ABS) norms which are of particular relevance and interest in the context of the current international debate.

The ITPGRFA entered into force in a context where multiple, sometimes overlapping and even conflicting policies and legislation on ABS are in place. It seems that existing ABS laws and policies such as the 1996 Decision 391 of the Andean Community on a Common Regime on Access to Genetic Resources and the 1998 Law of Biodiversity of Costa Rica may have to be adjusted and amended in order to prevent conflicts with overall ITPGRFA obligations and mandates.

Exchanging genetic resources and sharing the benefits

The ITPGRFA access provisions will operate through a Multilateral System of Access and Benefit Sharing. Under this System, standardized Material Transfer Agreements (MTAS), approved by the Treaty's Governing Body, will determine conditions and requirements to facilitate access to an initial number of 65 food and forage crops. The System is based on the fact that, in terms of plant genetic resources for food and agriculture in particular, interdependence among countries and regions prevails and no country is self sufficient individually to provide its agriculture system with plant genetic resources for breeding, conservation, and food security purposes.

Benefits from facilitated access under the ITPGRFA will

rights (IPRS), and other measures that can contribute to the implementation of Article 8(j).

While these working groups, member countries, and signatories of the CBD and ITPGRFA debate how to incorporate into national policies this relatively new and complex array of ABS concepts, some genetic resources are becoming more valuable as the agriculture, pharmaceutical, and biotechnology industries continue to provide improved means to assay and use them. The economic value of the information contained in the genes and biochemical compounds of genetic resources has increased with the development of novel technologies such as high-throughput analysis, combinatorial chemistry, bioinformatics, and genomics. In 1997, 11 of the top 25 best-selling pharmaceutical products were either biologicals, natural products or entities derived from natural products, or synthetic versions based on a natural template. Worldwide sales of these 11 products reached about $17,500 million USD (TEN KATE and LAIRD 1999). Most of the sales were made by multinationals such as Pfizer (USA), GlaxoSmithKline (UK), Merck and Co. (USA), Novartis (Switzerland), and Bristol Myers Squibb (USA). In 2002 and 2003, however, some pharmaceutical companies such as Merck have reduced or closed some of their natural products discovery programs (J. ROSENTHAL, pers. comm. February 2004, J. Cabrera, pers. comm. February 2004).

These multinationals have an important market share in developing countries such as Chile and the Philippines. However, countries such as China, Egypt, and India favor mainly their domestic pharmaceutical industries that manufacture almost exclusively generic drugs (TEN KATE and LAIRD 1999). Counterfeiting of pharmaceutical and

---

Box 1. Continued

be shared fairly and equitably among parties through: a) exchange of information; b) access to and transfer of technology; c) capacity building; and d) sharing of monetary or commercial benefits from the use of resources. Under current national ABS laws and policies, monetary benefits are negotiated bilaterally and they include royalty rates, up-front payments, and milestone payments. In the case of the ITPGRFA, the sharing of monetary benefits is an issue which still needs to be addressed and decided by the Governing Body. Being part of the System is already an important benefit for countries (Article 13).

Ex situ *conservation centers*

Ex situ conservation centers (especially the International Agriculture Research Centers), hold an important portion of the world's collections of plant genetic resources for food and agriculture. These are held "in trust" for the benefit of humankind and were obtained mostly prior to the CBD entering into force. These centers will sign agreements with the ITPGRFA Governing Body (to replace current agreements with FAO) which will determine the new policies and rules regarding access to and use of these materials. A specific MTA is under negotiation for this purpose.

Intellectual property (IP)

The ITPGRFA recognizes that "access and transfer [of plant genetic resources] shall be provided on terms which recognize and are consistent with the adequate and effective protection of intellectual property rights" (Article 13.2.b.iii). Clearly there is an express recognition of the need to respect IP. On the other hand, IP (whether patents or plant breeders' rights) shall not be applied to plant genetic resources in the form received from the Multilateral System (Article 12.2.d). It has not been decided whether this restriction of IP also applies to components or derivatives of these resources. If patents were allowed over isolated components and depending on how countries were to apply and interpret national and international IP rules, there could be certain restrictions regarding access to and use of plant genetic resources for food and agriculture containing these components or derivatives even if they are part of the Multilateral System.

Farmers' Rights

As part of the Undertaking, Farmers' Rights were to be implemented through an international fund to compensate small farmers for their conservation and development of plant genetic resources efforts. Under the ITPGRFA, Farmers' Rights will be implemented at the national level through individual government action (Article 9). This may be undertaken either through development of laws for the protection of traditional knowledge, the participation of indigenous peoples in the benefits derived from the use of plant genetic resources for food and agriculture, or through participation of indigenous peoples in decision-making processes pertaining to these.

In the last few years many countries may have actually been implementing their ITPGRFA obligation in regards to Farmers' Rights. The CBD, the WIPO Intergovernmental Committee on Genetic Resources and Intellectual Property, Traditional Knowledge and Folklore, and other initiatives have triggered a series of national and regional policy and legal processes oriented at the protection of traditional knowledge in general. In the case of Peru for example, the 2002 Law 27811 for the protection of indigenous peoples' traditional knowledge related to biodiversity will certainly be giving substantive content to the Farmers' Rights provisions of the ITPGRFA. Similarly, general provisions on the protection of traditional knowledge in ABS laws in Costa Rica, Philippines, and a few others, could also be indirectly addressing Farmers' Rights (see Chapter 1).

Final Word

Many countries are still analyzing the implications of the Treaty on their national access regulations and intellectual property rights. One simple but sometimes politically difficult way to overcome potential problems is for countries expressly to recognize (as they develop their ABS policies and laws) that the ITPGRFA Multilateral System as it applies to the list of crops is an exceptional regime, with its own set of rules and principles, which should not be affected by other laws and regulations.

many other products is a common practice in these and many other developing (and developed) countries that translates into significant economic losses for multinationals. Therefore, these multinationals have lobbied to prevent these activities and strengthen intellectual property protection for their products all over the world in order to recover their significant investments (SIEBECK et al. 1990, RYAN 1998). These multinationals were particularly effective during the 1986–1994 Uruguay Round of multilateral trade negotiations when the Agreement on Trade Related Aspects of Intellectual Property Rights (TRIPS)[2] was adopted. Unlike the Convention of the International Union for the Protection of New Varieties of Plants (UPOV) or any other intellectual property rights treaty[3], TRIPS establishes legal enforcement of minimum standards for all IPRs. According to TRIPS, member countries have to provide patent protection for microorganisms (as products) and for nonbiological and microbiological processes used for the production of plants and animals. Plants and animals themselves may be excluded from patentability. However, plant varieties must be protected by plant breeders' rights or another *sui generis* system. TRIPS has a timetable for compliance. For example, the least developed countries have until 2016 to provide patent protection for pharmaceuticals (WTO News 2002). Failure to comply with this timetable might bring trade sanctions (DUTFIELD 2000).

In November 2001, trade ministers from all over the world adopted the Doha Ministerial Declaration in order to facilitate the implementation of current agreements of the World Trade Organization (WTO), among other issues. The Declaration encourages the TRIPS Council to review the relationship between TRIPS and the CBD and the protection of traditional knowledge and folklore.[4] The outcome of this review is still unclear. However, several analysts suggest that the impact of TRIPS on the CBD is strong, and they have challenged the patent scenario promoted by TRIPS (SHIVA 1995). Indigenous communities and other sectors of society reject the idea of patenting life, and this position has had direct and indirect consequences that include the cancellation of bioprospecting[5] projects (SHIVA 1995, see Chapter 6). Others argue that patents should not be used to protect genes that have just been isolated *in vitro* because according to traditional patent law this is a discovery and not an invention[6] (CORREA 1999, DUTFIELD 2000, see Chapter 6). On the other hand, many argue that when patents are linked to bioprospecting agreements, they can support local capacity building and conservation (REID et al. 1993, TEN KATE and LAIRD 1999).

Bioprospecting projects are long-term efforts whose fruits could materialize perhaps 10 or 15 years into the future provided that products are developed and marketed. In the short run, however, these projects can provide and have provided research, training, and educational op-

portunities to biodiversity stakeholders from developing countries. They have also transferred technology required to carry out specific tests and have provided incentives for the development of *in situ* and *ex situ* conservation activities (ROSENTHAL et al. 1999, see Chapters 5, 7, and 11). However, it is unrealistic to pretend that current and future bioprospecting projects can be a significant source of funding for the conservation of biological diversity or a guaranteed means of generating, particularly in the short term, major levels of revenue (SIMPSON et al. 1994). Costa Rica, the only country in the world that has over a decade of documented experience implementing bioprospecting projects, has accumulated valuable data about the impact of these projects on conservation. Between 1991 and 2000, these projects channeled about $2.7 million USD to conservation purposes. This is equivalent to an average of $300,000 USD per year, an amount which is quite insignificant compared to the $650 million USD per year that Costa Rica gets from ecological tourism (see Chapter 5). Research and development for the production of pharmaceuticals and other biotechnology products derived from biodiversity can be a risky, costly, and time-consuming activity (DIMASI et al. 1991, REID et al. 1993).

Bioprospecting projects have been the target of heavy criticism in the last few years. Claims of biopiracy, unfair distribution of benefits, illegal appropriation of traditional knowledge, and the problem of the patenting of life have contributed to revive the old south-north debate that focuses on access to genetic resources on the one hand and the economic returns of using them on the other (SHIVA 1995, 1997, see Chapter 6). The essence of the debate is that industrialized countries are the primary users and economic beneficiaries of genetic resources and traditional knowledge that are "produced" in developing countries. The apparent solution to this disparity is to provide some legal and social mechanism for balancing inequities between the north and south in access to genetic resources and financial benefits from using them. This mechanism has to be the result of a participatory process that involves all sectors of society. Otherwise, as history has shown, ABS initiatives are likely to fail (see Chapter 6). This is the challenge faced by the policy makers and bioprospectors who are designing ABS policies (see Chapters 1, 2, and 3). These policies should promote the conservation, sustainable use, and equitable distribution of the benefits derived from terrestrial and marine biodiversity. But they also need to facilitate the access and exchange of genetic resources found in megadiversity countries that form the basis for the improvement of agricultural crops, for the development of key medicines and pharmaceutical products, and for crop-protection products that are fundamental to the survival of the world's population.

Regional Significance and ABS Frameworks

The Pacific Rim countries include 11 of the 17 so-called megadiversity countries or the biologically wealthiest nations of the world (MITTERMEIER et al. 1999). These 11 countries[7] cover only 7% of the world's continental surface but harbor about 48% of the world's biodiversity. Many of these nations are within centers of origin and diversity of crops such as maize (Mexico), potato (Peru and Bolivia), rice (Philippines), and soybean (China). The agricultural productivity of countries such as Australia and the USA is heavily dependent on a supply of genetic resources from the Pacific Rim region (FAO 1998).

Furthermore, Pacific Rim countries are also valuable sources of genes and biochemicals that are currently used by the pharmaceutical and biotechnology industries in healthcare and agriculture. In the USA, 79% of the top 150 prescription drugs used in 1993 were nature-inspired compounds, semisynthetics and their analogs, and natural products or chemicals found in nature. Only 21% were completely human-made drugs. Almost 74% of these drugs come from plants, 18% from fungi, 5% from bacteria, and 3% from snake venom (FANNING 1995). Most of the contributions of nature to the pharmaceutical industry come from plants, but only 0.1 to 0.5% of the 250,000 known species of flowering plants have been intensively examined for possible medicinal value (GRINDLEY 1993). The biotechnology industry has also used living organisms to clean up polluted sites, to provide energy, and to separate valuable minerals from ore, among other uses (TEN KATE and LAIRD 1999).

Two years after the CBD came into force, a handful of biodiversity-rich Pacific Rim countries pioneered the first comprehensive ABS frameworks in the world. In the Asian region of the Pacific Rim, the Philippines, a megadiversity country, developed in 1995 the first ABS regime (Chapter 7). Similarly, in mid-1996, the Andean Community of Nations[8] adopted Decision 391 (Chapter 4), the first instance in which a group of biodiversity-rich countries realized that they had to act as a unit to enact legislation to protect common traditional knowledge and ecological regions, in this case the Pacific Rim, the Andes, and the Amazon region. Two years later, on 23 April 1998, the Costa Rican government adopted the "Biodiversity Law" which established ABS rules and procedures for bioprospectors with commercial and academic purposes (Chapter 5).

Problem Statement

Since the CBD came into force in 1993, designing legal frameworks to regulate access to genetic resources has been a central task in the realm of international environmental policy. Political scientists, sociologists, economists, molecular biologists, ecologists, and scientists from many other disciplines have contributed to the debate on the CBD, IPRS, bioprospecting initiatives, and contractual arrangements, and this information has contributed to the development of the first ABS frameworks. For example, REID et al. (1993) and the CRUCIBLE GROUP (1994) presented valuable insights on the relationships among the CBD, the International Undertaking of the FAO, IPRS, benefit-sharing strategies, and bioprospecting initiatives for pharmaceutical and agricultural purposes. The debate on the impact of IPRS on biodiversity conservation and traditional knowledge promoted by VOGEL (1994), GREAVES (1994), SWANSON (1995), and BRUSH and STABINSKY (1996) also influenced the development of recommendations for ABS frameworks (MUGABE et al. 1997, TEN KATE and LAIRD 1999) that still need to be tested. Others such as GLOWKA (1998) and LAIRD (2002) have attempted to provide a menu for the development of ABS frameworks. In 2002, COP 6 of the CBD adopted the 2001 Bonn Guidelines on ABS designed to help countries develop their access regulations.

However, over eight years have passed since the first access framework was adopted by the Philippines, and there are still many questions regarding the impact of this and other policies regarding the exchange of genetic resources[9] and on the implementation of these policies at a national level. Some of these issues have been addressed. For example, in 1999, a workshop at Columbia University resulted in an interesting report that reviewed seven examples of bioprospecting agreements implemented in seven countries. Issues analyzed by the report included: a) stakeholders; b) property rights; c) prior informed consent; d) benefit sharing; e) compliance; and f) biodiversity conservation and sustainable use (EPSW 1999). Similarly, BASS and RUIZ (2000) analyzed access policies within the context of conservation and sustainable use in seven countries. GLOWKA et al. (2001) published case studies of ABS policy progress in 12 Southeast Asian countries and NNADOZIE et al. (2003) published a handbook that addresses laws, policies, and institutions that govern ABS issues in 10 African countries. But no comprehensive study has been conducted about the difficulties and successes that these and other nations experienced while developing their ABS frameworks. Moreover, no comparative analyses have been conducted on the experience this far of nations that have engaged in the development and implementation of ABS policies.

The Pacific Rim countries that pioneered the development of ABS frameworks have faced a wide variety of technical, political, social, and legal difficulties in designing and implementing novel ABS policies at a national level. The Andean Pact countries, the Philippines, and Costa Rica, for example, have had problems ensuring that these policies embody the principles of the CBD and at the same time take into account the beliefs and opinions of key sectors of society about how genetic resources and traditional knowledge should be used and administered. Today, most of the economic value of genetic resources comes from the information that they provide to the biotechnology industry, and regulating access to this information creates challenges that many countries have never faced before. These nations have also had conceptual, financial, and administrative difficulties in implementing their ABS policies at a national level (PONCE DE LEÓN 1998, CASAS 1999, CARRIZOSA 2000). Moreover, in countries such as Colombia, Ecuador, and Peru a lack of clarity about the implementation of key ABS laws has specifically prevented scientists from collecting plants and animals for noncommercial research purposes (GRAJAL 1999, REVKIN 2002).

There is also a lack of information about the role of access policies on IPR issues, benefit-sharing strategies, and bioprospecting initiatives for pharmaceutical, agricultural, and industrial purposes. The experience of these pioneer countries will certainly facilitate the development of balanced and sound ABS policies. These policies might in turn facilitate the exchange of genetic resources and benefits for many Pacific Rim countries whose unrestricted or mismanaged access to genetic resources has already led to unsound practices that have depleted a significant concentration of species and ecosystems crucial for the survival of many local cultures and industries. We have undertaken this study to determine and address the problems of development and implementation of ABS frameworks, the unexpected consequences of ABS frameworks on bioprospecting projects, and the lack of access to information among countries about ABS issues.

Study Design and Organization of this Report

Many Pacific Rim countries share ecological similarities in large terrestrial and marine regions, and they also share the need to regulate access to their rich genetic resources. There is already much experience in the region that can be shared not only among the Pacific Rim countries, but also between these countries and other non-Pacific Rim countries that may also be facing access concerns. Therefore, in early 2002, with financial support from the University of California's Pacific Rim Research Program, an effort was initiated to identify existing access frameworks, benefit-sharing strategies, IPR issues, and bioprospecting initiatives in the Pacific Rim region and develop a comparative analysis. Between 2002 and 2004, over 60 experts from 41 Pacific Rim countries that signed the CBD were identified and contacted. Thirteen of them were asked to develop in-depth reports about the ABS legislation status, IPRS, and bioprospecting projects of five countries that have these type of policies in place and three countries that are currently working on legal ABS frameworks. The forty-nine experts from the other 33 countries were asked to respond to a survey. Specific issues that all of the experts were asked to discuss included: a) the process that led to or will lead to the development of national ABS laws and policies; b) successes and concerns that countries experienced during the design of these regulations; c) successes and concerns experienced during the implementation of these regulations; d) influence of these frameworks and IPR issues on bioprospecting initiatives; and e) novel benefit-sharing strategies that have been implemented locally. This report presents comparative analyses of the above issues (Chapters 1 through 3) and a selection of eight case studies that show in detail the status and experiences of five countries that have ABS frameworks and three countries that are struggling to develop such frameworks (Chapters 4 through 11).

In October 2003, a preliminary overview of the results of the study was presented at a workshop at the University of California, Davis.[10] Forty-five experts on ABS issues from seventeen Pacific Rim countries, multilateral organizations involved in CBD implementation, nongovernmental organizations (NGOs) with CBD expertise, collections-based organizations, industry, and academia participated. The workshop provided an opportunity to identify the main elements and gaps of the existing international system of ABS governance, the main elements of what a future international regime on ABS should have, and measures that might be taken by the international community to enhance effective international governance. A summary of the workshop conclusions is presented in Appendix 1.

One of the participants was Tomme Young, Legal Officer at the Environmental Law Center of the World Conservation Union in Bonn, Germany. At the workshop she presented an analysis of elements for the future international regime and she contributed an amplification of that address here as Chapter 12. The chapter presents an overview of the existing system of international ABS governance, discusses the opportunities and challenges facing the international community in negotiation of an international regime, and suggests a potential blueprint, in the form of proposed areas of action to clarify ABS concepts and assumptions, upon which the international community may wish to focus in the development of an effective international system of ABS governance.

Finally, Chapter 13 summarizes the main lessons learned from the study and their implications for the development of ABS frameworks. Appendix 2 provides background information on authors and Appendix 3 provides contact information for authors and survey respondents.

References

BARTON J. 1993. Introduction: Intellectual property rights workshop. p. 13–19 *in* P.S. BAENZIGER, R.A. KLEESE, and R.F. BARNES (eds.) *Intellectual property rights: Protection of plant materials.* CSSA Special Publication No. 21, Crop Science Society of America, American Society of Agronomy. Soil Science Society of America, Madison, WI, USA.

BASS S. and M. RUIZ. 2000. *Protecting biodiversity: National laws regulating access to genetic resources in the Americas.* International Development Research Center, Ottawa, Canada.

BENT S., R. SCHWAAB, D. CONLIN, and D. JEFFREY. 1991. *Intellectual property rights in biotechnology worldwide.* Stockton Press, NY, USA.

BRUSH S.B. and D. STABINSKY (eds.) 1996. *Valuing local knowledge: Indigenous people and intellectual property rights.* Island Press, CA, USA.

CARRIZOSA S. 2000. *La bioprospección y el acceso a los recursos genéticos.* (Bioprospecting and access to genetic resources). Con la colaboración de Adriana Casas. La Corporación Autónoma Regional de Cundinamarca (CAR), Bogotá, Colombia.

CASAS A. 1999. *Recursos genéticos: Biodiversidad y derecho.* (Genetic resources: Biodiversity and law). Instituto Colombiano de Derecho Ambiental, Ediciones Jurídicas Gustavo Ibañez, Bogotá, Colombia.

CORREA C.M. 1999. Access to plant genetic resources and intellectual property rights. Background Study Paper No. 8. Commission on Genetic Resources for Food and Agriculture, FAO, Rome, Italy.

CRUCIBLE GROUP. 1994. *People, plants and patents: The impact of intellectual property on biodiversity conservation, trade and rural society.* International Development Research Center, Ottawa, Canada.

DUTFIELD G. 2000. *Intellectual property rights, trade and biodiversity.* Earthscan, London, UK.

FANNING O. 1995. New survey shows majority of drugs originate in nature as well as in laboratory. Internal Medicine. *World Report,* May 15–31.

DIMASI J.A., R.W. HANSEN, H.G. GRABOWSKI, and L. LASAGNA. 1991. Cost of innovations in the pharmaceutical industry. *Journal of Health Economics* 10:107–142.

EPSW. 1999. Access to genetic resources: An evaluation of the development and implementation of recent regulation and access agreements. Environmental Policy Studies Workshop, Working Paper #4, School of International and Public Affairs, Columbia University, NY, USA.

FAO. 1998. *The state of the world's plant genetic resources for food and agriculture.* FAO, Rome, Italy.

FAO. 2001. International treaty on plant genetic resources for food and agriculture. FAO, Rome, Italy.

GLOWKA L. 1998. A guide to designing legal frameworks to determine access to genetic resources. Environmental Policy and Law Paper No. 34. Environmental Law Center, IUCN, Gland, Switzerland, Cambridge, UK, and Bonn, Germany.

GLOWKA L., B. PISUPATI, and S. DE SILVA. 2001. Access to genetic resources and traditional knowledge: Lessons from South and Southeast Asia. IUCN, Homagama, Sri Lanka.

GRAJAL A. 1999. Biodiversity and the nation state: Regulating access to genetic resources limits biodiversity research in developing countries. *Conservation Biology* 13:6–9.

GREAVES T. (ed.) 1994. *Intellectual property rights for indigenous peoples: A source book.* Society for Applied Anthropology, OK, USA.

GRINDLEY J. 1993. The natural approach to pharmaceuticals. *Scrip Magazine,* **December**: 30-33.

LAIRD S. (ed.) 2002. *Biodiversity and traditional knowledge: Equitable partnerships in practice.* Earthscan, London, UK.

MITTERMEIER R.A., N. MYERS, P. ROBLES-GIL, and C. MITTERMEIER-GOETTSCH (eds.) 1999. *The hotspots.* CEMEX. USA.

MUGABE J., C.V. BARBER, G. HENNE, L. GLOWKA, and A. LA VIÑA (eds.) 1997. *Access to genetic resources: Strategies for sharing benefits.* Environmental Law Center, IUCN, Nairobi, Kenya.

NNADOZIE K., R. LETTINGTON, C. BRUCH, S. BASS, and S. KINGBY (eds.) 2003. *African perspectives on genetic resources: A handbook on laws, policies, and institutions.* African Union Scientific, Technical and Research Commission, the Southern Environmental and Agricultural Policy Research Institute, and the Environmental Law Institute, Washington DC, USA.

PONCE DE LEÓN E. 1998. Concepto sobre propiedad de recursos genéticos en la legislación colombiana (Opinion on the concept of property over genetic resources in Colombian law). p. 221–236 *in* Grupo ad hoc sobre diversidad biológica, ILSA, IGEA, and WWF (eds.) *Diversidad biologica y cultural: Retos y propuestas desde America Latina.* (Cultural and biological diversity: Challenges and proposals from Latin America). ILSA. Bogotá, Colombia.

Reid W.V., S.A. LAIRD, R. GÁMEZ, A. SITTENFELD, D.H. JANZEN, M.G. GOLLIN, and C. JUMA. 1993. A new lease on life. p. 1–52 *in* W.V. REID, S.A. LAIRD, C.A. MEYER, R. GÁMEZ, A. SITTENFELD, D.H. JANZEN, M.G. GOLLIN, and C. JUMA (eds.). *Biodiversity prospecting: Using genetic resources for sustainable development.* World Resources Institute, Washington DC USA.

REVKIN A.C. 2002. Biologists sought a treaty: Now they fault it. The New York Times, May 7.

ROSENTHAL J.P., D. BECK, A. BHAT, J. BISWAS, L. BRADY, K. BRIDBOARD, S. COLLINS, G. CRAGG, J. EDWARDS, A. FAIRFIELD, M. GOTTLIEB, L.A. GSCHWIND, Y. HALLOCK, R. HAWKS, R. HEGYELI, G. JOHNSON, G.T. KEUSCH, E.E. LYONS, R. MILLER, J. RODMAN, J. ROSKOSKI, and D. SIEGEL-CAUSEY. 1999. Combining high risk science with ambitious social and economic goals. *Pharmaceutical Biology* 37:6–21.

RYAN M.P. 1998. *Knowledge diplomacy: Global competition and the policies of intellectual property.* Brookings Institution Press, Washington DC, USA.

SHIVA V. 1995. *Captive minds, captive lives: Ethics, ecology and patents on life.* Research Foundation for Science, Technology and Natural Resource Policy, India.

SHIVA V. 1997. *Biopiracy: The plunder of nature and knowledge.* South End Press, MA, USA.

SIEBECK W.E., R.E. EVENSON, W. LESSER, and C.A. PRIMO

BRAGA. 1990. *Strengthening protection of intellectual property in developing countries: A Survey of the literature.* World Bank Discussion Papers No 112, The World Bank, Washington DC, USA.

SIMPSON R.D., R.A. SEDJO, and J.W REID. 1994. *Valuing biodiversity for use in pharmaceutical research.* Resources for the Future, Washington, DC, USA.

SWANSON T. (ed.) 1995. *Intellectual property rights and biodiversity conservation: An interdisciplinary analysis of the values of medicinal plants.* Cambridge University Press, Cambridge, UK.

TEN KATE T.K. and S.A. LAIRD. 1999. *The commercial use of biodiversity: Access to genetic resources and benefit-sharing.* Earthscan. London, UK.

VOGEL J.H. 1994. *Genes for sale: Privatization as a conservation policy.* Oxford University Press, NY, USA.

WTO News. 2002. TRIPS council approves decision on delaying pharmaceutical patents for LDCs. February 28. http://www.wto.org/wto/english/news_e/news02_e/news02_e.htm.

Endnotes

[1] The CBD was signed by 167 nations at the United Nations Conference on Environment and Development (UNCED) in Rio de Janeiro, Brazil, 1992.

[2] TRIPS is administered by the World Trade Organization (WTO).

[3] These include the Patent Cooperation Treaty, the Paris Convention for the Protection of Industrial Property, and the Bern Convention for the Protection of Literary and Artistic Works. These multilateral treaties are administered by the World Intellectual Property Organization (WIPO).

[4] See http://www.wto.org/wto/english/tratop_e/dda_e/dohaexplained_e.htm for additional details.

[5] In this chapter bioprospecting is defined as the search for plants, animals, and microbial species for academic, pharmaceutical, biotechnological, agricultural, and other industrial purposes.

[6] According to CORREA (1999) genetic engineering has "blurred" the distinction between "inventions" that can be patented and "discoveries" that cannot. An isolated and purified form of a natural product can be patented in countries such as the USA and Japan. So, "the unknown but natural existence of a product cannot preclude the product from the category of statutory subject matter" (BENT et al. 1991). Also, when patents are granted on genes, they usually cover the vector or plasmid that incorporates the sequence of the gene and the organism (i.e., plant or animal) that has been transformed by means of the vector (BARTON 1993).

[8] The Pacific Rim megadiversity countries are China, USA, Australia, Mexico, Indonesia, Peru, Colombia, Papua New Guinea, Malaysia, Philippines, and Ecuador (MITTERMEIER et al. 1999).

[8] The Andean Community of Nations (formerly known as the Andean Pact or Cartagena Accord) is based on an economic and social-integration treaty among Colombia, Peru, Ecuador, Venezuela, and Bolivia.

[9] Very restrictive access requirements may have also affected communities and industries from other Pacific Rim countries by excluding them from the benefits derived from biodiversity. In 1996, the American firm Andes Pharmaceutical applied for access to Colombia's genetic resources under Decision 391, and in 1998, after two years of negotiations, the application was rejected for various reasons. One of them was that the benefit-sharing compensation package presented by Andes Pharmaceuticals did not meet the requirements of their counterparts. It should also be noted that political motives and the lack of clear negotiation guidelines may have also contributed to this decision (CARRIZOSA 2000).

[10] The workshop was organized by the University of California Genetic Resources Conservation Program with financial and technical support provided by the University of California Pacific Rim Research Program, Ford Foundation, The Institute of International Education, Environmental Law Program–The World Conservation Union, Andean Finance Corporation, United Nations University–Institute of Advanced Studies. See Appendix 1, this volume, for a summary of the workshop's conclusions and see http://www.grcp.ucdavis.edu/projects/ABSdex.htm for Workshop agenda and roster of participants.

1

Diversity of Policies in Place and in Progress

Santiago Carrizosa

On 29 December 1993, one and a half years after its signing, the Convention on Biological Diversity (CBD) became international law and a binding legal document for the 37 countries that ratified it by that date. By October 1994, one month before the first meeting of the CBD Conference of the Parties, 88 countries and the European Community had ratified the convention. Today, there are 188 Parties (countries who have ratified, acceded, accepted, or approved the CBD), but only about 22% of these Parties have concluded or are developing laws and policies regulating access and benefit sharing (ABS).[1] The 41 Pacific Rim countries examined in this report harbor about 48% of the world's biodiversity (Mittermeier et al. 1999). These countries are: Australia, Cambodia, Canada, Chile, Colombia, Cook Islands, Costa Rica, Ecuador, El Salvador, Fiji, Guatemala, Honduras, Japan, Indonesia, Kiribati, Lao People's Democratic Republic (hereafter Laos), Malaysia, Marshall Islands, Mexico, Federated States of Micronesia (hereafter, Micronesia), Nauru, New Zealand, Nicaragua,

Niue, People's Republic of China (hereafter China), Palau, Panama, Papua New Guinea, Peru, Philippines, Republic of Korea, Russian Federation, Samoa, Singapore, Solomon Islands, Thailand, Tonga, Tuvalu, the United States of America (hereafter, USA), Vanuatu, and Vietnam. As of July 2004, 40 of these countries were Parties to the CBD, the USA is a signatory, not a Party[2]. Our findings indicate that only nine of these 41 Pacific Rim countries (22%) had developed some sort of ABS law or policy[3], 26 of them (63%) were working towards the development of ABS frameworks, and six (15%) were not involved in any systematic process leading to the development ABS frameworks (see Table 1). Before the CBD was signed, most, if not all, of these countries had a permit system to regulate the extraction and management of biological resources and the transition from these permit systems to more comprehensive ABS frameworks has proven to be difficult. Chapter 2 provides a detailed account of the problems faced by selected countries during the development process of their ABS laws and policies.

Overview of Regional and National ABS Policies and Laws

Several national and regional initiatives have been undertaken by Pacific Rim countries to develop ABS frameworks. The presence of common ecoregions (i.e., the Andes and Amazon) and ethnic and cultural beliefs were factors that promoted the development of a Common Regime on Access to Genetic Resources (Decision 391) of the Andean Community[4]. Following the lead of the Andean Community, countries of the Central American region developed a draft protocol on "Access to genetic and biochemical resources, and their associated knowledge" and the Association of Southeast Asian Nations[5] (ASEAN)

drafted the "ASEAN Framework Agreement on Access to Biological and Genetic Resources".[6] However, these drafts are not as comprehensive, detailed, and prescriptive as Decision 391. They were developed by each body knowing that their member countries already had or were about to develop national ABS laws and policies. In contrast, the Andean countries had no national ABS policies before Decision 391 was developed. Furthermore, when Decision 391 was approved under the Cartagena Agreement of the Andean Pact Countries it became binding and was automatically integrated into national legislation. Initially, the application by a country of Decision 391 did not require the development of any new national law, but only some additional dispositions and regulations might be needed. Venezuela applied this regime directly to several access applications[7] and Colombia attempted unsuccessfully to negotiate an access application under Decision 391. However, technical ambiguities, social protest, political concerns, and institutional limitations, among other factors, forced Bolivia, Ecuador, Peru, and recently Colombia to develop national policies to facilitate the implementation of Decision 391 into their national context. Peru, for example, should be approving the regulation of Decision 391 sometime in 2004 (M. Ruiz, pers. comm. January 2004) and Colombia is currently working on a proposal for a national ABS policy (see Chapter 4). Furthermore, traditional knowledge is part of the scope of protection provided by Decision 391, but the Andean Community has still to develop a regional policy to address this issue. On 10 August 2002 Peru became the first country in the Andean region that adopted a national comprehensive legal system (Law No. 27811) for the protection of indigenous communities' collective knowledge associated with biodiversity (PERUVIAN CONGRESS 2002). On 7 July 2002, the Andean Community adopted a Regional Biodiversity Strategy (Decision 523). This strategy includes an ABS component that describes some of the problems experienced by the Andean countries in implementing Decision 391 and proposes a course of action to facilitate its implementation (ANDEAN COMMUNITY 2002).

The only Pacific Rim country in South America that does not have any ABS policy is Chile. This country has been the research site of several bioprospecting[8] groups but so far this has not been a significant incentive for policy makers to develop a comprehensive ABS framework. In late 2003 the Ministry of Agriculture developed an ABS proposal that applies only to agricultural genetic resources. The proposal however, was discarded after much criticism, but efforts to develop a new proposal continue. Also, in 2003 the National Commission of the Environment published the country's National Biodiversity Strategy that called for the development of an ABS policy. The strategy is the guiding chart of the National Biodiversity Action Plan that was initiated in mid-2004.

Costa Rica, one of the main promoters of the Central American draft protocol on ABS, is the only country in that region that has a national law (the 1998 Law of Biodiversity No. 7788) which includes ABS provisions. In December 2003, the Costa Rican government published a general access procedure that functions as a bylaw of the Law of Biodiversity. Nicaragua has followed the example of Costa Rica and developed a proposal for a law of biodiversity that will be consistent with the protocol and should be sent to Congress in 2004 or 2005. Nicaragua's draft law of biodiversity responds to the mandate (Article 70) of the 1996 General Law of the Environment and Natural Resources No. 217 (GLENR). Similarly, Honduras is planning to develop a law of biodiversity that will include

ABS provisions and from there they will derive a more specific ABS framework. As a first step, however, Honduras is developing a proposal to assess national capacity and priorities regarding access to genetic resources. Some objectives of this proposal include: a) identification of advances in the area of genetic resources; b) identification of the importance of genetic resources at a national level; c) definition of priorities; and d) identification of local organizations that use genetic resources. Honduras has endorsed the Central American draft protocol on ABS and will likely ratify it once this country's priorities regarding this issue have been identified. Panama will ratify the draft protocol in 2004 or 2005 and it is currently working on an ABS policy that will complement existing natural resource use legislation that includes: a) Forestry Law No. 1 of 3 February 1994; b) Law No. 30 of 30 December 1994; c) Wildlife Law No. 24 of 7 June 1995; and d) Resolution 001-97-14 of January 1997. The legal mandate to develop an ABS policy in Panama is included in the 1998 General Law of the Environment No. 41 (GLE) that designates the National Authority for the Environment[9] (ANAM) as the competent authority for the regulation, management, and control of the access to and use of biogenetic resources. According to GLE, ANAM must elaborate legal instruments and economic mechanisms to facilitate ABS goals in Panama (Article 71). GLE also states that indigenous communities must have a share of the benefits derived from the use of natural resources found in their lands (Article 105) and clarifies that holders of rights granted for the use of natural resources do not hold rights for the use of genetic resources contained in them (Article 71) (LA ASAMBLEA LEGISLATIVA 1998). National initiatives to develop more specific ABS regulations include draft Law No. 36 that might create an Institute on Traditional Indigenous Medicine. This draft law includes some access, benefit-sharing, IPRS, and marketing provisions for products used in traditional indigenous medicine (see Chapter 2). El Salvador just completed ABS guidelines that are likely to provide a course of action about how to implement existing and future policy. Finally, Guatemala's 1999 Action Plan of the National Strategy for the Conservation and Sustainable Use of Biodiversity addressed the need to develop an ABS policy. But policy-makers from this country do not seem to be engaged in a systematic and participatory process to do so. Guatemala is also a signatory of the Central American draft protocol on "Access to genetic and biochemical resources, and their associated knowledge" and it will become national law once it is ratified by this nation.

In North America, Mexico has used Article 87 of the 1988 Ecological Equilibrium and Environmental Protection General Act (EEEPGA) to facilitate access for two bioprospecting projects (see Chapters 3 and 6). This article and Article 87 BIS were introduced in the 1996 reform of the act and they set forth principles regarding prior informed consent (PIC) and benefit-sharing issues for collections of biological species for scientific, economic, and biotechnology purposes. The 1999 Wildlife General Act (WGA) and the 2003 Sustainable Forestry Development General Act (SFDGA) regulate the collection of wildlife resources and forest biological resources respectively and address PIC and benefit-sharing issues as well. However, EEEPGA, WGA, and SFDGA lack details about how to achieve the implementation of PIC requirements and other ABS principles. Currently, there are two pieces of legislation in Congress that purport to fill this gap. One submitted by the Federal Representative Alejandro Cruz Gutierrez (Institutional Revolutionary Party) and the other by Federal Senator Jorge Nordhausen (National Action Party). The proposal of Senator Nordhausen, entitled "Law for Access and Use of Biological and Genetic Resources" (LAUBGR), is more comprehensive and may be approved sometime in 2004 or 2005 (Jorge Larson, pers. comm. February 2004). Therefore, it will be discussed in this report. Canada has undertaken some background research on ABS issues and held some preliminary discussions with provincial governments and some aboriginal groups. The USA is not a CBD Party and it does not have a national ABS policy. Access is usually regulated by the landowner. Multiple federal and state laws regulate genetic resources found on land owned by the federal or state governments. In contrast, genetic resources found on private lands are controlled by the owner unless these resources are protected by the Endangered Species Act or other relevant federal or state laws. The owner of genetic resources is relatively free to negotiate ABS conditions with the bioprospector.

The only European country that borders the Pacific Rim is the Russian Federation and, despite its high biological diversity, this country has not developed a comprehensive ABS framework. The Ministry of Industry, Science, and Technology is analyzing ABS issues such as ownership of genetic resources in the context of existing legislation. These issues have been addressed thanks to the momentum created by a 2001 national report on access to genetic resources.

In the Asian region of the Pacific Rim, the Philippines and Thailand are the only two countries that have completed national ABS frameworks. In 2001, the Philippines enacted Republic Act No. 9147, known as the Wildlife Resources and Conservation Act (hereafter Wildlife Act) that addressed many of the criticisms of an earlier policy, the 1995 Executive Order No. 247 (EO 247). The Wildlife Act is a codification of existing laws on the protection and conservation of wildlife resources. It includes only two provisions that deal with bioprospecting issues but it modifies EO 247 considerably and facilitates access to the country's genetic resources. In July 2004, draft "Guidelines for Bioprospecting Activities in the Philippines"[10] was released for review and comment. These guidelines outline detailed ABS requirements for commercial bioprospectors and facilitate the implementation of the Wildlife Act. The guidelines would also facilitate the implementation of those provisions of EO 247 that were not repealed by, or

are consistent with, the Wildlife Act. Even though Thailand did not become a CBD Party until January 2004, in 1999, this country adopted the following laws and regulations that cover ABS issues and apply to bioprospectors: a) the Royal Forest Department (RFD) Regulation on Forestry Studying and Research Conducting within Forested Areas (RFSRCFA); b) the Plant Variety Protection Act (PVPA); and c) Act on Protection and Promotion of Traditional Medicinal Intelligence (APPTMI). In addition, foreign bioprospectors have to comply with the regulation on the permission for foreign researchers to conduct research in Thailand that was enacted by the National Research Council of Thailand (NRCT) in 1982. These policies, however, present overlapping problems. Therefore, in 2000 the Prime Minister enacted a regulation on Conservation and Utilization of Biological Resources that is basically a mandate for all government bodies to coordinate the development and implementation of ABS rules and procedures, among other issues.

In Malaysia, the federal government is currently finalizing a bill on ABS that could be enacted in 2004 or 2005. This bill will complement ABS policies already enacted at a state level by Sarawak and Sabah. Singapore is also developing a national ABS policy and guidelines. Indonesia is currently working on an Act on Genetic Resource Management that includes a government regulation on ABS issues. In Cambodia, ABS issues are partially regulated by the 2002 Forestry Law. Laos, however, is not currently engaged in the development of national ABS frameworks. On the other hand Vietnam's 1995 National Action Plan on Biological Diversity addressed the need to develop an ABS policy. Therefore, in the last few years the government has been collecting and analyzing ABS literature and it is planning to start working actively on a national ABS policy in 2004 or 2005. The two Asian economic powers, China and Japan, also lack ABS policies but both countries are collecting information, conducting studies, and analyzing trends regarding ABS policies. The Environmental Protection Administration of China is also putting together a team to develop a comprehensive ABS law or policy. The Republic of Korea is currently amending its 1991 Natural Environment Conservation Act. The amended act will include specific ABS provisions and it is likely to be completed in 2004 or 2005. It should be noted that this act has been repeatedly amended since 1991. For example, the 1994 amendment included Article 25.4 that allowed foreigners to collect and use domestic biological resources for commercial, medical, or scientific uses. This article, however, was removed from the act by Law No. 5876 of 8 February 1999.

In addition to these national ABS policies, several Asian nations have been active in the development of a regional policy known as the ASEAN Framework Agreement on Access to Biological and Genetic Resources, scheduled to be adopted in 2004 or 2005 by the ASEAN countries. The ASEAN framework will cover the following Pacific Rim countries whose ABS frameworks are analyzed in this report: Thailand, Malaysia, Singapore, Indonesia, Laos, and Cambodia.

In Oceania, Australia has carried out an interesting process that resulted in the development of the 2001 Environment Protection and Biodiversity Conservation Amendment Regulations (EPBCAR) that will apply to ABS issues in the commonwealth areas of Australia. These regulations, which will reform the 1999 Environment Protection and Biodiversity Conservation Act, are likely to be introduced in Parliament in 2005. At a state level, Queensland and Western Australia are also undertaking activities to develop ABS laws. In mid-2004, Queensland adopted a Biodiscovery Bill and Western Australia is currently discussing a licensing regime for terrestrial bioprospecting activities that will be included in a draft Biodiversity Conservation Act. These states are consulting with Environment Australia to ensure that where jurisdictions overlap with commonwealth territories, these regulations are not duplicated. In addition to this, in 2002 the Natural Resource Management Ministerial Council adopted a federal agreement on a "Nationally Consistent Approach for Access to and the Utilization of Australia's Native Genetic and Biochemical Resources". This agreement includes 14 principles to facilitate the development or review of legislative, administrative, or policy ABS initiatives for a nationally consistent approach in each jurisdiction.

Australia's neighbor, New Zealand, has undertaken some key activities towards the development of a national ABS policy. In November 2002, the Ministry of Economic Development published a discussion paper on bioprospecting. The paper invited the public to submit comments by the end of February 2003. In May 2003 the Ministry posted a summary of the submissions on its website.[11] However, future efforts to develop ABS legislation can be complicated by a claim by a number of tribes (Iwi) of the Maori people to a tribunal in which they assert exclusive rights over both traditional knowledge and indigenous genetic resources under the Waitangi Treaty of 1840. This claim was presented to the tribunals in 1991 and is not likely to be settled in the near future. Nevertheless, government officials continue to debate bioprospecting issues together with this community and other stakeholders. In Samoa, in 2000, the Department of Lands, Surveys, and Environment adopted a preliminary regulation titled "Conditions for Access to and Benefit Sharing of Samoa's Biodiversity Resources" (CABSSBR). In addition, this department is working on a more comprehensive ABS regulation that will be appended to the 1989 Lands and Environment Act that is currently under revision. In March 2002, Micronesia finished its National Biodiversity Strategy and it is expected that the development of ABS policy will follow from the needs identified by the strategy.

Cook Islands, Fiji, Marshall Islands, Niue, Solomon Islands, and Vanuatu lack ABS policies but have working groups and committees in place analyzing existing legislation and proposing courses of action for the development of local policies. Vanuatu, for example, is analyzing ABS provisions that might be included in the draft of its Environment Act. Palau is planning to start working on ABS policies sometime between 2004 and 2005, depending on the availability of funding and technical capacity. In Papua New Guinea, the Department of Environment and Conservation is working closely with lawyers from the Department of Justice and Attorney General to develop a framework on intellectual property rights and ABS. Kiribati, Nauru, Tonga, and Tuvalu have received technical advice from the South Pacific Regional Environment Program, WWF-South Pacific Program, the Foundation for International Environmental Law and Development, and other local organizations, but these countries are not currently engaged in a systematic development process of ABS policies. The ABS laws and policies of these countries are in different stages of development and implementation and all of them provide valuable lessons. Table 1 summarizes the information provided in the preceding paragraphs and provides additional details.

Analyzing ABS Policies and Laws of Selected Countries

The remainder of this chapter focuses on national ABS policies and laws that are already in place and drafts of ABS policies and laws that are still going through an executive or legislative process and may still be modified. These drafts include interesting provisions that merit careful analysis and are useful for the purposes of this report. Colombia, Costa Rica, Ecuador, Mexico, Peru, Philippines, Samoa, and Thailand comprise the group that has already adopted national ABS laws and policies. Despite the fact that they may still be modified at a political and legislative level, these laws and policies can be used by bioprospectors. As noted above, the USA does not have a national ABS policy and it is not likely to develop one in the future. However, depending on the region where biological or genetic resources are found, there are certain regulations that bioprospectors have to follow in order to access genetic resources. This section examines the application of National Park Service (NPS) regulations to ABS activity (i.e., the Diversa/Yellowstone National Park bioprospecting project) and it suggests that these regulations are analogous to ABS laws and policies developed by other countries under the umbrella of the CBD.

Australia, Malaysia, and Nicaragua comprise the group that is in the process of developing or adopting ABS policies or laws. Australia's amendment regulations on access to genetic resources are likely to be passed by Parliament in 2004 or 2005 and Malaysia's federal bill on access to genetic resources is likely to be approved by Parliament in 2005. Nicaragua's Ministry for the Environment and Natural Resources recently concluded a final draft of the

Law of Biodiversity and it should be sent to Congress in 2004 or 2005.

This section discusses the main provisions of ABS laws and policies of these nations that have been inspired by the CBD and influenced by international and national social, economic, and political factors. These provisions are: a) ownership; b) scope; c) access procedure; d) prior informed consent; e) benefit sharing and compensation mechanisms; f) intellectual property rights and the protection of traditional knowledge; g) *in situ* biodiversity conservation and sustainable use; and h) enforcement and monitoring. Each of these issues will be presented as national laws and policies describe them. Then, a subsequent analysis will compare and contrast the main issues and implications for the main actors that play a part in bioprospecting initiatives, namely government authorities, bioprospectors, and the providers of genetic resources and traditional knowledge.

Ownership

Ownership of genetic resources determines access conditions, procedures, rules, and rights over these resources. Traditionally, the constitutions of countries define the concept of ownership of natural resources. The concept of ownership of genetic resources is novel and in some cases ABS laws have made the connection between natural and genetic resources. This section compares and contrasts ownership systems of natural and genetic resources proposed by the selected countries.

Australia: Draft EPBCAR

In the commonwealth areas of Australia, the Commonwealth owns the biological resources in the land in accordance with common law principles discussed by VOUMARD (2000). The Australian Constitution, however, does not explicitly provide for this. Rather, ownership flows from the common law. This provides that ownership of land includes the substrata. That being the case, natural things growing on it or in it are owned by the Commonwealth. Insofar as genetic and biochemical resources are physical elements found within biological resources then, where the Commonwealth owns the biological resources, then it must also own those constituent elements[12] (G. Burton, pers. comm. January 2003).

Colombia, Ecuador, and Peru: Decision 391

Decision 391 establishes that genetic resources and their derivatives found in the Andean Community are considered the goods or patrimony of the State, depending on the country's national legislation. This applies to resources found in private, public, and indigenous lands and in *in situ* and *ex situ* conditions (ANDEAN COMMUNITY 1996).

Costa Rica: The Law of Biodiversity

This law states that genetic and biochemical resources are considered to be in the public domain, independent of any private ownership of the land where they are located.

Therefore, these resources belong to the State and it can regulate access to them (see Chapter 5).

Malaysia: Draft federal bill on access to genetic resources

In Malaysia, ownership of biological, genetic, and biochemical resources is still a gray area. The Constitution allocates ownership of land and minerals to the thirteen states. Therefore, biological, biochemical, and genetic resources found in public lands belong to the individual state. However, in some states the ownership situation of resources found in indigenous and private land is under controversy and it is unclear whether these resources belong to the state or the owner of the land (see Chapter 11). The draft of the federal bill on access to genetic resources will apply to public, indigenous, and private lands, therefore ownership of resources found in these areas will have to be clarified before the law is adopted.

Mexico: EEEPGA, WGA, SFDGA, and draft LAUBGR

In Mexico, EEEPGA has been implemented to regulate ABS under the understanding that genetic resources are public property. The Constitution defines public property over certain natural resources, such as land, oil, and water. It does not mention genetic resources, but again as in other constitutions it can be implied that natural resources contain the biological, biochemical, and genetic components. In addition to this, WGA recognizes the rights of landowners to make a sustainable use of the wildlife resources found in their lands (SEMARNAT 2000) and SFDGA establishes that the owners of forest resources are the owners of the land where these resources are found (SEMARNAT 2003). Critics, however, argue that new legislation has to be developed to clarify public, indigenous, and private property status of genetic and biochemical resources (see Chapter 6). The draft LAUBGR may help clarify the ownership status of genetic resources (GACETA PARLAMENTARIA 2001).

Nicaragua: Draft Law of Biodiversity

In 1996, GLENR established that natural resources are patrimony of the state (MARENA 1996). The draft Law of Biodiversity takes a step forward by specifying that that wildlife, genetic, and biochemical resources are considered public domain. Therefore, these resources belong to the State which can regulate access to them. Nevertheless, it is important to note that the draft law acknowledges that indigenous peoples own the wildlife, biochemical, and genetic resources found in their territories. This, however, does not mean that they can access these resources for biotechnological purposes without State intervention. The State is still a party in any agreement established between an indigenous community and a third party (MARENA 2002).

Philippines: EO 247 and Wildlife Act

The Constitution states that all lands of the public domain, waters, minerals, coal, petroleum, and other mineral oils, all forces of potential energy, fisheries, forests or timber, wildlife, flora and fauna, and other natural resources are owned by the State. The exploration, development, and utilization of natural resources shall be under the full control and supervision of the State. This provision of the Constitution is the basis for EO 247 as stated in its Preamble. Although it is not categorically stated in EO 247 that ownership of biological and genetic resources belongs to the State, it is implied in some of its provisions such as the collection of royalties for the use of these resources. Furthermore, the claim of State ownership over these resources is expressly stated in commercial and academic research agreements that have been subsequently developed. Therefore, it is reasonable to assume that when the Constitution says "natural resources", the term includes all that is part or portion of the resource (tissues, genes, molecules, etc), plant or animal, living or preserved. Thus, exploration and use of these resources is under the full control and supervision of the State (P. Benavidez, pers. comm. January 2003).

Samoa: CABSSBR
Samoa's Constitution is not specific about ownership of natural, biological, or genetic resources. Also, the CABSSBR does not include information about ownership of these resources (DLSE 2000). Land is classified as private, freehold, and customary land[13] (the latter amounting to about 85% of the country's total land area) (C. Peteru, pers. comm. December 2003).

Thailand: PVPA, RFSRCFA, and APPTMI
The Constitution states that natural resources are owned by the State but it gives the authority to manage such resources to the people. Therefore, if natural, biological, and genetic resources are found in National Forests or any other public land, the owner is the State. If these resources are found in a private garden, the landowner will need the State's authorization to commercialize them. In any case, ownership issues is still a gray area in Thailand and the government is trying to develop laws such as the PVPA to clarify ownership issues regarding biological, genetic, and biochemical resources (J. Donavanik, pers. comm. January 2003).

USA: NPS research specimen collection permit
Title 36 of the US Code of Federal Regulation states that all specimens collected in a national park under research (or access) permits belong to that park. This is the case of the collection of samples carried out by Diversa in Yellowstone National Park (see Chapter 8).

Analysis: Ownership
The legal status of genetic resources depends on the rights upon an organism or its parts, and the information embodied in them. Evidently, the information component of genetic resources is the most valuable for bioprospectors. However, no State has created a property right system for this component. Therefore, countries still rely on the physical entity (i.e., organism or its parts) to define the

legal status of their genetic (and biochemical) resources. For example, wild fauna found in *in situ* conditions has been considered *res nullius*, or no one's property. This concept has been replaced by that of State's ownership which means that the State would have to authorize the use by others of this resource (DE KLEMM 1994). Plants can be considered as State, private, or communal property. In theory, the private owner and the co-owners have the discretion to use their resources the way they see fit. However, private and communal property of plants and other biological resources can be subject to government restrictions (GLOWKA 1998).

Two ownership systems can be identified from the case studies. In one system, priority is given to private or communal ownership of natural resources and the private or communal owner of the land does not need the State's approval to market his or her biological, biochemical, or genetic resources. Nevertheless, there may be restrictions to this system if the target species is protected by special legislation such as the Endangered Species Act in the USA. A second system considers natural resources (and the biological, biochemical, and genetic components) as property of the State. The main implication of such a regime is that access to these resources is regulated for public, communal, and private lands. Therefore, bioprospectors are required to have a permit from the State and the individual or collective owner or holder of the land or collection where the biological or genetic resource is found. Under either of these two systems, the State and the owner of the land have veto powers and may deny access to their resources.

Scope

A precise definition of the scope of ABS policies and laws facilitates their implementation. The concept of scope should address several questions about the types of genetic and biological resources covered by a given policy or law: Are they found in *in situ* or *ex situ* conditions or both? Does the policy apply to derivatives? Does it cover the traditional or scientific knowledge associated with the biological resources? Does it address the use of human genetic resources and the use and exchange of biological resources by indigenous communities? The scope should also include information about the geographic boundaries, context, and coverage of access activities and it may also identify access restrictions such as geographic sites, genetic and biological material, and actors that can use and mobilize biological material without having to apply for access.

Australia: Draft EPBCAR
These regulations will apply to Commonwealth areas which are lands owned or leased by the Commonwealth government and marine areas over which the Commonwealth has sovereignty. The regulations will not apply to the states and territories, which have their own legislation and policies governing access to biological resources. However,

in October 2002, the Natural Resource Management Ministerial Council proposed fourteen principles to promote the development or review of legislative, administrative, or policy frameworks for a nationally consistent approach for the Commonwealth, states, and territories (see Chapter 9).

The regulations also apply to the collection and use of native biological resources, genetic resources, and biochemical compounds for commercial, scientific, and conservation purposes. The scope also covers traditional knowledge associated with the use of these resources but it excludes human genetic resources and the use and exchange of biological resources by indigenous communities. The regulations will apply only to native species and not to exotic plants and animals. The regulations are not clear regarding application to genetic resources found in *ex situ* conditions. Under the regulations, permit provisions may not apply to biological resources in the following cases: a) if they are found in a collection of a Commonwealth department or agency and if there are reasonable grounds to believe that access to the biological resources is administered consistently with the purpose of the regulations; b) if access to these resources is controlled by another Commonwealth, self-governing territory, or state law, consistent with the purpose of the regulations (the purpose of this provision is to avoid duplication of any access arrangements applying in a Commonwealth area); and c) if an international agreement, to which Australia is a Party, applies (e.g., FAO International Treaty on Plant Genetic Resources for Food and Agriculture (ITPGRFA)) (see Chapter 9).

Colombia, Ecuador, and Peru: Decision 391

Decision 391 applies to all *in situ* and *ex situ* genetic resources (native and domestic) and their derivatives indigenous to each member country and to genetic resources of migratory species that are collected in any of these countries for bioprospecting, basic research, conservation, industrial, and commercial purposes. Derivatives are defined as molecules, a combination or mix of natural molecules, including crude extracts of living or dead organisms of biological origin, coming from the metabolism of living beings. Access may also be limited in cases of: a) presence of endangered, rare, or endemic species, subspecies, or races and b) fragile or vulnerable ecosystems. The scope of Decision 391 excludes all human genetic resources and their derivatives and the consumption and exchange of all genetic resources, their derivatives, associated knowledge, and biological resources among black, indigenous, and local communities (ANDEAN COMMUNITY 1996). The scope also applies to the collective and individual knowledge, innovation, or practice involving a species or its derivatives.

The scope of Peru's new Law No. 27811 on the protection of knowledge of indigenous peoples applies only to the collective knowledge of indigenous communities about uses and properties of biodiversity. Collective knowledge is

defined as accumulated and transgenerational knowledge developed by indigenous communities about properties, uses, and characteristics of biological diversity (PERUVIAN CONGRESS 2002). The scope does not apply to agricultural or marine practices or innovations. It is also limited to collective knowledge of the community and does not extend to the knowledge of individuals inside the community. The scope also poses practical difficulties that include defining guidelines to identify collective knowledge that applies to biological diversity and the boundaries of the community or communities that hold such knowledge.

Costa Rica: The Law of Biodiversity

This law regulates the use, management, associated knowledge, and the equitable distribution of benefits and costs derived from the utilization of all *in situ* and *ex situ* biological and genetic resources (native and domestic). The scope also extends to biochemical resources which are defined as any material derived from plants, animals, fungi, or microorganisms that contains specific characteristics or special molecules or leads to the design of them. The law excludes access to human genetic and biochemical resources and the exchange of genetic and biochemical resources that are part of traditional practices of indigenous peoples and local communities (see Chapter 5).

Malaysia:
Draft federal bill on access to genetic resources

The draft law will regulate access to *in situ* and *ex situ* biological and genetic resources and their derivatives and associated knowledge. These include native and domestic resources used by all industries and academia for commercial and noncommercial purposes. With respect to *ex situ* resources, the draft would apply only to those acquired after the CBD entered into force.

Access to genetic resources will be limited to the biological and geographical boundaries as defined by the federal government. These include genetic resources found on public lands, communal or customary lands, and private lands. The draft legislation also preserves the rights of indigenous and local communities to continue with their traditional customary practices of use, exchange, and marketing of biological resources. As an exemption, access to human genetic resources is prohibited by the draft legislation. It is not clear what will be the relationship between the scope of this law and that of access policies enacted by the Malaysian states of Sabah and Sarawak (see Chapter 11).

Mexico: EEEPGA, WGA, SFDGA, and draft LAUBGR

EEEPGA regulates access to native plant and animal species and other biological resources for scientific (noncommercial), economic (for reproduction and commercial objectives), and biotechnological (commercial) purposes. Biotechnology is defined as any application that uses biological resources, living organisms, or their derivatives for the creation or modification of products for specific uses (see Chapter 6). The EEEPGA does not cover traditional knowledge associated with the species nor access to *ex situ* genetic resources.

The scope of WGA includes the scientific, academic, or noncommercial collection of wild flora and fauna, their parts and derivatives, excluding aquatic and domestic species and traditional knowledge. WGA does not regulate *ex situ* collections directly. However, any scientific and museum collection of wildlife species, whether private or public, must be registered and permanently updated in an official record. Once registered, this collection can be exempted, under specific circumstances, from certain obligations regulating proof of legal provenance of wildlife species as long as they do not have any biotechnological or commercial purposes (SEMARNAT 2000). SFDGA regulates the collection and use of forest biological resources for scientific, economic, and biotechnological purposes. Forest biological resources are defined as species and varieties of plants, animals, and microorganisms and their biodiversity found in forest ecosystems. SFDGA states that commercial or noncommercial collectors of forest biological resources must acknowledge the rights of indigenous peoples on the ownership, knowledge, and use of local varieties (SEMAR-NAT 2003). The law, however, does not define the concept of local varieties nor does it differentiate between *in situ* and *ex situ* forest biological resources.

If approved, the draft LAUBGR will regulate access to biological, biochemical, and genetic resources and associated knowledge found in *in situ* and *ex situ* conditions. Access is regulated for bioprospecting, industrial, and any other economic use. The scope of the draft excludes access to human genetic resources and their derivatives and the exchange of genetic resources made by indigenous peoples and obtained from noncommercial uses, practices, and customs (GACETA PARLAMENTARIA 2001).

Nicaragua: Draft Law of Biodiversity
The scope of access activities will cover all *in situ* genetic and biological resources and their associated knowledge, innovations, and practices. The draft does not specifically refer to biochemical resources and it does not apply to *ex situ* genetic resources. However, the scope of the Central American Protocol on "Access to genetic and biochemical resources, and their associated knowledge" applies to these two issues. The protocol has already been signed by the Central American nations and it will become national law once it is ratified by them. Therefore, Nicaragua may invoke the protocol to facilitate access to biochemical and *ex situ* genetic resources.

The draft law excludes the following from its scope: a) human genetic resources and their derivatives; b) the utilization of genetic resources with purposes different from their use as source of genetic resources; c) the exchange of genetic resources and their associated knowledge made by indigenous and local communities according to traditional practices; d) biosafety for pharmaceutical products; and e) the use of domestic species, but not their protection and conservation (MARENA 2002).

Philippines: EO 247 and Wildlife Act
EO 247 regulates access to wild biological and genetic resources and their by-products and derivatives used for commercial and noncommercial purposes. By-products are defined as any part taken from wild biological resources such as hides, antlers, feathers, fur, internal organs, roots, trunks, branches, leaves, stems, flowers, and the like, including compounds indirectly produced in a biochemical process or cycle. Derivatives refer to something extracted from wild biological resources such as blood, oils, resins, genes, seeds, spores, pollen, and the like, taken from or modified from a product. Genetic resources are defined as genetic material of actual or potential value and genetic material means any material of plant, animal, microbial or other origin containing functional units of heredity. Access is regulated in the public domain and in the cases of natural occurrence in private or communal lands. EO 247 also recognizes the rights of indigenous communities to their knowledge when it is used for commercial purposes, but this policy does not apply to traditional uses of biological and genetic resources by indigenous and local communities in accordance with their traditional practices (see Chapter 7).

Under EO 247 bioprospecting was defined as the research, collection, and use of biological and genetic resources for commercial and noncommercial purposes. In 2001, however, the Wildlife Act stated that bioprospecting would be defined as those activities implemented only for commercial purposes. The act "covers all wildlife species including exotic species, which are subject to trade, cultured, maintained, bred in captivity, or propagated in the country". This act modified EO 247 extensively. It excluded academic and scientific collection and research activities from EO 247 coverage. Today, the Wildlife Act covers these activities. The scope of the 2004 draft Guidelines for Bioprospecting Activities in the Philippines (see endnote 10) will cover any commercial bioprospecting of biological species carried out in the Philippines (except for those accessed under international agreements where the Philippines is a party). The scope covers wildlife, microorganisms, domesticated or propagated species, exotic species and all *ex situ* collections of biological resources sourced from the Philippines. The guidelines, however, would not apply to collections related to traditional uses of biological and genetic resources, subsistence consumption, and conventional commercial consumption. The scope would also exclude logging or fishing, agrobiodiversity, and scientific activities such as taxonomic collections. Perhaps agrobiodiversity is being excluded to facilitate future implementation of the FAO ITPGRFA whose scope is restricted (for now) to the list of crops found in Annex I of the Treaty.[14] Access to human genetic resources and their derivatives is forbidden under the EO 247 (see Chapter 7).

Samoa: CABSSBR
The Samoan conditions cover access to biodiversity

resources and traditional knowledge for commercial or academic purposes. These include genetic resources, organisms or parts of them, populations, and any other component of ecosystems with potential use or value for humanity (DLSE 2000). The scope does not mention or define the biochemical component. However, taking into account that the conditions have been used to regulate benefits derived from the use of "prostratin" (a chemical compound derived from the plant *Homalanthus nutans*) (COX 2001), it is reasonable to assume that the biochemical component is included in the biological component of the scope. The scope of the conditions does not address the issue of access to *ex situ* genetic resources, and it does not include exclusions to the type of genetic resources sought by bioprospectors.

Thailand: PVPA, RFSRCFA, and APPTMI

Access to Thailand's *in situ* and *ex situ* biological and genetic resources and traditional knowledge is partially covered by these three laws. The PVPA regulates access to domestic and wild plant species (including mushrooms and seaweed) all over the country for commercial and noncommercial purposes (THAILAND CONGRESS 1999). The RFS-RCFA applies to natural, biological, and genetic resources[15] found in forest conservation areas administered by RFD and protected areas managed by the Department of National Parks, Wildlife, and Plant Conservation. (C. Hutacharern, pers. comm. June 2003). It is not clear whether the scope of the regulation applies to *ex situ* collections. APPTMI protects traditional knowledge about medicinal formulae derived from plants, animals, bacteria, minerals, and extracts of plants or animals used for diagnosing, treating, and preventing diseases, or promoting the health of humans or animals. This knowledge includes both that which has been passed on from generation to generation and that which is in the public domain and has been recorded in Thai books, palm leaf, stone inscription, or other materials (NITTM 2002). In case of conflict between RFSRCFA and the PVPA, the PVPA overrules RFSRCFA. Additional conflict issues between ABS policies are likely to be solved by a National Committee on Conservation and Utilization of Biological Diversity that was created by a Prime Minister Regulation on Conservation and Utilization of Biological Diversity. Thailand is also planning to develop a law specifically on medical research, which will be addressing human genetic resources and another law on endangered species (J. Donavanik, pers. comm. November 2003).

USA: NPS research specimen collection permit

Access to the biological diversity of USA national parks for research purposes (commercial and noncommercial) is governed by NPS specimen collection permit regulations. These regulations have been implemented since 1983 and permits for the collection of biological samples throughout the NPS are issued routinely. Permits regulate access to the biological resource and the genetic material it contains. Access, however, can be denied if the proposed research activity has any of the following characteristics (see Chapter 8): a) adverse effects on the experiences of park visitors; b) a potential for negative impacts on the park's natural, cultural, or scenic resources, and particularly to nonrenewable resources such as archeological and fossil sites or special-status species; c) a potential for creating high risk of hazard to the researchers, other park visitors, or environments adjacent to the park; d) extensive collecting of natural materials or unnecessary replication of existing voucher collections; e) need for substantial logistical, administrative, curatorial, or project monitoring support by park staff, or insufficient lead time to allow necessary review and consultation; f) conducting investigator lacks scientific institutional affiliation and/or recognized experience in conducting scientific research; and g) lacking sufficient scientific detail for justification.

Analysis: Scope

Despite the fact that the scope of the CBD is limited to materials of biological origin that include functional units of heredity such as DNA and RNA, in practice, the scope of most ABS laws examined in this section is broader, including biological (specimens and parts of specimens), genetic (DNA and RNA), and biochemical (molecules, combination of molecules, and extracts) resources. The scope of most of these ABS policies also applies to traditional knowledge and is adamant about restricting access to human genetic resources and their derivatives. This broad scope has caused difficulties in countries such as Colombia and the Philippines (see Chapters 4 and 6). Also most policies include provisions excluding the use and exchange of genetic resources made by indigenous communities.

The main implication of Article 15(3) of the CBD is that *ex situ* genetic resources collected before the CBD entered into force are not covered by it. Therefore, some experts argue that pre-CBD *ex situ* collections of genetic resources should not be covered by the scope of ABS laws or policies (TEN KATE and LAIRD 1999, see Chapter 11). However, in practice, most ABS policies cover these collections. In any case, procedures to access to pre or post-CBD *ex situ* collections have not been clearly defined by the ABS polices presented in this section. Ownership of these collections is still controversial.

Except for the Philippines (draft Guidelines for Bioprospecting Activities), access to agricultural genetic resources is covered by the scope of ABS polices of all of these countries. So far Australia, Colombia, Costa Rica, Ecuador, Malaysia, Nicaragua, Peru, and Thailand have signed or acceded to the FAO ITPGRFA. The USA also signed it, but there is little probability that the USA Congress will ratify it. In any case, the FAO ITPGRFA entered into force on 29 June 2004 and present evidence indicates that these countries (except for the USA) will exclude the food and forage crops listed in Annex 1 of the ITPGRFA from the scope of their national ABS laws and policies.

Access Procedure

Obtaining access can be a long, confusing, and cumbersome process. Access permits may have to be obtained from several regional and local agencies that administer the same resource. In addition, bioprospectors may have to negotiate with several providers of genetic resources and traditional knowledge. This bureaucracy and overlapping of functions can lead to high transaction costs and long processing times for required permits. This section discusses the main similarities and differences regarding access procedures of the selected countries and presents the access definitions proposed by some countries in their ABS laws and policies.

Australia: Draft EPBCAR

Access to biological resources is defined as the collection process and use of organisms, their parts, genetic material, and biochemical make-up for conservation, commercial, industrial, or taxonomic research purposes. According to the draft regulations bioprospectors (with commercial and noncommercial purposes) have to obtain a permit[16] to access biological resources in Commonwealth areas and establish benefit-sharing agreements with the providers[17] of these resources. Permits are valid for a maximum of three years and the cost of a permit is the same for all applicants (national or international, commercial or noncommercial): $50 AUD for access and no payment for a transfer of the permit or variation or revocation of a permit condition. Benefits are to be negotiated on a case-by-case basis and the benefit-sharing agreement takes effect only if a permit is issued. The regulations establish that bioprospectors have to submit applications for access permits to the Secretary of the Department of the Environment and Heritage.

Once the Secretary has received the benefit-sharing agreement (including the PIC requirement) and the permit application, he or she must give a report to the Minister for the Environment and Heritage within 30 days of their receipt. This time can be extended if the authorities require the following information: a) whether the environmental impact assessment (EIA) (if required) was undertaken and completed; b) relevant information from the Commonwealth department or agency; c) additional information about the proposed benefit-sharing agreement; d) whether bioprospectors complied with the regulations requiring consultation with the providers of genetic resources; e) the views of any representative of the Aboriginal and Torres Strait Islander body within the meaning of the Native Title Act of 1993; and f) whether the access provider has received independent legal advice about the regulation. If the Minister decides not to grant the permit, the bioprospector can appeal through the courts under the 1997 Administrative Decisions (Judicial Review) Act. Detailed administrative arrangements for the handling of access applications can be expected to be developed once the regulations are enacted

Under this regulation, the Minister may declare that the permit provisions do not apply to biological resources if: a) these resources are held in a collection by a Commonwealth department or agency and there are reasonable grounds to believe that access to this collection is administered consistently with the purpose of the regulations and b) there are reasonable grounds to believe that access to the resources is controlled by another Commonwealth department or agency, self-governing territory, or state law, consistent with the purpose of the regulations. Due to ownership issues access procedures to *ex situ* collections have not been defined yet. Holders of such collections and the Department will discuss potential solutions to this problem (see Chapter 9).

Colombia, Ecuador, and Peru: Decision 391

Access is defined as obtaining and using *ex situ* and *in situ* genetic resources, their derivatives, and associated knowledge with research, bioprospecting, conservation, industrial application, and commercial use, among others. Decision 391 proposes an access contract to be negotiated between the bioprospector and the Competent National Authority (CNA) in the member country where resources are sought. Prior to the negotiation of the contract the bioprospector has to present an application for access to the relevant CNA. The application must include: a) information about the applicant, including its legal capacity to enter into a contract; b) the identity of the supplier of genetic or biological resources and their derivatives and/or of the associated intangible component (or knowledge); c) the identity of the national support institution or individual; d) the identity and curriculum vitae of the project leader and team; e) the nature of the access activity being requested; and f) the area in which the access will be made including the geographic coordinates. The application must include a project proposal based on a model provided by the CNA. Then, the CNA has 30 working days (extendable to 60) to evaluate the application. If the CNA is satisfied with the application, it is placed on the official record and nonconfidential information is available for public scrutiny in the national official gazette. Otherwise, the application may be returned to the applicant for more information or denied.

A successful application will lead to the negotiation of the "access contract". The parties to the contract are the applicant and the CNA. The CNA also needs to take into account the interests of other Andean countries and of the suppliers of the biological resources and intangible component (traditional knowledge) in the negotiation of the access contract. Therefore, the applicant must negotiate an annex contract with the supplier of the knowledge and an accessory contract with the supplier of the biological resource that contains the biochemical or genetic component. The provider of the biological resource can be the holder of the land or the *ex situ* conservation center where the biological resource is found. Accessory contracts can also be signed with national support institutions that are not included in the access contract. Annex and accessory contracts cannot authorize access to the resource by themselves. Access is only granted through the access contract negotiated with the CNA (see Chapter 4). Peru's Law No. 27811 endorses the use of an annex contract or license.

Under this law, commercial bioprospectors have to identify the community or communities that hold the collective knowledge and sign a license with them. Such a license has to be registered before the Peruvian National Institute for the Defense and Protection of Traditional Knowledge (INDECOPI) (PERUVIAN CONGRESS 2002).

Costa Rica: The Law of Biodiversity
Access to biochemical and genetic elements is defined as the action of obtaining samples from *in situ* or *ex situ* elements of indigenous or domestic biodiversity and their associated knowledge, for the purposes of basic research, economic benefit, or bioprospecting. Bioprospecting is defined as the systematic search, classification, and research (with commercial purposes) of new sources of chemical compounds, genes, proteins, microorganisms, and other products that have present or potential economic value with commercial purposes.

Under this law local and foreign bioprospectors are required to obtain access permits to obtain genetic or biochemical resources and their associated knowledge. These are valid for three years and can be renewed, but are not transferable. First, in conformity with the "General Access Procedure" (GAP)[18] interested parties must register with the Technical Office (TO) of the National Commission for the Management of Biodiversity (CONAGEBIO). The application includes: a) identification of the interested party; b) identification of the responsible researcher; c) exact location of place where samples will be collected; d) the elements of biodiversity that will be the subject of the investigation; e) the owner and manager or holder of the premises; f) a list of activities, aims, and purposes; and g) an address for legal notifications. Later, the PIC must be negotiated between the applicant and the owner of the conservation area or indigenous land, resources, or *ex situ* collections.

The permits will contain a certificate of origin, permission or prohibition to extract samples, periodic reporting obligation, monitoring and control, conditions relative to resulting property, and any another applicable condition stated by the TO. Different requirements are established for those who request permits for noncommercial bioprospecting[19] and for those who need access permits for occasional or continuing economic utilization.[20] At this stage there is no information about the duration of these procedures. In any case, the current scheme empowers the owners of the lands where biological resources are found to negotiate contracts (by means of the PIC) with bioprospectors.

In case of *ex situ* collections, different rules will be proposed for framework agreements that authorize the transfer of multiple materials. In such cases material transfer agreements (MTAS) will have to be standardized and approved by the TO. The Law of Biodiversity also requires all holders of *ex situ* genetic resources to register with the TO. Bioprospectors will have to obtain a permit in order to access *ex situ* genetic resources. However, no procedure has been defined yet because of the complexi-

ties associated with the holders of genetic resources and also because there are other national laws not necessarily related to access that regulate *ex situ* collections. The GAP provides 6 months for the drafting of an access procedure for *ex situ* genetic resources and establishes a moratorium on the access of *ex situ* genetic resources until such procedure is adopted.

The Law of Biodiversity requires a determination of the administrative fee. The GAP states that this fee is a fifth of the minimum wage. After the TO issues a certificate of origin, it publishes the requests and final resolutions on its website within eight calendar days. An EIA can be requested by the TO. Its evaluation is the responsibility of the National Technical Secretariat (see Chapter 5).

Malaysia:
Draft federal bill on access to genetic resources
The draft bill defines access as all activities relating to bioprospecting, collection, commercial utilization, research, and development of biological resources or the associated relevant community knowledge and innovations. If the draft bill is adopted, both foreign and local bioprospectors will have to follow the same basic access procedure in order to obtain access to genetic resources for commercial purposes. But international bioprospectors will have additional conditions for approval of the access application. For example, the application will require foreign bioprospectors to have a local collaborating organization to both sponsor the collection and be responsible for actions of the collector. The local organization will also participate in the collection, research, and development of samples collected.

Both national and international bioprospectors will be required to sign an access agreement with the competent authority and the relevant resource provider. However, the relevant authority may decide that the restrictions relating to access to resources shall not apply to Malaysian researchers conducting noncommercial bioprospecting activities. The procedure for foreign scientists who want to obtain access for noncommercial purposes is still not clear at this point. The financial costs of applying for access have not been determined yet, but it is not likely to deter bioprospectors from applying.

There shall be no access to biological resources or community knowledge and innovation without an access license granted by the competent authority. Information required in the application for the license includes: a) identification of the collector; b) identification of material to be collected or knowledge to be accessed; c) identification of collection sites; d) quantity and intended use of the resource; e) time when the access activity is to be carried out; e) EIA; f) PIC certificate; g) benefit-sharing arrangements; and h) identification of the local collaborator or sponsor (a Malaysian institution). This information can be made available to the public. Once the application has been reviewed it can be approved, returned to the applicant if more information is required, or rejected. A decision can be appealed at any time within three months of the date of receipt of the decision. Access procedures to *ex situ* collections have not been defined yet (see Chapter 11).

Mexico: EEEPGA, WGA, SFDGA, and draft LAUBGR

EEEPGA, WGA, and SFDGA do not include an access definition. But collection of biological resources under any of these laws requires a permit from the Secretariat of Environment and Natural Resources (SEMARNAT). Under Article 87 and 87 BIS of EEEPGA, local and foreign bioprospectors have to apply to SEMARNAT in order to obtain access to genetic resources for scientific (noncommercial), economic (for reproduction and commercial activities) and biotechnology purposes. Under Article 87 of EEEPGA and Article 97 of WGA access for scientific or noncommercial purposes requires a permit or a license for a researcher with a specific line of work. Both laws require the PIC of the landowner, report submissions, and deposit of at least one duplicate of the material collected in a local institution or scientific collection. Authorization under these laws cannot be extended to commercial purposes, and nonconfidential research results must be available to the public. However, Mexican legislation recognizes that scientific or academic collections can later be used for industrial or commercial applications. If this is the case norm NOM-126-ECOL-2000 mandates a new declaration stating a change of purpose, thus setting the stage for new PIC and ABS contracts. Chapter 6 suggests that this measure has a low transaction cost because the change in the PIC and the negotiation of the ABS contract would happen only after a finding that the biological resource has a commercial application. However, an argument could be made that under controversial social and political circumstances (see Chapter 3) the costs of the delay that would be generated after a discovered commercial application could be very high.

Under Article 101 of SFDGA collectors and users of forest biological resources for scientific, economic, or biotechnological purposes have to apply for authorization to SEMARNAT. This application must include the PIC of the owner of the land that provided the resources. It should be noted that under SFDGA and article 87 BIS of EEEPGA collectors must present the PIC in order to obtain government authorization. In contrast, under article 87 of EEEPGA and WGA, the PIC is not required to obtain this authorization but it is required before collecting activities are initiated (see Chapter 6).

According to Article 102 of SFDGA, commercial and noncommercial bioprospectors that use traditional knowledge must submit an agreement to SEMARNAT that includes the PIC of the indigenous community that provided the knowledge. This agreement must also acknowledge the property rights of indigenous communities to their knowledge. SEMARNAT evaluates the application and ensures that a benefit-sharing agreement is negotiated with the providers of genetic resources. The 2001 Rural Sustainable Development Act (RSDA) gives priority rights to indigenous and local communities for obtaining permits and authorizations under either EEEPGA or WGA. Under SFDGA, collections of forest biological resources carried out by public entities of the federal, state, or municipal governments or the owner of the land, need only to submit a notification in accordance with the pertinent official Mexican norm and the consent of the owner of the land (SEMARNAT 2003).

On the other hand, the draft LAUBGR defines access as the action of obtaining samples from *in situ* or *ex situ* elements of indigenous or domestic biodiversity and their associated knowledge with economic or bioprospecting purposes. The draft law would regulate only commercial activities, leaving noncommercial applications to the current regulatory framework. The access procedure includes the following steps: a) the applicant must obtain an authorization from a Federal Executive Authority (SEMARNAT); b) an access contract must be signed with SEMARNAT, the provider of the biological and genetic resource, and the provider of the traditional knowledge; c) if relevant, an authorization must be obtained either for collection done by an *ex situ* conservation body, transport to any area not specified in the access agreement, export of the material collected, or transfer of the rights and obligations given by the access authorization. The draft bill, however, does not define the procedure and requirements for authorization for *ex situ* collections. Requirements for an EIA are not clearly regulated and the participation of Mexicans in research and development is required (GACETA PARLAMENTARIA 2001).

Nicaragua: Draft Law of Biodiversity

Access is defined as the action of obtaining samples from biological and genetic resources and their associated knowledge, practices, and innovations. Details about access procedures for genetic resources found in *ex situ* and *in situ* conditions have not been defined yet. However, the draft Law of Biodiversity states that all domestic and foreign bioprospectors will have to obtain an authorization from the National Biodiversity Institute in order to obtain access to biological and genetic resources. Such authorization must include: a) the PIC of the provider of the biological and genetic resource as well as the traditional knowledge and b) a description about the intent to sign accessory contracts with local or foreign organizations or a description of accessory contracts signed with these parties before the law came into force. The authorization will also require a permit showing that an EIA was carried out (if required). Access to genetic resources may be denied if: a) the access application is determined to include false information; b) the applicant has attempted to access genetic resources illegally in the country or overseas; c) access activities cause the endangerment or extinction of species; or d) access activities cause ecological, social, cultural, or economic impacts that cannot be mitigated. Bioprospectors will also have to deposit duplicates of specimens collected in local *ex situ* conservation centers. The draft law also states that "framework agreements" will be established between the government and universities or other users of genetic resources for noncommercial purposes (MARENA 2002). The draft law of biodiversity implements Article 63 of GLENR which requires an authorization for studies on biotechnology (MARENA 1996). This authorization has to be given by the national competent authority which in this case is the National Biodiversity Institute.

Philippines: EO 247 and Wildlife Act

EO 247 does not define the concept of access. However, it can be argued that this policy uses the concept "prospecting or bioprospecting" as a proxy for "access". Bioprospecting is defined as the research, collection, and utilization of biological and genetic resources for purposes of applying the knowledge derived from these resources to scientific and commercial purposes. Under EO 247, local and foreign bioprospectors must apply for access to genetic resources for commercial and noncommercial purposes. Applications for Academic Research Agreements (ARA) or Commercial Research Agreements (CRA) are submitted to the Technical Secretariat for an initial evaluation. Then, they are passed to the Inter-Agency Committee on Biological and Genetic Resources (IACBGR) and the IACBGR makes a recommendation to the pertinent agency. Foreign applicants must involve a local institution in the research process. EO 247 does not provide for a specific timeframe within which to process applications. However, it usually takes about five months or longer because the IACBGR is required to meet once every four months, although the chairman can call for special meetings. Also, the application process is often slow due to delays in obtaining the PIC. Depending on whether it is an ARA or a CRA that is sought, certain distinctions are incorporated in the application process (see Table 1 of Chapter 7).

The Wildlife Act, however, modified EO 247 substantially and excluded the collection and use of biological resources for academic or scientific purposes. Therefore, an ARA is no longer required. The Wildlife Act states that the collection and use of biological resources for academic or scientific purposes can be undertaken through a free permit. The Department of Environment and Natural Resources (DENR), the Department of Agriculture (DA), and the Palawan Council for Sustainable Development (PCSD) are in charge of implementing the Wildlife Act (P. Benavidez, pers. comm. February 2004).

Under the 2004 draft Guidelines for Bioprospecting Activities (see endnote 10) commercial bioprospectors must pay a fee of $3,000 USD for each Bioprospecting Undertaking (which replaces the CRA of EO 247) and such fee may be modified depending on whether the applicant is a national and other criteria. In addition, bioprospectors must pay $1,000 USD per collection site annually during the collection period. According to the guidelines access to biological resources does not imply automatic access to traditional knowledge associated with these resources. A bioprospector wishing to access associated traditional

knowledge must state this purpose in the research proposal. The draft Guidelines provide a detailed procedure for the negotiation and execution of the Bioprospecting Undertaking with an emphasis on standardizing and streamlining the procedure for access. The application must include the proposal and documentation that all required items (such as PIC and any benefit-sharing terms negotiated and approved by the resource providers) have been obtained. The agency receiving the application (the Protected Areas Wildlife Bureau (PAWB) of DENR, the Bureau of Fisheries and Aquatic Resources, or PCSD) will draft the Bioprospecting Undertaking incorporating the terms agreed upon by the applicant and the resource providers and forward it to their respective or joint technical committees for review. Their final evaluation must be completed within 15 days of receipt of application and it is forwarded to the appropriate agency signatories. The goal is for the agency decision to be made within one month from the submission of the application. If the Bioprospecting Undertaking is approved, the applicant will sign it along with the appropriate signatories, respecting the terms negotiated with resource providers, and including the standard terms and conditions under the guidelines. Bioprospecting may then proceed once the required performance and rehabilitation bond is posted.

Samoa: CABSSBR

This policy does not define the concept of access. Bioprospectors must submit an application form to the Director of the Department of Lands, Surveys and Environment (DLSE). There is an application fee of $500 USD and 75% of it is returned if the application is unsuccessful (the remaining 25% is used for processing costs). Upon receipt of the application, DLSE is required to consult with pertinent government bodies and publicize the application. The evaluation process can take up to 20 working days. The access permit is valid for a year and it can be renewed for an additional year. The applicant must also obtain an export permit in order to export any specimen out of Samoa (DLSE 2000). CABSSBR does not provide details about access procedures for *ex situ* genetic resources and it does not differentiate between commercial and noncommercial collectors of biological resources.

Thailand: PVPA, RFSRCFA, and APPTMI

These laws and policies do not define the concept of access. However, access procedures are quite detailed. Before entering the country foreign bioprospectors have to apply to NRCT for permission to conduct research in Thailand.[21] According to regulation B.E. 2525 of NRCT, bioprospectors have to fill out form NRCT-01 and submit it to NRCT no less than 90 days prior to entering the country. Together with this application NRCT requires two letters of endorsement from local researchers. A letter of permission from NRCT is required to obtain the visa at the Royal Thai Embassy or Consulate. Within 7 days of arriving in Thailand, the applicant has to report to NRCT, pay a processing fee of $200 Baht per researcher, and obtain an identification card. Then, the applicant can apply for access to genetic resources under the PVPA or RFSRCFA.

Under the PVPA, local and foreign commercial bioprospectors have to file a petition with the Department of Agriculture and then obtain a PIC from the holders of local genetic resources. When wild plant varieties are used, they have to establish a benefit-sharing agreement with the government and sometimes with the provider of the resource (J. Donavanik, pers. comm. January 2003). The act states that collectors of wild plant varieties that have commercial purposes have to present the following information to pertinent authorities: a) the purpose of the collection; b) the amount or quantity of samples of the intended plant variety; c) the obligations of the person to whom permission is granted; d) intellectual property rights which may result from the development, study, experiment, or research activities; e) the amount or rate of, or the term for, the profit sharing under the profit-sharing agreement with respect to products derived from the use of the plant variety thereunder; f) the term of the agreement; g) the revocation of the agreement; h) dispute settlement procedure; and i) other items or particulars as prescribed in the Ministerial Regulation. Collectors of plant material with noncommercial purposes will have to follow a regulation that has yet to be developed by the Plant Variety Protection Commission (THAILAND CONGRESS 1999).

Under RFSRCFA, national and foreign bioprospectors have to submit an application and a "full project proposal" (translated into Thai) to the RFD. RFSRCFA provides 60 days for the review of the application and proposal. A Research Proposal Reviewing Subcommittee (RPRS) and the director of the area where samples will be collected examine these materials and give a recommendation to the Director General of RFD. A positive recommendation will result in an access permit that is submitted to NRCT and then delivered to the applicant. It should be noted that if the proposal has a negative review from the director of the collection area, then the permit could be denied. The final access permit must include the signatures of the Director General of RFD, the secretary of the RPRS, and the Director of the Department of National Parks, Wildlife and Plant Conservation. The RFD will also inform the staff that must accompany bioprospectors during the site visits. Upon reception of the access permit and 15 days before entering the collection site, the applicant must notify the Director General of RFD and local forestry officials (C. Hutacharern, pers. comm. June 2003). The terms of the agreements can vary between one and five years or more, but each agreement has to be reviewed annually to ensure compliance. An application fee must also be paid (CHALERMPONGSE 2001).

Bioprospectors may have to use an MTA in order to obtain access to genetic resources found in *ex situ* collections or in geographical areas not covered by PVPA and RFSRCFA. However, procedures about how to apply for access to genetic resources under MTAS have not been officially stated and they may vary according to the holder of the resource

(J. Donavanik, pers. comm. January 2003).

Under APPTMI, whoever wishes to use traditional knowledge protected in the registrar must apply to the Permanent Secretary of the Ministry of Public Health. APPTMI also protects plants, animals, bacteria, and minerals that are of study and research value, have important economic value or may become extinct. The commercial use or export of these species requires a license from the Permanent Secretary of the Ministry of Public Health (NITTM 2002).

USA: NPS research specimen collection permit

Under NPS regulations, bioprospectors can access national park genetic resources through a collection permit process that has been in place since 1983. The regulations apply to commercial and noncommercial bioprospectors as long as they engage in scientific research activities. Researches must apply for a permit on the National Park Service's Research Permit and Reporting System website.[22] The following information is asked for to successfully complete the application process for such a permit: a) contact information about the applicant *(required)*; b) project title *(required)*; c) purpose of study *(required)*; d) study start and end dates *(required)*; e) identification of any federal funding agencies; f) location of activity in the park; g) method of access; h) names of co-applicants; i) if you are collecting specimens, contact information of repositories; j) a copy of the study proposal; and k) a copy of all peer reviews.

Once the application has been filed (this is equivalent to the PIC), NPS officials and outside experts review its content for issues that include: a) scientific validity; b) researcher and institutional qualifications; c) benefit to the NPS and the public; d) actual or potential impacts to park resources; and e) impacts on visitor experiences, wilderness, and safety. Reviewers may recommend denial or acceptance of the permit application at this stage. If accepted, the benefits and risks of the proposal are analyzed under the National Environmental Policy Act (NEPA). Then the reviewers make a recommendation to the Superintendent or designee to approve or reject the permit request. If the application is approved, the permit and attached conditions (including requirement for annual accomplishment report) are sent to applicant for signature. If the application is rejected, there is an opportunity for revising and resubmitting the application. This process usually takes less than three months (see Chapter 8).

Analysis: Access Procedure

Most of the above laws and policies define access as the action of collecting and using biological, biochemical, and genetic resources and their associated knowledge for commercial and noncommercial purposes. All of the laws and policies reviewed in this section have in common at least the following main steps for access: a) submission of an access application to a designated national competent authority; b) review of the application; c) approval or denial of the application (if denied there is a legal recourse to appeal); and d) negotiation of PIC and benefit-sharing requirements. However, the length of the access process varies across countries and depends largely on the length of negotiation of PIC and benefit-sharing agreements with the providers of genetic resources and traditional knowledge and in some cases with national authorities.

But should States be directly involved in the benefit-sharing negotiation of each bioprospecting project? Should they be parties to each benefit-sharing contract? Or should this negotiation be carried out only by the direct providers of genetic resources and traditional knowledge? This is a controversial issue. Social protest in countries such as Mexico demands the need for a strong State intervention not only in the negotiation of these benefits but also in all stages of implementation of bioprospecting projects (see Chapter 6). Involving the State's bureaucracy in the negotiation of benefit-sharing provisions may lead to inefficiencies and high transaction costs as suggested by Chapter 6. Perhaps, State intervention in the negotiation of benefits should be focused on an advisory and training role. For example, countries such as Australia have proposed independent legal advice and training programs to improve the negotiation capacity of local providers of genetic resources and traditional knowledge. In addition to this, States could be more efficient by setting a minimum amount of royalties and other benefit-sharing criteria (see the section on Benefit Sharing and Compensation Mechanisms) for those bioprospectors that are likely to obtain significant benefits from local genetic resources.

While most countries require the PIC (see next section) from local communities, one country (Thailand) does not require bioprospectors to obtain PIC from local communities, only from government officials. Evidently, obtaining the PIC from local communities increases not only the length of the access process but also transactions costs. This has been the case in the Philippines (see Chapter 7). Additional access requirements of countries such as Thailand and Malaysia are also likely to increase the length of application and transaction costs. However, since national ABS policies of these and many other countries require a local collaborator to be involved in the different steps of the research process, having a local counterpart that is familiar with local costumes and bureaucracy may not only help expedite the access process, but also bring legitimacy and transparency to the project.

Recently several scientists have argued that ABS policies restrict noncommercial scientific research activities such as taxonomic collections (GRAJAL 1999). Some countries such as Costa Rica, Mexico, Nicaragua, and the Philippines have been trying to differentiate between access for commercial and noncommercial purposes. The line between commercial and noncommercial bioprospecting is still blurred; however, these countries are taking steps in the right direction.

Most national and regional ABS laws and policies regulate access to biological, genetic, and biochemical components found in *in situ* conditions nationwide. The main

implication of such a comprehensive scope is that these ABS laws and policies apply to national and international representatives of the pharmaceutical, seed, crop protection, botanical medicine, food, and all other industries that use biological, genetic, and biochemical elements to develop processes and products. Therefore, to deal efficiently with a large number of applicants, these countries may have to design more practical access criteria. These criteria would translate into practical access procedures that differentiate between an industry that uses modern biotechnology techniques such as genetic engineering and combinatorial chemistry and one that uses standard procedures to extract aromatic oils. Otherwise, the policies may be unenforceable as they try to regulate access to millions of local small firms that use, for example, plant material for the development of oils, infusions, and other common remedies that can be developed rapidly with relatively unsophisticated technology.

Access procedures for *ex situ* genetic resources remain a gray area in all countries due to ownership issues. For now, it seems that applications for *ex situ* collections in the countries examined in this section will be considered on their own merits with respect to a range of factors. These include the ownership of the material from which the *ex situ* accessions were obtained and the circumstances under which the material passed into the possession of the *ex situ* holder, including possible terms and conditions proposed by the holder (i.e., gene bank or botanical garden) of the *ex situ* genetic resources. For example, *ex situ* conservation centers such as the ones administered by FAO have adopted MTAS as a standard practice to exchange genetic resources (C. Qualset, pers. comm. January 2004).

Prior Informed Consent (PIC)

The CBD states that access to genetic resources should be granted on mutually agreed terms and subject to PIC procedures and this principle is endorsed by the laws and policies reviewed in this section. Under most regional and national ABS laws and policies, in contrast to the CBD mandate, PIC must be obtained not only from the designated government authorities but also from indigenous peoples and the landowners concerned. For this summary and analysis, PIC is defined as the consent obtained by the applicant from the designated government authorities, local community, indigenous people, the protected area or *ex situ* collection manager, or private land owner after disclosing fully the intent and scope of the bioprospecting activity, in a language and process understandable to all, and before any collecting of samples or knowledge is undertaken.

Australia: Draft EPBCAR
In Australia, aboriginal groups own significant areas (42% of the Northern Territory and 27% of South Australia). Therefore, the regulations mandate the use of PIC in order to get access to genetic resources and knowledge provided by communities found in these areas. If the access provider is the owner of indigenous peoples' land or a native title

holder for the area, the access provider must have given informed consent to the agreement. Chapter 9 lists key issues that the Minister of the Environment and Heritage must take into account to ensure that bioprospectors will comply with PIC requirements. These include making sure that the access provider had sufficient time to review the application and to consult with relevant people about the pros and cons of the application.

Colombia, Ecuador, and Peru: Decision 391
Decision 391 requires PIC from the pertinent government authority and the provider of genetic resources, their derivatives, traditional knowledge, innovation, or practices. PIC from the providers of genetic resources or traditional knowledge is provided to the government authority in the access application (see previous section). When access to genetic resources includes access to traditional knowledge an annex contract signed by the provider of the knowledge will be integrated into the access contract. In certain cases, however, (subject to national legislation) the national authority may also sign the annex. In Peru, for example, Law No. 27811 requires academic and commercial bioprospectors to obtain the PIC from organizations that represent the interest of the community or communities that hold the collective knowledge (PERUVIAN CONGRESS 2002).

Costa Rica: The Law of Biodiversity
The legislation is not clear, but it is assumed that the PIC will be formalized in a private contract as described by the GAP. The role of the TO is to endorse the contract. A separate PIC will be obtained from individuals, government, or nongovernmental organizations that own lands or marine resources and provide traditional knowledge. Access to flora and fauna found on private lands may also need authorizations from state entities, particularly in cases of endangered species. In cases where collections are made in conservation areas, the PIC and the respective agreement are enough to obtain the access permit (see Chapter 5).

Malaysia:
Draft federal bill on access to genetic resources
The pertinent authority shall establish an appropriate process for securing PIC of the resource provider that may be affected by the access application. The authority shall prescribe the process after consultation with relevant parties in order to ensure and verify that PIC is properly obtained. The consultation procedure must include at least the following requirements: a) participation of representatives of the indigenous and local communities and b) wide and effective dissemination of relevant information to the providers of samples or traditional knowledge and other interested parties on the proposed access activity (see Chapter 11).

Mexico: EEEPGA, WGA, SFDGA, and draft LAUBGR
EEEPGA requires two PICs, one given by the Mexican Government in the form of a collecting permit and another given by the owners of the land. The first PIC protects the

interest of society and the second protects the interest of the owner of the land. EEEPGA does not regulate access to traditional knowledge, therefore it does not require any PIC from the provider of traditional knowledge (see Chapter 6). While Article 97 of WGA requires only the PIC of the owner of the land (SEMARNAT 2000), Articles 101 and 102 of SFDGA require the PICs from the owner of the property and from the indigenous community that provided traditional knowledge used for commercial and noncommercial purposes (SEMARNAT 2003). The draft LAUBGR includes a PIC requirement from the government and providers of both genetic resources and traditional knowledge (GACETA PARLAMENTARIA 2001).

Nicaragua: Draft Law of Biodiversity
Bioprospectors are required to obtain the PIC of the providers of traditional knowledge and the holders of the land where these resources are found. The consent has to be clearly stated in a PIC contract established between the bioprospector and provider of the genetic resource or knowledge. The contract does not give exclusive use over the resource or knowledge. The provider is the rightful owner of the knowledge and has the right to establish contracts over the same component with other parties. The bioprospector cannot transfer the knowledge to other parties without the prior consent of the community. This contract will be effective once the access contract established between the government and the bioprospector is signed (MARENA 2002). The PIC requirement of the draft Law of Biodiversity is consistent with Articles 62 and 63 of GLENR that protect the interests of the providers of genetic resources and traditional knowledge (MARENA 1996).

Philippines: EO 247 and Wildlife Act
According to EO 247 and the Wildlife Act, bioprospecting activities, under a CRA, can be allowed only upon obtaining the PIC of the community or individual that provides the genetic resource or the knowledge. Before conducting any actual bioprospecting activity at the site, the researcher must obtain a PIC certificate. Bioprospecting is permitted in protected areas with the PIC of the Protected Area Management Board (PAMB), in the lands of indigenous and local communities with their PIC, and on privately owned land with the PIC of the landowner. Under EO 247 the provider of the PIC had to issue the certificate within 60 days from the submission of the proposal. The Wildlife Act, however, removed this requirement.

Under EO 247, applicants for a CRA must complete the following steps in order to secure a PIC certificate: a) submit copies of the research proposal to the head of the local community, city, or municipal mayor of the local government unit, PAMB, or private landowner concerned in a language or dialect understandable to them; b) inform the local community, PAMB, or the private landowner concerned of the intention to conduct bioprospecting within the area through various media advertisements or direct communication; c) post a notice in a conspicuous place one week prior to the holding of a community assembly;

d) hold community consultation; e) obtain certificates of compliance from the head of the local community, municipal or city mayor, PAMB, or private landowner upon determination that applicant has undergone the process required by law; and f) submit PIC certificate to the IACBGR together with proofs of compliance with the PIC process. The research proposal presented to the provider of the genetic resource or traditional knowledge must include the purpose, methodology, duration of the activity; designate the species and quantity to be used or taken; describe the proposal for equitable sharing of benefits, if any, to all parties concerned; and state that the proposed activity will not affect traditional uses of the resource (see Chapter 7).

This procedure was slightly altered by the 2004 draft Guidelines for Bioprospecting Activities that will implement the Wildlife Act if approved. The necessary steps include notification through a letter of intent (including research proposal) to the resource providers and the holding of a community assembly at which the proposal is presented giving a very detailed description of the activity and assurances that traditional uses or consumption of the resource will not be affected. The next steps depend on the issuer of the PIC: for the PAMB, the chair will sign the PIC certificate upon authority granted through an appropriate Resolution passed within 30 days after the consultation favorably granting such consent; the private landowner, or other concerned agencies, must issue the PIC certificate within 30 days after the consultation; and in the case of indigenous peoples, the issuance of the PIC certificate is governed by pertinent rules and regulations under the Republic Act No. 8371 also known as the Indigenous Peoples' Rights Act. Access to traditional knowledge must be explicitly reflected in the certificate. The guidelines provide a standard PIC form. Under the Wildlife Act, collectors and users of biological resources for noncommercial purposes will also have to obtain PIC from the providers of these resources. No PIC procedure has been officially adopted yet for this kind of collections, but it is likely to involve fewer steps and requirements than the one proposed for collectors that have commercial purposes (P. Benavidez, pers. comm. February 2004).

Samoa: CABSSBR
PIC is obtained from the government when the access application is submitted to the Division of Environment and Conservation of the Department of Lands, Surveys, and Environment (DLSE 2000). A final decision on the application is made by the Minister of Lands, Surveys, and Environment who can require the applicant to provide evidence of the prior informed consent of the resource owner (or person in effective control of the resources). Bioprospecting activities carried out in private or customary land (85% of the land area of the country) will require PIC from the landowners.

Thailand: PVPA, RFSRCFA, and APPTMI
Foreign bioprospectors must obtain initial PIC from a designated government authority (i.e., NRCT) through the permission letter that is required to obtain a visa. Under

PVPA anyone who collects domestic plant varieties, wild plant varieties, or any part of such plant varieties for the purposes of variety development, education, experiment, or research for commercial interest shall obtain permission from the competent official in the Ministry of Agriculture (THAILAND CONGRESS 1999). Under RFSRCFA and APPTMI, bioprospectors obtain PIC from government officials by applying to the RFD and Ministry of Public Health respectively (C. Hutacharern, pers. comm. June 2003). It should be emphasized that the PVPA, RFSRCFA, and APPTMI do not require bioprospectors to obtain PIC from communities living in collection areas

USA: NPS research specimen collection permit
The PIC is implemented through the detailed permit application and approval process now instituted throughout the NPS (see previous section and Chapter 8).

Analysis: PIC
As interpreted from the CBD, bioprospectors must obtain PIC and this is incorporated in the policies and laws for all the countries reviewed in this section. Procedures for obtaining PIC in these countries are usually initiated when the access application is submitted to the designated government authorities (see previous section). ABS policies of these countries, except for Thailand and the USA, also require PIC from the providers of genetic resources and traditional knowledge. However, information about how to obtain PIC from traditional communities remains unclear in all countries except for the Philippines (EO 247 and Wildlife Act) and Peru (Law No. 27811). Thailand is the only country that requires foreign bioprospectors to obtain PIC twice from government authorities. The first one is obtained prior to entering the country through the letter of permission required for the visa. The second one is obtained through the application process made to the agency that administers the resource that will be accessed. Unlike the other countries, the USA does not have a designated government authority regulating access to genetic resources that provides the PIC of the State. In the specific case of the NPS lands, bioprospectors have to obtain the consent from the NPS and such consent, which is analogous to the PIC, is obtained through the permit application of the NPS.

Despite the fact that PIC requirements are likely to be expensive and cumbersome to obtain for many bioprospectors, the motive for the requirement is twofold: a) PIC is a direct consequence of countries being sovereign to determine whether or not to grant access to their genetic resources and b) PIC will help to ensure that benefits are shared equitably, give transparency to bioprospecting projects, and contribute to their success. However, bioprospectors are likely to run into difficulties and challenges while trying to obtain PIC from local communities and government agencies. These include: a) identifying the representatives of the communities and assessing their representation power and capacity; b) identifying all the parties affected by the project; c) presenting the bioprospecting project, legal concepts (IPRs, property, etc.), and benefits for the community in a form and manner understandable to the target group; d) identifying and presenting the implications of the project for the community; e) identifying communities who share the same knowledge; and f) obtaining the PIC from several local and national government agencies that administer the same biological resource. In any case, bioprospectors have to keep in mind that traditional communities and governments may choose to deny access (see Chapters 3, 4, and 6) and this is a legitimate decision based on the national sovereignty recognized by the CBD and the ABS laws and policies described above.

Benefit Sharing and Compensation Mechanisms

Biodiversity conservation and sustainable use, research and training opportunities, public education and awareness, transfer of technology, exchange of information, and technical and scientific cooperation are some of the key goals of the CBD that may become operational in the context of bioprospecting projects. These are also some of the benefits that are usually negotiated in access and benefit-sharing contracts[23]. Contracts formalize this relationship and attempt to ensure that pharmaceutical, seed, agricultural, biotechnology and other companies compensate researchers, collectors, and collaborators from countries with great biological, genetic, and cultural diversity. Trust funds have also been proposed as a mechanism to facilitate the equitable distribution of benefits.

Australia: Draft EPBCAR

Benefit-sharing agreements must be negotiated at the beginning of a project, rather than after a lead has been identified. In 2004 or 2005, the Minister is likely to present a model benefit-sharing agreement, but its use by bioprospectors will not be mandatory. These agreements must provide for reasonable monetary and nonmonetary benefit-sharing arrangements covering matters such as upfront payments for samples, royalties, milestone payments, and participation of Australians in research activities. They must also recognize and value any indigenous knowledge given by the access provider. A trust fund has also been proposed to facilitate the compensation of indigenous knowledge, but no decisions have been made so far to facilitate its development. The regulations also state that an agreement may be both a benefit-sharing agreement and an indigenous land-use agreement under the Native Title Act (see Chapter 9).

Colombia, Ecuador, and Peru: Decision 391

Commercial and noncommercial bioprospectors have to negotiate an access agreement with the government and an accessory or annex agreement with the providers of the genetic resource or the traditional knowledge respectively. These agreements have to address at least the following benefit-sharing issues: a) establishment of conditions for a just and equitable sharing of benefits generated from access; b) promotion of the participation of local scientists in order to enhance local scientific, technical, and technological capacities; and c) strengthening of mechanisms to transfer knowledge and technologies including environmentally sound biotechnologies. Bioprospectors are also obliged to deposit duplicates of samples collected in sites designated by the pertinent national authority (ANDEAN COMMUNITY 1996).

Under Decision 391, the national authority may also establish framework access contracts for projects carried out by universities, research centers, or researchers for noncommercial purposes. Details about requirements for this type of contracts are defined according to local legislation. For example, the draft of the Peruvian regulation on genetic resources states that universities and academic research centers (based in Peru) may use a framework access contract[24] to access genetic resources as long as they comply with the following requirements: a) participation of national professionals in collecting and research activities; b) indication by the research program of proposed methodologies for the collection of samples; c) commitment to inform local authorities about research advances, results, and publications generated from access activities; d) plan to restrict the transfer of samples to third parties; e) provisions about potential IPRs on products or processes derived from the use of genetic resources and their derivatives; f) background information about the situation of the genetic resources, their derivatives, and associated knowledge that are being accessed; g) information about access risks, including uses and value of the resource; h) provisions about collection and sample payments; and i) deposition of duplicates of collected samples in organizations identified by the national authority (these organizations may loan these duplicates to foreign partners only for taxonomy studies) (INRENA 2001).

Decision 391 recognizes the rights and decision-making capacity of indigenous, black, and local communities with regards to their traditional knowledge, practices, and innovations connected with genetic resources and their derivatives (ANDEAN COMMUNITY 1996). Under Peru's Law No. 27811 commercial bioprospectors have to sign an annex contract or license that provides at least the following benefit-sharing obligations: a) an up-front payment or its equivalent that contributes to the sustainable development of indigenous communities; b) royalties no less than 5% of the gross sale of products (before taxes) derived from the use of collective knowledge accessed by the bioprospector; and c) the strengthening of local capacities of indigenous communities in relation to their collective knowledge associated with biological diversity (PERUVIAN CONGRESS 2002).

Decision 391 states that the member countries shall set up trust funds or other financial mechanisms to distribute the benefits derived from bioprospecting initiatives. Neither Colombia, Ecuador, nor Peru has so far received economic benefits that can be channeled to a trust fund. Peru's Law No. 27811, however, creates a trust fund for the development of indigenous peoples. No less than 10% of the gross sales (before taxes) of products derived from the collective knowledge will go to the trust fund (PERUVIAN CONGRESS 2002).

Costa Rica: The Law of Biodiversity

This law regulates the equitable distribution of benefits and the protection of traditional knowledge. In addition to monetary and nonmonetary benefits negotiated among the parties to a bioprospecting initiative, the Law of Biodiversity mandates bioprospectors to pay 10% of the research budget and 50% of the royalties to the National System of Protected Areas, the indigenous representative, or the landholder that provided the genetic, biological, or biochemical resources (see Chapter 5).

Malaysia:
Draft federal bill on access to genetic resources

The draft bill regulates the sharing of benefits derived from the use of genetic resources and traditional knowledge. In determining the nature and combination of benefits from access to either biological resources or traditional knowledge, the pertinent authority shall take into account relevant factors that include: a) the conservation status of the biological resource; b) endemism or rarity of the biological resource; c) the existing, potential, intrinsic, and commercial value of the resource; d) the proposed use of the resource; and e) whether traditional knowledge is involved. In any case, since local organizations must be part of any bioprospecting venture, monetary or nonmonetary benefits are likely to be received by these entities.

Furthermore, a provision of the bill proposes the establishment of a common trust fund to channel benefits derived from the use of traditional knowledge. Therefore, bioprospectors will have to pay to the fund a percentage of the gross sales of any product or process utilizing or incorporating the traditional knowledge. The competent authority and the indigenous or local community will be jointly responsible for the equitable distribution of the monies solely for the benefit of the concerned indigenous or local community. The payment made to the fund will be administered by the national competent authority to promote the wellbeing of the indigenous and local communities and for the conservation and sustainable use of the biological resources (see Chapter 11).

Mexico: EEEPGA, WGA, SFDGA, and draft LAUBGR

Article 87 BIS of the EEEPGA states that owners of genetic or biological resources are entitled to receive a share of benefits derived from the use of these resources. Mexico's EEEPGA does not regulate access to traditional knowledge associated with genetic resources, but it recognizes the need to protect and disseminate the knowledge of indigenous communities in order to promote the conservation and sustainable use of biodiversity (see Chapter 6). Similarly, Article 24 of WGA states that conservation and sustainable use activities of wildlife resources must ensure the protection of traditional knowledge and the participation of rural communities. Furthermore, these activities must encourage the equitable distribution of benefits derived from the use of such knowledge. Under Article 102 of SFDGA bioprospectors that use traditional knowledge must sign a PIC agreement with the indigenous community that provided the knowledge. It is not clear whether this is also a benefit-sharing agreement, however, according to SFDGA this agreement must acknowledge the property rights of the community over its knowledge (SEMARNAT 2003).

Under the draft LAUBGR bioprospectors have to negotiate an access and benefit-sharing contract with SEMARNAT and the provider of the genetic resource and traditional knowledge. SEMARNAT can also negotiate access contracts with national universities and research centers. In any case, the access contract should include the conditions for the fair and equitable distribution of benefits derived from the commercialization of products derived from local genetic resources and traditional knowledge. It should also include the type of protection given to traditional knowledge. The protection of technologies derived from access activities will be shared by the parties and adjusted for IPR protection (GACETA PARLAMENTARIA 2001).

Nicaragua: Draft Law of Biodiversity

The main access contract that bioprospectors have to negotiate with the government has to include an accessory contract that provides details about benefits negotiated with the providers of the genetic resources and indigenous knowledge. The PIC contract described in the previous section is also used to protect and compensate indigenous knowledge and it includes the following requirements: a) identification of the parties; b) description of the collective knowledge that will be transferred; c) plans for up-front payment and a payment of a percentage of the net sales of products marketed as a result of the knowledge provided; d) the obligation to inform the provider about the objectives, risks, or implications derived from the use of the collective knowledge; and e) the obligation to inform the parties about progress in the research, industrialization, and marketing of products derived from the knowledge provided (MARENA 2002).

Philippines: EO 247 and Wildlife Act

EO 247 provides an ARA or CRA to facilitate the sharing of monetary and nonmonetary benefits. The Wildlife Act, however, does not require an ARA any longer. The ARA was intended primarily for academic purposes, so benefits shared included opportunities to publish research, access to information, and academic training. An ARA was valid for a period of five years, renewable upon recommendation of the IACBGR. Research intended for commercial use require a CRA that is valid for a period of three years and renewable for a period as may be determined by the IACBGR.

Although the introductory clause of EO 247 mentions traditional knowledge, nowhere in the text of the law has it been discussed. However, traditional knowledge of local and indigenous communities is linked with the PIC of the communities where the resources are taken.

Under EO 247 benefit sharing is required at two stages: at the time of collection and at the time of commercialization. At the time of collection, the minimum benefits that must be obtained are explicitly provided for in EO 247, while benefit sharing at the time of commercialization is not expressly required. The parties, however, are free to negotiate any kind of monetary and nonmonetary benefits (see Chapter 7).

However, the 2004 draft Guidelines for Bioprospecting Activities would repeal the benefits-sharing provisions of EO 247 and require bioprospectors to apply for a Bioprospecting Undertaking instead of a CRA. Under the guidelines, in addition to the fees discussed above in the Access Procedure section, applicants would have to be prepared to pay a minimum amount of 2% of the gross sales of products made or derived from collected samples. In addition, the applicant would have to provide minimum nonmonetary benefits such as equipment for biodiversity inventory and monitoring, supplies and equipment for resource conservation acitivities; arrangements for technology transfer; formal training and educational facilities, infrastructure directly related to management of the collection area; health care costs for persons involved; and other capacity building and support for *in situ* conservation and development activities. The guidelines include a model checklist of indicators (Annex V) for monitoring whether the benefit-sharing agreement is fair and equitable (see endnote 10 for access to the guidelines).

Samoa: CABSSBR

The conditions state that a benefit-sharing agreement has to be signed between the bioprospector and the government of Samoa. This agreement has to acknowledge all relevant traditional knowledge and practice that will be used by the bioprospectors. The conditions also state that the minimum royalty is 2%. However, it is not clear whether this is 2% of the net or gross sale of final products derived directly from collected samples or inspired by the chemistry of these samples. Bioprospectors also have to negotiate a legally binding agreement with the providers of biological resources. This agreement must include royalties, fees, and other payments for access to genetic resources and traditional knowledge (DLSE 2000).

Thailand: PVPA, RFSRCFA, and APPTMI

PVPA provides for two benefit-sharing models for commercial users of local domestic,[25] general domestic,[26] and wild[27] plant varieties. The first model applies to any bioprospector who collects or procures a local domestic plant variety or any part thereof for the purposes of variety development, education, experiment, or research for commercial purposes. If this is the case, the distribution of benefits derived from this activity is as follows: Twenty percent of the profits shall be allocated to the persons who conserved or developed the plant variety, 60% to the community as its common revenue, and 20% to the local government organization, the farmer's group, or the cooperative that signs the benefit-sharing agreement with

the bioprospector.

The second benefit-sharing model applies to collectors of general domestic plant varieties, wild plant varieties, or any part of such plant varieties for the purposes of variety development, education, experiment, or research for commercial interest. In this case the profits derived from any benefit-sharing agreement must be paid to the Plant Varieties Protection Fund. The main objective of this fund will be to promote the conservation, research, and development activities of plant varieties of local communities (THAILAND CONGRESS 1999).

Under RFSRCFA, commercial bioprospecting projects have to establish a benefit-sharing agreement with the RFD that includes a payment of royalties on all inventions derived from genetic resources. This agreement may include other forms of monetary and nonmonetary compensation strategies. The agreement must also state that Thai scientists will be involved in all collection and research activities. All Thai citizens and governmental organizations must have access to collected specimens and relevant data for research and studies. A duplicate of specimens collected must also be deposited at the Royal Forest Department (CHALERMPONGSE 2001). APPTMI states that users of traditional knowledge about medicines must submit an application to the licensing authority at Ministry of Public Health in order to initiate the negotiation process of potential benefits derived from such a use (NITTM 2002).

USA: NPS research specimen collection permit

The 1986 Federal Technology Transfer Act was invoked to develop a Cooperative Research and Development Agreement (CRADA)[28] that facilitated the distribution of benefits derived from the use of biological samples collected in Yellowstone National Park. The term of the CRADA was for an initial five-year period, but it provided that the benefit-sharing obligations survived termination which is very important since development of valuable discoveries can take more than ten years to achieve (see Chapter 8).

Analysis:
Benefit Sharing and Compensation Mechanisms

Contracts are the heart of bioprospecting initiatives. They are the main mechanism used by countries to ensure that monetary and nonmonetary benefits are negotiated under mutually agreed terms. Monetary and nonmonetary benefits have been thoroughly identified by the literature and include royalties, up-front payments, milestone payments, research funding, license fees, salaries and infrastructure, sharing of research results, biodiversity conservation, training, participation of nationals on research activities, technology transfer, and recovery of traditional knowledge. These and many other benefits should be negotiated on a case-by-case basis among parties directly involved in the projects. In some cases these parties must follow minimum benefit-sharing criteria. For example, Costa Rica, Peru, the Philippines, and Samoa have chosen to set a baseline or criteria for the benefits that they expect to receive. Samoa, for example, demands a minimum 2% royalty (no information is provided about whether this is taken from net or gross sales of products). Furthermore, Malaysia's draft bill proposes to use a set of criteria to identify the nature and combination of benefits. Unfortunately, most countries seem to be focused on the negotiation of royalties that might never materialize and they tend to give less importance to nonmonetary benefits that might contribute to build local capacity.

These benefit-sharing criteria, however, are merely a starting point. Whether agreements are fair and equitable is a subjective issue that lies in the eye of the beholder (or the negotiator). The fairness of contracts depends in large part on the skills of the parties to negotiate adequate benefit-sharing and compensation provisions. In the past, negotiators from developing countries may not have been as qualified as their counterparts from industrialized countries, but this is changing. The actors involved in the business of bioprospecting have increased in diversity and number. Information about the rights and obligations of bioprospecting parties and their collaborators has proliferated and it is reaching scientists and indigenous groups from developing countries. In any case, bioprospectors should keep in mind that a fair and equitable sharing of benefits derived from access activities is one of the three objectives of the CBD and a requirement of ABS. Article 15(7) of the CBD specifically refers to the aim of sharing the results of research and development" as well as the "benefits arising from the commercialization and other utilization of genetic resources".[29]

Contracts in combination with PIC requirements have also been proposed to protect and recognize indigenous knowledge in monetary and nonmonetary terms. ABS laws and policies of most countries propose access, annex, and accessory contracts to this purpose. In addition to this, most countries have endorsed trust funds as a useful mechanism to distribute benefits among several communities that share the knowledge used by bioprospectors. However, there is little experience and information on the practical operation of these trust funds and therefore on their usefulness.

IPRs and the Protection of Traditional Knowledge

Article 16(5) of the CBD recognizes the potential influence of patents and other IPRs on the implementation of the Convention and called on Contracting Parties to ensure that "such rights are supportive of and do not run counter to its objectives".[30] This statement reflects uncertainty and disagreement about the impact of patents and IPRs on the CBD objectives. This was probably due to the different political positions on this controversial issue during the negotiations of the CBD and the lack of agreement on the impacts of patents and other IPRs on biodiversity which led to such a broadly and ambiguous text. Even today there is great disagreement about the impacts of IPRs on biodiversity and traditional knowledge (CORREA 1999, DUTFIELD 2000, SHIVA 2001, see Chapters 6 and 7) and the issue will not be settled in the near future.

Under the CBD, Parties are not obliged to have a patent system for the protection of inventions derived from biological diversity and traditional knowledge. However, under the Agreement on Trade-Related Aspects of Intellectual Property Rights (TRIPS), member countries have to provide patent protection for microorganisms (as products) and for nonbiological and microbiological processes used for the production of plants and animals. The scope of patent protection does not have to include plants and animals. But, plant breeders' rights or another *sui generis* system must protect plant varieties. Furthermore under TRIPS, the World Trade Organization (WTO) can enforce minimum standards for all IPRs.

Sixty percent of the 41 Pacific Rim countries examined in this report are WTO members and have complied or are in the process of complying with TRIPS requirements, 20% are WTO observers, and the remaining 20% of countries do not fall in any of the above categories. Countries within this last 20% include Kiribati, Niue, and Solomon Islands which are planning to develop IPR laws and may apply for WTO membership in the future. In addition, they rely on IPR legislation of developed countries such as the United Kingdom and New Zealand with which they have post-colonial and economic ties (see Table 2).

Australia: Draft EPBCAR

Australia's patent law allows for the patenting of plants, microorganisms, genes, and related biological materials, provided that these meet the country's standards of proof for patentability.[31] Plant variety protection is also provided by plant breeders' rights. Therefore, Australia complies with the relevant TRIPS provisions. However, the country's intellectual property regime does not currently protect indigenous knowledge. On the other hand, it should be noted that the Nationally Consistent Approach states that legislative, administrative, or policy frameworks in Australian jurisdictions shall "recognize the need to ensure the use of traditional knowledge is undertaken with the cooperation and approval of the holders of that knowledge and on mutually agreed terms" (see Chapter 9). This may be a narrower principle than that which indigenous people appear to be asserting in Australia (see Chapter 9). The fact that the debate continues, however, suggests that there may be a need for a more rigorous attempt to identify the issues and to develop acceptable solutions.

The draft regulations do not refer specifically to IPR protection of inventions derived from genetic resources or indigenous knowledge. They do, however, include provisions requiring prior informed consent and adequate valuing of indigenous knowledge in the benefit-sharing contract. VOUMARD (2000) also recommended that patent law should be amended in order to include proof of source and, where appropriate, prior informed consent, as a prerequisite for granting a patent.

Colombia, Ecuador, and Peru: Decision 391

Decision 391 includes key provisions about IPRs that are strengthened by Decision 486, the Common Regime on Industrial Property that was approved by the Andean Community in 2000. Decision 391 states that member countries will not recognize intellectual property rights over genetic resources, derivatives, synthesized products, or related intangible components that have been obtained through access activities which do not comply with the provisions of the Decision. According to Decision 391 national intellectual property offices shall require applicants to submit the registration number of the access contract and a copy of it as a prerequisite for the granting of the IPR when there is reasonable evidence to suggest that the products or processes for which an IPR is being sought have been obtained from genetic resources of an Andean Member Country (ANDEAN COMMUNITY 1996). Decision 486 supports Decision 391 by requiring patent applicants to include a copy of the access contract, when products or procedures have been obtained or developed based on genetic resources from any of the members of the Andean Community (ANDEAN COMMUNITY 2000).

Decisions 391 and 486 also address the need to protect traditional knowledge. According to Decision 391, the Andean Community will prepare a proposal for a special regime to strengthen the protection of traditional knowledge, innovations, and practices of indigenous, black, and local communities that could take the form of a community intellectual right system (ANDEAN COMMUNITY 1996). So far, no regional initiatives to protect traditional knowledge have been proposed. In contrast, the 2002 Peruvian Law No. 27811 provides a *sui generis* system for the protection of indigenous peoples' collective knowledge about properties, uses, and characteristics of biological diversity and it has the following objectives: a) promotion, respect, protection, preservation, and development of collective knowledge of indigenous peoples; b) promotion of the just and equitable distribution of benefits derived from the use of collective knowledge; c) promotion of the use of collective knowledge for the benefit of indigenous peoples and humanity; d) assurance that collective knowledge is used with the prior informed consent of indigenous peoples; e) development of capacities of indigenous peoples and mechanisms traditionally used by them to share and distribute benefits derived and shared collectively; and f) prevention of the patenting of inventions derived from the collective knowledge of indigenous peoples without taking into account the novelty and inventive level of such knowledge. The law creates three registers for the protection of collective knowledge as follows: a) national register for collective knowledge that is in the public domain; b) national register for confidential collective knowledge; and c) local registers for either kind of collective knowledge. INDECOPI will be in charge of the first two registers and will provide support for local registers if requested by local communities. This organization will also submit to patent offices worldwide the public information registered by indigenous communities in order to block unauthorized patent applications of products and processes that may have been developed with such knowledge (PERUVIAN

CONGRESS 2002).

On the other hand it should be noted that Decision 486 will provide intellectual property protection as long as applicants prove that they complied with regulations that protect the genetic resources and knowledge of indigenous peoples and other local communities. Decision 486 also complies with TRIPS. It protects microorganisms but it does not provide protection to plants, animals, sequences of genes (that have been isolated), and essentially biological procedures for the production of plants or animals. Decision 486 also includes a compulsory licensing provision that allows member states the free use of any invention derived from biological resources in a situation of national emergency (ANDEAN COMMUNITY 2000).

Plant variety protection is provided by Decision 345, the Common Regime for the Protection of the Rights of Breeders of Plant Varieties, that establishes a *sui generis* property rights regime regulating plant breeders' rights, thus protecting farmers and regulating ownership of newly developed plant varieties. The regime complies with the provisions of the International Union for the Protection of New Varieties of Plants (UPOV) (see Chapter 4).

Costa Rica: The Law of Biodiversity
The Law of Biodiversity established that the State will use patents, trademarks, plant breeders' rights, copyrights, and *sui generis* systems to protect individual or collective traditional knowledge, innovations, practices, and inventions. This protection is extended to genetically modified microorganisms, but excludes biological processes for the production of plants and animals, plants, animals, sequences of genes, and any other organism as it exists in nature (this protection, however, was derogated by the Patents, Industrial Designs, and Utility Models Law as amended by Law No. 7979 of 31 January 2000). Protection is also excluded for any inventions derived from traditional knowledge or biological practices that are part of the public domain. The Law of Biodiversity also includes a compulsory licensing system that allows the State to use any invention derived from biological resources in a situation of national emergency.

Intellectual property right authorities must consult the TO before granting protection of intellectual or industrial property related innovations that involve biodiversity elements. The submission of the certificate of origin and prior informed consent will be required. The Law of Biodiversity also establishes that under *sui generis* community intellectual rights, the State protects traditional knowledge, practices, and innovations of indigenous communities. A participatory process mandated in the Law of Biodiversity is working on the *sui generis* community intellectual rights. Consultations with indigenous and peasant communities are expected to be completed in 2004.

The Law of Biodiversity also focuses on the protection of knowledge by means of a register. During the consultation process with local communities (and later), they may register their knowledge, traditional practices, or innovations. The service is voluntary and free of charge. This register will allow the TO to reject any claim of intellectual property derived from knowledge protected by this system.

Costa Rica has comprehensive legislation related to IPRs that include: a) the Patent, Drawings and Utility Models Law No. 6867, emended by Law No. 7979 of 31 January 2000 to make it compatible with TRIPS and b) Plant Breeders' Rights draft published in The Gazette on 10 August 1999 and yet to be approved. This draft was developed in accordance with the model law of UPOV and its 1991 Act (see Chapter 5).

Malaysia:
Draft federal bill on access to genetic resources
The draft does not recognize protection for: a) plants, animals, and naturally occurring microorganisms, including parts thereof and b) biological and naturally occurring microbiological processes. Approval of the competent authority is required in order to obtain a patent that involves the use of biological resources. The draft has to be consistent with the provisions of the Malaysian Patent Act of 1983. It is not clear, however, whether genes are patentable under the Act. It is necessary to harmonize the provisions of this Act with Malaysia's international obligations under TRIPS. To satisfy the requirements of TRIPS, Malaysia developed the draft Protection of New Plant Varieties bill. This is essentially a *sui generis* system for the protection of plant genetic resources. Congress has not passed the bill yet.

Moreover, there is no specific provision in the act to protect indigenous knowledge related to genetic resources. Malaysia has been discussing a proposal for a *sui generis* system of community intellectual rights. The system's objectives are to: a) recognize the ownership rights of communities over their knowledge, innovations, and practices; b) protect communities' knowledge, innovations, and practices; and c) ensure the equitable sharing of benefits derived from their genetic resources and knowledge. The proposal, however, was very controversial and it was not included in the draft Access to Genetic Resources bill (see Chapter 11).

Mexico: EEEPGA, WGA, SFDGA, and draft LAUBGR
Neither EEEPGA nor WGA includes provisions that protect intellectual property derived from genetic resources or traditional knowledge. However, SFDGA protects the knowledge of traditional communities about local forest biological resources found in their land. Article 102 states that collectors of forest biological resources for commercial and noncommercial purposes must acknowledge the rights of indigenous communities over the knowledge, ownership, and use of local varieties. Furthermore, any patenting of forest genetic resources and by-products will be legally void unless the collector acknowledges the aforementioned rights of indigenous communities. However, some exceptions may apply in the context of agreed relevant international agreements or treaties

(SEMARNAT 2003).

The 1991 Industrial Property Act protects inventions derived from genetic resources, but there is no protection for traditional knowledge. Furthermore, the act does not include requirements for disclosing the origin of samples or knowledge used for the invention of products or processes that are to be patented. Under the act patents must comply with the requirements of novelty, inventive step, and industrial application, and there is an exception to patenting biological and genetic material. However, the Mexican patent office considers that once biological or genetic materials have been isolated and characterized, it is no longer "as it is found in nature". Therefore, sequences of genes can be patented under Mexican law. Mexico's PVPA also gives property rights to plant breeders for plant varieties (see Chapter 6).

Under Article 176 of RSDA, the inter-secretarial commission together with the Mexican council must develop measures to defend IPRs of peasant and indigenous communities. However, no such measures have been adopted so far by the Mexican government. Mexico's current legislation does not provide a comprehensive protection to traditional knowledge. The draft LAUBGR, however, includes a provision that promotes the evaluation of the proportion of "relevant knowledge" given by each party in order to distribute the resulting IPRs. There are no details about how to implement this measure. The draft law also proposes a register system to protect traditional knowledge (GACETA PARLAMENTARIA 2001).

Nicaragua: Draft Law of Biodiversity
The draft law states that access contracts must refer to the type of IPR protection that will be sought for inventions derived under the agreement. This draft also proposes *sui generis* community intellectual rights to protect the knowledge, practices, and innovations of local communities. In addition, the draft promotes the development of a register to protect the knowledge of these communities. This register will be voluntary and confidential. The draft law also requires IPR authorities to ask for access authorization (including proof that PIC was sought) before IPR protection is granted on inventions derived from biodiversity or indigenous knowledge. In late 2000, the government developed a proposal for *sui generis* community intellectual rights to protect the knowledge, practices, and innovations of local communities

Nicaragua's IPR laws include the Patent Law 354 and plant breeders' rights to protect new plant varieties. Plants, animals, and biological processes to produce any organism are excluded from patent protection. But protection is given to sequences of genes that have been isolated and characterized and it can be extended to any product that includes such a sequence (J. Hernández, pers. comm. November 2002).

Philippines: EO 247 and Wildlife Act
EO 247 recognizes the rights of indigenous communities to their knowledge and practices when this information is

used for commercial purposes. The Philippines, however, has yet to pass a *sui generis* IPR system that will cover traditional knowledge associated with biological and genetic resources of local and indigenous communities. The 1997 Traditional Alternative Medicine Act protects knowledge of traditional medicine in a very limited way. The law provides for a policy for indigenous groups seeking to protect their knowledge. This policy, however, is still under development (P. Benavidez, pers. comm. July 2003).

Both the 1998 Intellectual Property Code and the 2002 Plant Variety Protection Law comply with TRIPS. The code excludes plant varieties, animal breeds, or essentially biological processes for the production of plants or animals from patent protection. However, microorganisms and nonbiological and microbiological processes can be protected by patents. The Plant Variety Protection Law allows compulsory licensing at any time after two years from the granting of the protection. This situation may occur if the variety is required for the production of any medicine or food preparation, among other reasons (see Chapter 7). Protection under the Law is patterned after the UPOV plant breeders' rights. EO 247 also includes a compulsory licensing provision that applies to products or technologies developed from the use of endemic species. In this case the invention must be available for use in the Philippines without paying royalty to the inventor.

The Indigenous Peoples' Rights Act of 1997 emphasizes that indigenous communities "are entitled to the recognition of the full ownership and control and protection of their cultural and intellectual rights" (BARBER et al. 2002). Under the act, bioprospectors have to obtain the PIC from indigenous communities. Unfortunately, there is no provision in the intellectual property code of the country that denies intellectual property right protection to bioprospectors who fail to present the PIC of the local community that provided the genetic resource or knowledge (P. Benavidez, pers. comm. March 2003).

Samoa: CABSSBR
The conditions provide that traditional knowledge has to be acknowledged in any benefit-sharing agreement (DLSE 2000). This includes the negotiation of access to IPRs or traditional knowledge owned by or vested in any individual, group of individuals, or representatives thereof, and the payment of fees, royalties, or license payments for such rights or access. The 1998 Intellectual Property Rights Law and the 1989 Village Fono Act also provide a general framework for the recognition of ownership of traditional knowledge. These regulations, however, are likely to be strengthened with future legislation (DIVISION OF ENVIRONMENT AND CONSERVATION 1998).

Thailand: PVPA, RFSRCFA, and APPTMI
Existing IPR laws have been revised to be in line with the requirements of the TRIPS Agreement. Thailand's 1979 Patent Act (amended in 1992 and 1999) protects inventions derived from biological resources except for plants, animals, or essentially biological processes for the production of plants and animals. Applications for gene sequences are accepted by the patent office, but there are still problems with interpretation of the law and they may be denied. Thailand's PVPA also protects new plant varieties, traditional varieties, community varieties, and wild varieties (J. Donavanik, pers. comm. January 2003). Under RFSRCFA bioprospectors must obtain the approval of RFD before they apply for intellectual property right protection (i.e., copyright, patent, trademark, etc.). Depending on particulars of the situation RFD may ask bioprospectors to share ownership of intellectual property protection (C. Hutacharern, pers. comm. June 2003).

The APPTMI provides a *sui generis* system to protect traditional knowledge associated with formulae of medicines derived from plants, animals, bacteria, and minerals. According to the act, such protection takes effect when such knowledge (oral or written) about formulae of medicines is registered at the National Institute of Thai Traditional Medicine. The act creates the following three categories of *sui generis* "medicinal intellectual property rights":

- *The national formula of traditional Thai drugs or the national text on traditional Thai medicine;*
- *general formula of traditional Thai drugs or general traditional Thai medicine document; and*
- *personal formula of traditional Thai drugs or personal text on traditional Thai medicine* (NITTM 2002).

National formula is defined as the one that has a special medical or public health value; general formula is the one that has been widely used, and personal formula is the one that is not national or general and has been developed by a person or group of persons. The inventor, improver, or inheritor of the personal formula may register such knowledge. The act protects registered knowledge for the lifetime of the bearer and 50 additional years from the time the owner or last owner (in case of joint ownership) of the registration has passed away (NITTM 2002).

USA: NPS research specimen collection permit
The Patent Act of 1793 defined patentable statutory subject matter as "any new and useful art, machine, manufacture, or composition of matter, or any new or useful improvement [thereof]". The Plant Patent Act of 1930 gave protection to clonally propagated varieties of plants such as fruit trees and tubers. In 1970, the PVPA granted protection to new, uniform, and distinct plant varieties. In 1980, the USA Supreme Court opened the door for patents to be applied to plants, animals, microorganisms, genes, and DNA sequences. In late 2001, the Supreme Court confirmed that plant varieties are eligible for protection by utility patents, as well as under the Plant Patent Act of 1930 and the PVPA of 1970. The distinction between what the law rewards (new, useful, and nonobvious discoveries based on research results) and what the law protects (naturally occurring life forms that remain free for all to use) is at

the core of the biodiversity prospecting access and benefit-sharing issues first pioneered in the USA at Yellowstone (see Chapter 8).

Analysis:
IPRs and the Protection of Traditional Knowledge

Traditional and *sui generis* IPR systems, registers, PIC requirements, certificates of origin, and benefit-sharing agreements are the main instruments used by most countries to protect scientific and the traditional knowledge at different levels. All of the countries reviewed above, except for Samoa and Malaysia, have IPR legislation that complies fully with TRIPS. They provide intellectual protection to inventions derived from biological resources that exclude plants, animals, and biological processes to develop these organisms. These countries, except for Costa Rica, also have legislation to protect new plant varieties and Thailand extends this protection to wild plant varieties. However, IPR protection depends on the application of the patentability test. In other words, inventions have to be novel, useful, and nonobvious. Unlike Australia, Costa Rica, Mexico, Nicaragua, and the USA, the Andean Community does not protect gene sequences that have been isolated and characterized. According to these countries, genes exist in nature and their mere isolation does not comply with the novelty and inventive steps of the patentability test. Thailand accepts applications for the protection of gene sequences, but patent clerks still have trouble interpreting the norm (J. Donavanik, pers. comm. February 2003). Bioprospectors may also object to the fact that the Andean Community (Decision 486) and Costa Rica (Law of Biodiversity) include a compulsory licensing provision that allows these nations to use any invention without having to pay royalties in case of national emergency or security.

Can traditional IPR systems be applied to protect inventions derived from the use of traditional knowledge? Patents, for example, protect only those inventions that can only be attributed to individuals or small groups of people. Some argue that in traditional societies the sources of knowledge can be traced to individuals, kinship, or gender-based groups. On the other hand, most traditional knowledge is in the public domain and cannot be attributable to a single community or geographical location making it ineligible for patent protection. In addition, many communities resent the fact that their traditional knowledge has been stolen to patent plants or inventions derived from plants. Examples include the ayahuasca (COICA 1996), the neem tree (DUTFIELD 2000), and the enola bean (see Box 1 of Chapter 6). Others have ethical concerns about the idea of monopolizing and commercializing their knowledge. These concerns and issues have discouraged most traditional communities from facilitating the use of knowledge for patenting purposes.

In the last few years there has been intensive debate at a national and international level to protect indigenous or traditional knowledge. This debate has reached international bodies like the World Intellectual Property Organization

(WIPO) which is examining proposals to protect traditional knowledge. Specifically, the Global Intellectual Property Division and the Intergovernmental Committee on Genetic Resources, Traditional Knowledge and Folklore of WIPO have been looking at the IPR needs of holders of traditional knowledge and the feasibility of establishing databases or registers to protect traditional or indigenous knowledge, among other issues.

WIPO can provide a space for the discussion of these issues but it does not have the power to oblige countries to develop legislation that protects traditional knowledge. WTO can utilize economic sanctions to advance these issues worldwide. However, there is still great disagreement among countries about fundamental issues such as the patenting of life and whether the TRIPS agreement should be amended in order to make it consistent with CBD obligations such as the protection of traditional knowledge and ABS requirements. For example, in early June 2003, at a meeting of the TRIPS council, the Africa Group emphasized that TRIPS should include some sort of international mechanism to ensure the effective protection of traditional knowledge. In contrast, the USA called for traditional knowledge to be removed from the agenda of the TRIPS Council. Furthermore, the Africa Group called for a ban on the patenting of life, a request that was opposed by the USA and the European Union. On the other hand, the Indian Group proposed that TRIPS should be amended in order to require patent applicants to disclose the source of origin of the biological resource and traditional knowledge and to provide evidence of PIC and benefit sharing. This issue was supported by the European Union, but it was not clarified whether it should be addressed by WIPO or WTO. Japan, Canada, and the USA argued that WIPO was already working on these issues and proposed to wait for the results before further action was taken (ANONYMOUS 2003).

More than 50% of the countries examined in this report are already addressing these issues in their national policies. These countries have either included in their ABS policies provisions that call for a *sui generis* community rights system to protect indigenous knowledge, or are examining options for the development of a similar system. Furthermore, these countries are already taking additional measures to protect traditional knowledge and to ensure that bioprospectors comply with ABS regulations. These include requirements for national IPR authorities to ask for access contracts, PIC evidence, or some certificate of origin when they receive applications for IPR protection of products and processes that have been derived from local biological resources or traditional knowledge. The Andean Community and Costa Rica already have this kind of provision in their ABS laws and Australia and Nicaragua are proposing similar measures in their draft regulations. Mexico's General Law of Sustainable Forestry Development also requires bioprospectors to provide PIC evidence when inventions derived from forest biological resources are patented. However, this requirement applies only to local varieties found in forests owned by indigenous communities. Requirements for registers of traditional knowledge have been included in the ABS law of Costa Rica and proposed by the draft ABS law of Nicaragua. According to DUTFIELD (2000), "failure to register does not surrender the innovation rights, but doing so may block a patent application". Blocking potential patent applications by advertising prior art is precisely the main objective of the register of the American Association for the Advancement of Science (Science and Human Rights Program) known as Traditional Ecological Knowledge-Prior Art Data Base.[32] The register has over 30,000 entries that include traditional knowledge about medicinal plants that has been collected mainly online from other websites. The system also gives the option to holders of traditional knowledge to submit information to the register. However, traditional knowledge under this register is available and of easy access to anyone, not only to patent examiners, and traditional communities may not want to share their knowledge with pharmaceutical companies and other users. Holders of traditional knowledge may want to maintain control over their knowledge and keep their options open for negotiation with potential bioprospectors. To this purpose Nicaragua proposes a confidential register and Peru, under Peruvian Law No. 27811, protects access to collective knowledge by a confidential register (one of the three registers provided by the law) requiring written consent of the holders of such knowledge. Under Thailand's APPTMI, a register protects traditional knowledge about medicinal formulae that are in the public domain and that is registered by individual or collective owners. However, the act is not clear about whether the register protects sensitive information in a confidential manner. The Philippine's 1997 Traditional Alternative Medicine Act that protects knowledge of traditional medicine is not operational yet, and it is uncertain whether it will use the register system to protect traditional knowledge (P. Benavidez, pers. comm. July 2003).

In situ Biodiversity Conservation and Sustainable Use

Some of the *in situ* biodiversity conservation and sustainable use activities listed by Article 8 of the CBD include: a) establishing a system of protected areas; b) promoting the protection of ecosystems, habitats, and populations; and c) adopting measures to avoid or minimize impacts on the use of biological diversity. Even before the CBD came into force, bioprospecting was identified as a potential source of funding and technical expertise to promote the conservation of biodiversity and its sustainable use (SCHWEITZER et al. 1991).

Australia: Draft EPBCAR
The purpose of the regulations is to provide for the control of access to biological resources in Commonwealth areas while promoting the conservation and sustainable use of biological diversity. Therefore, the regulations and a

model benefit-sharing agreement will include a requirement that at least some of the benefits under the contract should promote biodiversity conservation in the area where samples are collected.

The regulations will also require an EIA when bioprospecting activities are likely to have a significant impact on the environment. If this is the case, within 20 days after receiving the access application the applicant must provide the Minister of the Environment and Heritage with information about the potential environmental impacts of the proposed access. Within 10 days of receiving such information, the Minister must publish a notice inviting anyone to comment on the likely impacts, and within five days after the end of the period given in the invitation for comments, the Minister must give the applicant a copy of the comments received. Finally, the applicant must give the Minister a response to these comments. There is no timeframe for such a response, but presumably, it is in the applicant's interests to respond expeditiously. Then, at intervals of less than 12 months, the Minister must invite applications from anyone who wants to be informed of applications for access permits where an EIA by public notice is required. The Minister is also required to keep a register of information about permits. The register must be available for public scrutiny. However, information is not be included in it if the Minister believes the information is confidential or culturally sensitive (see Chapter 9).

Colombia, Ecuador, and Peru: Decision 391
Decision 391 regulates access to the region's genetic resources in order to promote the conservation and sustainable use of biodiversity, among other reasons. This law also encourages the development of projects and technologies that promote the conservation and sustainable use of biodiversity and its derivative products that contribute to the well being of local communities. Therefore, access applications, access contract, and accessory contracts must include conditions that support research activities that promote the conservation and sustainable use of biodiversity. Bioprospectors should be guided by the precautionary principle.

Under Decision 391, the Andean committee on genetic resources will also design and implement programs to ensure the conservation of genetic resources and will analyze the viability and convenience of an Andean fund for the conservation of these resources. This approach is already being followed at a national level. The Peruvian draft regulation on access to genetic resources proposes the creation of a national trust fund for the conservation, research and development of genetic resources.

Each country may also require an EIA from access applicants and this information will be included in a file that will be available for public scrutiny. In addition, member countries may also impose partial or full access restrictions if they identify that access activities may: a) endanger or threaten rare, endemic, or any other species, subspecies, variety, or race; b) endanger the structure or function of ecosystems; c) cause undesirable or uncontrollable environmental and socioeconomic impacts; d) cause biosafety impacts; and e) affect genetic resources or strategic regions. In Peru, under Law No. 27811, INDECOPI may reject the registration of the license signed between bioprospectors and representatives of indigenous communities if national environment authorities prove that access activities will cause damage to the environment and parties to the agreement refuse to mitigate such damage (PERUVIAN CONGRESS 2002).

Costa Rica: The Law of Biodiversity

The general goal of this law is to promote the conservation and sustainable use of biodiversity and to ensure the fair and equitable sharing of benefits derived from it. Therefore, the law establishes that up to 10% of the research budget and 50% of royalties of access projects will go to the national system of conservation areas, the private owner, or indigenous community. Conservation of ecosystems is also one of the criteria stated by the GAP for the evaluation or approval of the access applications.

The GAP also allows the imposition of restrictions on access to genetic resources to ensure their conservation and sustainable use. "To establish complete or partial restrictions some of the elements that will be considered are: a) the danger of extinction of the species, subspecies, race, or variety; b) reasons of scarcity and endemic conditions; c) vulnerable or fragile conditions in the structure or function of the ecosystems; d) adverse effects on human health, the species, and the ecosystems or on essential elements of the autonomy or cultural identity of peoples and communities; and e) strategic genetic resources or geographical areas qualified as such." (see Chapter 5). Access for military purposes is to be prohibited in all cases. An EIA can also be requested by the TO.

Malaysia:
Draft federal bill on access to genetic resources

Under this draft law, when an access application is made the official carrying out the evaluation of the application will take into consideration: a) the conservation status of the resource that will be collected or used; b) the contribution of the project to the conservation and sustainable use of the biological resources; and c) adverse impacts, risks, and dangers of the project to any component of biological diversity and its sustainable use. Bioprospectors are required to submit an environmental and socioeconomic impact assessment.

When traditional knowledge cannot be attributed to a particular community another provision of the bill proposes the establishment of a common trust fund. The purpose of the trust fund will be not only to promote the welfare of indigenous communities, but also for the conservation and sustainable use of biodiversity (see Chapter 11).

Mexico: EEEPGA, WGA, SFDGA, and draft LAUBGR

One of the goals of the EEEPGA is to promote the conservation of biological diversity. Access will not be granted

if bioprospecting activities are likely to compromise the viability of species, habitats, and ecosystems. Article 87 BIS states that any income received from permits, authorizations, and licenses (derived from bioprospecting projects) will be used to promote the conservation and restoration of biodiversity in the areas where specimens were collected. Also, the EEEPGA provides for the implementation of EIA studies when any activity is likely to cause damage to local ecosystems or public health. Furthermore, Article 106 of SFDGA states that any utilization of forest resources, either for commercial or noncommercial purposes, in areas which are habitats for endemic, threatened, or endangered species of native flora and fauna, must be done without altering the environmental conditions which allow their subsistence, development and evolution (SEMARNAT 2003). Similarly, Article 97 of WGA emphasizes that permits will not be granted if collecting activities affect the viability of populations, species, habitats, and ecosystems (SEMARNAT 2002).

Two of the main objectives of the draft LAUBGR are to regulate the access to genetic resources and to ensure the conservation of biological and genetic resources. The draft law also proposes the establishment of a trust fund for the conservation and use of genetic resources and requires an EIA of proposed activities including measures that will be taken to mitigate negative impacts (GACETA PARLAMENTARIA 2001).

Nicaragua: Draft Law of Biodiversity

The draft law regulates access to genetic resources while conserving biological diversity. Access to genetic resources will require an environmental permit that must be issued based on a previous analysis of environmental impacts and risks of access activities. The evaluation of access applications will take into account whether proposed activities contribute to: a) the conservation and sustainable use of biological and genetic resources and b) the preservation of endemic, threatened, or endangered species. Access will be denied when access activities: a) endanger or threaten one or more species and b) cause uncontrolled ecological, social, economic, and cultural environmental impacts. In any case, the National Biodiversity Institute will take into account the precautionary principle to ensure that access activities do not deplete biological diversity.

Philippines: EO 247 and Wildlife Act

Under EO 247, access applicants, the government, and local communities may define actions to ensure conservation of biological diversity as part of benefit-sharing agreements. However, this is up to the parties. There is no financing mechanism or trust fund in place to support biodiversity conservation objectives. The Wildlife Act provides such a mechanism. Under the act a wildlife management fund is created to finance restoration of habitats affected by activities committed in violation of the law. The fund also supports scientific research, enforcement and monitoring, and local capacity-building activities.

The act's objectives include: a) conserve and protect

wildlife species and their habitats to promote ecological balance and enhance biological diversity; b) regulate the collection and trade of wildlife; and c) initiate or support scientific studies on the conservation of biological diversity. Access applicants may be asked to prepare an EIA. This is usually required for projects that will carry out activities in environmentally critical areas. However, no EIA has ever been required from any applicant (see Chapter 7).

The 2004 draft Guidelines for Bioprospecting Activities (see endnote 10) state that local communities shall ensure that the funds received are used solely for biodiversity conservation or environmental protection, including alternative or supplemental livelihood opportunities for community members. Furthermore, any bioprospecting activity involving species listed under CITES and the IUCN Red List shall be governed by these guidelines in addition to specific regulations on the conservation of these species.

Samoa: CABSSBR

Samoa's conditions make no reference to the use of benefits from bioprospecting for conservation purposes. However, once the access application has been submitted the Minister of Lands, Surveys, and Environment may require an EIA to be conducted.

Thailand: PVPA, RFSRCFA, and APPTMI

PVPA and APPTMI provide for the establishment of trust funds called the "Plant Varieties Protection Fund" and the "Fund on Traditional Thai Medicine Intelligence" respectively, to promote activities related to the conservation, research, and development of plant varieties and the conservation and promotion of intelligence on traditional Thai medicine, respectively. PVPA requires EIA studies for access activities likely to have a negative environmental impact and APPTMI proposes the development of a "Plan for the conservation of herbs" to promote the conservation of areas where animals, plants, bacteria, and minerals used for the development of medicines are found.

RFSRCFA does not specifically promote the use of bioprospecting benefits for biodiversity conservation activities. However, conservation is one of the mandates of the Royal Forest Department and it is safe to assume that a share of potential profits will go to this purpose. RFSRCFA states that access permits may be cancelled if bioprospecting activities cause negative impacts to the environment and to natural, biological, and genetic resources. If samples are collected, one duplicate must remain in the facilities indicated by RFD. If there is only one specimen available, it must remain in Thailand (C. Hutacharern, pers. comm. June 2003).

USA: NPS research specimen collection permit

The NPS operates consistently with the main conservation principles provided in the CBD. Bioprospectors that profit from research involving national park resources are expected to invest the benefits resulting from their research in the conservation of the park's biological diversity. Under NEPA, NPS authorities may also require bioprospectors to

determine the environmental impact of proposed activities (see Chapter 8).

Analysis:

In situ *Biodiversity Conservation and Sustainable Use*

All of the ABS laws and policies mentioned above, except for Samoa's conditions, promote the conservation of biological diversity and trust funds are the main strategy to collect and distribute monies for conservation and sustainable use goals. But, in most of these countries, these are stated as general goals, and it is up to government authorities and access applicants to negotiate biodiversity conservation activities as part of benefit-sharing agreements. Costa Rica's Law of Biodiversity is the only policy that specifically states that bioprospectors must invest a percentage of the research budget and royalties in the areas where genetic resources are collected. If the collection site is part of the national system of conservation areas, benefits are likely to go into conservation initiatives. However, if collections take place in other public land, or in private or indigenous land there is no guarantee that benefits will go into conservation activities (see Chapter 5).

Article 15(2) of the CBD states that Contracting Parties must "create conditions to facilitate access to genetic resources for environmentally sound uses".[33] All of the countries examined above may require bioprospectors to present some sort of proof (i.e., EIA) that access activities will not have a negative impact on biological diversity and ecological processes. In some cases the scope of the EIA is broadly defined to include social and economic impacts. This is a justifiable concern given available evidence of negative impacts in the past. DAVIS (1993) and PINHEIRO (1997), for example, report that the collection of leaves from wild jaborandi (*Pilocarpus jaborandi*) by an American-Brazilian bioprospecting project had a negative effect on the shrub as well as on the local economy and community that had become totally dependent on the commercial exploitation of the species. Similarly, in Kenya the USA National Cancer Institute was responsible for harvesting the whole adult population (27,215 kg) of the shrub *Maytenus buchanii* that is the source of the cancer compound maytansine (OLDFIELD 1989). Furthermore, species such as *Trilepidea adamsii*, an endemic mistletoe of New Zealand, and *Tecophilaea cyanocrocus*, an endemic lily of central Chile, are extinct because they were overcollected (DE KLEMM 1994). It is uncertain whether these species were critical to the survival of other species and to the structure or function of the local ecosystem. But if this were the case, both the ecosystem and the species dependent on the target species may have been affected by these bioprospecting activities.

Enforcement and Monitoring

Enforcement and monitoring requirements are essential components of meaningful ABS laws and policies. The motivation for these requirements is important not only to ensure that benefits are distributed in a timely manner but also to monitor the ability of species and ecosystems to recover from negative impacts and their capacity to continue delivering ecological services to society.

Australia: Draft EPBCAR

Enforcement of access regulations is likely to be carried out by Environment Australia which manages compliance with the EPBCAR. Fifty penalty units[34] are set for contravening the regulation which requires a permit for access to biological resources. The draft does not include any monitoring activities but the outline of the model contract proposes a section titled "Monitoring and review of the contract" (VOUMARD 2000). The regulations also require an EIA when collections are likely to harm the environment and this may contribute to the development of baseline information about the status of biodiversity. But no details are provided about how to use this information in the context of a monitoring program of impacts caused by collections over time.

Colombia, Ecuador, and Peru: Decision 391

Under Decision 391, the national authority in coordination with other organizations will set up appropriate monitoring mechanisms to enforce contracts negotiated with bioprospectors. The national support organization will also be obliged to cooperate with the national authority in monitoring and reporting about activities that involve the use of genetic resources, derivative products, and traditional knowledge (ANDEAN COMMUNITY 1996). The national authority is also authorized to enforce Decision 391 according to national standards and mechanisms. For example, if approved, the Peruvian draft regulation on access to genetic resources would require bioprospectors to pay 15% of the total budget of the project as a bond or guarantee that there will be total compliance with the provisions agreed on the contract (M. Ruiz, pers. comm. January 2004). Under Decision 391, the national authority of each country will also have to monitor the state of conservation of biological resources. However, explicit provisions on monitoring biological and genetic resources for conservation purposes are not provided.

Costa Rica: The Law of Biodiversity

Once access is authorized, monitoring and control procedures begin at the expense of the TO and in coordination with the authorized representatives of the sites where access to the resources is taking place. The TO has not been established due to lack of budget, personnel, constitutional action, and political will, therefore monitoring procedures have not been carried out. Infringements of the Law of Biodiversity will be penalized according to Costa Rica's Penal Code and pertinent national laws. Penalties for violations of access activities will be used to finance activities of CONAGEBIO and the TO. An EIA can also be requested by the TO based on some general provisions of the LB related to EIA. The evaluation is the responsibility of the National Technical Secretariat. To date no EIA has been requested of the National Biodiversity Institute or any other bioprospector (see Chapter 5).

Malaysia:
Draft federal bill on access to genetic resources

Existing monitoring and enforcement authorities would be responsible for monitoring and enforcement of the provisions of this draft bill, within their respective sectors or jurisdictions. These authorities will also have "powers of arrests, entry, search, and seizure with respect to offenses under the law". Under this draft bill, when an access application is made the applicant is required to submit an EIA (see Chapter 11).

Mexico: EEEPGA, WGA, SFDGA, and draft LAUBGR

SEMARNAT enforces EEEPGA, WGA, and SFDGA and would enforce the draft LAUBGR as well. The recently amended Criminal Code regulates infringements to EEEPGA, WGA, SFDGA, and the draft LAUBGR (if adopted). Article 420 of the code punishes with prison sentences of between one and ten years and fines of between 300 and 3,000 minimum daily wages to those who "illegally execute any activity with traffic purposes, or capture, possess, transport, gather, introduce to the country, or extract from it, any specimen, its products, its subproducts, and other genetic resources, of any wild flora and fauna species, terrestrial species, or aquatic species on temporary prohibition, considered endemic, threatened, endangered, subject to special protection, or regulated by any international treaty of which Mexico has become a Party". Furthermore, "an additional punishment will be applied when the described activities are executed in or affect a natural protected area, or when they are executed with a commercial purpose". This punishment, for example, would include those using biological material for biotechnological applications without proper permits issued under 87 BIS. In addition to this, Article 122 of WGA punishes as an administrative infringement the use of biological material for biotechnological purposes without the acquisition of due permits. The EEEPGA also requires an EIA when bioprospecting or any other activities are likely to have a significant environmental impact (see Chapter 6).

Nicaragua: Draft Law of Biodiversity

Access contracts will include obligations for the establishment of an evaluation and monitoring system that will be financed by the access applicant. These contracts will also include penalties and sanctions for potential violations. The law also includes penalties that range between $1,000 and $10,000 USD to be paid to the national environmental trust fund. The draft law also requires and EIA of the ecological, social, economic, and cultural impacts (MARENA 2002).

Philippines: EO 247 and Wildlife Act

Under EO 247 the IACBGR is set up to monitor and enforce compliance with research agreements, as well as to coordinate further institutional, policy, and technology development. The respective member agencies of the IACBGR shall conduct monitoring of research agreements based on a standard monitoring plan to be proposed by this committee. The plan will include a monitoring team responsible for establishing a mechanism to ensure the integration and dissemination of the information generated from research, collection, and utilization activities. The PAWB shall be the lead agency in monitoring the implementation of the research agreement. The DENR regional offices shall also participate in the monitoring.

A second monitoring team headed by representatives of the Department of Science and Technology and the Department of Foreign Affairs monitors the progress of the research, utilization, and commercialization outside the country. The only commercial bioprospecting project that has been granted access is required to submit a report every four months and a government representative joins project scientists during every field visit. This project was not required to submit an EIA.

Under the Wildlife Act, applicants have to pay an ecological or performance bond. The 2004 draft Guidelines for Bioprospecting Activities (see endnote 10) state that the applicant must post a rehabilitation/performance bond, in the form of a surety bond, in an amount equivalent to 25% percent of the project cost as reflected in the research budget. The bond would have to be posted within a reasonable time after the signing of the Bioprospecting Undertaking. No collection of samples may be conducted until after the bond has been posted and failure to post the bond can be a basis for rescission of the Bioprospecting Undertaking.

Under the guidelines, reporting requirements are as follows: the resource user must submit an annual progress report to the implementing agencies covering the following items: a) status of the procurement of PIC; b) progress of collection of samples; c) benefit-sharing negotiations; d) progress on payment of benefits or other provisions of the Bioprospecting Undertaking. The annual report must be submitted not later than January 30 of the following year. For purposes of compliance monitoring, bioprospectors must issue the following certifications as proof of compliance, particularly on the proper procurement of PIC, delivery of benefit-sharing agreement, and collection quota: proper procurement of PIC; acceptance by resource providers of the monetary and nonmonetary benefits required by the undertaking; and compliance to the collection quota as set out in the undertaking.

Noncompliance with the provisions in the Bioprospecting Undertaking would result in the automatic cancellation the agreement and confiscation of collected materials in favor of the government, forfeiture of bond and imposition of a perpetual ban on access to biological resources in the Philippines by the violator. Such a breach would be considered a violation of the Wildlife Act and would be subject to the imposition of administrative and criminal sanctions under existing laws. Any person who conducts bioprospecting without an approved Bioprospecting Undertaking would be subject to sanctions for collecting without a permit. Furthermore, the violation would be published in national and international media and it would be reported by the agencies to the relevant

international and regional monitoring bodies. Collection, hunting or possession of wildlife, their by-products and derivatives without the necessary permit is penalized with imprisonment of up to four years and a fine of up to $300,000 P (see Chapter 7).

Samoa: CABSSBR

Bioprospectors have to submit a report on the status of the analysis of samples every six months. However, the conditions do not set up a monitoring structure or mechanism of proposed enforcement strategies, sanctions, or penalties (DLSE 2000). The Minister of Lands, Surveys, and Environment may ask bioprospectors to conduct an EIA.

Thailand: PVPA, RFSRCFA, and APPTMI

The Department of Agriculture and RFD oversee the PVPA and RFSRCFA, respectively, but no monitoring structure has been defined under these policies. However, the Prime Minister Regulation on the Conservation and Utilization of Biological Diversity created a National Committee on Conservation and Utilization of Biological Diversity that is likely to address this issue. On the other hand, RFSRCFA states that every six months, bioprospectors must submit three copies of a progress report to the RFD. In addition, bioprospectors that cause negative environmental impacts are liable and may be punished by Thai laws (J. Donavanik, pers. comm. January 2003). APPTMI provides for the creation of an enforcement force of officials from the Ministry of Public Health to enforce the provisions of the act. The act also includes penalties such as prison sentences and fines for breaches of the act (NITTM 2002).

USA: NPS research specimen collection permit

There are at least three main routes by which NPS can use its enforcement authority: a) regulations and related statutes; b) permit provisions that include regulations and contracts; and c) contracts. Collecting without a permit or poaching is theft of Federal property and in this case criminal sanctions can apply. Failure to comply with regulations and permit provisions (assuming a permit is issued) can be less serious; administrative penalties (possibly judicial) can apply (including a punitive 20% mandatory "royalty" payment in the context of the Diversa/Yellowstone National Park agreement). If there is an agreement violation or breach of contract; damages and injunctive relief can also apply. The Diversa/Yellowstone National Park CRADA also included audit clauses designed to promote compliance (P. Scott, pers. comm. February 2003). In addition, as part of the research permit terms, scientists are required to submit a yearly summary of their park research activities, known as an Investigator's Annual Report. In addition, the park may require copies of field notes and scientific publications (see Chapter 8). Besides, it may be that the potential negative publicity of being caught by the NPS is a significant deterrent itself (P. Scott, pers. comm. December 2004).

Analysis: Enforcement and Monitoring

All countries analyzed above, except for Samoa, have proposed measures to ensure that bioprospecting projects comply with ABS regulations. However, none of these monitoring mechanisms are operational yet. Not even the Philippines, which has granted access to a couple of bioprospecting projects under EO 247 (see Chapter 7), has a monitoring system up and running. This may be related to the fact that setting up this kind of system is an expensive endeavor. One strategy to finance monitoring activities is proposed by Nicaragua's draft Law of Biodiversity which requires access applicants to pay for an evaluation and monitoring system. This can be a practical and cost-effective measure as long as a third independent party runs the system to ensure its objectivity. Others looking to ensure compliance may want to ask bioprospectors for a bond as Peru and the Philippines propose in their national ABS policies.

In any case, the complexity of bioprospecting projects may make compliance and monitoring systems difficult to implement. Bioprospecting projects involve multiple activities that include: a) collecting samples; b) processing and shipping samples to research laboratories usually located in foreign countries; c) analyzing samples; d) transferring samples between research organizations; and e) developing and commercializing products. This is an oversimplified description of a complex chain of events where multiple actors interact with the samples and products derived from them. Therefore, final products or processes may not have a physical connection with the genetic resource collected. Products may have been manufactured from scratch based on the molecular structure of genetic resources collected. The samples may be stored in *ex situ* conservation centers for years before the appropriate technology is designed to take advantage of them. On the other hand, controlling or prohibiting illegal access activities can be impossible. A tourist can take samples back to his or her country with almost no difficulty. The likelihood of catching such a perpetrator is very slim. Furthermore, enforcement under statute is very complicated once the collector has left the area of jurisdiction. If a citizen of a country patents a product derived from a sample illegally collected in another country, the source country cannot compel anything to be done to the citizen of the country that patented the sample. The collector, however, may be deterred by bad publicity

and blacklisted with the subsequent loss of reputation and business opportunities in other countries.

Most ABS policies may also require bioprospectors to submit an EIA to ensure that project activities will not have significant ecological, social, or economic impacts. Such an assessment may provide baseline information that can be used to monitor the evolution of ecological, social, or economic conditions in sites where collections take place. However, so far no country has proposed standards, at least about biodiversity indicators and other procedures to monitor and evaluate the state of biological diversity and its sustainable use.

In the last decade, several indicator methodologies have been proposed to monitor the status of environmental issues and biodiversity conservation efforts at the level of the management of community and species (Noss 1990) and at the provincial, national, regional, or global policy-making level (SBSTTA 1997). Perhaps the most popular methodology for an environmental indicator system, among policymakers and scientists, has been the so-called pressure, state, response framework (SBSTTA 1997). According to this framework, pressure indicators measure the forces that development trends such as bioprospecting activities (i.e., collection of biological samples and traditional knowledge) exert on the environment; state indicators are those that inform about the present quality and quantity of an environmental variable (i.e., population size of species in the region where specimens are being collected or number of conflicts among local indigenous groups); and response indicators inform about the activities implemented to mitigate a situation (i.e., reforestation or restoration projects or conflict resolution meetings). Additional elements that a bioprospecting system of indicators should consider include: 1) the type of information that should be collected by scientists for the indicators proposed, such as number of species and hectares of habitat affected and 2) the frequency of collection of this information that should coincide with the workplan of a given bioprospecting project. Information fed to the indicator system could also be manipulated to assess whether bioprospecting initiatives are complying with the Convention on Biological Diversity and relevant access laws and policies.

Final Comments

The CBD's provisions on access to genetic resources, traditional knowledge, technology transfer, and benefit sharing (Articles 8(j), 15, 16, and 19) are closely linked to CBD articles that address biodiversity conservation, sustainable use, monitoring, and capacity building objectives (Articles 6, 7, 9, 10, 12, 13, 14, 17, 18, and 19). While countries such as Costa Rica and Nicaragua have established this connection directly through the design of comprehensive single laws and policies that implement all of the provisions of the CBD, other countries such as Australia, Colombia, Ecuador, Mexico, Peru, Philippines, Samoa, and Thailand have developed single ABS regulations that

are complemented by existing or future environmental, sustainable development, or biodiversity related laws or policies. In any case, ABS laws and policies of these countries aim at implementing the CBD and they share key similarities that include: a) the establishment of bilateral agreements between bioprospecting groups and the national government that must be negotiated on mutually agreed terms; b) the recognition of national sovereignty over biological and genetic resources within national borders; c) the establishment of procedures for obtaining PIC from government authorities and the providers of samples and traditional knowledge (except for Thailand which requires PIC only from government authorities); and d) the equitable sharing of benefits derived from the use of biological diversity. However, as expected, these laws and policies also present several differences that are simply the result of different policy or regulatory options taken by countries and the expression of different legal systems, cultural beliefs, and social and economic conditions. For example, countries with large percentages of indigenous population are still trying to figure out strategies to protect indigenous knowledge. Furthermore, most of the countries examined in this chapter are working on policies that show concern about the potential negative impact of on access activities on the environment.

This review also shows that most ABS laws and polices are comprehensive, but sometimes confusing, costly, and difficult to implement. They share provisions and principles that need further clarification. For example, countries such as Colombia, Peru, Ecuador, Costa Rica, and the Philippines that have had ABS laws in place since the mid-1990s are still trying to define the scope of their access laws, the strategies to protect the knowledge of indigenous peoples, and the conditions to facilitate access to noncommercial bioprospecting activities. In contrast, Samoa's ABS conditions consist of one page with an over-simplified proposal to facilitate access that will still need further clarification, but which is practical and refreshing. New proposals for ABS laws and polices are also dealing with similar issues and trying to resolve new ones (e.g., the ownership issue in Malaysia). In the USA, NPS regulations are analogous to some of the provisions of ABS laws and policies that other countries have proposed and these NPS regulations facilitate ABS goals in NPS land.

In synthesis, ABS laws and policies developed under the umbrella of the CBD have created a complex and comprehensive scenario for access and exchange of genetic resources. This is the result of a process marked with conceptual and operational concerns and difficulties that still continue even for countries that pioneered ABS regulations in the mid-1990s. The next chapter examines these issues and their influence on the development process of selected ABS laws and policies.

References

ANDEAN COMMUNITY. 1996. Decision 391: Common regime on access to genetic resources. http://www.comunidadandina.org/ingles/treaties/dec/d391e.htm.

ANDEAN COMMUNITY. 2000. Decision 486: Common intellectual property regime. http://www.comunidadandina.org/ingles/treaties/dec/D486e.htm.

ANDEAN COMMUNITY. 2002. Decision 523: Regional biodiversity strategy for the tropical Andean countries. http://www.comunidadandina.org/ingles/treaties/dec/D523e.htm.

ANONYMOUS. 2003. TRIPS, biodiversity and traditional knowledge. *Bridges* **7(5)**:11–12. http://www.ictsd.org/.

BARBER C.V, L. GLOWKA, and A.G.M. LA VIÑA. 2002. Developing and implementing national measures for genetic resources access regulation and benefit-sharing. p 363–414 *in* S. LAIRD (ed.) *Biodiversity and traditional knowledge: Equitable partnerships in practice.* Earthscan, London, UK.

CHALERMPONGSE A. 2001. Access and benefit sharing relating to forest genetic resources and traditional knowledge in Thailand. p. 119–142 *in* L. GLOWKA, B. PISUPATI, and S. DE SILVA (eds.). *Access to genetic resources and traditional knowledge: Lessons from South and Southeast Asia.* Proceedings of the South and Southeast Asia regional workshop on access to genetic resources and traditional knowledge, February 1998. IUCN.

COICA. 1996. Pueblos indígenas amazónicos rechazan el robo y la privatización de sus conocimientos. Press Release, 24 June. Coordinadora de las Organizaciones Indígenas de la Cuenca Amazónica, Quito, Ecuador.

CORREA C.M. 1999. Access to plant genetic resources and intellectual property rights. Background study paper No. 8. Commission on Genetic Resources for Food and Agriculture, FAO, Rome, Italy.

COX P.A. 2001. Ensuring equitable benefits: The Falealupo Covenant and the isolation of anti-viral drug prostratin from a Samoan Medicinal Plant. *Pharmaceutical Biology* **39**(Supplement):33–40.

DAVIS S. 1993. *Pathways to economic development through intellectual property rights.* Environment Department, World Bank, Washington DC USA.

DE KLEMM C. 1994. Conservation legislation. p. 189–204 *in* D.R. GIVEN (ed.) *Principles and practice of plant conservation.* Timber Press, OR USA.

DIVISION OF ENVIRONMENT AND CONSERVATION. 1998. Government of Samoa: National report to the Convention on Biological Diversity. Department of Lands, Survey, and Environment, Apia, Samoa.

DLSE. 2000. Conditions for access to and benefit sharing of Samoa's biodiversity resources. Department of Lands, Surveys and Environment (DLSE), Government of Samoa.

DUTFIELD G. 2000. *Intellectual property rights, trade and biodiversity.* Earthscan. London, UK.

GACETA PARLAMENTARIA. 2001. Del Sen. Jorge Rubén Nordhausen González, del Grupo Parlamentario del Partido Acción Nacional, la que contiene iniciativa de Ley para el acceso y aprovechamiento de los recursos biológicos y genético. N. 14. Senado de la República, México. http://camaradediputados.gob.mx/gaceta/.

GIFIS S.H. 1991. *Law Dictionary.* Third edition. Barron's Educational Series, New York, NY USA.

GLOWKA L. 1998. A guide to designing legal frameworks to determine access to genetic resources. Environmental Policy and Law paper No. 34. Environmental Law Center, IUCN, Gland, Switzerland, Cambridge, and Bonn.

GRAJAL A. 1999. Biodiversity and the nation state: Regulating access to genetic resources limits biodiversity research in developing countries. *Conservation Biology* **13(1)**:6–9.

INRENA. 2001. Proyecto de reglamento sobre acceso a los recursos genéticos. Instituto Nacional de Recursos Naturales

(INRENA), Ministerio de Agricultura, Lima, Perú.

LA ASAMBLEA LEGISLATIVA. 1998. Ley No. 41 (de I de julio de 1998): Ley general de ambiente de la Republica de Panamá. Diario Oficial No. 23,578, Panamá.

MARENA. 1996. Ley General del Medio Ambiente y los Recursos Naturales-Ley No. 217. Ministerio del Ambiente y los Recursos Naturales (MARENA), Managua, Nicaragua, http://www.marena.gob.ni/normas_procedimientos03.htm.

MARENA. 2002. Proyecto de Ley de Biodiversidad. Ministerio del Ambiente y los Recursos Naturales (MARENA), Managua, Nicaragua.

NITTM. 2002. Act on the Protection and Promotion of Traditional Thai Medicinal Intelligence, B.E. 2547. National Institute of Thai Traditional Medicine, Office of the Permanent Secretariat, Ministry of Public Health, Book Development Project, The Thai Traditional Medicine Foundation. Bangkok, Thailand.

NOSS R.F. 1990. Indicators for monitoring biodiversity: A hierarchical approach. *Conservation Biology* **4(4):**355–364.

OLDFIELD M. L. 1989. *The value of conserving genetic resources.* Sinauer Associates, Inc., Sunderland, MA USA.

PERUVIAN CONGRESS. 2002. Ley que establece el régimen de protección de los conocimientos colectivos de los pueblos indígenas vinculados a los resguardos biológicos. Poder Legislativo Congreso de la Republica, Ley 27811, Lima, Perú. URL: http://www.concytec.gob.pe/infocyt/ley27811.html.

PINHEIRO C.U.B. 1997. Jaborandi (*Pilocarpus* sp., Rutaceae): A wild species and its rapid transformation into a crop. *Economic Botany* **51(1):**49–58.

SBSTTA. 1997. Recommendations for a core set of indicators. Subsidiary Body on Scientific, Technical and Technological Advice (SBSTTA), Convention on Biological Diversity. URL: http://www.biodiv.org/doc/meetings/sbstta/sbstta-03/information/sbstta-03-inf-13-en.htm.

SEMARNAT. 2000. Ley General de Vida Silvestre. Secretaría de Medio Ambiente y Recursos Naturales (SEMARNAT), Diario Oficial, Ciudad de México, México.

SEMARNAT. 2003. Ley General de Desarrollo Forestal. Secretaría de Medio Ambiente y Recursos Naturales (SEMARNAT), Diario Oficial, Ciudad de México, México.

SCHWEITZER J., F.G. HANDLEY, J. EDWARDS, W.F. HARRIS, M.R. GREVER, S.A. SCHEPARTZ, G. CRAGG, K. SNADER, A. BHAT. 1991. Commentary: Summary of the Workshop on Drug Development, Biological Diversity, and Economic Growth. *Journal of the National Cancer Institute* **83(18):**1294–1298.

SHIVA V. 2001. *Patents: Myth or reality.* Penguin Group. USA.

TEN KATE T.K. and S.A. LAIRD. 1999. *The commercial use of biodiversity: Access to genetic resources and benefit-sharing.* Earthscan. London, UK.

THAILAND CONGRESS. 1999. Plant Variety Protection Act. Government Gazette, Vol. 116, Part 118a, 25 November. Thailand.

VOUMARD J. 2000. *Access to biological resources in Commonwealth areas.* Commonwealth of Australia. Canberra, Australia.

Endnotes

[1] TEN KATE and LAIRD (1999) report that the following 41 countries, which are Parties to the CBD, and the United States of America, which is a signatory, but not a Party, have developed or are developing access and benefit-sharing frameworks: Argentina, Australia (at the Commonwealth level and in the states of Western Australia and Queensland), Belize, Bolivia, Brazil, Cameroon, Colombia, Costa Rica, Ecuador, Eritrea, Ethiopia, Fiji, The Gambia, Ghana, Guatemala, India, Indonesia, Kenya, Lao People's Democratic Republic, Lesotho, Malawi, Malaysia (including the State of Sarawak), Mexico, Mozambique, Namibia, Nigeria, Papua New Guinea, Peru, Philippines, the Republic of Korea, Samoa, Seychelles, Solomon Islands, South Africa, Tanzania, Thailand, Turkey, Venezuela, Vietnam, Yemen, and Zimbabwe.

[2] See the CBD website for a roster of country status with respect to signing and becoming a Party to the CBD, URL: http://www.biodiv.org/world/parties.asp.

[3] All of the countries that developed these access and benefit-sharing frameworks are still working to improve their laws or to turn their policies or administrative measures into laws (see Chapter 2).

[4] The Andean Community (formerly known as the Andean Pact or Cartagena Accord) is an economic and social-integration treaty among Colombia, Peru, Ecuador, Venezuela, and Bolivia.

[5] The Association of Southeast Asian Nations or ASEAN is a regional organization that promotes economic growth, social progress, and cultural development in the region. Its member countries are Indonesia, Malaysia, Philippines, Singapore, Thailand, Brunei Darussalam, Laos, Myanmar, and Cambodia.

[6] The "African model law for the protection of the rights of local communities, and farmers and breeders, and for the regulation of access to biological resources" is another example of this type of regional initiatives.

[7] Between April 1998 and May 2004 Venezuela has invoked Decision 391 to facilitate access to 12 projects and has subscribed five framework agreements with national universities and research centers to carry out bioprospecting activities for noncommercial purposes (M.E. Febres, Pers. Comm. May 2004). Under Decision 391, a university, research center, or scientist that subscribes a framework agreement with the government is allowed to carry out several projects under such agreement.

[8] In this chapter bioprospecting is defined as the search for plants, animals, and microbial species for academic, pharmaceutical, biotechnological, agricultural, and other industrial purposes.

[9] ANAM regulates access to wildlife genetic resources and the National Institute for Agricultural Research (IDIAP) controls access to agricultural genetic resources (M. Dimas, pers. comm. August 2000).

[10] Draft *Guidelines for Bioprospecting Activities in the Philippines* (Joint DENR-DA-PCSD-NCIP Administrative Order No. 1). Available at URL: http://www.denr.gov.ph/article/view/2332/.

[11] URL: http://www.med.govt.nz/ers/nat-res/bioprospecting/index.html.

[12] The situation in Australian States and Territories is not consistent or clear. Resolving ownership issues in some states may well be controversial. Complicating the issue is that some people confuse ownership of biochemical and genetic material from individual examples of species with ownership of the species as a whole.

Furthermore, there is the misconception held by some people that the patent system somehow allows a patentee to assert control over the possession and use of biological resources from which the patented invention has been derived (G. Burton, pers. comm. January 2003).

[13] Customary land is held and used according to custom and it is owned by a family, clan, or tribe (C. Schuster, pers. comm. August 2002).

[14] Full text of the ITPGRFA and its Annex are available at URL: ftp: //ext-ftp.fao.org/waicent/pub/cgrfa8/iu/ITPGRe.pdf.

[15] Natural resources are defined as living and nonliving resources that include "soil, rock, sand, nutrients, water, air, forest, plants, animals, insects, microorganisms, and living residues"; biological resources are defined as "any living resources within the forested area" and genetic resources include "genetic units" and "different forms of genes".

[16] The EPBCAR currently provides for reserve and wildlife permits: a) reserve permits are for activities in Commonwealth areas that include reserves, parks, conservation zones, and external territories; and b) wildlife permits are for taking, keeping, and moving listed threatened migratory, marine, and cetacean species and communities in Commonwealth areas (VOUMARD 2000).

[17] Bioprospectors may find that there can be several access providers; for example, if a Commonwealth area is subject to native title, the Commonwealth and the native titleholders are both access providers. If the access provider is the Commonwealth, the Secretary to the Commonwealth department that has administrative authority for the Commonwealth area may, on behalf of the Commonwealth, enter into the benefit-sharing agreement (see Chapter 9).

[18] This is a draft bylaw of the Law of Biodiversity that was approved on 15 December 2003.

[19] According to the Law of Biodiversity public universities were exempted from control for a term of one year (until 7 May 1999) in order for them to establish their own controls and regulations for noncommercial projects that require access. So far only the University of Costa Rica has developed access controls and regulations. This is due to the fact that the law is not currently under implementation (J. Cabrera, pers. comm. January 2004). However, once the constitutional challenge is resolved, universities will have to develop these access controls and regulations in a predetermined period of time. Otherwise they will have to comply with the Law of Biodiversity just like commercial bioprospectors.

[20] If the TO authorizes the continuing use of genetic material or of biochemical extracts for commercial purposes, applicants are required to obtain a separate concession from the provider of the resource. The Law of Biodiversity does not provide information about the process, requirements, and length of time needed to obtain this concession.

[21] URL: http://www.nrct.net/modules.php?op=modload&name=Sectio ns&file=index&req=viewarticle&artid=181.

[22] URL: http://science.nature.nps.gov/research.

[23] GIFIS (1991) defines a contract as "a promise or a set of promises, for breach of which the law gives a remedy, or the performance of which the law in some cases recognizes as a duty".

[24] Several academic or scientific projects (noncommercial) can be included in one framework access contract (PERUVIAN CONGRESS 2002).

[25] A local domestic plant variety is one that exists only in a particular locality within the country and has never been registered as a new plant variety and which is registered as a local domestic plant variety under this Act.

[26] A general domestic plant variety refers to any plant variety originating or existing in the country and commonly exploited and shall include a plant variety which is not a new plant variety, a local domestic plant variety, or a wild plant variety.

[27] A wild plant variety refers to one that currently exists or used to exist in the natural habitat and has not been commonly cultivated.

[28] A CRADA is defined by the Federal Technology Transfer Act (FTTA) of 1986 as "any agreement between one or more Federal laboratories and one or more non-Federal parties under which the Government, through its laboratories, provides personnel, services, facilities, equipment, or other resources with or without reimbursement (but not funds to non-Federal parties) and the non-Federal parties provide funds, personnel, services, facilities, equipment, or other resources toward the conduct of specified research or development efforts which are consistent with the mission of the laboratory" (see Chapter 8).

[29] The complete text and annexes of the CBD are available at http: //www.biodiv.org/convention/articles.asp.

[30] The complete text and annexes of the CBD are available at http: //www.biodiv.org/convention/articles.asp.

[31] For further information about the law relating to the patenting of plants, microorganisms, and related biological materials, see IP Australia's website at http://www.ipaustralia.gov.au/.

[32] URL: http://ip.aaas.org/tekindex.nsf.

[33] The complete text and annexes of the CBD are available at http: //www.biodiv.org/convention/articles.asp.

[34] Regulation 8A. 05. of the Crimes Act; a penalty unit is currently set at $110 AUD.

Table 1. Access and benefit sharing (ABS) policy status of Pacific Rim countries signing the CBD

A. Countries with ABS laws and policies

1. Colombia

As a member of the Andean Community, Colombia is subject to the 1996 Decision 391 on ABS, a regional law, and is currently working on a policy to facilitate implementation of Decision 391 at a national level.

2. Costa Rica

In 1998, Costa Rica enacted the Law of Biodiversity No. 7788. In late 1998, the Attorney General of the Republic challenged the law, which prevented its implementation. In December 2003, a "General Access Procedure" that will operate as the bylaw of the Law of Biodiversity was published. Before the development of this law, there were some provisions in the 1992 Law of Wildlife Conservation (and its 1997 regulation) regarding flora and fauna collection permits. There were also some bylaws dealing with research, specifically referring to national parks.

3. Ecuador

As a member of the Andean Community, Ecuador is subject to the 1996 Decision 391 on ABS, a regional law. In 1996, a law for the protection of biodiversity was passed by Congress. The law includes only one article that determines the State's ownership of biological species as national and public goods. This article also states that the commercial exploitation of these species will be subject to special regulations issued by the President that will guarantee the rights of indigenous communities over their knowledge and genetic resources. Ecuador is also working on a draft regulation of Decision 391 that has been in the making since the ratification of Decision 391. A final draft was submitted in April 2001 to the Minister of the Environment. That draft received much criticism and was not approved by the Minister. There are also general provisions in the pending new draft National Law for the Conservation and Sustainable Use of Biodiversity debated by Congress in April 2002 and February 2003. The draft law is still under discussion among government officials (July 2004).

4. Mexico

Articles 87 and 87 BIS of the Ecological Equilibrium and Environmental Protection General Act (EEEPGA) regulate ABS issues in Mexico. This law incorporates the three main principles stated in the Convention on Biological Diversity (CBD): prior informed consent, mutually agreed terms, and benefit sharing. The EEEPGA is complemented by a norm (NOM-126-ECOL-2000) that facilitates a change of purpose from scientific (or noncommercial) to biotechnological (or commercial) uses. The 1999 Wildlife General Act (WGA) and the 2003 Sustainable Forestry Development Act (SFDGA) regulate the collection of wildlife and forest biological resources respectively. EEEPGA, WGA, and SFDGA set the principles but not the details that should regulate ABS initiatives. There are two ABS law proposals in the Federal Congress that purport to fill this gap: one submitted by Federal Senator Jorge Nordhausen (National Action Party), and another submitted by Federal Representative Alejandro Cruz Gutierrez (Institutional Revolutionary Party). So far Congress has not discussed these laws in the plenary.

5. Philippines

In 1995, the Philippines adopted the first ABS policy in the world, Executive Order 247 "Prescribing Guidelines and Establishing a Regulatory Framework for the Prospecting of

Biological and Genetic Resources in the Philippines, their By-Products and Derivatives for Scientific and Commercial Purposes and for other Purposes". In 2001, the Philippines enacted Republic Act No. 9147, also known as the Wildlife Resources and Conservation Act that addressed many of the criticisms made to the Executive Order 247. This Act includes only two clauses about bioprospecting issues but it modifies Executive Order 247 considerably. In July 2004, draft "Guidelines for Bioprospecting Activities in the Philippines" was released for review and comment by the Department of Environment and Natural Resources. If adopted, the guidelines would facilitate the implementation of the Wildlife Act and those provisions of EO 247 not repealed by the Wildlife Act. The Philippines has also been actively leading the development of the ASEAN Framework on Access to Biological and Genetic Resources that is scheduled to be adopted in 2004 or 2005.

6. Peru

As a member of the Andean Community, Peru is subject to the 1996 Decision 391 on ABS, a regional law. Peru has a draft regulation for Decision 391 that is being reviewed by the National Environmental Council. The government is also developing a second regulation targeted to facilitate access to genetic resources found in indigenous land. In August 2002, Peru adopted Law No. 27811 for the protection of indigenous communities' collective knowledge associated with biodiversity.

7. Samoa

In 2000, Samoa adopted the "Conditions for access to and benefit sharing of Samoa's Biodiversity Resources". This is a regulation that is being implemented to facilitate access, while the country completes a draft bioprospecting regulation. However, further progress on this regulation is on hold until the Department of Lands, Surveys and Environment completes a review of the 1989 Lands, Surveys, and Environment Act. The draft bioprospecting regulation is expected to be appended to the Act.

8. Thailand

ABS is regulated by the following two laws and two regulations: The 1999 Plant Variety Protection Act, the 1999 Act on Protection and Promotion of Traditional Medicinal Intelligence Act, the 1999 Royal Forest Department Regulation on Forestry Studying and Research Conducting within Forested Areas, and the 1982 Regulation on the Permission of Foreign Researchers of the National Research Council of Thailand.

9. United States of America (USA)

The USA signed the CBD but it has not ratified it yet. Access to natural resources in the United States is ordinarily managed by the private or public owner of the resource. For example, access to genetic resources found in national parks is governed by the National Park Service (NPS) regulations. Since 1983, the NPS has issued permits to facilitate the collection of specimens, and Cooperative Research and Development Agreements (CRADAS) can be used to address benefit-sharing issues. A CRADA is defined by the Federal Technology Transfer Act of 1986 as "any agreement between one or more Federal laboratories and one or more non-Federal parties under which the Government, through its laboratories, provides personnel, services, facilities, equipment, or other resources with or without reimbursement (but not funds to non-Federal parties)

Table 1. Continued

and the non-Federal parties provide funds, personnel, services, facilities, equipment, or other resources toward the conduct of specified research or development efforts which are consistent with the mission of the laboratory".

B. Countries working towards the development of ABS laws and policies

1. Australia

The draft Environment Protection and Biodiversity Conservation Amendment Regulations are expected to be enacted in 2005 and they will go under section 301 (Control of access to biological resources) of the 1999 Environment Protection and Biodiversity Conservation Act. These regulations will apply only to the "commonwealth area" of the country. The states and territories are also working on their own ABS regulations. For example, in mid-2004, Queensland passed a Biodiscovery Bill and Western Australia is currently discussing a licensing regime for terrestrial bioprospecting activities that will be included in a draft Biodiversity Conservation Act. In addition to this, in 2002 the Natural Resource Management Ministerial Council adopted a federal agreement on a "Nationally Consistent Approach For Access to and the Utilization of Australia's Native Genetic and Biochemical Resources" to facilitate the development ABS regulations nationwide.

2. Cambodia

In 2002 Cambodia adopted a new Forestry Law. While this law is not specific about regulating ABS issues in relation to forest genetic resources, it regulates the commercial and noncommercial use of timber that is extracted from all forests (natural and planted), including wild vegetation, wildlife products, and services provided by the forest. Also, in 2002, the Ministry of Environment made public the country's National Biodiversity Strategy and Action Plan. This document does not address the need to develop a comprehensive ABS policy, but it states as one of its goals to ensure the equitable sharing of benefits from the protection and sustainable use of biological resources. Furthermore, the strategy and action plan emphasizes that existing legislation concerning biodiversity conservation and sustainable use is currently under revision in Cambodia.

3. Canada

No official decision has been made as to whether Canada should have an ABS policy. However, this country has undertaken some background research on ABS issues and held preliminary discussions with the provinces, some aboriginal groups and stakeholders on ABS issues, especially with respect to the negotiation of the CBD Bonn Guidelines on ABS. The National Biodiversity Convention Office has been consulting aboriginal people on the Bonn Guidelines.

4. Chile

In late 2003, Chile concluded a proposal for a law to regulate access to agricultural genetic resources. This proposal was developed by the Ministry of Agriculture without the participation of all sectors of society and the government and it was discarded after much criticism. However, efforts to develop a new proposal continue within the Ministry. In December 2003, the National Commission of the Environment (CONAMA) published the National Biodiversity Strategy that was approved by CONAMA's Ministerial Council. Subsequently, in mid-2004 the National Biodiversity Action Plan was initiated. It should be noted that the strategy emphasizes the need to develop

legal instruments to regulate access to genetic resources and to ensure the fair participation in and equitable distribution of benefits derived from their use.

5. China

China, like many other countries, has policies that regulate access to genetic resources, but these policies lack benefit-sharing provisions. However, China's 1997 National Report on Implementation of the Convention on Biological Diversity states that a priority action for the country is to draft a genetic resources policy or law that regulates prior informed consent principles, benefit-sharing issues, and intellectual property rights, among other issues. So, in late 2002, the State Council of China authorized the Environmental Protection Administration (SEPA) to coordinate all ABS-related issues to ensure the implementation of the CBD. Therefore, SEPA is currently leading a national project to inventory all genetic resources in China. This includes the participation of experts from many organizations and universities from the agriculture, forestry, fishery, and medical sectors. Also, SEPA is assembling a team to develop a comprehensive ABS policy or law.

6. Cook Islands

The country is currently working on a national ABS policy that will go under a proposed National Environmental Act. Central government ministries regulate national laws such as this act. The island councils of the different inhabited islands and the municipal councils for the capital island may adopt by-laws. These by-laws are managed under the Island Council.

7. El Salvador

In El Salvador there is no integral biodiversity law or strategy that regulates the use of and access to genetic, biological, and biochemical resources. The current legal framework for the regulation of access to genetic resources is partially covered by some laws. For example, Article 66 of the Environmental Law states that any access, research, manipulation, and use of biological diversity can only be carried out with a permit, license, or concession granted by the authority in charge of managing the resource in question. Every time this permit is granted relevant communities have to be consulted. In 2002, however the Environment Ministry developed policy guidelines, administrative procedures, and a capacity-building strategy on access to genetic and biochemical resources. This information is currently being reviewed by the Presidency and constitutes the foundation for a national policy on access to genetic and biochemical resources that must be adopted by the government in 2004 or 2005.

8. Fiji

There is no legal or administrative framework in place on ABS. There is a draft administrative paper that forms the basis of an unwritten understanding between all stakeholders on the issue of ABS. A national committee is also working on the development of an ABS policy. Committee members include scientists at the local University of the South Pacific and legal officers from the state law office.

9. Guatemala

The 1999 Action Plan of the National Strategy for the Conservation and Sustainable Use of Biodiversity states the need to develop a national ABS policy. However, no participatory process has been initiated yet. Guatemala is a signatory of the Central American draft protocol on "Access to genetic and biochemical resources, and their associated knowledge" but it has not been ratified yet by this nation.

Table 1. Continued

10. Honduras

The country is currently working on a national law to regulate access and benefit-sharing issues. In 2001, the National Strategy on Biodiversity was adopted and one of its strategic themes was the ABS issue.

11. Indonesia

Indonesia is currently working on a law that is likely to be called Act on Genetic Resource Management. This act will include a government regulation on ABS issues. The government is also conducting an assessment of existing legal instruments that regulate ABS issues. Local officials estimate that ABS legislation will be concluded in 2004 or 2005.

12. Japan

The Japanese government initiated a survey to collect policies on ABS. Also, several ministries are involved in the discussion about ABS issues; currently, discussion is at individual ministry levels. The government has also been conducting studies on global issues and trends on ABS policies through research contracts or financial assistance with think tanks. For example, the Japan Bioindustry Association (JBI) has been actively participating in the meetings of the Conference of the Parties to the CBD. JBI has also conducted studies and seminars to help implement the CBD in Japan, and in 2000 this organization published a policy statement that provided general and voluntary prior informed consent and benefit sharing guidelines for its members.

13. Malaysia

The federal government is working on a national ABS bill that is likely to be adopted in 2005. However, states such as Sabah and Sarawak already have the 2000 Sabah Biodiversity Enactment, the 1997 Sarawak Biodiversity Center Ordinance and the 1998 Sarawak Biodiversity Regulations. The relationship between these policies that regulate ABS issues and the new federal bill is uncertain.

14. Marshall Islands

In 2000, the National Biodiversity Strategy and Action Plan acknowledged the importance of regulating access to the country's genetic resources and ensuring that the benefits derived from the use of these resources are shared equitably. Furthermore, the strategy calls for the development of IPR legislation that protects the rights of indigenous owners of genetic resources and traditional knowledge and facilitates access to and benefit sharing of these resources and knowledge under prior informed consent obligations. Plans to develop this legislation are in progress.

15. Micronesia

Micronesia finished its National Biodiversity Strategy and Action Plan in March 2002. It is expected that the development of ABS legislation will follow from the needs identified through this collaborative process between the National Government and the four states. The two national government departments that would be most involved in the process of developing access legislation are the Department of Justice and the Department of Economic Affairs, Sustainable Development Unit, National Biodiversity Strategy and Action Plan. Regional ABS model guidelines and legislation have been developed with the assistance of a number of multilateral bodies (Secretariat of the Pacific Community, WWF-South Pacific Program, and the Foundation for International Environmental Law and Development (FIELD) among them) that will assist

in this effort. However, under the Micronesia's Immigration law, Title 50 of the Micronesian Code, researchers entering the country are required to declare the purpose of their visit. The Department of Immigration then refers the request to the Division of Archives and Preservation. If acceptable to that Division, the Department of Immigration issues an entry permit under the category "researcher's permit" to the entrant.

16. New Zealand

The 2000 New Zealand Biodiversity Strategy addresses ABS goals and includes the following desired outcome for 2020: "There is an integrated policy for the management of all genetic material in New Zealand and for bioprospecting activities, in accord with international commitments. There is appropriate domestic and international access to indigenous genetic material, taking into account New Zealand's sovereignty and rights to the benefits from its genetic material, as well as rights and obligations under the Treaty of Waitangi." In November 2002, the Ministry of Economic Development published a discussion paper on bioprospecting. The paper invited the public to submit comments by the end of February 2003. In May 2003 the Ministry posted a summary of the submissions on its website (http://www.med.govt.nz/ers/nat-res/bioprospecting/index.html). Further consultation will follow with stakeholders such as the Maori people to examine key bioprospecting issues and a future national policy on ABS or bioprospecting will be drafted taking into account this consultation process. However, future efforts to develop such a policy can be complicated by a claim by a number of tribes (Iwi) of the Maori people to a tribunal. According to this claim the Maori have exclusive ownership rights over both traditional knowledge and indigenous genetic resources under the Waitangi Treaty of 1840 between the chiefs of most New Zealand Iwi at the time and the British Government (the Crown). This claim was lodged in 1991, and it does not appear that it will be concluded in the near future.

17. Nicaragua

The government developed a proposal for a law of biodiversity that addresses ABS issues. The proposal should be sent to Congress in 2004. Nicaragua's draft law of biodiversity responds to the mandate (Article 70) of the 1996 General Law of the Environment and Natural Resources No. 217.

18. Niue

The protection of traditional knowledge and ABS have been identified as priority issues in the National Biodiversity Strategy and Action Plan. Therefore, funds were used to conduct a consultancy to assess capacity needs in Niue related to this kind of work. Niue has experienced some access situations in the past year that suggest the urgent need for ABS legislation. In the absence of this legislation, access applications have been handled on a contractual basis. Village stakeholders are particularly interested about strategies to protect traditional knowledge. An Environment Bill was approved in 2003 and this will facilitate the insertion of ABS regulations and other regulations that protect traditional knowledge. ABS regulations may be modeled after the South Pacific Regional Environment Program (SPREP) framework legislation on access and benefit sharing.

19. Panama

Panama is currently developing and modifying existing laws and policies to facilitate ABS goals. For example, draft Law No. 36, includes ABS, intellectual property, and marketing pro-

Table 1. Continued

visions for products used in traditional indigenous medicine. Also, Panama is working on an ABS and indigenous knowledge policy that is likely to provide a course of action about how to implement existing and future ABS policies. The 1998 General Law of the Environment No. 41 (GLE) designates the National Authority for the Environment (ANAM) as the competent authority for the regulation, management, and control of the access to and use of biogenetic resources. ANAM shall also develop the legal instruments and economic mechanisms to this purpose. GLE clarifies that the holders of rights granted for the use of natural resources do not hold rights for the use of genetic resources contained in them.

20. Papua New Guinea
The Department of Environment and Conservation is working closely with lawyers from the Department of Justice and the Attorney General to develop a framework on ABS.

21. Republic of Korea
Comprehensive ABS provisions are proposed for addition to the 1991 National Environment Conservation Act No. 4492 by amendment. The 1994 amendment (Law No. 4783) of the act included one provision that facilitated access but it did not regulate benefit-sharing issues. Article 25.4 of the act applied only to foreigners and it regulated the use of domestic biological resources (excluding selected wild animals and plans) for commercial, medical or scientific use. This provision, however, was removed from the act by Law No. 5876 of 8 February 1999.

22. Russian Federation
An important problem for the country is the absence of coordinated measures towards conservation and sustainable utilization of biodiversity. In 1996, Russia started implementing the project of the Global Ecological Foundation Biodiversity Conservation. This project included three components: Strategy of Biodiversity Conservation (2001), Protected Natural Regions (2000), and Baikal Region (2003). The Supervisory Committee and Management Group, nominated for the project, have already begun preparing The National and Regional Strategy, and establishing ecological networks of protected areas (72 reserves and national parks). In mid-2001, the National Report of the Russian Federation on ABS was prepared for the Conference of the Parties of the CBD. The report states that prior to the development of an ABS policy it is necessary to establish a national coordination center for the problems related with access to genetic resources. Since 2003, the Department of Life and Earth Sciences of the Ministry of Industry, Science, and Technologies of the Russian Federation has been analyzing gaps, contradictions, and needs of existing national laws and policies that apply to ABS goals. Some of the challenges faced by policymakers include identifying land and genetic resources ownership rights and increasing awareness about ABS issues among local administrators, members of Parliament, policymakers, and the public in general.

23. Singapore
The country is currently formulating policy and guidelines that will regulate ABS issues. An ad hoc inter-agency committee is working on a strategy document on access to genetic resources. Member agencies of the committee include: the Intellectual Property Office of Singapore (Ministry of Law), Attorney-General's Chambers, Ministry of National Development, Agri-Food and Veterinary Authority of Singapore, Ministry of Trade and Industry, Economic Development Board, Trade

Development Board, and National Science and Technology Board. The country does not have indigenous peoples engaged in traditional practices, therefore issues such as the protection of traditional knowledge are not being discussed by policymakers. Singapore has also been actively involved in the development of the ASEAN framework agreement on access to biological and genetic resources.

24. Solomon Islands
In the last few years, this country has experienced a period of social and economic crisis on the island of Guadalcanal. The shortage of economic resources caused by this situation and a weak governmental structure has delayed efforts to develop access and benefit-sharing policies. However, they are beginning to examine ABS issues with the assistance of SPREP and other organizations such as WWF South Pacific Program that organized a workshop in May 2003. In the meantime, bioprospectors may apply for a research permit under the Research Act to the Ministry of Education and Training. The Ministry liaises with provinces and communities where research activity is to occur and a research committee decides whether to approve or reject the application. This decision takes into account the views of provincial authorities and communities.

25. Vanuatu
After a national consultation process, the country is analyzing ABS policies that might be included in a draft of its Environment Act. Vanuatu, however, has a Cultural Research Policy that regulates consultation with local communities, chief's councils, and women's groups.

26. Vietnam
In 1995 Vietnam developed a National Action Plan on Biological Diversity that addresses ABS issues. In the last few years the government has been actively collecting examples of ABS laws and policies and it is planning to start working on national ABS legislation in 2004 or 2005.

C. Countries not involved in any process leading to the development of ABS laws and policies

1. Kiribati
It is a high priority but the country lacks the funding needed to develop ABS policies. The National Biodiversity Strategy and Action Plan, however, may create momentum to begin the ABS development process. The plan was completed in February 2000 but it has not been tabled yet by the Cabinet for approval and endorsement.

2. Laos
Lack of financial support and technical expertise has prevented this country from developing an ABS policy.

3. Nauru
ABS is not a top priority, and there are budgetary constraints.

4. Palau
Palau should start working on an ABS policy in 2004–2005, depending on funding and capacity availability. However, this country is currently working on a national biodiversity strategy and action plan.

5. Tonga
This subject has not been raised with the government by the relevant government body, the Ministry of Labor, Commerce, and Industries. Tonga, however, is working on a national biodiversity strategy and action plan.

Table 1. Continued

6. Tuvalu

Tuvalu ratified the CBD in December 2002 and developing ABS regulations is not a top priority.

Table 2. Status of intellectual property rights in Pacific Rim countries signing the CBD

A. Countries with ABS laws and policies

1. Colombia

Colombia is a member of the World Intellectual Property Organization (WIPO) and World Trade Organization (WTO). It is also a signatory to the Agreement on Trade-Related Aspects of Intellectual Property Rights (TRIPS). All WTO members are de facto Parties to all WTO agreements. Colombia is also a member of the Andean Community and as a member of this organization, it is protected by the Common Regime on Industrial Property, Decision 486 of 2000. With this Decision, the Andean Community countries complied with TRIPS. Decision 486 and Decision 391 (i.e., the Andean ABS law) have a strong connection. Decision 486 requires patent applicants to present a copy of the access contract when the products or procedures of the patent requested have been obtained or developed from genetic resources or their derivatives of which any of the member countries are countries of origin. If applicable, a copy of the authorization for the use of traditional knowledge from indigenous, Afro-American, and local communities, when the products for which the patent is requested have been obtained or developed from such knowledge of which any of the member countries is a country of origin. Colombia does not have in place a comprehensive system to protect traditional knowledge. Decision 391 establishes that a norm to protect these rights has to be proposed at the Andean Community level, but this has not occurred. Colombia is also covered by the 1993 Decision 345 of Andean Community that protects plant breeders' rights.

2. Costa Rica

Costa Rica is a WIPO and WTO member and therefore a Party to TRIPS. Intellectual property right requirements and conditions are clearly stated in the Law of Biodiversity. The Law established diverse exclusions but the compatibility of some of these exclusions with TRIPS is debatable. Costa Rica has comprehensive legislation related to IPRs. The 1983 Patent, Drawings and Utility Models Law No. 6867 was reformed by Law No. 7979 of 2000 to make it compatible with TRIPS. The new law has no exclusions for microorganisms, biological processes, genes, and genetic sequences as long as the patentability requirements are met. A plant breeders' rights draft law is yet to be approved. A proposal for a *sui generis* system of intellectual community rights is being developed through a consultation process that begun recently. The National Commission for the Management of Biodiversity must propose policies on access to genetic and biochemical resources of *ex situ* and *in situ* biodiversity. It will also act as an obligatory consultant in procedures related to the protection of intellectual property rights on biodiversity. The General Access Procedure (bylaw of the Law of Biodiversity) states as one of the criteria: Intellectual property rights not affecting key agricultural products and processes for the nourishment and health of the country's inhabitants. This criterion also includes protection for the resources of local communities and indigenous populations. The Law of Biodiversity excludes DNA sequences from patent processes; plants and animals; unmodified microorganisms; essential biological processes for plant and animal production; the processes or natural cycles; inventions essentially derived from the knowledge involved or biological traditional practices or in public domain; the inventions that are produced monopolistically that may affect the processes or agricultural basic products used for feeding and health purposes (Article 78). There is a criterion that is based on the thesis that reforms to the Patent Law of 2000 tacitly derogated the exclusions of the Law of Biodiversity since they were promulgated later on; it excludes some, but not all, of the aspects provided in Article 78 from the patent process.

3. Ecuador

Ecuador is a WIPO and WTO member, a signatory to TRIPS, and a member of Andean Community. See Colombia for information about IPR legislation that covers all Andean Community countries.

4. Mexico

Mexico is a WIPO and WTO member and therefore a signatory to TRIPS. The 1994 Industrial Property Act (amended in 1997 and 1999) provides patent protection for products and processes that comply with the patentability test of novelty, inventiveness, and industrial application. It excludes protection for biological and genetic material as found in nature. The 1996 Federal Plan Variety Act protects varieties that are new, stable, distinct, and homogeneous.

5. Philippines

The Philippines is a WIPO and WTO member and therefore a signatory to TRIPS. This country is also member of the 1995 ASEAN Framework Agreement on Intellectual Property Cooperation. The 1998 Intellectual Property Code was enacted in compliance with the minimum standards set under TRIPS. As of 1999, more than 100 microorganisms have been granted patent protection in the Philippines. The law excludes from patent protection plant varieties and animal breeds. It also does not give protection to traditional knowledge, but allows for the creation of a *sui generis* protection system for community intellectual property rights. In 2002, Congress passed a plant variety protection bill (Republic Act No. 9168) that provides *sui generis* protection over plant varieties and Farmer's Rights. Patent protection over life forms including microorganisms remains a controversial issue in the Philippines. It is argued that life forms are not eligible for patents because nothing new is created and the process merely involves reorganizing something that already exists. In 1997, Republic Act No. 8423, also known as the Traditional Alternative Medicine Act was passed in order to protect traditional knowledge related to traditional medicine. This law is not operational yet. However, the Philippines has yet to pass a *sui generis* intellectual property rights system that will cover traditional knowledge associated with biological and genetic resources.

6. Peru

Peru is a WIPO and WTO member, a signatory to TRIPS, and as member of the Andean Community, it is covered by regional IPR legislation. See Colombia for details about these laws. In addition, the 2002 Peruvian Law 27811 provides a *sui generis* system for the protection indigenous peoples' collective knowledge about properties, uses, and characteristics of biological diversity. The law creates three registers for the protection of collective knowledge as follows: a) national register for collective knowledge that is in the public domain; b) national register for confidential collective knowledge; and c) local registers for either kind of collective knowledge.

7. Samoa

Samoa is a WIPO member and a WTO observer. Samoa has a 1972 Patents Act that will be strengthened in order to comply with the requirements of TRIPS.

Table 2. Continued

8. Thailand

Thailand is a WTO and WIPO member. The country's 1992 patent law (amended in 1999) complies with TRIPS. The 1999 plant variety protection law protects is considered a *sui generis* protection system. It protects new, traditional, community and wild varieties. Thailand is also member of the 1995 ASEAN Framework Agreement on Intellectual Property Cooperation.

9. United States of America (USA)

The USA is a WIPO and WTO member and therefore a signatory to TRIPS. Unlike the other countries examined in this report the USA is not a CBD Party. The Plan Patent Act of 1930 gave protection to clonally propagated varieties of plants such as fruit trees and tubers. In 1970, the Plan Variety Protection Act granted protection to new, uniform and distinct plant varieties. In 1980, the Supreme Court opened the door for patents to be applied to plants, animals, microorganisms, genes, and DNA sequences. In late 2001, the US Supreme Court also ruled that plant varieties are eligible for protection by utility patents, as well as under the Plant Patent Act of 1930 and the Plant Variety Protection Act of 1970.

B. Countries working towards the development of ABS laws and policies

1. Australia

Australia is a WIPO and WTO member and therefore a signatory to TRIPS. The 1990 Patent Act (amended in 2000 and 2001) allows for the patenting of plants, microorganisms, and related biological materials, provided that these meet the standards of proof for patentability. The 1994 Plant Breeders' Rights Act (amended in 2002) provides plant variety protection.

2. Cambodia

Cambodia is a WIPO member and it is in the process of becoming a WTO member. The 2002 Patents, Utility Model Certificates and Industrial Designs Act provides patent protection. In addition, Cambodia is completing a Plant Variety Protection Act.

3. Canada

Canada is WIPO and WTO member and therefore a signatory to TRIPS. The 1985 Patent Act (amended in 1992, 1993, 1994, 1995, 1996, 1999, and 2001) is compatible with TRIPS. No patents are granted on higher life forms. In December 2002 the Supreme Court of Canada ruled that the Harvard Mouse cannot be patented. The 1985 Plant Breeders' Rights Act (amended in 1994 and 1995) protects plant varieties.

4. Chile

Chile is a WIPO and WTO member. The 1991 Industrial Property Act provides patent protection. The 1994 Law N°19.342 protects new plant varieties. The current legislation only excludes expressly the patenting of plant and animal varieties. Currently, the Chilean intellectual property legislation is being modified in order to make it compatible with requirements of TRIPS. Regarding the modifications proposed for the patents system, the main changes are related to the period of protection of the rights conferred by the patent (it increases from 15 to 20 years) and procedural aspects for the concession of this right. Specifically in relation to the patentability of different forms of life the Bill excludes plants and animals from patent protection (with the exception of microorganisms).

5. China

China is a WIPO and WTO member and therefore a signatory

to TRIPS. The 1984 Patent Act (amended in 1992 and 2000) is TRIPS compatible. China also has the 1997 Regulation for Protection of New Plant Varieties. The patent system does not protect genes yet. However, China's patent authority is considering incorporating genes under patent protection in the future.

6. Cook Islands

This country is neither a WIPO nor a WTO member. It does not have any intellectual property right system.

7. El Salvador

El Salvador is a WIPO and WTO member and therefore a signatory to TRIPS. The 1993 Law on the Promotion and Protection of Intellectual Property and its 1994 regulation is TRIPS compatible. The country is currently working on a plant variety protection law, but it has not addressed the issue of a *sui generis* system to protect traditional knowledge.

8. Fiji

Fiji is a WIPO and WTO member and therefore a signatory to TRIPS. It is currently reviewing the Fiji Patent Act of 1967. There is no plant variety protection legislation.

9. Guatemala

Guatemala is a WIPO and WTO member and therefore a signatory to TRIPS member. The 2000 Industrial Property Law provides patent protection.

10. Honduras

Honduras is a WIPO and WTO member and therefore a signatory to TRIPS. The 2000 Law on Industrial Property provides patent protection. The country is also about to approve a draft law for the protection of new varieties of plants.

11. Indonesia

Indonesia is a WIPO and WTO member and therefore a signatory to TRIPS. Amendments to the 1989 Patent and Trademark Acts as well as membership to several international treaties were conducted between 1997 and 2001. The Patent Law is TRIPS compatible. Nonbiological genetic engineering technologies are also patentable. It excludes all living organisms and biological processes used for the production of plants and animals, except microorganisms and plant varieties. Indonesia's 2000 Law on Plant Variety Protection protects new varieties as well as local or indigenous varieties. This country is a member of the 1995 ASEAN Framework Agreement on Intellectual Property Cooperation.

12. Japan

Japan has the longest tradition of industrial property rights in Asia. This country is a WIPO and WTO member and therefore a signatory to TRIPS. The Patent Law was amended in 1999 and 2002. The 1998 Seeds and Seedlings Law (amended in 2002) provides protection for new plant varieties.

13. Malaysia

Malaysia is both a WIPO and WTO member and therefore a signatory to TRIPS. Intellectual property rights (nonpatentability, limitations, certificate of origin and PIC, compulsory licenses). The 1983 Patent Act (amended in 1986, 1993, and 2000) is TRIPS compatible. The draft Access to Genetic Resources Bill includes a nonpatentability provision which means that no patents shall be recognized with respect to: 1) plants, animals, and naturally occurring microorganisms, including the parts thereof and 2) essentially biological processes and naturally occurring microbiological processes. To satisfy additional TRIPS requirements there is a draft Protection of New Plant Varieties Bill that is essentially a *sui generis* system for the

Table 2. Continued

protection of plant genetic resources. Malaysia is also a member of the 1995 ASEAN Framework Agreement on Intellectual Property Cooperation.

14. Marshall Islands
At present there is no IPR legislation in the Marshall Islands. This country is neither a WIPO nor a WTO member. There are plans to develop legislation that protects the rights of indigenous owners of genetic resources and traditional knowledge, and to provide access to that knowledge and resources with the prior informed consent of the owners, provided that these owners have an equitable share of the benefits from the use of that knowledge and genetic materials.

15. Micronesia
This country is neither a WIPO nor a WTO member and does not have either patent legislation or *sui generis* systems in place that would protect inventions derived from genetic resources and traditional knowledge.

16. New Zealand
New Zealand is a WIPO and WTO member and therefore a signatory to TRIPS. The 1954 Patent Act (amended in 1999) provides patent protection for genetic resources. The 1987 Plant Variety Rights Act (amended in 1999) protects new plant varieties.

17. Nicaragua
Nicaragua is a WIPO and WTO member and therefore a signatory to TRIPS. The 1999 Plant Variety Protection Law and its 2000 regulation provide protection for new varieties of plants. The 2000 law on Patents, Utility Models, and Industrial Designs is compatible with TRIPS. The country is also developing a draft law for the protection of traditional knowledge.

18. Niue
Niue does not have legislation that protects intellectual property derived from biological resources. This country is neither a WIPO nor a WTO member.

19. Panama
Panama is a WIPO and WTO member and therefore a signatory to TRIPS. The 1996 Law on Industrial Property and its 1998 regulation provide patent protection. Decree No. 13 of 1999 and Law No. 23 of 1997 provide protection for new plant varieties. The 2000 Special Regime on Intellectual Property over Collective Rights protects collective rights of indigenous peoples over models, drawings, designs, symbols, petrogliphs, and other innovations.

20. Papua New Guinea
Papua New Guinea is a WIPO and WTO member and therefore a signatory to TRIPS. The 2000 Patent and Industrial Act protects inventions derived from genetic resources.

21. Republic of Korea
The Republic of Korea is a WIPO and WTO member and therefore a signatory to TRIPS. The 1961 Patent Law and the 1994 Law on the Promotion of Inventions comply with TRIPS. The 2001 Seed Industry Law protects plant breeders' rights.

22. Russian Federation
The Russian Federation is a WIPO member and a WTO observer. The 1992 Patent Law needs to be reformed in order

to comply with TRIPS. The 1993 Law on the Protection of Selection Achievements provide plant variety protection.

23. Singapore
Singapore is a WIPO and WTO member and therefore a signatory to TRIPS. The Patent Act (amended in 1994, 2001, and 2002) fully complies with TRIPS. The country also has a plant variety protection law and it is a member of the 1995 ASEAN Framework Agreement on Intellectual Property Cooperation.

24. Solomon Islands
This country does not have intellectual property right legislation. It is neither a WIPO nor a WTO member.

25. Vanuatu
This country is neither a WIPO nor a WTO member. Vanuatu is promoting a Traditional Property Rights Policy to protect traditional knowledge. The policy would protect information about names, designs or forms, oral tradition, practices and skills.

26. Vietnam
Vietnam is a WIPO member and a WTO observer. The 1995 Civil Code includes a chapter on industrial property. The Civil Code covers the basics of intellectual property, and has been supplemented by decrees on patents, trademarks, designs, utility models, and appellations of origin (1996), and copyright (1997). The Patent Act includes broad compulsory licensing provisions under public health or national security conditions. It is uncertain whether genetically modified organisms and particularly microorganisms can be protected. Vietnam is also a member of the 1995 ASEAN Framework Agreement on Intellectual Property Cooperation.

C. Countries not involved in any process leading to the development of ABS laws and policies

1. Kiribati
Kiribati does not have an intellectual property right system. This country is neither a WIPO nor a WTO member.

2. Laos
Laos is a WIPO member and a WTO observer. The 2002 Prime Minister Decree on Patents, Industrial Designs and Utility Models and its 2003 regulation provides for patent protection. Laos is also a member of the 1995 ASEAN Framework Agreement on Intellectual Property Cooperation.

3. Nauru
Nauru does not have an intellectual property right system. This country is neither a WIPO nor a WTO member.

4. Palau
There are no statutory or regulatory intellectual property rights at this time. This country is neither a WIPO nor a WTO member.

5. Tonga
Tonga is a WIPO member and a WTO observer. The 1994 Industrial Property Act provides patent protection, but it needs to be reformed in order to comply with TRIPS. The Bill on Seeds and Seedlings protects new varieties of plants.

6. Tuvalu
Tuvalu does not have intellectual property rights legislation. This country is neither a WIPO nor a WTO member.

2

Scenarios of Policymaking Process

Santiago Carrizosa

The 2001 Bonn Guidelines on Access to Genetic Resources and Fair and Equitable Sharing of the Benefits arising out of their Utilization (hereafter Bonn Guidelines on access and benefit sharing (ABS)) adopted by the Sixth Conference of the Parties of the CBD, have provided guidance for the countries embarked on the development of ABS frameworks. Several international bioprospecting[1] projects have directly and indirectly encouraged policymakers to develop national ABS policies. However, this has been a long and difficult process for many nations. Developing balanced ABS laws is a slow process in which multiple sectors of society with different interests, views, and backgrounds must play a role. Even countries that enacted ABS laws and policies in the mid-90s are still reforming such policies as

they encounter obstacles that prevent their effective and efficient implementation, affect the interests of local communities, and prevent the flow of genetic resources among nations. This chapter is divided into two main parts: the first part describes the policymaking process and main concerns experienced during the development of national ABS laws and polices in Australia, Chile, China, Colombia, Cook Islands, Costa Rica, Ecuador, El Salvador, Honduras, Indonesia, Malaysia, Mexico, Nicaragua, Panama, Philippines, Peru, Samoa, Thailand, and Vanuatu; and the second part analyzes the policymaking process and identifies key lessons and patterns derived from the case studies presented in the first part of this chapter.

Policymaking Process and Main Concerns: Case Studies

Australia

Process
Development of ABS policies in the Commonwealth areas began in 1993 when a consultative group of Commonwealth, State, and Territory environment ministers produced a report on the implementation and implications of ratification of the CBD. In 1994, First Ministers established the Commonwealth State Working Group (CSWG). The CSWG addressed the issue of establishing a nationally consistent system of access arrangements for the Commonwealth, States, and Territories and concluded that a nationally consistent system should focus on broad principles while allowing jurisdictions the freedom to apply those principles in ways which meet their needs and which take into ac-

count their existing policy frameworks.

The ABS development process continued in mid-1999 with the announcement of an inquiry into access to biological resources in Commonwealth areas. The inquiry, initiated by the Minister for the Environment and Heritage, was the most significant event in the development process of ABS regulations. Its main objective was to advise on a scheme that could be implemented through regulations under section 301 of the Environment Protection and Biodiversity Conservation Act of 1999 (EPBCA) to provide for the control of access to biological resources in Commonwealth areas. In January 2000 the inquiry was advertised in national, state, and territory newspapers. The inquiry received 80 submissions and held two public hearings and consultations with the traditional owners of the three national parks and their representatives (see Chapter 9).

In September 2000 the Minister released the inquiry report for public comment and promoted another one-year period of consultations with Biotechnology Australia departments and other agencies. In September 2001, the Minister for the Environment and Heritage released the draft of the regulations for a period of public consultation ending in October 2001. The regulations reflect the scheme proposed by the inquiry and they are likely to be enacted in 2005.

Another significant result of the inquiry was the reactivation of the idea of a nationally consistent system as it was proposed by the CSWG in 1996. This system would prevent the risk of a "price war" among Australian jurisdictions that could be caused by bioprospectors while shopping for the easiest and most accessible genetic resources. In October 2002, Australia's Natural Resource Management Ministerial Council released fourteen principles to promote the development or review of legislative, administrative, or policy frameworks for a nationally consistent approach in each jurisdiction (see Chapter 9). Therefore, in December 2002 the Government of Western Australia released a consultation paper to promote the idea of a new act (i.e., A Biodiversity Conservation Act for Western Australia). The new act would include a licensing regime for terrestrial bioprospecting activities to ensure that benefits arising from the exploitation of Western Australia's biological resources are shared with the Western Australian community, among other objectives. Australia's ABS policy will be compatible with the FAO's International Treaty on Plant Genetic Resources for Food and Agriculture (ITPGRFA) (see Chapter 9).

Concerns

The main concerns identified by the 1999 inquiry were: a) ownership of genetic resources; b) intellectual property rights (IPRS) and indigenous knowledge; c) benefit sharing; and d) exclusivity issues. Ownership to genetic resources found in *ex situ* conditions was a significant issue for scientists, nongovernmental organizations (NGOS), and indigenous groups. Under common law, however, neither a holder nor a buyer can claim ownership to a plant or to the species or genus to which it belongs. The lack of clarity about ownership also applied to *in situ* resources under state and territory jurisdiction. In this case, legislative details vary from state to state. Therefore the inquiry recommended that Biotechnology Australia and the Attorney-General's Department, in conjunction with the state and territory governments, ensure that information on the ownership of biological resources is compiled and made publicly available.

Indigenous groups were also concerned about the impact of ownership or exclusive rights over IPRS of these groups and on access for traditional uses. The inquiry stated that according to Australian law, IPRS on any products or processes derived from *ex situ* collections or resources

found in *in situ* conditions belong to the inventor. However, the inquiry stated that it is up to a Commonwealth agency to allow access only if ownership of products derived from genetic resources is shared jointly with the inventor, the Commonwealth agency, and a representative of indigenous communities that may own the resource. Many NGOs and indigenous groups also rejected the idea of patenting life, namely sequences of genes and the organisms that embody these genes. Australian patent law, however, allows this practice. Indigenous groups also argued that their cultural knowledge related to plants, animals, and the environment was being used by scientists, medical researchers, nutritionists, and pharmaceutical companies for commercial gain, often without their prior informed consent (PIC) and without any economic benefits flowing back to them. In the knowledge that these are significant and sensitive issues for indigenous people, the inquiry recommended further research and consultations with stakeholders.

Scientists were also concerned that the access scheme and the model contract might not be sufficiently flexible and effective to allow the negotiation of benefits in commercial and noncommercial access situations. In addition, the access process could inhibit noncommercial research activities. In this regard the inquiry recommended that provisions in the proposed model contract should anticipate that most contractual arrangements will be for commercial purposes but that in some cases, provisions should be flexible enough to address situations where access conditions for noncommercial initiatives are negotiated.

Exclusivity issues were also addressed during the consultation process. In theory parties to a contract should be able to negotiate exclusivity provisions freely. However, the Minister can also assess the fairness of exclusivity provisions in the contract against evidence of proper PIC, mutually agreed terms, and adequate benefit sharing. In addition, contractual provisions of an exclusive nature which benefit the bioprospector should be reflected in the amount of benefits payable to the provider of the genetic resource or traditional knowledge (see Chapter 9).

Chile

Process

Chile does not have an ABS policy yet. In early 2003 the Ministry of Agriculture developed a proposal for a law to regulate access to agricultural genetic resources that could have facilitated the implementation of the FAO's ITPGRFA[2], among other purposes. This proposal was developed without public consultation and it was discarded after much criticism. However, efforts to develop a new proposal continue within the Ministry with support from the National Commission of the Environment (CONAMA). In 2003, CONAMA published the country's National Biodiversity Strategy. It should be noted that the strategy emphasizes the need to develop legal instruments to regulate access to genetic resources to ensure fair participation in and equitable distribution of the benefits derived from their use.

The strategy was approved by the CONAMA's ministerial council (which is the highest environmental policy body in the country) and the National Biodiversity Action Plan was initiated in mid-2004.

However, Chile's recent experience in the access and benefit-sharing debate goes back to the early 1990s when the country's genetic resources were accessed by several bioprospecting projects (see Table 1 of Chapter 3). These projects were briefly scrutinized by the press and local NGOs and brought momentum for the analysis of ABS issues at workshops. Government authorities also established a working group to discuss the issue and several meetings were held. In the long run, there were no significant results from this initiative at a legislative or political level. This failure was due, in considerable part, to the complexity of the subject. The process was stalled by the inability to identify solutions to the issue of ownership of genetic resources and the absence of a national biodiversity policy. But the main problem was a lack of political support among legislative and executive decision makers to consider this a matter of importance for the country (see Chapter 10).

In mid-2004, the Foundation for International Environmental Law and Development (FIELD) and the Chilean NGO Fundación Sociedades Sustentables released the findings of a project for an ABS policy in Chile. Some of the project's conclusions revealed the lack of technical capacity and information about key ABS issues such as the protection of traditional knowledge. Furthermore, the project found great contradictions among those that see the need to regulate access to genetic resources and those that perceive such regulation as a strategy to legalize the misappropriation of genetic resources and traditional knowledge. One of the most important recommendations of this project is the need to develop a participatory process involving all government and nongovernment stakeholders to facilitate the development of an ABS policy for Chile.[3]

Concerns

Between 1996 and 1997, consultants were hired by CONAMA to assess legal and political circumstances and propose a strategy for developing a national regulation for genetic resources. After internal debate, it was concluded that the only way to initiate the development of ABS legislation was by addressing the issue of ownership of genetic resources through legislative changes in the property regime of Chile. This conclusion prevented the implementation of further efforts because the Chilean Constitution gives strong protection to private property and any modifications of this regime would require a legislative reform in Congress (see Chapter 10).

China

Process

China, like most countries examined in this report, has policies that regulate access to genetic resources[4], but these policies lack benefit-sharing provisions. Therefore, China's 1997 National Report on implementation of the

Convention on Biological Diversity states that a priority action for the country is to draft a genetic resources policy or law that regulates PIC principles, benefit-sharing issues, and IPRs, among other issues.

In late 2002, the State Council of China authorized the State Environmental Protection Administration (SEPA) to coordinate all issues regarding ABS issues to ensure the implementation of the CBD. Consequently, SEPA is currently leading a national project to inventory all genetic resources in China. This includes the participation of experts from many organizations and universities from the agriculture, forestry, fishery, and medical sectors. Also, SEPA is assembling a team to develop a comprehensive ABS policy or law. Access and benefit-sharing issues are a new topic for Chinese authorities and they are looking for experience and case studies in foreign countries. Governmental officials from different ministries and experts designated by the relevant ministries will participate in the ABS process development. However, indigenous representatives and foreign consultants are not likely to be invited to this process (D. Xue, pers. comm. December 2003).

Concerns

So far the main difficulties faced by the process have been the overlapping of functions and lack of coordination between the relevant ministries. SEPA is responsible for the implementation of the CBD, but ministries such as the Ministry of Agriculture want to be in charge of access and benefit-sharing issues pertaining to crops, livestock, and fishery production. In addition, there have been difficulties in defining beneficiaries from access activities. Should the state, ministry, organization, or individual receive benefits derived from the country's genetic resources? How should these benefits be allocated? IPRs are also likely to be a major concern and obstacle for the development and implementation of legislation development and implementation in the future. Chinese genetic resources have been used to develop inventions that have been patented in other countries. Channeling benefits derived from these inventions back to China is a problem that will be addressed by future legislation (D. Xue, pers. comm. December 2003).

Colombia, Ecuador, and Peru

Process

Colombia, Ecuador, and Peru, along with the other members of the Andean Community, participated in the development process of Decision 391. Initial discussions for a regional ABS law included the participation of NGOs, government organizations, and indigenous groups. The Secretariat of the Andean Community commissioned the World Conservation Union, which subsequently involved the Peruvian Society for Environmental Law, to develop a first draft of the issues that should be addressed by a regional access regulation. In mid-1994, a draft was completed. It received strong criticism and some governments were opposed to having such a document as the basis for discussion. Besides, other proposals had already emerged from various groups. In August 1994, a Colombian non-governmental initiative developed a different proposal for a regional access and benefit-sharing law. These documents were discussed in a regional workshop in Colombia and included wide participation (NGOs, academic institutions, private sector, intergovernmental institutions, and indigenous organizations) from the Andean countries. Nevertheless, there was increased tension in the debate about whether the proposal should implement the CBD as a whole or just its specific ABS goals. Failure to come to an agreement about this and other issues encouraged government representatives in charge of the initiative to pull away from this participatory process. In addition, most governments disliked the idea of discussing the development of an access norm based on an NGO proposal.

Consequently, in November 1994, the Colombian and Venezuelan governments jointly presented a new proposal for discussion. The following year, the governments of Bolivia and Ecuador proposed two different texts of draft decisions and the discussions between government officials evolved around these three governmental drafts. A total of six meetings resulted in a final proposal that was presented to the Commission of the Cartagena Agreement for its approval in July 1996.

In synthesis, Decision 391 lacked the input of a participatory process where local NGOs, indigenous groups, and other stakeholders could have contributed to key issues such as the protection of traditional knowledge. The conflicting attitude between local NGOs and other stakeholders led Andean governments to pull away from the broad debate that characterized the early stages of the development of the ABS law. In addition, not all participating experts had adequate legal, technical, scientific, and economic experience to develop an access regime (see Chapter 4).

While Venezuela has been applying Decision 391, Colombia, Ecuador, and Peru have been working on national policies to facilitate the implementation of Decision 391 with varying results. Colombia is working on a proposal for an ABS policy that will be concluded in 2004 (see Chapter 4). Peru developed a policy that was presented to its National Environmental Council for approval in 2000 and it could be adopted in 2004 (M. Ruiz, pers. comm. January 2004). Ecuador developed a policy in 2001, but it was not approved and there are no initiatives to reactivate the process (J. Vogel, pers. comm. April 2003). In addition to these efforts, Peru and other Andean countries have proposed a general review of the text of Decision 391 to facilitate its implementation (M. Ruiz, pers. comm. April 2004). In 2002, the Andean Community adopted a Regional Strategy on Biodiversity that includes an ABS component. The strategy identifies some of the problems of Decision 391 and proposes measures to facilitate the identification of solutions (ANDEAN COMMUNITY 2002). The Andean Community is currently working on an action plan for the strategy that might bring new momentum to ABS discussions and consolidate regional efforts to reform Decision 391 and facilitate its implementation.

Concerns

Should a regional ABS policy emphasize the biodiversity conservation and sustainable development goals? Or should this policy focus on ABS issues in order to take advantage of millions of dollars that could be obtained from genetic resources? This was one of the dilemmas faced by stakeholders and policymakers at the beginning of the policymaking process and it was one of the sources of conflict that stopped the participatory process. The potential loss of benefits was a major incentive for government officials to develop an ABS proposal as soon as possible.

Protecting both traditional and scientific knowledge was also a major concern addressed by some NGOs which advocated for a special access process and treatment for the cases that involved traditional knowledge. In the end, the governments proposed a solution that considers traditional and scientific knowledge as an intangible component associated with genetic resources and a weak definition of the protection of traditional knowledge. Decision 391 provides a contractual approach to protect traditional knowledge but delegates the development of a law to protecting traditional knowledge to future negotiations. The issue, however, is very controversial and no regional proposal dealing specifically with traditional knowledge has been officially discussed yet among the Andean countries. In the last stages of the development process of Decision 391 there was intense discussion among government representatives about the scope of access activities. The agreed-upon definition was based on a Colombian proposal, which is very close to the current definition found in Decision 391 (see Chapter 4).

Cook Islands

Process

Although this country has most of its traditional knowledge associated with agricultural resources, these genetic materials are rarely endemic to the region. The main potential that can be used by the pharmaceutical industry is associated with marine resources. Therefore any new ABS law will be targeted to this sector.

Currently there are no national ABS policies that regulate agricultural and marine resources. There is, however, a code-of-conduct in effect under the taro germplasm project, a regional genebank of taro (*Colocasia esculenta*) collected throughout the Pacific Islands under the auspices of the Secretariat of the Pacific Community (SPC).[5] This code stipulates that the samples may not be used for commercial purposes without PIC.

At present the only national attempt to regulate access to bioprospectors is through a National Research Committee. The secretariat for this committee is the Prime Ministers Office and its key governmental authorities in charge of agricultural, marine, cultural, and other issues. However, it rarely meets. The National Research

Committee issues a pre-research permit that is presented by the bioprospector to immigration authorities (normally at the international airport) who issue a final research permit allowing access. However, few researchers go through this process. Some exceptions include university students who wish to reside in the country for periods that exceed three months. Most researchers simply enter on a visitor's visa (which actually restricts activities of research under the Immigration Act) issued at the port of entry.

In the last few years, organizations such as the South Pacific Regional Environment Programme (SPREP), the World Wildlife Fund–South Pacific Program (WWF-SPP), and FIELD have created awareness about the CBD and the need to develop a national ABS law. In March 2000, these organizations promoted a regional workshop on the implementation of the CBD in the Pacific Islands region that produced a draft list of guidelines on ABS issues adopted by participants from 12 Pacific Island countries that included government organizations, NGOs, and academic institutions.

A year later, SPREP, WWF-SPP, and FIELD organized a national workshop on ABS in the Cook Islands that developed a list of recommendations for a national ABS law. The meeting had widespread representation and publicity and became an important turning point. Consequently, Cook Islands, under the leadership of the Ministry of Marine Resources, is currently working on a national ABS policy that will go under a proposed National Environmental Act. The law is likely to be enforced by an Environment Ministry, established under the Act or alternatively by the Office of the Prime Minister. Central government ministries regulate this type of national law. The Island Councils of the different inhabited islands and the municipal councils for the capital island may adopt by-laws that are managed under the Island Councils.

This process will probably take about three years. It has benefited from the input of the Prime Ministers Office, Environment Service, Agriculture, Marine, Culture, Education, and Justice sectors, Attorney General Office, Representatives of Island Councils and Municipal Councils, indigenous bodies (traditional healers and carvers), and private sector lawyers. SPREP also provided a technical staff familiar with CBD issues and a legal consultant (B. Ponia, pers. comm. February 2002).

Concerns

Major concerns include how to regulate access to *ex situ* collections and the perception that creating an access regulation actually encourages bioprospecting and the loss of traditional knowledge. There are also mixed views on ownership of genetic resources and the protection of traditional knowledge associated with medicinal plants.

A major problem that also complicates the development of this participatory process is the lack of technical capacity. There is a great need to educate people about key ABS issues. But the main obstacle to this process is getting the Environment Act passed. At present the Environment

Service only operates on the main island (Rarotonga). The remaining islands, managed by Island Councils, are reluctant to have the central government apply an Environment Act to them. There has been a process of decentralizing government in order to give Island Councils as much autonomy as possible. Perhaps the alternative to the Environment Act would be a separate Access and Benefit-Sharing Act. But this has not been decided yet (B. Ponia, pers. comm. February 2002).

Costa Rica

Process

The development process of the Law of Biodiversity No. 7788 took about two years and revealed two opposing positions. Some regarded legislating access as a way of promoting bioprospecting and legitimizing biopiracy while others defended the law as a way to promote the sustainable use of genetic resources. In 1996, the first draft of the law was developed by Luis Martínez, a former president of the Environment Commission of the Legislative Assembly with technical support provided by the regional office for Mesoamerica of the World Conservation Union. The draft law was widely distributed to the public by mail and it was also made available on the internet (J. Cabrera, pers. comm. April 2003). Many stakeholders considered this first version to be particularly restrictive and opposed both to the public good and scientific research.

The Environment Commission made the second draft available in January 1997. Even though this draft addressed some of the objections made to the first draft, it also repeated several of the contentious concepts stated in the initial version of the document. Therefore, it received similar opposition. This situation led to the creation of a Special Commission in the Legislative Assembly. Its mandate was to create a new draft, taking into consideration the previous ones. The Assembly promised to respect the outcome.

The Commission, led by Jorge Mora, Rector of the National University, was established in April 1997. It included the main political parties (National Liberation and Social Christian Unity), the Advisory Commission on Biodiversity, the National Small Farmers Forum, the National Indigenous Forum, the Union of Chambers of Private Business, the University of Costa Rica, the National University, the Costa Rican Federation for Environmental Conservation, and the National Biodiversity Institute. The Commission met until December 1997 when the new draft was sent to Congress. It received the favorable opinion of the Environment Commission, and after a few modifications, the Legislative Assembly approved the draft law in April 1998 during the last days of the administration of President Figueres Olsen. The Law of Biodiversity entered into force as Law of the Republic No. 7788 on 6 May 1998 (see Chapter 5).

Concerns

Time constraints for completing the draft law prevented in-depth discussions of some of the most controversial aspects such as ownership of genetic resources and IPRs. In addition, there were internal difficulties among the members of participating stakeholder groups. For example, representatives of the industry sector stated that since they were incapable of negotiating on behalf of all their associates, they would not vote for any of the proposals but would limit themselves to taking part in the debates of the Commission. Since the law covered multiple policy objectives, the possibility of dedicating sufficient time to ABS issues was diminished due to the pressing need to finalize a comprehensive draft.

One of the most controversial issues was ownership of genetic resources. Stakeholders such as representatives of the farming sector criticized the fact that under the Law of Biodiversity these resources were considered to be in the public domain, independent of private ownership of the land. There were also concerns about integration between intellectual property and the procedures of the Law of Biodiversity, since diverse exclusions have been established. Compatibility of some of these exclusions with the Agreement on Trade-Related Aspects of Intellectual Property Rights (TRIPS) is an issue that needs careful consideration. In the end, some of the patentability exclusions were eliminated and others remained, in spite of warnings about their possible unconstitutionality (see Chapter 5).

The development process for the Law of Biodiversity revealed a lack of technical expertise from certain sectors such as academic, indigenous, rural, political, and entrepreneurial groups. Many of them used the process to make political rather than technical statements. Therefore, some of the issues that may have needed a larger discussion forum were addressed and defined by a few technocrats. For example, IPR issues were debated by representatives from business and academic groups in a Special Subcommittee in charge of drafting the law. Concerns of indigenous peoples that opposed the use of IPRs were disregarded.

In addition, discussions evolved around conceptual issues and ignored procedural, operative, or administrative issues that have impaired the full implementation of the law (see Chapter 5). Several stakeholders argued that since the National System of Conservation Areas had a close relationship with the National Biodiversity Institute it should not be in charge of granting access permits and authorizations. Instead, this duty should have been given to a new commission able to represent the wider interest of society. Other provisions such as the creation of a National Commission for the Management of Biodiversity (CONAGE-BIO) were accepted under different proposals. According to the Law of Biodiversity, CONAGEBIO's duties include the formulation of biodiversity and ABS policies and the management of public funds. However, the Minister of the Environment and Energy considered these functions unconstitutional and asked the Attorney General's Office to submit a constitutional challenge that is currently under review. The suit does not suspend the execution of the Law of Biodiversity. However, politically, it has definitely delayed CONAGEBIO's implementation of the law.

El Salvador

Process

ABS issues were placed on El Salvador's institutional agenda by the 1999 National Biodiversity Strategy. The strategy provided a participatory arena for the debate of ABS issues among various sectors of society. In 2002, with financial support from the Global Environment Facility (GEF), the Environment Minister developed the following four reports: a) national assessment of genetic and biochemical resources; b) capacity-building strategy for access to genetic and biochemical resources associated with wildlife; c) administrative procedures for access to genetic and biochemical resources; and d) policy guidelines on access to genetic and biochemical resources. These reports were developed by a variety of actors from government, peasant, and academic institutions. Then, these reports were submitted to the Presidency for review, approval, and adoption under a national policy on access to genetic and biochemical resources. The Presidency should be adopting the policy sometime in 2004. Subsequently, government sectors in charge of administering biological resources (e.g., Agriculture Ministry) will develop rules and procedures that must be followed by bioprospectors in order to get access to these resources. The policy will also be consistent with and supported by the Central American Protocol on Access to Genetic and Biochemical Resources and their Associated Knowledge. The scope of the policy will exclude genetic resources covered by the FAO's ITP-GRFA that was already signed and ratified by El Salvador (J.E. Quezada-Díaz, pers. comm. January 2004). The 1998 Environment Law provides the legal framework for the new ABS policy. Article 66 of the law states that access, research, manipulation and use of genetic resources are allowed under permit, license, or concession granted by the government agency in charge of administering and managing the resource.

Concerns

Opportunities for stakeholders to participate in the development process are limited by their lack of expertise. Many sectors of society do not realize the implications of a policy that regulates access and benefit-sharing issues. There is lack of information and misinterpretation about concepts such as equitable sharing of benefits, protection of traditional knowledge, and IPR issues. The country has yet to begin a process to address these issues properly and carefully. Biological resources are owned by the State. However, there is on-going debate about ownership issues related to genetic resources. Financial support for the development of the policy was provided by the GEF and additional funding will be required to build local capacity to facilitate its implementation (J.E. Quezada-Díaz, pers. comm. January 2004).

Honduras

Process

In 2001, under the leadership of the Natural Resources

and Environment Secretariat, the National Strategy on Biodiversity was officially presented and one of its strategic components was the ABS issue. The strategy was the product of nine regional workshops that included the participation of indigenous communities, industry, peasants, and government organizations. The strategy created momentum for additional discussions on ABS issues. But it is not clear how ABS goals will be incorporated into national law. Some advocate for a comprehensive law similar to the Costa Rican Law of Biodiversity. However, there is also a possibility to develop a single ABS law. This is one of the issues to be discussed in future meetings. An initial discussion of ABS issues already begun at a government level and a preliminary draft has been developed. Next steps will include developing a final draft together with relevant stakeholders consulted at a national level (J.A. Fuentes, pers. comm. June 2003).

Concerns

The lack of technical capacity is one of the main obstacles that the ABS development process will face in the future. The relationship between traditional property rights and indigenous knowledge was one of the main concerns addressed during initial discussions of the draft ABS policy. A great deal of debate went also into details about how to protect indigenous knowledge. Issues debated included: a) the number of years of protection provided by the system; b) the individual or collective nature of indigenous knowledge; c) strategies to protect indigenous knowledge; and d) the relationship between trade secrets and traditional knowledge. This discussion included also procedural issues such as identifying the characteristics of the government agency in charge of administering this system (J.A. Fuentes, pers. comm. June 2003).

Indonesia

Process

Indonesia is currently working on a draft law, the Act on Genetic Resource Management that includes a regulation on ABS issues. This law will be comprehensive and the provisions will be consistent with existing laws on agriculture, forestry, and biodiversity. The government is also conducting an assessment of existing legal instruments that regulate ABS issues. Local officials estimate that ABS legislation will be concluded in 2004.

The act will have a national scope, but provincial or district level governments should develop their own regulations that must be formulated in line with the national law. The law will apply to the pharmaceutical, agricultural, botanical medicine, biotechnology, and other pertinent sectors. The Act will also be compatible with the FAO's ITPGRFA that Indonesia should be signing and ratifying soon.

As the focal point for the CBD, the Ministry for the Environment established an inter-ministerial working group to formulate this law. This working group was organized into smaller groups in charge of technical tasks

including the analysis of ABS laws enacted by other countries. The working group has also organized workshops to facilitate the debate and contribute to the identification of key issues. Participants include representatives from the Ministry of Agriculture, Ministry of Forestry, Ministry of Justice and Human Rights, Ministry of Environment, Ministry of Research and Technology, Indonesian Institute of Science, local universities, NGOs, and national experts. There are no foreign consultants involved in the process, but the 2001 Bonn Guidelines on ABS are being used to guide the process. Before the draft law is sent to Congress it should be available for public comment (B.S. Wardhana, pers. comm. March 2004).

Concerns

The main challenge is likely to be the resolution of controversial issues that include ownership of genetic resources, indigenous knowledge, and the relationship between traditional IPR systems and traditional knowledge. For example, the national constitution states that natural resources (including genetic resources) are owned by the State. However, since local communities have used these resources traditionally without major restrictions they believe that they hold ownership over them (B.S. Wardhana, pers. comm. March 2004).

Malaysia

Process

The development of the draft law on Access to Genetic Resources has promoted an interesting cooperation among federal and state authorities. This process began in 1994 with the establishment of the National Committee on Biological Diversity, which supported by the Attorney-General, played a significant role in the development of the draft law (see Table 2 of Chapter 11). The process received ample input during a National Workshop on Access and Benefit Sharing of Genetic Resources held in 1997 (see Box 2 of Chapter 11). Two years later a task force, established by a National Technical Committee on Biological Diversity, completed the final text of the draft law.

Presently, the Ministry of Science, Technology, and the Environment (MOSTE), in close collaboration with the Attorney-General's Chambers, is handling the whole process from the final draft bill to the passing of the draft bill into law. This draft bill was scheduled to go through the national consultation process in 2000 and 2001, then to the Cabinet for approval, and finally to the Parliament for the bill to be passed into law. However, the process has progressed at a relatively slower pace particularly with regard to national consultation. Furthermore MOSTE gave priority to enacting the Biosafety Bill into law. Consequently, the draft is not expected to be adopted by the government until 2004 or even later. Favorable comments from the states of Sabah and Sarawak[6] among others, is crucial to facilitate the completion and adoption of the draft law (see Chapter 11).

Concerns

A major issue debated during the development process that needs to be clarified further is ownership of genetic resources. In Malaysia, there are biological resources found on public lands that belong to federal and state governments. In some states, ownership rights of biological resources found in indigenous or community-held land, belong to the community and ownership rights over traditional knowledge and innovations still need to be clarified. IPR systems for the protection of biological organisms and traditional knowledge were also major points of discussion. A *sui generis* system of community intellectual rights was proposed but it was not included in the draft bill because it turned out to be very controversial. In addition, stakeholders opposed the use of patents to protect genes, plants, and other organisms.

In addition, several procedural and conceptual issues discussed during the design of the draft law remain unresolved. Tasks that remain to be tackled before the draft bill is passed into law include: a) determining the federal authority in charge of matters relevant to biological diversity; b) ensuring uniformity in relevant state laws; c) determining the institutional structure for the implementation of the draft bill; d) determining the competent authorities and negotiating partners to identify and address the interests of the holders of indigenous knowledge; and e) ensuring adequate participation of indigenous representatives in the development of PIC procedures and benefit-sharing requirements (see Chapter 11).

Mexico

Process

The 1996 reform of the 1988 Ecological Equilibrium and Environment Protection General Act (EEEPGA) introduced article 87 BIS that regulates access and benefit sharing for biotechnology purposes. This reform was carried out in 18 months by the Commissions of Ecology and Environment of the Senate and House of Representatives and the Secretariat of Environment and Natural Resources (SEMARNAT). The reform promoted by these organizations was the result of a small process of consultation that included few stakeholders. This process, nonetheless, facilitated the approval of one ABS provision and other measures that reformed the EEEPGA (J. Larson and C. López-Silva, pers. comm. January 2004).

Concerns

Issues such as ownership of genetic resources and the protection of traditional knowledge were not properly discussed and addressed by the reform of the EEEPGA. These legal gaps and the lack of a nation-wide participatory process of discussion of the reform may have provided impetus for the public opposition that led to the cancellation of access granted under the law to several bioprospecting projects (see Chapter 6).

Nicaragua

Process

The process of developing the draft Law of Biodiversity was initiated in 1995 by the national strategy for the conservation of biodiversity and briefly supported in 1996 by a proposal from the Ministry for the Environment and Natural Resources (MARENA). In 2000, MARENA reactivated the 1996 proposal with financial support from the World Conservation Union, the United Nations Development Programme, the Mesoamerican Biological Conservation Corridor, and the government of Nicaragua. Subsequently, an interdisciplinary team of national and international experts from Peru, Mexico, Argentina, Costa Rica, and Nicaragua developed the draft Law of Biodiversity. Representatives of more than 50% of Nicaraguan indigenous communities participated in this process. They played a pivotal role in the development of one of the most controversial and novel provisions of the draft Law of Biodiversity that calls for the development of a *sui generis* system for the protection of the knowledge, practices and innovations of local communities. In 2001, the draft was available for comment to a group of 40 specialists from NGOs and government organizations that suggested the inclusion of biosafety, wildlife, and environmental issues into the proposal. Most recently, indigenous communities, NGOs, and industry representatives had the opportunity to provide additional input and contribute to the final draft. In late 2003, Government officials completed a final draft that should be sent to Congress in 2004 (J. Hernandez, pers. comm. February 2004).

Concerns

Traditional knowledge, IPRs, ownership of genetic resources, biosafety, and procedural issues have been the main topics of heated discussion during the development process of the law. The protection of traditional knowledge was so controversial that some government officials from the Ministry of Industry and Commerce opposed its inclusion into the draft law. In June 2000, however, resolutions of the CBD and guidelines of the World Intellectual Property Organization endorsing strategies to protect traditional knowledge provided convincing arguments and this provision remained in the draft law.

While the draft law states that genetic resources are in the public domain, it provides indigenous communities with ownership rights to genetic resources found in their lands. This property right distinction is likely to be controversial when the draft law reaches Congress. Policymakers are also uncertain about how to address the new commitments of the FAO's ITPGRFA that was acceded to by Nicaragua in November 2002.

But perhaps the main problem is a current disagreement between the Environment Ministry and the Agriculture and Forestry Ministry about jurisdictional powers over access to genetic resources for agricultural purposes and biosafety issues. The Agriculture and Forestry Ministry argues that they handle biosafety issues and that a stand-alone law of biosafety just like the Peruvian proposal should address them. The Environment Ministry responds that biosafety is one of the main provisions of the CBD and as such it should be included in the Law of Biodiversity. In addition, there is overlapping between the draft Law of Biodiversity and existing laws. The draft law includes provisions about invasive and domestic species, issues that are already regulated by the Law of Production and Commerce of Seeds and the Law of Animal and Plant Sanitation (J. Hernandez, pers. comm. February 2004).

Panama

Process

Currently, Panama does not have a clear and comprehensive ABS law. However, in the last few years the National Authority for the Environment (ANAM) has been using a contractual approach to facilitate access to bioprospecting projects. The 2001 Bonn Guidelines on ABS have been employed in the negotiation of these projects and will be followed in the development of future national ABS regulations.

The development process of ABS laws and policies started with the 1998 General Law of the Environment No. 41 (GLE) that designated ANAM as the competent authority for the regulation, management, and control of the access to and use of biogenetic resources. According to GLE, ANAM had to develop the legal instruments and economic mechanisms to facilitate ABS goals in Panama (LA ASAMBLEA LEGISLATIVA 1998). In 1999, ABS discussions reached new momentum with the adoption of the National Strategy for the Environment that proposed a long-term vision for biodiversity issues. This vision was reinforced by the 2000 National Biodiversity Strategy that proposed the implementation of ABS principles. In addition to this effort, the National Biodiversity Action Plan proposed, as one of the 10 goals for year 2005, the equitable distribution of benefits derived from the use of biological diversity among all sectors of society. Actions to implement this goal have been focused on three main fronts: a) the ratification of the Central American Protocol on Access to Genetic and Biochemical Resources and their associated knowledge that should take place in 2004; b) the development of a national wildlife trust fund that will facilitate the distribution of benefits derived from the use of genetic resources; and c) the development of new ABS procedures that will be adopted by the executive branch. Since late 2002 Panama has been working on a policy to fill the gaps present in existing legislation regarding ABS and indigenous knowledge issues. Representatives from the agriculture, biotechnology, industry, and indigenous groups have been participating in workshops. Foreign consultants from the Central American Commission on Environment and Development have also supported this process.

In parallel with the above process, there has been an initiative promoted by the Commission of Indigenous Affairs since 2000, to complete draft Law No. 36. This includes the establishment of a system to regulate access to genetic resources in indigenous lands and a mechanism to ensure the equitable sharing of benefits derived from the use of these resources. The draft law also includes penalties, PIC requirements, the right of indigenous groups to deny access to their genetic resources, and the intellectual protection of indigenous knowledge. According to the draft law, indigenous knowledge or genetic resources used by traditional communities will not be entitled to IPR protection. IPR protection such as patents for any product derived from access activities in indigenous lands will require the authorization of indigenous leaders and the proposed institute. The process to pass draft Law No. 36 is currently on hold due to several factors that include budgetary constrains. However, in late 2003 the Ministry of Health created a unit on traditional indigenous medicine that will address some of the issues proposed by the draft law.

In 2000, Panama adopted a *sui generis* system for the protection of community intellectual rights that is among the first in the region. Law 20 of 26 June 2000 established a special regime for the intellectual protection of community rights, cultural identity, and traditional knowledge. The law provides protection to traditional knowledge of indigenous groups that include customs, models, drawings, music, art, and other inventions, through a registry system. The Division of Industrial Property of the Ministry of Commerce and Industry administers the system. Registration is voluntary, free of charge, and there are no time limits for the protection provided by the registry. The registry will not prevent the continuous use of traditional knowledge but it will protect it from being used by others without previous authorization or compensation. Policymakers are currently working on a regulation for the law that will include monitoring requirements and compensation provisions such as royalties and up-front payments if indigenous knowledge is used by third parties. Additional work is also taking place on a draft law for the protection of the collective rights of local communities to protect the biological, medical, and ecological knowledge of indigenous peoples (M. Dimas, pers. comm February 2004).

Concerns

Lack of technical capacity, pertinent information, and mistrust from indigenous groups are some of the concerns and obstacles facing the development process of ABS laws in Panama. These issues have contributed to controversial and heated debates about ownership of genetic resources, traditional knowledge, and IPRs. There are still many overlapping issues and judicial obstacles that policymakers will have to overcome in order to develop a comprehensive and cohesive ABS system. Panama has not signed the FAO's ITPGRFA and it is uncertain how national laws and policies will assimilate the treaty requirements (M. Dimas, pers. comm. February 2004).

Philippines

Process

The history of ABS policies in the Philippines has been

marked by two significant events: the adoption of the 1995 Executive Order 247 (EO 247) and the enactment of the 2001 Wildlife Resources and Conservation Act (hereafter, Wildlife Act). The act included only two articles about access and benefit-sharing issues, but it addressed many of the criticisms made of EO 247 and modified it substantially. However, EO 247 is still quite relevant for the regulation of bioprospecting activities (see Chapters 1 and 7).

The development process of EO 247 can be traced back to the 1992 Seventh Asian Symposium on Medicinal Plants, Species, and Other Natural Products held in the Philippines. Two of the main outcomes of the Symposium were the Manila Declaration entitled "The Ethical Utilization of Asian Biological Resources", and the "Code of Ethics for Foreign Collectors of Biological Samples and Contract Guidelines". These two documents and the CBD created great awareness about the issue of bioprospecting in Asian countries and encouraged the Philippine Network for the Chemistry of Natural Products in Southeast Asia (with financial support from UNESCO) to develop the first draft of EO 247. Subsequently, in October 1993, Antonio G.M. La Viña, a legal consultant, was invited to revise the draft with input from members of the Philippine Network and representatives of key government departments. The EO 247 was adopted by the Philippines in 1995. In 1996, implementing rules and regulations for EO 247 were developed under the aegis of La Viña who was appointed under-secretary of the Department of Environment and Natural Resources (DENR). Drafts were circulated for comments to stakeholders that included government agencies, universities, private organizations, and NGOs. The secretary of DENR signed a final version in mid-1996. The high level of participation in the development of EO 247 was quite unusual for an executive order in the Philippines, which usually requires only limited consultation. In this case, representatives of government, scientists, nongovernmental organizations, community organizations, and the business community were actively involved in the drafting through a number of consultative meetings (A.G.M. La Viña, pers. comm. March 2003).

In 2001, the 11th Congress passed the Wildlife Act. The process began in 1998, when five House bills were filed and consolidated into one bill. A similar bill was filed in the Senate. The lower house version was used as a working draft during the bicameral committee sessions. Since the Wildlife Act is actually a codification of existing laws on the protection and conservation of wildlife resources, experience with the implementation of existing laws helped greatly in the design of the Wildlife Act. Concerns and issues raised against old laws such as EO 247 were addressed in the act.

The following sectors participated during the discussion process: government (Bureau of Customs, Philippine National Museum, Department of Science and Technology, Bureau of Aquatic Resources, National Bureau of Investigation, Protected Areas and Wildlife Bureau, Ecosystems Research and Development Bureau,

Department of Trade and Industry, National Committee on Biosafety in the Philippines, and the ASEAN Regional Center for Biodiversity Conservation); academia (University of the Philippines (UP) Marine Science Institute and the Institute of Plant Breeding-UP Los Baños); business (Floratrade/Philippine Horticultural Society and Southeast Asian Fisheries Development Corp); and NGOs (Kalikasan Mindoro Foundation and Conservation International).

Participants were in full support of the Wildlife Act and acknowledged its potential to facilitate and streamline ABS procedures. Most of the concerns or criticisms against EO 247 were considered and accommodated. There were also no controversial provisions or issues. DENR redrafted the Wildlife Act's provisions on bioprospecting. This is the same agency primarily in charge of implementing EO 247 (See Chapters 1 and 7). In July 2004, the draft "Guidelines for Bioprospecting Activities in the Philippines" were released by DENR for public review and comment. These guidelines were based on national consultations and interagency meetings. If adopted, the guidelines would facilitate the implementation of the Wildlife Act and those provisions of EO 247 not repealed by the Wildlife Act.

Concerns

The main difficulty experienced during the design of EO 247 was the lack of experience of policymakers, both domestically and internationally. Another concern was its impact on domestic research. Getting all the agencies and stakeholders that should be engaged and involved in drafting EO 247 to commit the time and resources for the process was difficult. As noted above, the first draft of EO 247 came from a group of scientists (a network of Natural Chemistry professors and researchers), and promoting subsequent support of the initiative by government agencies was difficult.

The process had to overcome several procedural and technical issues and perhaps the most difficult one was determining the scope of the regulation. Other challenges included funding and sanctions. In addition, it was difficult to determine a strategy to encourage self-regulation within the domestic academic community so that EO 247 would not become a bureaucratic nightmare for legitimate researchers. The Academic Research Agreement was conceptualized as the way to deal with this concern. Under this concept, researchers within an institution need apply for access only with that institution and not separately with the government. Putting together the administrative machinery for implementation was also a difficult problem as there are many agencies with some aspect of jurisdiction over bioprospecting activities (A.G.M. La Viña, pers. comm. March 2003).

Some of the concerns voiced during discussion of the Wildlife Act included: a) the need to simplify the permitting system for noncommercial research and development; b) the need to provide a list of species that are banned and restricted for prosecution purposes; c) government agencies mandated to do research had to be exempted from securing permits for collection; e) species listed under the Convention on International Trade in Endangered Species of Wild Fauna and Flora should be prohibited from exploitation except for scientific, education, experimental breeding, and propagation purposes; and f) the need to ensure that bioprospectors comply with the Cartagena Protocol on Biosafety when samples are imported (see Chapter 7).

Samoa

Process

Since the mid-1990s, Samoa has been carrying out initiatives to implement the CBD. In 1996, policymakers initiated development of a draft National Biodiversity Strategy that was not completed due to lack of funding[7]. In 2001, however, thanks to financial support provided by the GEF, the draft was revised, improved, and completed becoming part of the National Biodiversity Strategy and Action Plan (NBSAP). The NBSAP was adopted by Samoa in April 2001 and provided the conceptual and strategic foundation for the parallel and future efforts on ABS issues that have been supported since 1998 by WWF-SPP and SPREP. In March 2000, these organizations and FIELD held in Fiji a regional workshop on the implementation of the CBD in the Pacific Islands region. Participants at the workshop included government organizations, NGOs, and academic institutions.

The workshop produced a draft list of guidelines on ABS issues that was adopted by participants from 12 Pacific Island countries. As a result of this workshop and the regional guidelines the Department of Lands, Surveys, and Environment of Samoa adopted the 2000 "Conditions for Access to and Benefit Sharing of Samoa's Biodiversity Resources". The conditions, however, are likely to be replaced by a draft bioprospecting regulation that will become part of the 1989 Lands and Environment Act (C. Schuster and D.M. Clarke pers. comm. November 2003).

Concerns

Lack of funding and local capacity, ownership of genetic resources and traditional knowledge, and the impact of IPRs are some of the concerns and difficulties faced by stakeholders and policymakers of Samoa. Many stakeholders oppose the patenting of knowledge and have concerns about the impact of IPRs on the conservation of biodiversity (C. Schuster, pers. comm. November 2003).

Thailand

Process

Origins of the development process of the 1999 Plant Variety Protection Act (PVPA) and the Royal Forest Department (RFD) Regulation on Forestry Studying and Research Conducting within Forested Areas (RFSRCFA) go back to 1994 when the working group on genetic resources (established under the National Committee on the Convention on Biological Diversity) examined legal issues associated with access to and benefit sharing of genetic resources. Early discussions on the Act on the Protection and Promotion of Traditional Medicinal Intelligence (APPTMI) also took place in 1994 when TRIPS was concluded and Thailand learned about its commitments regarding the need for a protection mechanism of plant varieties.

The development process of the PVPA took two years. The drafting process was initiated by the Ministry of Agriculture and Cooperatives in 1997 during the government of Prime Minister Chavalit Yongchaiyudh and it was passed into law in 1999 while Prime Minister Chuan Leekpai was in office. The process was initiated with brainstorming sessions among government officials resulting in a working group that brought together policymakers, NGOs, researchers, private sector representatives, lawyers, and academics to work on the drafting of the act. The first draft was discussed at a public hearing, amendments were made, and it was sent off to the Parliament. A major obstacle to the process was that Parliament was dissolved while the draft law was being discussed. The draft law was sent back to government and officials used this opportunity to modify some of the provisions unilaterally. However, in the end, compromises were made between government officials and stakeholders, the draft was resubmitted to the next Parliament and passed into law (J. Donavanik, pers. comm. January 2003).

Between 1998 and 1999, RFD officials that included forestry experts and lawyers developed the RFSRCFA. Prompted by complaints from researchers about extremely long application times for access permits, among other reasons, RFD set up a Technical Committee in October 1998 to advise the Director General. The Technical Committee met several times in 1998 and early 1999 and discussions focused on developing a regulation to facilitate access for researchers to state-owned forested areas. In April 1999, a Research Proposal Reviewing Subcommittee (RPRS) was set up under the Technical Committee to examine issues related with the upcoming access regulation. In September 1999, the RFD released and adopted the RFSRCFA. In 2002, a second unit was split out from the RFD, the Department of National Parks, Wildlife, and Plant Conservation (DNWP). In late 2003, both departments were put under the aegis of the Ministry of Natural Resources and Environment. Under the new scheme the general directors of RFD and DNWP regulate access to natural, biological, and genetic resources found in forest and protected areas of Thailand (C. Hutacharern, pers. comm. December 2003).

In 1998, the Institute of Traditional Thai Medical Practice (Ministry of Public Health) initiated the development process of the APPTMI. The process included the participation of traditional healers, specialists in herbal medicines, and experts in the development process of traditional medicines. Other participants included lawyers, scholars in the field of traditional medicine, doctors, chemists, and government officials. Stakeholders discussed different ideas and strategies to ensure the protection of medicinal knowledge about plants and animals. The debate also addressed Article 8 (j) of the CBD on the protection of traditional knowledge, innovations, and practices. The draft went through several public hearings, it was sent to Parliament, and became law in 1999 (J. Donavanik, pers. comm. January 2003).

Concerns

The development process of the PVPA was marked by rivalry between domestic NGOs and government officials. Ownership of genetic resources, indigenous knowledge, and IPRS were controversial issues. For example, NGOs did not want modern IPR protection such as patents on life forms or traditional knowledge. The private sector stressed the potential of genetic resources as a source of monetary and nonmonetary benefits to society. Compromise regarding this point was reached by providing a minimum standard of protection to allow the protection of inventions (J. Donavanik, pers. comm. January 2003).

The development process of the RFSRCFA had to overcome conflicts about details involving monitoring strategies, application proposals, and progress reports among the members of the technical committee. RFD officials where also concerned about potential biopiracy and they proposed prevention strategies such as assigning a co-researcher to every bioprospecting project. Some officials who were concerned about biopiracy issues also attempted to put additional restrictions in the access process.

In the early stages of the development process of the APPTMI, the government was not open to the idea of this act because its scope had not been clearly defined (see Chapter 1). Furthermore, there were concerns about compatibility issues between the act and TRIPS. These concerns were echoed by the American Embassy in Thailand. However, the scope was refined, compatibility issues were addressed, the government accepted the draft bill, and it was passed into law (J. Donavanik, pers. comm. January 2003).

Vanuatu

Process

In 1997, the Ministry of Lands, Natural Resources, Energy, and Environment established a National Biodiversity Advisory Committee that promoted a process of discussion of biodiversity issues to facilitate the implementation of the CBD. This committee had ample participation by representatives of government, academic institutions, and NGOs that, together with the Ministry, facilitated the completion of the National Biodiversity Action Plan in 2000. In 2001, the momentum created by this plan was channeled by the Ministry to establish four working groups to have discussions on access and benefit sharing, traditional knowledge and rights, and capacity building. Priority has also been given to the discussion of the protection of traditional knowledge and innovation and the fair and equitable sharing of benefits derived from biodiversity.

Regional and international organizations such as SPREP, WWF-SPP, and FIELD have supported these initiatives with regional and national workshops held in Fiji and Vanuatu in March 2000 and April 2001, respectively. The workshops have provided a valuable arena for stakeholders to discuss a great variety of issues ranging from ownership of biological and genetic resources to definitions of access to genetic resources. Discussions among stakeholders still continue but access and benefit-sharing regulations are expected to be incorporated into a draft Environment Act that should be introduced into Parliament in 2004 (C. Schuster, pers. comm. August 2003).

Concerns

In the absence of national regulations, government agencies have negotiated ad hoc arrangements with bioprospectors that include a standard application form, not legally binding, that has been used since 2000 to regulate foreign bioprospectors. Kava (*Piper methysticum*) and other biological resources have been heavily exploited in Vanuatu and there is a perception that local communities have not been adequately compensated for their resources and traditional knowledge. Local researchers and institutions have not been invited to collaborate in bioprospecting initiatives and the government does not monitor the use of samples once they leave the country. In addition, there are concerns that samples initially collected for one purpose are stored and then used for another purpose. For example, blood samples originally collected for malaria experiments were later used for the human genome project. The unauthorized use of blood samples resulted in protests from indigenous groups (C. Schuster, pers. comm. October 2003).

Ownership of land and genetic resources is a complex issue. According to the constitution, traditional communities own all the land in Vanuatu. Therefore, PIC procedures are particularly important, but researchers have shown resistance to follow them. Land cannot be alienated but the government may own land acquired by it in the public interest. Parliament, after consultation with the national Council of Chiefs, may allocate land according to different use categories. Lack of financial aid, technical information, and expertise are also major concerns in Vanuatu. Efforts to complete the National Biodiversity Strategy and Action Plan would have not been possible without funds from the GEF and technical assistance from organizations such as SPREP and WWF-SPP (C. Schuster, pers. comm. October 2003).

Policymaking Process: Analysis

For the countries reviewed in this chapter, ABS policymaking has been an incremental process, a sequence of events influenced by many actors with different interests, values, information roles, perspectives, and agendas. Since the CBD came into force, each nation has followed different policy timelines driven by its unique social, economic, and political circumstances. While a few countries have concluded the policymaking process, most are still conducting it, and some have not yet found the conditions to initiate it.

The policymaking process can be visualized in many ways. BREWER and DELEON (1983) propose that a framework composed of three stages: a) initiation, b) estimation, and c) selection can be used to characterize policymaking efforts. Initiation consists of problem identification and agenda setting, estimation involves expert analysis and technical consideration, and selection refers to the fact that someone, based on technical and political input, has to make a decision about the best course of action or policy. This framework facilitates the identification and understanding of key patterns and lessons from our case studies.

Policy Initiation

ABS issues have been poorly defined by the CBD. Most of the work has been passed to the member countries that have received key input from the CBD secretariat, Conference of the Parties, and other bodies. As CBD members, countries have responsibilities that include identifying relevant ABS issues, putting them on the agenda, identifying the stakeholders, ensuring equal opportunities to participate, initiating the debate, and addressing policy and value conflicts.

The agenda of the policymaking process can be divided into systemic and institutional (BUCK 1991). The systemic agenda includes all issues that the "attentive public" agrees need to be resolved. The "attentive public" is the informed, political, intellectual, and more educated layer of society. This public is usually composed of representatives of academic, research, advocate, or grassroots organizations. They are vocal about recurring issues that are problematic and cannot be ignored. When this public can convince its government about the importance of these issues, then policymakers place these issues on the institutional agenda. Sometimes, however, issues bypass the systemic agenda and simply originate at the institutional level. The institutional agenda includes issues that the government plans to consider seriously and actively. The problem is clearly identified, solutions are proposed, and financial resources are allocated. Issues placed on the institutional agenda are also subject to time constraints

When the CBD came into force, ABS issues were placed on the institutional agenda of the international community of countries. More than 160 countries agreed on the need to implement the CBD in order to ensure the conservation and sustainable use of biological diversity and the equitable distribution of benefits derived from this diversity, among other issues. Many countries, however, have been unable to address several CBD issues comprehensively and effectively. ABS, for example, has not been a priority for 15% of the Pacific Rim countries examined in this report. Lack of technical expertise, budgetary constraints, weak government structures and political support, local social conflict, and conflict over ownership of biological resources are some of the reasons cited by ABS experts that have prevented Kiribati, Lao People's Democratic Republic, Nauru, Palau, Tonga, and Tuvalu from working actively towards the development of ABS policies. The remaining 75% of Pacific Rim countries have managed at least to initiate policy processes to incorporate ABS provisions into national laws and policies (see Table 1 of Chapter 1). They have allocated scarce financial and technical resources needed to begin the collection of key information and the identification of the range of possible responses, policy choices, and stakeholders.

The controversial nature of ABS issues demand the involvement of potential providers, users, and intermediaries of genetic resources in the initiation process of ABS policies. If these stakeholders appropriate the policy development process as their own, this will increase the legitimacy of the policy outcome and facilitate its implementation process. Government agencies, legislative commissions, industry and academic groups, NGOs, and regional economic and social integration organizations have been some of the loci for initiation of processes for countries that have completed or are currently working on ABS policies. Industry groups, NGOs, and academia played varying roles in the initiation process of pioneer ABS laws such as the Andean Decision 391, the Philippines's EO 247, and Costa Rica's Law of Biodiversity. The process that resulted in the adoption of Decision 391 by the Andean Community was initiated by the Secretariat of the Andean Community with technical support from domestic NGOs, international agriculture research centers, and government agencies. At the initial stage of the policy debate these actors attempted to democratize the process by holding a workshop but conflict and controversy arose among participants and thwarted the continuation of the participatory process. Some NGOs, for example, advocated a policy instrument focused on biodiversity conservation and sustainable use goals, while government actors insisted on the importance of keeping the commercial perspective of ABS issues. No middle ground was found and government officials assimilated the policymaking process that resulted in the commercial orientation of Decision 391. This outcome suggested that the concern of government agencies had the tendency to dominate the process conceptually and administratively to the exclusion of concerns of some environmental NGOs and other participants that should have shared the focus of attention. Years after the adoption of Decision 391 and criticism about its restrictive nature (GRAJAL 1999), Andean countries such as Colombia are still working on national policies to facilitate its implementation.

In the Philippines, an academic/industry group initiated the policy process that resulted in the adoption of EO 247. In spite of the participatory process launched by this group, involving and making government and other sectors support the process was a difficult and long undertaking. Similarly, the first draft of Costa Rica's Law of Biodiversity was developed by a Costa Rican ex-politician with technical support provided by the World Conservation Union's Regional Office for Mesoamerica. The process included the participation of a wide variety of sectors, but interestingly enough the Costa Rican Ministry of the Environment and Energy was not deeply involved into the process and no one within the Ministry appropriated the new law as a government initiative (J. Cabrera, pers. comm. February 2004). Therefore, when the new Minister came into power, she submitted a constitutional challenge that has prevented the full implementation of the law. Costa Rica's Law of Biodiversity has influenced other Central American nations such as Nicaragua. In this case, however, Nicaragua's Ministry for the Environment and Natural Resources provided leadership to initiate and advance a participatory development process of a draft Law of Biodiversity that addresses ABS issues and other biodiversity related goals. Presently, however, the draft law is stalled because the Agriculture Ministry argues that biosafety issues fall under the jurisdiction of this body, hence an independent law enforced by the Ministry should address them. This brings up the point that ABS policy goals are typically under the jurisdiction of multiple government organizations that must be actively involved into the policymaking process.

Processes to include ABS principles into existing laws have also been initiated by governmental bodies with varying degrees of success. For example, Mexico's SEMARNAT and the commissions on ecology and environment promoted the reform of EEEPGA. The reform, however, was not significant and only two articles (87 and 87 BIS) were included into the Act to facilitate access and benefit-sharing goals. Legal gaps and a lack of a nationwide participatory process during the development of the law questioned its legitimacy (see Chapter 6). Thailand's RFSRCFA, was developed by RFD officials without input from other stakeholders. So far the regulation has not been tested by commercial bioprospectors. Similarly, Chile's Ministry of Agriculture completed in isolation a draft for a law to regulate access to agricultural genetic resources that was discarded after severe criticism (see Chapter 10). In contrast, the process initiated by Environment Australia to include ABS provisions into the EPBCA involved the participation of biotechnology, indigenous, environmental, government, and academic groups through a national inquiry and several public hearings. A key factor that contributed to the strength and momentum of the process was the establishment in 1999 of Biotechnology Australia, a multi-departmental government agency, responsible for coordinating nonregulatory biotechnology issues for the Commonwealth Government (see Chapter 9). A different but equally effective process to develop a federal ABS policy was initiated by a task force integrating federal and state representatives from government and NGOs of Malaysia. The sufficiently diverse composition of the task force provided technical expertise and legitimacy to the process. Government and nongovernment agencies with strong technical capacities on biotechnology and biodiversity research together with environment ministries have proven to be an effective combination to advance the incorporation of ABS goals into national policies. This pattern is clear not only in Australia and Malaysia, but also in Costa Rica and the Philippines.

SPREP, WWF-SPP, and FIELD have held a series of workshops among Pacific Island countries that initiated ABS processes in countries such as Cook Islands, Marshall Islands, Niue, Samoa, and Vanuatu. A direct impact of a workshop held in Fiji was Samoa's adoption of ABS conditions as an executive provisional measure to regulate ABS goals. These conditions have been turned into a bioprospecting regulation that will complement an upcoming Land and Environment Act (see Chapter 1). Other countries such as Cambodia, China, El Salvador, Honduras, Indonesia, Japan, New Zealand, Papua New Guinea, the Republic of Korea, the Russian Federation, Singapore, and Thailand have different processes under way that have been initiated by central government bodies in charge of judicial and environmental duties (see Table 1 of Chapter 1). All of them are still at initial or intermediate stages of discussing ABS.

Policy Estimation

Policy initiation and estimation are usually parallel processes (BREWER and deLEON 1983). Estimation is essential not only to analyze risks, costs, and benefits of ABS goals but also to facilitate the selection of the ABS policy (Law of Biodiversity, stand-alone national ABS policy, etc.) that fits legal, social, administrative, economic, and political conditions of the country. Estimation also involves the analysis of empirical and theoretical characteristics of ABS issues that apply to PIC, biodiversity conservation, ownership of genetic resources, and the protection of traditional knowledge (see Chapter 1). Sometimes these policy goals are in conflict with each other and with existing policies and forms of government. An example of this is the incompatibility between Chile's current strict private property right system and the issue of ownership of genetic resources which prevented initial efforts to develop an ABS policy in that country. Malaysia's initiatives to adopt a national ABS policy have also been delayed by a property rights conflict. The federal government claims ownership over genetic resources found in federal land that are also claimed by state governments and indigenous communities. Similarly, New Zealand's Maori people have claimed exclusive rights over genetic resources, thereby delaying efforts to initiate an ABS policy (see Table 1 of Chapter 1). Ownership of genetic resources found in *ex situ* conditions has also been a concern for Australia, Cook Islands, and Nicaragua.

Policy estimation also has to take into account political agendas, misperceptions, value conflicts, and different levels of information and expertise. For example, organizations such as ETC (formerly known as RAFI) label any kind of bioprospecting (even if it involves benefit-sharing agreements) as biopiracy[8] and this message has reached many indigenous and grassroots organizations worldwide. Some level of opposition to bioprospecting and concerns about the inequitable distribution of benefits was identified in all the countries addressed in this chapter. The protection of traditional knowledge and patenting of life are also major concerns, particularly in countries such as Australia, Ecuador, Honduras, Malaysia, Mexico, Panama, Peru, and Thailand that have significant indigenous populations.

The essential role of policy experts and facilitators of explaining the multiple dimensions and implications of ABS policies is certainly needed in all the countries that are attempting to implement the CBD. ABS issues have presented new conceptual, political, and operational challenges to stakeholders. Technical guidance and support by the Conference of the Parties of the CBD, the *ad hoc* group of experts on ABS, and regional organizations such as SPREP have been instrumental to further key national efforts. Countries such as Panama and Indonesia have welcomed and are using the Bonn Guidelines on ABS. SPREP workshops and technical assistance together with technical expertise provided by FIELD, WWF-South Pacific Programme, and the United Nations University have supported ABS initiatives of Pacific Island countries. Efforts advanced by these organizations, however, do not have an impact unless they are assimilated and appropriated by strong and proactive national agencies and NGOs. Building local capacity to improve policy initiation and estimation is a priority for all the countries reviewed in this chapter but particularly so for the Pacific Island countries.

Policy Selection

Selection involves the most political step in the policymaking process. A decision maker or decision makers select a course of action based on available technical, social, and political information gathered and analyzed during the initiation and estimation stages (BREWER and DELEON 1983). If previous analyses present technical contradictions or political conflicts, policymakers may decide not to select any policy. For example, in the early 1990s, Chile's National Commission of the Environment examined the possibility of developing a national ABS law, but this effort was thwarted by an inability to resolve technical issues, lack of political support, and the unwillingness of government officials to promote a participatory process to discuss the issue (see Chapter 10).

The Mexican experience also shows that the simplistic focus of ABS policy incorporated into the EEEPGA diverted attention from the short- and medium-term problems that arise with implementation of the policy (see Chapter 6). A more comprehensive perspective of ABS issues can be addressed within the context of NBSAP, which is the first step followed by most countries that want to implement the CBD as a whole (MILLER and LANAU 1995). There is not sufficient evidence that NBSAP can lead to successful ABS policies. But Chile's recent National Biodiversity Strategy and future NBSAP may provide the needed framework, resources, political support, and momentum to overcome old difficulties in developing an ABS policy. Countries such as Australia, Cook Islands, El Salvador, Honduras, Marshall Islands, Micronesia, New Zealand, Niue, Palau, the Russian Federation, and Tonga have also followed this approach. On the other hand, China, Colombia, Ecuador, Peru, Philippines, and Thailand, among other countries, have developed or are developing ABS policies independently of any process triggered by an NBSAP.

Policy options identified in this report that address ABS goals include:

- Regional and national stand-alone ABS laws and policies (Andean Community, China, Malaysia, and the Philippines);

- Laws of biodiversity, sustainable development, or environment acts that include biodiversity conservation and sustainable use provisions and ABS guidelines. These laws are usually designed to implement the CBD as a whole (Costa Rica, Cook Islands, Honduras, Indonesia, and Nicaragua);

- Existing environmental, sustainable development or ecological laws that have been amended (by national legislative bodies) or modified (through executive regulations) to include ABS provisions (Australia and Mexico);

- ABS policies that may be developed further into more comprehensive ABS laws (El Salvador, Samoa, and Panama).

It is not realistic to suggest that any one of the above policy approaches is a magic wand that can facilitate the incorporation of ABS principles into national policies. Each of them has advantages and disadvantages. For example, the Costa Rican experience shows that the debate of a multi-objective regulation such as the Law of Biodiversity may not provide the time or resources to debate adequately the intricacies of ABS issues. Also, Nicaragua's draft Law of Biodiversity overlaps with existing laws and presents a jurisdictional conflict to government agencies. Policy approaches should be carefully analyzed and selected according to national social, political, and institutional characteristics, priorities, and local expertise.

In some countries that share common ecosystems and cultural backgrounds, national ABS policies have been supported by regional initiatives such as the Central American

Protocol on Access to Genetic and Biochemical Resources and their Associated Knowledge and the ASEAN framework agreement on access to biological and genetic resources. One of the goals of these regional frameworks is to ensure that national ABS requirements are consistent to prevent bioprospectors from shopping for the best deal in countries that share similar ecosystems. All Central American countries already signed the Protocol and when approved it will become national law in each of them. The ASEAN framework is expected to be adopted in 2004 or 2005.

Final Comment

Ideally, the policy process has to be initiated and appropriated by the highest number possible of providers, users, and intermediaries of genetic resources to ensure its legitimacy during its development and implementation. This is the main lesson identified from ABS policy processes carried out in countries that include Colombia, Costa Rica, Mexico, the Philippines, Australia, and Malaysia (see Chapters 4, 5, 6, 7, 9, and 11). The advantages of carrying out a wide participatory process lie in the collection of key practical and theoretical information about ABS issues (see Chapter 1), in the identification of potential problems and concerns (this chapter), and in the opportunity to involve key stakeholders that bring legitimacy to the policy process, its final outcome, and implementation process. This is certainly a long, difficult, and expensive process and there are no guarantees about the efficacy and efficiency of the policy outcome. However, our case studies suggest that ABS polices that reflect and involve the needs and desires of all stakeholders have a higher probability of being successful than those that are developed by a minority of technocrats.

References

ANDEAN COMMUNITY. 2002. Decision 523: Regional biodiversity strategy for the tropical Andean countries. URL: http://www.comunidadandina.org/ingles/treaties/dec/D523e.htm.

BREWER G.D. and P. deLEON. 1983. *The foundations of policy analysis*. The Dorsey Press, IL USA.

BUCK S.J. 1991. *Understanding environmental administration and law*. Island Press, CA USA.

FAO. 1998. *The state of the world's plant genetic resources for food and agriculture*. Rome, Italy.

GRAJAL A. 1999. Biodiversity and the nation state: Regulating access to genetic resources limits biodiversity research in developing countries. *Conservation Biology* 13(1):6–9.

LA ASAMBLEA LEGISLATIVA. 1998. Ley No. 41 (de 1 de julio de 1998): Ley general de ambiente de la Republica de Panamá. Diario Oficial No. 23,578, Panamá.

MILLER K.R. and S.M. LANOU. 1995. *National biodiversity planning: Guidelines based on early experiences around the world*. World Resources Institute, Washington, DC USA.

Endnotes

[1] Consistent with my use in Chapter 1, I define bioprospecting as the search for plants, animals, and microbial species for academic, pharmaceutical, biotechnological, agricultural, and other industrial purposes.

[2] In March 2002 the Ministry of Agriculture started a process of consultation and analysis within government agencies to determine the consequences and benefits that signature and ratification of the ITPGRFA may have for Chile. After a few months of discussions Chile signed it on 4 November 2002 (see Chapter 10).

[3] See the FIELD website at URL: http://www.field.org.uk/biodiversity_pg4.php.

[4] These policies and laws are: a) the 1989 Wild Animal Protection Law; b) the 1997 Wild Plant Protection Regulation; c) the 1998 Regulation for Protection of New Plant Varieties; d) the 1989 Regulation for Seeds Administration; e) the 2000 Seeds Law; f) the 1993 Regulation for Protection of Chinese Herb Medicine Varieties; g) the 1994 Administrative Regulation for Breeding Livestock, Animals, and Poultry; h) the 1994 Regulation for Nature Reserves; i) the Provisional Regulation for Seeds Importing and Exporting;

j) the 1998 Provisional Regulation for Human Genetic Resources; and k) the 2001 Regulation for Safety of Agricultural Genetically-Modified Organisms (D. Xue, pers. comm. December 2003).

[5] "One of the oldest regional organizations in the world, SPC celebrated its 50th anniversary on 6 February 1997. It is a non-political, technical assistance and research body, and fills a consultative and advisory role." URL: http://www.spc.org.nc/history.htm.

[6] While the above process was taking place at the federal level, the states of Sarawak and Sabah were working on their own access and benefit-sharing regulations that culminated in the enactment of the Sarawak Biodiversity Center Ordinance of 1997 and the Sabah Biodiversity Enactment of 2000 (see Chapter 11).

[7] This preliminary draft was developed with technical support provided by the New Zealand Official Development Assistance (known today as the New Zealand Agency for International Development).

[8] See http://www.etcgroup.org/article.asp?newsid=432.

3

Implementation Pathways

Stephen B. Brush and Santiago Carrizosa

The drafting and implementation of national policies and laws to facilitate access to genetic resources and ensure the equitable sharing of the benefits of access is still very much a work in progress. Only 22% of Pacific Rim countries have established access and benefit-sharing (ABS) laws and policies (see Chapter 1) and their experience in implementing them is uneven. Costa Rica, the Philippines, Mexico, Samoa, and the USA (National Park Service (NPS) policy)[1] are the only Pacific Rim countries that have approved access applications under ABS laws and policies developed or reformed after the Convention on Biological Diversity (CBD) came into force in 1993 (see Table 1 of Chapter 1). The novel and sometimes experimental nature of some of the policy tools employed affects our ability to distill definitive lessons or guidelines that can be used to improve existing or pending ABS frameworks. Nevertheless, the range of experiences among Pacific Rim countries in processing bioprospecting[2] project proposals is useful in anticipating obstacles and suggesting pathways to policy implementation. Under the ABS laws and policies of these countries a total of 22 bioprospecting projects[3] have been approved between 1991 and July 2004 (see Table 1). The purpose of this chapter is to use the information gathered in the Pacific Rim case studies (Chapters 4 through 8) to illustrate some critical lessons about the implementation of ABS regimes.

We will analyze the implementation of ABS policy by focusing on three steps in the process of initiating a bioprospecting project: a) application to a competent authority, b) review and negotiation of acceptable terms such as prior informed consent (PIC) procedures and benefit-sharing obligations with the government and providers of genetic resources and traditional knowledge, and c) initiation of approved projects for the collection of biological materials and the return of benefits related to collecting. It is impossible at this time to determine whether the implementation of ABS policies has been successful in meeting the overarching goals of the CBD beyond providing access to biological resources (i.e., providing benefit sharing and achieving conservation of biological diversity). Our evaluation of the extent to which these goals have been met is limited by the following considerations: a) many projects which have been initiated under ABS regimes are still in progress, b) a delay is expected in identifying, using, and perhaps commercializing useful genetic resources, and c) a long time is needed to determine whether biodiversity conservation and adequate benefit sharing have indeed been achieved.

The Road Towards Implementation of ABS Laws and Policies

The CBD and biopiracy claims prompted governments around the world to draft national ABS policies. Because the CBD recognized that countries have sovereign rights over their genetic resources, it did not specify or suggest model policies for nations to emulate[4], but a few noteworthy experiments in fashioning ABS agreements have provided ideas for national policy frameworks. Parties from several countries that lack ABS frameworks have used Letters of Intent (LI), Letters of Collection (LC), Memoranda of Understanding (MOU), and benefit-sharing or material transfer agreements to facilitate access and define benefit-sharing obligations (see Table 1). Since the late 1980s, in response to the reluctance of biodiversity-rich countries to allow bioprospectors to conduct collections freely, the National Cancer Institute (NCI) in the United States of America (USA) developed three standard agreements to facilitate the sharing of monetary and nonmonetary benefits. The first agreement, a 1990 LI, was later improved by a 1992 LC and a 1995 MOU. Under these instruments NCI collectors (e.g., the New York Botanical Garden, the Missouri Botanical Garden, the University of Illinois at Chicago, and the Coral Reef Research Foundation) were able to get access to biological samples found in many Pacific Rim countries (see Table 1, CRAGG et al. 1994, ten Kate and Laird 1999). Many of these samples were obtained in collaboration with scientists from local research and academic organizations. Perhaps the primary example of a comprehensive and influential benefit-sharing agreement was the Merck–National Biodiversity Institute (INBio) contract negotiated in Costa Rica in 1991 (REID et al. 1993). This agreement not only inspired subsequent contracts signed by INBio with many organizations worldwide (see Chapter 5), but also the agreements established under the International Cooperative Biodiversity Group (ICBG)[5] program. From 1993 to 2003, the ICBGs used benefit-sharing agreements that facilitated access to the genetic resources of the following Pacific Rim countries: Chile (1993), Costa Rica (1993), Mexico (1994 and 1998), Panama (1998), Peru (1993), Laos (1998), and Vietnam (1998) (see Table 1).

The timing and publicity of the 1991 Merck–INBio and ICBG agreements helped make them models for creating national policies and laws to reach the general goals of the CBD (ROSENTHAL et al. 1999). Among the elements of these agreements that are replicated in ABS policies are a bilateral and contractual approach, well-defined parties to the contract, exchange of tangible short- and long-term benefits for the right to access, biodiversity conservation and sustainable use, and an intellectual property framework for deriving benefits (REID et al. 1993, ROSENTHAL et al. 1999). These elements are found in many ABS policies (see Chapter 1), but in some contexts, they are associated with difficulties in the implementation phase.

While much of the period following the 1992 United Nations Conference on the Environment and Development that gave rise to the CBD has been devoted to creating policies and administrative frameworks for access and benefit sharing, there is still only a limited number of cases where a national ABS law or policy has been tested in terms of applications, negotiations to establish acceptable terms, and the initiation of activities under agreements for access and benefit sharing.

Case Studies

Our survey of national laws and policies for access and benefit sharing relating to biological resources and the case studies done in the Pacific Rim region illustrate two general facts. First, relatively few countries have entered fully into the implementation stage of their national ABS laws and policies, in terms of processing applications for biological collections, reviewing and negotiating the terms of access and benefit sharing, and carrying out bioprospecting activities. Second, the experience of countries that have implemented bioprospecting projects is very uneven and information on countries' experience is difficult to find. At one extreme, some countries have succeeded in launching bioprospecting projects after negotiating with parties wishing to collect and use biological resources, while at the other extreme, some countries have failed, with the result that neither access nor benefit sharing has occurred. In this chapter, we will illustrate three types of experience in implementing ABS laws and policies as characterized by experiences in launching bioprospecting projects under them: successful implementation, mixed success and breakdown, and thwarted implementation.

Successful Implementation

Two rather different countries, Costa Rica and the USA have succeeded in signing and entering into bioprospecting agreements. It is interesting and important to note the initiation of projects in these countries is not an instance of implementing ABS policies that were formally developed as a government response to the CBD. Rather, these projects grew out of personal networks and collaboration between researchers, government officials, and private firms and preceded the CBD or emerged outside of its framework.

Costa Rica. Success in initiating bioprospecting projects preceded the creation of a legal framework governing biodiversity (the 1998 Law of Biodiversity No. 7788) in response to the CBD mandate. The Law of Biodiversity created a national framework that includes the National Commission of the Management of Biodiversity (CONAGEBIO). CONAGEBIO's role includes the formulation of ABS policies. For example, CONAGEBIO developed a General Access Procedure that was approved through an executive decree in December 2003 (see Chapter 5).

The initial agreement that triggered subsequent ones is the Merck–INBio agreement reached in 1991 (REID et al. 1993). INBio grew out of Costa Rica's unique environmental, social, scientific, and political context. Scientific leadership in Costa Rica and the networks between this leadership and scientists outside of Costa Rica also were instrumental in developing a model ABS framework. INBio was established in 1989 with the support of the Ministry of Natural Resources, Energy, and Mines (MIRENEM[6]) as part of Costa Rica's efforts to improve environmental protection for its notable biological diversity (GÁMEZ et al. 1993).

INBio's novel approach financed conservation through debt-for-nature swaps. INBio grew out of the Biodiversity Office, which was a dependency of MIRENEM, but it was created as a private, not-for-profit, public-interest association dedicated to carrying out research and conservation activities for the protection of biological diversity in Costa Rica. While INBio was created prior to the 1992 Law of

Wildlife Conservation (LWC) No. 7317, the LWC opened a window of opportunity for INBio because an element in Costa Rica's regulatory framework under the LWC permitted MIRENEM to allocate biodiversity prospecting concessions in national conservation areas (SITTENFELD and GÁMEZ 1993). INBio became the agent for that allocation by means of a 1992 formal agreement between MIRENEM and INBio that authorized INBio to negotiate subsequent agreements that provided access to genetic resources in national parks in return for financial support for INBio's national biodiversity inventory and the National Parks Fund of MIRENEM (SITTENFELD and GÁMEZ 1993).

The Merck–INBio agreement prompted other international companies and research institutions to seek similar arrangements for access to genetic resources in Costa Rica by collaborating with INBio and other national institutions such as the University of Costa Rica. A total of 15 bioprospecting projects have been granted access to Costa Rica's biological and genetic resources under the 1992 LWC and its 1997 regulations. The Merck–INBio agreement was renewed three times before expiring in 1999. INBio has negotiated 14 other agreements with international and national research institutions and private firms for prospecting activities that include chemicals from insects, fragrances and aromas, nematicides, and extremophilic organisms, in addition to bioassays of plants. Nine of these agreements are with private firms, one is with a multilateral organization, three are with universities in the United Kingdom, USA, and Canada, and one is with a local university and hospital.

The level of activity reached under the LWC has helped make Costa Rica a model for ABS strategies based on bioprospecting. The success in carrying out bioprospecting projects in this framework is due to the special position of INBio as a nongovernmental institution with high scientific and administrative capacity and the 1992 agreement with MIRENEM which allows INBio to broker contracts for access to resources on certain public lands as long as INBio obtains the permits mandated by the LWC. Furthermore, the 1992 MIRENEM/INBio agreement sets a target for bioprospecting projects that 10% of a project's annual research budget and 50% of future royalties from the project that accrue to INBio must be donated to the National Parks Fund to be reinvested in conservation (SITTENFELD and GÁMEZ 1993). Between 1991 and 2000, $2.7 million USD have been invested in conservation (see Chapter 5). By working in designated conservation areas, such as the Guanacaste National Park, INBio is alleviated from the need to negotiate with landholders and local communities. Likewise, the sharing of benefits is facilitated by INBio's scientific and educational role and by its special relation to the National Park system and MIRENEM. These factors help INBio and its international partners to minimize transaction costs in negotiating for access and distribution of benefits. By acting as a singular and nongovernmental authority in negotiating access and benefits, INBio reduces the complexity of negotiating with private firms and universities. Finally,

its focus on national parks and designated conservation areas directly connects benefits to accepted conservation activities.

However, and despite the apparent success of this model, Costa Rica went beyond the framework provided in the LWC by enacting the Law of Biodiversity in 1998 (see Chapter 5). The new law is a response to the mandate of the CBD to draft national ABS policies, and it replaces the nongovernmental approach utilized by INBio with a centralized process of issuing access permits through the Technical Office of CONAGEBIO. INBio is not a member of CONAGEBIO.

Although the implementation of the Law of Biodiversity is not yet fully tested, as Chapter 5 suggests, it faces some severe obstacles. These include lack of clarity about the role and power of key elements in the proposed ABS provisions, ambiguity about the relation to the ABS framework established previously under the LWC, and obscurity and complexity in the application procedures. The general atmosphere of the new ABS regime under the Law of Biodiversity is to be more restrictive and controlling of the process of negotiating access and benefits. Furthermore, the constitutional challenge requested by the Ministry of Environment and Energy (MINAE, the former MIRENEM, see endnote 6) in 1998 and made by the Attorney General against the law's article that created CONAGEBIO (among other articles) has brought political uncertainty to the role of this commission. The brief record of receiving applications under the new law appears to validate these concerns. Furthermore, none of the three applications submitted to date have been finalized (see Chapter 5).

The case of Costa Rica suggests that success in implementation of ABS policy is best achieved in a decentralized system with flexible norms of negotiating benefits, a simple and direct system whereby the entity empowered to grant access negotiates directly with the organization seeking access, and where the number of parties in the negotiation and permitting process is minimized. The process envisioned in the Law of Biodiversity appears to move Costa Rica away from these norms.

USA. Similarly to other countries, the USA has a brief history regulating ABS with regard to its own genetic resources. The country's experiment with ABS of national biological resources is represented in this report by a single case, the contract between the Yellowstone National Park and Diversa Corporation for access to thermophilic bacteria found in the hot springs of Yellowstone National Park. The Yellowstone–Diversa contract (i.e., a Cooperative Research and Development Agreement (CRADA)) is similar to the Merck–INBio agreement in several ways. Both were negotiated outside of the specific CBD context. In Costa Rica's case, the deal was agreed to before the CBD, and the USA case involves a country that is not party to the CBD. Like INBio, Yellowstone National Park was created before any ABS policy was conceived, and both the park and the institute had well-defined conservation missions before entering into bioprospecting contracts.

The Merck–INBio and Yellowstone–Diversa cases differ in their genesis. In Costa Rica, negotiations over access and benefits preceded bioprospecting activities, while in Yellowstone, bioprospecting preceded negotiations over access and benefits. The Yellowstone–Diversa CRADA, negotiated in 1997, followed the commercial success of using biological specimens from Yellowstone to create an essential tool for the biotechnology industry. The Cetus Corporation obtained samples of the *Thermus aquaticus* bacteria that had been collected in 1966 and deposited with the American Type Culture Collection (ATCC), a nonprofit organization established in 1925 as a resource center for biological products. ATCC acquires, authenticates, preserves, and distributes biological materials. Biological specimens, such as *Thermus aquaticus*, are held as public goods by ATCC, and ATCC does not claim intellectual property over them.

Cetus had acquired the original sample of *Thermus aquaticus* from ATCC in 1985 as a public good. The specimens of *Thermus aquaticus* were deposited with ATCC before it had established a special collection and material procedure with the USA National Park Service (NPS). ATCC now maintains a special collection of biological materials from the NPS, including *Thermus aquaticus* from Yellowstone and has a material transfer agreement for the NPS collections which requires that the person requesting material acknowledge ownership by the federal government, agree to use the material, its replicates, and derivatives for research only and not commercial purposes without authorization, and agree to inform the NPS of findings from the material, its replicates, or derivatives.

Thermus aquaticus proved to be highly valuable because it included a heat-stable enzyme named *Taq* polymerase that facilitated efficient, controlled replication of DNA. The commercial success of patenting, sale, and licensing of *Taq* led to recommendations from several groups and political leaders in the USA that the NPS begin to regulate access and to seek benefits from its biological resources (see Chapter 8).

The ABS approach followed by the NPS was to adopt the framework of the 1986 Federal Technology Transfer Act (FTTA) whose purpose was to facilitate access by the private sector to knowledge and technology developed by government agencies or with public funding. The emphasis of this act is on access rather than benefit sharing (APEN et al. 1994). Increased access was meant to increase the rate of return on public investment and thus provide increased social benefit. The underlying logic of FTTA is that access to knowledge, for instance through exclusive licensing of patents held by government laboratories, will facilitate the development and diffusion of new technology and thereby provide for benefit sharing by enhancing social welfare. FTTA was one of several laws passed to enhance commercial development of publicly owned knowledge or resources and to increase private investment in research that had been initiated by public agencies (APEN et al. 1994). Although the FTTA emphasized access, it also

anticipated the possibility of a benefit stream back to the federal partner (See Chapter 8). The vehicle that the FTTA promoted for increasing ABS goals between federally funded programs and private businesses was the CRADA[7]. The 1997 Yellowstone National Park–Diversa CRADA provided access to thermophilic and other biological resources of Yellowstone National Park to Diversa in return for short- and long-term financial returns (see Chapter 8). While the Yellowstone–Diversa agreement was challenged as a violation of the public trust and the conservation mission of Yellowstone National Park, the challenge was dismissed by a federal court in 2000. The Yellowstone–Diversa agreement has led both to new products for the company and to financial support from the company to the park for its conservation work (see Chapter 8).

The success of this project is noteworthy because it occurred outside of the CBD framework. Success in this case owes to the legislative context of technology transfer in the USA that was created to enhance private access to publicly owned knowledge and resources. Benefit sharing was not unimportant, and it clearly was one intended outcome of access, but it was secondary. As in the Merck–INBio case, the negotiations were confined to immediate parties—the company and Yellowstone National Park. Success was also due to the decentralized nature of the federal government's approach. Rather than a centralized system for negotiating agreements, by default the USA has a de facto loose framework that allowed and encouraged these agreements. Chapter 8 notes the "dizzying array of laws, regulations, and policies" that exists in the USA at different political levels and jurisdictions and prevents a centralized approach. Moreover, Chapter 8 reminds us that the NPS followed a pragmatic approach that emphasized efficiency in reference to ABS goals and resulted in conservation benefits for the national park rather than a philosophical approach based on disputing private benefit from access to public goods. As in the case of Costa Rica's early bioprospecting experience, decentralization favored the success of the Yellowstone–Diversa project.

Mixed Success and Breakdown
The case studies of Mexico and the Philippines offer examples of ABS regimes that had initial implementation success but also saw the implementation process breakdown with the closing of nascent bioprospecting projects. These cases show the difficulties inherent in involving different institutions and communities in a national program to meet the general goals of the CBD.

Mexico. Unlike the Costa Rica and USA cases, Mexico created a post-CBD national legislative ABS framework as part of environmental protection before the negotiation of specific agreements. This framework is primarily outlined in articles 87 and 87 BIS of the 1996 Ecological Equilibrium and Environmental Protection General Act (EEEPGA) that regulate access to all species for commercial and noncommercial purposes. In addition, the 1999 Wildlife General Act (WGA) and the 2003 Sustainable Forestry Development

General Act include relevant ABS provisions that apply specifically to wildlife and forest resources, respectively. While Articles 87 and 87 bis provide general ABS principles, national legislation does not specifically address details about how to implement these principles (see Chapter 6). Article 87 outlines authorization for the collection of wildlife species for scientific and economic[8] purposes and Article 87 bis provides authorization for the collection of wildlife species and other biological resources for commercial utilization. A key aspect of Article 87 bis is the obligation for bioprospecting projects to obtain PIC from the Mexican government as well as from the landowner where collection is anticipated. Moreover, this article also requires applicants to share benefits with the owners of the land where collections are made.

Like the Merck–INBio and Yellowstone–Diversa agreements, the four Mexican projects we discuss were negotiated outside of a national legal ABS framework or centralized approach. However, after negotiation, the first three of these four projects, summarized below, were granted access permits under environmental legislation that did include ABS principles (i.e., Article 87 and 87 bis of the EEEPGA). The fourth project was authorized before ABS principles were incorporated into the EEEPGA.

The first project was between the National Autonomous University of Mexico (UNAM) and the Diversa Corporation to access biological materials from public lands and natural protected areas in Mexico. UNAM's rights to collect under this agreement were accepted and facilitated by three federal agencies with responsibility for federal public land and protected areas. In this case, UNAM was the Mexican beneficiary.

The second project, known as the Maya ICBG, was negotiated and launched in the southern Mexican state of Chiapas. The direct partners were a group of participating Mayan communities in the Chiapas highlands, a national educational and research institution (ECOSUR), the University of Georgia in the USA, and Molecular Nature Limited, a biotechnology company from the United Kingdom. The aim of the project was to access biota in highland Chiapas that the Maya knew to have medicinal properties and to ensure the equitable distribution of benefits derived from that utilization. The Mexican beneficiaries of the project were to be ECOSUR and the participating Mayan communities.

The third project, known as the Latin American ICBG, focused on collecting plant material from arid ecosystems in the states of Chihuahua, Oaxaca, and San Luis Potosí, but it also sampled xerophytic plants available for sale in local markets. Colleting in local markets also permitted the analysis of each region's medicinal plant trade network and the evaluation of the collection pressure upon wild populations of plants. The University of Arizona in the USA coordinated this project, UNAM was again the main Mexican beneficiary, and plant material was screened by UNAM in Mexico and by three organizations in the USA: G.W.L. Hansen's Disease Center,

American Home Products Corporation's Wyeth-Ayerst Research Laboratories, and American Cyanamid Company (TIMMERMANN et al. 1999). This project also sought the participation of local communities and associations such as the Association of Traditional Healers of Oaxaca (TIMMERMAN et al. 1999), although they were not parties to the main agreement. Nevertheless, these communities received nonmonetary benefits that included urban and rural health centers and training for the cultivation of medicinal plants (TIMMERMANN et al. 1999).

The fourth project involved a civil society organization representing indigenous communities (the Zapotec and Chinantec Communities Union–UZACHI) in the state of Oaxaca and the Sandoz Corporation to access microscopic fungi. The member communities of UZACHI were the Mexican beneficiaries.

The UNAM–Diversa and the Latin American ICBG agreements are the most similar to the Merck–INBio and Yellowstone–Diversa agreements. Like these, the UNAM–Diversa and Latin American ICBG agreements involved an independent institution that was given permission to facilitate access to public resources by a private company and that would benefit from commercialization of discoveries resulting from this access. In all four cases, the negotiation of the contract took place with a minimum of different parties and a lack of major constraints by a centralized framework for reviewing the contract. In addition, the UZACHI–Sandoz and Maya ICBG agreements involved civil society organizations and rural communities of indigenous people. Of all the agreements discussed so far, the Maya ICBG is the most complex in terms of the number and diversity of actors and source of financial backing.

Three of the Mexican agreements faced political challenge, legal uncertainties, and termination before accomplishment. The challenge to each was made in a different way. The UNAM–Diversa agreement was challenged as a vehicle for the inappropriate expropriation of publicly owned resources (see Chapter 6). Even though the project had been granted access under Article 87 bis of EEEPGA (which regulates collection of samples for biotechnological purposes), it had a specifically noncommercial scientific goal not a biotechnological one. Collection activities under the UNAM–Diversa agreement were suspended after a legal challenge to the Federal Attorney for the Protection of the Environment (PROFEPA) resulted in additional PIC requirements under Article 87 bis from the providers of genetic resources. The project expired in 2001.

The Maya ICBG project initiated collection activities for scientific purposes but it was vigorously challenged by civil society organizations in Chiapas and by international organizations that claimed the project was relying on its ties to a limited number of communities to expropriate resources that were widely shared among many other communities (NIGH 2002). These organizations further objected to the possibility of patents being obtained on products derived from biological collections from Chiapas. National and international political pressure resulted in the withdrawal of ECOSUR and funding from the consortium of USA agencies, before the ICBG could obtain the full PIC from local communities that was required for authorization under Article 87 bis of EEEPGA. However, BERLIN and BERLIN (2003) document the extensive effort made by the project participants to obtain PIC and the belief by them that it had been obtained. They conclude that PIC may always be ambiguous and open to challenge. The samples collected by this ICBG under Article 87 never left the country (J.C. Fernandez, pers. comm. April 2004).

The Latin American ICBG was granted access under Article 87 of EEEPGA. However, because of the commercial and biotechnological nature of the project, access should have been granted under Article 87 bis that regulates the collection of samples for biotechnological purposes (see Chapter 6). This legal inconsistency, the controversy raised by the fact that samples were being collected at local markets, and fears that this project might be as controversial as the Maya ICBG prompted the decision to deny access under article 87 bis (J.C. Fernandez, pers. comm. April 2004).

The most successful Mexican project was the UZACHI–Sandoz project. Although that project was also challenged politically locally and internationally, the challenges did not result in suspension or closure because of the support by indigenous communities and the recognition that UZACHI was acting within its legal rights to enter into and execute the agreement. The UZACHI–Sandoz agreement was not renewed due to the unclear regulatory power of the national ABS framework (see Chapter 6).

Issues that played in the uneven experience of Mexico include an incomplete legal ABS framework, uncertainty over local authority to grant access, social controversy, and institutional complexity within the bioprospecting projects. The legal framework that confronted the UNAM–Diversa agreement involved a "popular denunciation" to the PROFEPA office, but that office averred that it did not have the authority to void the agreement. Nevertheless, the PROFEPA office asked that the parties of the agreement revisit the issue of PIC under Article 87 bis of EEEPGA even though this appeared to have been adequately negotiated in the original agreement with the intervention of the Secretariat of Environment and Natural Resources and other federal authorities. The PROFEPA decision left the agreement in an indeterminate state that ultimately led to its expiration without fulfillment. The problems caused by legal ambiguity are exacerbated in situations where bioprospecting agreements are associated with social controversy. This situation is typified by the two ICBG projects, which were also encumbered by institutional complexity because of the involvement of different types of national and international organizations and the reliance on extramural financing.

Philippines. This nation's response to the ABS provisions of the CBD is embedded in the 1995 Executive Order No. 247 (EO 247), its 1996 implementing rules and regulations, and the 2001 Republic Act No. 9147, also known as the Wildlife Resources Conservation and Protection Act (hereafter, Wildlife Act). Prior to this legal framework, in 1990

the Philippines established an MOU for collecting biological specimens, although this framework was not specifically designed to facilitate ABS goals, it allowed the signing of an agreement (i.e., LI) between the Philippine National Museum and the USA National Cancer Institute that accomplished both access and benefit sharing to a degree (see Chapter 7). In contrast, the framework established under EO 247 employs a contractual approach and entails two types of collecting agreements depending on whether they are Commercial Research Agreements (CRA) or Academic Research Agreements (ARA), a centralized review process, PIC stipulations, and environmental protection requirements. The Wildlife Act modified this by freeing academic and scientific research from commercial bioprospecting requirements. The 2004 draft Guidelines for Bioprospecting Activities in the Philippines, that will implement the Wildlife Act, require commercial bioprospectors to apply for a Biopropsecting Undertaking instead of a CRA. According to the draft guidelines, commercial bioprospectors may have to pay a bioprospecting fee of $3,000 USD for each Bioprospecting Undertaking and $1,000 per collection site annually during the collection period. Furthermore, commercial bioprospectors must be prepared to pay a minimum amount of 2% of the gross sales of products made or derived from collected samples, in addition to some minimum nonmonetary benefits (see Chapters 1 and 7). A major issue in the Philippines' ABS policies is to protect the interests of indigenous people and their traditional knowledge; the draft guidelines outline detailed PIC procedures to this effect.

Two out of 33 projects presented between 1996 and 1998 have been approved under EO 247 (Chapter 7). The fact that no projects have been presented since October 1998 implies that the frameworks developed under EO 247 have discouraged collectors from initiating new activities. Of the 33 projects presented between 1996 and 1998, eight were from foreign universities or companies, one was from an international agricultural center located in the Philippines, and 24 were submitted by Philippine institutions. The large majority of both foreign and national projects involved academic and research institutions rather than commercial interests. The only approved foreign application came about with a CRA under EO 247 and appears to be nearing accomplishment. This is a collaboration between the University of Utah in the USA and the University of the Philippines Marine Science Institute. None of the foreign projects that have moved successfully through the review process involve collection of biological specimens on land or involve indigenous people or traditional knowledge. Six of the eight foreign projects and the project of the international agricultural research center have either been withdrawn, required to submit further material, or are pending, sometimes several years after the original application date. The same low rate of approval characterizes projects submitted by Philippine institutions. Only one ARA has been approved for the University of the Philippines. It should be noted that while the CRA was approved in a bit more than a year, the ARA took two and a half years until the Technical Secretariat gave its approval.

It is difficult to know exactly why there is such a low approval rate and lengthy application procedure for bioprospecting projects in the Philippines. It may be related to the fact that PIC requirements under EO 247 involve a lengthy application process and the national framework presents a complex system of different types of application procedures and levels of approval that feed into a centralized system. Although EO 247 and the Wildlife Act seek a contractual approach, the role of the centralized review and permitting process mean that the two parties interested in a contract are not acting alone. If adopted, the Guidelines for Bioprospecting Activities are likely to reduce transaction costs by streamlining application and negotiation requirements for commercial bioprospectors (see Chapter 1 for detailed access procedures).

Thwarted Implementation

Colombia. This nation has experienced great difficulty in launching bioprospecting projects since negotiation in 1996 of the Common Regime on Access to Genetic Resources (Decision 391) of the Andean Community. None of the projects that were submitted since Decision 391 came into force have been approved or implemented. Chapter 4 provides information on 15 bioprospecting projects submitted between February 1997 and February 2004. One was declined, three withdrawn, and 11 are still pending. Only one of the 15 projects submitted was commercial in nature and the rest were for academic and conservation

purposes, predominantly by Colombian scientists. Only two of these projects involved the participation of international organizations.

Several factors thwarted Colombia's ability to move these projects forward, and among these, three stand out. First is the evident lack of knowledge and confusion on both the access and benefit side. Second was the transaction costs of obtaining information and negotiating agreements under Decision 391. Third was unreasonably high expectations about economic benefits, especially when most of the projects were academic rather than commercial. These problems were exacerbated by Colombia's lack of technical capacity and expertise to handle access applications and interpret key provisions of Decision 391. Furthermore, there is confusion and uncertainty about policy and institutional needs required to implement Decision 391. Perhaps the sharpest contrast between Colombia's approach and the approach taken in the more successful efforts discussed above is centralization through Decision 391. The application of this ABS law occurred before individual negotiations between potential partners could occur, and this deeply affected negotiations. In contrast, the successful instances of negotiating and initiating bioprospecting projects discussed above occurred in contexts characterized by the presence of organizations with mutual interests and objectives that were able to operate under decentralized and flexible national policy frameworks. Examples of these are Costa Rica's INBio agreements, the USA Yellowstone–Diversa agreement, and Mexico's UZACHI–Sandoz agreement.

Lessons

A decade after the promulgation of the CBD, the prospects for creating successful national ABS policies are guarded. Although there are several cases of successful bioprospecting projects, closer examination of these suggests that the actors and interests who join in them still face serious obstacles to forming effective partnerships. Five lessons can be drawn from this review of Pacific Rim case studies.

First, agreements are most likely to succeed when the number of parties is minimized. Two immediate parties in projects are the collector and the agency or social entity that is recognized as being the competent authority to grant access. For example, in Costa Rica, INBio was authorized to negotiate access to biological resources in certain areas, and in the USA, the National Park Service granted Yellowstone National Park authority to negotiate access to resources within the park. Likewise in Mexico, the UZACHI–Sandoz agreement involved only local interests. Moving the locus of negotiation and agreement away from the immediate parties, for instance by setting up a complex national ABS framework with multiple participants and interests, tends to encumber negotiation, agreement, and accomplishment. The most successful bioprospecting projects were established outside of focused national frameworks corresponding to the CBD. A prime example

of this are the numerous agreements signed in Costa Rica under the 1992 LWC and its 1997 regulation but before the 1998 Law of Biodiversity was enacted. In December 2003 the ICBG program approved a planning grant for a project that will be carried out by Harvard University and INBio in Costa Rica. This project will test the efficiency and effectiveness of the ABS provisions of the Law of Biodiversity. Colombia's difficulties stem to some degree from the fact that this country not only had to address national interests and policies in reviewing access proposals, but it also had to harmonize its national policies with Decision 391. Furthermore, difficulties in regionwide implementation of Decision 391 have led Colombia and the other members of the Andean Community of Nations to a revision of this law (M. Ruiz, pers. comm. April 2004). In summary, simplicity and directness in negotiating and approving agreements under ABS laws and policies is a strong virtue.

Second, the determination of a competent authority or local focal point in granting access is critical, and ambiguity in this is problematic. The INBio, Yellowstone, and UZACHI agreements mentioned above illustrate this conclusion.

Third, the determination of clear access procedures and particularly PIC requirements are essential to expedite the approval of applications and the negotiation of benefits. The tendency for successful projects in Costa Rica, the Philippines, and elsewhere to focus on biological resources that are not controlled or used by local people suggests that decisiveness in defining effective PIC requirements is crucial. The efforts of the Maya ICBG project in Mexico to acquire PIC proved insufficient to ward off a challenge. BERLIN and BERLIN (2003), who were leading participants in the Maya ICBG project, observed that PIC is inevitably ambiguous and open to challenge.

Fourth, governments need to build local capacity to facilitate the effective and efficient implementation of ABS laws and policies. Lack of trained evaluators and negotiators result in delayed responses for project applications and missed opportunities for benefit sharing as demonstrated by the Philippines and Colombian experiences. This capac-

ity needs to be transferred to local organizations that may be involved in the negotiation of benefits.

Fifth, creating a forum for balanced discussion of controversial ABS concepts and implications may facilitate the application process and accomplishment of bioprospecting projects. As demonstrated by the Mexican experience the novel, complex, controversial, and experimental nature of ABS concepts make bioprospecting projects particularly open to challenge. While some organizations may be against bioprospecting initiatives, other groups like the UZACHI may have a different perspective. Positive experiences where the primary users and stewards of biological diversity are clear beneficiaries of bioprospecting projects are likely to create a favorable political and social environment for accomplishing them.

References

APEN P.G., B.C. BENICEWICZ, and J.R. LAIA. 1994. A new model for public-private partnerships. *Technology in Society* **16**:398–402.

BERLIN B. and E.A. BERLIN. 2003. NGOs and the process of prior informed consent in bioprospecting research: The Maya ICBG project in Chiapas, Mexico. *International Social Science Journal* **55**:629–638.

CARRIZOSA S. 1996. Prospecting for biodiversity: The search for legal and institutional frameworks. Ph.D. Dissertation, The University of Arizona, UMI Dissertation Services, A Bell & Howell Company. URL: http://wwwlib.umi.com/dissertations/fullcit/9720602.

CRAGG G.M., M.R. BOYD, M.R. GREVER, and S.A. SCHEPARTZ. 1994. Policies for international collaboration and compensation in drug discovery and development at the United States National Cancer Institute, The NCI Letter of Collection. p. 83–98 *in* T. GREAVES (ed.) *Intellectual property rights for indigenous peoples: A source book.* Society for Applied Anthropology, Oklahoma City, USA.

GÁMEZ R., A. PIVA, A. SITTENFELD, E. LEÓN, J. JIMÉNEZ, and G. MIRABELLI. 1993. Costa Rica's Conservation Program and National Biodiversity Institute (INBio). p. 53–67 *in* W.V. REID, S.A. LAIRD, C.A. MEYER, R. GÁMEZ, A. SITTENFELD, D.H. JANZEN, M.G. GOLLIN, and C. JUMA (eds.) *Biodiversity prospecting: Using genetic resources for sustainable development.* World Resources Institute, USA.

NIGH R. 2002. Maya medicine in the biological gaze: Bioprospecting research as herbal fetishism. *Current Anthropology* **43**:451–476.

REID W.V., S.A. LAIRD, R. GÁMEZ, A. SITTENFELD, D.H. JANZEN, M.G. GOLLIN, and C. JUMA. 1993. A new lease on life. p. 1–52 *in* W.V. REID, S.A. LAIRD, C.A. MEYER, R. GÁMEZ, A. SITTENFELD, D.H. JANZEN, M.G. GOLLIN, and C. JUMA (eds.) *Biodiversity prospecting: Using genetic resources for sustainable development.* World Resources Institute, USA.

ROSENTHAL J.P., D. BECK, A. BHAT, J. BISWAS, L. BRADY, K. BRIDBOARD, S. COLLINS, G. CRAGG, J. EDWARDS, A. FAIRFIELD, M. GOTTLIEB, L.A. GSCHWIND, Y. HALLOCK, R. HAWKS, R. HEGYELI, G. JOHNSON, G.T. KEUSCH, E.E. LYONS, R. MILLER, J. RODMAN, J. ROSKOSKI, and D. SIEGEL-CAUSEY. 1999. Combining high risk science with ambitious social and economic goals. *Pharmaceutical Biology* **37**:6–21.

SITTENFELD A. and R. GÁMEZ 1993. Biodiversity prospecting by INBio. p. 69–97 *in* W.V. REID, S.A. LAIRD, C.A. MEYER, R. GÁMEZ, A. SITTENFELD, D.H. JANZEN, M.G. GOLLIN, and C. JUMA (eds.) *Biodiversity prospecting: Using genetic resources for sustainable development.* World Resources Institute, USA.

TIMMERMANN B.N., G. WÄCHTER, S. VALCIC, B. HUTCHINSON, C. CASLER, J. HENZEL, S. RAM, F. CURRIM, R. MANAK, S. FRANZBLAU, W. MAIESE, D. GALINIS, E. SUAREZ, R. FORTUNATO, E. SAAVEDRA, R. BYE, R. MATA, and G. MONTENEGRO. 1999. The Latin American ICBG: The first five years. *Pharmaceutical Biology* **37**:35-54.

Endnotes

[1] In the USA, NPS regulations are analogous to some of the provisions of ABS laws and policies that other countries have proposed and these NPS regulations facilitate ABS goals in NPS lands (see Chapter 1).

[2] Consistent with our use in Chapters 1 and 2, we define bioprospecting as the search for plants, animals, and microbial species for academic, pharmaceutical, biotechnological, agricultural, and industrial purposes.

[3] National ABS laws and policies have approved 15 projects in Costa Rica, three in Mexico, two in the Philippines, one in Samoa, and one in the USA. It must be noted that this account does not include projects that have been negotiated following a contractual approach in countries that lack national ABS laws or policies such as Chile, Laos, and Vietnam.

[4] Recently, however, several countries, such as Panama and Indonesia, have found guidance in the Bonn Guidelines on Access to Genetic Resources and Fair and Equitable Sharing of the Benefits Arising out of their Utilization (see Chapter 2). These guidelines were adopted by the Sixth Conference of the Parties to the CBD in April 2002.

[5] The ICBGs are an international bioprospecting approach initiated in 1992 and financed by the USA National Institutes of Health, National Science Foundation, and Department of Agriculture that is guided by the following objectives: 1) to uncover new knowledge that will lead to improved therapies; 2) to enhance scientific capacity building in developing countries; and 3) to ensure sustained economic growth and the conservation of genetic resources in the countries where collections of organisms are made. These groups are international partnerships composed of universities, NGOs, pharmaceutical companies, and other organizations from the USA and the countries that provide the genetic resources, and in some cases, traditional knowledge. The first five-year phase of the program started in 1993 and 1994 with five groups. In 1998, three new groups won awards and three of the previous groups were renewed for a second five-year period until 2003. One of the new projects, the Maya ICBG was terminated in 2001 (see this chapter and Chapter 6). In December 2003, the new round of awards supported five-year-long projects for five groups (three of these were renewals) and two-year planning grants for seven groups (ROSENTHAL et al. 1999, http://www.nih.gov/news/pr/dec2003/fic-16.htm).

[6] In November 1995, the Environment Organic Law defined a more specific range of activities for MIRENEM regarding the field of natural resources and MIRENEM became the Ministry of Environment and Energy (MINAE).

[7] The CRADA has been used as a vehicle to promote ABS goals in other bioprospecting projects. For example, in 1994 a CRADA was used by one of the ICBGs to facilitate the negotiation of benefit-sharing provisions between the Walter Reed Army Institute of Research and other public and private organizations (CARRIZOSA 1996).

[8] This purpose applies to use of wild flora and fauna specimens in economic activities that involve their controlled reproduction or captivity and semi-captivity management.

Table 1. Bioprospecting in Pacific Rim countries. This table provides information about all bioprospecting projects approved under national access and benefit-sharing (ABS) laws and policies until January 2004. However, not all bioprospecting projects implemented outside the scope of these laws and policies or in countries without ABS laws and policies are listed here.

A. Countries with ABS laws and policies

1. Colombia

Decision 391 has been in place since 1996 and until February 2004 not a single access contract has been approved under it. Also, the number of access applications has been extremely low. Between 1996 and 2002 the Ministry for the Environment received 15 access applications. One of them was denied and the rest are on hold (see Chapter 4). The New York Botanical Garden, the University of Antioquia, University of Medellin, and the Botanical Garden Juan Marin Cespedos of Tulua collected biological samples for the USA National Cancer Institute (NCI) before Decision 391 became national law.

2. Costa Rica

The 1998 Law of Biodiversity is not operational yet. Access applications involving bioprospecting have been approved under the 1992 Law of Wildlife Conservation No. 7317 (and its 1997 regulation) and in accordance with a cooperation agreement between the National Biodiversity Institute (INBio) and the Ministry of the Environment and Energy. Since 1991, 15 bioprospecting projects have been granted access (see Chapter 5). In December 2003, the USA-based International Cooperative Biodiversity Group (ICBG) program approved a planning grant for a new project that will be implemented by Harvard University and INBio. This project will be negotiated under the 1998 Law of Biodiversity framework.

3. Ecuador

No bioprospecting projects have been negotiated under Decision 391.

4. Mexico

Three bioprospecting projects were granted access under the Ecological Equilibrium and Environmental Protection General Act. These are: 1) The USA Maya ICBG, 2) The Latin American ICBG, and 2) the Diversa/National Autonomous University project. However, these projects were terminated due to social protest and legal inconsistencies (see Chapter 6).

5. Philippines

Two out of 32 proposed bioprospecting projects have been granted access under Executive Order 247. The University of Utah/University of the Philippines project, and the University of the Philippines system project. In late 2003, the USA ICBG program approved a planning grant for a project coordinated by the USA Michigan State University in collaboration with the University of the Philippines and local indigenous communities. This project will be granted access under the 2001 Wildlife Resources and Conservation Act (see Chapter 7).

6. Peru

No bioprospecting project has been negotiated under Decision 391. Between 1993 and 1998 the USA ICBG program provided funding for bioprospecting activities in Peru. This project was coordinated by Washington University in collaboration with the Museum of Natural History and other organizations. The New York Botanical Garden, in collaboration with the Research Institute of the Peruvian Amazon Region, collected samples for the USA NCI before Decision 391 came into force.

7. Samoa

In 1995, Nonu Samoa Enterprises began export of nonu (*Morinda citrifolia*), a tree with medicinal properties, to the USA. In 2001 the administrative directive entitled "Conditions for access to and benefit sharing of Samoa's biodiversity resources" was invoked to negotiate a benefit-sharing agreement between the government of Samoa and the AIDS Research Alliance for the use of a compound called prostratin derived from the mamala plant (*Homalanthus nutans*). This compound may be used together with other drugs for the treatment of AIDS. In late 2003, the USA ICBG program approved a planning grant for a project coordinated by the USA National Tropical Botanical Garden in Hawaii in collaboration with the Samoan Ministry of Trade and Tourism and other organizations. It is uncertain what legal ABS framework will apply to this project as Samoa is currently developing an ABS framework.

8. Thailand

So far no projects have been approved under the new access framework because the government is still developing lower level regulations to facilitate the implementation of ABS laws. However, the University of Illinois at Chicago in collaboration with the Thailand Forest Herbarium has collected plant samples for the USA NCI. In the 1990s, Chris Deren of the University of Florida announced plans to develop a USA version of Thailand's Jasmine rice. Germplasm for this experiment was obtained from the Philippines-based International Rice Research Institute through the USA Department of Agriculture. In 1975 Sankyo of Japan extracted the active ingredient (plaonotol) of the tree plaonoi (*Croton sublyratus*) to produce Kelnac, a tablet to treat ulcers.

9. United States of America (USA)

The owner of the land (public or private) where the genetic resource is found defines access and benefit-sharing issues. So, far the most public and documented bioprospecting initiative negotiated under federal regulations that are analogous to ABS policies is the agreement signed between Yellowstone National Park and the pharmaceutical company Diversa Corporation (see Chapter 8). In 2000, Diversa also signed an agreement with the USA-based Arctos Pharmaceuticals, Inc. giving Diversa rights to bioprospect in Alaska and neighboring territories. Through this agreement, Diversa obtains access to genetic resources found in habitats covered by agreements Arctos has signed with Alaskan landholding native corporations, individuals and other entities. In 2002, Diversa announced the signing of an access and benefit-sharing agreement with the Marine Bioproducts Engineering Center at the University of Hawaii in Honolulu. This agreement gives Diversa the right to study genes from existing collections and from environmental samples collected by the Hawaiian center. Pfizer has screened medicinal plants provided by the New York Botanical Garden and Phytera has carried out bioprospecting activities in Hawaii and the Virgin Islands.

B. Countries working towards the development of ABS laws and policies

1. Australia

There is a long history of benefit-sharing agreements negotiated by bioprospectors in Australia. These include AstraZeneca R&D and Griffith University; the USA NCI and the

Table 1. Continued

Australian Institute of Marine Science; Cerylid Biosciences Ltd. and Royal Botanic Gardens; and BioProspect Ltd. and the Department of Conservation and Land Management of Western Australia (see Chapter 9).

2. Cambodia
N/A

3. Canada
Several bioprospecting projects have been implemented in the last few years in Canada. Researchers from universities such as the University of British Columbia and private companies such as Accutec Technologies (Vancouver, British Columbia), Semgen (St. Nicolas, Québec), and Ecopia Biosciences (Montréal, Québec) have carried out bioprospecting activities in marine and terrestrial environments. Cubist Pharmaceuticals is also bioprospecting in Western Canada.

4. Chile
Some of the bioprospecting projects implemented in this country include a USA ICBG project (1993–2003) coordinated by the USA University of Arizona in collaboration with Catholic University of Chile and other organizations; the Institute for Agriculture Investigation (INIA) and the Royal Botanical Gardens, Kew bioprospecting project; and the INIA and C.M. Rick Tomato Genetics Resource Center of the University of California, Davis (see Chapter 10).

5. China
China's extensive information about medicinal plants has been examined by many bioprospectors. These include American Biosciences, the USA National Institutes of Health and New York University that have patents on several Chinese medicinal species. Also, the USA NCI has screened plants collected in collaboration with the Kunming Institute of Botany. Pfizer is also relying exclusively on traditional medical practices to identify potential pharmaceuticals.

6. Cook Islands
Current bioprospecting initiatives include projects related to pharmaceutical research for marine products, marine toxins, whale research, and marine/terrestrial flora and fauna taxonomy (national heritage project).

7. El Salvador
Some local universities and research centers extract chemical compounds from plants for pharmaceutical purposes. No major findings have been reported.

8. Fiji
The most documented bioprospecting agreement in Fiji is the one established between the University of South Pacific and the Strathclyde Institute of Drug Research in Scotland. Biological samples were collected in collaboration with the Verata community. The community was not a partner to the main agreement, but ABS was provided in a separate agreement signed between the university and the community. Kava (*Piper methysticum*), a medicinal plant native to the South Pacific region was traded and used widely before the CBD was adopted. The cultivation of the plant has brought economic benefits to Fiji and many other South Pacific countries. Kava extracts and active compounds have been patented by companies in Europe and the USA. However, no royalties have flowed to Pacific Island countries. In any case, the Kava market has declined in recent years in Europe and the USA due to allegations that the plant causes liver damage. However, it should be noted that Fiji and other Pacific Island countries

have enjoyed the benefits of this plant for generations and its consumption remains strong casting doubts over the alleged detrimental health effects. American Home Products also holds a patent on a Fijian sponge that has anti-tumor properties. In late 2003, the USA ICBG program approved a planning grant for a project coordinated by the USA Georgia Institute of Technology in collaboration with the University of South Pacific and other organizations.

9. Guatemala
Local universities and research centers carry out several bioprospecting projects. But there is no information available about them.

10. Honduras
There are no more than three projects involving local universities. But there is no information available about them.

11. Indonesia
The USA-based pharmaceutical company Diversa Corporation and Bogor University have been implementing a bioprospecting project since 1997. The project was renewed in 2002. Also, the USA NCI has screened samples of marine and terrestrial organisms that have been collected by the Coral Reef Research Foundation, the University of Illinois, the Indonesia Herbarium Bogoriense, and the Indonesian Institute of Science.

12. Japan
Multiple Japanese biotechnology companies are engaged in many bioprospecting projects in Japan. However, there is no information available about these initiatives.

13. Malaysia
In the late 1980s and early 1990s, the USA NCI discovered that two naturally occurring compounds (Calanolide A and B) were effective against HIV. In 1996, this discovery led to the establishment of a joint venture between the State Government of Sarawak and MediChem Research to develop and market Calanolide A as an anti-HIV medicine. In 1999, MediChem's share in the company was transferred to Advanced Life Sciences, Inc. Other bioprospecting initiatives include: 1) the Universiti Kebangsaan Malaysia that tested 51 samples of marine sponges on human tumor cell lines in cytotoxic tests, and found 20 samples to be toxic to the tumors and 2) the Universiti Sains Malaysia that tested sea cucumbers for bioactive compounds (see Chapter 11).

14. Marshall Islands
No bioprospecting projects are currently being implemented in the Marshall Islands. However, in the past, the Palauan-based Coral Reef Research Foundation has collected samples of marine organisms for the USA NCI.

15. Micronesia
The Coral Reef Research Foundation has collected samples of marine organisms for the USA NCI.

16. New Zealand
The Coral Reef Research Foundation has collected samples of marine organisms for the USA NCI. The University of Canterbury (Christchurch) has also collaborated in the collection of biological samples for NCI. The University also has collaborative links with the Danish Technical University and the School of Pharmacy, University of London, among others. Other local companies such as Global Technologies, and Biodiscovery New Zealand look for bioactive compounds from deer/sheep and bacteria respectively. Tairawhiti

Table 1. Continued

Pharmaceuticals extracts manuka and kanuka oils. Phytomed Medicinal Herbs manufactures and supplies plant extracts and dried herbs to health practitioners and other herbal manufacturers.

17. Nicaragua

N/A

18. Niue

In 2002, the Ministry of Tourism signed an agreement with the Zoological Parks Board of New South Wales based in Sydney, Australia. Under the agreement, three sea snakes (*Laticauda schistorynchus)* were given to the Taronga Zoo for display purposes only. The agreements states that the sea snake's venom, skin, or any other genetic component will be protected during display and that no genetic material will be extracted from the sea snakes for scientific research or any other purpose. In 2002, a project of the South Pacific Commission (SPC) collected samples of 40 varieties of taro (a root crop and staple of the Pacific diet).

19. Panama

In recent years this country has used a contractual approach to facilitate bioprospecting activities and this strategy has been supported by legislation that regulates the collection of natural resources. Since 1998 a USA ICBG project has been carrying out bioprospecting activities in Panama and funding for this project was renewed in late 2003 for five additional years. This project is coordinated by the Smithsonian Tropical Research Institute in collaboration with the National Secretariat for Science, Technology, and Innovation and other organizations. Local academic and research centers also have carried out bioprospecting projects.

20. Papua New Guinea

In late 2003, the USA ICBG program approved funding for a five-year project coordinated by the USA University of Utah in collaboration with the University of Papua New Guinea and other organizations. The Australian National University and the Tillegerry Habitat Association, New South Wales, Australia have implemented projects in coordination with the Australian-based Cerylid Biosciences Ltd and the Kelam People of the Kaironk Valley in Papua New Guinea. Also, the Palauan-base Coral Reef Research Foundation and the University of Illinois have collected samples of marine and terrestrial organisms for the USA NCI in collaboration with the Papua New Guinea Forest Research Institute, the Lae Herbarium, and the Papua New Guinea Department of the Environment and Conservation, Boroko. Sponges growing on a coral reef off the coast of Papua New Guinea are the source of a powerful antifungal compound papuamine. The sponges yield only minute quantities of the compound. Therefore, Myco Pharmaceuticals (USA) is now attempting to synthesize papuamine in the laboratory.

21. Republic of Korea

N/A

22. Russian Federation

In 2000 the USA-based Diversa Corporation signed a biodiversity access agreement giving the company rights to obtain, identify, and commercialize genes collected in unique Russian habitats. Diverse will work with Russia through the

USA Department of Energy's Idaho National Engineering and Environmental Laboratory to obtain samples from Russian habitats.

23. Singapore

N/A

24. Solomon Islands

In the 1980s, marine collections were made for cancer research (pharmaceuticals). In the early 1990s, the University of California made plant collections for pharmaceutical purposes. Collections of taro are being carried out by SPC. In the early 1990s, a human sample resulted in a patent application in the USA. The Research Committee denied two access applications of the Coral Reef Foundation that was planning to collect samples for the USA NCI. The Lauru Land Conference and communities opposed plant collection made by the University of Hawaii in Choiseul province for pharmaceuticals and other industrial purposes. Applications for native orchid exports by nationals have been turned down. Kava has been collected in the 1980s and 1990s and exported worldwide.

25. Vanuatu

The Coral Reef Research Foundation has collected samples of marine organisms for the USA NCI. Kava has been collected in the 1980s and 1990s and exported worldwide.

26. Vietnam

The USA ICBG project of Vietnam has been carrying out bioprospecting activities since 1998 and its funding was renewed in late 2003. This project is coordinated by the USA University of Illinois at Chicago in collaboration with the Vietnam National Center for Natural Sciences and Technology and other organizations.

C. Countries not involved in any process leading to the development of ABS laws and policies

1. Kiribati

Taro varieties have been collected by a project of SPC.

2. Laos

The USA ICBG of Laos has been bioprospecting since 1998 and its funding was renewed in late 2003. This project is coordinated by the USA University of Illinois at Chicago and includes the participation of several local organizations.

3. Nauru

N/A

4. Palau

The Coral Reef Research Foundation has collected samples of marine organisms for the USA NCI.

5. Tonga

The Coral Reef Research Foundation has collected samples of marine organisms for the USA NCI. In late 2003, the USA ICBG program approved a planning grant for a project coordinated by the USA National Tropical Botanical Garden in Hawaii in collaboration with the Tonga Ministry of Agriculture and Forestry and other organizations.

6. Tuvalu

The Coral Reef Research Foundation has collected samples of marine organisms for the USA NCI. Taro varieties are been collected by a project of SPC.

4

Colombia: Access and Exchange of Genetic Resources

Paola Ferreira-Miani

Colombia is characterized by high levels of biodiversity and endemism (CHAVES and ARANGO 1997, DNP 1997). Colombia has a land surface of 114,174,800 ha, which constitutes approximately 0.7% of the earth's continental area. This area contains 10% of the world's biodiversity. This is why Colombia is considered among the megadiverse countries of the world.

Of the land surface of Colombia, 53.2 million ha are covered by natural forests: 21.6 million ha by other types of vegetation which include savanna, arid areas, and wetlands; 1.1 million ha by continental water, snow peaks, and human settlements; and at least 38.4 million ha are under agricultural use and colonization processes. These general categories of land cover and use host the ecosystem diversity typical of Colombia. The richness in ecosystem types has been attributed to a variety of factors including the following: the country's localization between the two tropics, the variety of soil and climatic conditions that results in a wide array of geographic spaces, and the existence of areas that have been geographically isolated. The country's ecosystem diversity is of such importance that only a few of the world's ecosystems are not represented in Colombia.

Ecosystem diversity is related to species diversity, which is the most common way to refer to biodiversity. It represents the number of species in any given area. Approximately 35,000 vascular plants are known to be present in Colombia, a large number for the size of the country, especially considering that all Africa south of the Sahara contains in total 30,000 species, and that Brazil, which has a surface 6.5 times larger, has 55,000 species of vascular plants. Colombia has between 3,000 and 3,500

species of orchids that represent approximately 15% of the world's total. Other extremely diverse plant families are Araceae, with one sixth of the world's known species; Heliconiaceae with approximately 95 species; and Ericaceae with 267 species. Studies in the Caribbean region regarding seaweeds have shown it is one of the richest areas of the Atlantic Coast with approximately 430 species. The Pacific coast has a lower diversity with 133 identified species of seaweeds.

Regarding vertebrates (excepting fish), Colombia holds third place with 3,278 species (Table 1). Richness in mammals, and in particular bats (151 species) and rodents (94 species) is noteworthy. There are 27 primate species, which represent one third of those found in tropical America, surpassed only by Brazil, which has 55 primate species. Colombia is commonly classified as the country with the largest number of birds. It contains 60% of all identified South American birds and approximately 60 of these species are endemic to Colombia. Information on fish diversity is extremely scarce and large areas of the country have not

Table 1. Number of vertebrate species (excluding fish) in Colombia compared to the number described worldwide

Group	Colombia	World	Proportion in Colombia (%)
Mammals	454	4,629	9.8
Birds	1,766	9,040	19.5
Reptiles	475	6,458	7.3
Amphibian	583	4,222	13.8
Total	3,278	24,394	13.5

Source: IAVH PNUMA inédito, cited in FANDIÑO and FERREIRA (1998).

been surveyed. Along the Caribbean coast, species richness in coral reefs is particularly noticeable, with 326 species identified out of an estimated total of 700 marine species. Surveys have been less complete on the Pacific coast. Insects are also particularly relevant because of their endemism and rarity.

Biodiversity, and in particular genetic diversity, has been considered a potential source of wealth for the country. As a party to the Convention on Biological Diversity (CBD), Colombia has the responsibility of setting the conditions for giving access to its genetic resources to other parties, upon mutually agreed terms, while respecting the sovereign rights of the state over these resources.

Colombia and the other countries of the Andean Community[1], motivated by factors such as the need to comply with the CBD, to support by regional integration,

and to create opportunities for access activities, negotiated and approved legislation on access to genetic resources covering the five nations. As a result of this process, Colombia is now a participant in an Andean regional policy governing access to genetic resources and derivatives: "Decision 391 of the Cartagena Agreement" or "Common Regime on Access to Genetic Resources". This legislation constitutes the main legal framework regarding access to genetic resources in Colombia.

It is important to understand this legislation in the context of Colombia's biological diversity and the larger picture of the country's biodiversity policy. The threats to the country's biodiversity are also very real (Box 1). Following is a section regarding the country's policy principles and goals that are relevant for understanding the access and benefit-sharing (ABS) policy framework.

National Biodiversity Policy and National Biodiversity Strategy and Action Plan

Colombia, as a party to the CBD, has been committed to conservation and sustainable use of its biological resources. Therefore, in 1997 the Colombian Government approved a National Biodiversity Policy (NBP) which determined the country's policy priorities for the future (DNP 1997). The policy has three major goals:

- Conservation of the components of biodiversity;

- Greater knowledge of biodiversity; and

- The promotion of sustainable use of biodiversity and the equal distribution of benefits of that use.

These three goals were further developed in ten strategies. The guidelines for the development of the policy were approved by the National Environmental Council, which is the highest advisory authority to the Ministry of Environment (MOE). These initial guidelines were further developed by the Instituto de Investigación en Recursos Biológicos "Alexander von Humboldt"[2], (Research Institute on Biological Resources), the National Planning Department (DNP)[3], and the MOE.

The NBP set forth eight principles that are relevant for its interpretation and orientation (DNP 1997):

1. Biodiversity is a national patrimony and has a strategic value for the nation's current and future development.

2. Biological diversity has tangible components at the level of molecules, genes and populations, species and communities, and ecosystems and landscapes. There are also intangible components that include knowledge, innovation, and associated cultural practices.

3. Biodiversity has a dynamic character both in space and time, and its components and evolutionary processes must be preserved.

4. The benefits derived from its use must be distributed in a fair and equitable manner and in an agreed-

upon fashion with the community.

5. The importance of the protection of individual and collective property rights is recognized.

6. The conservation and sustainable use of biodiversity must be addressed globally. It thus requires international commitment between nations.

7. The conservation and sustainable use of biodiversity requires a cross-sectoral approach and must be addressed in a decentralized manner, including the participation of all levels of government and society.

8. The precautionary principle must employed, especially with respect to genetic erosion and biosafety.

The NBP proposes the following ten strategies, aligned with the three basic goals described earlier (FANDIÑO and FERREIRA 1998):

- Distribute the benefits derived from biodiversity equitably.

Knowledge

- Characterize the components of biological diversity.
- Recover, protect, and publicize traditional knowledge.

Conservation

- Develop and consolidate the National System of Natural Protected Areas.
- Reduce the processes that deteriorate biodiversity.
- Restore ecosystems and species.
- Promote *ex situ* conservation.

Use

- Promote sustainable management systems of renewable natural resources.
- Promote sustainable development of the economic potential of biodiversity.

- Develop economic valuation systems of biodiversity components.

Since the NBP proposes a set of strategies meant to provide a long term view of Colombia's policy objectives regarding biodiversity, it was necessary to develop a strategy to implement them. This strategy should determine specific goals and objectives to be reached and identify those who should be involved in its implementa-tion. Therefore, in 1996 the MOE of Colombia formulated a project to finance such an endeavor and received a grant from the United Nations Environmental Program (UNEP) to develop the National Biodiversity Strategy and Action Plan (NBSAP). This project was initially comprised of two stages. In the first stage, a technical proposal of the NBSAP was developed. This task was assigned to the Humboldt Institute and the DNP, with the collaboration of the MOE.

Box 1. Causes of Biodiversity Loss (DNP 1997)

Direct Causes

The country has been under an accelerated rate of destruction of its habitats and natural ecosystems due to such causes as inadequate land use policies that lead to colonization and land clearing for agricultural use. Other causes of habitat destruction are the establishment of illicit crops, construction of infrastructure and service works, mining activities, land works to transform wetlands for pasture, firewood consumption, occurrence of fires in natural ecosystems, and in some cases wood production. This transformation results in habitat reduction or fragmentation.

Between 1960 and 1995 the main causes of land use changes can be summarized as follows: there was a decrease in land for agricultural use from 5 million ha to 4.4 million; land under pasture increased from 14.6 million ha to 35.5 million ha; and there was a decrease in forest cover and other uses from 94.6 to 72.4 million ha. There is no consensus on what the country's yearly deforestation rate is. Nevertheless, there are estimates that 40% of the cover of natural ecosystems has disappeared, with some specific areas under more critical conditions. For example, the Andean Cordilleras have lost 74% of their forest cover, and dry tropical forests have only 1.5% of their original surface.

Another main cause of biodiversity loss is due to introduction of invasive species that have competed with and eventually displaced native species. This displacement has often imperiled the viability of populations or caused them to become extinct. Often the introduction of species is promoted by government policies, particularly in the case of fisheries. For example, in the watersheds of the Amazon, Cauca, Orinoco, and Catatumbo rivers at least 32 species have been introduced, substantially reducing naturally occurring populations.

On the other hand, the over-exploitation and unsustainable management of wild species of fauna and flora for domestic consumption or commercialization is also having important effects on biodiversity. In Colombia, fauna is under severe pressure due to hunting, mainly to provide specimens, skins, and products for the illegal international market. The fisheries are also affected by over-exploitation and by the use of inadequate fishing practices. For example, the watershed of the Magdalena River has lost 78.4% of its yearly production. Similar numbers have been reported for other watersheds.

Wood production by industry has also led to unsustainable forest use, affecting substantial forested areas. Additionally, wood provision comes from the most biodiverse areas in the country: the Amazonian and the Pacific Coast. Estimates for 1987 accounted that between 40,000 and 68,000 ha of natural forests had been negatively affected because of wood extraction. Nevertheless, in the past years, wood industries have increased their wood planting activities as well as their imports, decreasing their direct pressure over natural forests.

Another cause of biodiversity loss is domestic and industrial contamination. Contamination has affected natural environments when their carrying capacity has been surpassed. The damages due to contamination have not been quantified, but their impact can be foreseen by the following data. In 1998, only 65% and 27% respectively of urban and rural areas had disposal systems. Also, solid waste production was estimated to be 15,903 tons per day, of which only 32% was disposed of in adequate waste facilities, 3% was buried, 50% was left without any treatment in open air spaces, and 15% went to water bodies. Contamination is also produced by insecticides and plague control substances.

Indirect Causes

Underlying the direct causes of biodiversity loss described above are a set of political, social, demographic, technological, institutional, and economic factors that are indirect causes of biodiversity loss. The importance of biodiversity and its relevance in achieving development goals has traditionally being ignored by decision-makers and the mainstream development policies of governments. Even though there is a growing consciousness of its importance, it is far from being seriously considered by leaders in government or the private sector.

Another major indirect cause is land distribution that has often led to inappropriate land use patterns. Likewise, the lack of real land reform has led to the use of forest reserves by peasants in need of additional land. Further, policies regarding illicit crop eradication have induced their shift from one place to another, increasing land clearing to establish these crops, and having an enormous impact on the country's biodiversity. The areas where these crops have been established coincide largely with the location of the more vulnerable ecosystems in the Andes and Amazonia.

Also, a major cause of biodiversity loss is the very low institutional capacity to reduce impacts. Even though there is a complex environmental system in place, with a Ministry of Environment, 34 regional corporations that act as environmental authorities, and four research institutes, their responsibilities surpass their capacity. Additionally, the government presence in remote areas of the country has traditionally been very low and the local empowerment weak, which has not contributed to biodiversity conservation.

The second stage required wide consultation at the national and state level, in order to discuss, modify and develop an strategy able to be implemented.

The first phase of the NBSAP developed the ten strategies of the NBP, building upon the same principles of the policy. Nine working groups were established, which included more than 90 persons from different backgrounds, representing various interests and stakeholders. These groups worked for a period of eight months, and the final edited result was published in 1998 (FANDIÑO and FERREIRA 1998).

The second phase (the consultation phase) of the project never occurred due to institutional and political circumstances. Since the technical proposal was developed during the final year of a government administration, it was finished just as a new government with a new Minister of the Environment and a new senior staff took office. Even though assigning the responsibility of further development of the proposal was decided by the same Ministry, it finally opted not to adopt it formally and not to undertake the required political consultations. The following are the main factors that may have led to this outcome:

- There was a new political establishment that inherited a process already under development, and the MOE was reluctant to undertake a consultation on a proposal that was developed "outside" the Ministry.

- Biodiversity was not a political priority. In fact, the environmental priority at the time was water, and all environmental policy was supposed to revolve around this topic, including biodiversity actions.

- There was a lack of understanding of the scope of the ENBPA. At the time, the government did not perceive the need to develop and implement a strategy and action plan focusing only in biodiversity. It preferred to put all of its environmental goals under a sole policy document, which is much more general than an action plan.

- There was lack of clarity of the role of different institutions. Unlike other countries (Peru, for example, which has an institution devoted to the implementation and development of a national biodiversity strategy and action plan), in Colombia there is confusion about institutional responsibilities regarding biodiversity. Even though the law is clear that the MOE is in charge of approving environmental policies and the Humboldt Institute is a research institution that cannot assume political responsibilities, the prominent role that Humboldt has played has created some confusion. Therefore, the Ministry does not perceive biodiversity as one of its main responsibilities, even though a large amount of its work pertains to biological resources.

As a result Colombia does not have to date an officially approved National Biodiversity Strategy and Action Plan. Neither does it have a governing body directing and following its implementation. Nevertheless the published document of the proposal has been *de facto* used by the government as a policy framework for several of its actions regarding biodiversity. Therefore, it is worthwhile to consider it in any policy analysis related to biodiversity in Colombia.

Identification and Definition of Access Laws and Policies

Policies Related to Access to Genetic Resources[4]

On 7 July 2002, the Andean Community adopted a Regional Biodiversity Strategy (Decision 523) under the auspices of the Inter-American Development Bank. This strategy includes an ABS component that provides a brief assessment of the problems experienced by the Andean Community in implementing Decision 391 and proposes a course of action to facilitate its implementation. According to the strategy, Decision 391 presents ambiguities that have prevented not only its implementation at a national and regional level, but has also prevented the advancement of science and the involvement of traditional communities in access and benefit-sharing projects. Thus, the Regional Biodiversity Strategy encourages the Andean Community to develop a common strategy on access to genetic resources that includes a better definition of the scope of Decision 391 and benefit-sharing issues, an increase in local scientific capacity, and the development of a regional communication system on national access and benefit-sharing initiatives. The Andean Community is currently working on an action plan to facilitate the implementation of the Regional Biodiversity Strategy.[5]

From 1998 to 2002 the main governmental environmental policy in Colombia was called the "Proyecto Colectivo Ambiental" ("Environmental Collective Project"). This policy's Biodiversity Program did not consider the issue of ABS as a central aspect. This trend continues in the present (2002–2006) governmental environmental policy. In 2003, the executive branch was partially reorganized and MOE was assigned housing responsibilities (among other duties) that became a high priority for the Ministry. Furthermore, MOE's name was changed to Ministry of Environment, Housing, and Land Development. ABS issues continue to have a low priority within MOE. The NBP and ENBPA, however, provide more specific policy elements on the topic. The NBP and NBSAP contain five strategies related directly or indirectly to the issue of ABS. These strategies, including a description of the policy objectives and goals pertaining to ABS, and a brief qualitative assessment of their implementation, are as follows:[6]

- Promote sustainable development of the economic potential of biodiversity. This strategy directly addresses the issue of ABS as one of the nine possible areas of economic potential of biological resources. The strategy's objective is to promote bioprospecting for the development and sustainable use of genetic resources. It sets the following goals:

- Increase the knowledge of wild flora, fauna, and microorganisms with current and potential uses as active principles in the development of drugs, plague and illness control agents, etc.

- Develop technologies, promote uses, and develop national and international markets that allow for the maximization of added value to these resources locally and nationally.

- Promote a national industry for the development of products that require more sophisticated processes.

- Improve the negotiation capacity of the MOE and relevant agencies in issues related to ABS and their derivatives.

- Consolidate a national industry of pharmaceutical products that originate from biodiversity to compete in national and international markets.

- Develop and apply various techniques of economic valuation of biodiversity to incorporate the results in frameworks for decision making.

Main accomplishments: The development of the Colombian Biotrade Initiative (Biocomercio) has helped in developing markets and strengthening the entrepreneurial capacity to develop new biodiversity products (not limited to genetic resources).

- Distribute benefits from biodiversity equitably. This strategy includes the equitable distribution of benefits derived from biodiversity in general, including, but not limited to, genetic resources. Its approach aims at strengthening the negotiation capacity for a more equitable distribution of benefits. There are no specific indications of how fair and equitable distribution of benefits should be included in ABS agreements.

Main accomplishments: There are few advances in this area.

- Characterize the components of biological diversity. There is an important relationship between this strategy and ABS since it is oriented at improving the knowledge of Colombian biodiversity, including genetic resources. Its goals include increasing biological inventories, organizing available and new information, and improving national research capacity for the characterization of biological resources. Its development will allow for a better understanding of what the country has to offer in terms of genetic resources.

Main accomplishments: This strategy has achieved more tangible results. The Humboldt Institute has

a Program with the main task of undertaking the country's biological inventory, which has substantially advanced implementation the strategy's goals.

- Recover, protect, and publicize traditional knowledge. This is a key policy strategy related to ABS, even though the strategy's scope goes beyond genetic resources. On the specific topic of access, the goal is to establish and implement norms and mechanisms for the protection of knowledge, wisdom, innovations, and traditional practices.

Main accomplishments: The debate over the way to protect and recover traditional knowledge is highly controversial, and substantial discussions are still required to reach a consensus at the national level. This is particularly true for knowledge related to genetic resources. The Humboldt Institute carried out a study specifically related to the protection of traditional knowledge in the context of ABS, and outlined a proposal on the topic: "Protección al conocimiento tradicional. Elementos conceptuales para una propuesta de reglamentación—El caso de Colombia" (Protection of traditional knowledge. Conceptual elements for a norm proposal—Colombia's case). This proposal provides a relevant first step in continuing the national debate, before entering negotiations at the Andean level.[7]

- Promote *ex situ* conservation. This strategy is closely related to the topic of ABS. Its goals include completing the inventory of existing taxa in *ex situ* collections; selectively incorporating into *ex situ* collections strategic components of biodiversity depending on their vulnerability or their cultural, economic, ecological or evolutionary importance; strengthening of *ex situ* conservation banks; strengthening human resources for *ex situ* conservation and related research; creating a national information system of *ex situ* collections and; obtaining verifiable economic, social and ecological benefits from *ex situ* conservation banks. The development of this strategy will significantly affect the way access to genetic resources occurs in Colombia.

Main accomplishments: There are substantial results in the implementation of this strategy nationwide, mainly in terms of information management. There are still insufficient efforts to incorporate species of particular strategic importance in *ex situ* collections.

Legislation on Access to Genetic Resources

Identification of Relevant Access Laws

Although the most comprehensive piece of legislation for Colombia regarding ABS is Decision 391, there are several other key laws and statutes related to genetic resources. Table 2 includes the names of the pertinent ones in chronological order. The more relevant aspects of laws and statutes and their relationship to ABS will be highlighted in this section. Additional information on how these laws and decrees relate to genetic resources may be obtained from Instituto Humboldt (Pardo 1999a).

The CBD is considered the central piece of legislation regarding biodiversity in Colombia. One of the objectives of the CBD is to promote the fair and equitable sharing of

Table 2. Laws and norms related to genetic resources

Norm	Title
Decree Law 2811 of 1974	Natural Resources Code
Decree 622 of 1977	Regulates the Natural Resources Code (Decree 2811/74)
Decree 1608 of 1978	Regulates the Natural Resources Code (Decree 2811/74) regarding wild fauna.
Law 47 of 1989	ITTO Agreement
Decree 1974 of 1989	Regulates the Natural Resources Code (Decree 2811/74) regarding issues of natural protected areas (Integrated management districts).
Political Constitution of 1991	
Law 21 of 1991	Convention No. 169 on Indigenous people and tribes in independent countries
Law 70 of 1993	Develops the 55 transitory article of the Constitution (black communities)
Law 99 of 1993	Creates the MOE and organizes the National Environmental System
Decision 345 of 1993	Common Regime for the Protection of Plant Variety Breeders' Rights.
Law 165 of 1994	Convention on Biological Diversity
Decree 1745 of 1995	Regulates the law of Afro-Colombian communities
Decree 1397 of 1996	Creates the National Commission of Indigenous Territories and the permanent harmonization table with Indigenous Organizations.
Decision 391 of 1996	Common Regime on Access to Genetic Resources
Law 299 of 1996	For the protection of Colombian flora, and regulates botanical gardens.
Decree 730 of 1997	Determines the National Competent Authority in the matter of access to genetic resources.
Resolution 620 of 1997	By which some functions of Decision 391 are delegated and the internal procedures for access to genetic resources and their derivatives requests are set.
Decree 309 of 2000	Regulates scientific research about biological diversity.
Decision 486 of 2000	Common Regime on Industrial Property

Adopted from Pardo (1999) and updated.

benefits arising out of the utilization of genetic resources. The CBD also encourages the transfer of relevant technologies, through appropriate funding, taking into account all rights over those resources and technologies (UNEP/CBD 1998). Additionally, the CBD recognizes the sovereign rights of nations over their natural resources and their authority to determine access to genetic resources. It also establishes that each contracting party should endeavor to create conditions to facilitate such access by other contracting parties and should not impose restrictions that run counter to the intentions of the Convention. It further states that when access is granted it should be given under mutually agreed upon terms. Additionally, it indicates that each contracting party shall endeavor to carry out scientific research based on genetic resources provided by another party with the providing party's full participation, and, if possible, to conduct that research in the country of origin. Finally, it establishes that each party should take legislative, administrative, or policy measures, as appropriate, with the aim of sharing in a fair and equitable way the results of research and development. The agreement also requires that benefits arising from the commercial or other utilization of genetic resources shall be shared with the contracting party providing such resources and such sharing should be upon mutually agreed terms. The CBD thus sets a comprehensive policy framework for ABS and requires countries to take the appropriate measures to facilitate it.

Of the national legislation summarized in Table 2, it is worth highlighting the contents of the Colombian Political Constitution and of Law 99 of 1993. The Political Constitution establishes in Article 81, second paragraph, that the State will regulate the entry and exit of genetic resources and their use according to national interests. Since the Colombian State is sovereign over its genetic resources, it is entitled to legislate their conservation, use, import, export, and any other activity related to this resource.

Law 99 of 1993 also creates the MOE and organizes the National Environmental System. Two relevant provisions regarding ABS that develop the mandate of the Constitution are given to the MOE. Article 5, numeral 20, gives the MOE the function of regulating the securing, use, management, research, import, export, distribution, and commerce of species and genetic lineages of fauna and flora; regulating import/export and commerce of such genetic material; establishing the mechanisms and procedures of command and control; and arranging for the necessary claim of payments or acknowledgements of the rights or privileges bestowed on the Nation due to the use of genetic material. In numeral 38 of the same article, law 99/93 indicates that the MOE must ensure that the study, exploitation, and research, both national and foreign, relating to Colombia's natural resources respects national sovereignty and the rights of the Colombian Nation over its genetic resources. This law gave the MOE major responsibilities regarding ABS before the adoption of Decision 391.

Common Regime on Access to Genetic Resources— Decision 391

Decision 391 is a regional regime that was negotiated and adopted in 1996 under the Cartagena Agreement of the Andean Community. Decisions adopted under the Cartagena Agreement are binding, and once approved, they are automatically integrated into national legislation for their execution, without requiring any approval by the legislative apparatus of the member states (GTZ/FUNDECO/IE 2001). Therefore, their application does not necessarily require the establishment of a new law, and can be implemented with only a few additional dispositions (CAILLAUX et al. 1999). Additionally, it is commonly understood as a general norm that establishes minimal rules applicable to all member states, which countries can individually decide to develop further on their own or apply immediately (GTZ/FUNDECO/IE 2001). Therefore, this agreement is binding for all countries of the Andean Community: Bolivia, Colombia, Ecuador, Peru, and Venezuela.

By the end of 1993, the Andean Community approved Decision 345 regarding a Common Regime for the Protection of Plant Variety Breeders' Rights. This decision establishes that the member countries would adopt "a common regime on biogenetic resources, biosafety measures for the Sub region, in concordance with the Convention on Biological Diversity". After the approval of Decision 345, the first steps for the development of an access decision were initiated. Decision 391 was adopted on 2 July 1996, and became officially binding on 17 July 1996, when it was published in the Official Gazette of the Cartagena Agreement. It is considered a major development of the CBD on ABS. The following three major characteristics of this Decision make it noteworthy:

- Decision 391 regulates the access[8] to genetic resources[9] as well as to their derivative products[10]. Therefore it is not limited to genetic resources *per se*, but also includes other molecules of biological origin produced by living beings, with a broader scope than the specific provisions of the CBD.

- The agreement explicitly recognizes the importance of knowledge associated with the genetic resources by considering it a central part of access under the name "intangible component".[11] Here again it goes beyond the original scope of the CBD.

- The Decision makes a reiterative separation between biological resources on one hand and the genetic resources and their derivative products on the other, by indicating that the former contains the latter.

The following are the objectives and goals of Decision 391:

- Provide conditions for a fair and equitable participation in the benefits derived from access.

- Establish the basis for the recognition and valuation of genetic resources, their derivative products, and their intangible associated components, especially when referring to indigenous, Afro-Colombian, and local communities.

- Promote the conservation of biological diversity and the sustainable use of biological resources that contain genetic resources.

- Promote the consolidation and development of scientific, technological, and technical capacities at the local, national, and subregional levels.

- Strengthen the negotiating capacity of member countries.

The Decision indicates the minimal requirements that must be taken into account when making an access application. It also stipulates the need to establish a contract agreement between those interested in the access activities and the National Competent Authority (NCA) in order to guarantee the objectives of the decision. This contract should take into account the rights and interests of the providers of the genetic resources and its derivative products, the providers of the biological resources that contain them, and the providers of intangible components, if applicable (PARDO 1999a). The principal contract should be supplemented with an appendix when access to genetic resources or derivative products with an intangible component are requested. This appendix should be signed by the provider of the intangible component and the applicant to access, even though it may also be signed by the MOE (PARDO 1999a). Additionally, the Decision includes the need for an accessory contract to protect the rights of the owners of the biological resources and of the landowners where the resources are located. These aspects will be expanded upon later.

Legal Developments of Decision 391 and Norms that Contribute to its Implementation

In Colombia two main additional legal dispositions were adopted in order to facilitate the implementation of Decision 391 (Table 2):

- Decision 391 establishes that every country must determine an NCA for ABS purposes. This authority is a public entity authorized to provide genetic resources or their derivative products, to subscribe to and oversee the contracts on ABS, and to comply with the provisions of the decision. Decree 730 of 1997 determined that the NCA is the MOE, thus empowering the Ministry as the unique authority in all access issues in Colombia.[12]

- Resolution 620 of 1997 clarifies the internal procedures to be undertaken by the MOE to process access applications. These procedures will be detailed later.

Another legal development, adopted by Decree 309 of 2000 that regulates scientific research relating to biodiversity, contributes to the implementation of Decision 391 and was partially developed with this intent.[13] This

85

Decree basically simplifies the permits, authorizations and safe conducts that were required to undertake scientific research regarding biological diversity in Colombia by establishing a unique "study permit with the purpose of scientific research"[14]. This permit is required for activities of collection, recollection, capture, hunting, fishing, manipulation of the biological resources, and their mobilization through the national territory. It is worth noting that the decree explicitly excludes issues pertaining to health and agriculture except when these involve specimens or samples of wild fauna or flora (Article 1). It also indicates that foreigners willing to undertake scientific research in Colombia must present a Colombian co-researcher(s) to participate in the research activities. The decree has specific provisions related to access to genetic resources, and the following should be highlighted:

- Any scientific research which requires obtaining and utilizing genetic resources, their derivative products, or their intangible components is subject to the decree and to all other norms pertaining to access to genetic resources (Article 15).
- The granting of a study permit by an environmental authority does not require the MOE to authorize access to genetic resources.

The Autonomous Regional Corporations (i.e., regional environmental agencies) thus may have an indirect role in the application of Decision 391 when they grant a study permit that may involve ABS with respect to the activities regulated by Decree 309 of 2000 or any other activity that the access project may require that may lie within the Corporation's functions. However, the Regional Corporations do not have any major authority, nor do they take part in the evaluation of ABS or the granting of access contracts. Nevertheless, the MOE may consult the Regional Corporations if it considers this useful and may even involve them in follow up and oversight activities of a given ABS contract, through specific agreements.

No future legal reforms to implement the Decision have been proposed to date. Still required is the development of policies (as will be analyzed below) and of additional legislation for the protection of traditional knowledge. In fact, Decision 391 establishes that a special regime or harmonization norm should be established for the protection of knowledge, innovations, and traditional practices of indigenous, Afro-Colombian, and local communities.

Ex Situ Conservation Entities, Industries, and Activities Regulated by Decision 391

Ex situ conservation organizations

The Common Regime on ABS clearly indicates that it is applicable to those countries that are countries of origin of genetic resources, their derivative products, and their intangible components. Additionally, access is defined as the obtainment and utilization of genetic resources in *ex situ* or *in situ* conditions, their derivatives, and, if it is the case, their intangible components, with the purpose of research, bioprospecting, conservation, industrial application or commercial use, among other activities. Finally, the Decision explicitly indicates that *ex situ* conservation centers or other entities that undertake activities relating ABS or their derivative products or, if applicable, their intangible components associated must sign access contracts.

Therefore, the Decision explicitly includes all genetic resources and derivative products under *ex situ* conditions, thus including botanical collections, seed banks, zoos, breeding centers, botanical gardens, aquariums, tissue banks, collections in natural history museums, herbaria, *in vitro* collections, and any other instance, center, or collection that may possess genetic resources or derivative products that will be used for ABS purposes. This implies that Decision 391 is also applicable to The International Center for Tropical Agriculture, a research institution under the Consultative Group on International Agricultural Research located in Colombia.

Industries and activities regulated by Decision 391

The access definition of Decision 391 is very broad. It refers to access as related to the intent of those who wish to use the genetic resources, derivative product, or intangible component, in specifying that the purpose must be for "research, bioprospecting, conservation, industrial application, or commercial profit, among others" (Article 1, Decision 391). Therefore, a wide range of activities may lie within this definition, but exactly which activities should be regulated under the Decision is still unclear.

The Decision also makes a clear distinction between genetic resources and derivative products, and biological resources, thus limiting the scope of the Decision by excluding biological resources that are not used or acquired with the intent of access to genetic resources or their derivative products. This exclusion is nonetheless difficult to understand as all biological material contains genetic material or derivative products.

However difficult the interpretation of the Decision may be regarding what activities are covered, it is necessary to keep in mind both the intention of the Regime and the practical aspects of its application. It would be a mistake to require access contracts for a wide range of activities that require the use of biological material, under the premise that biological materials contain genetic material.

An example to illustrate this point, even though controversial, is the exchange of botanical collections for taxonomic identification. Botanical samples not intended for ABS purposes are frequently sent to experts for the purpose of taxonomic identification. Nevertheless, an NCA may believe that since a biological resource containing genetic resources is exchanged, an access contract is required. This is even more of an issue if the sample is exported to a foreign collection. The NCA is correct that access can occur, but it is mistaken in requiring an access contract, because the intent is taxonomic identification and not access to genetic resources. Nevertheless, the access definition of Decision 391 allows for this ample interpretation of the norm.

Even more difficulties arise when other types of activities are analyzed. For example should biological resources from which botanical extracts are obtained, purified, or processed for commercial purposes be included? Under a strict interpretation of Decision 391 they can be included, but it is unclear whether this is the right policy choice.

The activities and industries that should definitely be covered by Decision 391 are thus difficult to identify. Therefore it is the duty of each of the countries of the Andean Community to reflect upon this complex subject in order to determine the appropriate interpretation of the Decision. Ideally, this interpretation should be agreed upon by all countries, and the appropriate forum to discuss this topic would be the Andean Committee on Access to Genetic Resources, which was created by Decision 391. In fact, within the Andean Regional Biodiversity Strategy, such discussions have already begun at a very general level.

In Colombia, the Humboldt Institute has begun to analyze the subject. One of its publications regarding Colombian legislation states:

> It is important to acknowledge that there are practical differences between using biological resources and accessing genetic resources, because the access to a biological resource implies the physical action of collecting, taking, hunting or cultivating. Biological resources can be used and profited as a whole. On the contrary, to access a genetic resource, the biological resource must undergo a transformation process that allows separating and isolating the genetic resources or derivative products, through technologies developed for that purpose. Thus, in order to access genetic resources it is necessary first to access the biological resource. Nevertheless, the access to a biological resource does not necessarily imply the access to a genetic resource. In this sense, the object of the access is completely different and must be taken into account to determine the applicable legislation (PARDO 1999a).

Even though there is a relevant advancement in the analysis of the topic, this interpretation has not been officially adopted by the MOE, nor has it been debated. This issue thus requires further analysis and development in Colombia, as well as in the other Andean nations. In Colombia the project "Design of a Policy on Access to Genetic Resources and their Derivatives for Colombia" which the Humboldt Institute will complete in 2004, will likely address this central issue. The implications of the interpretation of the norm over scientific research should be carefully analyzed, in order to avoid creating unjustifiable obstacles to research efforts in the region.

Therefore, bioprospectors from the pharmaceutical, agricultural, botanical medicine, and biotechnology fields may be included in the scope of Decision 391, because it covers all access activities without particular considerations or exclusions of any given sector. Nonetheless, until more specific guidelines are developed, these activities must be analyzed on a case-by-case basis based on the activity they will undertake in order to determine whether they are covered or not by Decision 391.

Regulation of Access Activities in a Given Place

For the purpose of covering access activities in a given place, Decision 391 established the form of accessory contracts. It indicates that accessory contracts are those that, for the completion of activities related to access to genetic resources or their derivative products, must be established between the applicant to such access and:

- The owner, possessor, or administrator of the estate where the biological resource containing the genetic resource is located;
- The *ex situ* conservation center;
- The owner, possessor, or administrator of the biological resource containing the genetic resource; or
- The national support institution[15] for activities that may be undertaken that are not part of the access contract.

Other characteristics of such accessory contracts are that their establishment does not grant the access to genetic resources or its derivative products, and their content is subject to whatever is established in the access contract. Also they do not enter into force unless the access contract is valid. Similarly, if the NCA judges that the accessory contract is vital to obtaining access, it may terminate the access contract when the accessory contract is declared null.

These are the main provisions covering access activities in a given place or land. The purpose of the accessory contract is to protect the legally acquired rights and interests of the owners of the estates and biological resources that contain the desired genetic resources. Therefore, the Colombian state cannot disregard the rights of third parties or interfere in the free exercise of the property rights of individuals (PARDO 1999a). Rarely, if national interest surpasses private interest, the government may decide to expropriate a given property and make it public in order to grant an access contract. Nevertheless, this would be an extreme situation and is very unlikely to occur.

The provisions of the accessory contract apply to access activities on all types of properties, and identifying the appropriate parties to the contract depends on who is the owner, possessor, or administrator of the estate where the biological resource containing the genetic resource is located. In the case of public lands or marine areas, or national protected areas, for example, the owner is the State. The owners of private or community owned lands are the private individuals or the community; therefore, the applicant to access must enter into contracts with them.

In Colombia, the use of biological resources has a distinctive applicable legislation, and there are diverse laws over the use of wild resources. Additionally, it is now clear that genetic resources are State property by inalienable right and cannot be seized, or proscribed as stated by the Colombian State Court (Sentence 977 of August 1997). Therefore, the access applicant must agree on a contract with the state as owner of the genetic resource. Additionally, it must enter into an agreement with the owner of the biological resource if the resource is privately owned, and with the owner, administrator, or possessor of the land where the biological resource containing the desired genetic resource is located.

Enforcement of Decision 391

Decision 391 gives the NCA a major role in its evaluation, monitoring and enforcement (Article 50, Decision 391). It is the entity responsible for formulating the dispositions required to comply with the Decision at the national level. It must receive, evaluate, admit, or reject access applications; negotiate, subscribe to, and authorize access contracts and issue the corresponding access resolutions[16]; watch over the rights of the providers of biological resources that contain genetic resources and the intangible components; keep records of access applications and accompanying technical material; modify, suspend, resolve, or rescind access contracts and nullify them if necessary; decide on national support institutions and their suitability; supervise and control compliance with the conditions of the contracts and of the dispositions of the Decision, establishing the mechanisms of supervision and evaluation it considers necessary; review previously granted access contracts and adjust them as necessary; delegate supervision activities to other entities while maintaining control and responsibility over such supervision according to internal legislation; supervise the state of biological resources containing the genetic resource; carry out the national inventory on genetic resources and its derivative products; and maintain appropriate communication and information exchange with intellectual property right (IPR) authorities at the national level.

Decree 730 of 1997 determines that the MOE of Colombia is the NCA, thus giving this Ministry all of these responsibilities. Additionally, Law 99 of 1993 had already given the MOE several major functions in related genetic resources topics.[17]

Decision 391 also defines a set of parameters for infringement and sanctions. It states that anyone undertaking access activities without due authorization will be sanctioned. This also applies to persons undertaking transactions related to derivative or synthesized products[18] from genetic resources or to their intangible associated components. The NCA must apply the sanctions according to the country's national laws and such sanctions will apply without affecting other sanctions such as access or payment of damages for harm caused.

Standards for Evaluation of Access Applications

Decision 391 does not establish any specific standards for the evaluation of access applications.[19] It only establishes a set of prerequisites for an application to be accepted. It also indicates that compliance with environmental legislation must be considered when evaluating the request (Article 31, Decision 391).

Nevertheless, NBSAP may provide some guidance in the type of access applications that the country may favor, even though this is by no means an evaluation standard. Similarly, Decision 391 in article 17 indicates that the access applications and contracts, and, if applicable, the appendices, should include parameters such as those specified in the Article. These are not evaluation standards, but they indicate the type of access applications that may be favored. Such parameters are:

- The participation of citizens from the region in research activities of access to genetic resources, their derivative products, and intangible components;
- The support of research within a member country that is the country of origin of the genetic resource or any other country from the region that contributes to the conservation and sustainable use of biodiversity;
- The strengthening of mechanisms of transfer of knowledge and technologies, including biotechnologies, that are culturally, socially, and environmentally safe and healthy.
- The supply of background information and state of the art or science that may contribute to a better knowledge of the situation of a given genetic resource, its derivative or synthesized product, and the associated intangible component that originates from a given member state;
- The strengthening and development of the institutional national or sub regional capacity associated with genetic resources and its derivative products;
- The strengthening and development of the capacity of indigenous, Afro-Colombian, and local communities in relation to intangible knowledge associated with the genetic resources and their derivative products;
- The deposit of duplicates of all collected material in institutions determined by the NCA;
- The obligation of providing the NCA with the results of the research undertaken; and
- The terms of the transfer of the accessed material to third parties.

Even though the above parameters may help the access applicant develop its access proposal, they are insufficient from a policy point of view. The NCA needs to adopt policy guidelines with this in mind in order to facilitate the access process and to make it more clear and efficient.

Description of Legislation Relevant to ABS

Because there was no specific policy on ABS in Colombia as of July 2004, this section will be completely devoted to a description of the relevant existing legislation.

Steps to Obtain Access to Genetic Resources

The steps required for an applicant interested in obtaining access to genetic resources, their derivative products, and the associate intangible components (i.e., knowledge) are clearly described in Decision 391. In this section these steps will be described, along with an analysis of the difficulties that may arise in their implementation and suggestions of how they could be improved. None of the suggestions require any legal reform of Decision 391; most of them call for the development of policies defining key aspects of the access process.

It is worth noting that the procedures of Decision 391 are exactly the same for Colombians and for foreigners. Also, there are no differences between applications for scientific research and for commercial purposes.

Presentation of an Access Application

The process to access genetic resources or their derivatives begins with the presentation by the applicant of a request to the NCA, (i.e., the MOE). The request must include the prerequisites that are indicated in Decision 391, Article 26. There is no government fee for the presentation of the application.[20] Of these prerequisites it is worth highlighting the following: the identification of the provider of the genetic and biological resources, their derivative products, and intangible components; the identification of the person or national support institution; the identification and curriculum vitae of the responsible leader of the project and of its working group; the access activity that is requested; and the locality or area where the access will take place, indicating its geographic coordinates. In addition, the request must be accompanied by a project proposal.

If the proposal and all additional materials are complete, the NCA will accept it, and the process will be officially initiated. If the application is incomplete, the applicant will be notified without delay and apprised of the missing items, in order for the application to be completed. If accepted, an abstract of the application will be published within five days in a media source of wide national circulation, as well as in a media source in the locality where the access is requested.

One major aspect of this access application may be unclear: the requirement to present a "project proposal". This project proposal, along with the credentials of research group, should be a key element in evaluating the access application. However there are no guidelines, either in the Decision or any other policy document, as to what its content and scope should be. The only references that may be used by the applicant are the parameters described in Article 17 of the Decision. Guidelines for the content and scope of this project proposal need to be defined by the NCA in an official policy document that can be used as a reference by applicants. The definition of such parameters would substantially facilitate the access process both for the applicant and for the NCA.

Evaluation of the Access Application and Project Proposal

Within 30 working days of its official acceptance, the NCA will evaluate the proposal and will undertake the inspections it regards as necessary. The NCA will issue a legal and technical statement indicating whether the request is or is not approved. This time frame may be expanded up to 60 working days at the NCA's discretion.

Taking into account the legal and technical statement, the compliance with the Decision, and other analysis, the NCA will accept or deny the request. Applicants will be notified of the acceptance of the application and project proposal within five working days of the NCA's decision. If the request and project proposals are accepted, the NCA will proceed to negotiate and elaborate the terms of the access contract. If the request and project proposals are not accepted, the NCA will communicate its decision to the applicant by resolution stating the reasons of such denial and will terminate the procedure. The applicant may appeal this decision through a process determined by national legislation.

Even though this step is straightforward, the difficulty lies in the fact that the evaluation criteria are not defined or even outlined in an officially adopted policy document. This makes it more difficult for the applicant to submit a successful proposal and for the MOE to evaluate it. Even though there is a learning curve in evaluating the access proposals on a case-by-case basis, the NCA must use this learning process in order to outline the basis for evaluation criteria.

Elaboration of the Access Contract

Decision 391 indicates that after the request has been officially accepted a period of negotiation between the NCA and the applicant will occur, after which an access contract is signed. The terms or other characteristics of the negotiation and the time frame in which it is to take place are not specified by the Decision. The negotiation stage is one of the major hurdles of the access process, again because of the lack of a government policy. Additionally, the scope of the negotiation is not completely clear, given that the request and project proposal have already been accepted. This aspect should be clarified and developed. It is implicit that the negotiation should address issues such as the distribution of benefits and take into account the compliance with the Decision and its intent, etc. Nevertheless, the parameters provided by the Decision in this respect are insufficient because they do not specify the interests of the government of Colombia when entering into an access contract. These interests should be defined in a policy on ABS.

The legislation indicates that a contract agreement must be entered into between the NCA and the applicant, and it also indicates the requirements for the appendix to the contract and the accessory contract already described in this paper. It is not clear whether these documents must precede or follow the signing of the access contract.

Enactment of the Contract

Once the access contract has been adopted and signed, the NCA will issue and publish an access resolution, accompanied by an abstract of the contract, in the official gazette or newspaper of wide national circulation. The contract will be considered as perfected once this step is taken.

The length of the whole procedure depends on the duration of the negotiation between the applicant and the NCA. All other legal steps described above require a maximum of 65 working days.

Government Capacity to Negotiate ABS Agreements

The current capacity for evaluating, negotiating, and monitoring ABS proposals is very low, mainly because the MOE and other institutions have diverse responsibilities in many areas. In addition, there are no experts in the specific topics of ABS involved in the evaluation process. Resolution 620 of 1997 establishes that the evaluation and negotiation stages must be coordinated with the Ministry of Interior, the Ministry of Foreign Commerce, the Ministry of Agriculture, and other entities related to the MOE, as well as private and public universities, in particular the National University of Colombia (Universidad Nacional de Colombia) and the Amazonian University.

Relationship between Decision 391 and International Laws and Policies

The issue of ABS is central to Colombian foreign policy regarding biodiversity. This policy is centered on three aspects: 1) the application of the CBD, 2) restrictions on the application of IPRs, and 3) promotion of the sustainable use of genetic resources and equitable distribution of monetary and nonmonetary benefits.[21]

There were two main motives for the development of an agreement on ABS at the Andean level: implementing the CBD and regional integration between Andean countries. Both are international policies of the Colombian government. Also, within the Andean Community, there has been a strong interest in environmental issues as a key element of the integration process. Environmental issues have been addressed in eight presidential Councils of the Cartagena Agreement, and the commission has developed at least six Decisions related to agricultural and biological resources. The agreement to develop an Andean

Biodiversity Strategy is also a clear indication of the commitment of Andean countries to strengthen their capacity to implement the CBD.

Additionally, Decision 391 has supported the Colombian government's position in several international negotiations and forums related to genetic resources. It provided the government with a solid political basis to construct the country's position for the FAO International Undertaking,[22] the CBD, World Trade Organization forums, as well as for the negotiation of Decision 486 or Common Regime on Industrial Property. Table 2 shows the laws that relate to ABS. In this section, a brief reference to their relationship to Decision 391 will be provided.

The relationship between Decision 391 and Law 165 of 1994 of CBD has already been established. Nevertheless, it is worth highlighting again that Decision 391 was basically adopted to comply with the provisions of the CBD, and it follows the spirit of the Convention.

The ITTO agreement shares a common purpose with the Decision because it has the objective of promoting the conservation and sustainable use of the tropical forests and of its genetic resources (Law 47 of 1989, cited by PARDO (1999)). The same is true of Convention No. 169 on Indigenous People and Tribes in Independent Countries, which states that the rights of the people over the natural resources existing in their lands must be specially protected. These rights include the right to participate in the use, management, and conservation of these resources. It also indicates that when the state has ownership or rights over the resources existing in these lands, the government must establish procedures for consulting with the interested communities before allowing any exploration on their lands. The people must always participate in the benefits that these activities produce and receive equitable indemnification for any harm they may suffer as the result of these activities (Law 21 of 1991, cited by PARDO 1999a). Decision 391 embraces the intent of Law 21 by creating provisions protecting the rights of the people over their lands and protecting their knowledge through accessory contracts and the appendix to the contract.

Decision 345 or Common Regime for the Protection of Plant Variety Breeders' rights is closely related to access to plant genetic resources, because it establishes a *sui generis* property rights regime regulating plant breeders' rights, thus protecting the farmers and regulating ownership of newly developed plant varieties. The regime complies with the provisions of the International Union for the Protection of New Varieties of Plants.

Decision 486 or Common Regime on Industrial Property has the strongest relation to the topic of ABS and thus with Decision 391. There is a direct assertion that the elements of industrial property must safeguard and respect the genetic patrimony of the states, as well as the knowledge of indigenous, black, and local communities. Any patent granted using genetic material or knowledge from a country of the region requires the material to have been acquired according to international, regional, and national norms (in the case of Colombia, according to Decision 391 and related regulations). Therefore, the applicant must present the access contract, appendix, and accessory contracts, if applicable; otherwise, the patent will be null. Additionally, the Decision explicitly excludes the granting of patents on parts of live resources as they exist in nature, including the genome or germplasm of any natural living organism. Therefore, it prohibits patents over accessed genetic material if it exists as such in a living organism. The relationship between access and Decision 486 will be analyzed later.

Provisions that Promote the Conservation of Biodiversity, its Sustainable Use and the Fair and Equitable Distribution of Benefits

The central spirit of Decision 391 is the conservation and sustainable use of biological and genetic resources, and the fair and equitable distribution of benefits. Two of its five goals are related to these concepts: "to provide the conditions for a fair and just participation in the benefits derived from access to genetic resources" and "to promote the conservation of biological diversity and the sustainable use of the biological resources containing genetic resources" (Decision 391 1996).

Decision 391 states that the applicant for access must comply with the applicable environmental legislation. Additionally, it indicates that member states can establish limitations to access and their derivative products by a special legal norm, in the following cases:

- Endemism, rarity, or danger of extinction of species, subspecies, varieties, or lineages;
- Conditions of vulnerability or fragility in the structure or function of ecosystems that may be aggravated because of access activities;
- Adverse effects over human health or over essential elements of the cultural identity of the people;
- Undesirable or uncontrollable environmental impacts caused by access activities on ecosystems;
- Danger of genetic erosion due to access activities;
- Biosafety regulations; and
- Genetic resources or geographic areas determined as strategic.

Finally, in addition to these specific references, the access, appendix, and accessory contracts are the main instruments to promote the conservation and sustainable use of biodiversity and to seek the equitable and fair distribution of benefits. There are no specific indications on how these objectives should be reached, and they should be further developed by the Andean Committee on Genetic Resources and by national policies.

Process that Led to the Development of Decision 391

National discussions over ABS increased in Colombia soon after the Biodiversity Convention was ratified by the country. In particular there was a nongovernmental organization (NGO) initiative named the "National Biodiversity Strategy" (NBS) which was important in these discussions. From a legal standpoint, by the end of 1993 the Andean Community approved Decision 345 (Common Regime for the Protection of Plant Variety Breeders' Rights). In this regime, the countries already indicated their interest in developing an Andean norm related to ABS and agreed to adopt a common regime on biogenetic resources and biosafety for the region. Soon after that, the formal discussions of such a norm were initiated.

An analysis of the process that led to the decision has identified two main motivations that resulted in the negotiation of Decision 391 (CAILLAUX et al. 1999): 1) The need to develop legislation to protect genetic resources in order to gain control over the inventions derived from them, given the increased strength of IPR regimes after Decision 345 had been approved, and 2) the fact that Andean countries share, in general terms, a great amount of their biodiversity. The countries thus wanted to avoid competition between themselves and opted for the adoption of a common set of rules and the promotion of cooperative mechanisms between countries. At the Andean level, the initial discussions on the ABS norm had the ample participation of various sectors of civil society. Moreover, the Secretariat of the Andean Community asked the World Conservation Union (IUCN), which lately involved Peruvian Society for Environmental Law (SPDA)[23], to develop a first draft of the elements that should be considered in an access regime. This draft was presented to the countries in October 1994 under the title "Possible Elements for a Decision of the Andean pact about Access to Genetic Resources" (JUNTA ACUERDO DE CARTAGENA 1994). In September 1994, there were already deep differences with the IUCN/SPDA proposal, as well as resistance from some governments even to have such a document as a basis for discussion. Also, a number of other draft norms emerged from various groups. In Colombia, in August 1994, the NBS produced an alternative draft, "Proyecto de Decisión Andina sobre Acceso a Recursos Genéticos—Propuesta de Colombia".[24] These various documents were discussed in a regional workshop in Villa de Leyva, Colombia. This workshop had wide participation (NGO's, academic institutions, private sector, intergovernmental institutions, and indigenous organizations) from the Andean countries. Nevertheless, there was increased tension in the debate between "conservation" and "commercialization", which led government representatives to decide to isolate themselves from the NGO process (CAILLAUX et al. 1999). As a result, the NGOs and others contributing to the debate lost their opportunity to participate in the development of the Decision (CAILLAUX et al. 1999).

Most governments felt uncomfortable discussing the development of an access norm based on an NGO draft proposal. In fact, after this phase of active civil society participation, a number of government proposals were put forth, and the formal instances of debate and negotiation began to be called "government expert meetings". In November 1994, the Colombian and Venezuelan governments jointly presented a new draft Decision for discussion. The next year, the governments of both Bolivia and Ecuador proposed two different texts of draft decisions. Finally, the discussions between government officials developed around these three governmental drafts. There were six expert meetings which led to the elaboration of a final proposal that was presented to the Commission of the Cartagena Agreement for its approval in July 1996.

Analyses of the process indicate that the opportunity for wider participation in the debate and groundwork on a topic of such relevance as ABS was lost. Indeed, some argue that the conflicting attitude between NGOs led the governments, and particularly the Colombian government, to shy away from the broad debate that characterized the early stages of the development of the decision. As a result, some feel that topics such as traditional knowledge and the equitable distribution of benefits were not developed enough. An additional perception is that not all participating experts had adequate legal, technical, scientific, and economic experience to develop an access regime, which is partially explained by the fact that there is no strong experience within Colombia in the biotechnology, pharmaceutical, or agricultural industries either in research or business development (CAILLAUX et al. 1999).

From the reading of the official reports of these meetings, it is possible to observe that there was a sense of urgency to approve a decision. There were also extensive proposals regarding the definition of access and what it should cover. The group finally adopted a wide-ranging definition based on a Colombian proposal, which is very close to the current access definition of Decision 391. It is worthwhile noting that the negotiators possessed much less information than we do now regarding the activities and opportunities that ABS offers. Therefore, they tried to do their best using a very wide definition that can cover all types of activities. Unfortunately, the result of the application of this norm has been the opposite of its intent.

Difficulties During the Design of Decision 391

A number of issues were controversial during the development of Decision 391. The main ones will be highlighted:

- **Conservation vs. Commercialization.** The main controversial issue was the tension between a conservationist decision and a norm targeted at controlling the flow of genetic resources with a more "commercial" perspective (CAILLAUX et al. 1999). Some NGOs, in particular, wanted a broader norm aimed at the conservation and sustainable use of biodiversity from a larger perspective. The other group thought that there were other instruments to do this, including the CBD. Finally, governments opted for a focused regime solely oriented at ABS issues.

- **Scientific and Traditional Knowledge.** The treatment of knowledge involves both scientific and traditional knowledge. There was the intent to protect traditional knowledge and to respect scientific knowledge simultaneously. Some NGOs wanted a special access process for the cases that involved traditional knowledge. Additionally, there was interest in protecting traditional knowledge from a larger perspective, and there were not any other forums to do so. The governments opted for a midpoint solution that treats both types of knowledge as intangible components associated with genetic resources and a weak definition of the protection of traditional knowledge. In fact the Decision creates the basic instruments to protect traditional knowledge but delegates the solution to future negotiations. It indicates that the Cartagena Board must elaborate a proposal of a special regime or harmonization norm oriented to the protection of traditional knowledge, innovations, and practices within three months of July 1996. The issue is so controversial that such a proposal has not emerged, nor have the countries pursued all the steps indicated by the norm (i.e., to undertake national studies on the topic and carry out training workshops in communities) in order to develop such a proposal.

- **The "green gold" perception.** The other issue that was a cause of debate was the perception by some government officials that genetic resources were the "green gold" of the Andean countries. Some people gave genetic resources an extremely high economic value and expected an immediate high economic return from their use (CAILLAUX et al. 1999). This perception was not accepted by all participants and was a cause of tension in the debates. Finally, the governments opted for a norm aimed at strictly controlling the flow of genetic resources and their export to third countries, under the premise that important sums of money were at stake.[25]

Implementation of Decision 391 in Colombia

Even though Decision 391 has been in place since 1996, by February 2004, not a single access contract had been signed in Colombia. Also, the number of access applications has been low: in total the MOE has received 15 access applications, which are summarized in Table 3. Overall, a similar situation is occurring in the other Andean countries. Between July 1996 and July 2001, Venezuela, Ecuador, Bolivia, and Peru received only 26 applications. Of these, one was approved, four were denied, two did not require access contracts, and the others are under evaluation (GTZ/FUNDECO/IE 2001). Simply put, there has been very little implementation of Decision 391. The Decision has been useful to the subregion in setting up strong positions in international forums such as the FAO International Undertaking negotiations, but it has not been particularly useful at the national level. It has served mainly as a framework to analyze the access proposals that have been presented. One must suspect that most access activities in Colombia, and in other Andean countries, both for research and commercial purposes, are currently conducted illegally. Potential applicants for access do not understand the decision, or they ignore it, perceiving it as an obstacle to research and development.

Table 3 summarizes the access proposals that have been submitted to the MOE, and provides information about the applicant, the objective of the project, and its status. Most of the applications are solely for scientific research and do not have commercial purposes. It is worth noting that in several cases the applicant withdrew from the access process. Box 2 summarizes the case of BioAndes, which has been the only application with commercial purposes.

Several of the implementing obstacles for Colombia have been identified already in this document. At the Andean level the main difficulty is the interpretation of the Decision 391 (GTZ/FUNDECO/IE 2001) both by governments and access applicants. A summary of other implementing difficulties is the following (GTZ/FUNDECO/IE 2001):

- Confusion over which activities require access contracts;
- Lack of knowledge of the norm by potential users;
- Lack of experienced and qualified personnel to inform the public;
- Insufficient information regarding access procedures;
- Confusion over the most important terms of the norm and the role of different parties;
- Lack of interest by potential applicants to get involved in a complicated, expensive, and uncertain procedure;

- Uncertainty regarding issues related to the protection of traditional knowledge and whether they will be defined or not;
- Expectations of high economic benefits on the part of governments and indigenous communities;
- Difficulties in the negotiations of accessory contracts with the providers of the biological resources (excessive expectations of economic remuneration);
- Lack of an appropriate information system;
- Lack of compliance with the terms and timetable established by Decision 391; and
- Lack of sufficient economic resources for implementation.

On the other hand, the Decision has not yet reached the main purposes for which it was developed. First of all, the countries do not have a unified access policy, one of the initial motivations of the norm (FERREIRA and PARDO 2001), because they have given the Decision such a wide range of interpretations. Another main purpose was to be able to control the flow of genetic resources. This has not occurred due to the lack of implementation of the Decision. Finally, the norm could have provided favorable conditions for promoting interesting access agreements. This has not happened because applicants do not feel sufficient legal certainty or clear negotiation conditions (FERREIRA and PARDO 2001). As was pointed out before, the Andean Committee on ABS provides a valuable forum to discuss and develop implementing solutions.

In the case of Colombia, there is the perception from the MOE, the Ministry of Commerce, and research institutions such as the Humboldt Institute that the norm can be successfully applied without legal reform. There is an agreement that the current legal framework can work, even to actively promote ABS activities in Colombia, if the appropriate procedures and policy developments are set in place. In fact, the lack of a clear and publicized government policy has had three grave results: the lack of application of the norm, leading to illegal access[26], the insufficient active promotion of access activities, and a weak and unclear response to the few access applications that have been submitted. The result: a net loss of opportunities for the sustainable use of genetic resources. There are currently two major efforts to address these needed developments. First, the MOE hired a research institute of the National University of Colombia to develop key access concepts and procedures. Secondly, the Humboldt Institute is undertaking a research project that will lead to a policy proposal on ABS.

Intellectual Property Rights and Bioprospecting

The Andean countries in general, and Colombia in particular, have comprehensive IPR legislation, some of which is specifically related to biodiversity. Table 4 summarizes the legal norms related to IPRs and biodiversity in Colombia (PARDO 1999b).

Of this group of norms, two are particularly relevant in the context of ABS and bioprospecting. These are Decision 345 and Decision 486. Decision 345, Common Regime for the Protection of Plant Variety Breeders' Rights, establishes the intent of Andean Community to develop a common regime on ABS. This Decision has the following objectives (GTZ/FUNDECO/IE 2001):

- Recognize and guarantee the protection of the rights of breeders of new plant varieties through a certificate.

- Encourage research activities in the Andean region.
- Promote technology transfer activities within and outside the subregion.

Decision 486 of 2000 is the newly approved Common Regime on Industrial Property. With this Decision, the Andean Community complied with the Agreement on Trade-Related Aspects of Intellectual Property Rights (TRIPS) requirements. In fact, this is why Decision 344 was replaced. Furthermore, the process leading to the common regime on industrial property was largely promoted by the Colombian Government (MINISTERIO DE COMERCIO EXTERIOR 2001).

Decision 486 has critical provisions related to ABS:

- Article 3 establishes that member countries will guarantee that elements of industrial property be

Table 3. Access proposals presented to the MOE of Colombia between 1997 and early 2004

Project name	Applicant	Project objective	Status
1. Access application to all of Colombian genetic resources in all Colombian territory (February 1997). Revised proposal: Access to all of genetic resources in natural protected areas (May 1997). Second proposal: access to all genetic resources excluding park areas contested by civil law or inhabited by indigenous or Afro-Colombian communities.	BioAndes de Colombia (Joint venture between Andes Pharmaceuticals Inc. – USA and ERS Associates – Colombia).	Research of *in vitro* bioactive compounds for the treatment of cancer and other diseases.	After several resolutions and new proposal by BioAndes the request was denied in December 1998.
2. Identification of the importance of hibernating sites of four North America migrating bird species (*Catharus ustulatus, Seiurus noveboracensis, Setophaga ruticilla,* and *Dendroica striata*), by using genetic markers and census in the National Natural Park of Tinigua.	Alejandro Calixto	Research to identify hibernating sites of migrating species.	The application was submitted in July 1998 and filed after the applicant withdrew.
3. Genetic analysis of Fungi Ustilaginales from the collection of the Colombian National Herbaria.	Adriana Mercedes, Gil Correa	Determine phylogenetic relationships among the fungi analyzed. Research for academic purposes.	In February 1999 the applicant withdrew and the application was filed.
4. Analysis of the genetic variation and degree of genetic isolation in the populations of *Inia geoffrencis* in the Amazon and Orinoco basins.	Eulalia Banguera Hinestroza	Contribute to the taxonomic knowledge of this river dolphin species by using genetic markers. Provide information to contribute to the development of policies and conservation strategies for the dolphin populations.	The access request was accepted in 1999. The process has not concluded and the negotiation phase and signing of the access contract are pending.

granted protection while respecting their biological and genetic patrimony, as well as the traditional knowledge of their indigenous, black, and local communities. It further states that patents for inventions developed from material obtained from this patrimony or such knowledge will only be granted if this material has been acquired in conformity with the international, subregional, and national legal systems. It states that member countries recognize the rights and authority of indigenous, black, and local communities over their collective knowledge. It also indicates that Decision 486 will be applied and interpreted in such a manner that it should not contravene Decision 391.

• Article 20 establishes restrictions to patents. In particular, it indicates that plants, animals, and essentially biological procedures for the production of plants or animals that are not nonbiological procedures will not be subject to patents.

• Article 26 regarding the requirements for obtaining a patent establishes that the applicant must present: a) a copy of the access contract when the products or procedures of the patent requested have been obtained or developed from genetic resources or their derivatives of which any of the member countries are countries of origin and b) if applicable, a copy of the authorization for the use of traditional

Table 3. Continued

Project name	Applicant	Project objective	Status
5. Analysis of the genus *Trianopiper*. Expedient No. 2413.	María Alejandra Jaramillo	Request for taxonomic scientific research. The objective was to pursue a taxonomic revision of the species of the *Trianopiper* genus using genetic tools.	Additional information was requested by MOE in December 2000.
6. Study of genetic diversity of the genus *Cattleya* of the Andean Region of Colombia using AFLP. Expedient No. 2378.	María Eloisa Aldana	Study of the genetic structure of the orchid genus *Cattleya* of the Colombian Andes, including the extraction of DNA. The study would allow for a better understanding of the genus classification and provide strategies for its *ex situ* and *in situ* conservation.	The applicant withdrew its request in June 2001.
7. Export permit of samples of tissue and blood from the marine turtles, genus *Caretta*. Expedient No. 2490.	Diego Amorocho	Genetic study for the conservation of the turtle in the Department of Magdalena. The objective is to determine the size and structure of the populations of the marine turtles.	Additional information and permits have been requested by MOE in 2001.
8. Expedient 2294.	Not publicly available	Not publicly available	Under evaluation
9. Access to genetic resources and their derivatives of the "Mono Titi" (*Sanguinus oedipus*). Expedient No. 2571.	Disney's Animal Kingdom	The access requested is aimed at determining the hormonal levels of several females, through sampling of feces. Additionally the genetic variability within a population will be determined, including paternity and relationships between the individuals of each conservation group through skin and hair samples. The main purpose of the research is the ecology and behavioral traits of the populations of the cotton-top tamarin, *Sanguinus oedipus*, in their natural environment.	Under evaluation.

knowledge from indigenous, black, and local communities, when the products for which the patent is requested have been obtained or developed from such knowledge of which any of the member countries is a country of origin, according to Decision 391 and its developments.

There is a very strong connection between the two regimes, as Decision 486 strengthens the relevance of ABS procedures. Therefore, it is extremely important for Andean countries to promptly implement Decision 391 in order not to block the IPR regulation.

As for other proposals made in terms of IPR, the Latin American and Caribbean Group have proposed to include the issue of traditional knowledge in the negotiations of the Free Trade Area for the Americas and TRIPS[27]. These propositions are still under development and debate.

As was explained above, Colombia does not have in place a comprehensive system to protect traditional knowledge. In fact, this has been a major hurdle to access because most communities feel they do not have sufficient protection of their rights. Decision 391 establishes that a norm to protect these rights has to be proposed at the Andean level, but this has not occurred. The issue is so controversial at the national, subregional, and international levels that there is not a clear foreseeable outcome. In Colombia there has been some conceptual progress with the development of elements for the elaboration of a protection regime for traditional knowledge, innovations, and practices (SÁNCHEZ et al. 2000). Nevertheless, this is an academic proposal that may serve as an initial basis for discussion but that still requires wide opportunities for debate, discussion, and modification from Colombian traditional communities.

Recommendations to Facilitate Access to Genetic Resources in other Countries

The most relevant recommendations to facilitate access in Colombia were outlined in previous sections of this paper. Some lessons can be derived from the Andean experience, and in fact developers of several of the new laws and policies worldwide regarding access have already benefited from these lessons. The recommendations that emerge from the Andean and Colombian process can be summarized as follows.

The main problem with Decision 391 is its lack of implementation. This problem has many origins, but two are outstanding:

- The country lacks the capacity to put the norm in place due to institutional limitations, insufficient budget, and lack of appropriate expertise.
- The scope of the norm is not clearly defined. After almost six years there is no consensus on what access to genetic resources means and includes, what type of activities it covers, and what relationship it has to the use of biological resources. The defini-

Table 3. Continued

Project name	Applicant	Project objective	Status
10. Isolation and identification of a microorganism with "levansacarasa" activity. Expedient No. 2571	Director, Institute of Biotechnology (National University of Colombia)	Study of a microorganism with "levansacarasa" activity.	The application was filed in January 2001.
11. Bird malaria in Colombia. Expedient No. 2572.	Medicine Department, University of Antioquia	Study of malaria present in the bird population of Colombia	Additional information was requested by the MOE on 20 February 2002.
12. Genetic diversity of three populations of *Colombobalanus excelsa.* Expedient No. 2573	Eliana Gonzales Valencia	Analysis of genetic diversity of the endangered tree species, *Colombobalanus excelsa* (Fagaceae)	Additional information was requested by the MOE on 21 November 2003.
13. Study of amphibians and reptiles in eastern Colombia	Taran Grant, American Museum of Natural History	Analysis of the diversity of amphibians and reptiles in eastern Colombia	Additional information was requested by MOE on 15 March 2002.
14. Request for three research projects. Expedient No. has not been assigned yet.	Director	Humboldt Institute	Unknown, additional information was requested by MOE on 20 August 2002.
15. Genetic characterization of the South American dolphin. Expedient No. 2788	Susana Caballero	Analysis of the genetic diversity of the South American dolphin for scientific (noncommercial) purposes.	MOE should be making a decision in 2004.

tion of access in the Decision is too wide, impeding its implementation and creating confusion both in the NCA and among persons interested in access activities.

The lessons derived are straightforward:

- Put in place legislation that can effectively be implemented, even if it is less ambitious in its scope than may be ideal: at least some of the access activities will be undertaken under legal terms, and the country can gradually learn from the process and advance to more complicated schemes if necessary. It is necessary to guarantee that the appropriate resources (institutional, human capacity, budget, etc.) are available to put the norm in place.

- Clearly define a reasonable scope of what the legislation covers, thus minimizing confusion from government and the users. Also, it is necessary to define the relationship with other natural resource uses that very likely have their own legislation in place and should be dealt with separately.

The Colombian experience also demonstrates that the lack of policy on ABS issues has exacerbated the low rate of implementation of Decision 391. If the Colombian government had a policy framework to implement the decision, most of its difficulties could be overcome. Within the definition of the policy the most important task is to identify the country's policy objectives: Does the country want to control all flows of genetic resources? Does it want to promote technology transfer and increase

its scientific and technical capacity through access activities? Does it want to promote foreign investment or does it want more stringent norms on foreigners to discourage their ABS activities? What is the role of the government? Should the government determine what technology transfer takes place? These policy choices have to be evaluated and properly debated. Once defined, they will provide a useful framework for the implementation of the norm and/or the promotion of access activities. As in the case of the Andean countries, it is clear that the existence of the decision alone is not enough.

Another lesson that can be derived from the Andean process is that these governments rushed to have a decision in place, in their urgency to protect their genetic patrimony. The net result so far has been the opposite of what they intended. Even though the negotiations surrounding Decision 391 began with open debate, they ended with a very limited group of so called "government experts".[28] Apparently not all "government experts" had sufficient expertise in access issues, and none of the countries had practical experience in pharmaceutical or other relevant areas. As a result, they developed a norm with their best knowledge and certainly with good intentions, but with considerable implementation difficulties. The negotiation process could have benefited from the following:

- A wider consultation with experts from different fields, including international experts with practical experience on access activities;

- A more sustained discussion, not limited to NGOs, with the different stakeholders, including academic interests and the private sector; and

---

Box 2. The case of BioAndes (Information from COLUMBIA UNIVERSITY (1999) and from the MOE Public Expedients and Resolutions)

The BioAndes case has been the only access application with commercial purposes that has taken place in Colombia. In February 1997 BioAndes formally submitted an ABS request for drug discovery in all Colombian Territory. This initial request was later modified to focus on the National Natural Park System, excluding contested areas or areas inhabited by indigenous or black communities. The application was for the collection of random biological materials for the elaboration of extracts for the research of *in vitro* bioactive compounds for the treatment of cancer and other diseases. This first application was denied by the MOE in November 1997 arguing the following:

- Geographic inaccuracy: it was proposed to sample sites in all protected areas of the system.

- Taxonomic inaccuracy: the application included a request to sample all taxonomic groups in Colombia, both marine and terrestrial.

- Absence of strategic alliances with local partners for technology transfer and lack of a National Support Institution (BioAndes did not meet the requirements since it was the applicant to access).

- Absence of cash-sharing benefit schemes, although BioAndes had asked for a principle of equitable treatment.

Later BioAndes appealed the MOE decision, arguing that the ample application scope was necessary to warrant the viability of the enterprise, and that the taxonomic breadth was justified by the bioassay method to be used. It also argued that strategic alliances were not required because the elaboration of the extracts was common practice. It also claimed that Decision 391 did not require monetary compensation as part of the application process.

Afterwards the MOE reiterated its decision, but it did emphasize some positive aspects of the initial application. BioAndes appealed, and in May 1998 presented a second access application, this time limiting research to 10-15 protected areas, excluding all parks inhabited by traditional communities. The taxonomic scope was still wide; and the group planned to "examine plants with known medicinal activity… purchased at market places" and to use "popular literature" to gather information about useful plants. This second request was again denied in November 1998, and the MOE gave its final negative response in December 1998.

- Lengthier discussions on the purpose and philo- sophical intent of the Decision. Even though the negotiation process took two and a half years, op- portunities for debate were not sufficient.[29]

A related lesson is that the issue of traditional knowl- edge was not properly addressed. As was stated before, this issue is so controversial and sensitive that the countries opted to postpone the discussions. This has, in practical terms, left the topic undeveloped, creating a major difficul- ty for the implementation of the norm, not to mention the discomfort and discontent of traditional communities.

Other more specific rescommendations to governments that arise from this analysis are the following:

- Provide legal certainty to all stakeholders.
- Do not put in place a law with an access model that is too rigid. Set a more flexible scheme that allows learning from the process and benefiting from technological innovations in biotechnology

and molecular biology.

- In the access application, ask for detailed informa- tion about the research project that is proposed. That will provide useful information for the evalu- ation process and orient the applicant in developing a more appropriate access proposal.
- Do not overestimate the economic benefits to the government that will arise from access activities. Rather, promote other non-economic benefits such as technology transfer and scientific devel- opment.
- Minimize the role of the government and promote more active participation from the private sector, NGOs, and local communities. After a few initial basic steps, the role of the government should be to oversee the access activities, not to control every flow of genetic resources.

Table 4. Legal norms that address IPR issues related to biodiversity in Colombia

Norm	Title	Norm	Title
Political Constitution of 1991[30]		Law 173 of 1994	Approves the Paris Convention for the Protection of Industrial Property.
Law 21 of 1991	Convention No. 169 on Indigenous People and Tribes in Independent Countries (Articles 23 and 25)[31]	Decree 1745 of 1995	Develops chapter 3 of Law 70 of 1993, adopts the recognition of the collective property of the land of Afro-Colombian communities and other dispositions.
Decision 344 of 1993	Common Regime on Industrial Property (substituted for by Decision 486).		
Decision 345 of 1993	Common Regime for the Protection of Plant Variety Breeders' Rights	Law 191 of 1995	Frontiers Law (Articles 3 and 8).[33]
Law 70 of 1993	Develops the 55th Transitory Article of the Constitution (black communities)	Law 243 of 1995	International Convention for the Protection of Plant Varieties.
		Decision 391 of 1996	Common Regime on Access to Genetic Resources.
Law 99 of 1993	Creates the MOE and Organizes the National Environmental System (Article 5 # 21).[33]	Decree 1397 of 1996	Creates the dNational Commission on Indigenous Territories and the Permanent Agreement table with the People and Indigenous Organizations (Article 12)[34]
Decree 117 of 1994	Develops Decision 344.		
Decree 533 of 1994	Develops the Common Regime on the Protection of Plant Varieties.		
Law 165 of 1994	Convention on Biological Diversity.	Law 463 of 1998	Approves the Cooperation Treaty in Patents.
Law 170 of 1994	Adopts an Agreement related to IPR issues related to Commerce.	Decision 486 of 2000	Common Regime on Industrial Property.

References

CAILLAUX, J., M. RUIZ, and B. TOBIN. 1999. *El Régimen Andino de Acceso a los Recursos Genéticos: Lecciones y experiencias.* SPDA, Lima, Perú and WRI, Washington DC USA.

CHAVES S., M.E. and N. ARANGO V. (eds.). 1997. *Informe Nacional Sobre el Estado de la Biodiversidad Colombia, 1997. Tomo I. Diversidad biológica.* Instituto Humboldt. Colombia.

COLUMBIA UNIVERSITY. 1999. *Access to genetic resources: An evaluation of the development and implementation of recent regulations and access agreements.* School of International and Public Affairs, Unpublished manuscript. Working paper # 4, prepared for the Biodiversity Action Network.

DNP. 1997. *Política Nacional de Biodiversidad, Colombia.* Departamento Nacional Planeación, Colombia.

FERREIRA P. and M.P. PARDO. 2001. *Estrategia de Colombia frente a la negociación de la Estrategia Andina en Biodiversidad. Documento de Soporte Técnico, Informe Final.* Unpublished manuscript. Comunidad Andina de Naciones, Ministerio de Medio Ambiente de Colombia.

FANDIÑO, M.C. and P. FERREIRA MIANI (eds.). 1998. *Colombia Biodiversidad Siglo XXI. Propuesta técnica para la formulación d un Plan de Acción Nacional en Biodiversidad.* Instituto Humboldt, Ministerio del Medio Ambiente, and Departamento Nacional Planeación, Colombia.

GTZ/FUNDECO/IE. 2001. *Acceso a recursos genéticos— Documento preliminar para revisión por parte de los países.* Manuscript. Comunidad Andina de Naciones, Estrategia Regional de Biodiversidad. Bolivia.

MINISTERIO DE COMERCIO EXTERIOR. 2001. Informe de avance del Plan Nacional de Desarrollo de Julio 2000 a Junio 2001. URL: http://www.mincomex.gov.co.

JUNTA ACUERDO DE CARTAGENA. 1994. *Hacia un marco legal para regular el acceso a los recursos genéticos en el Pacto Andino. Posibles elementos para una Decisión del Pacto Andino sobre acceso a los recursos genéticos.* Unpublished manuscript. Peru.

PARDO M.P. 1999a. *Biodiversidad: Análisis normativo y de competencias para Colombia.* Instituto Humboldt. Legis Editores, Colombia.

PARDO M.P. 1999b. *Compilación y análisis normativo sobre propiedad intelectual.* Unpublished manuscript. Instituto Humboldt. Colombia.

SÁNCHEZ E., M.P. PARDO, M. FLORES, and P. FERREIRA. 2000. *Protección del conocimiento tradicional. Elementos conceptuales para una propuesta de reglamentación—El caso de Colombia.* Unpublished manuscript. Instituto Humboldt. Colombia.

UNEP/CBD. 1998. Convention on Biological Diversity. UNEP/CBD/94/1. URL: http://www.biodiv.org/convention/articles.asp.

Endnotes

[1] The Andean Community, a subregional organization endowed with an international legal status, is made up of Bolivia, Ecuador, Venezuela, Peru and Colombia.

[2] The institute is linked to the MOE and is in charge of promoting, coordinating and undertaking research leading to the conservation and sustainable use of Colombia's biodiversity.

[3] The National Planning Department is the central government office responsible for designing and setting economic, social and environmental policies in coordination with other ministries and territorial entities.

[4] Separate sections will be used to describe and analyze policies and laws related to ABS due to the different nature and intent of these two instruments. Biodiversity related policies in Colombia are aimed at providing an orientation and defining actions from government and also from civil society regarding the conservation and sustainable use of biological resources. One of their main purposes is to group efforts from diverse societal interests regarding biodiversity. On the other hand, legislation defines rules that have the force of authority by virtue of their promulgation by an official branch of the state or other organizations. Even though laws and norms are set in a policy environment, they do not replace policies; they are mere policy instruments.

[5] Further information is available in the Andean Community web page at: http://www.comunidadandina.org.

[6] Since there is no official follow up on the implementation of the NBP or the NBSAP a precise report on their accomplishments cannot be provided. The information offered is largely based on the consultant's assessment and knowledge of the latest developments.

[7] As will be explained below, the Andean Community has agreed to develop a special regime or norm to strengthen the protection of traditional knowledge, innovations, and practices, as a stated in Decision 391 on ABS.

[8] Access is defined in Decision 391 as the obtainment and utilization of genetic resources conserved in *ex situ* or *in situ* conditions, of their derivatives, or, if it is the case, of its intangible components, with the purpose of research, bioprospecting, conservation, industrial application, or commercial use, among others.

[9] Genetic resources are defined in Decision 391 as all material of biological nature that contains genetic information of real or potential value or usefulness.

[10] Derivative product is defined by Decision 391 as molecules or a combination of natural molecules, including crude extracts of living or dead organisms of biological origin, coming from the metabolism of living beings.

[11] Intangible component is defined by Decision 391 as every knowledge, innovation, or practice, whether individual or collective, with real or potential value associated with the genetic resource, their derivative products, or the biological resource that contains them, whether protected or not by intellectual property regimes.

[12] The MOE can not delegate any functions to the Regional Corporations, either on this or any other topic. Nevertheless, it can make agreements with the Corporations to undertake supervision responsibilities under Decision 391 Article 50 or to participate in the process as National Support Institutions.

[13] No other laws or regulations have been formulated to facilitate the implementation of Decision 391. Decree 309 of 2000 modifies and renders null several previous regulations affecting scientific biodiversity research.

[14] Before promulgation of the Decree, separate permits were required for the activities that the decree regulates, often provided by diverse environmental authorities. The unification under a unique permit considerably simplifies the legal requirements for scientific research on biological resources.

[15] National support institution is defined by Decision 391 as a person or national legal entity dedicated to technical or scientific biological research that accompanies the access applicant and participates in the access activities. All access contracts requests must include the identification of the person or national support institution. Also, national support institutions must be approved by the NCA.

[16] Access resolution is defined by Decision 391 as the administrative act issued by the NCA that perfects the access to genetic resources and their derivative products, after having complied with all the prerequisites and conditions established in the access procedure.

[17] Nevertheless, the MOE has not developed monitoring procedures.

[18] Synthesized products are defined by Decision 391 as substances obtained by means of an artificial procedure from genetic information or from other biological molecules. It includes semi-processed extracts and substances obtained from a derivative product by an artificial process.

[19] It only indicates that the NCA will evaluate the request and will undertake the necessary inspections.

[20] Even though there is no government charge for the presentation of the access application, there are transaction costs involved due to the legal requirements and the length of the process. These transaction costs have not been calculated.

[21] A.M. Hernández, MOE, pers. comm., 5 February 2002.

[22] Colombian negotiators supported the FAO International Treaty on Plant Genetic Resources for Food and Agriculture and used the CBD and Decision 391 to back up their negotiation position. Colombia has not signed the treaty yet, and it has not been debated yet what the relationship with Decision 391 will be. In fact the MOE and the Humboldt Institute are currently researching this issue, which is unclear due to the *supra* national nature of Decision 391.

[23] Sociedad Peruana de Derecho Ambiental, a Peruvian think tank.

[24] This proposal was elaborated with the representation of indigenous organizations, Afro-Colombian communities, NGOs, Academic Centers, and central and regional government institutions.

[25] In fact, Law 99 of 1993 states that Colombia has the right of economic compensation for the use of its genetic resources.

[26] Decision 391 has not been necessarily an obstacle to access activities and research initiatives. They continue to take place without the required access contracts.

[27] A.M. Hernández, MOE, pers. comm. 5 February 2002.

[28] This problem is augmented in the Andean case due to the nature of Andean Decisions, which do not require going through congress before their adoption. This minimizes the debate, even though it may prevent a prolonged interest-oriented political debate.

[29] This difficulty may have appeared due to the nature of Andean negotiations that require the travel of numerous negotiators around the five Andean countries, increasing costs of meetings, etc.

[30] Articles 61, 150 # 24, 189 # 27. These articles are about IPR in general; they are not specific to biodiversity.

[31] These articles relate to traditional arts, rural industries, and health issues related indirectly to IPRs.

[32] This article is about the functions of the MOE regarding access to genetic resources, including the function given to the Ministry with respect to the rights of the nation over its genetic resources.

[33] These articles are about technology transfer to local, indigenous and Afro-Colombian communities (Article 3), and about the protection of traditional knowledge associated with genetic resources and the need to have prior informed consent before its use (Article 8).

[34] This article indicates the functions of the "permanent agreement table", including the adoption of principles, criteria, and procedures concerning protection of indigenous collective knowledge related to biodiversity and genetic resources; it also discusses and develops

5

Costa Rica:
Legal Framework and Public Policy

Jorge Cabrera-Medaglia

Access to genetic resources and the distribution of benefits were two of the most controversial topics debated in the development of the Convention on Biological Diversity (CBD). The sustainable use of genetic resources by means of bioprospecting or other forms of economic utilization (REID et al. 1993) represents for many an important promise to obtain economic benefits while insuring biodiversity conservation and the well being of local communities and indigenous peoples. Articles 3 and 15 of the CBD have reaffirmed countries' sovereignty over their own genetic resources and the right to regulate and facilitate access to those resources for environmentally sound uses. This has imposed upon countries, especially suppliers, an enormous responsibility.

This chapter provides basic information on the Costa Rican experience in the matter of access to genetic resources, distribution of benefits, and establishment of *sui generis* systems. In it I will examine and share the lessons and merits of the Costa Rican process of adoption and implementation of the Costa Rican national Law of Biodiversity.

The biological wealth in the tropical countries of our region and the alternatives for using genetic and biochemical resources and traditional knowledge constitute a day-by-day reality. The advances achieved in relation to organism exploration techniques and the feasibility of 'new biotechnologies' have opened the doors to a new vision of the 'hidden' values of our resources and traditional knowledge. Frequently, we hear about the interest of agrochemical, seed, and pharmaceutical companies in carrying out research using our natural wealth and traditional knowledge in their investigations. However,

based on the existing legal norms, access to Costa Rica's resources and knowledge should comply with the following requirements:

- Obtain prior informed consent (PIC) from the State and other stakeholders, including owners of traditional knowledge or biological, genetic, and biochemical resources.

- Include sharing of benefits generated from access to biodiversity and traditional knowledge by means of agreements or contracts that broadly embrace "mutually agreed terms".

- Promote biodiversity conservation and capacity building aimed at adding value to each country's natural resources.

These requirements do not deal only with controlling the access to biological, genetic, and biochemical resources. They deal with the fact that (in compliance with the prevailing regulatory standards) the traditional knowledge, innovations, and practices of local communities and indigenous peoples must also be protected in the countries of our region. Modern societies acknowledge that for centuries most indigenous peoples have developed their own agricultural systems, practices and knowledge, plague-fighting methods, handling of natural resources, and traditional medicine and that this knowledge is undoubtedly valuable and useful for those in other sectors of society who are not the intellectual creators and developers of those practices.

For many years, biological diversity, traditional works aimed at improving animal life and cultivation, and indigenous knowledge involved in these activities were considered a public good and a "Common Heritage of Mankind". Nevertheless, based on the genetic resources freely obtained, a great variety of natural products were developed such as new vegetable varieties, pharmaceutical products, and pesticides, which were classified as private property and subject to intellectual property rights (IPRS) (basically, plant breeders' rights, patents, and trade secrets). In this way, natural products based on free genetic resources were available at a high cost for developing countries. The asymmetry of this relationship between genetic resources that were freely provided by the South and the final products using those resources that could only be acquired at a certain price from the companies of the North should have been justified in some manner.

This asymmetry resulted from the application of a concept that allows for the extraction of our countries' genetic wealth without granting any compensation. This concept stated that biological diversity was considered the common heritage of mankind; that is, it was declared a public good and no payment should be made for its use. Naturally, pesticides, medicines, and improved seeds belong to the private sector and were not affected by this concept.

Simultaneous with the rising international consciousness rejecting the concept of the common heritage of mankind, the advance of modern biotechnology (such as the recombining of DNA and cellular fusion) are advances in the field of microelectronic technical screening of biological materials that have strengthened the interest of many pharmaceutical, chemical, and biotechnology companies and seed producers in the wild or domesticated genetic resources and traditional knowledge of indigenous peoples and local communities.

Identification of Relevant Access Laws and Policies

Key Features of Laws and Policies and Current Status of Implementation.

The national legislation that regulates access to genetic material, biochemical resources, and traditional knowledge for the whole country is the Law of Biodiversity (LB), No. 7788 of 30 April 1998. Before the enactment of this law, there were some provisions in the Law of Wildlife Conservation (LWC) No. 7317 of 21 October 1992 regarding flora and fauna collection permits. There were also some bylaws dealing with research, specifically referring to national parks. No modern regulations on agricultural materials existed at the time. Currently, there is a General Access Procedure (GAP) in place that will function as a bylaw of the LB. The GAP was approved on 15 December 2003 by the Minister of Environment and Energy and the President through an executive decree. The GAP was proposed by the National Commission for the Management of Biodiversity (CONAGEBIO) in conformity with LB Article 62 with the participation of personnel of the National System of Conservation Areas (SINAC)[1], universities, nongovernmental organizations (NGOs), and industry.

In relation to access policies, there is a National Biodiversity Strategy that contemplates a set of actions to be taken in the area of access to genetic resources.[2] Additionally, there is a National Environmental Policy draft (Conservation and Sustainable Development Strategy) that includes biodiversity as one of its components, in particular the topic of access to genetic resources and distribution of benefits. Finally, SINAC concluded a National Research Strategy that would be applicable to its officials and to joint ventures between SINAC officials and officials from other entities wishing to access genetic resources for research purposes.

During the development of the LB, a series of topics were considered for the formulation of the dispositions relative to access, distribution of benefits, and protection of traditional knowledge. These included basic definitions, scope, the procedure for prior informed consent (PIC), mutually agreed terms, competent authority, distribution of benefits, and sanctions. Some relevant topics such as the need to distinguish between access with agricultural or pharmaceutical purposes or between research with commercial or academic purposes and the need of prompt and special mechanisms for *ex situ* collections were scarcely considered. These areas constitute some of the deficiencies of the legislation that must be corrected with appropriate regulations.

The LB, whose application and interpretation still remains uncertain in several areas, sets up the basis for access permits and contracts. The law contains clear definitions on crucial topics (LB Article 7) such as access to biochemical and genetic elements, bioprospecting, PIC, innovation, and access permits. Likewise, it has clarified the genetic and biochemical resources property regime by stating that these resources belong in the public domain to be managed by the State (LB Article 6). Also, two types of properties were distinguished: that of the biological or organic resource and that of the genetic and biochemical resource.

According to LB Article 117, the law has been fully in force since its publication in April 1998. However, an action to declare this law unconstitutional was brought by the Attorney General's Office. This claim was admitted for study by the Constitutional Chamber (Unconstitutionality Action Number 98-006524-007-CO-M, admitted by October 1998 Resolution). According to Articles 81 and 82 of the Law of the Constitutional Jurisdiction No. 7135, the suit does not suspend the execution of the LB. However, from the political point of view it has definitely delayed implementation of CONAGEBIO.

This action was brought specifically against LB Articles 14 and 22. In relation to access, Article 14 is of supreme importance. It creates the CONAGEBIO, one purpose of which is to define the national policies for biodiversity, including access to genetic resources. The chapters dealing with access to genetic resources (procedural and substantive aspects) have not been questioned. As a consequence, if the action succeeds it would only affect the legal competencies of CONAGEBIO in this matter, not the remainder of the applicable dispositions.

The Ministry of Environment and Energy (MINAE) considered these legal competencies unconstitutional; thus the Ministry requested the Attorney General to submit a constitutional challenge. Fundamentally, the following powers have been questioned:

- CONAGEBIO's legal authority to formulate national policies and to coordinate them (clauses 1, 2, 3, 4, and 5 of LB Article 14) and its authority to exhaust the administrative route in case of challenges presented against the resolutions of the Technical Office (TO) of the Commission (clause 6 of LB Article 14). In both cases this would run counter to the exclusive power of the Executive Branch in these areas.

- Independent management of public funds (as provided by LB Articles 19 and 20), running counter to Articles 121, 176, and 180 of the Constitution.

As indicated, the constitutional challenge, although not preventing the implementation of the regulations, has had the effect of slowing down many of the necessary decisions to make the law operational. For example, the CONAGEBIO was not put into effect until January 2000, almost two years later than initially foreseen by the law. Equally, there is a legitimate concern that if the action succeeds, CONAGEBIO's role could turn out to be that of a simple adviser and not a public policy maker. To date, the action has not been resolved by the Constitutional Chamber.[3]

Scope of the LB, Exceptions and Specific Treatment for Some Sectors

The legislation is applied "...on the elements of the biodiversity under the State's sovereignty, as well as on the processes and the activities carried out under its jurisdiction or control, independently of whether the effects of the actions are manifested inside or outside the national jurisdiction". The LB will regulate specifically the use, management, associated knowledge, and distribution of benefits and costs derived from the utilization of the elements of the biodiversity (LB Article 3). LB Article 6 establishes that "The biochemical and genetic properties of the components of biodiversity, wild or domesticated, belong to the public domain. The State will authorize the exploration, research, bioprospecting, and use of the components of biodiversity which constitute part of the public domain, as well as the utilization of all the genetic and biochemical resources, by means of the rules of access established in chapter v of this law." Also, in conformity with LB Articles 62 and 69, every research program or bioprospecting effort on genetic material carried out in Costa Rican territory requires an access permit, unless covered by one of the exceptions foreseen by the LB.

These exceptions (LB Article 4) refer fundamentally to access to human genetic resources and the exchange of genetic and biochemical resources that are part of traditional practices of indigenous peoples and local communities and that have a commercial purpose. In addition, public universities were exempted from control for a term of one year (until 7 May 1999) in order for them to establish their own controls and regulations for noncommercial projects that require access. Apart from this, all the remaining sectors (pharmaceutical, agriculture, biotechnology, ornamental, and medicinal herbs) are subject to the LB and must follow its access procedures. There is only one access procedure to be followed by all users. The GAP regulates access for commercial and noncommercial bioprospecting (including teaching), occasional economic utilization, constant use of genetic and biochemical resources, and traditional knowledge. The law indicates that a concession will be required in case of access to genetic resources for commercial use, without defining steps or requirements.

The LB is applied equally to genetic agricultural resources. It establishes the possibility of fixing, by means of a separate regulation, the procedures for access permits to the *ex situ* collections duly registered before the TO of CONAGEBIO (LB Article 69). To a great extent, access to genetic agricultural resources is realized by means of *ex situ* collections, though in Costa Rica there are some requests to make use of agricultural resources found *in situ*.

The LB foresees specifically that in the case of duly registered *ex situ* collections, the regulation of the law will set the authorization procedure for access permits (LB Article 69). It would include any type of collection. The above-mentioned procedure was supposed to be determined by means of the GAP. However, the draft still does not have rules on this point. On the contrary, the GAP establishes a moratorium on the access to genetic resources found in *ex situ* conditions, unless the specific regulations are approved. The GAP provided six months for the drafting of these regulations. These regulations are especially complex due to the institutional structures that keep genetic resources in *ex situ* conditions. Furthermore, other applicable dispositions to *ex situ* collections can be found in different regulations, without direct relation to access, but in relation to conservation and maintenance (e.g., see the decree of creation of the National Commission of Plant Genetic Resources, No. 18661-MAG of 9 September 1988 and the Law of Seeds No. 6289 of 4 December 1978 and its bylaw). There is no official record of the *ex situ* collections in the country.

As mentioned, the LB applies to all the elements of biodiversity found under the sovereignty of the State (LB Article 3) and to all basic research and commercial bioprospecting projects conducted in Costa Rican territory (LB Article 69). In this respect, access regulations are applied to genetic resources in public or private land, terrestrial or marine environments, *ex situ* or *in situ* collections, and indigenous territories.[4] Nevertheless, there are some omissions relative to resources in marine areas. Hence, other legal rules can be applicable to obtain access to these biological resources. Specifically, the Costa Rican Institute of Fishing and Aquaculture (IFA) is the entity entrusted with granting fishing licenses, including research permits, but excluding permits for resources found in marine regions of wild protected areas (Law of Creation of IFA No. 7384 of 29 March 1994, Article 5 and Attorney General's Opinion C-215-95 of 22 September 1995). In this case, access permits by the TO are also required. Regarding access to indigenous land there are other applicable laws, besides the LB, such as the Convention on Indigenous Peoples of the International Labor Organization and the rules of the *sui generis* system of intellectual community rights that are being developed through a consultation process that began recently.

Monitoring Mechanisms

The LB creates a self-governed CONAGEBIO (LB Article 14) as a separate legal entity, but belonging to the MINAE. CONAGEBIO's duties include: To formulate the policies and responsibilities established in LB chapters IV, V, and VI. Furthermore, it has to coordinate these policies with the relevant institutions. Additionally, it has to formulate and coordinate the policy for access to elements of biodiversity and associated knowledge, ensuring a suitable transference of science and technology, as well as the distribution of benefits, which are general procedures under Title V of the LB.

CONAGEBIO will execute its agreements and resolutions and will design its internal procedures by means of its TO's Executive Director (LB Article 16). The composition of CONAGEBIO is set forth in LB Article 15: MINAE, which presides over it, the Ministries of Agriculture, of Health, and of Foreign Trade, SINAC, IFA, the National Small Farmers Board, the National Indigenous Peoples Board, National Council of Rectors, the Costa Rican Federation for the Conservation of the Environment (FECON), and the Costa Rican Union of Chambers of Commerce. NGOs are represented by FECON. The National Biodiversity Institute (INBIO) is not a member of the CONAGEBIO.

In addition, CONAGEBIO must formulate policies on access and distribution of benefits. It can also revoke the TO's resolutions regarding access matters (LB Article 14). In conformity with LB Article 62, CONAGEBIO must propose policies on access to genetic and biochemical resources of *ex situ* and *in situ* biodiversity. It will also act as an obligatory consultant in procedures related to the protection of IPRS on biodiversity.

The Executive Director will appoint CONAGEBIO's TO, as well as other personnel indicated in the regulation of the LB. The TO will grant or deny access requests (LB Article 17, clause a); coordinate access issues with conservation areas, the private sector, indigenous peoples, and rural communities (LB Article 17, paragraph b); organize and keep an updated record of access requests and *ex situ* collections, as well as a record of the individuals and legal entities that devote themselves to genetic manipulation (paragraph c); and compile and update regulations relative to the fulfillment of its agreements and directives (paragraph d).

The TO has not been established due to lack of budget, personnel, constitutional action, and political will. Nevertheless, CONAGEBIO's budget in 2002 was $250,000 USD, which allowed for the establishment of an Executive Director and some support personnel such as a secretary, a technician, an attorney, and a bookkeeper.

CONAGEBIO's activities are regulated by means of MINAE decree No. 29680, published in The Gazette of 7 August 2001, and its modifications. Its members are designated for a two-year period. The Commission's responsibilities include granting of access permits and implementation of monitoring and evaluation procedures. To date, evaluation and monitoring procedures have not been carried out because of the lack of implementation of LB. Due to absence of human and technical resources, it is improbable that these monitoring procedures will be implemented in the short run. Probably, those who undertake the access procedure will be subject to monitoring for the obligations assumed under the PIC agreement and the TO's resolution approving their access permit.

Evaluation of Commercial and Noncommercial Bioprospecting Initiatives

According to LB Article 71 (characteristics and conditions of access permits), the access requirements will be determined differently depending on whether the research has or does not have a commercial purpose. In the latter case, the noncommercial purpose will have to be verified. Nevertheless, the GAP does not contemplate different requirements for bioprospecting projects with commercial and noncommercial purposes in spite of the fact that GAP Article 9 (permits for basic research) establishes that if a project has commercial purposes, the interested party will have to fulfill additional requirements. In general, there is no clarity on the form this distinction would take. This issue has been a constant in the critiques of diverse regulations and reports, as in the case of The Philippines' Executive Order on Bioprospecting, as well as in the conclusions of the CBD's Experts Panel on Access to Genetic Resources.

Main Characteristics of the Law of Biodiversity

Main Steps Outlined by the LB

The LB regulates the basic requirements for access, including the PIC, transfer of technology, equitable distribution of benefits, the protection of associated knowledge, and the definition of the ways in which the above-mentioned activities will contribute to the conservation of species and ecosystems. It also mandates the designation of a legal representative in the country, when the person or organization requesting access is domiciled abroad (LB Article 63). The procedure to follow is clearly outlined in LB Article 64. It includes proof of the PIC of the owner of the property where the activity will be developed, whether it is an indigenous community, a private owner, or public entity. Other interesting provisions incorporate the right of cultural objection (LB Article 66), the registry of access applications, and the protection of confidential information, except in the case of biosafety concerns (LB Article 67).

The LB also regulates in detail commercial and non-commercial bioprospecting permits (Article 69). These are valid for three years and can be renewed. They are given to specific persons or entities and are therefore not transferable. The permits are limited to the genetic and biochemical elements expressly authorized for specific areas or territories (LB Article 70). The permits will contain a certificate of origin, permission or prohibition to extract samples, periodic reporting obligation, monitoring and control, conditions relative to resulting property, and any another applicable condition deemed relevant by the TO (LB Article 71).

The access request requirements are name and identification of the interested party, name and identification of the responsible researcher, exact location of the place, and the elements of biodiversity that will be the subject of the investigation, indicating the owner and manager or holder of the premises. The applicant will also have to submit a descriptive chronology of activities, aims, and purposes as well as place for legal notifications. The application must be accompanied by the PIC (LB Article 72) and a record of individuals or legal entities who are to conduct the bioprospecting (LB Article 73). The TO must also authorize those agreements contemplating access to genetic and biochemical elements (LB Article 74) signed between individuals, natives, or foreigners, or between them and the institutions registered for such purposes. There is also a possibility to establish framework agreements with universities and other duly authorized centers (LB Article 74). It is established that up to 10% of the research budget and 50% of royalties will have to go to the conservation area, the private owner, or indigenous community (LB Article 76). In cases in which the TO authorizes the continuing use of genetic material or of biochemical extracts for commercial purposes, applicants are required to obtain a separate concession from the interested party (LB Article 75). There are no further guidelines in the LB

about the process, requirements, and length of time needed to obtain this concession (Figure 1).

First, in conformity with access procedure norms, interested parties must register with the TO using a specific form (LB Article 12). Later, the PIC must be negotiated in conformity with a guide which stipulates the minimal points for discussion (LB Article 19) between the applicant and owner of the conservation area or indigenous land, resources, or *ex situ* collections. This would include not only individuals, but other government entities such as municipal governments, the Agrarian Development Institute, and the IFA.

The PIC is supposed to contain mutually agreed-upon terms that represent the fair and equitable distribution of benefits. Once obtained, this agreement must be endorsed by the TO. Even though the legislation is not clear, it is assumed that the PIC will be formalized in a private contract. The TO limits itself to endorsing the contract rather than negotiating it. The TO's approval authorizes three fundamental aspects: the PIC's fulfillment of the requirements established in the Technical Guide, the number of samples to be taken, and the time frame for the reports to be presented (LB Article 13).

A request form and completed Technical Guide (LB Article 9) must be submitted to the TO. In both cases there are requirements and documents that must be presented jointly. Additionally, the documents established in GAP Article 14 must be attached. Additional requirements are established for those who request permits for basic research or bioprospecting (GAP Article 9.4) and for those who need access permits for occasional or continuing economic utilization (GAP Article 9.5).

LB Article 76 requires a determination of the administrative fee. The GAP also refers to this payment (GAP Article 27 on administrative rates). After the TO extends a certificate of origin (GAP Article 19), it proceeds to publish the requests and final resolutions on its website within eight calendar days (GAP Article 15).

Once access is authorized, the monitoring and control phase begins (GAP Article 20) at the expense of the TO and in coordination with the authorized representatives of the place where access to the resources is taking place. Applicants will have to follow applicable sanitary and phytosanitary rules for the exportation of the materials.[5]

In case of *ex situ* collections, special rules may be established allowing framework agreements that authorize the transfer of multiple materials. In such cases Material Transfer Agreements would have to be duly standardized and approved by the TO. The TO's resolutions can be revoked or appealed by the CONAGEBIO (GAP Article 16).

Finally an environmental impact assessment (EIA) can be requested by the TO based on some general provisions of the LB related to EIA, but not specific to bioprospecting activities (LB Article 92). The evaluation is the responsibility of the National Technical Secretariat (a body of MINAE).

To date no EIA has been requested of INBio or any other bioprospector.

At this early stage the approximate duration of the above procedures is unknown. The current system is based on the LWC No. 7317 of 21 October 1992 and its regulation No. 26435-MINAE of 3 December 1997, as well as permits for flora and wildlife collection (LWC Article 36 and subsequent articles). These collection permits are granted by SINAC after the submission of an administrative form and a consultation in the conservation area where the research and collection will take place. This procedure is relatively simple and takes approximately one month for processing.

Up to now, SINAC has had only five full-time employees, untrained in the topic of the bioprospecting agreement negotiations. Research permits are being granted by the SINAC Director. LB Article 18 establishes that the Executive Director of the TO must be a suitable profes-sional, without any further specifications and LB Article 16 allows CONAGEBIO to name *ad hoc* expert committees in complex cases.

In any case, the current scheme would leave the ne-gotiation of contracts (by means of the PIC), in the hands of the managers of conservation areas and eventually of other public authorities, insofar as they are the owners of the lands or of the biological resources.

Characteristics of the Access Requirements

The procedures for access are not completely clear, espe-cially under the GAP. On the other hand, the requirements are clearly established in Articles 63 and 72 of the LB, as well as in the GAP's Articles 9 to 20. Only the TO and eventually the CONAGEBIO shall grant access permits. A separate PIC should be obtained from other entities such

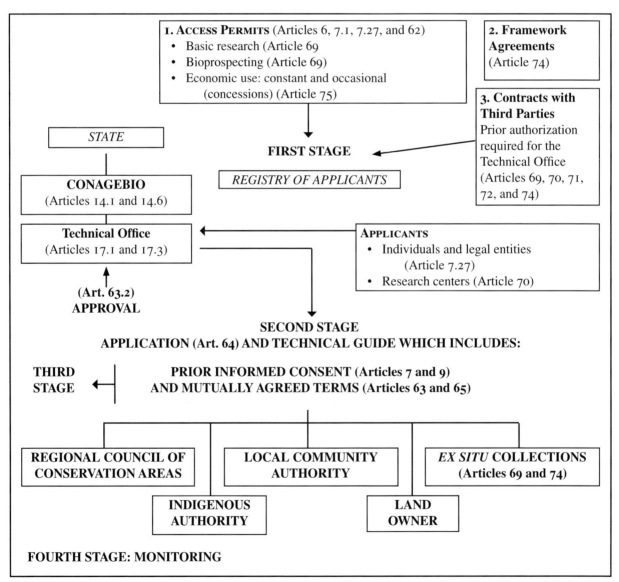

Figure 1. Access procedure.

as conservation areas, indigenous territories or public authorities who are owners of lands, or, in the case of marine resources, other authorities such as IFA.

In this respect, access to flora and fauna found on private lands would eventually need other authorizations from state entities like the MINAE, particularly in cases of species in danger of extinction or with reduced populations. Access would be granted in conformity with the technical and scientific arrangements stated by SINAC. Thus, even if the flora were in private lands (e.g., orchids), the SINAC would give the permits for the manipulation of the resource (LWC No. 7317, Articles 14, 18, and 25 and its regulation No. 26435, Article 20.). In such a case it is not clear whether there should be a double authorization: from the TO for the genetic resource and from the SINAC for the biological one, as well as the landlord's consent regarding private property.

In cases where collections are made in conservation areas, the PIC and the respective agreement are enough to obtain the access permit. The main difficulties arise when there is a question of privately owned wild, threatened flora.

All interested parties can access genetic and biochemical resources. Nevertheless, GAP's Article 24 establishes the following "Criteria for the evaluation or approval of the request" based on the public environmental interest criteria embodied in the LB (Article 11.3):

- Development options for future generations;
- Food safety and sovereignty;
- Conservation of ecosystems;
- Protection of human health;
- Improvement of citizens' quality of life;
- Gender issues; and
- IPRS not affecting key agricultural products and processes for the nourishment and health of the country's inhabitants. This criterion also includes protection for the resources of local communities and indigenous populations.

Also, GAP's Article 24 allows the imposition of total or partial restrictions on access to the resources to ensure their conservation and sustainable use. These restrictions are issued by the TO in the resolution approving access. In this way, it can prohibit access, set limits, and regulate the methods of collection, in application of the precautionary principle mentioned in LB's Article 11.2. To establish complete or partial restrictions some of the elements that will be considered are:

- The danger of extinction of the species, subspecies, races, and varieties.
- Reasons of scarcity and endemic conditions.
- Vulnerability or fragility conditions in the structure or function of the ecosystems.
- Adverse effects on human health, the species, and the ecosystems or on essential elements of

the autonomy or cultural identity of peoples and communities.

- Strategic genetic resources or geographical areas qualified as such.
- The prohibition of access for military purposes or for denaturalization of the resources.

Relationship to Other Laws

In theory it is possible to foresee some reforms to other national laws as a result of new access regulations. Reforms to the Patent Law may be made to include the presentation of the certificate of origin in cases where an invention using genetic resources or traditional knowledge is being patented. Some similar regulations may be necessary in the Plant Breeders' Rights draft that is currently being discussed in the Legislative Assembly. Eventually, the LB's dispositions on patentability exclusions (Article 78) might be integrated with the Law of Patents (see below).

Some laws that govern asssccess to biological resources, such as LWC or Law of the IFA, might be reformed to establish the necessary coordination between the access permit to genetic resources and the access permit to biological resources (wild flora and fauna are in some cases marine resources), with the intention of simplifying the steps and respective procedures to obtain access.

The laws relative to customs control (General Customs Law No. 7557 of 8 November 1995) and the export of sanitary or phytosanitary material (Phytosanitary Protection Law), could be reformed to include a clause like the one stated by Decision 391 (Common Regime on Access to Genetic Resources of the Andean Community), which expressly mentions that the authorization to export biological material does not imply the authorization for the use of the genetic component (Fourth Complementary Disposition). There could be a need to reform the Phytosanitary Protection Law as it deals with other topics such as biosafety.

Provisions that Promote the Conservation of Biodiversity, its Sustainable Use, and the Fair Sharing of Benefits Derived from Biodiversity

The LB was designed to implement the CBD in Costa Rica. LB Articles 15, 16, and 19 are of paramount importance in access to genetic resources. The LB established that, without prejudice to the fulfillment of regulations relative to the trade of endangered species of flora and fauna, the application of sanitary and phytosanitary measures and technical procedures and biosafety, the disposition on access to genetic resources will constitute neither a concealed restriction nor an obstacle to trade (LB Article 68, general rule of interpretation). There are also similarities between LB and other laws such as the LWC, the Law of the IFA, the Law of Phytosanitary Protection No. 7664 and its regulation No. 26921-MAG, and the Convention on

International Trade of Endangered Species, Law No. 5605 of 22 October 1974.

The general goal of the LB is to promote the conservation and sustainable use of biodiversity and to ensure the fair and equitable sharing of benefits derived from it (Article 1). The entire LB responds to this goal as put forth by the CBD. For example, it establishes the environmental function of the land (Article 8), general principles of the law (Article 9), objectives (Article 10), criteria for applying the law (Article 11), SINAC's administrative structure (including the administration of the national wild protected areas, Articles 22 to 43), the guarantee of environmental safety (biosafety and exotic organisms, Articles 44 to 48), the conservation and the sustainable use of the ecosystems and species (Articles 49 to 61), the regulations on access to genetic resources (Articles 62 to 76), IPRS (Articles 77 to 85), education and public awareness and research and transfer of technology (Articles 86 to 91), environmental impact assessment (Articles 92 to 97), incentives (Articles 98 to 104), and procedures and sanctions (Articles 105 to 113). All of these elements are in accordance with the three objectives of the CBD.

Specifically relating to access, LB Article 63 also mentions the transfer of technology and equitable distribution of benefits, the protection of associated knowledge, and the definition of the ways in which the project's activities will contribute to the conservation of species and ecosystems. Other regulations mentioned in LB Article 76 also contain parameters for distribution of benefits. All monetary and nonmonetary benefits to be distributed are not listed but a generic rule is set forth with some specific indications regarding royalties, operation budget (Article 76), and technology transfer (Articles 63 and 76).

There are no binding requirements that benefits must go towards the conservation of the resources. It is perfectly possible that a private owner, public institution, or indigenous territory could grant the PIC without allocating benefits towards conservation since the legal authority of the TO is limited to endorsement. In these circumstances, it is valid to ask whether the TO would have the legal authority to revoke a previous consent because of a lack of benefits towards conservation derived from the access (Article 63). As one might expect, in those cases in which a conservation area grants the permits, it is assumed that the benefit will go in its entirety towards biodiversity conservation.

Analysis of the Process that Led to the Development of the LB

The formulation process of the LB and the discussion of matters related to access, the protection of associated knowledge, and IPRS are particularly relevant. The first draft of the LB was developed in 1996. It generated a negative reaction from different stakeholders that considered it to be especially restrictive and opposed to both the public good and scientific research. Multiple suggestions were made to the Legislative Assembly, including a complete new draft prepared by the Advisory Commission on Biodiversity which was never formally incorporated by the legislative course (CABRERA MEDAGLIA 1999).

The second draft of the law appeared in January 1997. Even though this draft considered several of the objections made to the first draft, it also repeated several of the concepts and dispositions stated by the first version of the document. Therefore, it met with the same opposition. This situation led to the creation of a Special Commission in the Legislative Assembly. Its mandate was to create a new draft, taking into consideration the old one. The Assembly promised to respect the outcome.

The Commission, led by the National University, was installed in April 1997. It included the main political parties (National Liberation and Social Christian Unity), the Advisory Commission on Biodiversity (COABIO), the National Small Farmers Forum, the National Indigenous Forum, the Union of Chambers for Private Business, the University of Costa Rica (with two representatives), the National University (with two representatives), FECON, and INBio. The group was composed of twelve representatives and their alternates, named by sectors including the nongovernmental sector, representatives of indigenous peoples and farmers, the private sector, the academic sector, and the government (by means of the Advisory Commission on Biodiversity). The Special Commission met until December 1997 when the new draft was sent to the Parliament. It received the favorable opinion of the Parliament's Commission on Environment, and after minor modifications, the text was finally adopted as law. It was published in The Gazette, the Official Diary, in May 1998 and entered into force as law of the republic the same year. As mentioned before this was comprehensive legislation and access was only one of the topics covered. No foreign consultants participated in this process.

Main Difficulties and Successes Experienced During the Design of the LB

The most controversial aspects of the process can be summarized in the following points:

- There was disagreement about the access process and the entity entrusted with granting the permits and authorizations. Diverse sectors thought that the current system, with authorizations granted by the SINAC, was inappropriate and should have had a wider representation. It was alleged that the SINAC's close relationship to INBio might put the permits into question. These groups argued that the creation of a wider Commission to deal with access and related topics (e.g., National Biodiversity Strategy and CBD negotiations), integrated with diverse sectors, would propitiate a more suitable space and greater credibility concerning the control of the state over genetic resources.

- The public character of the genetic resources made them subject to a public property regime, independent of private ownership of the land where they were located, and created legal consequences to the rights of applicants of access.

- TO's approval of contracts and agreements that INBio had previously signed with national and foreign companies created problems which will be described later in this report.

- The integration of procedures regarding intellectual property with the procedures of the LB, since diverse exclusions have been established (Article 78), needs to be accomplished. The compatibility of some of these exclusions with the Agreement on Trade Related Aspects of Intellectual Property Rights (TRIPS) is debatable.

- There was opposition between those who considered access as a way of legitimizing biopiracy and those who, on the contrary, were defending the mechanism as a way to promote the sustainable use of the genetic and biochemical resources.

- The LB involved wide public participation in its design process, a necessity in a matter affecting the activities and interests of many sectors. The law functioned as a comprehensive initiative to deal with different challenges imposed by the CBD, such as access, technology transfer, *ex situ* and *in situ* conservation, biosafety, environmental impact assessment, education, and public awareness.

- There was a lack of information and participation by some groups such as indigenous communities, peasants, and private sectors, who were only able to express their points of view in relation to certain specific issues. It became clear that capacity building in the design of these legal frameworks is critical. The lack of sufficient information on comparable international experiences also pre-vented an understanding of real difficulties found elsewhere.

- There was a need for both open discussion on topics of national interest that affect many different interested parties and eliminating the habit of deciding these issues by a small group.

- Due to the fact that the main policy aspects of the negotiation were included in the law, while the operative aspects were deferred to the by-laws (due to the representative character of the Legislative Assembly versus the regulatory duty of the Executive Power), the drafting process dealt with the main topics and their complexities without reference to a discussion of the regulations.

The most troubling points were solved through a process of negotiation, but due to time constraints to achieve an agreement, many of the points were sent to the Parliament's Plenary without a final resolution. On the other hand, some of the most controversial aspects, such as IPRs, were strongly debated by the business and academic representatives in a Special Subcommittee in charge of drafting the law. Other aspects, such as the public character of genetic resources and the existence of a CONAGEBIO, were accepted, under different proposals. For example, the CONAGEBIO would work through a TO composed of government employees who would make the legal decisions, with power of review at the expense of the Commission. In order to ensure the TO's independence, a maximum self-government statute was granted to it.

Some of the patentability exclusions were eliminated and others remained, in spite of warnings on their possible unconstitutionality. Finally, the public character of the resources was accepted. This point still provoked protest and review by representatives of the farmers' sector, who even considered the possibility of asking for a hearing by the Department of Technical Services of the Parliament. Eventually, this Department decided to reject this submission.

Although the access process was simplified in relation to the first proposal, some of the most controversial dispositions were kept, such as the TO's power of reviewing contracts with third parties (LB Article 76). Some of the difficulties and incongruities that became apparent after approval, were problems that had been pointed out by the members of the CONAGEBIO during the drafting process of the GAP.

Main Obstacles to the Completion of the LB

There was a lack of information on access. In spite of the fact that some members of the Commission had experience in the matter, several of the interested sectors were only able to formulate very general positions that did not include the range of topics that access entails. Some academic, indigenous, rural, and entrepreneurial sectors, as well as political party representatives, made general statements, but when the moment for deeper technical debates arose, these stakeholders were not prepared to make concrete propositions.

There were time limitations for completing the draft of law and sending it to the Legislative Assembly. Due to time constraints imposed by Parliamentary procedures for approval of laws and the need to submit a final text, topics were sent to the Parliament's Plenary. This prevented a real discussion of the some of the most controversial and relevant aspects.

The legislation needed to be comprehensive. Since the LB covered the multiple mandates expressed by the CBD, the possibility of dedicating sufficient time and effort to access to genetic resources was diminished due to the need to finalize a comprehensive draft (more than 117 articles).

Stakeholder involvement was of primary importance.

Probably one of the most relevant elements of the elaboration process was the opportunity granted to different interested groups, such as the indigenous populations and farmers, to take part in the negotiating process. It was an exercise on how processes work in reality, especially in those cases in which opposite points of view exist. Additionally, this procedure allowed a real exercise of environmental democracy in a strategic area of national development.

There were internal difficulties within participating stakeholder groups. During the negotiation several proposals and issues arose on which representatives had to consult their constituencies. For example, the representatives of the industry sector stated that they would not vote for any of the proposals but would limit themselves to taking part in the debates of the Commission, since they were incapable of negotiating on behalf of all their associates.

Identification and Analysis of the Difficulties and Successes in the Implementation of the LB

In spite of the fact that the LB was adopted in 1998, it has not been implemented due to the action of unconstitutionality filed against it. Neither have the positions within the TO nor access procedures that would function as regulations of the law been created. For this reason there have been no requests. Informally, several access requests have been submitted, but none have been processed or resolved.

The informal requests made to date are:

- University of Wisconsin, Madison requested the right to gather wild potato material in some areas of the Bi-National Park "La Amistad". This group withdrew their request since they could not get any response from Panama where they also wanted to collect.

- The Firenze Institute, Italy requested access to "Cyanobacterias". Only a preliminary document was submitted and no follow-up communications were obtained.

- The National University requested access to wild material of the *Sechium* genus in some protected areas and in an *ex situ* collection. The response is pending.

To date, the requests involving bioprospecting, namely those of INBio, are dealt with in accordance with the cooperation agreement between INBio and the MINAE, and with regard to conservation areas, by means of the LWC.

Bioprospecting Projects

INBio's Biodiversity Prospecting Program[6]

INBio was created in 1989 as a nongovernmental and nonprofit association. Its mission is to promote a new awareness of the value of biodiversity in order to achieve its conservation and use it to improve the quality of life.

In 1991, INBio developed the concept and practice of "bioprospecting" as one of the answers to the need for the sustainable use of Costa Rican biodiversity to benefit society. This concept, which refers to the systematic search for new biological sources of chemical compounds, genes, proteins, microorganisms, and other products that possess a current economic value or potential, continues to gain acceptance in government, scientific, academic, and managerial circles. The use of the biodiversity presents opportunities and challenges to promote and to organize the infrastructure investments and human resources that add value and contribute to its conservation.

INBio has a formal agreement with MINAE, which allows carrying out specific activities related to the identification and use of biodiversity in the government's protected areas. INBio actively develops biodiversity prospecting in the protected wild areas of the country under that agreement, with the participation of the national and international academic and private sector. Research is carried out in collaboration with research centers, universities, and national and international private companies, by means of research agreements that include key elements, such as:

- Access that is limited in time and quantity.
- Equity and compensation.
- Research budget.
- Benefit sharing.
- Technology transfer.
- Nondestructive activities.

The agreements also called for up-front payment for conservation. They specify that 10% of the research budgets and 50% of the future royalties shall be donated to MINAE to be reinvested in conservation (Table 1). The research budget supports the scientific infrastructure in the country, as well as activities of added value aimed at conservation and sustainable use of biodiversity. Until now no royalties have been paid nor has any product reached the market, but there are some products under development, particularly in the ornamental and herbal areas.

INBio Agreements with Industry

A brief summary of the most outstanding research agreements to date including the benefits accrued to INBio is as follows:

INBio-Merck Agreement: Search for Sustainable Uses of the Costa Rican Biodiversity. Signed in October 1991, this was the first agreement with a commercial company to search for sustainable uses of Costa Rican biodiversity with potential for the pharmaceutical industry and veterinary science. It was renewed in 1994, 1996, and 1998 upon similar terms and expired in 1999. The agreement covered the study of a limited number of extracts of plants, insects, and environmental samples to determine their potential use. The agreement has given INBio access to technology, technical expertise, and training.

Chemical Prospecting in a Costa Rican Conservation Area. This project began in 1993 and ended in September 1999. It is one of the five International Cooperative Biodiversity Groups (ICBGs) financed by three units in the USA: the National Institutes of Health (NIH), the National Science Foundation, and the Department of Agriculture. It was located in the Guanacaste Conservation Area and was carried out in collaboration with the University of Costa Rica, Cornell University, and Bristol Myers Squibb. Its objectives were to incorporate tropical insects in the search for new pharmaceutical products and to increase the capacity of human resources in the fields of ecology, taxonomy, and ecochemistry.

INBio-Givaudan Roure Agreement: Fragrances and Aromas. In 1995, as a result of the constant search for new options, INBio began an association with the company Givaudan Roure to explore potential fragrances and aromas from Costa Rican biodiversity. These fragrances and aromas were taken directly from the air surrounding fragrant objects in the forest. The objective was to determine the feasibility of new products from volatile compounds in Costa Rican biodiversity and to promote technology transfer in this area. A royalty rate was established. This project concluded its activities in Costa Rica by the middle of 1998.

INBio-British Technology Group (BTG)-Ecos La Pacífica Agreement. In the agricultural area, INBio seeks to integrate the result of bioprospecting activity with the economic development of the country. This process began with the signing of the INBio-BTG agreement in 1992 that allowed INBio to begin the research into characterization of and production of a chemical compound with nematicidal activity known as DMDP that was derived from a tree of the Costa Rican dry tropical forest (*Lonchocarpus felipei*). Parallel investigations have been developed jointly with the corporation Ecos La Pacífica, aimed at determining the growing conditions of the species and the production of the DMDP, as well as the effectiveness of this nematicide in tropical crops. The greenhouse and field trials began in 1999 and continue being carried out to date with satisfactory results. BTG has paid a small amount of money to both INBio and Ecos La Pacifica due to the licensing of a patent related to the DMDP use.

INBio-Diversa Agreement: Search for Enzymes from Extremophilic Organisms with Applications to the Chemical Industry. For the exploration of new enzymes in aquatic or terrestrial microorganisms of Costa Rican biodiversity under extreme conditions, INBio signed a research agreement with Diversa Corporation in 1995. This agreement was renewed in 1998 and 2002, and it will expire in 2007. It involves the gathering of bacteria in different conservation areas of Costa Rica that will be studied for the identification and isolation of new enzymes useful in industry. The agreement also guarantees the training of Costa Rican scientists in collection methods, isolation, and molecular biology, specifically in cloning and characterization of genes associated with enzymes. A third negotiation is currently being carried out.

INBio-Indena S.p.A. Agreement: Search for Compounds with Antimicrobial and Antiviral Activity. With the objective of obtaining compounds with antimicrobial potential to be used as active ingredients in cosmetics, INBio and the phytopharmaceutical company Indena S.p.A., with headquarters in Milan, Italy signed a collaboration agreement in 1996, with a second phase that started in 2000 and concluded in 2002. Extracts of selected plants were

Table 1. Contributions made to biodiversity conservation in Costa Rica as a result of bioprospecting agreements signed by INBio with various organizations from 1991 until 2000. All values in $ USD.

Organization	1993*	1994	1995	1996	1997	1998	1999	2000	Total
MINAE by 10%	110,040	43,400	66,670	51,092	95,196	24,160	38,793	82,797	512,148
Conservation areas	86,102	203,135	153,555	192,035	126,243	29,579	0	0	790,649
Costa Rican public universities	460,409	126,006	46,962	31,265	34,694	14,186	7,123	4,083	724,728
Other groups in INBio	228,161	92,830	118,292	172,591	129,008	0	0	0	740,882
Total	884,712	465,371	385,479	446,983	385,141	67,925	45,916	86,880	2,768,407

*Estimated amounts since 1991.

evaluated in bioassays to determine their antimicrobial activity. The final process is carried out by Indena.

INBio-Phytera Inc. Agreement. Traditionally, drugs have been developed from extracts of leaves, roots, bark, and other parts of plants. Today, with the advances in biotechnology, medicines can be derived from cell cultures, and new techniques can create a variety of chemical substances from these cultures. In 1998, INBio signed an agreement with this company, which continued in effect until the year 2000.

INBio-Eli Lilly Agreement: Search for New Compounds. This project started in 1999 and concluded in 2000. It was carried out in collaboration with the pharmaceutical company Eli Lilly and Co. with an objective of searching for botanical compounds with pharmaceutical application.

INBio-Akkadix Corporation Agreement: Search for Compounds with Nematicidal Activity. This project was carried out with the company Akkadix Corporation from 1999 to 2001. Its main objective was the search for alternatives for the control of nematodes.

INBio Agreements with Academia

These research agreements of an academic nature with national and international universities vary considerably in their focus, but they are all guided toward the solution of problems and the search for knowledge and products.

INBio-University of Strathclyde Agreement. This agreement allows access to new technologies and methodologies. The University of Strathclyde, UK also facilitates interaction between INBio and the Japanese private sector. INBio provided a limited number of extracts of plants that were evaluated during a limited time by several industries of that country. This agreement was implemented between 1997 and 2000.

INBio-University of Massachusetts Agreement: Search for Potential Insecticides. Through a collaboration with the University of Massachusetts, USA, with the support of NIH, this joint venture carried out research to find compounds with insecticidal activity. This project began in October of 1995 and concluded in 1998. Its objective was the development of enzymatic bioassays of extracts derived from plants, insects, bryophytes, and mollusks.

INBio-University of Guelph Agreement: Development of New Technologies for Medicines Based on Plants, an International Interdisciplinary Initiative. This agreement is being carried out with the University of Guelph, Canada. It was signed in 2000 and will conclude in 2004. Its main objective is the search for new pharmaceutical products through techniques such as plant tissue culture.

Other Agreements

Validation of Promising Plants. This project was financed by the Costa Rican USA Foundation. It contemplated three subprojects that allowed obtaining information to improve the quality of life of Costa Ricans. In collaboration with the

University of Costa Rica Research Center of Parasitology, two plants were studied to isolate active components against malaria. This project built upon the encouraging results of the ICBG project.

Also, in collaboration with the Unit of Electronic Microscopy, the Laboratory of Biological Assays, and the National Children's Hospital, these plants were validated for gastritis treatment by their anti-*Helicobacter pylori* activity. Finally, some species were validated by their alkaloid content to explore their economic feasibility. This project was implemented between 1999 and 2001.

The Chagas Project. INBio, together with EARTH, the National University of Costa Rica, other Latin American institutions of Brazil, Mexico, Chile, Argentina, Uruguay, and NASA in the United States, are part of "The Chagas Space Project", a research project that is looking for a solution to one of the most serious health problems of Latin America: the Chagas disease or American Tripanosomiasis. INBio carried out some research activities on plants with inhibitory activity towards the disease in 1997. In 2001, the USA Congress approved a fund dedicated to refinance this project which has allowed resumption of the bioassays. The project was renewed in 2002.

INBio-Inter-American Development Bank (IDB) Agreement: Program for Support of the Development of the Use of Biodiversity by Small Enterprises. In February 1999, INBio signed an agreement with the IDB with the purpose of formalizing the terms of a technical cooperation grant to support the development of the use of biodiversity by small companies. The project is likely to expire in 2004; however, in the first phase of the project, six projects were approved:

- Agrobiot S.A: Propagation of Costa Rican tropical plants to be commercialized as eco-educational souvenirs (started in 2001);
- Laboratorios Lisan S.A: Pharmaceutical products based on medicinal plants (started in 2000);
- La Gavilana: Development of a model of eco-friendly practices for vanilla production (started in 2001);
- Industrias Caraito S.A: Generation of added value on the carao agro-industry;
- Bougainvillea S.A: Research for development and production of a biocide from *Quassia amara* wood; and
- Follajes Ticos S.A: Native ornamental plants with market potential.

Negotiation of Selected Access Requests.

In access negotiations with companies, INBio has taken the most active role, so it has learned a great deal from the process. The State has limited its participation to granting collection permits through the SINAC in accordance with the LWC and the Cooperation Agreements with INBio.

In this section I would like to establish the lessons learned from the process of negotiating agreements and contracts, based on the experiences of INBio. Several publications have been written (GÁMEZ and SITTENFELD 1993) concerning the structure, policies, and programs of INBio. In general, significant experiences in benefit sharing have been obtained since the signing of the agreement with Merck and Co. in 1991. These, and other contractual relationships, have resulted in the following benefits:

- Monetary benefits by means of direct payments;

- Payment for specific samples;

- Coverage of research budgets;

- Transfer of important technology that has allowed the development of infrastructure in INBio is the laboratory of biotechnology, which has been used for research and development of local products;

- Capacity-training for scientists and technicians, in relation to state-of-the-art technologies;

- Experience in market negotiations, knowledge, and research for finding more intelligent uses of biodiversity resources;

- Support of conservation efforts by means of payments to MINAE to strengthen the National System of Conservation Areas;

- Transfer of equipment to other institutions, such as the University of Costa Rica;

- Future royalties and milestone payments, which will be shared on a 50-50 basis with MINAE; and

- Creation of national skills in order to add value to biodiversity resources.

According to my experience as INBio's legal adviser, the lessons learned by INBio in access negotiations are as follows:

- It is essential to have a defined institutional policy on the requirements and criteria to be included in the biodiversity prospecting agreements.

- The national scientific capacity facilitates adding value to biodiversity resources and enhances the country's position in the negotiation of benefits to be incorporated in the contract (e.g., higher royalty rates).

- It is necessary to develop a good understanding of the operation and evolution of biodiversity markets and to be aware of the technical and scientific changes that support them.

- The existence or the development of institutional capacity for the negotiations in legal, scientific, and business areas) is a necessity. The terms of the agreements are often challenging and complex.

- Innovation and creativity add considerable weight to compensation and benefit-sharing negotiations.

- Mastering of key issues is crucial: IPRs, warranties, determination of royalty rates, transfer of materials to third parties, definitions (products and extracts), ownership of IPRs, joint research, confidentiality, dispute resolution, and the survival of obligations. These are some of the key issues that are negotiated with bioprospectors.

- Proactive approaches to business development according to the needs of the country and a defined institutional policy (biodiversity prospecting strategy) enhance the opportunities for new and innovative agreements. The existence of a Business Development Office at INBio with a highly qualified expert staff; attending seminars and activities with the industry the distribution or sharing of information and material, and direct contacts all enable an answer to be given, to a larger or smaller extent, to institutional challenges. The current policy is based on the idea that it is not enough to wait to be contacted, or to be available at the behest of the company, but one must assertively have and maintain one's own approach. Even if no formal market survey has been made, the identification of potential partners in the field of biotechnology has been developed.

- Coordination with other national and international institutions devoted to biodiversity R&D and understanding of technology transfer needs and capacity building at the country level are important requirements in the process.

- Good political support, an appropriate legal framework, and legal certainty (e.g., who is entitled to grant permits) create a positive environment for success.

- The development of macro-policies such as national biodiversity inventories, information management systems, investment in science and technology, and well-defined protected areas provide a smoother scenario for biodiversity prospecting.

The Role of the LB in Hampering or Facilitating
Access to the Country's Genetic Resources

Although this role cannot be precisely defined due to the lack of application of the LB, several difficulties, including the lack of clarity of certain clauses, the obscure and complex system proposed by the GAP, the lack of qualified personnel versed in the functioning of the genetic resources market, the terms of the contracts and agreements, the absence of practical experience in the applicability of the law and the time it will take to enforce it, and certain sectors' resistance to new rules for the academy and research, suggest a difficult future for bioprospectors. For instance, some provisions of the LB may actually prevent access.

The legislation is not clear in relation to the TO's powers. The TO has to endorse the PIC and, according to the GAP, some other functions are bestowed upon it (LB Article 13, authorization of the number of samples to obtain or export and the periodicity of the activity reports; LB Article 20, control and follow-up activities, etc.). Notwithstanding this fact, the TO does not have the power to negotiate access terms with the applicant, since it can only endorse them without the possibility of modifying them. This literal reading of the GAP creates some difficulties. For example, what happens if there is no third party from whom to obtain physical access? If a university possesses its own *ex situ* resources and wants to make use of those resources in bioprospecting[7] the PIC prescribed in articles 63, 65, and 74 of the law and in the GAP would not be necessary. In this case, should the TO grant the PIC? Apart from this, access to genetic resources does not overrule existing norms on access to biological resources. In this case, even if an access permit is granted by the TO, would an additional permit under the LWC be required?

Article 74 governs the cases in which once the former conditions are met, 10% of the research budget and up to 50% of the royalties are given to the conservation area or private or indigenous owner. This terminology excludes other relevant actors since the phrase "private owner" is even more restrictive than, for example, "landlord" or "tenants". Nevertheless, aren't the latter supposed to be included in the PIC? In this case, the phrase can be disregarded. Or, we can also interpret that when these monetary benefits have not been considered in the prior informed consent, the TO can demand their inclusion. This implies that the TO could interfere in the negotiation process. But the parties could have excluded a monetary provision on purpose, since, for example they could have stipulated different benefits to be shared. In this connection, it is not clear whether these two stipulations have to be included in both the contracts (PIC) and the TO resolutions. This is aggravated by the fact that according to LB Article 76, and in conformity with rules issued by CONAGEBIO, the TO has to dictate the deposit of up to 10% of the research budget and 50% of the royalties. This detail seems to make this requirement mandatory in all cases. This generates some complications since there will not always be a research budget or controversies may arise in relation to the scope of the language. For example, does the budget include sampling and export costs?[8]

The approval of third-party contracts also raises several doubts. In this case we would be in the presence of intermediaries or joint research agreements involving foreign counterparts. In this example, the contracts have been previously signed. Should the TO limit itself to endorsement, given its inability to examine the negotiation process? In this state of affairs, under which criteria can the TO disapprove the contract, perhaps an insufficient technology transfer?[9]

Should the authorization process be initiated before the procedure for getting the prior informed consent is started? Or, which seems more logical, should both procedures be initiated at the same time? It is obvious that the applicant negotiates its relationship with the owner based on the fact that the TO's approval is pending. This can create uncertainties for the negotiators since the TO can eventually request further requirements that would have to be distributed between the applicant and the company.

Confidentiality is a little obscure. Article 74 states that the procedure should follow Articles 69, 70, and 71. (This is another argument in favor of the simultaneity in the third-party contract approval and the presentation of the PIC.) On the contrary, it would be senseless to apply these articles to third-party contract authorizations. Yet, the only reference to confidentiality is found in article 67. This article mandates confidentiality for all the information submitted to the TO, unless biosafety concerns override this norm. Confidentiality is one of the main protections companies seek. (See paragraph 59 of the CBD Expert Panel's First Report.) Furthermore, the recently approved Non-Disclosed Information Law establishes criminal sanctions for those who reveal confidential information. In spite of this, CONAGEBIO's multi-sector character can create confidentiality for companies.

The rights granted to those who perform bioprospecting are crucial. There is a tendency to grant to the term "public domain" a scope difficult to sustain. Some think that when the State grants an access permit this only implies custody of the material for research purposes. Which are the recipient-user's rights? In particular, are there any transforming or protection rights such as the ones embodied in the intellectual property rules? Can the user patent an improved material or an invention derived from a given genetic material? Can a gene be isolated, characterized, and patented? This is linked to the discussion under the aegis of the FAO in relation to the Multilateral Access System for Plant Genetic Resources for Food and Agriculture. According to it, delivered genetic resources, parts, and components cannot be protected under intellectual property. From a commercial point of view, this kind of restriction can be very important in the determination of whether a company will conduct bioprospecting or not.

A reasonable solution would be to give free access to the genetic material but without the possibility of protecting it, if there is no modification. In such a case, we would be in the presence of an invention and protection would be requested over a whole organism (obviously including the genetic component associated with the rest of the organism).

In the same way, can microorganisms, genes, enzymes, and diagnostic agents obtained from genetic material by means of incorporating new genes obtained elsewhere be patented? It must be remembered that some material transfer agreements from the Centers of the Consultative Group on Agriculture Research include a clause preventing patentability of transferred material and related information. This is also the case in the transfer agreements of the MOSSAIC project (Micro-Organism Sustainable Use and Access Regulation International Code of Conduct) and other equivalent agreements. This point deserves a detailed analysis linked to the next topic to be discussed.

What are the implications of considering genetic resources in the public domain if this means IPRs cannot be acquired, since applicants will be considered as holders? Would a company agree to be granted custody only? The use restriction over the material should be clarified. Normally the materials (dry samples, etc.) are not sent as such. Instead bioprospectors send extracts, stock with genetic resources, isolated genetic sequences, etc. The degree of restrictions over these materials is another important point.

The framework agreements constitute an adequate mechanism to regulate access. Nevertheless, their real dimension is still to be assessed, since they are limited to basic research, excluding bioprospecting. Maybe in the present state of affairs this makes sense, since universities can conduct their teaching activities (molecular taxonomy, etc.) without requiring individual permits for each project. Would a similar approach be valid for the INBio? Apart from this, since according to the access procedure each sampling has to be approved by the respective conservation area, perhaps the best option would be to negotiate a framework agreement. This possibility is not contemplated in the present draft. Also, a framework agreement could be a possible way out for third-party access to *ex situ* collections.

The proposed GAP distinguishes four related situations: basic research access (including teaching, since the molecular taxonomy courses require access permits), bioprospecting (commercial exploration), and occasional and constant economic use. The last two are differentiated from bioprospecting (related to the idea of exploration). For the occasional or constant economic use situations, the user tries to access a genetic resource because of its demonstrated commercial utility. For instance, taxol and DMDP provide good examples.

Taxol is the active ingredient with anticancer properties isolated from the bark of the Pacific yew (*Taxus brevifolia*,

a tree). Large amounts of the bark were needed for small yields of taxol and, initially, the demonstrated efficacy of the drug in the absence of being able to synthesize it or domesticate the tree, meant that the only source was extraction from the native genetic resource. Fortunately, synthesis of the chemical became possible, removing the need for extractive harvest. In the Costa Rican case, due to the necessity of extracting more DMDP, attempts at domesticating *Lonchocarpus felipei* were made on a private farm. If this experiment is successful, the interpretation of the norms prompts at least three questions:

1. When does commercial usage begin? In the DMDP case, the decision to domesticate the tree on a farm was made to avoid one of the common allegations against bioprospecting: over-exploitation due to market pressures. Nevertheless, this action does not imply the presence of a commercial phase. The planting serves an initial research purpose with no certain economic benefits. According to the proposed regulation, would this imply a constant economic use, thus requiring a public concession? It is my belief that this is not the case. Even in the case in which genetic material is required for clinical tests (a provision that is often included in bioprospecting contracts), it is only in the exploratory phase. Commercial use takes place only when it is in the presence of a final commercialized product. This would require a grant or concession following the dispositions of the Law.

2. Some regulators believe that the bioprospecting permit and the permit for economic use should be separate. This is derived from the oral explanation from the members of CONAGEBIO about the USA National Cancer Institute's experience in Africa. In this view, whenever a product is achieved, a new negotiation process leading to an "economic use approval" should be started. This implies that the research phase requires one permit and the commercialization another one. This interpretation artificially divides bioprospecting, since from the beginning it looks for economic gains. Obviously this point of view is incorrect, and the placement in the market of derived products should be considered in the initial agreement where the sharing of benefits rules was agreed upon.[10]

3. Which is the concession procedure and how it is differentiated from the access permit? For example, in the case of DMDP, once its commercial potential is identified, does the supplier have to obtain a concession to send the material? It must be acknowledged that inappropriate rules could lead interested parties to look for the materials elsewhere. In this case, the communities and local entrepreneurs could lose the possibility of profiting from their genetic materials, and scientists could lose the chance to conduct certain scientific procedures in the country. Finally,

there is a thin line between constant and occasional economic use. The initial phase of resource extraction should guarantee the rational exploitation of the biological diversity.

Finally, as in every process of change, new regulations bring uncertainties about the interpretation and application of the law, as well as for the duration of the process. This could produce delays due to the absence of experience and current capacities in the field.

Based on my own experience, bioprospectors and other access applicants (for basic research, teaching, etc.) can have the following concerns in relation to the legislation:

- It is a subject matter where regulation is new. Besides, the main focus of this regulation is to control the flow of information, something complex and full of difficulties. The first national regulations were put forward in the Philippines in 1995. After this, several norms have been designed at the national or regional level achieving different levels of success in their implementation. However, with only nine years since the first legislation, there are few examples related to achievements and failures that could be used as a guide.

- Because of historical inequalities in access and benefit sharing, the regulatory authorities tend to be suspicious and try to impose strong control mechanisms in order to avoid past injustices. Suspicion and mistrust appear to be the main motivators behind this tendency. The bioprospector is not regarded as an ally but as a suspect. As with any partner, bioprospectors should be governed by legal and contractual mechanisms, without omitting good faith in the negotiations. The tendency in some of the existing access regulations is to control rather than to promote, an aspect that will be dealt with properly later on. I should also point out the emotional aspect embodied in terms such as "National Patrimony" and "Sovereignty", an aspect that transcends any juridical consideration.

- In general, there is uncertainty over the application of new rules, the control character of the TO, the will to promote access or not, authorities' expertise on genetic research topics, the excessive bureaucratic procedure, the high transaction costs, etc.

Due to the difficulties explained above it is probable that basic research and teaching will be affected as, for example, in the molecular taxonomy technique, which is useful for national inventories.

The economic cost of applying for access is imprecise. Article 76 indicates that the TO will determine the amount to be paid on a case-by-case basis. However, it is unlikely that it will be an important amount (probably less than $100 USD). Other costs would depend on the hiring of a lawyer (not mandatory).

Finally, there are no specific conditions and costs for national and international bioprospectors. In practice, the existence of national bioprospectors as individuals or partners with foreign entities would enable access, since there would be a responsible party in the country.

Intellectual Property Rights

The list below documents Costa Rica's comprehensive legislation related to IPRs. In addition, new laws have been enacted on integrated circuits, trademarks, and industrial drawings, and there is an amended Copyrights Law.

- The Patent, Drawings and Utility Models Law No. 6867 was reformed by Law No. 7979 of 31 January 2000 to make it compatible with TRIPS. Supposedly, there are not exclusions for microorganisms, biological processes, genes, and genetic sequences as long as the patentability requirements are met. Yet, there is no administrative or judicial practice in the field.

- The Non-Disclosed Information Law No. 7975 was passed on 18 January 2000.

- The Plant Breeders' Rights Draft was published in The Gazette on 10 August 1999, but is yet to be approved.

- The Intellectual Property Rights Compliance Procedure No. 8033 was passed on 27 October 2000.

- A draft has been completed on plant breeders' rights in accordance with the model law of the International Union for the Protection of New Varieties of Plants (UPOV) and its 1991 Act reform. In that area an important group composed of NGOs supported by local politicians has expressed their disagreement with the legislative draft on the implications for farmers' seed reutilization. In the same way, the scheme for community rights protection should make some references to plant breeders' rights in order to guarantee compatibility between the texts. However, the specificities of the proposal are still unknown since the participatory process that will determine those community rights has only recently begun. No concrete proposals have been made to the TRIPS Council.

Articles 82 and subsequent articles of LB are related to the *sui generis* community intellectual rights. A participatory process mandated in the law is working on the *sui generis* community IPRs. The consultations are expected to be completed by 2004.

In general, the Costa Rican System for the Protection of Traditional Knowledge is based on the following items:

- A legal structure on access that guarantees prior informed consent and benefit sharing in relation to traditional knowledge. The TO and, eventually, the CONAGEBIO are granted with powers of control, authorization, and supervision (LB Articles 63, 65, 66, and 72, among others).

- A combination of specific mechanisms for accessing, contracting, and licensing processes and *sui generis* structures based on registries.

- Different forms of knowledge and innovation such as patents, commercial secrets, copyrights, plant breeders' rights, *sui generis* community intellectual rights, etc. (Article 78) protected through the use of appropriate mechanisms (LB Article 77).

- Legislation focused on the protection of knowledge using a system of registration. This aspect is supported by the doctrine itself, which, in practical terms, has been implemented in India (KAUSHIK 2000, DUTFIELD 2000), and in Venezuela. It was also included in the draft of the Peruvian Regime Proposal for the Protection of the Collective Knowledge of the Indigenous Peoples and Access to Genetic Resources, among others. Therefore, it promotes the protection of the *sui generis* community intellectual property and inventions of the communities that request such protection (LB Article 84). Nevertheless, these guidelines for registration have been criticized due to some adverse effects they may produce (DOWNES and LAIRD 1999, RUIZ 1999). Some of the adverse judgments expressed are: the need to define access to information, the control required thereto, the possibility that communities not involved in the access will grant prior informed consent, registering knowledge in the name of third parties, etc.

To define the scope, nature and requirements of these rights, a participatory process should begin to consult indigenous communities and peasants (LB Article 83) on the subject. Likewise, the process will determine the form in which the intellectual community right will be used, who will be vested with powers of representation, and who the corresponding beneficiaries are (LB Article 85). Based on the aforementioned, and concerning the assignment of rights and responsibilities, either collective or private, the following items must be explained:

- The object of protection;

- The protection process;

- The rights granted and the party responsible for compliance thereof; and

- Monitoring systems.

Definitely, the success of the proposed scheme will depend to a great extent on the existence of the bylaw and the outcome of the participatory process called to examine it.

Impact of IPRs on Biodiversity and Traditional Knowledge

During the process of drafting the LB and, as part of the definition of regulations on access and benefit sharing, the topic of IPRs and their relationship with biodiversity inevitably arose. Article 16 of the LB states that these rights should support, and should not be opposed to, the objectives of the agreement.

Thus, the LB establishes that IPRs shall be congruent with its objectives by virtue of the principle of integration (Article 79). The LB excludes the following: DNA sequences from patent processes, plants and animals, unmodified microorganisms, essential biological processes for plant and animal production, the processes of nature or natural cycles, inventions essentially derived from the knowledge of biological traditional practices or in the public domain, inventions that are produced monopolistically that may affect the processes, and basic agricultural products used for food and health purposes (Article 78).[11] Authorities should consult the TO before granting protection of intellectual or industrial property-related innovations that involve biodiversity elements. The submission of the certificate of origin and prior informed consent shall be required. A well-grounded opposition by the TO shall prevent protection from being granted (Article 80). It has been stated that particular beneficiaries granted protection of intellectual or industrial property rights regarding biodiversity must cede to the State a legal obligatory license. In the event of a justified emergency, this license will allow the use of such rights for the benefit of the community. This provision is aimed at solving an emergency, without involving compensation or royalty payment (Article 81). Some have affirmed that there are contradictions in certain clauses with respect to TRIPS (CARVALHO 2000) and therefore, based on the Costa Rican structures, with the Constitution itself; pursuant to our judicial system, Treaties have a superior value over ordinary law and shall not be disregarded by the law. Furthermore, it is important to emphasize certain questions that are fundamental because, to some extent, they were the express or implicit cause of these regulations (CABRERA MEDAGLIA 2000, CABRERA MEDAGLIA and ALARCÓN 2000):

- Are traditional IPR systems insufficient in relation to the protection of knowledge, innovations, and practices, such as it is affirmed by the doctrine? Or, on the contrary, could they be used in order to protect important sectors involved, for example, in using trademarks and denominations of origin?

- What possibilities exist for IPR to add value to biodiversity and the associated knowledge, in an indirect manner, by protecting a market of protected products? If there are possibilities, how could such mechanisms be useful to claim such value (LESSER 1998)?

- Is it possible and viable to establish the so-called Certificate of Origin (TOBIN 1997) so that it is a requirement to present a record or document on the legality of the access and benefit sharing? This requirement is contemplated in the Peruvian regulation on Plant Breeders' Rights, in Decision 391 of the Andean Community Common Regime on Access to Genetic Resources, in Decision 486 of the same regional entity on a Regime of Industrial Property, and in the LB of Costa Rica (Article 80), among others. This topic has been discussed in the World Trade Organization, mainly in the Council of TRIPS and the Committee for Trade and Environment, where different countries and groups have presented proposals to include this requirement in the revised text of these proposals. Furthermore, other forums like the Patent Treaty of WIPO and its Working Group on Biotechnology, have touched upon the topic. Different objections have been presented from incompatibility with the fixed patent requirements of the WTO (Article 27 of TRIPS) to practical criticisms (difficulties with respect to plant varieties originating in different countries, or from crosses and retro-crosses; the fact that a product or patent process does not necessarily reach the market; the additional workload for the Intellectual Property Offices; and the lack of patents of multiple products derived from tropical biota, etc.).

- In what way do IPRs impact biodiversity, for example, through restrictions on the exchange of seeds through patents, plant breeders' rights, contracts or technology to control the expression of genes? Up to what point can impediments be produced in traditional practices given patents and other awarded rights on inventions that claim the use of genetic resources even when, from a legal point of view, these rights, many of which have been revoked in the United States or Europe, never should have been granted because the processes weren't new or because they lacked invention char-

acteristics (as has been the argument with respect to the neem, turmeric, and ayahuasca plants). Can IPRs restrict the exportation of traditional products (beans in Mexico, for example), claiming the existence of plant breeders' rights or patents granted in the importation market to third parties on the characteristics of these products?

- Up to what point do IPRs have a direct impact on the environment and on the conservation and sustainable use of genetic resources and traditional knowledge? For example, up to what point do they facilitate or hinder the transfer of safe environmental technologies or create undesirable effects such as genetic erosion? To what extent do they increase the use of synthesis chemicals (especially given the sale of seeds that are transgenic and resistant to herbicides) or orient research and development to areas that are not desired and create a homogenous agriculture that is not adapted to local needs?

- The *sui generis* system for plant variety can be used, which was foreseen in TRIPS Article 27.3b that protects traditional knowledge and stipulates benefit sharing, despite the fact that, in the TRIPS framework, this statement takes on a singular meaning (LESKIEN and FLITNER 1997).

- Does the stipulation of IPRs in access contracts guaranteeing larger returns to the countries of origin or local contractors, including communities, actually entail greater returns for the companies involved, given the lack of competition and copies? Are they a marketing mechanism that allows greater royalty payments for the company and therefore contributes even more to benefit sharing?

- Finally, has the International Undertaking had any influence on national access laws? The LB does not mention the possibility of including a clause on genetic and biochemical resources used for food and agriculture, subject to easy access as prescribed by the recently approved International Treaty on Plant Genetic Resources for Food and Agriculture (that substitutes for the Undertaking).

Lessons Learned and Recommendations

The Costa Rican experience has provided some of the most relevant examples in terms of obstacles as well as achievements with respect to the regulation on access to genetic resources, intellectual property, and traditional knowledge. We must indicate that there are two views, to some extent opposed, with respect to the underlying idea behind regulation of access (CAILLAUX et al. 1999). On the one hand, protection of traditional knowledge and access to genetic resources is seen as a conservation strategy and as a way to avoid the theft and inappropriate use of these resources, especially through the system of IPRs. On the other hand, access is seen as a mechanism that, besides

offering such protection, plays an important role in benefit sharing and compensation for the commercial use of the knowledge and resources. In the first view, registries would be enough to conserve and safeguard the information, publications, and other mechanisms and to avoid its inappropriate use (destruction of the novelty requirement of the patents, nondisclosed information laws, etc.). The other view, although recognizing this reality, seeks to create or provide mechanisms for the distribution of benefits. The following sections summarize the main lessons and recommendations that are provided by the Costa Rican experience.

The Myth of Biodiversity Prospecting Programs and the Expected Values in Return

For years, prospecting was associated with the exploration for ore and hydrocarbons. In the early nineties, Thomas Eisner is credited with using the term, or at least popularizing it, for the exploration for biodiversity. Both types of exploration present different levels of risk; therefore, distribution of benefits will depend on the understanding of how these activities operate. The bioprospector, despite different studies that show the existing potential benefits, is unaware of what exactly he will find in the rich tropical jungles. The wealth in terms of biodiversity does not necessarily translate into marketable products such as new medicines and seeds.

In this sense, those who believed that bioprospecting would become a "green mine of gold" have had to modify or moderate their observations. In Costa Rica the income contributed by the biodiversity prospecting program reaches several million USD overall and makes important contributions to technology, capacity training, equipment, the National System of Conservation Areas, and, most importantly, to the creation of national capacities and negotiation capacities. Although this last aspect stands out as the most important in relation to acquired benefits, it is important to point out that ecological tourism contributed $650 million USD in just one year, making bioprospecting's return seem relatively small with respect to the amount of money obtained. From this perspective, biodiversity prospecting is a component of a much larger strategy of conservation and sustainable use of biodiversity rather than a solution for the immediate needs of conservation.

Without Access There is no Benefit Sharing

Our historical background on this matter has shown that there was a perceived need for stricter controls on access to avoid so-called biopiracy. Some regulations to date have concentrated more on controlling than on promoting access. Such a regulatory focus can inadvertently result in the ignoring of the objectives of the CBD and individual national laws, despite the good intentions of those who proposed the regulations. Such regulations are creating high transaction costs and complicated bureaucratic procedures leading to an absence of access applications without which it is not possible to speak about benefit sharing. If the idea persists that access represents a form of colonialism, instead of a mechanism to generate joint initiatives adequate for all participants, the possibility of generating reasonable experiences will be limited. Besides the necessary legal guarantees, it is important to foresee regimes that are sufficiently flexible and transparent. Furthermore, there must be a balance between confidentiality and transparency and the access of third parties to the results of negotiations.

Linking Access with National Biodiversity Strategies for Conservation and Sustainable Use

Unfortunately, the evolution of legal regulations on access to genetic resources has been separate from the definition of national policies on conservation and sustainable use of biological diversity. As a result, the contribution of monetary as well as nonmonetary benefits barely touches upon the conservation process. When nations, through mechanisms that are highly participatory, establish public policies on this matter, concrete negotiations to allow access could reach wider objectives. Ultimately, these National Strategies must serve the development and strengthening of the national and institutional capacities that give the resources added value.

Definition of Property Rights

It is urgent that property rights on genetic and biochemical resources be defined. The CBD only mentions the sovereignty of the State over them without considering the existing property rights. With this in mind, the clear differentiation among the concepts of property, sovereignty, and national patrimony is necessary for legal certainty. The uncertainty over who owns the genetic resources leads to difficulties in the process of obtaining the PIC and in determining who should participate in the access negotiations. In turn, this creates difficulties in reaching agreements on access that are appropriate given the existing doubts and companies' requirements to have adequate guarantees on the legality of the procedures and to avoid public and judicial problems.

Access and Technological Change

According to REID (1997) we can affirm that technology plays a relevant and contradictory role in the process of access. On one hand, new screening techniques and recombinant biotechnology have opened doors to the use of biodiversity elements never known before and have greatly increased the value of these resources and knowledge. But on the other hand, the reduction of operational costs and the ability facilities to work with fewer samples have reduced the concrete value of each resource and have facilitated the illegal trade of resources.

It is essential to follow the changes in technology. Eventually, technological advances such as combinatory chemistry could result in a reduction of interest in biodiversity, access, and the use of traditional knowledge. It is important to be aware of these transformations.

Impact of Access on National Basic Research

The regulations on access are based on the idea of conserving biological diversity, its sustainable use, and the fair distribution of its benefits. An indispensable component to reach these objectives lies in basic research, especially when there is no essential information on ecosystems and species. Research conducted by universities and research centers represents in itself an element that contributes to this process. The rules on access could interfere with this research, for example, by controlling nonscientific activities in order to regulate the resulting commercial benefits and thereby affecting the attainment of the CBD's objectives. This negative impact must be avoided through adequate procedures that favor basic research.

Participatory Processes

Participatory processes are important in an area of great national importance such as biological diversity. Notwithstanding this fact, participation requires enough information to avoid an "observer only" role for certain stakeholders. This need is increased by the complex nature of the topics. At the same time, greater participation involves transactions, internal negotiations, and compromises that could result in weaker legislation.

Conclusion

The Costa Rican experience has shown interesting details that are worthy of mention, although it does not necessarily constitute an example to follow in other countries. Peculiar circumstances of the national reality (read about these particular situations in MATEO 1996), the size of the country, a central government, and its political, educational, and social situation have led it to establish its own terms. It is the example of a nation that decided to choose a path instead of arguing about existing problems that impeded advancement. From this point of view, the practical experi-

ence on access and benefit sharing presented at the level of contracts and collaboration agreements with the public, private, national, and international sectors, the formulation of a Law on Biodiversity that seeks answers to the challenges proposed by the CBD, and the regulation of the main principles of the *sui generis* model are elements that provide valuable information for future debate on access laws and policies. This is, possibly, the most valuable aspect of the Costa Rican experience.

References

CABRERA MEDAGLIA, J. 1999. Premisas, principios y contenidos de una ley marco sobre la diversidad biológica. *Revista Ivstitia*, San José, Costa Rica.

CABRERA MEDAGLIA, J. 2000. Soberanía, derechos de propiedad intelectual y biodiversidad, *Revista Mensual de Gestión Ambiental*. Universidad Carlos III, Madrid, Spain.

CABRERA MEDAGLIA, J. and E. ALARCÓN. 2000. *Acceso a los recursos genéticos y el papel de los derechos de propiedad intelectual*. Investigación Agrícola y Propiedad Intelectual, PROCITROPICOS, Brasilia, Brazil.

CAILLAUX, J., M. RUIZ, and B. TOBIN. 1999. *El Régimen Andino de Acceso a los Recursos Genéticos: Lecciones y experiencias*. SPDA, Lima, Perú and WRI, Washington DC USA.

CARVALHO, N. 2000. Ley de Biodiversidad de Costa Rica: Compatibilidad entre el Convenio de Diversidad Biológica (CBD) y el TRIPS. Document prepared for the UPOV-OMPI National Seminar on Vegetal Obtentions and Bioqdiversity Protection, San José, Costa Rica.

DOWNES, D. and S. LAIRD. 1999. Registries of local and indigenous knowledge relating to biodiversity. Prepared for the UNCTAD Biotrade Initiative.

DUTFIELD, G. 2000. *Intellectual property rights, trade and biodiversity*. Earthscan, London, UK.

GÁMEZ, R. and A. SITTENFELD. 1993. Biodiversity prospecting by INBio. p. 69–98 *in* W.V. REID, S.A. LAIRD, C.A. MEYER, R. GÁMEZ, A. SITTENFELD, D.H. JANZEN, M.A. GOLLIN, and C. JUMA (eds.) *Biodiversity prospecting*. World Resources Institute, Washington DC USA.

KAUSHIK, A. 2000. Protection of biodiversity and traditional

knowledge: The Indian experience. Unpublished manuscript.

LESKIEN, D. and M. FLITNER. 1997. Intellectual property rights for plants: Options for a *sui generis* system. *Issues in Plant Genetic Resources*, No 6.

LESSER, W. 1998. Propiedad intelectual y biodiversidad. p. 15–23 *in* A.G. RODRÍGUEZ (ed.) *La conservación y el uso sostenible de la biodiversidad para el desarrollo sostenible*. SINADES, San José, Costa Rica.

MATEO, N. 1996. Wild biodiversity: The last frontier? The case of Costa Rica. p. 73–82 *in* C. BONTE-FRIEDHEIMAND and K. SHERIDAN (eds.) *The place of agricultural research*. ISNAR, The Hague, Netherlands.

REID, W. 1997. Technological change and regulation of access to genetic resources. p. 53–70 *in* J. MUGABE, C.V. BARBER, H. GUDRUN, L. GLOWKA, and A. LA VIÑA (eds.) *Access to genetic resources: Strategies for sharing benefits*. ACTS Press, WRI, ELC-IUCN, Nairobi, Kenya.

REID, W.V., S.A. LAIRD, C.A. MEYER, R. GÁMEZ, A. SITTENFELD, D.H. JANZEN, M.A. GOLLIN, and C. JUMA (eds.) 1993. *Biodiversity prospecting*. World Resources Institute, Washington DC USA.

RUIZ, M. 1999. Protecting indigenous peoples knowledge: A policy and legislative perspective from Perú, Sociedad Peruana de Derecho Ambiental, Policy and Environmetal Law Series, No 3, Lima, Perú.

TOBIN, B. 1997. Certificates of origin: A role of IPR regimes in securing prior informed consent. p. 329–340 *in* J. MUGABE, C.V. BARBER, H. GUDRUN, L. GLOWKA, and A. LA VIÑA (eds.) *Access to genetic resources: Strategies for benefit sharing*. ACTS Press, WRI, ELC-IUCN, Nairobi, Kenya.

Endnotes

[1] The SINAC is a department of the Ministry of Energy and Environment.

[2] The Strategy proposes thirteen strategic elements. The last one is called "Establishment of the mechanisms needed to facilitate access to genetic resources of biodiversity and the fair and equitable distribution of the benefits derived from them." It establishes the technical, normative, and organizational frame to guarantee the just and equitable access to the elements of biodiversity, along with a set of strategies and concrete actions.

[3] The Unconstitutionality Action was presented against other dispositions of the Law related to the managing and specific destiny of public funds, as well as to the juridical status of the SINAC. These issues will not be commented upon since they deal with matters foreign to this report. Nevertheless, it must be indicated that the action presented against the National System has contributed to the lack of implementation of the Legislation in its entirety.

[4] Article 2 (Area of Application) of the GAP establishes that it will apply to *in situ* and *ex situ* genetic and biochemical elements of wild or domesticated biodiversity that are under the sovereignty of the State, whether in public or private property.

[5] See the Law of Phytosanitary Protection and diverse decrees applicable to the exportation of materials.

[6] Information provided by the Bioprospecting Program of INBio.

[7] An article of the LB establishes that the public universities have one year to design internal procedures and internal controls only applicable to academic and research activities, when this implies not-for-profit access to biodiversity. The universities that fail to do this in the elapsed time will have to abide by the ordinary procedure embodied in the law. Up to now only the University of Costa Rica has submitted its internal rules, but according to the CONAGEBIO these are too general. Consequently, the Commission's rules will still be applicable for specific matters not contemplated in the general norms. Without wanting to go in deep in the discussion, I have to say that the meaning of "not-for-profit" is not always clear. The CONAGEBIO has not provided any guideline to the universities on the content and conditions of these internal procedures.

[8] These articles have as background the cooperation agreement between MINAE and INBio, which established this percentage of the budget and royalties to the transferred to the MINAE. However, the agreement mentions that when the budget cannot be used as a basis for calculations, other formula for the distribution of benefits should be designed.

[9] The Access Norms contemplate a series of restrictions (Article 34), some of which are found in comparative law (e.g., danger of extinction, endemism, fragility or ecosystem vulnerability, access for military ends, etc). Other restrictions are not so clear like "denaturalization of the resources". It is not clear which additional limitations can be used by the TO for nonendorsement of a contract.

[10] The fact that this is the thesis of the GAP proponents is even more evident in Article 9.5, "Additional requirements for requesting an occasional or constant economic use permit". It establishes the obligation to pay to the conservation area, landowner, or indigenous community where access took place up to 50% of the royalties obtained by the interested party.

[11] One thesis holds that reforms to the Patent Law of 2000 tacitly derogated the exclusions of the Law of Biodiversity since they were promulgated later on; it excludes some, but not all, of the aspects provided in LB Article 78 from the patent process.

6

Mexico: Between Legality and Legitimacy

Jorge Larson-Guerra, Christian López-Silva, Francisco Chapela,
José Carlos Fernández-Ugalde and Jorge Soberón

Should access to genetic resources be regulated differently from other biological resources? Yes, because the objective of appropriation is different. The essence of the difference is that once the information in the genetic resource has been accessed, once the key value is outside the hands of the owner of the land or the genetic resource (be it a farmer, an ethnic group, or a country), there is no need for further access. The biological material or individual accessed has been used or transformed, and the value is beyond the control of the provider. On the other hand, to hunt deer, cut trees, or fish tuna implies the harvesting of individuals again and again. In contrast, the main source of value from genetic materials is the "information" contained in the genetic resource; once it has been accessed there is rarely a need for additional extractions, and the information can be shared with others without necessarily requiring more genetic material. In addition, the degree of redundancy found in genetic information across taxa implies that users may need to prospect only a small subset of Earth's species before finding most of the information they need. This does not imply that genetic resources are valuable only because of the information they contain; in fact, we think they are much more than that. But we cannot hide the fact that much of the debates related to bioprospecting and biopiracy implicitly view genetic resources as valuable information. In Mexico, the conventional use of biological resources is now regulated more precisely and with sustainability criteria by the Ecological Equilibrium and Environmental Protection General Act (EEEPGA), the Wildlife General Act (WGA, MEXICAN CONGRESS 2000) and the Sustainable Forestry Development General Act (SFDGA) and within the complex institutions of fisher-

ies and plant health[1]. Relevant regulation designating certain species as strategic[2] was passed in the 2001 Rural Sustainable Development Act (RSDA). However, genetic resources lack a specific and comprehensive regulatory framework. Currently, there are two formal legal initiatives in Congress that purport to fill this gap. Their content will be addressed later, but it is fair to say that that they have not been widely discussed and they are not a priority in the legislative agenda.

The process of extracting genetic resources from species with the aim of developing an industrial application, either within or outside the jurisdiction in which access took place, must be regulated through specific provisions for legal use within access and benefit-sharing agreements and in compliance with Convention on Biological Diversity (CBD) obligations. Access and benefit sharing (ABS) requires regulating a complex set of actions and interests whose legal, institutional, and commercial framework has been well described by TEN KATE and LAIRD (1999). Once access to a genetic resource has occurred the steps between appropriation and industrial innovation may be complicated and difficult to follow. This is the basic reason why there should be legally binding agreements that should clearly state the rules of the game and explicitly include present and future benefits for all those involved.[3]

Adding to this complexity is the use of traditional knowledge (TK) in the development of products that may be patented. If the contribution of the genetic resource itself to a biotechnological invention is not yet fully recognized, then a respectful development of new products involving TK seems even more difficult to implement. The so-called nontangible component of the genetic resource may be even more important culturally and ethically to local communities than the genetic resource itself. Thus, ABS in cases where TK is a component of the agreement tends to be much more complicated. Inequity between the recognition given to collective and diffuse knowledge and that given to individual invention property rights (HERSCH and LARSON 2002) is often an additional complication. Therefore, this added complexity stresses the importance to analyze ABS and TK issues in a separate way but always keeping in mind its close interdependence (FERNÁNDEZ et al. 2002).

These are some of the fundamental reasons why access to genetic resources should be differentiated from the simple use of biological resources. This difference is clearly recognized in the CBD objectives: "the conservation of biological diversity, the sustainable use of its components[4], and the fair and equitable sharing of the benefits arising out of the utilization of genetic resources, including by appropriate access to genetic resources and by appropriate transfer of relevant technologies, taking into account all rights over those resources and to technologies, and by appropriate funding".

Despite the apparent clarity and simplicity of the stated objective, institutions have been slow in responding to this new reality. The potential economic value of a genetic resource depends substantially on further investments in research and development. Of course the genetic resource itself must be paid for, but this accounts only for part of the value that a product or production process can generate. Translating the conceptual notion of evolutionary value into a concrete rule to estimate a fair share of the benefits for the genetic resource is not easy (SWANSON 1997). Developing a drug and obtaining a legitimate patent requires time and resources. As a result, ensuring that a share of the benefits is received by the provider of genetic resources and/or associated traditional knowledge requires complex institutional designs. Thus, legitimate and legal bioprospecting projects usually have high transaction costs. The cases described in this chapter will reveal some of the many forms that these costs can take.

Seeds, vegetative parts, and other reproductive materials including larvae or sperm, have been collected systematically and exchanged under the aegis of the Food and Agriculture Organization (FAO) as common heritage resources or, in other words, as biodiversity in trust (FUCCILLO et al. 1997). Until a decade ago these resources were rarely subject to patent claims, but with the advent of modern biotechnology there is a need to update and clarify the legal situation of these resources. The recently adopted[5] International Treaty on Plant Genetic Resources for Food and Agriculture (ITPGRFA) is a step forward in this direction. This is one of the most important multilateral events taking place after Rio and before Johannesburg and it endorses the CBD principles. The implications of ITPGRFA for bioprospecting in the food and agriculture sector are hard to evaluate yet, but there is an opportunity for greater coordination among ministries

of different sectors. Surprisingly, while our country played an important role since the negotiations started ten years ago it has not signed the treaty yet.

Most genetic resources have not been collected yet, as is the case for most FAO-related crops, and this is a relevant difference in terms of the negotiating position of megadiverse countries with respect to ABS. If we harvest a biological resource, the territory or land ownership can be a logical criterion for property rights, but when genetic resources are separated from their territory, land property as a criterion is clearly limited. If someone sells a permit for deer hunting, he does not necessarily invade the rights of others. But if he offers access to the genes of a plant living on his land and on his neighbors' land, he faces the possibility of incurring moral or patrimonial damage to third parties. This fact clearly justifies the need of State involvement in these processes[6]. By analogy, Mexico's Constitution, like many other legal frameworks around the world, takes an approach that justifies State intervention when dealing with the issue of water sources emanating from a property the use of which impacts the availability of water downstream. It is very important to have a clear solution to this issue of wider interest in the case of genetic resources and to have in mind that it involves complex institutional designs and the need to face difficult and diverse social and cultural realities. Developing countries tend to have weak law enforcement in general, particularly within natural resource use and conservation. Thus, it is naïve to think that the solution is only legal. The development of policies regarding genetic resources has to include careful consideration of diffuse property rights, common goods, and collective rights and innovations.

Prior to the CBD, genetic resources flowed freely among countries, but also biotechnology inventions such as genes were rarely protected by patents. After the CBD came into force, there has been a slow adjustment to the new regime. Since the appropriation processes for different natural resources are different, the rights and obligations related to them are also different (Figure 1).

Since legal change is not usually retroactive, we have to face the situation of materials collected pre-CBD and deposited in *ex situ* collections. Whether public or private, their legal status has not been fully clarified. This is also an area where the ITPGRFA will have important consequences. On the other hand, there has been further collecting post- CBD without prior informed consent (PIC) and benefit-sharing agreements. When, in addition to that, those possessing the materials claim intellectual property rights on dubious inventive and industrial application grounds, the result is what we call biopiracy. Biopiracy, is probably one of the major threats to the viability of legitimate bioprospecting agreements. Thus, although this report deals mainly with ABS, we firmly believe that illegitimate and/or illegal patenting practices, particularly in the United States, remain a fundamental obstacle to the legitimacy of bioprospecting. Such patenting practices have to stop. Otherwise, those who see biopiracy and bioprospecting as the same

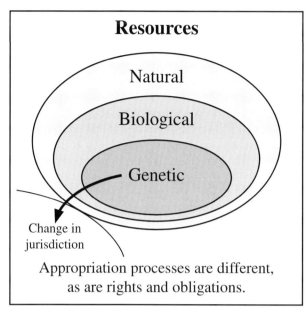

Resources

Natural

Biological

Genetic

Change in
jurisdiction

Appropriation processes are different,
as are rights and obligations.

Figure 1. Natural, biological and genetic resources. Although genetic resources are a part of biological resources and these are a central component of natural resources, the fact remains that the processes of appropriation are different and so are the rights and obligations related to them.

thing will have a relevant point. As an example, consider the case of the USA patent granted on the Enola bean in which initial access was from a public market in Mexico. The biological materials were taken into the United States without permission. In addition, the patent lacks innovation worthy of qualifying as invention. A definitive legal decision will not be reached until after the request to re-examine posed by the Center for International Tropical Agriculture is settled. The ayahuasca case is another example of this issue, because a clearly illegitimate patent was re-examined and finally reinstated by the USA Patent and Trademark Office (USPTO), after a costly process.[7] This is worrying precedent that should alert academics and civil society within the USA.

There are many other patents in the United States and Europe that involve Mexican genetic resources and/or traditional knowledge or make use of them in their development. Some of them are clearly illegal and illegitimate, but the picture is far from being black and white. Box 1 presents examples of patents to illustrate some of these issues. SARUKHÁN et al. (1996) recognized that the issue of genetic resources is the «subject of debate since it involves intellectual property rights, strong economic interests, the ethics of human legacy and the limits to the commercialization of life». These debates are far from being settled and current activities within the CBD, FAO, the World Trade Organization (WTO), and the World Intellectual Property Organization (WIPO) will have to deal with the full extent of these issues in a comprehensive manner in order to achieve coherence at the multilateral level. Interesting work is being developed by WIPO in relation to traditional knowledge and genetic resources (WIPO 2001).

For the authors of this report, biopiracy means the appropriation of genetic resources through noninventive patents, without the prior informed consent of the owners of the resource or knowledge involved, and without effective distribution of contractually agreed benefit sharing. Bioprospecting, on the other hand, may be composed of a superficially similar set of actions, but it declares its intention, it registers patents with clear inventive steps, claims, and industrial applications, and it seeks and obtains previous informed consent and proposes specific schemes for benefit sharing. There are those who assume that biopiracy and bioprospecting are the same thing (see CUADERNOS AGRARIOS 2001, a volume fully dedicated to the issue that reflects part of the social perception on bioprospecting in Mexico). This sets a complex political scene for ABS projects, not only in our country but in other regions of the world as well.

To begin with, we will briefly describe the national legal landscape and comment on the social and cultural context of ABS projects in Mexico. We will then review three projects implemented in Mexico. Finally, we describe current legal initiatives on access to genetic resources, followed by conclusions and recommendations.

Legal Basis for Access and Benefit Sharing in Mexican Law

The Constitution[8]

The basic Constitutional framework related to ABS is found in four articles, because the issue crosses sector boundaries. It is important to note that in Mexico, CBD obligations are above sector-specific federal laws but below the Constitution (Supreme Court 1999). The most relevant Constitutional article in this context is 27, which establishes the basis of land tenure and natural resource use (MEXICAN CONGRESS 1992). This article regulates land property rights, be they private or collective, and it defines public interest over specific elements. In its third paragraph it states that "the nation shall have at anytime the authority

to impose upon private property the conditions dictated by public interest, and to regulate, for social benefit, the use of the natural elements susceptible of appropriation, with the aim of distributing fairly public assets, [and] care for its conservation…. Therefore, the necessary measures will be dictated to …preserve and restore ecological equilibrium… and to avoid the destruction of the natural elements."[9]

Despite the fact that this article indeed explains the sovereignty of the State over certain natural resources, such as oil or water, for example, it is far from clear that this includes all natural resources. The concept of eminent domain over property on behalf of the State (the concept of original public property) is not sufficient to determine *a priori* public property over any natural resource[10]. When not explicitly stated, Article 27 delegates such decisions to ordinary legislation (see Figure 2). If, in turn, subsidiary instruments do not make an explicit decision, then there is an "apparent gap" that is solved by going back to the concept of original property of the State. Thus, there are two complementary arguments to affirm that genetic resources are public property but private individuals have the right to use them. One is the applicability of the WGA that recognizes the right to make a sustainable use. The other

is a constitutional interpretation relating to the concept of original public property.

Article 28 regulates antitrust rules, one of the exemptions being intellectual property rights: "The privileges that, for a certain period of time, are granted to ...inventors and innovators of any addition shall not constitute a monopoly" (MEXICAN CONGRESS 1995). This article, along with article 25 (MEXICAN CONGRESS 1999) indicates three ways in which an activity can be affected by a special public regimen. These are the strategic areas,

---

Box 1. Examples of USA patents related to Mexican genetic resources or traditional knowledge

In most biotechnological development with an industrial purpose, the usual final step in the appropriation process is the granting of a patent. Problems in this important link of the chain weaken the whole structure of bioprospecting practices proposed by the CBD framework. The issuing of patents on living organisms, DNA sequences, enzymes, etc., with doubtful invention involved and broad industrial application claims is one of the facets that polarize and confuse discussions on bioprospecting.

Both recent and older patents involving Mexican genetic resources or traditional knowledge show some of the gray areas in which we have to deepen our understanding and enhance and tighten the criteria of novelty and invention in patent evaluation related to life systems. Following are three examples that illustrate important issues. Regretfully, they are only a part of the picture of a much wider, more complex process of granting temporal privileges to so-called inventions that only redistribute capital investment or simulate creativity through ideological discourse and technical jargon. Although living resource-related patents are particularly problematic in this regard, SHULMAN (1999) has nicely described other "absurdities" that should also worry USA society (civil, industrial, and academic).

The comments on the patents reflect our opinion, and the examples are intended to illustrate some of the issues and represent a spectrum of patenting practices. At least one of the patents, the so-called Enola bean, is currently in review in response to an objection. Regretfully, examples such as this abound, but this is not the place to suggest a thorough revision. It is, in fact, one of our recommendations to establish an interdisciplinary and intersectorial group to evaluate the extent of this situation regarding Mexican genetic resources and traditional knowledge in the patent offices of several countries. Collaboration among countries on this issue would certainly reduce the costs of monitoring.

These examples show that we need to ask if it makes sense to recognize patents at all. Invention is hard to distinguish from discovery, and many patents have unclear industrial applications, use genetic resources without recognizing third-party rights over them, or fail to recognize the contribution of genetic resources and traditional knowledge.

USPTO 5 894 079, 3 April 1999. Field bean cultivar named Enola. *Larry Proctor.*
This patent "relates to a new field bean variety that produces distinctly colored yellow seed which remain relatively unchanged by season". Seeds were bought in a Mexican

market and belong to a local landrace named Mayocoba of common bean (*Phaseolus vulgaris*). Two generations of self pollination fixed the yellow color but inbreeding produced problems of pod shattering or adherence to the plants. Selection was directed to eliminate this problem rather than to produce a bean of different color. However, the claims of the patent are only related to the germplasm deposited and to the color of the bean. This patent is being re-examined in response to an official request by the International Center for Tropical Agriculture, a member of the Consultative Group on International Agricultural Research. More information is available at http://www.ciat/cgiar/org.

USPTO 5 750 828, 12 May 1998. Method and materials for conferring Tripsacum genes in maize. *Mary Wilkes Eubanks.*
This patent shows inventive steps that seem original and non-obvious but which are impossible to achieve without the germplasm of an endemic species from Manantlán, Mexico that is at the core of the germplasm of maize. Setting aside the validity of the invention, access to the genetic resource occurred prior to CBD and relatively independent of the use of traditional knowledge and practices. This patent raises the issue of the legal situation of biological materials collected before the entry into force of the CBD and the possibilities of negotiating benefit sharing even after a patent has been granted.

USPTO Plant Patent 4759, 18 August 1981. Camote plant. *Steven Pollock.*
The abstract speaks by itself: "A new and distinct camote plant has been discovered. The novel psychotropic plant is a variety of the subtropical terricolous Basidiomycete fungus *Psylocibe tampanensis*", and it shows the subtleties of the use of traditional knowledge as a guide. The description recognizes existing Mazatec knowledge and practices relating to the "derrumbe" fungus and builds upon Pollock's own knowledge as a mycologist. He also refers to collaboration with Mexican mycologist Guzman. It is important to note that germplasm involved with the patent was not collected in Mexico, but in Tampa, Florida. Thus this patent did not involve access to Mexican genetic resources but involved Mazatec traditional knowledge. The question is whether it really constitutes an invention or a discovery (as the abstracts indicates) and if the description and isolation of a plant (fungus) constitute inventive steps. This patent has expired already, and we are not aware of further inventive developments deriving from it, nor do we know if it gained its owner economic benefits.

the priority areas and the public services. The areas considered strategic and of exclusive State participation are oil extraction, postal services, and extraction and use of radioactive minerals. On the other hand, some priority areas are satellite communications and train transport. These priority areas are given special public scrutiny, but private individuals can join in their commercial exploitation. The use of genetic resources is not affected by any of these public regimes. Although many people think that genetic resources should be considered a priority area by Mexico, this is not yet reflected in the legal framework. We agree that genetic resources should be regarded at least as a priority. Furthermore, these resources, after careful thought and debate, could be regarded as strategic, because our megadiversity indicates that there is important "wealth" involved, because of the fundamental role that genetic resources has played in our survival as cultures, peoples, and a nation, and because of their enormous value for biotechnology development. However, Article 25 of the Constitution recognizes that such consideration may be included in ordinary legislation. The rights of indigenous peoples over their knowledge and natural resources add complexity to this issue. Rights relating to them should recognize at least four nested levels of autonomy: com-

munity, municipality, people, and multiethnic region (STAVENHAGEN 1999). These rights should also recognize the specific characteristics of traditional medicine and traditional ecological knowledge, among others. Ongoing work is taking place on issues derived from Article 8j of the CBD and the International Labor Organization Agreement 169 related to tribal and indigenous peoples in independent countries. In Mexico, the indigenous uprising of 1994 confronted the nation's conscience, and subsequent negotiations and mobilization led to the recent amendments of Article 2 of the Constitution in the year 2001. According to COSSIO-DIAZ (2001) the amendment recognized two new categories of subjects of the law: indigenous "peoples" and "communities" (MEXICAN CONGRESS 2001). This type of community is different from that established in Article 27 as an agrarian community, which refers to a collective land-ownership regime, in which decisions have to be taken by the Assembly. Under the amendment, section A of this article establishes that "this Constitution recognizes and warrants the right of indigenous peoples and communities to self determination and therefore the autonomy to ...preserve and enrich their languages, knowledge, and all the elements that constitute their culture and identity". Section B of this same article adds that the

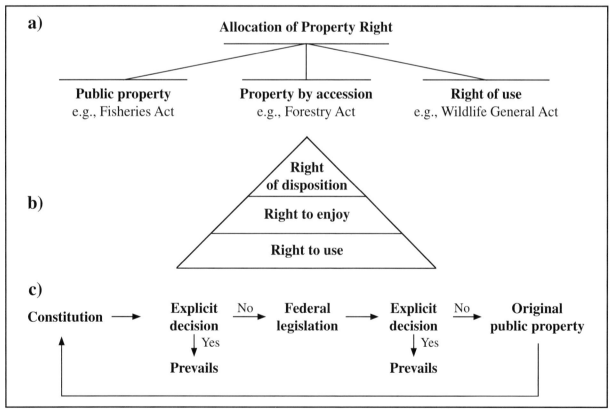

Figure 2. Allocation of property rights and natural resources. a) Sectorial legislation uses three basic techniques to allocate property rights, each of them set forth by different Acts. b) Property rights are comprised of three basic components, which can be separated, therefore, it is possible to allocate to private individuals the rights of the lower category. c) Decision schemes to determine the rights that exist over a natural resource: If the Constitution yields no explicit decision, then Federal legislation is applied; if that still does not resolve the issue, then we face an apparent gap, but legal hermeneutics resolves it by relying on the concept of original public property.

Federation, the States and the Municipalities[11] "in order to reduce the needs that affect the indigenous peoples and communities, shall have the obligation to …support the productive activities and sustainable development of the indigenous communities through actions that will enable them to reach the sufficiency of their economic incomes; the application of incentives for private and public investment that would foster job source creation; the introduction of technologies for raising their own productive capacity; as well as to ensure the equitable access to distribution and commercialization systems". Despite the fact that the amendment is a step forward, the reform will be merely a programmatic list if it is not properly defined in secondary legislation. Although the reforms superficially indicate a move towards recognition of collective rights to indigenous peoples in Mexico, the fact remains that part of the beneficiaries oppose to this reform and are currently demanding cancellation of the amendments and respect for the original reform proposed after the peace talks with the Zapatistas.[12] The outcome of these legal and political objections might have important implications for ABS in Mexico, particularly when it involves genetic resources related to traditional knowledge or indigenous lands and territories.

Thus, the Constitution establishes a set of general rules regarding land property, natural resource management, indigenous peoples, and intellectual property rights that must be elaborated further since new realities need to be faced. Although in many cases practical decisions can be made in ordinary legislation, there are some issues that are too important to be dealt with in secondary legislation, such as the clarification of property rights over genetic resources and the recognition of the collective rights of indigenous peoples.

Federal Legislation

In Mexican legislation, ABS only began to be explicitly regulated in 1996. Article 87 BIS of the EEEPGA was the first step in this direction (MEXICAN CONGRESS 1996b), setting the principles but still lacking specific guidelines, regulations, or standards.

Currently there are three federal environmental laws that regulate access to genetic resources (Table 1): the EEEPGA, the WGA, and SFDGA (MEXICAN CONGRESS 2003). In addition, there are three relevant federal laws that relate directly to this issue: the Industrial Property Act, the Plant

Table 1. Overview of existing laws and regulations with relevance to ABS issues

Constitution

Article 2. Recognizes legal standing for two new categories: indigenous "peoples" and "communities".

Article 25. Defines scope of strategic and priority areas and public services, in which genetic resources are not included.

Article 27. Grants and regulates the right to private property and defines public property over certain natural resources. Does not explicitly define proprietary rights over genetic resources.

Article 28. States the antitrust rule and intellectual property rights as an exemption.

Article 73 (XIX-G). Empowers the State to regulate the use of natural elements and empowers the Federal Congress regarding Environmental Legislation.

Ecological Equilibrium and Environmental Protection General Act (EEEPGA)

Article 2 (III). Use of genetic resources is recognized as "of public interest". Scope includes all species, but regarding aquatic species, coordination with other sectors is ordered.

Article 87. Scientific collection requires authorization, not extended to biotechnological purposes. Economic use of biological resources requires authorization and the explicit consent of the owner of the land has to be obtained.

Article 87-BIS. Biotechnological use requires authorization, subject to the explicit prior informed consent of the owner of the land, who has the right to an equal share of benefits.

Wildlife General Act (WGA)

This law regulates collecting activities for scientific purposes. Its scope limited to wild flora and fauna, excluding aquatic and domesticated species. It also excludes access to genetic resources for biotechnological development and refers this kind of use to other national or international legal instruments.

Sustainable Forestry Development General Act (SFDGA)

Scope related to forest resources. Regulates collecting

for scientific, commercial and biotechnological purposes. Requires an authorization or a notification, both subject to the PIC of the owner of the land. It declares void any registration including patents that do not acknowledge the rights of indigenous people on the ownership, knowledge or use of local varieties. If traditional knowledge is to be used there must be recognition of the ownership on behalf of the communities, an access agreement and proof of PIC. It calls for the promotion and respect of biological traditional knowledge and gives special protection to endemic and threatened species.

Industrial Property Act (IPA)

Article 16 (II). Establishes the positive requirements for patenting (novelty, inventive step, and industrial application), and states an exclusion of patenting over biological and genetic material "as found in nature".

Article 19. Excludes from patenting any discovery.

Plant Varieties Federal Act

Grants rights to plant breeders for varieties that are new, stable, distinct, and homogeneous. Does not address ABS.

NOM-126-ECOL-2000

Regulates scientific collecting. Follows WGA and EEEPGA with technical detail, explicitly excludes forestry related germplasm, and contemplates possible change of purpose from scientific to biotechnological applications.

Criminal Code

Article 420 of the code punishes with prison and a fine any individual who illegally "executes any activity with traffic purposes, or captures, possesses, transports, gathers, introduces to the country or extracts from it, any specimen …and other genetic resources …regulated by any international treaty of which Mexico (is) Party". Furthermore, "additional punishment will be applied …when the …described activities …are executed with commercial purpose".

Variety Federal Act, and the Criminal Code (MEXICAN CONGRESS 2002). Furthermore, there are dispositions in the RSDA that are relevant to traditional knowledge. Likewise, most of the novel provisions of the SFDGA are related to traditional knowledge rather than to ABS in general (see Table 1).

In the EEEPGA, the use of genetic resources is considered of public interest,[13] which means that the State can exercise an authority that supersedes any individual interest on behalf of the higher interest of society. This public interest must be protected and exercise of individuals' rights prejudicial to it must be avoided. This translates into an area of State discretion in which the authority can affect a specific activity, as the State does when declaring a Natural Protected Area over private or collectively owned land.

Thus, the regulation of access to genetic resources is within the jurisdiction of Federal authorities. However, some transfer of faculties to regulate these resources could be agreed upon between federal and state governments through coordination agreements, which would have to meet certain requirements. There are no current examples of such agreements regarding ABS.

The scope of the EEEPGA includes the use of all species, but aquatic species are also regulated by the Fisheries Act, the National Water Act, and relevant international treaties. The few provisions of the SFDGA related to ABS in general (and not to traditional knowledge) do not change the basic scheme of access stated by the EEEPGA and the WGA. Likewise, an authorization is required as well as the PIC of the owner of the land[14]. It only adds a simplified procedure in case of collections done by the owner of the land or by public agencies where only a notification and the PIC are required. There is however, an interesting feature of the SFDGA. By means of definitions it includes in its scope the ABS for biotechnological purposes of wild animals and microorganisms found in forest ecosystems which include a significant proportion of Mexico's terrestrial biodiversity.

General Regulation of Collecting Activities[15]

Collection activity can have three main application purposes: scientific, economic, and biotechnological[16]. In particular, the WGA (MEXICAN CONGRESS 1999) contemplates a wider and more explicit classification of objectives or purposes that exclude biotechnology.[17] Collection with economic purposes is regulated in Article 87 of the EEEPGA, which states that the use of wild flora and fauna specimens in economic activities will be authorized when the individuals guarantee their controlled reproduction or captivity and semi-captivity management, or, in the case of wild populations, the extraction rate should be less than the natural increase (a simple definition of sustainable use). Such use requires the explicit consent of the proprietor or legitimate possessor of the land where the individuals of a species or population are located. Thus, this regulation clearly intends biological resource use.

Collecting for Scientific Purposes

Scientific collection is also regulated in Article 87 of EEEPGA, which states that collection of wild flora and fauna specimens, as well as other biological resources (which by definition include genetic resources), requires an authorization. This authorization cannot be extended to biotechnological purposes, and it shall be ensured that research results will be available to the public, a provision that needs to be evaluated with regard to intellectual property.

As for the WGA article 97 states that before any collecting can be carried out the explicit PIC of the owner of the land (where the resources is located) must be obtained. Scientific collection authorizations shall not include biotechnology applications, nor commercial purposes and will be granted only when the viability of the populations, species, habitats, and ecosystems is not compromised. These authorizations are granted in two modalities: a permit by specific project or a license for a researcher with a specific line of research. Both require report submissions and deposit of at least one duplicate of the collected material in a Mexican institution or scientific collection.

Complementing Article 87 there is an Official Mexican Standard that regulates scientific collection (NOM-126-ECOL-2000). It basically follows the regulations of the WGA (with technical detail that it is not relevant here), with the exception that it contemplates a change of purpose from scientific to biotechnological applications, recognizing that scientific collections can later be used for industrial applications. In this case it mandates a new declaration stating a change of purpose, thus setting the stage for new PIC and ABS agreements. It is interesting to note that this simple measure may prove to have a low transaction cost because the change in the PIC and the negotiation of the ABS agreement would happen only after a finding that merited further development of the genetic resource. Thus, scientific collection is regulated and differentiated from collecting with biotechnological or economic purposes, but the distinction is not always easy to follow. The possibility of a future change of purpose is realistic, but it could create a sort of loophole in which ABS and PIC are not faced at the onset but are postponed. This Official Mexican Standard also confirms that for collecting aquatic species a special fishery permit is required, pursuant to other applicable legislation.

Collecting for Biotechnological Development Purposes

Biotechnological purposes are regulated in Article 87 BIS of the EEEPGA, which states that "the use of flora and fauna specimens, as well as other biological resources, requires an authorization, which can only be issued if the explicit PIC is granted by the owner or legitimate possessor of the land where the resources are located who shall have the right to the equal sharing of the benefits arising from the use of the resources". It is important to note that until recently this was the only article within the entire Mexican legal framework that directly regulated bioprospecting. Despite the fact that it comprises two elements stated by the CBD (the PIC and the benefit- sharing provisions), there are many aspects of ABS that at the national level are left to the authorities for interpretation and effective implementation. This article does not make any reference to the third fundamental element of access outlined in the CBD, the "mutually agreed terms" which is commonly understood to have a contractual nature. Due to this lack of reference the law reserves this element for private development which constitutes an important signal to the market. This feature of the current legal framework has been criticized and can be read in contrast with the proposed initiatives of law.

It is worth noting that while the CBD establishes rights and obligations among parties, Article 87 BIS also gives the right to grant PIC (and therefore to receive the benefits) to the owners of land. This transfer of benefits has intrinsic problems, because it amplifies the consequences of ownership of the resource, which is resolved in Mexico by granting rights of use. However, the problem of the transboundary nature of genetic resources is not acknowledged. Under such conditions, when the owners of the land grant a PIC, they may be affecting rights over genetic resources also found in neighboring fields. Furthermore, with regard to the distribution of benefits, attaching them to the granting of PIC has exclusion implications, since benefit-sharing arrangements compensate only the person(s) granting the PIC and not other custodians of genetic resources. It could be argued that this means that in Mexican Law there are two PICs, one given by the Mexican Government in the form of a collecting permit and another given by the owners of the land. In the first case the interest of society is protected and in the second, the interest of the owner(s) of the land. Thus, it is fundamental to address this situation in depth for any future comprehensive legislative effort.

As already indicated, the other environmental law regulating access to genetic resources is the WGA. It establishes that the right to make a sustainable use of the wildlife specimens found within the boundaries of a property is granted to the owner of the land.[18] This is important regarding the property status of genetic resources because the Constitution does not define them as private or public and ordinary legislation does not take a classic or strict property decision but assigns a right to sustainable use on behalf of landowners.

The WGA requires *proof of legal provenance* for registration and authorizations related to biological materials of wild species outside their habitat.[19] This disposition exemplifies the use of legal provenance as an instrument to regulate possession of biological materials such as wildlife cargo or hunting trophies. By analogy, a similar approach could be taken in the process to obtain intellectual property rights such as patents: including proof of having complied with the ABS conditions of the provider country or region. It is interesting to note in this regard the emergence of proposals to extend the disclosure requirements in intellectual property right applications, such as the one proposed by the Swiss, which calls for a requirement to disclose the origin, if known, of the genetic materials and traditional knowledge used in the inventions. These amendments are fully compatible with existing intellectual property rights principles since they constitute part of the description of the invention. However, these proposals stop short of requiring evidence of prior informed consent, which tends to be considered too complex and costly to be feasible. The development of a certificate of legal provenance would aid in this regard, facilitating the implementation of stricter and more comprehensive disclosure requirements in a more cost effective way. The decisions adopted by the Seventh Conference of the Parties (COP) to the CBD in Kuala Lumpur in 2004 indicate the political willingness to start development of some sort of international certificate for genetic resources which could facilitate the proof of legal acquisition of genetic materials at various stages of their use.

Ex Situ Collections

The EEEPGA does not regulate *ex situ* collections. Regarding the WGA, a few articles regulate access to *ex situ* collections indirectly: any scientific and museum collection, whether private or public, must be registered and permanently updated in an official record. Once registered, they can be exempted, under specific circumstances, from certain obligations regulating proof of legal provenance as long as they do not have any biotechnological or commercial purposes. In addition to severe punishments outlined by the Criminal Code in the next section, article 122 of WGA punishes as an administrative infringement the lack of due permits for the use of biological material for biotechnological applications.

The Criminal Code

The Criminal Code (MEXICAN CONGRESS 2002) punishes with prison from one to ten years and a fine of 300 to 3,000 minimum daily wages to those who "illegally execute any activity with traffic purposes, or capture, possess, transport, gather, introduce to the country, or extract from it, any specimen, its products, its subproducts, and other *genetic resources*, of any wild flora and fauna species, terrestrial species, or aquatic species on temporary prohibition, considered endemic, threatened, endangered, subject to special protection, or regulated by any international treaty of which Mexico has become a Party".[20] Furthermore, "an additional punishment will be applied when the described activities are executed in or affect a natural protected area, or when they are executed with commercial purpose".

Considering the models of criminal behavior proposed by Economic Analysis of Law (POSNER 2002) a person is assumed to act rationally on the basis of costs and benefits of legal and illegal opportunities. Particularly, most studies corroborate the hypothesis that the probability of punishment is more important than its severity as a deterrent effect on crime. Therefore, in theory, this regulation should promote compliance with current legal obligations. However, collecting seeds or microorganisms is almost impossible to control (a tourist can take samples back to his country with almost no difficulty). If caught in Mexico, he would face the aforementioned punishment, but the likelihood of such an event happening is so slim that his chances are good of taking the material without complying with our regulation.

On the other hand, and as will be seen below, if those who try to comply with the law face social objections, legal confusions, and high transaction costs, then the message that Mexico is sending to the world is that to ask for permission can be much more costly than simply taking the material. The punishment in the Criminal Code should help prevent such actions, but the reality of the distribution of living species and the ease with which they can be collected makes it unlikely that it will be an effective measure by itself.

Plant Breeders' Rights and Patents

The Plant Variety Protection Act (MEXICAN CONGRESS 1996a) gives property rights to plant breeders for a plant variety that is new, stable, distinct, and homogeneous. This is relevant in the ABS context because it is possible to obtain plant breeders rights without requiring an "inventive step" and under a more relative standard of "novelty". Thus, obtaining these rights may be easier and more flexible than obtaining a patent and the issue of access regulation becomes much more important. In most cases there are traditional and time consuming collective practices involved in the domestication or initial selection of wild germplasm. In Mexico this Intellectual Property Rights (IPR) approach is particularly undeveloped, but it will be important to monitor the granting of plant breeders' rights in other countries that use Mexican germplasm.

The Industrial Property Act (IPA) (MEXICAN CONGRESS

1994) in Mexico is relevant because it includes the possibility of obtaining patents over genetic resources. In any case, patents should comply with the requirements of novelty, inventive step, and industrial application, and there is an exception to patenting of biological and genetic material "as it is found in nature". The criterion with which this exception is applied is highly relevant: the current practice by the patent office in Mexico is to consider that once biological or genetic material has been isolated and characterized, it is no longer "as it is found in nature".[21] Such interpretation is not shared by the authors of this work nor do we think that it should be a common practice (this position is also found in CORREA (1999) and WTO (1997)), because isolating and characterizing biological materials is not an activity directly relevant to the creativity of the invention and such protections really recognize capital investment rather than invention. Therefore if a patent is granted on isolated and characterized materials then protection is being granted to discoveries, which are expressly excluded by Article 19 of the IPA. This is an issue of the in-depth patent review process that has to be resolved.

What needs to be clearly defined is that a product derived from isolating and describing the functions of biological materials does not comply with the inventive step requirement, and that inventions worthy of patents should involve modifications to the original material that are novel, nonobvious, and contribute decisively to the claimed industrial application.[22] This is a complex matter in itself. In Box 1, three examples are given of patents related to "Mexican" genetic resources or traditional knowledge.

The legal principles and regulations described are those in force at the time this paper was written. However, it should be kept in mind that the different ABS experiences described occurred when some of these regulations did not even exist. This has to be taken into account when reading the cases because not all legal aspects described above were already in place when the bioprospecting projects developed.

Social and Cultural Context for ABS

Compliance with laws and regulations is only a part of what is needed to achieve the general objectives of ABS: contributing to sustainable development and *in situ* conservation of biodiversity. Institutionality in a wide sense is the framework in which ABS can contribute to these objectives. When the genetic components of biodiversity are seen as resources, the question of value creation and recognition becomes fundamental, and the social and cultural realities in which this happens are of high importance.

Mexico faces severe social and political contradictions and tensions in rural areas. This is part of the institutional context that has to be considered when evaluating the potential contribution of ABS to development and conservation in our country. For instance, between

1988 and 1994, there were close to 18,000 documented human rights violations of different degrees in rural and indigenous Mexico; 38% of them were related to agrarian conflict (RAMÍREZ-CASILLAS 2000). This shows the degree of polarization present in rural and indigenous land in Mexico in regard to land tenure and natural resource use. Furthermore, half of the agrarian-related human rights violations mentioned above happened in Chiapas in the years before the Zapatista uprising. Although Mexico is in a process of democratic change, this does not mean that we have solved the agenda of poverty and land and resource use or created mechanisms to solve conflict in rural areas. This is a reality that has to be taken into account when thinking of bioprospecting in rural Mexico.

An additional issue to consider is that a contract that involves transferring biological materials to another country is seen by many sectors as a violation of the country's sovereign rights over its resources. This is a fundamental point in terms of political legitimacy for bioprospecting. Although we think that the experiences described below are proposals that precisely indicate a sovereign way in which to implement ABS, others see them as another form of piracy or as the ongoing sale of the country's resources. In fact, the National Indigenous Congress, one of the two main indigenous peoples coalitions in Mexico, has called for a total moratorium on all prospecting (including minerals, water, and biodiversity) in their territories (HARVEY 2002).

In many of these discussions and conflicts the main issue is one of value: neglected, appropriated, built, or recognized. Value creation and recognition is a complex process that involves many different activities. With the risk of oversimplifying, Figure 3 shows some of the important components. On top of the value creation and recognition arrow are the "informal" contributions made collectively and through generations by peasants and indigenous peoples that we are only beginning to fully recognize. Below the arrow are the contributions made by "formal" institutions, which are commonly recognized through State support or even by granting intellectual property rights to guarantee a return of the investment in innovation. This inequality between forms of innovation that have been valued since the industrial revolution and the contributions, both past and present, that we are just beginning to recognize is one of reason that ABS institutional designs tend to be so complex. Leveling the playing field among all stakeholders can be very difficult; consequently, short-term, nonmonetary benefits are very important when future benefits are, in a sense, meaningless to rural societies that are dealing with basic survival and subsistence

issues. Indigenous and peasant communities own most of the land where biodiversity is distributed in Mexico. Contributions by rural population have been historically neglected. Bioprospecting seeks to recognize these contributions and to generate mechanisms to reward them. To do so with legitimacy requires a social and cultural context in which peasants and indigenous communities have already begun the full appropriation of the values of their own resources.

The objective of ABS is to design institutional collaboration schemes that can address the recognition of the values that each part contributes in the development of a commercially viable product and to distribute the benefits that may be obtained according to their relative contributions. Thus, most ABS proposals include components of both the "formal" and the "informal" component of value creation and recognition. A strict definition of bioprospecting focuses on the value of "formal" components and speaks of retribution and benefit sharing from the value created by industrial development and commercialization. However, a wider definition of bioprospecting, such as the one used below in describing the activities of an indigenous organization in Oaxaca, is useful in leveling the ground because it recognizes the contribution of less intense biotechnological activities to value creation.

In general, the principal parties in ABS are the owners of the biological resource (the State and the landowners, be they private or collective), those intending to access the resource for technological development (researchers, research centers, and private companies), and a number of third parties involved in the ABS activities (in country collaborators). These third parties may probe to have a primary role in terms of technology transfer due to the need to have a suitable recipient in order for the transfer to occur (GOLLIN 1993). Hence, the roles each of the parties

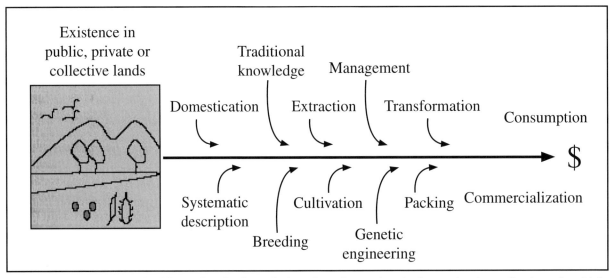

Figure 3. Recognizing and adding value. In the end, the value of a product in the market is a reflection of multiple processes that involve traditional or "informal" innovation and labor (above the arrow) and "formal" contributions to the value of the product (below).

play changes significantly from case to case, but the basic issue to be addressed is that each transaction among them must be known and fully understood by all parties and must involve a full recognition of the contribution of each. The knowledge, understanding, and trust that is needed to reach this level of communication between parties is not easy to achieve in a polarized political environment,

and the transaction costs can be very high. The following examples will show that Mexico is far from reaching such a level of understanding and trust between sectors. Thus, as they were ten years ago, awareness raising and capacity building are still at the top of the agenda in order to enhance the social and cultural environment for ABS projects in rural Mexico.

Three Bioprospecting Projects in Mexico

The following sections deal with three projects implemented in Mexico during the nineties. They are not the only ones that occurred, but they are by far the ones better documented and in which the authors had first-hand experience and information. Other experiences involve early attempts by Shaman Pharmaceuticals (CAMBERROS 1999), a company that evolved into Shaman Botanicals, and also an International Cooperative Biodiversity Group (ICBG)[23] related to arid zones and implemented through coordinated activities in several Latin American countries (TIMMERMANN et al. 1999).[24]

Of the three cases selected, the first one, based on ecological and evolutionary knowledge, excluded bioprospecting in socially owned land. It precipitated a "popular denunciation" that was presented before the Federal Attorney for the Protection of the Environment (PROFEPA) and triggered a set of recommendations that effectively suspended the bioprospecting activities. The second one included indigenous territories in Northern Oaxaca, but excluded traditional resources and knowledge. This project was completed successfully. The third case involved plants and traditional knowledge in the complex region of the Chiapas Mayan Highlands. This project was cancelled, proving that the basic issues surrounding bioprospecting have not been resolved in Mexico.

UNAM-Diversa: Bioprospecting in Extreme Environments

Brief Overview
This was the first ABS project in Mexico that went through a legal administrative process; it is rich in legal documentation and also underwent academic and press scrutiny. Therefore, it reflects the legal issues as well as the multiple conflicting views of different sectors on these matters. The project is also less complex than others in that it excludes traditional knowledge and collecting was designed to be made only on Federal Public Land, a fact that brought into one legal entity, the roles of the landowner subject of PIC and of the authority granting the permits.[25]

Institutional Context
On October 15, 1998, the Biotechnology Institute (IBT) of the National Autonomous University of Mexico (UNAM) and the United States-based Diversa Corporation Inc. (Diversa) signed a bioprospecting agreement whose purpose was the "collection, isolation, and extraction

of nucleic acids from biological samples obtained from lands owned by the Federation and located within Natural Protected Areas". The major benefits shared were "technologies and know-how transfer related to the extraction and cloning of DNA", plus "equipment transfer, payment of fees, and payment of royalties on products patented and sold by Diversa". While the royalties attracted most of the attention, the main dispositions of the bioprospecting agreement are shown in Table 2, which reveals the symmetry of the institutions involved regarding activities and benefits shown in Table 3. The aim was to obtain microorganisms and nucleic acids from samples from extreme environments and to seek subcomponents of industrial interest (PERSIDIS 1998).

It is worth noting that the relationship between UNAM and Diversa in no way included the potential asymmetries involved in agreements between indigenous communities and international organizations. Thus, the mutually agreed terms were fully understood by both parties. Particularly, the IBT was a suitable recipient of the negotiated technology transfer. An example of IBT's existing capacities to

Table 2. General aspects of the mutually agreed terms between the IBT of UNAM and Diversa

IBT of UNAM	Diversa
Obligations	
Obtain the PIC from the owner of the land. Collect and provide samples. Ensure that monetary benefits are deposited in the Biodiversity Trust Fund, on behalf of the owner of the land, and channeled to the National Protected Areas.	Provide technical assistance to establish a Mexican collection of wild microorganisms and DNA sequences. Provide equipment and training to collect and process samples. Provide technology and "know-how." Pay fee for samples. Provide corresponding benefits depending on the activities developed by UNAM.
Rights	
Receive technology and "know-how", technical assistance, fee for samples, monetary benefits, and IPRs.	Intellectual property rights and property rights over the components depending on the innovation activities developed.

133

produce useful drugs is the development of a product for noncoagulation of blood derived from the saliva of the common bat (*Desmodus rotundus*) in a biotechnological project with plenty of innovation and with clear industrial applications (ALAGÓN-CANO 1999). IBT was basically playing on a level field. Furthermore, a search in the USPTO internet database on patents shows that Diversa is the assignee of 45 patents as of 24 May 2002, and a brief review of these patents shows that Diversa's intellectual property policy involves inventions with clear industrial applications. Both of these factors are important in evaluating this agreement between two strong biotechnological institutions, one private and one public.

One of the objectives of collecting on public lands inside natural protected areas was that this contract would be carried out in a setting of clear property rights for the State. This contributed to the Mexican experience in negotiating access agreements without the complexity inherent in diffuse settings of property and traditional knowledge of indigenous peoples.

On 13 November 1998, the Secretariat of Environment and Natural Resources (SEMARNAT), through the National Institute of Ecology (INE), the National Commission for the Knowledge and Use of Biodiversity (CONABIO), and UNAM, through IBT, signed a Collaboration Agreement to facilitate the execution of UNAM's obligations under the bioprospecting agreement. The main dispositions of this agreement were that:

- INE would select the collection sites located within Federal Public Land and within the boundaries of Federal Natural Protected Areas.

- UNAM would be responsible for ensuring that monetary benefits arising from the bioprospecting agreement would be deposited in CONABIO's Trust Fund for Biodiversity[26], according to the guidelines jointly issued by the INE and CONABIO.

- To implement the above, UNAM would keep a record of collection sites, collected samples, materials transferred to Diversa, and the derived products.

Table 3. UNAM-Diversa agreement: joint and separate activities, intellectual property, and benefit sharing. Diversa does not collect material in any of the four different scenarios recognized by the agreement.

			Scenario			
			1	2	3	4
Activities	**Separate**	**UNAM**	Collection Isolation Extraction	Collection	Collection Isolation Extraction Identification	Identification
		Diversa		Isolation Extraction Identification		Identification
	Joint		Identification			Applying for patent over the same component
Intellectual Property and Benefit Sharing	**Separate**	**UNAM**	Technology transfer to pursue its activities	Royalties over products' net sales (0.3% and 0.4%)	Owns any rights over: - Sample materials - Derived products - Sales revenues - Intellectual property rights	
		Diversa		Owns any rights over: - Sample materials - Intellectual property rights		
	Joint		Obligation to negotiate a proportional share over: - Sample materials - Derived products - Sales revenues (Intellectual property rights)			First to identify prevails if patents derive from the same component. Other party will have right to: - a nonexclusive free license - grant scientific research sublicenses

- INE and CONABIO would take adequate measures to ensure that income from this source would be used in the same Natural Protected Areas where the materials had been collected.

Social Controversy

This bioprospecting project was seeing as a capacity-building experience to establish minimums for this type of contract. Press coverage showed that some saw this contract as a genetic resources "sale" and failed to recognize the value of the agreement as an important "know-how" transfer between parties with similar scientific and technical capabilities. On 28 September 1999, in *La Jornada*, a Mexico City newspaper, Alberto Székely and Alejandro Nadal each wrote articles about the UNAM/Diversa project. While Székely's article ("First effective effort to stop the plundering of the genetic resources") supported the project, Nadal's article ("The plundering of genetic resources") argued that the project had several legal and conceptual problems. If both of these authors are reasonable analysts, why do they have totally opposite positions in this matter? The answer probably lies in the fact that multiple assumptions are being made by each of them. For example, Székely values the "know-how" transfer, while Nadal disregards it and even calls it "a mask".

The main arguments in the press against the agreement ran as follows: legal gaps must be attended to before any agreement is signed; the agreement infringed national legislation, as well as the CBD; UNAM had no rights over the genetic material to be transferred to Diversa; the benefits shared were ludicrous, and the contractual obligation to share benefits was ambiguous and difficult to enforce.

Another of the main opposing arguments stated that industrial property legislation excluded discoveries of natural phenomena, such as the discovery of the information merely hidden in genetic material, from patent protection. Thus, all of the agreement's clauses regarding the possibility of obtaining patents were void. This argument is important because it shows the perception that patents on discoveries are being granted, and although they are not the general rule, they undermine the very grounds of bioprospecting agreements in which genetic resource value is recognized and innovation is protected.

As a result of the UNAM-Diversa controversy in Mexico, some provisions of international agreements, such as Article 27.3.b of the Agreement on Trade Related Intellectual Property Rights (TRIPS) which recognizes patents on microorganisms, were brought into the public arena as a vehicle for protesting the international expropriation of genetic resources. Thus, a long-postponed debate started. Despite the legal and technical inaccuracies and inconsistencies found in its coverage, the press did reflect social concerns that must be fully considered to create legislation that has legitimacy.

Press scrutiny raised doubts regarding the legality of the UNAM-Diversa agreement, and on 7 June 2000 a group of individuals and nongovernmental organizations[27] submitted a "popular denunciation"[28] against UNAM, INE, and CONABIO, for activities derived from the agreement (PROFEPA 2000). Figure 4 describes the parties to the controversy and gives an overview of the project.

The "popular denunciation" sought that the competent authority, PROFEPA, should declare the nullity of the agreement and should also declare a general *moratorium* on any bioprospecting activities in the country, based on the following arguments:

- Genetic resources rest within the sovereignty of the Mexican State; therefore UNAM cannot carry out acts of disposition of such resources.

- Collecting would take place in Federal Land, and the bioprospecting agreement did not take into account the Federation's interests since it was not a party to the agreement.

- The collection was done in Natural Protected Areas subject to several property regimes, social or private, and the PIC of all right holders had not been obtained.

- Benefit sharing was not equal due to the insignificant monetary fees.

- Some authorizations were issued for scientific purposes; therefore, some activities could have been done without authorization for biotechnological purposes.

- On the date of signature there was no proof of the PIC by the owner of the land.

After a thorough review of the documents and facts, on 29 November 2000, PROFEPA issued recommendation 01/2000 on Access to Genetic Resources, in which it reasoned that it did not have the authority to declare the agreement void. Further reasoning for the PROFEPA decision is described in Table 4.

Current Situation

As a consequence of this line of reasoning, PROFEPA recommended to the issuing authority (INE) that it should take the necessary measures to ensure that Diversa requested the adequate authorizations, that if so determined, the president of INE issue the PIC separately from the authorization. Finally, it recommended that a wide public consultation should be undertaken regarding access to genetic resources. As a result of the above recommendations and of the uncertainties surrounding access conditions, all bioprospecting activities were stopped, but collaboration between the two institutions continued in capacity building, training and technology transfer. Since the contract was not declared void, the ABS agreement finally expired on 14 October 2001.

Mexico had no prior experience in negotiating a contract with so many advantages in "know-how" transfer. If even these forms of benefit distribution are regarded as lacking value by those objecting to bioprospecting, the road to legitimate bioprospecting in Mexico will still be a long one.

UZACHI-Sandoz: A Bioprospecting Experience in Indigenous Territories without Providing Traditional Knowledge

For the purpose of this section we will use "bioprospecting" in a broad sense as in "the process of developing new uses for living organisms or their derivatives" and not only for using genetic resources (CHAPELA 1997). Bioprospecting also includes the learning of new processing techniques or uses, or more sophisticated *biotechnologies*[29], including fermentations and plant tissue culture or genetic manipulation techniques.

UZACHI is the Spanish acronym for "Zapotec and Chinantec Communities Union". It includes a Chinantec community of three settlements with 1,529 inhabitants (Comaltepec, La Esperanza, and Soyolapan) and three Zapotec communities (Xiacuí, Capulalpam, and Trinidad) with a population of 3,162. The area is recognized for its world-level biological importance, an example being the presence of *Papilio esperanza*, a microendemic swallowtail butterfly species named after the community mentioned above (TYLER et al. 1994). These and other Zapotec communities were the cradle of nineteenth century progressive and liberal thinking. Benito Juarez, the only self-conscious indigenous president that Mexico has had in its national history, was born in this region. Progressive Chinantec and Zapotec minds have led these communities in several social movements throughout their history. In recent times they have claimed legal rights to manage their own forests. During the 1980s they filed a lawsuit against the Minister of Agriculture and the President and recovered forest management and use rights that were previously under concession to a decentralized government paper company. Since then sawn wood has become their main source of income.

UZACHI has developed several initiatives to protect "their natural endowment" and to develop their customary stewardship institutions, using updated technologies when possible. They developed the first computerized forest production control systems in the area, started a microbiology laboratory, and were the first indigenous organization in Oaxaca connected to the Internet. Recently, they set up their own plant tissue culture and DNA analysis facilities. These processes were fostered by their traditional governing bodies. Their view is that the natural endowment within their territories is to be responsibly used and developed to improve their living standards and to assure the well being of their children and grandchildren.

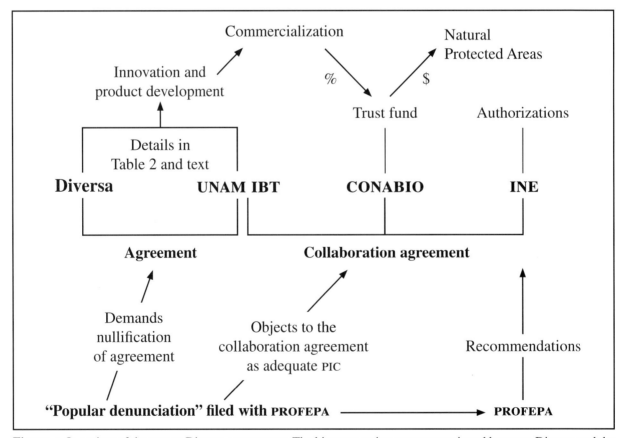

Figure 4. Overview of the UNAM-Diversa controversy. The bioprospecting agreement signed between Diversa and the IBT of UNAM was followed by a Collaboration Agreement between INE, CONABIO, and UNAM. After months of press scrutiny, a "Popular Denunciation" was submitted to PROFEPA with the demands indicated. The process concluded with a set of recommendations to INE.

The prevalence of traditional governance structures and a strong sense of the territory do not mean physical or cultural isolation in this case. Apparently, the use of modern technologies is not seen as a threat to their customary management systems, but rather as tools to control their resources under traditional governance and stewardship structures. UZACHI had fully appropriated its territory before bioprospecting was even considered. This approach was, in a sense, wise management of its resources, as long as UZACHI had the cultural capacity to control them and to get tangible benefits from them. For instance, in 1993 they contacted *matzutake* mushroom brokers to benefit from a valuable market. *Matzutake,* meaning "pine mushroom" in Japanese, is an interesting delicatessen item. One fresh kilogram is worth about $65 to 70 USD. Brokers were given the following conditions: buyers would have no access to UZACHI's forests; they would go to a community delivery point and purchase from community-authorized collectors; and they would pay them a previously publicly agreed price and pay an extra 10% fee to the community for control and protection activities. As *matzutake* had no previous use for these communities, these contracts enabled them to benefit from a "new" biological resource. This is a simple but effective way to bioprospect, developing a component of biodiversity into a biological resource and its derived products. After this experience, UZACHI's bioprospecting activities expanded. In 1994, they started their own studies on local edible mushrooms and on their traditional knowledge, which was vanishing. One year later, they started to train their own personnel in ecology and plant tissue culture.

With its "ethno-oriented sustainable development" approach, UZACHI tried to contact pharmaceutical industries to develop other biological resources. Their previous *matzutake* success gave them confidence to explore a new area. After considering several options, and after a three-year negotiating process (1990–1993), they finally signed a three-year (1995–1998) contract with the Switzerland-based Sandoz-Pharma.[30] A local nongovernmental organization, Estudios Rurales y Asesoría Campesina (ERA), assisted them in the negotiation process, mainly as translators and as technical advisors. As the negotiating process took place at the same time as the CBD was discussed, this contract was one of the first in the world to test and set in practice the main principles of this new international framework.

It is very important to underline that the signatories from the biological resources supply side were the indigenous communities. A Sandoz-Pharma high-level officer and the president of the indigenous organization signed the contract (see Figure 5 for an overview of the agreement). In recent times, this component of UZACHI's activities has received public attention, so we will address the issue, but it must be kept in mind that the UZACHI-Sandoz contract was only part of a more comprehensive strategy of indigenous communities to control their resources, develop new uses for them, and expand their own knowledge and resource transformation capacities.

Institutional Context

An interesting feature of the property system in Mexico is the right of rural and indigenous communities recognized by the Constitution to own land collectively. However, communities have struggled to exercise this property right. For their bioprospecting activities, they claimed in a sense, this full or broad property right.

In fact, environmental law was the only legislation available to regulate rights over biological resources. It used basically the same framework: the landowner has the right to develop the biological resources, as long as he/she does not threaten biodiversity, vegetation or the soil. This legal framework made it possible for an indigenous organization to sign a legally binding contract with an international firm.

Building on experience, UZACHI negotiated with Sandoz carefully considering the following hierarchically structured items:

- Minimize potential risks to their common natural endowment. Under no circumstance would access to communal lands be granted to Sandoz collectors, and no herbal traditional knowledge would be provided under any agreement.

- Maximize their own ability to manage biodiversity-related transactions and to capture as much as pos-

Table 4. PROFEPA's analysis of the UNAM-Diversa agreement regarding the authorization, the collecting role, the PIC, and the benefit-sharing issue

Authorization	Collecting role	PIC	Benefit sharing
Diversa must obtain the authorization because it has the biotechnology purpose (not the IBT)[31]. Although they were based on Article 87 BIS, they were specifically issued "for scientific purposes". Thus, no authorizations for bioprospecting existed.	The intermediary role of the collector must be exercised through a previous and explicit mandate of the Federation.	The PIC must be explicit and cannot be confused with the authorization, nor with the collaboration agreement. It must be included in the bioprospecting agreement. Thus, the bioprospecting agreement was not the final agreement, but merely part of the negotiations.	This could only be evaluated once the joint guidelines for making deposits were clearly defined.

sible the benefits from their biological resources.

- Maximize collective benefits in the medium term.
- Maximize short-term benefits.

The institutional framework to negotiate the agreement within UZACHI was a nested scheme where each community discussed the issues related to their biological resources in a general assembly. Then, the communities gathered and let the organization know their concerns and interests through three delegates. The delegates assembly set their priorities as explained above, and a negotiating team was then formed to contact Sandoz. This multi-layered process included technical and information support provided by ERA, which in turn had a formal agreement to collaborate with UZACHI.

ERA also served as a communication path between the UZACHI negotiating team and Sandoz, translating messages to Switzerland and back to the communities. This translation function was not merely changing words from one language to other, but making the messages understandable to both Sandoz officers and the Zapotec and Chinantec communities. To do this work, ERA had financial support from private foundations and was not a contracting party. It had no benefit from the contract besides previously agreed upon honoraria.

Access
One of UZACHI's goals for the negotiation was to develop as far as possible the communities' capacities to add value to their resources and products. This goal is consistent with the priorities outlined above, and it made the issues of infrastructure and social capital building more important to the negotiations than the royalties issue. This contrasts with most ABS initiatives, where royalties play a central role in the contractual design.

Another negotiating goal was to retain any right of access to the community lands. Thus, access for Sandoz was only indirect, and UZACHI offered value-added products. This approach gave them room to receive benefits other than royalties and enable them to demand infrastructure investments, training, collection fees, laboratory work, and collaboration fees. Of course, a share of the benefits in case a new product would be developed and marketed was also negotiated.

From the Sandoz perspective, the main interest was not pharmacological but a more strategic one. They wanted to understand how they could engage in long-term bioprospecting activities. They were also exploring the potential risks and benefits of the CBD's new legal framework. In contrast with other bioprospecting firms, Sandoz is not a natural products business and is not interested in traditional knowledge. Their approach is not to find "active principles" in medicinal herbs and convert them into drugs. Most of their products come from chemical synthesis and their expertise relies in combinatory chemistry. However they had observed competitors, such as Merck or Schering, investing in bioprospecting, and their administration wanted to have first-hand understanding

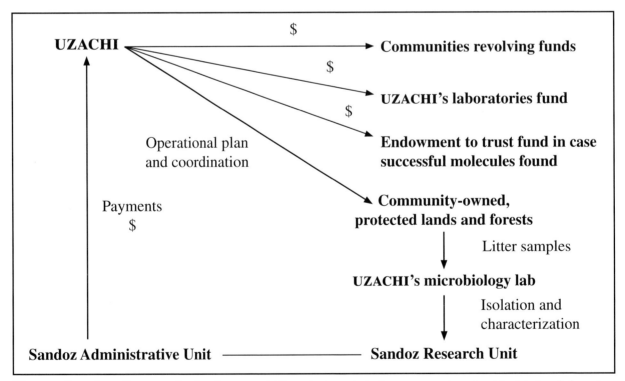

Figure 5. Overview of UZACHI-Sandoz Agreement. The private party in the agreement received isolated and characterized samples and did not have access to the territory. On the other hand, the organization and its communities received upfront short-term benefits in the form of capacity building and direct financing of prospecting activities.

of the opportunities and risks involved in this emerging area. The main interest for Sandoz in bioprospecting was that if the chemists in Switzerland had hints from ecologists collaborating with in-field organizations in tropical areas these chemists might find strategic paths for their combinatory chemistry capacities.

On the other hand, for a high-tech industry like Sandoz, the most interesting taxonomic groups are not plants or animals, where knowledge has accumulated for centuries and the most interesting compounds are already in the market, but instead: the microscopic world, which only began to be explored at the end of nineteenth century and which is one of the most promising field for future discoveries.

Under the agreement, UZACHI took care of all field operations, under mutually agreed standards and under precise and stringent field and laboratory protocols. This ensured useful results for Sandoz at their chemistry labs in Switzerland. UZACHI sent their people to Basel to be trained on the protocols, and then started collecting forest debris samples which they processed in their lab, isolating and characterizing microscopic mushrooms and actinomycetes, selecting those that seemed to be involved in ecological relationships such as commensalism, symbiosis, or parasitism, filing strains into their collection, and mailing duplicates to Basel for chemical analysis without disclosing the biological identity of the samples.

Benefit Sharing

From the start it was evident that the asymmetry between Sandoz and UZACHI was huge. Hence, the scheme of a partnership based on a percentage of net earnings as royalties seemed very unlikely to benefit UZACHI, whose strategy was not to include sensitive information, such as traditional knowledge, in the agreement and to take, as soon as possible, their benefits: increased human, social, and physical capital.

Hence they ensured that most benefits would materialize in the short term. This proved wise, because near the end of the contract Sandoz merged with Ciba, the lead research laboratory in Basel was restructured, and the new administration did not give high priority to long-term chemical innovation processes. This decision has unpredictable consequences to the competitiveness of Novartis-Pharma, but in any case UZACHI accomplished its main short-term objectives.

This case is also peculiar in terms of ABS because they did not need a long chain of intermediaries. The infrastructure was owned by Sandoz during the three-year contract and then passed to UZACHI ownership. UZACHI has since used the lab for its own activities. Payments for sampling and laboratory jobs were deposited directly into UZACHI's account, and were first used to cover operational expenses. Three years after the contract expired, the earnings that remained were used to finance further prospecting activities. Payments to communities were transferred from UZACHI's bank account to each community's account on a revolving basis after they had their own administrative system to use these funds to finance small projects. In this way each community's financial assets increased a little, and UZACHI increased its capacities.

Although the contract was basically a research endeavor, in which Sandoz tried to understand how bioprospecting could help its own pharmaceutical research, there is a chance that some compounds, within the thousands that the project yielded, may be interesting and lead to the development of novel pharmaceutical products. In that case, UZACHI would receive a previously agreed-upon fixed royalty. The amount negotiated was an endowment big enough to finance their technical staff in perpetuity. It will take years to see if any compound or molecule will yield such a result, but at present, UZACHI feels that the benefits it received were fair.

Social Controversies

Social objections to this project have to be placed into context at the local, regional, and national/international levels. Locally, the project had wide support from UZACHI's communities because they proposed it. Their basic concerns were met: control over access to their lands and resources and benefits from their biological resources. However, controversies did arise. There was a tendency to give more jobs to youth from the south (Zapotec) area, and the Chinantec people asked for a more equitable job policy. Unfortunately, the project did not expand enough to provide more employment. Two communities had problems agreeing on how to manage the community fund and set the priorities for using it, which delayed the transfer of funds to one community for a couple of months, and to the second one for a couple of years. This situation provoked tensions, but finally all community funds were transferred.

At the regional level, the project had little or no attention despite efforts made. Two regional information meetings had a very weak response from neighboring communities, and UZACHI also asked the local radio station to broadcast information about the project. The people in charge said the issue had insufficient interest to expend airtime on it. Much later, two years after the contract expired and Sandoz disappeared as such, some people at the radio station realized the importance of the UZACHI-Sandoz project. Indigenous communities directly prospecting on their own lands and receiving Swiss Francs to their bank account now seemed unusual and interesting. Unfortunately, the door for more bioprospecting activities was already closed, at least for the moment, because negotiations with Switzerland were suspended until a clear legal access framework was available in Mexico.

This situation upset the people at the radio station, who then used their airtime to discuss UZACHI's selfish attitude. They also charged UZACHI with "biopiracy", because, as they understood the contract, UZACHI gave Sandoz seeds, herbs, and traditional knowledge that was not their property, but a natural and cultural endowment that belonged to the Zapotec and Chinantec peoples. However, these components had been explicitly excluded from the very beginning and for the same reasons.

At the national and international level, the claims from the local radio were magnified through the newspaper "La Jornada" with aid from the Rural Advancement International Foundation (RAFI) (known today as the action group on Erosion Technology and Concentration (ETC)). RAFI posted the "biopiracy" accusation on the Internet and circulated it via many international email networks. These claims were stopped by UZACHI leaders, who asked representatives of neighboring communities to clarify things. UZACHI publicly showed that they were using their legitimate rights over their territories, and that they did not commit to the project any plant, animal, or any traditional knowledge. Regarding other communities' interest in benefiting from bioprospecting, UZACHI let them know that they hoped more communities would benefit from their biological resources, and that they would be willing to develop a new bioprospecting contract along with other communities whenever that might be possible. In response, two dozen community representatives from the region signed a letter of support of UZACHI and published it in the state newspapers. They did not have the money ($3,000 USD) to publish it in a national journal so it was never known at the national or international levels.

An interesting fact is that indigenous communities in Oaxaca's Sierra Norte are deeply interested in gaining control over their biological resources and in obtaining tangible benefits from them on their tables and their pockets. Bioprospecting projects in their broadest sense, including "soft" biotechnology, are only one of several ways in which to achieve these aims.

Current Situation

UZACHI's international activities are on stand-by because there is legal confusion regarding the current ABS legal framework in Mexico. Under current circumstances, both the industry and the communities' organization cannot commit to long-term ABS contracts. However, the interest of local communities in bioprospecting is high, and they would be willing to negotiate a new contract under the basic principles outlined above and within a comprehensive regulatory framework.

On the "internal front" UZACHI is still developing its biological resources potential. It has become the main supplier of mushroom "seeds" to other communities in the region, concentrating on the saprophytes *Pleurotus ostreatus* and *Lentinus edodes*. UZACHI does not seek to profit from the mushrooms themselves, but from the technical advice they can give to other communities to set up their own rustic mushroom production units. This initiative has helped recover mushroom traditional knowledge that was very fragmented and had nearly vanished; this reappropriation process is helping mushrooms to reappear on Oaxacan tables.

In the near future, UZACHI may expand its local bioprospecting activities aimed at regional consumption and self-sufficiency. The organization has collected the main edible mushrooms found in its communities and can develop the technological package to cultivate them. Again, the main approach is not to profit from supplying biomass, but from technical services.

Another bioprospecting area being developed by UZACHI is tissue culture for the reproduction of ornamental plants with two purposes: The first is to commercialize orchids, cycads, ferns, and bromeliads, internalizing in the price the tissue culture costs and a fee to support the conservation areas. Hence, plants obtained through "soft" biotechnologies may help pay the costs of stewardship of mother plants and their natural habitat. Technical assistance contracts with other communities could be the second purpose. In the long run, this activity may support the development of a market for sustainably produced ornamental plants and a network of indigenous communities producing and marketing these "exotic" plants internationally. Regarding plant variety protection the visualized strategy could be to publish the characteristics of the varieties so the materials may be regarded as "previous art" and not subject to patent or plant variety claims. This could help prevent biopiracy. The benefits from these activities will come directly from marketing plants and not from proprietary claims over germplasm or the royalties produced by such rights.

Among many other lessons, this experience shows that bioprospecting agreements can reach legitimacy if they are a part of a much wider process of social and cultural appropriation of territories and resources. Thus, full implementation of CBD objectives at the local and national level is a precondition for the development of locally and regionally legitimate ABS projects in Mexico.

The Maya International Cooperative Biodiversity Group (ECOSUR-University of Georgia-Molecular Nature Limited): Bioprospecting Resources and their Associated Traditional Knowledge

Brief Overview

The Maya International Cooperative Biodiversity Group was one of the ICBGs approved in 1998. The Maya ICBG was created on the premise that biological resources and traditional knowledge can be effective motivators for community development and resource conservation through the development of natural products such as phytomedicines and agroecological programs, as well as through the development of patentable pharmaceuticals (ROSENTHAL et al. 1999). The participating institutions in this ICBG were El Colegio de la Frontera Sur (ECOSUR) in Mexico, the University of Georgia (UGA) in the USA, and a small United Kingdom based biotechnology company named Molecular Nature Limited (MNL) that was funded in 1999. The study area for the project was the Chiapas highlands, in southeast Mexico, a region with political conflict, extreme poverty, and cultural erosion. For an overview of the agreement, see Figure 6.

In terms of access to genetic resources, the Maya ICBG undertook an important effort to obtain PIC from the communities, both in terms of time and resources dedicated to the task. The benefit-sharing provisions in the Maya ICBG contained some of the most comprehensive packages, including co-ownership of patents, technology transfer, and dissemination of "science-validated" traditional knowledge (BERLIN et al. 1999). Unfortunately, these were not enough to give the project viability in the Chiapas' highlands. Early in its development, opposing regional organizations of traditional healers coupled with radical organizations at the international level rendered the project politically infeasible, forcing the definitive shut down of

the project in October 2001. Thus, this section outlines the proposal and the process, but does not describe a finished and implemented bioprospecting project.

Institutional Context

The traditional medicine of the Chiapas' highlands is unusual in that the communities do not systematically cultivate medicinal plants. The Tzotzil and Tzeltal typically use fresh plants to produce remedies and do not use cultivated species dried or bought in local markets. Communities obtain the most common plants at the sides of roads and paths or in secondary forests, and, although some species are found in restricted habitats, the system appears to have

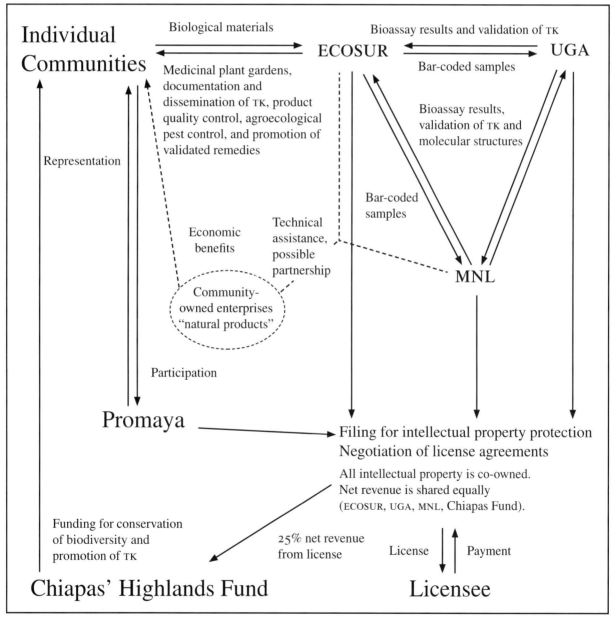

Figure 6. Overview of Maya ICBG. The complexity of the institutional design is self evident from the figure. Although ECOSUR, UGA, and MNL agreed on the terms of the collaboration, and on the side of the Mayan collaborators there was agreement with individual communities, second and third level social organizations (such as OMIECH and COMPITCH) objected to the agreement.

worked well until recently, when population growth and its ecological impact affected the availability and distribution of some species. In addition, the poverty in which most of the population of the region lives has created great pressure on their cultures and traditions, leading to cultural erosion and loss of knowledge. Preventing the irreversible loss of traditional knowledge is one of the greatest challenges for the region. The Maya ICBG was an attempt to advance in this area in the field of ethnomedicine and ethnobotanical knowledge. The Maya ICBG's choice of Chiapas for the project could be considered risky, but given the social needs, it was definitely worthwhile.

Poverty, culture, and indigenous rights are issues of great social and political relevance in contemporary Chiapas and Mexico. The Zapatista movement uprising began in 1994 and after a decade no profound and peaceful solution has been found.

In terms of the academic context, this project had an ideal platform, with more than three decades of work on ethnobotanical knowledge by Drs. Brent and Eloise Berlin and with ECOSUR, a regional research center well equipped and committed to make science one of the driving forces towards sustainable development in the region. Many of the communities where the project was promoted had done previous work with ECOSUR.

Access

The Maya ICBG sought to respect the rights of the communities over their plants and knowledge. To that end, the PIC of the communities was essential before collecting with biotechnological development purposes could take place. All channels available were used to transmit the project's aims: leaflets in Mayan languages, meetings in community assemblies, radio broadcasts, and plays. By "community", the project meant the *paraje*, a sub-unit of agrarian communities that traditionally maintained a high degree of independence in their decisions. The high number of *parajes* within agrarian communities has rendered them unable to handle a number of issues relevant for communal life, but the *paraje* seemed like the right choice as the basic unit of social involvement with the project. Eventually, to comply with national legislation that does not recognize this legal unit, the permits would have to be revalidated before the general communal assembly, which in most cases respects the decisions of the individual *parajes*. However, the political turmoil generated by the project prevented its efforts and the validation of the individual community decisions before the general assemblies did not take place.

Benefit Sharing

Equitable benefit sharing is one of the objectives of the CBD, and the Maya ICBG attempted to implement it fully. Of particular importance was to provide short-term as well as long-term benefits, recognizing that communities could not adjust to the timeframes typically found in pharmaceutical research. Proposed benefits in different time frames included:

Short term
- Assistance in developing medicinal plant gardens and information leaflets about medicinal plants in local languages;
- Production of documents and databases on traditional knowledge that, if desired by local communities, could be used to defend traditional knowledge against misappropriations;
- Generation of a sound biological and ethnobotanical information base, including a dissemination strategy at the local level and among academic centers in Mexico, thus directing research efforts to the region and making them more efficient;
- Work on agroecological experiments directed at exploring the potential of medicinal plants for the control of disease in local crops, which if successful, could reduce the damage caused by disease and by mitigation practices, since these technologies would be freely available;
- Dissemination of traditional knowledge among the communities in the highlands through workshops and other means;

Mid-term
- Studies on the biological activity of traditional remedies aimed at identifying the most active and effective and creating a constructive bridge between formal and traditional health systems, increasing the interest of the former in the latter;
- Evaluation of the technical and economic potential of species as phytomedicines in national and international markets, as well as assistance for small local cooperatives interested in the sustainable production of these species and remedies;

Long term
- Assessment of chemical compounds found in plants with the potential to become commercial products, with communities benefiting from a share in the net revenue obtained. In case a biotechnological product was developed as part of the Maya ICBG; and
- Explicit agreements to split the net revenue equally among the partners (ECOSUR, UGA, MNL, and a Chiapas Highlands Development Fund). to guarantee that 25% of direct net revenue would be invested in the region, and both UGA and ECOSUR commiting their share, an additional 50%, to ethnobotanical research in the region.

Moreover, with a view to safeguarding the rights of communities, the Maya ICBG considered the creation of a participation mechanism for the communities as partners in the project. Promaya was conceived as a social organization with representatives from the communities in the Chiapas highlands to help them coordinate their participation in the Maya ICBG. This organization would not only participate in the Maya ICBG's decisions, but would also be co-owner of any intellectual property arising from the project, with the right to propose and veto proposed uses and to negotiate licenses on the products of the project. This aspect represents one of the most significant innovations of the Maya ICBG in comparison with other bioprospecting projects.

Social Controversy

Representatives from the ICBG approached OMIECH[32] in January 1998, before the response to the request for applications was submitted to the USA National Institutes of Health, to assess their interest in participating. At that meeting, they showed little interest and expressed some opposition to the involvement of a private commercial partner and to Dr. Berlin, as a leader of the group, with whom there was some pre-existing antagonism. This first encounter was intended to invite them to participate as one of many organizations in Chiapas. The ICBG believed that OMIECH, COMPITCH[33] and other organizations could benefit from the natural products laboratory to improve quality control, production processes and marketing.[34] In addition, these organizations could assist in disseminating the results of the Maya ICBG in the region. Assurances were given that the project would not start without the proper legal framework in place, either contractual or legislative.

No further contact was made until after the grant was awarded and the Maya ICBG organized a workshop and forum on Mexican experiences on ABS in March 1999 as one of their initial activities. Representatives of nongovernment organizations, government, the Senate and academic institutions attended the forum where discussions centered around Mexican experiences that could help both the legislative and regulatory process in Mexico and also contribute in the design of the Maya ICBG. OMIECH participated at that forum as an observer, sending two representatives from their board of directors. The presence of representatives of different sectors was intended to enhance understanding and communication regarding ABS. However, these efforts did not achieve specific commitments by legislative or government representatives. On the legislative front, advances were slow. However, the initiatives mentioned in the following section are, in a general sense, a response to this and other efforts, including the 1997 Senate Seminar and social and legal objections to other bioprospecting projects that have altogether raised the level of this discussion in Mexico.

Other project activities did not start immediately for various reasons. Of fundamental importance was that bioprospecting activities could not start before PIC was obtained from the communities and the permit for collecting under Article 87 BIS of the EEEPGA was issued. However, activities that could start without delay included training of research assistants, information and negotiation meetings with the communities from which consent was sought, setting up of the natural products laboratory at ECOSUR, establishment of medicinal plant gardens at the community level, and scientific collecting for ECOSUR's

herbarium as well as the associated taxonomic work as part of the biodiversity survey. By May 1999, the decision was taken to initiate plant collecting for scientific purposes and the trainees started work that summer. Since no bioassays were involved and no extracts were to be derived from the collected plants, this part of the work fell within what is commonly referred to as scientific research, which was already authorized by the government under the responsibility of the herbarium's principal researcher. Also in May 1999, an agreement on minimal principles regarding Intellectual Property Rights was signed between ECOSUR, UGA, and MNL.

Work on the legal framework of the project also continued, including the design of Promaya as a fund and as an organization. OMIECH was also invited to provide comments and to be involved in Promaya, and a meeting was set for mid-September with them. Unfortunately, the meeting never took place, since OMIECH's first press release opposing the project was published on 11 September 1999. This first attack on the project was followed by a series of letters between ECOSUR and OMIECH; however, no formal meeting could be arranged. To avoid any misunderstandings regarding the activities of the Maya ICBG, the project halted all plant collecting activities in early November 1999.

From that moment on, the conflict escalated on several fronts: OMIECH started to distribute *communiqués* to the municipalities and communities as well as to transmit radio broadcasts, seeking to halt the project. RAFI also got involved, and a campaign opposing the project was launched at the national and international level. While the local campaign did not change the minds of the communities who had granted consent, it did start to cause problems for other projects at ECOSUR. At the same time, RAFI's campaign put pressure on SEMARNAT. Meetings at ECOSUR and in the communities were organized by the Maya ICBG as a strategy to clarify the project's intent and activities.

The situation did not improve during the following year, despite efforts by SEMARNAT to serve as mediator in the conflict and two meetings of a negotiating committee that were held in mid-2000. The institutional efforts naturally slowed down towards the end of the federal administration in December 2000, without resolving the conflict.

Current Situation

During its efforts to obtain PIC from the communities, the Maya ICBG obtained written consent from 46 *parajes* in 15 of the 28 municipalities in the study area. Eight medicinal plant gardens were established upon community request and some $50,000 USD had been secured in funds towards the Chiapas' Highland Maya Fund. The ethnobotanical collection database contains almost 6,000 records representing 1,047 species. Numerous academic exchanges and workshops were held. Scientific work was carried out on a number of related issues, including propagation of native species, pest damage to medicinal plants, potential of medicinal plants as a means to control cabbage pests, cultural transmission of ethnobotanical knowledge, Maya soil classification, and veterinary ethnomedicine. Of course, no results from bioassays exist since those activities never took place.

An example taken from a leaflet shows the kind of information being disseminated in Chiapas during the discussions. Under the heading "What is a patent?" is this explanation: "A patent is when a person, industry, business, university, research center, or government becomes owner of cultural heritage, biodiversity, ecosystems, and genetic resources, saying it discovered something in them and it is the only one that can use them. A patent is taking away the sacred and the spiritual in our lands, plants, animals, and lives." The level that discussions in the press and internet reached is beyond description and shows the risks of unaccountability in "communications".

During 2001, the USA government suspended funding for a year, giving time for the conflict to be resolved and the permits obtained. However, the application for a plant-collecting permit for biotechnological purposes was finally denied in the midst of political pressures. ECOSUR decided to withdraw from the Maya ICBG indefinitely in October 2001.

Lack of clarity and inadequate adaptation of the principles set out by the CBD into Mexican national legislation are part of the reason for the suspension of the project. An alternative solution would have been the recognition of the customary rules of these traditional communities which is a constant call in all the forums where traditional knowledge

is discussed. As mentioned above, the granted consent of the local communities would in time have to be reflected in the mechanisms of formal agrarian law which is currently the only means to canalize PIC issues, despite the fact that the decisions of the *parajes* are generally recognized by the legally defined *agrarian community*. However, due to political pressures the process towards obtaining the formal document of PIC was interrupted and the formal application was prematurely submitted to the authority. In the absence of such formal document the authority had clear technical grounds to deny the authorization and thereby finally burry the controversy. While it may seem that the project was therefore halted due to a technical deficiency, it seems clear that the lack of enforceability of a federal decision to upheld the validity of the consent of some of the communities or *parajes* meant that the granting of the collection permits for biotechnological purposes could lead to a deepening of the social conflict. Behind the technical deficiency there was rather an attempt to halt confrontation and alleviate the political tensions generated by the project.

Beyond the particularities of the social conditions in Chiapas that led to the heated controversy around the project and that could not have happened in other parts of the country, the project also highlighted the fact that the existing regulatory framework did not consider the traditional knowledge associated to genetic resources nor the rights of their holders, an issue that needs to be addressed at the national level.

Future Access and Benefit-Sharing Regulatory Framework

Regarding future legislation there are at least two initiatives in Federal Congress: one submitted by Federal Representative Alejandro Cruz Gutierrez (Institutional Revolutionary Party (PRI)) and the other by Federal Senator Jorge Nordhausen (National Action Party). Both initiatives are undergoing evaluation by the corresponding Congress Committees[35] and have not yet been discussed in the plenary, but they have been published in the Parliamentary Gazette[36]. The Nordhausen initiative has been partially discussed both by the legislative and some executive branches of government. Since a Committee already discussed a draft of the law, Congress is likely to consider this initiative during the 2004 parliamentary sessions.

Although these initiatives may never become laws, briefly describing and commenting on them is useful to show some of the issues that must be dealt with in order to achieve a comprehensive framework and a legitimate environment in which to comply with CBD rights and obligations at the national level.

The PRI Initiative

This text is an attempt to gather into one comprehensive regulatory framework both access to genetic resources and

biosafety. ABS regulation is comprised of eleven articles related to access conditions and intellectual property, which are summarized in the following paragraphs. The law initiative is of federal jurisdiction and proposes the creation of two competent authorities: a Biosafety Technical Counsel comprised of scientists and technicians and a Biosafety Mixed Committee including representatives of the Ministries of Agriculture, Environment and Health, as well as representatives of consumers, industry, and professional associations. Thus, it emphasizes biosafety and not ABS.

The initiative defines the property issue by declaring genetic resources as a Patrimony of the Nation, and it reaffirms that biodiversity conservation and the sustainable use of genetic resources are of public interest. These principles could help clarify and simplify State participation in ABS agreements. The scope of the law explicitly includes both wild and domesticated species, but no reference to aquatic species is made. Under this law, access to genetic resources would require an authorization from the Biosafety Mixed Committee. A minor contradictory disposition states that bioprospecting requires authorization from the Biosafety Technical Counsel. Access pursued in collectively owned land (communities and *ejidos*) would require the previous consent of the General Assembly, notwithstanding the fact that this approach still does not solve the resource distribution problem. The applicants must sign an Access Agreement, which must contain: a) the identification of the resource, its use, and any risks derived from its use; b) the material transfer agreement; c) the participation of national researchers; d) the obligation to share the results of the research; and e) a fee to guarantee compliance. The Committee shall publish in the Official Federation Gazette any resolution regarding access applications and will manage a record of related activities. This principle of information and public registry is important and should remain in any future legislation on ABS.

The authorizations could be denied whenever: a) there may be adverse effects on human health or on the essential elements of peoples' and communities' cultural identity; b) the species or geographic areas involved are considered strategic for national security; c) an uncontrollable impact on the environment may occur; d) the species involved are endemic, rare, or endangered; e) ecosystem vulnerability conditions might increase; and f) there is a risk of genetic erosion. The proposed regulation of intellectual property is confusing because it excludes from protection any living form and any genetic material (while allowing for process patents) but later gives protection to discoveries. It also confuses patents with plant breeders' rights when referring to patenting requirements (new, homogeneous, stable, distinct, and generic designation). Thus, the regulation will need technical clarification. It excludes from protection the genetic sequence information of a gene in order to eliminate barriers to biotechnological research. If not well defined and delimited, this proposal may, in turn, be in violation of trade-related obligations that Mexico has acquired. It mandates that no rights will be recognized whenever the collected samples were illegally acquired or whenever collective knowledge of indigenous communities or peoples was used. This last principle may seem a reasonable protection but on closer inspection it raises the question of whether prohibition is valid or if indigenous communities and peoples should be granted the right to say yes or no to such forms of protection.

The regulation mandates the Biosafety Mixed Committee to review patents or any other intellectual property right granted outside the country but based upon national genetic resources in order to allow claims for royalties or nullity. The exercise of patent review will be useful, and it is needed input for future legislation; however, it is not easy to see how this is a matter of biosafety (at least in the way the concept is implemented in the context of the CBD).

The Nordhausen Initiative

This initiative has a better structure, reflecting a more careful discussion developed by an interdisciplinary group before submitting it to the Senate, although information on the extent of consultations is not available.

The proposed law is meant to be federal to achieve coherence and certainty, but implementation can be executed locally. Once a law has allocated jurisdiction, transfer of some power can be coordinated between federal and state governments. The industries the law is to regulate are not listed but it is likely to regulate commercial activity as a whole. Certain provisions could affect specific industries; for instance, the biotechnology industry is affected both by IPR provisions and access provisions of the initiative. The proposed law is not likely to modify the current segregated agricultural framework, but since it includes domesticated species, it will fill many gaps and standardize regulation over different species. Simultaneously, however, it ignores its relationship with the International Treaty on Plant Genetic Resources for Food and Agriculture, signed in November 2001.

With regard to *ex situ* collections, the proposed law states the types of authorizations required. Germplasm banks seeking to pursue collection in Mexican territory must obtain a specific authorization. On the other hand, "*Ex Situ* Conservation Centers" are recognized by the law and must notify SEMARNAT of all Material Transfer Agreements related to Mexican resources. However, many aspects are not regulated and therefore WGA provisions and the NOM-126-ECOL-2000 regarding scientific collections would be applicable.

The enforcement authorities are meant to be SEMARNAT and its dependent and related agencies (INE and PROFEPA), CONABIO, the Secretariat of Agriculture, Livestock, Rural Development, Fisheries, and Food (regarding plant breeders' rights), and the Mexican Industrial Property Institute.

The differences between commercial and noncommercial purposes are defined by exclusion. Furthermore, differences are only evident regarding *ex situ* regulation; the proposed law does not regulate scientific collection since its scope is determined by the definition of "access" which only comprises commercial and economic activities. If properly developed, this initiative would regulate only commercial activities, leaving scientific applications to the current regulatory framework. The main characteristics of the access procedure would run as follows:

- The applicant must obtain an authorization from a Federal Executive Authority (SEMARNAT).

- An "access agreement" must be signed with the Federal Government (SEMARNAT, which has jurisdiction), the resource provider, and the intangible component (traditional knowledge) provider, if any.

- If relevant, an authorization must be obtained either for collection done by a germplasm bank, transport to any area not specified in the access agreement, export of the material collected, or transfer of the rights and obligations given by the access authorization.

The issue of State participation in ABS activities is a grey area. Particularly, having the State as a party to the access agreement is an example where the justification is somewhat blurry and might prove to be counterproductive. Despite the fact that the initiative is carefully designed, there are some issues that should be addressed in order to obtain greater clarity and coherence. These elements also show the complexities involved in reaching a harmonious transectorial regulation: the procedure and requirements for authorization are not defined for germplasm banks; for general-access authorization, the environmental impacts requirement is not clearly regulated; and the participation of Mexicans in research and development is required but not defined. Regarding IPRS, a provision involves the evaluation of the proportion of "relevant knowledge" given by each party in order to distribute the resulting IPRS. This obligation will be difficult to estimate and may overemphasize the role of patents over short-term benefits. It also undermines the intrinsic value of the genetic resource in the overall ABS scheme because it attends only to the added value.

The proposed law does not resolve the issue of ownership of the genetic resource because its provisions concerning consent are sometimes based upon the owner of the land and sometimes upon the federal government (probably assuming that it is the owner of the resource). The initiative should outline the issue more carefully.

One provision states that any protection of derived technologies must be shared between the parties. This could represent a form of compulsory license that might be contrary to international agreements (such as TRIPS).

Another provision requires that intellectual property authorities verify the presentation of documentation proving legal access, prior to the granting of any right. This does constitute an incentive for sustainable use, but unfortunately, as phrased this measure allocates the burden of proof to the intellectual property authority and not to the applicant, as it should in order to be effective.

Also, giving burden of proof to the victims of an alleged infringement through "conducting acts contrary to the usage and customs of indigenous people, *ejidos,* and communities that affect their cultural rights" eliminates any advantage the measure could have in promoting access to justice. This kind of inequity will have to be dealt with. Furthermore, regarding traditional knowledge (referred to as "intangible component"), the stated public record does not grant any specific positive right to its holders and the stated certification system is not regulated. Thus, the overview of this initiative shows that it has a chance of being reviewed and transformed into a workable law if it is enhanced technically and if its proponents manage to overcome the current impasse into which it has fallen.

The three cases of bioprospecting projects and agreements described above showed that it is urgent to develop a comprehensive regulatory framework. As this latest section shows, the task is far from complete, and it is not only a matter of legislation. The law has to be built in a coherent manner relating to the institutional framework that will enforce it, and this is not an easy task in Mexico. Even if these institutional problems can be properly addressed by the proposed law, there is still the issue of legitimacy. This can only be achieved if the process of building a regulation involves wide public consultation and addresses some basic concerns: the privatization of common and/or sacred resources and knowledge and the patenting of discoveries, among the most obvious and deeply felt social demands. If limits and criteria can be clearly set, both in access and intellectual property regulation, then the framework for bioprospecting activities can be built on a more rational, simple, and legitimate fashion. If patents continue to be granted around the world on sequences and organisms with no clear inventive steps, then the whole of bioprospecting is put on the stand and accused of biopiracy. The difference between discovery and invention has to be clear cut if social legitimacy is to be gained for bioprospecting in the medium term.

It is difficult to assess at this point what will emerge from the current analysis and discussion of the initiative within the Senate and the executive branch, but it is most likely that substantive changes will be made before it is passed to the lower chamber. Needless to say, the process of public consultation involved in a law of this nature may also be time consuming. Both of these factors may imply that it will yet take some time for Mexico to have specific access legislation

Multilateral Level

At this level, there are relevant initiatives related to ABS. In particular, a group of countries met in Mexico in 2002 and jointly issued The Cancun Declaration of Like-Minded Megadiversity Countries, hereby they created the "Group of Like-Minded Megadiverse Countries" with the following objective: "to jointly explore ways to ...harmonize our respective national laws and regulations on the protection of biological diversity, including related knowledge as well as access to biological and genetic resources, and the sharing of benefits arising from their sustainable use".[37] Furthermore, these countries targeted 15 specific objectives that broaden the agenda beyond access to genetic resources and benefit sharing to include coordination in international forums, promotion of *in situ* and *ex situ* conservation and investment in endogenous technologies, food safety, cultural integrity, regulatory harmonization, traditional knowledge and innovation, and trade and intellectual property rights (including patents, a *sui generis* system, trademarks and geographical indications). In direct relation to ABS and "modern" biotechnological development, the Declaration moves forward in relation to patents when it states the intent to "Seek the creation of an international regime to effectively promote and safeguard the fair and equitable sharing of benefits arising from the use of biodiversity and its components. This regime should contemplate, *inter alia,* the following elements: certification of legal provenance of biological materials, prior informed consent and mutually agreed terms for the transfer of genetic material, as requirements for the application and granting of patents, strictly in accordance with the conditions of access agreed by the countries of origin."

Such a regime might be declared incompatible with some international trade agreements, such as TRIPS, but it is precisely in these forums, where the presence and common understanding between these countries must be consolidated. The group of "Like-minded Megadiverse Countries" was formally presented at the Sixth COP of the CBD, on April 2002. The effect among other countries and regional groups was significant, because it modified the ongoing block negotiation scheme and was perceived as strong and innovative.

The most significant contribution of the group was the introduction of a call for action to "negotiate within the framework of the Convention on Biological Diversity, bearing in mind the Bonn Guidelines, an international regime to promote and safeguard the fair and equitable sharing of benefits arising out of the utilization of genetic resources" within the Plan of Implementation adopted by the World Summit on Sustainable Development in Johannesburg. These efforts culminated recently in the decision of the Conference of the Parties of the CBD to start negotiation of an international regime on ABS of genetic resources, at the heart of which are the development of user measures and coordination mechanisms among legal systems, primarily through the development of the Certificate of origin/source/legal provenance of genetic resources.

Conclusions and Recommendations

The transboundary nature of the distribution of genetic resources and its implications for ABS can be summarized in the following question: in what role does the owner of the land grant any PIC if the genetic resources are also found in other regions? Furthermore, attaching the benefit distribution to the granting of PIC has exclusion implications, since it would only compensate the person granting PIC and not other custodians of the resource. Thus, the approach of the landowner as the only relevant right holder may create more problems than benefits.

A good solution may be the concept of mutually agreed terms, once it has been clearly distinguished from the PIC in the national legislation and provided that the owner of the resource (the State) is given the right to grant it. This is one of the justifications for the CBD's demand for PIC from the providing country, and it should remain the same when translated to national legislation. In turn, the right to negotiate the mutually agreed terms of the specific access agreement could be the right granted to the owner of the land which could be justified as a right to make a sustainable use of the genetic resources found in his property. Obviously, this proposal implies a deep change in the perception of the role of the landowner and will require some other adjustments.

The only articles directly regulating biotechnological bioprospecting in Mexico are Article 87 BIS of EEEPGA and articles 101 and 102 of SFDGA. Despite the fact that the SFDGA does make the CBD's comprehensive recognition of the undeniable relationship between environmental regulation, rural development, traditional knowledge and practices, industrial applications, trade, and intellectual property, it has a limited scope. Therefore, even though both instruments incorporate the two main principles stated in the CBD: (prior informed consent and benefit sharing), the ABS legal framework as a whole lacks that important recognition. Since access to genetic resources is different from other processes of appropriation of biological resources, it seems reasonable to continue the efforts to develop a comprehensive Law on Access to Genetic Resources and Benefit Sharing that contributes clarification, principles, and operative mechanisms, including derived standards for specific sectors and material transfer agreement models.

The use of genetic resources is considered of public utility in Mexico, and this simple statement is of great importance because it empowers the State to defend a public interest. It also has the advantage that the concept of public interest has been properly defined in courts and literature; thus, it is not a new concept to regulate and control. Whereas there is a common understanding that genetic resources belong to the State, the "fragmentation of the property right" into a right of disposition (on behalf of the State) and right of use (on behalf on private individuals) is helpful in considering different levels of legal interest in the resource. Such an approach, taken by the WGA is of great importance (DÍAZ y DÍAZ 2000) because it allows for an evaluation based on both the requirements of the owner (the State) and those of the holder of the right to a sustainable use of the resource. Furthermore, it provides the basis for having the owner of the land as negotiator of the mutually agreed terms.

We must consider if a sector-specific approach is more convenient than a comprehensive approach. Due to the importance of the issue, an initial comprehensive regulation, comprising all species, is necessary in order to achieve coherence, and then continuing with a sector-by-sector specific regulation through official standards.

The development of policies regarding genetic resources has to consider scenarios of diffuse property, of common goods, and of collective innovation. To address these issues, profound changes in legal principles have to be considered, since most property rights are recognized for individuals and not for collective entities. Many legal concepts whose validity is taken for granted may be in serious contradiction with collective rights. Traditional knowledge and genetic resources are some of the areas in which collective rights have a clear and positive contribution to make in the development of the rights of farmers and indigenous peoples.

The discussions of biopiracy and bioprospecting have taken place and found their way into regulation in many countries for more than a decade now (e.g., India). In the Pacific region, countries like the Philippines and Malaysia (see Chapters 7 and 11) have made strong steps forward in regulating access, as has the Andes region (see Chapter 4) with its debates and common regulation. Mexico is lagging behind in the participation in these debates. Mexico's megadiversity is principally distributed in indigenous and peasant lands, and the political perception these sectors have of bioprospecting is fundamental for its future legitimacy. Appropriate access and transfer of relevant technologies are tied together and by definition need an actor to give or receive the technology.

Further discussions on the use of genetic resources in Mexico may well lead to the consideration of these resources as a priority area for the nation. If such an ap-proach reaches a consensus, it will probably prove useful to consolidate a public policy on these issues, setting the stage for a deeper discussion on the path Mexico will take in terms of biotechnological development and the prospecting and appropriation of our own biological and genetic resources. Such an approach need not affect private investment or property. The CBD is an international agreement, but countries adhering to it need to adjust to local conditions. The contradictions implicit in this process touch the fibers of nationalism and radicalize reactions against the commodification of life (GÖRG and BRAND 2000).

It is interesting to note that many of the social demands against bioprospecting can be read as demands for a stronger State involvement. In Mexico, in the last three decades, we have seen the systematic withdrawal of the State from the rural sector and the costs are visible. The lack of presence in terms of support and technical advice for development in these areas is a central component of

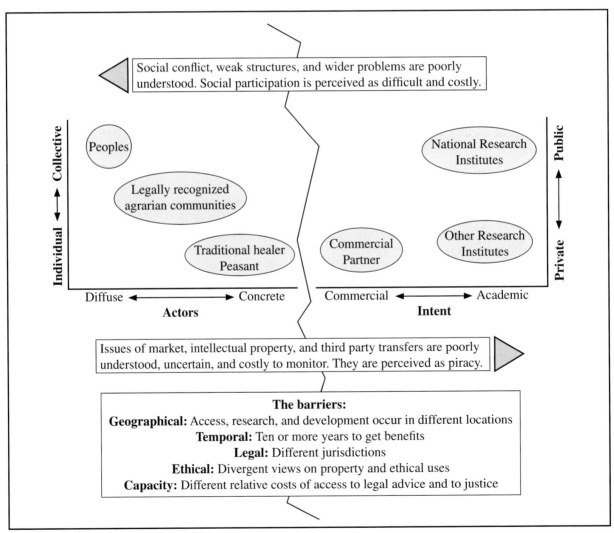

Figure 7. The barriers between providers and developers. Two differing paradigms that fail to understand each other's realities and concerns are divided by their own views on genetic resources, innovation, and commercial development. Strong efforts in capacity building and awareness are needed to breach the gap that is currently being widened mostly by misunderstandings.

the perception of social sectors towards bioprospecting, in a sense, saying to the State, "you have not been here for 30 years and now you are here to sell our resources". In a general sense they are right, and Mexico needs to face its own contradictions. However, the implementation of the CBD in all its components, particularly Articles 7, 8, and 9 may help alleviate some of them. Thus, the extent of the State involvement is a difficult issue. Having the State involved in all ABS activities might create excessive inefficiency in the ABS management and might be read as a system that does not facilitates access but hinders it.

The implications of property rights and commercial privileges implicit in patent rights must be fully comprehended in order to achieve a wider understanding that the part of knowledge being "taken" from the public domain (the part related to innovation) is only a small fraction of the whole, is only for a limited period of time, and is subject to several exceptions or limitations. This emphasis on the temporal limitation of the privileges of patents is much too often overlooked. Besides this temporal limitation to the appropriation process, it is also important to consider carefully the patenting criteria in specific innovation and industrial sectors, particularly in discussions of the revision of Article 27.3.b of the TRIPS Agreement within the WTO. This review, and the adoption of more stringent criteria for inventions, is a key factor in resolving adverse public perception to patent practices and in developing responsible practices in biotech-related IPR.

The approach of demanding proof of legal provenance of the biological material in applications for patents has been discussed for many years now (DUTFIELD 2000) and has been examined in working groups of the CBD. In fact, decision VI/24 of the 6th COP to the CBD mandates further study of the "feasibility of an internationally recognized certificate of origin system as evidence of prior informed consent and mutually agreed terms". The same decision states that "Parties are invited to encourage the disclosure of the origin of genetic resources and traditional knowledge in application for intellectual property rights".

This articulation between intellectual property rights and ABS can only be resolved with legitimacy if the process of building a regulation involves wide consultation and limits and criteria can be clearly set, both in access and intellectual property regulation. If so, the framework for bioprospecting activities can be built in a more rational, simple, and legitimate fashion.

A future law on access has to face the situation of ex situ collections and develop a creative solution to the problem; the legal situation of these collections bears directly on the issue of ABS and cannot be overlooked during the consultation process. This includes the legal status of material collected prior to the CBD's entry into force, of intellectual property rights, and of biosafety, since reference collections can be used to monitor and develop policy related to these issues. *Ex situ* collections are costly, and it is important to develop them as institutions that serve at the same time the purposes of conservation, access to genetic resources, and reference material for monitoring genetically modified organisms and IPRs.

The development of a comprehensive legal framework is urgently needed. The single most important issue to consider is that these frameworks have to be achieved through wide consultation and discussions if they are to be legitimate; in particular, there must be consultation with indigenous peoples, peasant organizations, and civil society. The temptation of legal reform without social legitimacy has dominated many processes in Mexico. Such a process may be complex but it has to be undertaken seriously by the different political parties in Congress and by executive authorities working on these issues. A former official of SEMARNAT (1994–2000) declared to Nature magazine that "Mexico lacks a legal framework for bioprospecting. I would not advise undertaking one of these projects now" (DALTON 2000). Is such a recommendation still valid? Probably yes, particularly if the project involves indigenous territories or traditional knowledge. The main issues to be addressed are not technical or regulatory, and we cannot afford to be politically naïve about these processes. Figure 7 delineates the barriers that polarize positions on ABS projects. Breaching these barriers is a priority. As simple as they may seem, capacity building and awareness raising on the issue of genetic resource conservation, access, and prospecting has to be taken seriously so that a policy that deals with these problems with legitimacy can be built.

Acknowledgements

This text is dedicated to Brent and Eloise Ann Berlin, with the certainty that when we are all gone and a young Maya of the highlands is in search for the knowledge of his forefathers, he will inevitably find himself among their written work.

References

ALAGÓN-CANO A. 1999. El rDSPAI: Un ejemplo de utilización de un recurso genético. p. 177–181 *in* A. ARROCHA y J. LARSON (ed.) *Senado de la República, Seminario sobre Legislación de Acceso a los Recursos Genéticos.* Memoria, México.

BERLIN B., E.A BERLIN, J.C. FERNÁNDEZ-UGALDE, L. GARCÍA-BARRIOS, D. PUETT, R. NASH, and M. GONZÁLEZ-ESPINOSA. 1999. The Maya ICBG: drug discovery, medical ethnobiology, and alternative forms of economic development in the highland Maya region of

Chiapas, Mexico. *Pharmaceutical Biology* **37**:127–144.

CAMBERROS S. 1999. El pasado como un prólogo, haciendo puentes entre el mundo moderno y el mundo tradicional. p. 85–90 *in* A. ARROCHA y J. LARSON (ed.) *Senado de la República, Seminario sobre Legislación de Acceso a los Recursos Genéticos.* Memoria, México.

CHAPELA I. 1997. Bioprospecting: Myths, realities and potential impacts on sustainable development. p. 79–90 *in* M.E. PALM and I. CHAPELA (eds.) *Mycology in sustainable development: Expanding concepts, vanishing borders.* Parkway Publishers Inc., North Carolina, USA.

CORREA C. 1999. Access to plant genetic resources and intellectual property rights. FAO–CGRFA, Rome, Italy. URL: http://www.fao.org/ag/cgrfa.

COSSIO-DIAZ J. 2001. *La Reforma Constitucional en materia indígena.* Cuadernos de Trabajo del Departamento de Derecho, Vol. 21, ITAM, México.

CUADERNOS AGRARIOS. 2001. *Biopiratería y bioprospección.* Número especial de Cuadernos Agrarios Nueva Época Número 21, México.

DALTON R. 2000. Political uncertainty halts bioprospecting in Mexico. *Nature* **408**:278.

DÍAZ y DÍAZ M. 2000. El aprovechamiento de los recursos naturales. Hacia un nuevo discurso patrimonial. *Revista de Investigaciones Jurídicas*: **Vol. 24**, Escuela Libre de Derecho, México.

DUTFIELD G. 2000. *Intellectual property rights, trade and biodiversity: Seeds and plant varieties.* IUCN, Earthscan Publications, London, UK.

FERNÁNDEZ J., A. ALDAMA, and C. LOPEZ-SILVA. 2002. Conocimiento tradicional de la biodiversidad: conservación, uso sustentable y reparto de beneficios. *Gaceta Ecológica*: Número 63, Instituto Nacional de Ecología, México.

FUCCILLO D., L. SEARS, and P. STAPLETON. (eds.) 1997. *Biodiversity in trust.* CGIAR and The Cambridge University Press, Cambridge, UK.

GOLLIN M. 1993. An intellectual property rights framework for biodiversity prospecting. p. 159–197 *in* W.V. REID, S.A. LAIRD, C.A. MEYER, R. GÁMEZ, A. SITTENFELD, D.H. JANZEN, M.G. GOLLIN, and C. JUMA (eds.). *Biodiversity prospecting: Using genetic resources for sustainable development.* World Resources Institute, Washington DC USA.

GÖRG C. and U. BRAND. 2000. Global environmental politics and competition between nation-states: On the regulation of biological diversity. *Review of International Political Economy* **7**:371–398.

HARVEY N. 2002. Globalization and resistance in post-cold war Mexico: Difference, citizenship and biodiversity conflicts in Chiapas. *Third World Quarterly* **22**:1045–1061.

HERSCH P. and J. LARSON. 2002. Traditional medicine, biological resources and intellectual property rights: A view from Mexico. Paper presented at the APEC Symposium on Traditional Medicine, Hong Kong, China. Unpublished manuscript.

MEXICAN CONGRESS. 1992. Constitution of the United States of Mexico. Last amendment to Article 27 published in the Federation Official Gazette on 28 January 1992.

MEXICAN CONGRESS. 1994. Industrial Property Act. Major amendment published in the Federation Official Gazette on 2 August 1994.

MEXICAN CONGRESS. 1995. Constitution of the United States of Mexico. Last amendment to Article 28 published in the Federation Official Gazette on 2 March 1995.

MEXICAN CONGRESS. 1996a. Plant Varieties Federal Act. Published in the Federation Official Gazette on 25 October 1996.

MEXICAN CONGRESS. 1996b. Ecological Equilibrium and Environment Protection General Act. Published in the Federation Official Gazette on 28 January 1988 and amendment published on 13 December 1996.

MEXICAN CONGRESS. 1999. Constitution of the United States of Mexico. Last amendment to Article 25 published in the Federation Official Gazette on 28 June 1999.

MEXICAN CONGRESS. 2000. Wildlife General Act. Published in the Federation Official Gazette on 3 July 2000.

MEXICAN CONGRESS. 2001. Constitution of the United States of Mexico. Last amendment to Article 2 published in the Federation Official Gazette on 7 August 2001.

MEXICAN CONGRESS. 2002. Criminal Code. Amendment published on the Federation Official Gazette on 6 February 2002.

MEXICAN CONGRESS. 2003. Sustainable Forestry Development General Act. Published in the Federation Official Gazette on 25 February 2003.

PERSIDIS A. 1998. Extremophiles. *Nature Biotechnology* **16**.

POSNER R. 2002. *Economic analysis of law.* Aspen Publishers, USA.

PROFEPA 2000. Popular denunciation regarding UNAM-Diversa Agreement. File No. 006/150/09. Federal Attorney for the Protection of the Environment.

RAMÍREZ-CASILLAS V.M. 2000. *Tierra, diferencia y poder. Violaciones a los derechos humanos indígenas en México: 1988-1994.* Universidad Iberoamericana A.C. México.

ROSENTHAL J.P., D. BECK, A. BHAT, J. BISWAS, L. BRADY, K. BRIDBOARD, S. COLLINS, G. CRAGG, J. EDWARDS, A. FAIRFIELD, M. GOTTLIEB, L.A. GSCHWIND, Y. HALLOCK, R. HAWKS, R. HEGYELI, G. JOHNSON, G.T. KEUSCH, E.E. LYONS, R. MILLER, J. RODMAN, J. ROSKOSKI, and D. SIEGEL-CAUSEY. 1999. Combining high risk science with ambitious social and economic goals. *Pharmaceutical Biology* **37**:6–21.

SARUKHÁN J., J. SOBERÓN, and J. LARSON-GUERRA. 1996. Biological conservation in a high beta diversity country. p. 246–263 *in* F. DI CASTRI and T. YOUNES (eds.) *Biodiversity, science and development: Towards a new partnership.* CAB International, Oxford, UK.

SHULMAN, S. 1999. Patent absurdities. *The Sciences* **Jan/Feb**: 30–33.

STAVENHAGEN R. 1999. Hacia el derecho de autonomía en México. p. 7–20 *in* C. BURGUETE and A. MAYOR (Coord.) *México: Experiencias de autonomía indígena.* Documento IGWIA 28. Dinamarca.

SUPREME COURT. 1999. *Hierarchy of international treaties in relation to other laws*, Ninth Epoch, Federation Judicial Weekly Publication, Vol. X, November. Thesis P.LXXVII/99.

SWANSON T. 1995. The appropriation of evolution's values: An institutional analysis of intellectual property regimes and biodiversity conservation. p 141–175 *in* T. SWANSON. *Intellectual property rights and biodiversity conservation:*

An interdisciplinary analysis of the values of medicinal plants. Cambridge University Press, UK.

TEN KATE K. and S.A. LAIRD. 1999. *The commercial use of biodiversity: Access to genetic resources and benefit sharing.* Earthscan Publications Ltd., London, UK.

TENA-RAMIREZ, F. 1985. *Derecho constitucional mexicano.* Editorial Porrúa, México.

TIMMERMANN B.N., G. WÄCHTER, S. VALCIC, B. HUTCHINSON, C. CASLER, J. HENZEL, S. RAM, F. CURRIM, R. MANAK, S. FRANZBLAU, W. MAIESE, D. GALINIS, E. SUAREZ, R. FORTUNATO, E. SAAVEDRA, R. BYE, R. MATA, and G. MONTENEGRO. 1999. The Latin American ICBG: The First Five Years. *Pharmaceutical Biology* **37**:35–54.

TYLER H., K.S. BROWN JR. and K. WILSON. 1994. *Swallowtail butterflies of the Americas: A study in biological dynamics, ecological diversity, biosystemaitcs and conservation.* Scientific Publishers, Gainesville, FL USA.

WIPO 2001. *Intellectual property needs and expectations of traditional knowledge holders.* Report on Fact-finding Missions on Intellectual Property and Traditional Knowledge. Geneva, Switzerland.

WTO 1997. The Convention on Biological Diversity and the Agreement on Trade Related Aspects of Intellectual Property, Committee on Trade and Environment, Secretary Note, WT/CTE/W/50.

Endnotes

[1] Although this sector has provisions vaguely related to genetic resources and biotechnology, they were not developed in response to a changing legal framework in access and benefit sharing.

[2] Nonetheless, the regulatory meaning of characterizing species as "strategic" is still unknown.

[3] This is evident from the recently agreed upon text of the Bonn Guidelines on Access and Benefit Sharing. The Bonn Guidelines, document UNEP/CBD/COP/6/20, is available at http://www.biodiv.org, as are other CBD documents referred to in the text.

[4] The components of biological diversity that we use are, in a simple interpretation, biological resources. For the complete definition see CBD, Article 2. Within the objectives, biological resources are differentiated from genetic resources.

[5] Adopted by Resolution 3/2001of the FAO Conference on 3 November 2001.

[6] The extent of such involvement is a contentious issue. It could be argued that the degree of participation currently covered in the legislation is sufficient. However, some would like to see a stronger presence of the State in the ABS process. An example of this has been found in the recent discussion regarding the Nordhausen initiative.

[7] See the web site of the group on Erosion Technology and Concentration (ETC) for further information.

[8] The text of the Constitution and other legal references are available at http://www.juridicas.unam.mx/infjur/ and http://www.cddhcu.gob.mx.

[9] Latest amendment published in the Official Federal Gazette.

[10] In fact it is something different. This concept of *eminent domain* derives from the notion of *sovereignty* of a State over its *territory* and has traditionally rendered thus some confusion between the concepts of sovereignty and property (TENA-RAMIREZ 1985). This also justifies the understanding that the CBD does not take any decision on property rights.

[11] *Municipios* are the lower or primary category of state organizational authority in Mexico that reproduces the three branches of government, with some restrictions.

[12] The San Andrés Agreements and the legal reform proposed by the Comisión de Concordia y Pacificación.

[13] According to article 2, subsection III.

[14] There is a key difference regarding the relationship between the PIC and the authorization. The SFDGA requires having the PIC as a prior condition to grant the authorization for both biotechnological and scientific purposes. The WGA regulation on scientific collection does not have that precedence requirement and the EEEPGA only has the requirement for biotechnological purposes, but not for scientific ones.

[15] The definition of bioprospecting is problematic: two activities are confused. Biotechnological use assumes economic objectives, and the presence of intellectual property considerations usually is perceived in association with biotechnological purposes. Regarding scientific collection regulation, WGA and the NOM-126-ECOL-2000 explicitly exclude economic and biotechnological purposes.

[16] Biotechnology is defined in article 3 of the EEEPGA, incorporating the text of the CBD.

[17] Article 83 includes three activities: collection, capture, and hunting; it classifies purposes in economic, reproduction, restoration, repopulation, reintroduction, translocation, and environmental education (although the economic purposes are not defined).

[18] According to articles 4, 5 and 18.

[19] According to articles 50 to 55.

[20] Article 420 of the Criminal Code.

[21] The interpretation of the Mexican Institute of Industrial Property is stated in the document responding to a consultation made by CONABIO (DDAJ.2000.232, 7 September 2000).

[22] Isolation and description of gene sequences complicates the issue further since some see them as an inventive step and some would still view them as insufficient steps.

[23] In 2001, the Latin American ICBG suspended collecting activities in Mexico. Access to this project was granted under article 87 of the EEEPGA that authorizes the collection of organisms for scientific purposes. However, because of the commercial and biotechnological nature of the project, access should have been granted under article 87 BIS that regulates the collection of samples for biotechnological purposes. When this contradiction became clear the project suspended activities and no collections have occurred in recent years.

[24] The director of the Latin American ICBG in Mexico, Robert Bye, presented, in the VII Latin American Botanical Congress in 1998, a round table called "The Convention on Biological Diversity: Opportunity or Limitation for the Use of Germplasm", reflecting the sentiment of the complications that the new framework imposes upon scientists.

[25] The applicable legislation states that the National Institute of Ecology (INE) has the authority to act, upon delegation of SEMARNAT's faculties, as representative of the Federation where Federal Land is involved. On the other hand, the applicable legislation also stated (bearing in mind that administrative regulations have changed since then) that the responsibility to issue authorizations to use wild flora and fauna fell within INE faculties.

[26] For which CONABIO acts as trustee. This was envisioned as a means to exercise the right to benefit sharing by the owner of the land where the genetic resource is located.

[27] Signed by the National Association of Trading Enterprises of Rural Producers, the National Union of Regional Autonomous Peasant Organizations, the National Association of Democratic Lawyers, the Group of Environmental Studies, Greenpeace Mexico, the Studies Center for Change in Rural Mexico, the Permaculture Network (Red de Permacultura), the Citizen Committee for the Defense of Mexico's Cultural and Natural Heritage, and four individuals belonging to research institutions.

[28] This legal procedure, analogous to a suit, recognizes that protecting the environment with society's participation requires the widening of the concept of legal interest and extends it to any individual.

[29] As stated in the CBD, "biotechnology" is any technological application that uses biological systems and living organisms or their derivatives to create or modify production processes or for specific uses. This includes a wide set of technologies, such as tissue culture, genetic engineering, and fermentations, among others.

[30] Sandoz-Pharma does not exist anymore as such; in 1993, it merged with Ciba to form Novartis. A couple of years later, the agriculture branch of Novartis was sold to other firms in order to concentrate their business in the pharmaceutical area. The UZACHI-Sandoz contract ended in 1998, almost at the same time that Sandoz merged with Ciba.

[31] The authority neglected proper consideration of the IBT as an essential part of the bioprospecting agreement which has an impact upon the existence of a suitable recipient of possible technology transfers.

[32] OMIECH is the Organization of Indigenous Healers of the State of Chiapas.

[33] COMPITCH is the Council of Indigenous and Traditional Medicine Men and *Parteros* (Birth supervisors) of Chiapas.

[34] COMPITCH currently markets a limited number of herbal remedies and nutritional supplements.

[35] For the Senate there are two relevant committees: the Committee of Health, Social Security, Environment, Natural Resources, and Fishery and Committee of Legislative Studies. For the House of Representatives, it is the Committee of Rural Development.

[36] In the Senate on 26 April 2001. Available at URL: http://www.senado.gob.mx/gaceta/51/index.html. In the House on 29 April 2002. Available at URL: http://camaradediputados.gob.mx/gaceta/.

[37] According to Decision 1, subsection d) of the Cancun Declaration, issued by Ministers in charge of the Environment and Delegates from Brazil, China, Colombia, Costa Rica, Ecuador, India, Indonesia, Kenya, Mexico, Peru, South Africa, and Venezuela, who convened in Cancun, Mexico, on 18 February 2002.

7

Philippines: Evolving Access and Benefit-Sharing Regulations

Paz J. Benavidez II

Biological and genetic resources are precious commodities which have long been accessed and exchanged by individuals and States, sometimes under government restrictions or regulations, and often "freely shared and given". However, the continuous, unbridled utilization and exploitation of these resources, the rapid advances in science and technology, the economic value of potential cures and applications from these resources, and the inequitable sharing of benefits derived from them have put increasing pressure on resource-rich countries to rethink their policies on access to and exchange of these resources.

The Philippines is one of the richest countries in the world in terms of wildlife species. It is home to a very impressive biological and genetic diversity and endemicity. The plants in Philippine forests consist of at least 13,500 species which represent 5% of the world's flora. There are 185 species of Philippine terrestrial mammals (115 or 62% of which are endemic). About 558 species of birds have been found of which 171 (31%) are endemic. There are 95 amphibian species, 54% of which are endemic. Over 2,782 species of mollusks, 54 species of millipedes, 44 species of centipedes, and more than 20,000 insect species are found in the Philippines (PAWB-DENR 1998).

There are 1,616 species of flora and 3,675 species of fauna in Philippine freshwaters, a record considered impressive. Inventories are yet to be made on the 78 lakes, 421 major rivers, four major swamps/marshes, and the many bays, estuaries, and mudflats of the country. From the FishBase (1997) data of the International Center for Living Aquatic Resources Management, the Philippines has a total of 230 freshwater fish species. Of these 228 are reportedly threatened species, 31 are endemic, while 53 are used in fisheries. There are 1,703 species of invertebrates and 1,764 species of insects, of which 1,146 are endemic (PAWB-DENR 1998).

In the Philippine coastal and marine ecosystems, there are at least 4,951 species of marine plants and animals. In terms of distribution among the ecosystems along the Philippine coasts, coral reefs are the most diverse with 3,967 species. Next to these are seagrass beds with 481 species. Its 16 taxa of seagrasses make the Philippines the second highest in seagrass species in the world. The diversity of mangroves is also high, with 370 species (PAWB-DENR 1998).

Studies show that there are 1,210 plant species important to agriculture populations of domesticated exotic animal species. In 1991 these totaled 2,766,000 carabaos, 1,991,000 cattle, 286,000 horses, 7,479,000 hogs, 2,403,000 goats, and 56,000 other domesticated exotic animal species. The aggregate poultry population reached 101,235,000 head (PAWB-DENR 1998).

The rate of biodiversity loss in the Philippines has been rapid due to the high rate of population growth; economic systems and policies that fail to put value on the environment and its resources; inequity in the ownership, management, and flow of benefits from the use and conservation of biological resources; deficiencies in knowledge and its applications; and legal and institutional deficiencies and constraints (BARBER and LA VIÑA 1997). Philippine forest cover has been reduced from more than 50% to less than 24% over a period of 40 years; only about 5% of the country's coral reefs remains in excellent condition; 30 to 50% of its seagrass beds have been lost in the last 50 years; and about 80% of its mangrove areas have been lost in the last 75 years. About 50% of national parks is estimated to be no longer biologically important (BARBER and LA VIÑA 1997). As of 1994, 45 species of birds and 30 species of terrestrial mammals are either extinct in the wild, critical, or endangered, and three species of reptiles and two species of amphibians are internationally recognized as threatened (DE LEON 1998).

This increasing threat to biodiversity has led both the government and nongovernmental organizations (NGOs) to seriously take up the challenge of conserving and protecting biodiversity, developing these resources, and utilizing them in a sustainable manner for the benefit of present and future Filipinos.

Pursuant to Executive Order No. 192, the Department of Environment and Natural Resources (DENR) formulated the Philippine Strategy for Sustainable Development which aims to balance economic growth and biodiversity conservation. In 1992, the Philippine Council for Sustainable Development (PCSD) was established with a Sub-Committee on Biodiversity (PAWB-DENR 1998).

On 1 June 1992, Republic Act No. 7586, otherwise known as the National Integrated Protected Areas System (NIPAS) Law, was enacted. It provides for the establishment and management of a comprehensive protected area system encompassing areas that are habitats of rare and endangered species of plants and animals, biogeographic zones, and related ecosystems in order to secure the perpetual existence of all native plants and animals.[1] The law recognizes that effective administration of these areas is possible only through cooperation among national government, local government, and concerned private organizations. The use and enjoyment of the same must be consistent with the principles of biological diversity and sustainable development.[2]

In 1993, the Philippines ratified the Convention on Biological Diversity (CBD). In response to the CBD, Executive Order No. 247 (EO 247)[3] was signed into law on 18 May 1995. Its implementing rules and regulations,[4] DENR Administrative Order No. 20 (DAO 20) was issued on 21 June 1996[5]. On 30 July 2001, the Philippine Legislature enacted Republic Act No. 9147, otherwise known as the "Wildlife Resources Conservation and Protection Act" (hereafter Wildlife Act) which provides for new measures relative to bioprospecting in the Philippines.

This paper will discuss the legal regime for access to and exchange of biological and genetic resources in the Philippines. It will analyze Philippine access regulations in the context of the goals of the CBD, the standards set by the Agreement on Trade-Related Aspects of Intellectual Property Rights (TRIPS) and other relevant international agreements, and the promises of the Wildlife Act as a relatively new access regulation and conclude with recommendations for the enhancement of regulations for access to and exchange of biological and genetic resources.

Pre-EO 247 Access Regulation

Prior to 1987, the National Museum of the Philippines was the primary government agency regulating collection of biological samples pursuant to Republic Act No. 4846, as amended by Presidential Decree 374 (BARBER and LA VIÑA 1997). In 1987, the Protected Areas and Wildlife Bureau (PAWB) under the DENR was given a bigger role in regulating collection activities. Requests for collection involving endangered species of fauna became the responsibility of PAWB. Collection of marine species was handled by the Bureau of Fisheries and Aquatic Resources, while requests for collection involving animals needed the approval of the Bureau of Animal Industry. Plant collection is within the mandate of the Bureau of Plant Industry. The National Museum, however, continued to be the "official clearinghouse for all requests to collect biological specimens" (BARBER and LA VIÑA 1997).

In 1990, a memorandum of agreement (MOA) was executed by various government agencies, which contained the "Guidelines for the Collection of Biological Specimens in the Philippines" for both local and foreign collectors of biological specimens, including materials for bioprospecting. It aimed to provide restriction and control mechanisms for the entry and exit of biological specimens to prevent technical smuggling under the guise of educational, scientific, or research purposes.[6] Among its salient features were: approval of collection was obtained from the Director of the National Museum or the head of a collaborating local research institution or university; a complete set of voucher specimens was deposited at the Museum and collaborating local institution; and a local counterpart had to accompany every field visit/collection. It also contained a code of ethics for collectors of biological specimens in the country. Other relevant provisions of the MOA included: protection from wanton exploitation of biological resources by limiting collections to the minimum possible number (MOA Subsection 3.3a); recognition and respect for indigenous communities, including their customs, traditions, and folk knowledge (Subsection 3.2b); participation of local counterparts in the collection and sharing of authorship in publications arising from these activities (MADULID 1995).

The MOA, however, proved to be inadequate in terms of compliance with the provisions of the CBD, because it was primarily an administrative coordination and permitting system and not a regulatory framework for bioprospecting. It is "not explicit in aspects such as equitable return of benefits to the country and to the local community in case a drug is developed from a local plant or animal, transfer of technology, and protection of Intellectual Property Rights of the indigenous communities" (MADULID 1995). Thus, the bioprospecting agreement between the USA National Cancer Institute (NCI)[7] and the National Museum only vaguely touched the issue of indigenous rights. Binding provisions for concrete compensation to communities and for their active participation in the collecting activities are lacking. The agreement was also inadequate regarding provisions on compensation to the government (BARBER and LA VIÑA 1997). Nevertheless, immediate benefits such as technology transfer, research collaboration, and complete sample collections have been obtained by the country through this agreement.[8]

In February 1992, the Seventh Asian Symposium on Medicinal Plants, Species and Other Natural Products (ASOMPS), which was held in the Philippines, issued *The Manila Declaration* concerning "The Ethical Utilization of Asian Biological Resources", together with the Code of Ethics for Foreign Collectors of Biological Samples and Contract Guidelines. ASOMPS "was largely instrumental in heightening awareness among Asian scientists on the issue of bioprospecting" (LA VIÑA et al. 1997).

After the Manila Declaration and the CBD, the Philippine Network for the Chemistry of Natural Products, with funding support from the UNESCO Regional Network for the Chemistry of Natural Products in Southeast Asia, took the initiative to draft the executive order. In October 1993, Atty. Antonio G.M. La Viña was commissioned to draft EO 247 with input from members of the Philippine Network nationwide and representatives of key government depart-

ments. Academic groups were also consulted on the draft before it was submitted to the Department of Science and Technology (DOST) for further consultation meetings with other sectoral groups including the Sub-Committee on Biodiversity of the Committee on the Conservation and Management of Resources for Development of the PCSD (LA VIÑA et al. 1997). The level of participation in the development of EO 247 was said to be unprecedented for an executive order in the Philippines, which usually requires only limited consultation. In this case, representatives of government, scientists, NGOs, community organizations, and the business community were actively involved in the drafting of EO 247 through a number of consultative meetings. "The process ensured that the capacity building priorities of scientists were addressed in the provisions on benefit sharing, and that the interests of local communities were taken into account in the provisions on local prior informed consent (PIC)" (SWIDERSKA 2001).

In 1996, the implementing rules and regulations of EO 247 were drafted by a small group composed of the legal staff of DENR, PAWB, DOST, and scientists. This draft was circulated for comment to the PCSD, scientific organizations, industry groups, and national pharmaceutical companies before its approval in June 1996 (SWIDERSKA 2001).

Executive Order 247

EO 247 was issued on the basis of the 1987 Philippine Constitution and the CBD. Specifically, section 16, Article II of the 1987 Philippine Constitution vests in the State the ultimate responsibility to preserve and protect the environment. Section 2, Article XII of the Constitution provides that plants and animals are owned by the State, and the disposition, development, and utilization thereof are under its full control and supervision. The CBD, on the other hand, calls for member countries to take appropriate measures with the aim that countries providing genetic resources are given access to and transfer of technology that uses those resources, on mutually agreed terms.

It was the perceived urgency for a comprehensive regulatory framework for access to biological and genetic resources, along with the slow pace of congressional legislation, which led policy makers to come up with an executive order (BARBER and LA VIÑA 1997). Executive Orders are "acts of the President providing for rules of a general or permanent character in implementation or execution of constitutional or statutory powers" (AGPALO 1990). Although a law passed by Congress is more permanent, may be broader in scope, and may appropriate funds and impose penalties, it may take longer to enact, amend, or repeal. On the other hand, an executive action is limited in scope because it covers only matters delegated by Congress to the President under a particular law, the Constitution, or international conventions, but it is faster and easier to promulgate. It can also be modified immediately in case of serious flaws.

The basic State policy set out in EO 247 is "to regulate the prospecting of biological and genetic resources to the end that these resources are protected and conserved, are developed and put to the sustainable use and benefit of the national interest. Further, it shall promote the development of local capability in science and technology to achieve technological self-reliance in selected areas".[9]

EO 247 has four basic elements (BARBER and LA VIÑA 1997):

- A system of mandatory research agreements between the collectors and the government containing minimum terms concerning provision of information and samples, technology cooperation, and benefit sharing;

- An interagency committee to consider, grant, monitor and enforce compliance with research agreements, as well as to coordinate further institutional, policy, and technology development;

- A requirement and minimum process standards for obtaining PIC from local and indigenous communities where collection of materials is carried out; and

- Minimum requirements to conform with environmental protection laws and regulations.

Scope of Application

EO 247 covers prospecting of all biological and genetic resources, their by-products and derivatives, in the public domain[10], including natural growths in private lands, which is intended to be utilized by both foreign and local prospectors.[11] "Bioprospecting" is defined as "the research, collection, and utilization of biological and genetic resources, for the purpose of applying the knowledge derived therefrom for scientific and/or commercial purposes".[12] Traditional uses[13] are excluded. This definition was severely criticized by the academic and scientific sectors for being too broad and vague. As defined in EO 247, bioprospecting refers to all kinds of collection and sampling of biological and genetic resources which, for some sectors, was not really the intention. This prompted policy makers to attempt to clarify in DAO 20 the scope of EO 247 by stating that the term refers only to "activities aimed at discovering, exploring, or using these resources for pharmaceutical development, agricultural, and commercial applications".[14] The Inter-Agency Committee on Biological and Genetic Resources (IACBGR) members agreed that research and collection activities associated with pure conservation work, biodiversity inventory, taxonomic studies, and the like shall not be processed under EO 247 but should follow an existing permitting system.[15] However, no further guidelines were issued and the IACBGR will decide the matter on a case-to-case basis. For example, collections of resources made for taxonomic studies are generally excluded, but if the study goes beyond studying the morphology of specimens, EO 247 would apply depending on the methods being used by the researcher. Also, internal guidelines were formulated to guide the Technical Secretariat (TS) in processing applications.

It is not clear if EO 247 covers *ex situ* collections and other domesticated resources because of the qualification placed in the implementing rules and regulations that it covers "only natural growths in private lands".[16] The implication of this provision is that such collections and resources are not covered by EO 247. It is interesting to note, however, that among the applications for research agreements pending before the IACBGR, one involves collection of resources in the commercial plantations of the proponent.[17] It appears, thus, that, though not stated in EO 247, the IACBGR regulates all biological resources in the country whether or not outside their natural environment, domesticated or wild.

Although the introductory clause of EO 247 mentions traditional knowledge, nowhere in the text of the order has it been discussed. However, traditional knowledge of local and indigenous communities is very much linked with the PIC of the communities where the resources are taken.

Administrative Mechanism

The administrative body charged with implementing EO 247 is the IACBGR. Its membership consists of the following: a) an Undersecretary of DENR as chairperson; b) an Undersecretary of DOST as co-chairperson; c) a permanent representative of the Department of Agriculture, who must be knowledgeable about biodiversity or biotechnology;

d) two representatives of the local scientific community from the academy who must be experts in biodiversity, biotechnology, genetics, natural products chemistry, or similar disciplines; e) a permanent representative of the Department of Health who is knowledgeable about pharmaceutical research and development with emphasis on medicinal plant/herbal pharmaceudynamics; f) a permanent representative of the Department of Foreign Affairs who has to facilitate international linkage relative to bioprospecting; g) a permanent representative of the National Museum who has expertise on natural history and/or biodiversity; h) a representative from the NGOs active in biodiversity protection; and i) a representative from a People's Organization with membership consisting of indigenous cultural communities, indigenous peoples,[18] and/or their organizations.[19] The members serve for three years and a term may be renewed for another three years.[20] Among the functions of the committee are: to process applications for research agreements and recommend their approval/denial; to ensure strict compliance with the agreements; to determine the quantity of collection; to ensure protection of the rights of indigenous peoples (IPs)/indigenous cultural communities (ICCs) where bioprospecting is undertaken.[21] The IACBGR meets at least once every quarter, but the chairperson/co-chairperson may call special meetings as she/he deems necessary. All decisions must be by a majority of its members.[22] The final approval, however, rests with the head of the government department that has jurisdiction over the resources and/or activity.[23]

Mandatory Research Agreements

One conducts bioprospecting by applying for a research agreement with the IACBGR. The research agreement may be an Academic Research Agreement (ARA) or a Commercial Research Agreement (CRA).

An ARA covers research undertaken by duly recognized Philippine universities and academic institutions, domestic governmental entities, and intergovernmental entities and their affiliates[24] intended primarily for academic and scientific purposes.[25] It may be comprehensive in scope and cover as many areas as the applicant proposes to work in.[26] Local academic institutions and intergovernmental research agencies with an ARA are given flexibility and allowed to exercise self-regulation. Any local scientist/researcher who is an affiliate of any of these institutions[27] with a valid ARA is allowed to conduct research under the aegis of the said ARA. However, before conducting any actual bioprospecting activity in the site, the researcher must secure the required PIC certificate. Compliance with the requirements of the ARA, including the PIC, is the responsibility of the institution.[28] These institutions are also mandated to enforce a Code of Conduct for researchers. Failure by the principal to monitor compliance with the ARA by their affiliates may result in the cancellation of the ARA.[29] An ARA is valid for a period of five years, renewable upon recommendation of the IACBGR.[30]

Research and/or collection intended, directly or indirectly, for commercial use requires a CRA that is valid for a period of three years, renewable for a period as may be determined by the IACBGR.[31] Under EO 247, all research agreements with private persons, including foreign international entities, shall conform to the minimum requirements of a CRA even if the bioprospecting activity is purely scientific.[32] In addition to the bioprospecting fees, the collector under a CRA is also required to pay a performance, compensation, or ecological bond to be determined by the IACBGR.[33]

Since 1996, the IACBGR has processed eight[34] applications for CRA and 17[35] for ARA. Only one CRA[36] and one ARA[37] have been approved so far (Boxes 1 and 2).

Application Process

EO 247 requires the applicant to satisfy certain requirements and to undergo an application process. EO 247 does not provide for a specific time within which to process applications. It is estimated to be at least five months. However, the process takes longer because the IACBGR is required to meet only quarterly, although the chair can call for special meetings. It is also difficult to secure a common schedule for IACBGR meetings. Also, the process is often stalled because the applicant cannot immediately submit the PIC. Under EO 247, action on the PIC can only be taken after the lapse of 60 days from the submission of a research proposal to the community (Box 3). This 60-day requirement has been removed in the Wildlife Act, and the law provides that action on the proposal shall be made within a reasonable period from submission of all requirements.

Considering the varying nature of the ARA and CRA, certain distinctions are incorporated in the application process corresponding to the characteristics of the ARA or CRA (Table 1). A new application procedure, however, is being drafted and will be enforced upon the approval of the implementing rules and regulations of the Wildlife Act.

Prior Informed Consent

Pursuant to Article 15 of the CBD, EO 247 mandates that prospecting, under either an ARA or a CRA, can be allowed only upon the prior informed consent of the community from which the resources are taken.[38] Unlike the CBD, the concept of PIC under EO 247 refers not only to the consent of the State but extends to the IPS, the local community, the Protected Area Management Board (PAMB), and the landowner concerned. PIC is defined as "the consent obtained by the applicant from the local community, indigenous people, the PAMB, or private land owner concerned, after disclosing fully the intent and scope of the bioprospecting activity, in a language and process understandable to the community, and before any bioprospecting activity is undertaken".[39] It is through the PIC process that IPS and local communities

are given the opportunity to negotiate for benefits with the applicants. Although representatives of IACBGR are present during negotiations for a PIC, the decision is left entirely to the community and its leaders.

Where the prospecting of biological and genetic resources and the indigenous knowledge related to their use, preservation, and promotion is done in ancestral domain[40] or ancestral land[41], the applicant must obtain the *free and prior informed consent* (FPIC) of the IPS in accordance with their customary laws.[42] In this case, FPIC means the consensus of all members of the ICCS/IPS, arrived at through customary law, free from external manipulation or interference. The process should involve disclosure of intention and extent of the activity in a transparent manner and in understandable language.[43]

Under EO 247, the process for securing a PIC certificate shall be as follows:

- Submit copies of the research proposal to the recognized head of the IP, City or Municipal Mayor of the local government unit, PAMB, or private landowner concerned.[44]

- Inform the local community, IP, PAMB, or the private landowner concerned of the intention to conduct bioprospecting activity within the area through various media advertisements or direct communication.

- Post a notice[45] in a conspicuous place one week prior to the holding of a community assembly.

- Hold community consultation.[46]

- Recognized head of the IP, Municipal or City Mayor, PAMB, or private landowner issues certificate upon determination that applicant has undergone the process required by law, but only after the lapse of 60 days from submission of the proposal.

- Submit PIC certificate to the IACBGR together with proofs of compliance with the PIC process.

Subsequent recanting by the community of the PIC shall not cause rescission of the agreement. However, if it was obtained through fraud, stealth, false promises, or intimidation, or if the continuance of the agreement shall impair the rights of the IPs to the traditional uses of the resources, the research agreement may be rescinded.

Minimum Terms and Conditions of Research Agreements

The following terms and conditions are incorporated in the CRA and ARA:

Ownership, Transfer, and Use of Materials.
The research agreement states that ownership of materials used and/or taken remains with the State[48] and complete access to specimens deposited abroad shall be allowed to all Filipino citizens and the government.[49] A report of

collections made, listing all depositories that have used or are currently using Philippine species and their database and information, shall be submitted to the IACBGR by the principal.[50] Transport of materials shall be subject to existing laws, rules and regulations, treaties, and international conventions.[51] For CRA, the researcher shall collect only the kind and quantity of resources originally listed in the agreement and only within the designated collection sites.[52]

Terms of Collaboration

Transfer of technology is encouraged by requiring compliance with certain conditions, namely: a complete set of voucher specimens for the collected material must be deposited at the National Museum or duly designated depository; holotypes must be labeled properly and retained at the National Museum; a complete set of all living specimens collected must be deposited in mutually agreed and duly designated depositories;[53] there must be collaboration with a Philippine scientist in all bioprospecting research by foreign persons, including technological development of a product derived from the collected resources;[54] and, for

a CRA, a donation must be made by the principal of some of the equipment used in the conduct of the research to the Philippine government agency, institutions, or universities concerned.[55]

Subsequent Transfers

Where the collector is merely an agent, the agreement between the collector and the principal must be reviewed by the IACBGR.[56] A Material Transfer Agreement (MTA) shall accompany every transfer for the purpose of retaining control over materials.[57]

Prior Informed Consent of Communities

No bioprospecting activity shall be conducted without the prior informed consent of the local community, PAMB, and the landowner concerned and the free and prior informed consent of IPS.

Environmental Protection

EO 247 provides that bioprospecting activities and their results must not directly or indirectly harm the biologi-

---

Box 1. Commercial Research Agreement applications (Information provided by the Technical Secretariat)

Applicant	Research title/Activity	Date	Status	Remarks
Dr. Gerard L. Penecilla Biological Sciences Dept., West Visayas State University, Iloilo City Collaborator: Univ. of Ghent, Belgium	"Collaborative Exploitation of Phyto-chemical Resources": This will involve collection of 200 species of flowering plants and bryophytes for purposes of: a) bioassay of medicinal plants with anti-cancer potential and other pharmaceutical properties, and b) bioprospecting of different plant species for pharmaceutical, pesticidal and other industrial purposes.	06/02/97	Application was withdrawn.	
Philippine National Museum, Department of Agriculture (DA), Bureau of Fisheries and Aquatic Resources (BFAR), National Cancer Institute, and the Coral Reef Research Foundation	"Investigations of Marine Species Diversity of the Philippines and the Search for New Anti-cancer Drugs from the Sea": This will involve collection of marine invertebrates and marine plant samples with potential cancer and anti-AIDS activity for extraction and isolation by the USA National Cancer Institute of Marine Natural Products.	01/09/96	Gratuitous Permit No. 01-97 issued by BFAR expired on 10/14/97.	Documents for CRA application referred to BFAR to draft the CRA.
University of California-Silliman University c/o William Fenical	"Research on Marine Organisms as Possible Sources of Novel Natural Products Including New Drugs Projects"	12/26/96		Documents were referred to BFAR.
UP Marine Science Institute-Utah University, USA	"Anti-Cancer Agents from Unique Natural Products Sources": This Project will involve collection of funicates, sponges and other invertebrate samples for biological assays to screen for potential bioactive compounds.	02/26/97	Approved/signed on 06/30/98 by DA Secretary Salvador Escudero III.	Collection report submitted to PAWB on 05/31/99.

cal diversity, ecological balance, or the inhabitants of the area where collection is undertaken. Also, collection under a research agreement must comply with all applicable environmental laws, regulations, and procedures such as the Environmental Impact Assessment Law and the NIPAS Act.[58]

Benefit Sharing

EO 247 provides for minimum benefit-sharing arrangements that must be met by the bioprospector. It mandates that all discoveries of commercial products derived from the resources shall be made available to the Philippine government and the local community concerned.[59] Likewise, all benefits resulting directly or indirectly from the bioprospecting activities conducted shall be shared equitably and upon mutual consent among the government, the communities concerned, and the principal.[60] The use of technologies, commercially or locally, developed from research on Philippine endemic species must be made available to the Philippine government without paying royalty to the principal unless other agreements may be negotiated by the parties, where appropriate and applicable.[61] Under a CRA, regarding technology or a commercial product developed and marketed any equity or remittance, in the amount to be mutually agreed upon by the parties, shall

be equitably shared with either of the following parties: a) the Philippine government, b) the Integrated Protected Areas Fund (IPAF), c) the concerned IPs or local communities, or d) the individual who modified such resource that came from private property.[62] A separate agreement shall be made for the transfer of royalty, benefits, technology, and agreements.[63]

Penalties and Sanctions

As an executive issuance, EO 247 does not provide for penal sanctions against violators of the law. However, activities undertaken without the required research agreement and PIC certificate shall be subject to criminal prosecution under relevant statutes such as the NIPAS Act.[64] Also, administrative sanctions are imposed, such as immediate termination of the agreement and a perpetual ban on undertaking prospecting in the Philippines in cases of noncompliance with the provisions of the research agreement.[65]

Implementation and Monitoring

The respective member agencies of the IACBGR shall conduct monitoring of research agreements based on a standard monitoring scheme to be devised by the IACBGR

Box 1. Continued

Applicant	Research title/Activity	Date	Status	Remarks
Mr. Tim M.A. Utteridge, Department of Ecology and Biodiversity, The University of Hong Kong, Pokfulam Road, Hong Kong	"Systematics of the Genus *Maesa* (Myrsinaceae) in the Philippines"	01/07/97	Pending.	Awaiting submission of necessary documents, e.g., PIC.
Dr. Lourdes J. Cruz, Marine Science Institute University of the Philippines, Diliman, Quezon City	"Neuroactive Peptides from Venomous Gastropods": This project aims to make use of animals that would otherwise be discarded by the shell craft industry. Selected gastropods (*Conus* and related groups of turrids and terribrids) will be studied.	10/29/98	Pending.	Submitted on 17 March 1999 original and notarized copies of the PIC certificates issued by Mun. Mayor of Mabini, Batangas and other documents required under DAO 96-20 and by the IACBGR not yet received.
Kagoshima University Research Center for the South Pacific Kagoshima, Japan	"Man and the Environment in Palawan, Philippines": Aims to conduct research expedition and collection of biological specimens in Palawan.	11/96		Application was withdrawn.
Rizal Technological Colleges c/o José Macabbalug	"Development/Establishment of Center for the Conservation of Philippine Native Orchids": Establishment of in-vitro culture bank for research, production, and commercialization of Philippine orchids.	11/18/96		Forwarded letter dated 06/03/98 requesting documents for the CRA application. No response yet.

for that purpose.[66] There shall be an IACBGR monitoring team responsible for establishing a mechanism to ensure the integration and dissemination of the information generated from research, collection, and utilization activities.[67] Another monitoring team headed by DOST and Department of Foreign Affairs representatives monitors the progress of the research, utilization, and commercialization outside the country.[68] A draft guideline on monitoring is now under review by the IACBGR.

Issues and Concerns

Since the issuance of EO 247 in 1995, several issues have been brought up which, in a way, affected the full implementation of the law. The issues and concerns that have confronted EO 247 are as follows:

Scope and Coverage[69]

Two relevant points were raised at the workshops[70] held in 1998:

Box 2. Academic Research Agreement applications (Information provided by the Technical Secretariat)

Applicant	Research title/Activity	Date	Description	Status
UP System		09/01/98	Conservation-related research, including studies as part of thesis requirements.	Approved
International Rice Research Institute c/o Ronald Cantrell and Dr. Mew		09/09/98	Conduct scientific research on rice varieties and wild species, rice-associated vegetation, fauna, and microorganisms.	For further evaluation/review by the TS and IACBGR.
Research Institute for Tropical Medicine (RITM) c/o Dr. R.M. Olveda	Development of an immunodot dipstick for the detection of circulating *Schistosoma japonicum* antigens in the urine using locally produced monoclonal antibodies.	05/29/98	Collection of snails' urine samples for *S. japonicum* antigen production. Evaluation of test assay.	Recommended for ARA between DENR and RITM. Additional requirements/ information submitted to PAWB 9 August 1999.
— " —	*S. japonicum* reinfection after treatment in domestic animals and impact of animal chemotherapy on transmission.	— " —	Collection of snails and stools, blood, and urine of animals and human to monitor *S. japonicum* infection in animals and man before and after treatment.	— " —
— " —	Biased short-term surveillance for Bat Lyssavirus.	— " —	Collection of blood and brain samples from species of bats to determine the presence of virus variants in bat populations.	— " —
— " —	Molecular epidemiology of canine rabies in the Philippines.	— " —	Collection of dog brain samples to describe the epidemiology of canine rabies virus variants.	— " —
— " —	Expanded surveillance of Ebola Reston Virus in the Philippines: Investigation of possible natural hosts.	— " —	Collection of blood, liver and other tissue samples from monkeys to describe the epidemiology of Ebola Reston Virus in indigenous macaque populations.	— " —
— " —	Epidemiologic survey of Hantavirus infection among rodent populations in the Philippines.	— " —	Collection of urban & rice field rats (*Rattus* spp.) to determine the presence of extent of transmission of Hantivirus infection.	— " —

- The scope of EO 247 is too broad due mainly to a vague definition of the term "bioprospecting". The term "prospecting" means to explore or to look for, but EO 247 covers not only just "looking for". The law regulates the act of collecting and sampling. As such, the definition appears to cover almost all kinds of collection, research, and utilization of biological and genetic resources, including conservation research that many scientists, academic institutions, and NGOs undertake and which have nothing to do with prospecting. This stifles and discourages all kinds of research in the country.

- EO 247 is ambiguous as far as *ex situ* collections are concerned, but the IACBGR regulates them. DAO 20 further muddles the issue by explicitly stating that only natural growths in private lands are covered by the law, thus implying that domesticated resources are not regulated. This ambiguity may be used to circumvent the law. Similarly, some people are not comfortable with the exclusion of traditional uses from the law's coverage. There is apprehension that bioprospectors can simply obtain resources from

Box 2. Continued

Applicant	Research title/Activity	Date	Description	Status
RITM continued	Specimen banking for future reference of other unknown or emerging zoonotic pathogens.	09/09/98	Collection of monkey and rat specimens for identification of other possible emerging zoonotic diseases from primates and rodents.	Recommended for ARA between DENR and RITM. Additional requirements/ information submitted to PAWB 9 August 1999.
— " —	Agusan del Sur Malaria Control Program.	— " —	Collection of mosquito adults and larvae to identify the vector breeding sites, to determine peak biting time, to test susceptibility to insecticides.	— " —
— " —	Application of radio nuclide technique in the detection of *Wuchereria bancrofti* infected mosquitoes for assessing filarial transmission.	— " —	Collection of mosquitoes to detect *W. bancrofti* infection in mosquitoes.	— " —
Aurora State College of Technology	Aurora Biodiversity Assessment Conservation Program.	05/98	Collection of certain species of birds, mammals and plants to assess biodiversity resources of Aurora, and establish a database and knowledge-base for its conservation.	Recommended for ARA by TS during the 08/28/98 meeting.
Emilio Aguinaldo College c/o Dr. Cecilia P. Reyes	Destructiveness and Potential to Transmit Microbial Diseases by *Scirtothrips dorsalin.*	06/22/98	Collection of both male and female insects to determine the degree of destructiveness of adults on larval instars of *S. dorsalis,* and to determine the role of adults and larval instars of *S. dorsalis* in transmitting microbial diseases.	
— " —	Identification of insect scavengers and their potential as biological agent of reclamation and management of organic household garbage.	— " —	Collection of 0.5 kg of garbage for arthropod extraction to identify different species on insect scavengers associated with household garbage, and to determine the preference & rate of consumption of garbage by insect scavengers.	

public markets or gather them under the guise of traditional use.

Application Process

The period from filing of the application to final approval of the agreement is estimated to require at least five months. For most local scientists and researchers, the process is cumbersome, costly, and considered a deterrent to research growth and development (EO 247 WORKSHOP 1998).

At the initial stage of the application process, the researcher is required to pay a minimal amount of $1,000P for Filipinos or $2,000P for foreign nationals as an application fee. As soon as the research agreement is approved, a bioprospecting fee is remitted to the national government.

For a CRA, the collector also posts a bond.[71] However, it is the cost of securing the PIC certificate that is the source of most complaints. For example, if the research would require utilization or collection of resources from 12 regions of the Philippines, the collector will have to go to 12 sites to secure 12 PIC/FPIC certificates. Each community will have different demands, terms, and conditions that must be complied with. Also, because negotiations for PIC are left entirely to the community and the applicant, collectors are worried that communities, IPs, politicians, and others who must give consent will hold the bioprospector and the activity hostage by asking outrageous and excessive demands (EO 247 WORKSHOP 1998). Because of the dire

Box 2. Continued				
Applicant	**Research title/Activity**	**Date**	**Description**	**Status**
Pamantasan ng Lungsod ng Maynila (PLM)		08/13/98	Conduct of conservation-related studies as part of thesis requirements, etc.	The PLM had been requested to submit the requirements for ARA; The Gratuitous Permit for the studies to be conducted by the PLM students for thesis requirements will be prepared by PAWB.
Central Mindanao University c/o Prof. Joel Almeror	Diversity of Vascular Plants in Mt. Kinasalapi, Kitanglad Range Natural Park.			Recommended for ARA by the TS during the 08/28/98 meeting.
Central Mindanao University c/o Mr. Jaime Gellor	Institute for Terrestrial Biodiversity and Conservation Studies in Mindanao.	08/12/98	Collection of endemic/endangered flora and fauna in Mindanao for research and instruction purposes.	Submitted in 11/98 copies of the research proposals on the ongoing, as well as future studies to PAWB for TS and IACBGR review.
New Samar Aquatic Resources Development Corp.	Scientific Study for the Protection and Preservation of Corals.		Experimental gathering of precious corals in the Philippines waters through the use of HAKUYO manned vehicle. After one year, the development of processing plant.	Referred to BFAR.
Miami University c/o Alycia Baybayan	An investigation of plant utilization (medicinal and home gardens) on the island of Igbayat, Batanes.		Collection of plants in pursuit of master's thesis.	Requested to submit the requirements for CRA between DENR and Miami University.
Central Luzon State Univ. c/o Annie Paz-Alberto			Institutional research.	Requested to submit the requirements for ARA.

economic situation, EO 247 is seen as the solution to the communities' socio-economic difficulties, leading them to focus on short-term and immediate benefits (PERIA 1998). Local scientists and researchers who normally rely only on financial grants consider this unreasonable, and the economic costs involved stifle their research. This is especially true for scientists who are not affiliated with any Philippine scientific, academic, governmental, or intergovermental institution which would only have to comply with the minimum terms and conditions of a CRA under EO 247.

Prior Informed Consent

The PIC requirement under EO 247 is seen as administratively tedious and burdensome, especially the 60-day period requirement before PIC is issued. As earlier stated, most collectors also dread the PIC requirement due to economic costs. Identifying which community should give consent is often problematic, especially in the case of pelagic or migratory species.

Another issue raised concerning PIC deals with full disclosure of the intended activity and its impact on intellectual property rights (TANTIA 1998). There are some who propose that disclosure should be limited to collection activity only rather than the entire process, so as not to prejudice patent rights and the confidentiality of information (EO 247 WORKSHOP 1998).

Nevertheless, many still believe that the PIC requirement should not be discarded because it is the only means for the inclusion of the communities' concerns in the research agreement. Also, it is the only opportunity for the community to negotiate equitable sharing of benefits with the proponent. The process for securing the PIC, however, should be properly studied (PERIA 1998).

Institutional Mechanism

An interagency body consisting of representatives of various agencies of the government and other sectors is advantageous because of the multidisciplinary nature of the issues relating to bioprospecting. Expertise and logistics are shared. However, an interagency approach has many inherent problems as well. It is difficult to get a quorum of the members; resolution or decision-making takes a long time because of irregular attendance of members; and coordination between member agencies is difficult. Also, responsibilities of the member agencies are not clearly delineated in EO 247 (EO 247 WORKSHOP 1998). Funding requirements have always haunted the implementers of EO 247 because there is no specific source of funds provided, except from the savings of the concerned government agencies and the fees collected by the IACBGR.

Box 2. Continued

Applicant	Research title/Activity	Date	Description	Status
Municipal Government of Lopez Jaena, Misamis Occ. c/o Mayor Melquirades Azcuna Jr.	Proposed Community-based Biodiversity Conservation and Management Program for Lopez Jaena Mis. Occ.	05/02/97	A collaborative pilot research and development program.	Required to submit requirements for ARA.
Ms. Julie Tan c/o VISCA, Leyte		12/03/97		Referred to Dept. of Health on 03/24/97.
UP Marine Science Institute c/o Dr. Suzanne Licuanan	Marine Biodiversity Enhancement and Sustainable Livelihood Program for the Hundred Islands Natural Park in the Lingayen Gulf.	11/03/97	Conservation oriented activities.	Referred to BFAR on 01/02/98.
Zambasul Mercantile Exotic Skins Tannery c/o Mr. Reynaldo Chua	Utilization of *Bufo marinus* for leather products.	09/02/97	Collection of Cane Toad for utilization-leather products for direct trade and biological control to cull toad population.	Referred to BFAR on 10/09/97.
Conservation International Philippines c/o Mr. Antonio de Castro	Marine Rapid Assessment in Western Busuanga, Palawan.	12/23/97	Collection of marine specimens for taxonomic/proper identification purposes and inventory of marine biological resources in the area.	Referred to BFAR.
St. Paul University c/o Mr. Maximo Roger Pua			Studies as part of thesis requirements.	

Box 3. Research proposal format

___Academic ___ Commercial

1. Project title
   _____

2. Project/Research objectives
   2.1 _____
   2.2 _____
   2.3 _____

3. Places of collection
   _____
   _____

   Projected date of implementation and reason
   _____
   _____

4. Bioresources and quantity (if possible) (indicate live or dead specimen, specify if by-products or derivatives)
   _____
   _____

5. Methodology (use separate sheet if necessary)
   _____
   _____

6. Manner data to be gathered (recorded, photographed, video, collected, observed, etc.) and format (notes, specimens, photographs, etc.)
   _____
   _____

7. Anticipated intermediate and final destination of bioresources, etc.
   _____
   _____

8. How bioresources obtained are to be used initially (i.e., national collection) subsequently (e.g., drug exploration, field guide preparation, etc.)
   _____
   _____

9. Description of funding support with budget (use separate sheet if necessary)
   _____
   _____

10. Analysis of the research of foreseen impact on biological diversity
   _____
   _____

11. Detailed description of immediate compensation anticipated
   _____
   _____

12. Detailed description of long-term compensation anticipated
   _____

13. List of in-country entities likely to receive compensation enumerated in #11 and reasons (logical and legal)
   _____

Benefit sharing

Local scientists view the benefit-sharing requirements under EO 247 as too demanding. They also worry about the involvement of local scientists in research which may invade the confidentiality of information and may jeopardize the chances for intellectual property rights protection on commercially viable products (TECHNICAL SECRETARIAT 2001).

There are others, however, who believe that the benefit-sharing provisions of EO 247 are not enough. Other questions posed which they feel should be answered include: How do we ensure equitable sharing, who should get what, how much, and for how long, what are the forms of benefit sharing, and will the community benefit? (EO 247 WORKSHOP 1998). Some believe that the community should be given a bigger role in negotiating benefit sharing (PERIA 1998). EO 247 merely provides for the minimum terms and conditions so as to give the parties enough leeway to negotiate. The problem is that effective bargaining and negotiation have not yet been given much attention by the implementers.

Biodiversity Conservation

Some also raise the issue that EO 247 does not provide for a mechanism to ensure that its goal to protect and conserve biological and genetic resources is achieved. The functions of the IACBGR do not even include resource protection, and conservation and technology transfer are merely second-

Table 1. Application process for research agreements. Requirements for ARAS and CRAS differ in steps 3 and 9.

Steps

1. Submission of Letter of Intent and three copies of research proposal to the Technical Secretariat
2. Initial screening by TS whether or not activity is covered by EO 247[72]
3. Submission of additional requirements
   ARA: Application form; Institution profile; Code of conduct; Environmental Impact Assessment,[73] if necessary; Processing fee[74]
   CRA: Application form; Company/institution/organization profile; Environmental Impact Assessment, if necessary; Processing fee; PIC certificate[75]
4. Initial evaluation by TS of application
5. Submission of evaluation result to IACBGR within 30 days from receipt of all requirements[76]
6. Final evaluation by IACBGR
7. Submission of IACBGR's recommendation to the Agency concerned[77]
8. Approval/Disapproval by the head of the Agency
9. Payment of fee and/or posting of bonds, if approved
   ARA: Bioprospecting fee
   CRA: Bioprospecting fee and Performance, compensation, ecological rehabilitation bond[78]
10. Transmittal of copies of agreement to applicant, IP, local community, Protected Areas Management Board (PAMB), or private landowner concerned

ary as a form of benefit sharing. There is no financing mechanism or trust fund in place to support biodiversity conservation objectives (OCHAVE 1999). Although EO 247 allows the proponent and the government and/or local community to agree on possible arrangements that would ensure protection and conservation of biological diversity as part of the benefit-sharing agreement or tied with the PIC, this is not always guaranteed because there are no concrete programs or mechanisms in place.

In response to the clamor for modification or revision of EO 247, new measures relative to bioprospecting were incorporated into the Wildlife Act.

The Wildlife Act

On 30 July 2001, the Philippine Legislature enacted the Wildlife Resources Conservation and Protection Act. As a legislative act of the Philippine Congress, it passed through the regular process of enacting a statute in the Philippines. The act was initiated in the 10th Congress (1995–1997) but it was not passed into law at that time. In 1998, five House bills were filed and consolidated into one House bill. A similar bill was filed in the Senate of the Philippines. The bills passed through several committee meetings before they were discussed and voted on in the plenary sessions of both houses of Congress. Subsequently, the Lower House version was used as a working draft during the bicameral committee sessions. During the various committee meetings the following sectors were represented: government (Bureau of Customs, Philippine National Museum, Department of Science and Technology, Bureau of Aquatic Resources, National Bureau of Investigation, Protected Areas and Wildlife Bureau, Ecosystems Research and Development Bureau, Department of Trade and Industry, National Committee on Biosafety in the Philippines, ASEAN Regional Center for Biodiversity Conservation); the academy (University of the Philippines (UP) Marine Science Institute, Institute of Plant Breeding-UP Los Baños); business (Floratrade/ Philippine Horticultural Society, Southeast Asian Fisheries Development Corp); and NGOs (Kalikasan Mindoro Foundation and Conservation International).

Based on the congressional records, there was a consensus that the passage of the Wildlife Act had been long overdue. All participants (both congressmen and resource persons) were in full support of the legislation, because existing laws on wildlife protection and conservation are outmoded and the penalties contained therein are very minimal. The new law will also enable the Philippines to meet its commitments to the Convention on International Trade in Endangered Species of Wild Fauna and Flora (CITES) (Spot Report on the Meeting of the Committee on Ecology, 2 December 1998). The Wildlife Act is actually a codification of existing laws on the protection and conservation of wildlife resources. As such, experiences in the implementation of existing laws helped a great deal in the design of the Wildlife Act. Concerns and issues that have been plaguing lawmakers and that were raised against the old laws were responded to in the law, such as minimal penalties and unclear provisions relative to CITES. As far as bioprospecting is concerned, the act addressed most of the concerns or criticisms made against EO 247. Thus, the discussions of the draft act in the committee level were not too heated. There were also no controversial provisions or issues. It would appear that the participants who were the implementers of existing laws shared their experiences and offered solutions to the problems that they encountered in the enforcement of these laws.[79] The provisions on bioprospecting were drafted by the Department of Environment and Natural Resources–Protected Areas and Wildlife Bureau which is the same agency primarily in charge of implementing EO 247.

The basic policy of the State in the Wildlife Act is "to conserve the country's wildlife resources and their habitats for sustainability". In the pursuit of said policy, the law has the following objectives:[80]

- Conserve and protect wildlife species and their habitats to promote ecological balance and enhance biological diversity.

- Regulate the collection and trade of wildlife.

- Pursue, with due regard to national interest, the Philippine commitment to international conventions on the protection of wildlife and their habitats.

- Initiate or support scientific studies on the conservation of biological diversity.

The law covers all wildlife species found in all areas of the country, including protected areas and critical habitats. It also governs "exotic species which are subject to trade, are cultured, maintained, and/or bred in captivity or propagated in the country".[81]

Although there are only two provisions in the Wildlife Act dealing with bioprospecting[82], these provisions modified EO 247 considerably. Most of the changes that were introduced try to address the issues and concerns that were raised against EO 247. These are as follows:

- Bioprospecting for purposes of scientific or academic research is no longer subject to the requirements of the law for commercial bioprospecting. Under the Wildlife Act, "bioprospecting" is now defined as "the research, collection and utilization of biological and genetic resources for purposes of applying the knowledge derived therefrom solely for commercial purposes".[83] Collection and utilization of biological resources for scientific research is covered by a gratuitous permit[84] issued upon securing prior clearance[85] from concerned bodies. This is a welcome development for local scientists and researchers who have longed for the exclusion of academic/scientific research from EO 247's coverage.

- The law governs all wildlife species found in all areas in the country. "Wildlife" is defined as "wild forms and varieties of flora and fauna, in all developmental stages, including those which are in captivity or are being bred or propagated".[86] Under the proposed "Guidelines for Bioprospecting Activities in the Philippines", wildlife, microorganisms, domesticated or propagated species, and exotic species are covered (Section 2, 2.1).[87]

- An undertaking signed by the applicant binds him/her to comply with certain terms and conditions as may be imposed.[88] The proposed Guidelines require the applicant to apply for a Bioprospecting Undertaking (BU) before access to biological resources for bioprospecting purposes is allowed (Section 6, 6.1, see endnote 87).

- The Secretary or its representative, in consultation with the concerned agencies, grants a permit to conduct prospecting. This responds to the problems inherent in the interagency approach established under EO 247. However, consultations with concerned agencies are still necessary before any grant for bioprospecting is allowed.

- Prior informed consent from concerned IPs, local communities, PAMB, or a private individual entity is still required in accordance with existing laws, but the 60-day requirement, which had been widely criticized, has been removed.[89]

- In case the applicant is a foreign entity or individual, a local institution shall actively participate in the research, collection, and, if applicable and appropriate, the technological development of the products derived from the resources.[90]

- A wildlife management fund is created which shall finance rehabilitation or restoration of habitats affected by acts committed in violation of the law and support scientific research, enforcement and monitoring activities, and enhancement of capabilities of relevant agencies.[91] This answers the need for a funding mechanism specifically intended for the conservation and protection of biological resources.

- Unauthorized collection, hunting, and possession of wildlife is punishable with imprisonment of up to four (4) years and a fine of up to $300,000P depending on the species illegally collected, hunted, or possessed.[92] The law, however, is silent on the liability of a person illegally conducting bioprospecting.

With the passage of the Wildlife Act, EO 247 has been repealed by implication or amended accordingly[93] and a new set of implementing rules and regulations on bioprospecting is currently being formulated by the DENR.[94] Thus, provisions in EO 247 which are clearly contradictory to and irreconcilable with the Wildlife Act are now deemed repealed.[95] However, the question as to what provisions of EO 247 will remain in force and effect will be answered only after the implementing rules and regulations have been issued, inasmuch as the administrative interpretation of the law will have to be considered. New guidelines in accordance with the Wildlife Act and, perhaps, some of the still-effective provisions of EO 247 will be formulated to replace DAO 20. Until such time, applications for a CRA will continue to be processed under EO 247.

Undoubtedly, the intention of the Wildlife Act is to simplify and facilitate access to biological and genetic resources. This is apparent in the very definition it has provided for "bioprospecting". Since one of the complaints against EO 247 is that it stifles scientific research, the scope of bioprospecting has been limited to commercial purposes only. Also, the minimum terms and conditions found in EO 247 were not legislated; instead, the Secretary

is given the option to impose reasonable terms and conditions which are necessary to protect biodiversity. This gives the Secretary of said agencies great flexibility in the conditions to be imposed. This clearly responds to the claim of local scientists that the minimum terms and conditions of EO 247 are unreasonable.

Equitable sharing of benefits derived from the utilization of biological and genetic resources is not mentioned in the law. It is unclear if the government, as a pre-condition for the approval of the application, shall still require the adoption of benefit-sharing arrangements. It is possible, though, that any benefit-sharing option will now be tied up with the PIC certificate.

Intellectual Property Rights (IPRs): Protection for Biological and Genetic Resources and Traditional Knowledge

The present intellectual property law in the Philippines is Republic Act No. 8293, also known as the Intellectual Property Code of the Philippines (IPC). It took effect on 1 January 1998 and was enacted in compliance with the minimum standards set under TRIPS.[96]

Among the "intellectual property rights" under the IPC, the patent is more relevant to the protection of biological and genetic resources and traditional knowledge associated with these resources. Section 21 of the IPC provides that "patentable invention" refers to "any technical solution of a problem in any field of human activity which is new, involves an inventive step, and is industrially applicable. It may be, or may relate to, a product, or process, or an improvement of any of the foregoing." Plant varieties or animal breeds or essentially biological processes for the production of plants or animals, except microorganisms[97] and nonbiological and microbiological processes cannot be the subject of a patent. However, the Philippine legislature may consider the enactment of a law providing *sui generis* protection for plant varieties or animal breeds and a system of community IPRs protection.[98] In short, the IPC chooses to categorically exclude from patent protection plant varieties and animal breeds. It also does not give protection to traditional knowledge but allows the creation of a *sui generis* protection for community IPRs.

Patent protection over life forms, including microorganisms, remains a controversial issue in the Philippines. It is argued that life forms are not eligible for patents because nothing new is created, and the process merely involves reorganizing something that already exists (BAUTISTA 1999). Some civil society groups clamor for total exclusion of any life form from patenting or even from *sui generis* protection due to moral and ethical issues. They consider it intrinsically wrong to patent any living organism. For them, it violates the belief that only the divine creator can bring forth life (BAUTISTA 1999).

Other reasons given for distrust, if not rejection, of the patent system as applied to life forms are the following: a) the Philippines suffers from a serious lack of visible

science culture; b) patent law applied to genetic resources represents a fusion of two fields, law and science, which people, generally, do not understand; c) patent law is another imposition of the developed countries on the developing countries, a view held by a number of NGOs which has some basis in history; and, d) the wide chasm separating the scientific and legal communities in the Philippines has caused even some scientists and technologists to have some aversion toward patent law (OCHAVE 1997).

There is also a growing concern that IPR systems under TRIPS as applied to life forms run counter to the goals of the CBD in the following aspects: a) IPRs hinder full realization of Art. 3 on national sovereignty and Article 8j on Farmers' Rights[99]; b) conservation of biodiversity is not compatible with a global regime of private monopoly rights; and c) TRIPS undermines the implementation of access and benefit-sharing provisions because the resource will be under the control of the IPR-holder (MUSHITA 1999). In particular, Article 27.3 (b) is said to be in conflict with goals of the CBD and the International Undertaking on Plant Genetic Resources insofar as conservation of biological diversity, specifically plant varieties, and equitable sharing of benefits are concerned. Granting exclusive IPRs to breeders will prevent certain established practices among farmers and indigenous communities, including common access to seeds and varieties, and most probably will be subject to infringement sanctions (CALIMON 1999).

Nonetheless, others believe that the conflict is not between the CBD and TRIPS but arises only from the legislation of individual member States, as in the case of plant varieties' protection. It is said that under TRIPS, IPRs need not involve exclusive rights. Both international agreements require member States "to provide protection to plant varieties consistent with their obligation to conserve biological diversity, the sustainable use of its components, and the fair and equitable sharing of the benefits arising out of the utilization of genetic resources". (CALIMON 1999). What is relevant for any plant protection law is the need to balance the protection of the IPRs of breeders and the interests and IPRs of farmers and local indigenous communities. To interpret TRIPS's Article 27.3b as not requiring balancing of rights will run counter to the objectives of the CBD (CALIMON 1999).

And yet, this so-called "balancing of rights" may be easier said than done. It would be very difficult to balance rights that are not equal to begin with. IPR-holders are usually moneyed and backed by powerful and rich governments while most farmers and IPs are not. In fact, even in their own countries, IPs and farmers' rights are, more often than not, not recognized or protected. Even if some balancing of rights is established through national legislation, the problem of asserting their rights will still persist because IPs and farmers have fewer resources or none at all.

The aversion to patenting life forms or even providing *sui generis* protection that grants proprietary rights over these resources to a single individual or corporation has been evident in how civil society and other interest groups view the 2002 Philippine Plant Variety Protection (PVP) law. In compliance with the country's obligations under TRIPS, the Philippine legislature passed a law which gives protection to new plant varieties.[100] Republic Act No. 9168, entitled "An Act to Provide Protection to New Plant Varieties, Establishing a National Plant Protection Board and for other purposes"[101], recognizes that "an effective intellectual property system in general and the development of new plant variety in particular is vital in attaining food security for the country". As such, the law aims to protect and secure the exclusive rights of breeders with respect to their new plant variety.[102]

Protection under Republic Act No. 9168 is patterned after the International Union for the Protection of New Varieties of Plants (UPOV) plant breeders' rights. The law provides that any breeder may be granted a Certificate of Plant Variety Protection for a particular plant variety upon showing that said variety is new, distinct, uniform, and stable. A variety covered by a PVP certificate is protected for 20 years, or 25 years in case of vines and trees, from date of issuance of the certificate.[103] The holder of the certificate has the right to authorize production or reproduction; conditioning for the purpose of propagation; offering for sale; selling or other marketing; exporting; importing; and stocking for any purpose mentioned above. Also, he may make his authorization subject to conditions and limitations.[104] Protection under the act extends to varieties which are essentially derived from the protected variety, where the protected variety is not itself an essentially derived variety; those which are not clearly distinct from the protected variety; and those whose production requires the repeated use of the protected variety.[105] It does not, however, extend to acts done for noncommercial, or experimental purposes; the purpose of breeding other varieties; and to traditional right of small farmers to save, use, exchange, share, or sell their farm produce of a protected variety, except when a sale is for the purpose of reproduction under a commercial marketing agreement. The act also exempts the exchange and sale of seeds among and between small farmers, but only for purposes of reproduction and replanting in their own land.[106]

The law also allows compulsory licensing at any time after two years from the grant of the PVP when it is for public interest and the reasonable requirements of the public, overseas market for sale of any part of the variety are not met or when the variety relates to or is required in the production of medicine and/or any food preparation. The duration of the compulsory license ends when the ground for its issuance no longer exists as determined by the government.[107]

Any of the following acts constitutes infringement of the plant breeders' plant variety protection: a) sell, offer, expose for sale, deliver, ship, consign, exchange, solicit an offer to buy, or any other transfer of title or possession of the novel variety; b) import into or export from the country of the novel variety; c) sexually multiply the variety as a step in marketing (for growing purposes); d) use the novel variety in producing (as distinguished from developing) a hybrid or different variety therefrom; e) use seed which had been marked "unauthorized propagation prohibited" or "unauthorized seed multiplication prohibited" or progeny thereof to propagate the novel variety; f) dispense the novel variety to another, in a form which can be propagated, without notice as to being a protected variety under which it was received; g) fails to use a variety denomination, the use of which is obligatory under the act; h) perform any of the foregoing acts even in instances in which the novel variety is multiplied other than sexually; and i) instigate or actively induce performance of any foregoing acts.[108]

The passage of Republic Act No. 9168 has been criticized by civil societies and farmer groups. They believe that the law highlights multinational corporations' control over the course of the Philippines' agriculture. Concern about the survival of small farmers has been rising because the law "prohibits them to continue with their traditional practices of seed utilization". Farmers have always been engaged in the art and science of plant breeding and selection long before scientists and agribusiness corporations came into being. They also freely store and exchange seeds among themselves, a process which played a major role in development of new varieties (MORDENO 2002). All these practices are now being endangered by the act.

Also, although PVP is not strictly patent protection, many consider the UPOV-kind of protection as a "soft" kind of patent regime which should likewise be rejected because it is just as "threatening as industrial patents on biodiversity and also represent an attack on the rights of farming and other communities at the local level". Anti-UPOV groups have listed the following reasons why UPOV should be opposed: a) UPOV denies farmers' rights; b) rich Northern countries will take over national breeding systems in poor Southern countries and get ownership of the latter's biodiversity with no obligation to share benefits; c) UPOV criteria for protection will exacerbate erosion of biodiversity; d) privatization of genetic resources affects research negatively; e) moves to keep biodiversity under negotiated access systems will be undermined as PVP laws grant private ownership of resources that fall under national and community sovereignty; and f) joining UPOV means accepting a questionable system that supports the rights of industrial breeders and disregards farmers and communities (DOYO 2002).

Furthermore, IPR systems under TRIPS, specifically patent laws and even PVP, are inadequate to protect traditional and community knowledge as well as inappropriate for defending the rights and resources of local communities and indigenous peoples. Traditional knowledge associated with biological resources may not meet all the requirements under traditional IPR regimes such as novelty, inventive step, and industrial applicability (AD HOC WORKING GROUP ON ACCESS AND BENEFIT SHARING 2001). The innovations, practices, and knowledge systems of IPs "were developed collectively, accretionally over time, and inter-generationally" (DAOAS 1999). Thus, the conditions of novelty and innovative steps for the granting of patent may be questionable. Also, knowledge is often held by different independent communities (AD HOC WORKING GROUP ON ACCESS AND BENEFIT SHARING 2001). It does not belong exclusively to one individual which is what a patent is all about (DAOAS 1999). TRIPS is an embodiment of western legal philosophy: norms, values, and mindset that are contrary to many IPs' cosmologies and values (TAULI-CORPUZ 2000). Moreover, the existing IPR system "promotes the misappropriation of indigenous knowledge, with the result that the benefits derived from the commercialization of this knowledge do not flow back to the source communities who freely shared the knowledge with outsiders" (TAULI-CORPUZ 2000).

Other reasons cited for the inadequacy and inappropriateness of IPR systems under TRIPS for the protection of traditional knowledge associated with biological resources are the following (CHAO 1999, AD HOC WORKING GROUP ON ACCESS AND BENEFIT SHARING 2001):

- Patents do not provide incentives for innovations generated at the community level. The recognition of value added through the IPR regime appears limited to the input of formal innovation (made by

scientists/academics) even if the end product or process was arrived at through informal innovation of the community.

- IPR systems do not compensate the custodians of biological resources even when these resources are used for commercially profitable and legally protected inventions and end products.

- IPR protection is said to favor those with ready access to economic and legal resources that local communities often find hard to obtain.

EO 247 and the Wildlife Act, and even the Republic Act No. 8371 also known as the Indigenous Peoples' Rights Act (IPRA), however, are not dependent on IPR protection of biological resources, traditional knowledge, and benefit sharing. Access to traditional knowledge associated with biological and genetic resources is not conditioned upon recognition of IPR rights of the source community (CHAO 1999). While the benefit-sharing provisions of EO 247 for the utilization of biological and genetic resources mandate payment of royalties, EO 247 does not require that IPRs be shared. In this sense, the regulation merely requires sharing a portion of the proceeds (e.g., licensing fees). The emerging view is that local counterparts should share in IPRs only if they have actual participation in the innovations developed (PAWB-DENR 1998).

Moreover, many believe that patent ownership is not the only form of benefit sharing and that contract law, not patent law, is the key to ensuring that source countries or communities share in whatever benefits are derived from the use of genetic resources. Thus, as correctly pointed out by José Maria A. Ochave, "if source countries or communities are to capture some of the benefits resulting from the utilization of their genetic resources, they should focus their attention not on the patent system, but on the nature and content of their contractual relations with prospective bioprospectors" (OCHAVE 1997).

What is important for us is that any access to our resources and traditional knowledge must have the approval of the government through research agreements or undertakings, and the prior informed consent of the local and indigenous communities obtained under existing laws, rules, and regulations.

Access to Indigenous Peoples' Biological Resources and Traditional Knowledge

Access to biological resources within ancestral lands and ancestral domain is allowed under EO 247. Under IPRA, the free and prior informed consent of the IPs is required prior to any access to these resources and their traditional knowledge. Moreover, under IPRA, the rights of the IPs to their ancestral domains and lands, to self-governance and empowerment, to self-justice and human rights, and to cultural integrity have been recognized.[109] The law also acknowledges the rights of the IPs to full ownership, control, and protection of their cultural and intellectual

property rights. Included under this is the "right to special measures to control, develop, and protect their sciences, technologies, and cultural manifestations, including human and other genetic resources, seeds, including derivatives of these resources, traditional medicines and health practices, vital medicinal plants, animals and minerals, indigenous knowledge systems and practices, knowledge of the properties of fauna and flora, oral traditions, literature, designs, and visual and performing arts".[110] Further, Sec. 35 of said law provides that "access to biological and genetic resources and to indigenous knowledge related to the conservation, utilization, and enhancement of these resources, shall be allowed within ancestral lands and domains of the ICCS/IPS only with a free and prior informed consent of such communities, obtained in accordance with customary laws of the concerned community". Under these provisions, a form of community IPRS of the IPS has been recognized. IPS have the right of restitution if these property rights are taken without their free and prior informed consent and in violation of their customary laws.

To safeguard the indigenous knowledge systems and practices, the following guidelines have also been adopted pursuant to the law: a) researchers and research institutions, etc. shall secure the free and prior informed consent of the ICC/IPS before access to indigenous peoples and resources can be allowed; b) a written agreement shall be entered into with the ICC/IPS concerned regarding the research, including its purpose, design and expected output; c) all data provided by the ICC/IPS shall be acknowledged in whatever writings, publications, or journals produced as a result of such research and the ICC/IPS will be named as sources in all such papers; d) copies of outputs of all such research shall be freely provided to the ICC/IPS community; and e) ICC/IPS shall be entitled to royalty from income derived from any research conducted and resulting publications (DAOAS 1999).

Also in 1997, Republic Act No. 8423, also known as the Traditional Alternative Medicine Act was passed which, in a very limited way, protects traditional knowledge of traditional medicine. The law sets out the policy of, among others, seeking a "legally workable basis by which indigenous societies would own their knowledge of traditional medicine. When knowledge of traditional medicine is used by outsiders, the indigenous societies can require the permitted users to acknowledge its source and can demand a share of any financial return that may come from its authorized commercial use."[111] To date, however, the Philippines has yet to pass a *sui generis* IPR system that will cover traditional knowledge associated with biological and genetic resources of local and indigenous communities.

Equitable Sharing of Benefits

The Wildlife Act is silent on benefit sharing. Therefore, the provisions of EO 247 on sharing of benefits are still relevant and effective. EO 247 employs a contractual approach in ensuring equitable sharing of benefits. This gives it flexibility. Benefit sharing is required at two stages: at the time of collection and at the time of commercialization. At the time of collection, the minimum benefits that must be obtained are explicitly provided for in EO 247, while benefit sharing at the time of commercialization is not expressly stated. However, the parties are free to negotiate on the kind of benefit-sharing arrangement/option that will be established.

The proposed Guidelines for Bioprospecting Activities also employ negotiation for benefits where the resource user negotiates with the resource providers for the benefit-sharing arrangements that will govern them. However, the Guidelines impose minimum benefits that must be obtained from the resource user. These are as follows (Secs. 15 and 16, see endnote 87):

- Bioprospecting fee of $3,000 USD for each BU, which may be increased or tempered based on certain criteria;
- Minimum amount of 2% of total global gross sales of the products made or derived from collected samples to be paid annually; and
- $1,000 USD per collection site annually for the duration of the collection period.

Nonmonetary benefits, which may be agreed upon in addition to the minimum benefits, may include (Sec. 17, see endnote 87):

- Equipment for biodiversity inventory and monitoring;

- Supplies and equipment for resource conservation activities;
- Technology transfer;
- Formal training including educational facilities;
- Infrastructure directly related to the management of the area;
- Health care; and
- Other capacity building and support for *in-situ* conservation and development activities.

Under the DA-Utah-UP CRA[112], the parties agreed to the "equitable sharing of benefits, direct or indirect, short or long term, including, but not limited to direct assistance, technology transfer, profit sharing, co-ownership of intellectual property".[113] Aside from the minimum terms and conditions on benefit sharing stipulated in EO 247 and DAO 20, the following arrangements have been agreed upon by the parties:[114]

- Utah-UP shall share 5% of the net revenue received and derived from any invention such as licensing fee, milestone payments, or royalty from the commercialization of any material to the DA (or the IPAF, if material was taken from the protected area) and the concerned community who gave the PIC.

- All materials and products derived therefrom, all data, documents, and publications shall contain a compulsory attribution recognizing the country and community of the origin of the materials used.

- UP shall develop an information/education module on resource conservation and environmental protection especially geared for the community where the collections are to be made.

- UP shall provide technical expertise to enable the

IACBGR to develop/implement a monitoring scheme for marine bioprospecting.

- UP shall help train at least one government representative in sponge/ascidian taxonomy or natural products chemistry through short-term internship/observation programs.

- UP shall conduct an information campaign on the protection/conservation of coastal resources and the value of coastal resources.

- In case inventions are derived from the use of materials, Utah-UP shall provide training in a marine-related discipline if there is a qualified candidate from the community.

There are a lot of possible benefit-sharing options, but under a contractual scheme, everything will depend on effective bargaining. How much, how long, how many, and who will benefit will rely heavily on the negotiating teams for the community and the government, on one hand, and the bioprospector, on the other. The following proposals (OCHAVE 1997) may be considered in strengthening the bargaining position of the source country:

- Alternative ways for protecting community resources should be explored.

- The scientific and legal communities should work together to increase understanding of each other's field. Contract negotiations should not be left to lawyers who know nothing about genes, or to scientists who may not appreciate the ramifications of seemingly innocuous contract terms.

- Regional cooperation, in various forms, will enable the entire region to present a common front in negotiations.

ASEAN Protocol on Access to Genetic Resources

Regional cooperation has long been the call of NGOs, government agencies, and scientists. Such cooperation is necessary because, it is not only the Philippines that has endemic species; there are species endemic to the entire southeast Asian region as well.

During the eighth meeting of the ASEAN[114] Senior Officials on Environment (ASOEN) in September 1997, the Philippine delegation proposed the formulation of a common protocol among ASEAN member countries on access to genetic resources and IPRs. Thereafter, ASOEN asked the ASEAN Working Group on Nature Conservation and Biodiversity to spearhead the drafting of said protocol. The Philippines was given the lead role in formulating a legal framework to regulate access to genetic resources for ASEAN. The first Technical Expert's Meeting was held in December 1998 to discuss and draft the framework. It was composed of technical experts from the member countries, NGOs from the region and representative of the ASEAN Secretariat. The second Technical Expert's Meeting was held in February 2000 (MOLINYAWE 2001).

Although the ASEAN Framework on Access to Biological and Genetic Resources is still being developed, it may already have created the regional cooperation that has long been desired in the region. In the 24 February 2000 draft of the Framework[115], the objectives include, among others, ensuring the conservation and sustainable use of these resources and equitable sharing of benefits consistent with the principle of PIC, giving recognition and protection to traditional knowledge, promotion of regional cooperation in the utilization of and access to these resources, ensuring uniform and consistent access regulations within the region, the setting of "minimum standards in regulating access to genetic resources and strengthening national initiatives towards this objective", promotion of technology transfer and capacity building, and establishment of "effective and participatory measures for the grant of PIC".[116]

The Framework covers all genetic and biological resources, including associated traditional knowledge. *Ex situ* materials collected prior to the CBD are considered held in trust and IPR shall not be allowed.[117] Patenting of life forms and traditional knowledge as well as IPR on genetic materials of human origin shall not be allowed.[118] Prior informed consent of member countries is necessary before access to these resources shall be allowed. Countries shall establish a legal process to ensure that fair and equitable sharing of benefits shall accrue to IPs and local communities who are considered as the legitimate users and custodians of biological and genetic resources.[119] The negotiation of benefit-sharing arrangements is left to the discretion of member States and may come in the form of technology transfer, capacity building, and monetary or nonmonetary benefits subject to certain requirements.[120]

The Framework also establishes a Common Fund for Biodiversity Conservation consisting of a share in the revenues derived from any commercialization of the use of common and shared resources among the member States as well as from a portion of the fees and charges imposed by the member States. Additional support shall be derived from other benefit-sharing arrangements that may be negotiated.[121] According to the ASEAN Ha Noi Action Plan (1999–2004) the ASEAN Protocol was scheduled to be adopted in 2004.

Conclusions and Recommendations

Ultimately, the legislative and institutional framework for access to genetic resources that any country develops will only be as good as the process through which it is developed. To actually work once established, the legislative framework must have the broad support of all relevant sectors of government and society; fit within the country's larger strategy for conserving and sustainably using biodiversity; and must be supported by institutional processes and capabilities sufficient to implement it (Mugabe et al. 1997).

Executive Order 247 has been faithful to the provisions of the Convention on Biological Diversity on access regulation. It is the world's first comprehensive policy framework that provides for access to biological resources on mutually agreed terms, subject to prior informed consent, and the equitable sharing of benefits. Since its issuance, the Philippines has approved only one commercial research agreement and one academic research agreement. The fees and bonds are still undetermined and a monitoring scheme is not yet in place. However, for the only CRA that has been approved so far, bioprospectors are asked to submit a quarterly report and a government representative joins them during every field visit. At present, a draft administrative regulation on collection and monitoring of bioprospecting activities is being reviewed by IACBGR. Benefit-sharing arrangements are yet to be tried. The other terms and conditions are still to be threshed out. All these have been compounded by a new law (the Wildlife Act) radically modifying EO 247.

This does not mean, however, that EO 247 has failed in its purpose. It only shows that the road towards the establishment of an ideal framework for access to and exchange of biological and genetic resources is long and tedious. However, the Philippines is learning a lot along the way. In fact, the passage of the Wildlife Act confirms that the process is dynamic, and the country intends to succeed in finding a better legislative and institutional framework on the subject.

Derived from the years of Philippine experience on access regulation under EO 247, the following recommendations may help other countries in their quest for the best and most suitable mode of regulating access to and exchange of biological and genetic resources:

There is a need to be clear as to the scope of the access regulation. States should know what they want to regulate in order to avoid over-regulation. They should conduct assessments of their genetic resources and their capacities to regulate access to their resources and make a realistic decision on the coverage of their regulation.

The prior informed consent (PIC) of communities should be nonnegotiable and measures that would guarantee compliance with the PIC process must be established. The PIC of communities and IPs, and the process of obtaining the

PIC, is a must in any access regulation, because it is the only way for States to help and support the IPs' capacities and efforts to protect their indigenous/traditional knowledge and resources. "Effective, on-the-ground mechanisms to ensure the PIC and protection of the rights of affected communities" are necessary (Barber and La Viña 1997). Nevertheless, the PIC process should be simple and fast.

There is a need for an effective and efficient implementing mechanism and monitoring scheme. A single but effective, efficient, and well-funded implementing agency must be established. Lack of funds and personnel to implement the access regulation will surely mean failure of whatever system that is implemented.

The procedure must be simple and fast. A straightforward application procedure will lessen the transaction cost for the collector. Documentary requirements should be minimal and only that information necessary for evaluation purposes should be required. "If requests for access are poorly administered—too bureaucratic, confusing, involving too many steps, too slow or too onerous—or based on benefit-sharing policies that seem unreasonable to the user, partnership will seem unattractive, and providers will price themselves out of the market" (Ten Kate 1995).

Biodiversity conservation and access must go hand-in-hand. The access regulation should provide for measures to guarantee that bioprospecting activities will not be detrimental to biodiversity conservation. Benefit-sharing arrangements should also include benefits accruing to environmental protection and conservation programs.

There must be regional cooperation among countries sharing the same resource. This will help create a united and strong position during negotiations for optimum benefits. "A consortium of suppliers could pool their expertise and equipment, offer a greater quantity and diversity of resources and services and agree to share among themselves, in proportion to the samples supplied, the royalties derived from any single marketed product. Others suggest that regional cooperatives could provide a mechanism for sharing the benefits from access to species common to the region" (Ten Kate 1995).

Effective guidelines or mechanisms to attain equitable benefit sharing and technology transfer must be developed. Identification and implementation of benefit sharing and technology transfer options must be incorporated. If the State decides to adopt contractual relations, it has to create an effective bargaining program in order to ensure optimum benefits for its people. Also, in the long run, the market for raw genetic material will be increasingly competitive (made more so by a growing black market) as a result of technological changes in the field of biotechnology. It is imperative, therefore, to develop stable, long-term partnerships with product development firms and institutions (Ten Kate 1995).

References

AD HOC WORKING GROUP ON ACCESS AND BENEFIT SHARING. 2001. *Report on the role of intellectual property rights in the implementation of access and benefit-sharing arrangements.* First Ad Hoc Open-ended Working Group on Access and Benefit Sharing, 22-26 October 2001, UNEP/CBD/WG-ABS/1/4. Bonn, Germany. URL: http://www.biodiv.org/doc/meetings/abs/abswg-01/official/abswg-01-04-en.pdf.

AGPALO R. 1990. *Statutory construction.* Rex Bookstore, Inc., Manila, Philippines.

BARBER, C.V. and A.G.M. LA VIÑA. 1997. Regulating access to genetic resources: The Philippine experience. p. 115–141 *in* J. MUGABE, C.V. BARBER, G. HENNE, L. GLOWKA and A. LA VIÑA (eds.). *Access to genetic resources.* WRI, ELC-IUCN, ACTS Press, Nairobi, Kenya.

BAUTISTA L.R. 1999. TRIPS agreement revisited: Focus on article 27.3 (b). *World Bulletin* **15**:343–354.

CALIMON D.J.L. 1999. Plant variety protection and rights of breeders, farmers and indigenous peoples under Philippine law. *World Bulletin* **15**:212–238.

CHAO I.M.C. 1999. Foraging for a fair share: Strategies for minimizing inequity between bioprospectors and Philippine local communities. *World Bulletin* **15**:161–211.

DAGDAGAN V.L. 1999. To catch the "biopirates." PCHRD *Bulletin* **15**:1–2.

DAOAS D. 1999. Efforts at protecting traditional knowledge: The experience of the Philippines. Roundtable on Intellectual Property and Traditional Knowledge, World Intellectual Property Organization. URL: http://www.wipo.int/documents/en/meetings/1999/folklore/pdf/tkrt99_6.pdf.

DE LEON J.L. 1998. *Wildlife resources in the Philippines and government efforts to conserve them.* Manila, Philippines.

DOYO M.C. 2002. Set free the seeds (2): A sovereignty issue. Human Face. Philippine Daily Inquirer. 14 February 2000.

EO 247 WORKSHOP 1998. Compilation of issues, comments, and suggestions reached during the EO 247 seminars/workshops sponsored by Southeast Asia Regional Institute for Community Education.

LA VIÑA A.G.M., M.J.A. CALEDA, and M.L.L. BAYLON. 1997. *Regulating access to biological and genetic resources in the Philippines: A manual on the implementation of Executive Order No. 247.* Foundation for Philippine Environment and World Resources Institute, Quezon City, Philippines.

MADULID D.A. 1995. On bioprospecting and collection of biological specimens in the Philippines. *Philippine Biodiversity Information Center Plant Unit Newsletter* **2**:1.

MOLINYAWE N. 2001. *Chronology of events/status of draft ASEAN framework on access to biological and genetic resources.* Department of Environment and Natural Resources, Protected Areas and Wildlife Bureau. Manila, Philippines.

MORDENO H.M. 2002. Seeds of discontent: Republic Act 9168 in perspective. MindaNews **I**:16. URL: http://www.mindanews.com/2002/08/3rd/vws12mordeno.html.

MUGABE J., C.V. BARBER, H. GUDRUN, L. GLOWKA, and A. LA VIÑA. 1997. *Access to genetic resources: Strategies for sharing benefits.* WRI, ELC-IUCN, ACTS Press, Nairobi, Kenya.

MUSHITA T.A. 1999. Access, benefit sharing and trade in genetic resources. Paper presented at ICTSD/ART Regional Seminar on Trade and Environment, 10–12 February 1999. Harare, Zimbabwe. URL: http://www.ictsd.org/dlogue/1999-02-10/mushita.pdf.

OCHAVE J.M.A. 1997. Barking at the wrong tree: Intellectual property law and genetic resources. Paper presented at the Regional Workshop on Sustainable Utilization of Genetic Resources in Southeast Asia and the Pacific, 7–11 July 1997, Grand Men Seng Hotel, Davao City, Philippines.

OCHAVE J.M.A. 1999. The anticommons in bioprospecting: Regulation of access to genetic and biological materials in the Philippines. *World Bulletin* **15**:150-160.

PAWB-DENR. 1998. The First Philippine National Report to the Convention on Biological Diversity. Protected Areas and Wildlife Bureau-Department of Environment and Natural Resources. Manila, Philippines. URL: http://www.biodiv.org/doc/world/ph/ph-nr-01-en.pdf.

PERIA E.V. 1998. *Can't we stop and talk awhile? A Philippine NGO perspective on Executive Order No. 247.* Paper presented at the 10th Global Biodiversity Forum in Bratislava, Slovakia, 1–3 May 1998. Southeast Asia Regional Institute for Community Education (SEARICE), Philippines.

SWIDERSKA K. 2001. Stakeholder participation in policy on access to genetic resources, traditional knowledge and benefit-sharing case studies and recommendations. *Biodiversity and Livelihood Issues* **4**:17.

TANTIA E.M. 1998. Position paper of the Pharmaceutical and Healthcare Association of the Philippines (PHAP) on access to genetic resources and benefit-sharing policies. Paper presented at the East Asia Forum on Genetic Resources Access and Benefit Sharing Policies. Cavite, Philippines.

TAULI-CORPUZ V. 2000. TRIPS and its potential impacts on indigenous peoples. Indigenous Peoples' International Centre for Policy Research and Education, Philippines. URL: http://www.wcc-coe.org/wcc/what/jpc/trips2.html.

TECHNICAL SECRETARIAT. 2001. Status of Executive Order 247 implementation. Inter-Agency Committee on Biological and Genetic Resources, Philippines.

TEN KATE K. 1995. *Biopiracy or green petroleum?: Expectations and best practice in bioprospecting.* Overseas Development Administration, Environment Policy Department London, UK.

Endnotes

[1] RA 7586, Sec. 2.

[2] Ibid.

[3] EO 247 is entitled "Prescribing Guidelines and Establishing a Regulatory Framework for the Prospecting of Biological and Genetic Resources, Their By-products and Derivatives, for Scientific and Commercial Purposes and For Other Purposes". The full text is available at URL: http://www.chmbio.org.ph/eo247.html.

[4] Implementing rules and regulations "issued by administrative or executive officers in accordance with, and as authorized by, law have the force and effect of law or partake of the nature of a statute. All that is required for their validity is that the rules should be germane to the objects and purposes of the law; that the regulations be not in contradiction with, but conform to, the standards that the law prescribes; and that they be the sole purpose of carrying into effect the general provisions of the law" (AGPALO 1990).

[5] Full text of Administrative Order No. 20 is available at: URL: http://www.chmbio.org.ph/dao20-96.html.

[6] Guidelines for the collection of biological specimens in the Philippines (hereinafter Guidelines), Part II, Section 3.

[7] The letter of agreement between the NCI and the National Museum is an open-ended contract that is still enforceable but no activity has been undertaken by them in the last five years (D.A. Madulid, pers. comm., 28 February 2002). Also, according to the TS of IACBGR, there is no information that NCI is doing bioprospecting activity with other institutions in the Philippines.

[8] Interview with Dr. Madulid, Head, Philippine National Herbarium, 28 February 2002 at the National Museum, Manila, Philippines.

[9] EO 247, Sec. 1.

[10] *Public domain* refers to water and lands owned by the State that have not been declared alienable and disposable (DAO No. 96-20, Sec. 2 (z)).

[11] DAO 96-20, Sec. 3 (3.1) (a).

[12] EO 247, Definition of Terms.

[13] *Traditional use* refers to customary utilization of biological and genetic resources by the local community and indigenous people in accordance with written or unwritten rules, usages, customs, and practices traditionally observed, accepted, and recognized by them (DAO 96-20, Sec. 2 (bb)).

[14] Id., Sec. 3 (3.1) (b).

[15] The applicant for these kinds of research and collection is given a gratuitous permit under a MOA. Some of the minimum terms and conditions under EO 247 are, however, incorporated in the MOA so as to avoid circumvention of the law.

[16] DAO 96-20, sec. 3.1 (a).

[17] Application of Pascual Laboratories, Inc. (PLI) for a Commercial Research Agreement in connection with its desire to work with Oxford Natural Products in standardizing Lagundi and Sambong Tablets using the latter's technology called "Total Quality Profiling". The application is now undergoing IACBGR's final evaluation.

[18] *Indigenous people* refers "to a group of people sharing common bonds of language, customs, traditions, and other distinct cultural traits, and who have since time immemorial, occupied, possessed, and utilized a territory except when such possession is either prevented or interrupted by war, *force majeure*, displacement by force, deceit, or stealth, or other usurpation" (EO 247, Definition of Terms).

[19] DAO 96-20, Sec. 10.1.

[20] DAO 96-20, Sec. 6.

[21] DAO 96-20, Sec. 7.

[22] DENR Special Order No. 97-323 dated 18 March 1 1997.

[23] DENR Special Order No. 97-323, Sec. 6.2.6.

[24] *Affiliate* refers to a registered student or scientist/researcher who is formally appointed to a staff or faculty position in a university or other academic institution acting as principal, or a representative of a domestic academic or governmental institution or a representative of an inter-governmental institution assisting in the bioprospecting research by virtue of a formal agreement duly signed by both the principal and the affiliate or a certified true copy of his enrollment form in the case of a registered student (DAO 96-20, Sec. 2.1, b).

[25] EO 247, Definition of Terms.

[26] EO 247, Sec. 5 (m).

[27] The institution with an ARA with the government is referred to as the principal.

[28] DAO 96-20, Sec. 8 (8.3) (2).

[29] Id., Sec. 8 (8.3) (4 & 5).

[30] Id., Sec. 8 (8.3) (7).

[31] EO 247, Definition of CRA and DAO 96-20, Sec. 8 (8.2) (5).

[32] Ibid.

[33] Id., Sec. 8 (8.2) (4).

[34] IACBGR has received 14 applications for CRA but 6 of those applications are exempt from EO 247 coverage. The pending CRA applications are still being processed under EO 247 until new implementing rules and regulations pursuant to the new Wildlife Act are issued.

[35] IACBGR has received 20 applications for ARA but 3 of those applications are exempt from EO 247 coverage. With the passage of the Wildlife Act, all pending applications for ARA shall not be processed anymore but shall undergo the MOA gratuitous permit system.

[36] The CRA between the Department of Agriculture (DA) and the University of Utah (principal collector) and the University of the Philippines (UP) was approved on 30 June 1998 (seven months after the project applied for access) (DA-Utah-UP CRA). The CRA expired on 1 July 2001 and was renewed until 2004. The project involves the collection of tunicates, sponges, and other invertebrate samples for biological assays to screen for potential bioactive compounds. So far, no products have been developed, but some organisms have yielded interesting results. Also, the project has been academically productive because of the publications derived from it.

[37] ARA of the University of the Philippines System was approved in 1999.

[38] EO 247, Sec. 2.

[39] DAO 96-20, Sec. 2 (w).

[40] *Ancestral domain*, subject to existing property rights, refers "to all areas generally belonging to IPs comprising lands, inland waters, coastal areas, and natural resources therein, held under a claim of ownership, occupied or possessed by IPs, by themselves or through their ancestors, communally or individually, since time immemorial, continuously to the present except when interrupted by war, *force majeure*, or displacement by force, deceit, stealth or as a consequence of government projects or any other voluntary dealings entered into by government and private individuals/corporations, and which are necessary to ensure their economic, social and cultural welfare. It shall include ancestral lands, forests, pasture, residential, agricultural, and other lands individually owned whether alienable and disposable or otherwise, hunting grounds, burial grounds, worship areas, bodies of water, mineral and other natural resources, and lands which may no longer be exclusively occupied by IPs but which they traditionally had access to for their subsistence and traditional activities, particularly the home rangers

of IPS who are still nomadic and/or shifting cultivators" (DAO 96-20, Sec. 2.1, c).

41 *Ancestral land*, subject to existing property rights, refers "to land occupied, possessed and utilized by individuals, families, and clans who are members of the ICCS/IPS since time immemorial, continuously to the present except when interrupted by war, *force majeure*, or displacement by force, deceit, stealth or as a consequence of government projects or any other voluntary dealings entered into by government and private individuals/corporations, and which are necessary to ensure their economic, social, and cultural welfare" (Id., Sec. 2.1, d).

42 RA 8371, Sec. 35.

43 RA 8371, Sec. 3 (g).

44 The research proposal must be presented in a language or dialect understandable to them stating therein the purpose, methodology, duration, species/specimen, and number/quantity to be used and/or taken, equitable sharing of benefits, if any, to parties concerned, and a categorical statement that said activity will not affect their traditional use of the resource (DAO 96-20, Sec. 7 (7.1.1)).

45 The notice includes a statement that copies of a summary of the research proposal and other information regarding the proposed activity have been filed with the recognized head of the IP, the local government unit, PAMB, or the private landowner concerned and that an application is pending with the IACBGR, or that the research is covered by an existing ARA (Id., Sec. 7 (7.2.1)).

46 Undergraduate, masters, and doctoral students carrying out research strictly for the purpose of complying with academic requirements and who do not receive any funding from a commercial entity are exempt from holding community consultation unless requested. The consultation shall be held in the presence of representatives of the IACBGR/NGOS/POS. (Id., Sec. 7(7.2.5)).

47 Id., Sec. 9 (9.1) (1&2).

48 Id., Sec. 8 (8.1)(16).

49 EO 247, Sec. 5 (b).

50 DAO 96-20, Sec. 8 (8.1) (10).

51 Id., Sec. 8 (8.1)(7).

52 Id., Sec. 8 (8.2)(1).

53 EO 247, Sec. 5 (b).

54 Id., Sec. 5 (h).

55 DAO 96-20, Sec. 8 (8.2)(3).

56 Id., Sec. 8 (8.1)(17).

57 MTA is not provided for in EO 247 or DAO 96-20 but it has been made part of the research agreement.

58 EO 247, Sec. 5 (a); DAO 96-20, Secs. 6 (6.1.4), 8 (8.1) (1), 8 (8.1) (5), 8 (8.1) (7), 8 (8.1) (14).

59 DAO 96-20, Sec. 8 (8.1)(9).

60 Id., Sec. 8 (8.1) (11).

61 EO 247, Sec. 5 (l). This remains to be threshed out and is subject to further study. (NATIONAL REPORT 1997).

62 DAO 96-20, Sec. 8 (8.2)(2).

63 Id., Sec. 8 (8.1)(14).

64 Id., Sec. 14 (14.1).

65 Id., Sec. 14 (14.3).

66 Id., Sec. 12 (12.1).

67 Id., Sec. 12 (12.2).

68 Id., Sec. 12 (12.3).

69 "Determining the coverage of EO 247 was from the start the most difficult issue" (Antonio La Viña, pers com. 7 January 2002).

70 In 1998, the Southeast Asia Regional Institute for Community Education sponsored a series of seminars/workshops to review/

assess EO 247. Various stakeholders participated in these workshops where issues and concerns affecting the implementation of EO 247 were identified and solutions/recommendations were formulated. The results were later transmitted to the IACBGR.

71 Under the DA-Utah-UP CRA, Utah/UP paid $10,000P bioprospecting fee and posted $10,000P bond ($1 USD = $51P).-

72 If the research is not covered by EO 247, the TS shall issue a Certificate of Exemption and refer the proposal to the government agency that has jurisdiction over the project.

73 Under the Philippine Environmental Impact Statement System, an Environmental Impact Assessment (EIA) is required for any activity that affects the quality of the environment. An EIA is a systematic study of the relationship between a proposed project and its surrounding environment. In particular, environmentally critical projects or those located in environmentally critical areas are required to undergo the process established under the system. (Presidential Decree No. 1586 and its implementing rules and regulations). Here it is important to note that no EIA was required for the DA-Utah-UP CRA.

74 Processing fee for Philippine nationals is $1,000P while for foreign national it is $2,000P per application for both ARA and CRA.

75 For ARA, the applicant submits the PIC Certificate after the signing of the agreement. (See discussion on PIC).

76 A draft ARA/CRA shall be included if the evaluation is favorable.

77 The Agency head/s who will sign the agreement will depend on the type of research (pharmaceutical, agricultural, etc.) and the nature of the resources (terrestrial, marine, etc).

78 Fees and bonds required under EO 247 are still undetermined. A draft "Guidelines on the Collection and Monitoring of the Prospecting of Biological and Genetic Materials and Prescribing the Fees, Bonds, Royalties and Benefit-Sharing Scheme thereto" is still under review.

79 The following are some of the issues that were raised during the discussions on the Wildlife Act:
- Simplification of a permitting system for science and technology research and development.
- The need to provide a list of species that are banned/restricted for prosecution purposes.
- Add and define the term "cultured species" to distinguish from captive-bred or propagated species.
- Government agencies mandated to do research must be exempt from securing permits for collection.
- A sound scientific study should be conducted before any re-stocking activity is performed as well as before any importation and introduction of exotic species.
- Those listed under the CITES should be exempted from exploitation except for scientific, education, and/or experimental breeding/propagation purposes.
- Include compliance with biosafety protocol as one requirements for importation.
- There is a need to enhance institutional capability to execute and handle biosafety procedures, hence the need to provide for institutional development.

80 RA 9147, Sec. 2.

81 Id., Sec. 3.

82 Id., Secs. 14 and 15.

83 Id., Sec. 5 (a).

84 *Gratuitous permit* means "a permit issued to any individual or entity engaged in noncommercial scientific or educational undertaking to collect wildlife" (Sec. 5 (l), RA 9147).

85 The law does not define "prior clearance". It will be clarified in the implementing rules and regulations.

86 Sec. 5 (x), RA 9147.

87 Draft *Guidelines for Bioprospecting Activities in the Philippines*

(Joint DENR-DA-PCSD-NCIP Administrative Order No. 1). Available at URL: http://www.denr.gov.ph/article/view/2332/.

[88] Sec. 14, RA 9147.

[89] Ibid.

[90] Ibid.

[91] Sec. 29, RA 9147.

[92] Sec. 27 (f) and Sec. 28, RA 9147.

[93] The repealing clause provides "Act Nos. 2590 and 3983, Commonwealth Act No. 63, as amended, Presidential Decree No. 1219, as amended, Republic Act No. 6147, and other laws, orders and regulations inconsistent herewith are hereby repealed or amended accordingly."

[94] Within 12 months following the effective date of the law, rules and regulations shall be promulgated (Sec. 37, RA 9147).

[95] There are two categories of repeals by implication. The first is where provisions in the two acts on the same subject matter are in irreconcilable conflict, the later act, to the extent of the conflict, constitutes an implied repeal of the earlier one. The second is if the later act covers the whole subject of the earlier one and is clearly intended as a substitute, it will operate similarly to a repeal of the earlier act (AGPALO 1990).

[96] The TRIPS Agreement has not been difficult to accept. Philippine patent and trademark laws needed only some adjustments and the country is also a signatory to the relevant conventions identified in the Agreement (BAUTISTA 1999).

[97] As of 1999, more than 100 microorganisms have been granted patent protection in the Philippines (BAUTISTA 1999).

[98] RA 8293, Sec. 22.

[99] In the Philippines, some groups are urging the government to protect its national interest "by strongly lobbying against patenting of plant varieties which will give power to the 10 giant world seed producers to violate farmers' and indigenous peoples' rights and culture" (DAGDAGAN 1999).

[100] At present, no Philippine law has yet been enacted providing *sui generis* protection for animal breeders and community intellectual rights.

[101] It took effect on 7 June 2002.

[102] RA 9168, Sec. 2 (a).

[103] Id., Sec. 32.

[104] Id., Sec. 36, 37 and 38.

[105] Id., Sec. 39.

[106] Id., Sec. 43.

[107] Id., Secs. 57 and 59.

[108] Id., Sec. 47. The violator may be charged before a court of justice and penalized with imprisonment of not less than 3 years but not more than 6 years and/or a fine of up to 3 times the profit derived by virtue of the infringement but in no case should be less than one hundred thousand pesos ($100,000P) (RA 9168, Sec. 56).

[109] Id., Secs. 2 (b) and (c) & 7.

[110] Id., Secs. 32 and 34.

[111] RA 8423, Sec. 2.

[112] The CRA is now up for renewal under the same terms and conditions as the original CRA.

[113] DA-Utah-UP, CRA Item IX.

[114] The Association of South East Asian Nations (ASEAN) includes the Philippines, Thailand, Indonesia, Malaysia, Singapore, Brunei Darussalam, Cambodia, Vietnam, Myanmar, and Laos.

[115] The text of the draft is available at URL http://www.iprsonline.org/legalinstruments/docs/asean_framework_agreement.pdf

[116] Draft ASEAN Framework Agreement on Access to Biological and Genetic Resources., Art. 2.

[117] The Philippines also shares this position.

[118] Draft ASEAN Framework Agreement on Access to Biological and Genetic Resources., Art. 4.

[119] Id., Art. 10.

[120] Id., Art. 11.

[121] Id., Art. 12.

8

The United States of America:
The National Park Service Experience

Preston T. Scott

The biological diversity and related genetic resources existing in the United States of America (USA) is vast. The USA spans a continent bordered by two oceans, and includes territory stretching from the Arctic Circle to the tropics. While much of the country has been industrialized and developed, the wide range of ecosystems found in the USA contributes to an equally wide range of representative samples of diverse life forms.

In light of the great diversity of life found in the various ecosystems that exist throughout the USA, scientists have begun to study the nation's biodiversity in more systematic ways. Such studies have begun to result in new appreciation for the value of biodiversity to environmental and social well being, as well as to the potential economic value that can result from important discoveries rooted in biological material. The value of biological material (particularly at a molecular and genetic level) is increasingly recognized, and the value of related discoveries and product inventions is growing rapidly (primarily as a result of the application of intellectual property rights and other research-related laws). While there are no reliable nationwide statistics on the number of so-called "bioprospecting" projects currently underway in the USA, reports suggest that the number is growing but affected by many different factors.

Access to genetic resources in the USA is governed by a dizzying array of laws, regulations, and policies that apply at various different local, state, regional, and national levels. Although the recognition and refinement of the principles related to access, sustainable use, and the equitable sharing of benefits arising from the utilization of biological resources has become increasingly sophisticated since adoption of the Convention on Biological Diversity (CBD)

in Rio de Janeiro in 1992, efforts to deal with some of the same issues have been part of the legal landscape in the USA for decades (albeit in a less systematic way). For example, formalized regulations relating to access to biological resources found in USA national parks for scientific research purposes date back to the 1960s. Since the 1980s, the USA Public Health Service (led by the National Institutes of Health and other major research agencies) has developed and implemented standardized approaches concerning the management of biological material for research purposes. These particular examples arose from perceived needs for new management tools to be applied in specific contexts and to respond to specific sets of circumstances.

Accordingly, much of the experience in the USA concerning the regulation of access to genetic resources actually pre-dates much of the international discussion as it has evolved in connection with the CBD. However, the USA experience has not been characterized by the "top-down" central-government approach often reflected in CBD-related texts. It also has evolved independently from the non-self-implementing framework agreement approach reflected most notably in the CBD. Instead, it has developed in response to various specialized sets of needs and circumstances often existing at very local or specific institutional levels.

The fundamental issues relating to access to natural resources in the USA are ordinarily managed by the owner of the resource (whether private or public). In the USA, such fundamental issues relating to ownership of property and resources are typically managed at very local and individualized levels. For example, in cases of wild biodiversity living on private lands, access is subject to the approval of the individual landowner. Where areas are managed by governmental authorities, access is usually subject to regulation (whether local, state, or federal). Marine areas may be subject to special regulations and laws enforced by both federal and state authorities. In addition, access to tribal lands in the USA are subject to tribal authorities and associated federal and state laws relating specifically to Native Americans.

All of this complexity is amplified by the fact that jurisdictional authority is divided not only within the federal (national) government, but also among the 50 individual states. Within the federal government alone, lands and associated biological resources may be managed by any one of a wide range of departments (such as Interior, Agriculture, and Energy) and separate agencies within departments (such as the Bureau of Land Management, the Fish and Wildlife Service, the USA Geological Survey, and the National Park Service—all within the Department of the Interior). In addition, access to genetic resources that have been isolated by a laboratory or other institutional research entity may be subject to certain contractual arrangements such as biological material transfer agreements or commercial use licenses, which may or may not be standardized. There also are several *ex situ* culture collections located in the USA (including the American Type Culture Collection (ATCC), which is often described as the world's largest).[1] In all cases, however, the first step is to determine who is in charge of the resources and to ascertain precisely what is expected or required to obtain legitimate access.[2]

In light of this complexity—and in order to present an illustrative example of genetic resource management in the USA that takes a more national approach—this chapter will focus on perhaps the most instructive case study arising in the USA concerning both access and benefit-sharing issues. Specifically, the case study provides a detailed overview of the background, experience, and status of genetic resource management in USA national parks, with focus on the particularly illustrative experience at Yellowstone National Park (YNP).

The chapter begins with an overview of the diversity of ecosystems protected by the USA National Park Service (NPS) and the fundamental natural resource management principles they use. The NPS experience has important nationwide relevance inasmuch as NPS protects and manages

representative samples—and in many cases the best examples—of virtually every type of ecosystem found in the USA. The chapter continues with a look back at the history of scientific research at Yellowstone, including a description of the natural resources that have attracted scientists to the park for more than a century. This is followed by an overview of the development and status of the laws and regulations that relate to the value of biological research in the USA, and that now govern access to the NPS genetic resources for scientific purposes. The chapter includes a discussion of the development of the first bioprospecting benefit-sharing agreement in the USA, which involved Yellowstone and the Diversa Corporation of San Diego, California, and concludes with information about possible future developments relating to genetic resource management issues at Yellowstone and other NPS units.

While the USA still has not ratified the CBD, much of the biological resource management experience reflected in the NPS is very consistent with the main conservation principles provided in the CBD. In April 2002, the Sixth Conference of the Parties to the CBD meeting in The Hague adopted a set of voluntary guidelines specifically concerning access and benefit-sharing issues.[3] Much of the voluntary guidelines concern pragmatic approaches to issues relating to prior informed consent (PIC) and mutually agreed terms as they pertain to access and benefit sharing.

While a section-by-section analysis is beyond the scope and purpose of this chapter,[4] it should be noted that the research specimen collection permit requirements developed and implemented by the NPS provide an excellent example of how many of the concerns associated with PIC can be very pragmatically addressed. Likewise, although NPS is currently conducting a study of the potential environmental impacts of implementing various benefit-sharing approaches throughout the NPS, the issues under study also reflect many of the concerns associated with "mutually agreed terms" that are included in the voluntary guidelines. While no single national experience can respond to or satisfy the interests and needs of a very diverse world, the NPS experience may provide some instructive examples about ways to implement many of the biodiversity conservation management principles that the international community is continuing to refine—a very long-term work-in-progress.

National Parks as Living Laboratories

Background

The USA National Park Service comprises more than 375 separate protected areas in every state of the USA (except Delaware) plus the District of Columbia, American Samoa, Guam, Puerto Rico, and the Virgin Islands, and encompasses approximately 33.4 million ha. Taken together, these areas protect examples of virtually every type of ecosystem found in North America, even though these areas cover less

than two percent of the total land area of the USA. Because of the importance attached to their relatively intact representative diversity, the ecosystems protected and managed by the NPS are of increasing interest to researchers and are often described as living laboratories.[5]

Access to genetic resources found in USA national parks is managed by NPS, a federal agency within the USA Department of the Interior. NPS was created by the USA Congress in 1916 specifically to *promote and regulate the use of the federal areas known as national parks, monuments, and reservations... by such means and measures as conform to the fundamental purpose of the said parks, monuments, and reservations, which purpose is to conserve the scenery and the natural and historic objects and the wild life therein and to provide for the enjoyment of the same in such manner and by such means as will leave them unimpaired for the enjoyment of future generations.*[6]

In order to understand how NPS approaches the issues of access to and use of USA national parks, it is important to understand NPS' overall natural resource management standard. While the USA Congress has given NPS broad management discretion to allow certain impacts within parks, that discretion is limited by the statutory requirement that NPS must leave park resources and values unimpaired to ensure they will continue to exist in a condition that will allow present and future generations opportunities to enjoy them.

The enjoyment of national park resources contemplated by NPS is broad and includes deriving benefit (including scientific knowledge). However, NPS has explained that by recognizing that the enjoyment of national parks by future generations can be ensured only if the superb quality of park resources and values is left "unimpaired", conservation of park resources is to be predominant when there is a conflict between conserving resources and values and providing for enjoyment of them.[7]

NPS works to maintain as parts of the natural ecosystems found in national parks all native plants and animals[8] and the full range of genetic types of native plant and animal populations. In carrying out this over-arching natural resource management approach, NPS aims to maintain all the components and processes of naturally evolving park ecosystems, including the natural abundance, diversity, and genetic and ecological integrity of the plant and animal species native to those ecosystems.

Accordingly, the way that NPS manages access to national park resources (including genetic resources) is based on the agency's fundamental duty to conserve national parks in an unimpaired condition for the enjoyment (broadly interpreted) of present and future generations.

Diversity of National Park Resources

The diversity of land ecosystems protected and managed by NPS includes tundra, boreal forest, Pacific forest, dry coniferous forest, eastern deciduous forest, grassland, chaparral, and deserts. Tropical ecosystems are found in USA national parks in Hawaii and the southern tip of Florida, Puerto Rico and the USA Virgin Islands, and American Samoa and Guam. NPS-protected tropical ecosystems include lowland rain forest, summer-deciduous forest, swamp and mangrove formations, as well as montane rainforest. Aquatic ecosystems protected in USA national parks are as diverse as the land ecosystems, and include marine environments, estuaries, underground systems, lakes and ponds, and streams. NPS units also include pro-

tected areas of volcanism, hot water phenomena, mountain systems, and mesas.

The largest national park in the USA is Wrangell-St. Elias National Park and Preserve in Alaska. At 5.3 million ha, it makes up 16.3% of the entire system. The largest unit in the 48 contiguous states is Yellowstone National Park, comprising 0.9 million ha. The smallest unit in the system is Thaddeus Kosciuszko National Memorial in Pennsylvania, comprising only 0.008 ha

Genetic Resource Diversity and Management at Yellowstone

Generally recognized as America's (and the world's) first national park, YNP was created by an act of the USA Congress[9] that was signed into law by President Ulysses S. Grant on 1 March 1872. It is located in the northern Rocky Mountain region of the USA in the northwest corner of Wyoming with territory overlapping into Montana to the north and Idaho to the west.

Yellowstone remains the largest national park in the continental USA outside Alaska. It covers 8,990 km² approximately 0.9 million ha), which is larger than the states of Rhode Island and Delaware combined. Its terrain includes 3,350-meter peaks and high plateaus; deep canyons and broad sweeping valleys; lakes, rivers, and waterfalls; and a variety of archeological and cultural sites. Yellowstone also is surrounded by wilderness areas protected by six national forests, Grand Teton National Park, and two national wildlife refuges.

YNP forms the core of the Greater Yellowstone Ecosystem, considered the largest remaining intact ecosystem in Earth's temperate zone. In view of its ecological significance, Yellowstone was declared a Biosphere Reserve under the UNESCO Man and the Biosphere Program in 1976 and was designated as a World Heritage Site by the United Nations in 1978.

Yellowstone protects vital habitats for a variety of wildlife, including bison, grizzly and black bears, moose, elk, bighorn sheep, eagles, cutthroat trout, and several endangered or threatened species, including the gray wolf. Yellowstone is the only area of its size in the 48 contiguous states that has never been farmed or fenced, and it remains the only place in the USA where continuously free-ranging wild bison have survived since prehistoric times. With the restoration of the gray wolf to the park in the mid-1990s, Yellowstone's ecosystem now includes all members of the mammalian biotic community that were present in the area at the time when Europeans first arrived in America.

Yellowstone also is a volcanic "hot spot" located in part of the most seismicly active region of the Rocky Mountains. Underground magma which formed an immense caldera approximately 40 kilometers wide and 70 kilometers long still provides the heat for the park's famous thermal features that are an important part of Yellowstone's ecosystem.

There are approximately 10,000 thermal features

at YNP—the single greatest concentration on Earth. Yellowstone's most charismatic thermal features are well known by names such as Old Faithful, Excelsior, Morning Glory, and Grand Prismatic, but the overwhelming majority of the park's thermal features are still unnamed and unexplored. Taken together, Yellowstone's hot springs, geysers, fumaroles, and mud pots comprise one of the world's most intriguing but still largely unexplored biological habitats.

Yellowstone and other USA national parks have cooperated and worked to support scientific activities involving park resources since the 19th century. In August 1898, the first research permit was issued at Yellowstone to W.A. Setchell from the University of California at Berkeley. The permit—written on a sheet of stationary from Mammoth Hot Springs Hotel and authorized by Captain James B. Erwin of the USA Cavalry, which then was administering Yellowstone—authorized Setchell "to collect and carry away such specimens of algous [sic] growth as he may deem necessary to carry out the investigation for which he is now visiting the Yellowstone National Park".[10]

A century later, the park's thermal features are increasingly recognized as providing rare habitat for many new forms of microscopic life only recently discovered—life too small to see outside of their sometimes richly colored colonies (or "mats"), but reflecting biological diversity that rivals the tropical rainforests and thrives in habitats once thought far too extreme to allow life to exist.

Like the early explorers, many of the contemporary scientific researchers at Yellowstone remain interested in the discovery of new forms of life and in the valuable information associated with such research. While Lewis and Clark identified 178 new plants and 122 new animals never before seen by inhabitants of European origin from east of the Mississippi during their historic 1804–1806 expedition, the discovery of new life continues in unexpected places like Yellowstone's hot springs that were first described by the early 19th century explorers as places where "Hell bubbled up". With tools of science not available to 19th and earlier 20th century explorers of the area, contemporary scientific researchers are beginning to open windows on the heretofore unexplored microbiological worlds found among the 10,000 thermal features at Yellowstone.

Discovery of *Thermus aquaticus*

Much of the first 100 years of research on thermophilic (heat-loving) life at Yellowstone tended to focus on trying to identify the upper temperature limits of different forms of life, and much of that research was based on what could be seen by the naked eye. The early "color-temperature" correlation observations of some 19th century scientists working at Yellowstone were being refined throughout the 20th century by observations made by many other scientists working with the benefit of accumulated data and increasingly sophisticated equipment. For example, as a result of these ongoing studies at Yellowstone and

elsewhere, by the early 1960s it was believed that the optimum temperature limit for thermophilic bacteria was 55°C, while the upper temperature limit for life was 73°C (KEMPNER 1963).

In the mid-1960s, Professor Thomas Brock, who was then working at Indiana University, undertook a series of studies on the distribution of photosynthetic microorganisms in the thermal gradients that flowed gently out of several hot springs at Yellowstone. During his studies, Brock observed that while the upper temperature limit of photosynthetic life clearly appeared to be around 73°C, there was evidence of life in the flow of some springs where the water was much hotter. At Octopus Spring, for example, Brock observed pink filaments alive with bacteria in waters with temperatures ranging as high as 88°C (dramatically suggesting the existence of life above the commonly accepted upper temperature limit) (BROCK 1998). This simple observation opened the door to the possibility that other types of nonphotosynthetic organisms might be discovered alive at Yellowstone at temperatures and in conditions previously unknown to support life.

On 5 September 1966, Brock collected a sample of bacteria from Yellowstone's Mushroom Spring which he subsequently isolated, cultured, and named *Thermus aquaticus*. Brock identified the culture of *T. aquaticus* as YT-1. While Brock's cultures of *T. aquaticus* grew best at around 70°C, cultures also grew at temperatures as high as 79°C (clearly surpassing the previously assumed upper-temperature-limit of 73°C) (BROCK 1997).

Significantly, Brock's observations of *T. aquaticus* were not limited just to temperature or other environmental factors. Laboratory analyses also led to new observations about the organism's characteristics. For example, Brock knew that most of the heat-loving bacteria that had been described by earlier researchers belonged to a group of spore-forming bacteria that produced heat-resistant spores. Brock's studies of *T. aquaticus* revealed that the organism did not produce spores. This suggested that *T. aquaticus* was some form of life that had not been discovered previously. Based on taxonomic methods, Brock concluded that it was a member of a genus of organisms not previously known to science (BROCK and FREEZE 1969).

The discovery, isolation, and culturing of *T. aquaticus* at Yellowstone effectively lifted the lid on human understanding (and curiosity) about the upper temperature limits of life. Thereafter, Brock identified the existence of an abundance of previously unknown microscopic life in boiling waters at Yellowstone (water boils at 92.5°C at Yellowstone because of the altitude). With a microscope, he was able to see bacteria alive on glass slides that had been immersed in hot springs located in various places throughout the park.

While observations dating back to the 19th century suggested that the colorful formations surrounding many thermal features at Yellowstone indicated the presence of life, Brock's discovery of life too small to see in waters too hot to touch confirmed that the diversity of life protected by the park (but still unexplored) was far greater than anyone had imagined. Since the discovery of *T. aquaticus* in 1966, many other previously unknown organisms have been discovered thriving in Yellowstone's thermal environments. Some scientists now estimate that perhaps less than one percent of all the organisms living in Yellowstone's thermal features have been discovered and identified to date.

Taq and PCR

In the 1980s, scientists from the Cetus Corporation were conducting research on ways to replicate DNA. Their work ultimately resulted in development of the polymerase chain reaction (PCR). A polymerase is an enzyme that replicates DNA. By incorporating the DNA-copying activity of the polymerase, PCR permits the duplication of batches of DNA from only tiny samples, a development so important to science that its discoverers were awarded a Nobel Prize. Now, PCR is used in a host of important applications ranging from diagnosing diseases to identifying criminals from their DNA fingerprints.

The early PCR experiments were not satisfactory, however, because the polymerase that was being used by the Cetus scientists was unable to withstand the heat required by the PCR process. The researchers theorized that perhaps a thermophilic microorganism could produce a thermostable enzyme that could tolerate the heat used in the PCR process and thereby fix the problem. Accordingly, they ordered samples of *T. aquaticus* (YT–1) from the ATCC that had been collected at Yellowstone and deposited by Brock approximately 20 years earlier.

From a sample of the YT–1 culture of *T. aquaticus*, the Cetus scientists identified and isolated a heat-stable enzyme that they named *Taq* polymerase. Subsequently, they discovered that incorporating the *Taq* polymerase into the PCR process satisfactorily fixed the "overheating" problem, which meant that the PCR process could efficiently replicate DNA as desired. USA patents were awarded to the scientists in 1989 on *Taq* polymerase and in 1990 on the PCR process.[11]

The value of the PCR process was quickly recognized, and in 1991 the patent rights were acquired by the pharmaceutical firm Hoffmann-LaRoche for a sum widely reported to be in excess of $300 million USD.[12] Subsequent revenues earned by Hoffmann-LaRoche from licensing rights to the use of PCR technology are estimated in excess of $1 billion USD and growing.

The importance of the research involving *T. aquaticus* and the *Taq* polymerase was summarized in 1991 in Congressional testimony offered by D. Allan Bromley (then Director of the White House Office of Science and Technology Policy and Science Advisor to President George H.W. Bush):

Different kinds of research and development tend to have different kinds of returns. With basic research—the majority of which is done by individual scientists and small groups of scientists at universities—it is very difficult to predict when, where, and to whom the returns will eventually accrue. Yet even work that can seem highly abstract can have surprisingly immediate impacts. To take just one example, in 1968 Thomas Brock, a microbiologist at the University of Wisconsin, discovered a form of bacteria in the thermal vents of Yellowstone that can survive at very high temperature. From these bacteria an enzyme was extracted that is stable at near-boiling temperatures. Nearly two decades later this enzyme proved to be vital in the process known as the polymerase chain reaction, which is used to duplicate specific pieces of DNA. Today, PCR is the basis of a multimillion dollar business with applications ranging from the rapid diagnosis of disease to forensic medicine.[13]

The success associated with *Taq* was coupled with additional reports of other important biological discoveries at Yellowstone. The more scientists learned, the more it appeared that the extreme environments characterized by Yellowstone's thermal features comprised a hothouse full of undiscovered microorganisms with many new potentially valuable uses precisely because of their ability to withstand such extreme conditions (MARRS and MADIGAN 1997). Although there was no definitive comprehensive report of all of the valuable discoveries associated with research involving Yellowstone's microbial resources, some journalists reported multiple applications that included development of new bioremediation technologies, "clean" fuels research, and uses involving paper, textiles, and plastics.[14] Other potentially valuable applications also were sometimes identified in scientific papers relating to the initial discovery, identification, and isolation of new microorganisms at Yellowstone. Taken together, these developments suggested that Yellowstone ranked as high as some other celebrated environments as a source of still undiscovered valuable biological information.

As a result of the research interest in the biological materials being discovered in Yellowstone's extreme thermal environments, the park was asked by the Director of the National Park Service to explore development of a pilot "benefit-sharing" program. Such a program would supplement permitted research use of research specimens collected at the park (with special focus on developing and implementing a cooperative research mechanism that would allow the park to benefit from any valuable discoveries resulting from research activities involving specimens already lawfully collected at YNP). The NPS Director asked Yellowstone to take this action because of public perceptions (fueled in large measure by media reports) that private sector entities were enjoying substantial economic and scientific benefits from research involving Yellowstone resources without sharing those benefits for the conservation of the park.

Not unlike the early 19th century explorers who were amazed by the rich diversity of megafauna such as bear, elk, and bison found in the Yellowstone area, the recent and ongoing discovery of previously unknown microscopic life forms in Yellowstone's hot springs has sparked a renaissance of scientific interest in the park. The rich diversity of previously unknown life at Yellowstone is presenting important new opportunities to manage scientific research activities that require access to genetic resources found at the park. By linking scientific and economic incentives associated with research activities with other incentives for conserving the park's valuable biological diversity, Yellowstone is exploring ways that it can strengthen research so that it also will rebound benefits to the park for sustainable resource conservation.

The Value of Biological Research and the Law

As knowledge and the tools of science have advanced, so too has the range of scientific inquiry at Yellowstone. When Professor Brock visited Yellowstone in the early-1960s, the definitive upper temperature limit of life was widely believed to be 73°C. Brock and his team of researchers at Yellowstone, however, were making observations that suggested that some forms of life appeared to thrive at higher temperatures—observations that ultimately led to the discovery of *T. aquaticus*.

It is simple to see that the more detail that Brock and his team learned about the newly discovered organism, the greater would be the value associated with their discoveries and ongoing research program. The term "value" does not necessarily imply monetary or economic value. Discoveries as significant as *T. aquaticus* generally help a researcher's appeals for funding and other support, often simply as part of the natural fall-out of a successful project. Nonetheless, it was the connection between the discoveries associated with the isolation of the *Taq* polymerase and its utility in the PCR process that generated the multimillion dollar revenues that in turn generated the headline-making news.[15] Typically, economic value attaches to discoveries that have some "useful" application in human society; the use of *Taq* in the development of PCR technology is but one of countless examples. Likewise, value rarely attaches to discoveries or other forms of creativity that simply are not useful in human society.

The value of such discoveries in biological research was recognized (and effectively amplified) by a landmark ruling of the USA Supreme Court in 1980. The case concerned the question of whether inventions that relate to certain "living things" are eligible for protection under the USA patent law. While the scientific value of advancing developments in biological research was clearly recognized and not in dispute, the issue of whether the economic value that attaches to inventions as a result of patent protection turned on the Court's decision. In retrospect, the case is seen as having provided the legal foundation for the phenomenal growth and development of the biotech industry in the USA since the early 1980s.

The case (*Diamond v. Chakrabarty*) concerned a patent application filed in 1972 by a microbiologist who asserted 36 claims related to a genetically engineered "bacterium from the genus Pseudomonas containing therein at least two stable energy-generating plasmids, each of said plasmids providing a separate hydrocarbon degradative pathway".[16] The Court's ruling in *Chakrabarty*, which held that a human-made living microorganism is patentable subject matter under USA patent law, was based on the Court's interpretation of the language of the patent statute. Commencing with a review of the legislative history of the Patent Act of 1793 that was drafted by Thomas Jefferson, the Court noted that the patent law defined patentable statutory subject matter as "any new and useful art, machine, manufacture, or composition of matter, or any new or useful improvement [thereof]"[17] and reflected Jefferson's view that "ingenuity should receive a liberal encouragement".[18]

From the Court's rationale, the focus of relevant inquiry for purposes of determining whether something "biological" qualifies as patentable "subject matter" under Section 101 of the USA patent statute is shifted away from the simple question, "Is it living?" Instead, the Court's rationale in *Chakrabarty* placed controlling emphasis on whether the living matter is the result of the intervention of human ingenuity and creativity.

The Court noted that Mr. Chakrabarty had "produced a new bacterium with markedly different characteristics from any found in nature and one having the potential for significant utility… not nature's handiwork, but his own".[19] Therefore, the Court ruled, "it is patentable subject matter" under Section 101 of the USA patent statute.[20] Elsewhere, still focusing on legislative intent, the Court reemphasized: "Congress thus recognized that the relevant distinction was not between living and inanimate things, but between products of nature, whether living or not, and human-made inventions".[21]

The USA Supreme Court's ruling in *Chakrabarty* paved the way under the existing USA patent statute for new patent claims on biological "inventions," which in turn accelerated development of the economic benefits that attach to useful patented discoveries.[22] The Court's rationale also emphasized that the "value" in biological discoveries recognized and protected by the patent statute resides in beneficial research results, not in naturally occurring phenomena "free to all men and reserved exclusively to none".[23]

Applying the rule announced by the Court in *Chakrabarty*, the USA Patent and Trademark Office (USPTO) has explained that "it is clear from the Supreme Court decision and opinion that the question of whether or not an invention embraces living matter is irrelevant to the issue of patentability", emphasizing that "the test set down by the Court for patentable subject matter in this area is whether the living matter is the result of human intervention".[24]

USPTO also has explained that it "will decide the questions as to patentable subject matter under 35 USC 101 on a case-by-case basis following the tests set forth in *Chak-*

rabarty, e.g., that 'a nonnaturally occurring manufacture or composition of matter' is patentable, etc.", emphasizing that "it is inappropriate to try to attempt to set forth here [USPTO policy guidance on patentability of living subject matter] in advance of the exact parameters to be followed".[25]

Not surprisingly, the number of patents pertaining to "living subject matter" approved by the USPTO increased dramatically after the Supreme Court's ruling in *Chakrabarty*. For example, only one patent was approved by USPTO in 1979 (the year before the ruling in *Chakrabarty*) for a Class 800 invention ("Multicellular Living Organisms and Unmodified Parts Thereof and Related Processes").[26] A decade later, 22 Class 800 patents were approved.[27] By 1996, the number had increased dramatically to 253, after which it rose to 281 in 1997 and

then leapt to 446 in 1998.[28] Similar trends occurred in Class 435 ("Chemistry: Molecular Biology and Microbiology") even though substantially more Class 435 patents already were being approved before *Chakrabarty*. In 2001, the USA Supreme Court also ruled that plant varieties are eligible for protection by utility patents issued pursuant to 35 USC 101, as well as under the Plant Patent Act of 1930 (35 USC 161 et seq.) and the Plant Variety Protection Act of 1970 (7 USC 2321 et seq.).[29]

The distinction between what the law rewards (new, useful, and nonobvious discoveries based on research results) and what the law protects (naturally occurring life forms that remain free for all to use) is at the core of the biodiversity prospecting access and benefit-sharing issues first pioneered in the USA at Yellowstone.[30]

NPS Genetic Resource Access Management

The search for potentially useful biological compounds in Nature (sometimes popularly referred to as "biodiversity prospecting" or "bioprospecting") involves two distinct sets of issues: access to biological resources and benefit sharing. Issues relating to access concern the terms and conditions associated with collection and sampling of biological research specimens. These issues also may relate to the purpose underlying collection and sampling, or to how the research specimens are to be used. Issues relating to benefit sharing concern the terms and conditions under which the provider of biological research specimens may be positioned to share in the beneficial results of research involving biological specimens provided to a research user.

While research specimen collection and related scientific research activities in USA national parks certainly is not new, the USA Congress enacted a law in 1998 that mandated increased scientific research in the national parks and use of the results of scientific study in park management decisions.[31] The new law encourages the development of cooperative research initiatives between individual national parks and scientific researchers (public as well as private), and mandates the integration of research results into park management decisions. It also mandates development of long-term inventory and monitoring activities that provide baseline information and document trends relating to the condition of resources protected by the national parks. Implementation of these new statutory directives clearly can accelerate cooperative development and management of the wealth of biological resource information flowing from Yellowstone's hot springs as well as from other national parks.

By linking scientific and economic incentives associated with research activities with other incentives for conserving valuable biological diversity, research initiatives can encourage sustainable resource conservation and management in accordance with the new mandates enacted by Congress in the National Parks Omnibus Management Act of 1998. Effective implementation of these provisions,

however, requires clear focus on the two sets of core issues that relate to biodiversity prospecting: access and benefit sharing.

Access

Access to the biological resources of USA national parks for research purposes is governed by NPS regulations. The NPS research specimen collection permit regulations have been implemented since 1983, and permits for the collection of research specimens throughout the NPS are issued routinely.[32] Issuance of an NPS research specimen collection permit is based on a determination by a park superintendent that "public health and safety, environmental or scenic values, natural or cultural resources, scientific research, implementation of management responsibilities, proper allocation and use of facilities, or the avoidance of conflict among visitor use activities will not be adversely impacted" by issuance of a permit.[33] Based on public comments filed at the time the regulations were promulgated, NPS concluded that these determinations are "adequate to ensure protection of park resources".[34]

A park superintendent's express regulatory authority to issue permits for the collection of research specimens (with terms and conditions deemed necessary to protect park resources) provides the mechanism for each NPS unit to govern access to its own biological resources for research purposes. "Permit" is defined under the regulations to mean "a written authorization to engage in uses or activities that are otherwise prohibited, restricted, or regulated".[35] The regulations also provide that a superintendent "shall include in a permit the terms and conditions that the superintendent deems necessary to protect park resources".[36] Collection of any biological material in an NPS unit without a permit is strictly prohibited.

NPS regulations provide that specimen collection permits

may be issued only to an official representative of a

reputable scientific or educational institution or a State or Federal agency for the purpose of research, baseline inventories, monitoring, impact analysis, group study, or museum display when the superintendent determines that the collection is necessary to the stated scientific or resource management goals of the institution or agency and that all applicable Federal and State permits have been acquired, and that the intended use of the specimens and their final disposal is in accordance with applicable law and Federal administrative policies.[37]

The regulations do not discriminate against for-profit or other corporate research firms provided they engage in reputable scientific research activities. This reflects the reality that some of the very best science is practiced by private corporations while some of the most entrepreneurial research activities are carried out by universities and other academic institutions.

Permits are issued after a researcher has submitted a permit application that provides the information required by the park and is deemed by the park superintendent to be consistent with the park's mission, applicable regulations (particularly 36 CFR 2.5), and NPS policy. The permit application process helps ensure that the permit applicant discloses the information required to enable the park to determine that the proposed research activities are consistent with NPS regulations and policy[38] (Figure 1).

In the review of applications for research projects, NPS considers it a "favorable" characteristic if the proposed research

- Contributes information useful to an increased understanding of park resources, and thereby contributes to effective management and/or interpretation of park resources;

- Provides for scheduled sharing of information with park staff, including any manuscripts, publications, maps, databases, etc., which the researcher is willing to share;

- Addresses problems or questions of importance to science or society and shows promise of making an important contribution to humankind's knowledge of the subject matter;

- Involves a principal investigator and support team with a record of accomplishments in the proposed field of investigation and a demonstrated ability to work cooperatively and safely and to accomplish the desired tasks within a reasonable time frame;

- Provides for the investigator(s) to prepare occasional summaries of findings for public use, such as seminars and brochures;

- Minimizes disruption to the park's natural and cultural resources, park operations, and visitors;

- Discusses plans for the cataloging and care of collected specimens;

- Clearly anticipates logistical needs and provides detail about provisions for meeting those needs; or

- Is supported academically and financially, making it highly likely that all fieldwork, analyses, and reporting will be completed within a reasonable time frame.[39]

NPS considers it "unfavorable" for a permit review, if the proposed research

- Involves activities that adversely affect the experiences of park visitors;

- Shows potential for adverse impact on the park's natural, cultural, or scenic resources, and particularly to nonrenewable resources such as archeological and fossil sites or special-status species (the entire range of adverse impacts that will be considered also includes construction and support activities, trash disposal, trail conditions, and mechanized equipment use in sensitive areas);

- Shows potential for creating high risk of hazard to the researchers, other park visitors, or environments adjacent to the park;

- Involves extensive collecting of natural materials or unnecessary replication of existing voucher collections;

- Requires substantial logistical, administrative, curatorial, or project monitoring support by park staff, or provides insufficient lead time to allow necessary review and consultation;

- Is to be conducted by a principal investigator lacking scientific institutional affiliation and/or recognized experience conducting scientific research; or

- Lacks adequate scientific detail and justification to support the study objectives and methods.[40]

Currently, as part of the research permit terms, scientists are required to submit a yearly summary of their park research activities, known as an Investigator's Annual Report. In addition, copies of field notes and scientific publications may be required by the park.

Microbial research projects at Yellowstone require access to the government-owned biological resources that are controlled by these research specimen permit regulations. There have been approximately 275 research projects permitted annually at Yellowstone since the mid-1990s that cover a wide range of natural resource subjects. Not all of these projects involve the collection of biological or other natural resource samples from the park for research purposes. In 1999, there were more than 50 research projects relating to thermophilic microbial resources at Yellowstone that involved the issuance of research specimen collection permits.

Projects also benefit from cooperative guidance and data provided by the Yellowstone Center for Resources in connection with resource-relevant information for the researcher. Researchers are frequently accompanied in the field by Yellowstone staff, who monitor specimen collection procedures and provide assistance on information relevant to the specific research project. This assistance from the park often makes the best use of research time and resources. Likewise, Yellowstone benefits from the researchers' own research-relevant information (some of which may be proprietary and protected by Federal intellectual property laws).

There is an important distinction between "sale or commercial use" of natural products collected from national parks (which is prohibited under 36 CFR 2.1(c)(3)(v)) and the discovery of valuable useful applications from "research results" that could bring the park potential benefits (whether commercialized or not). The facts and circumstances surrounding permitted research at Yellowstone and throughout the NPS system reflect this important distinction. This distinction also has been upheld as valid by the federal judiciary.[41] Significantly, the standardized permit

terms and conditions also specify that collected specimens remain NPS property.[42]

There are several additional important standardized research specimen collection permit terms and conditions that relate specifically to access issues. First, the permits provide that permittees shall comply with all applicable NPS and other federal and state laws and regulations, and that "[n]o specimens (including materials) may be collected unless authorized on the Scientific Research and Collecting permit".[43] Second, the permits prohibit unauthorized third-party transfers of any specimens collected, which effectively limits legitimate access to NPS resources that have been collected to specifically authorized persons only. Third, the permits require that "[c]ollection methods shall not attract undue attention or cause unapproved damage, depletion, or disturbance to the environment and other

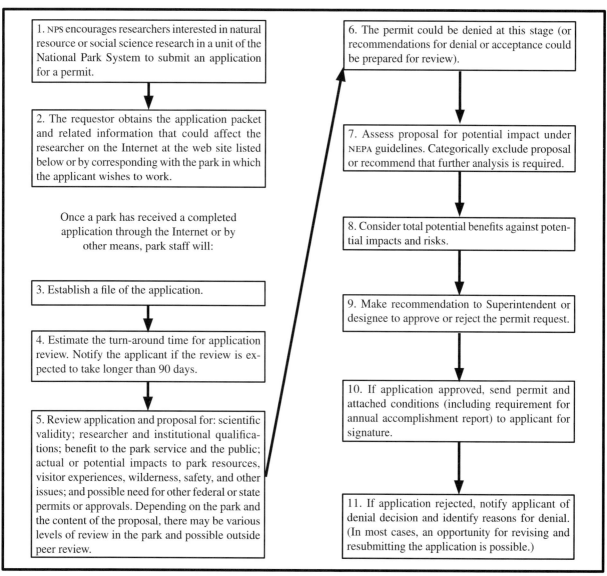

Figure 1. NPS Standardized Review Procedures for Scientific Research and Collecting Permit Applications. The chart illustrates the general order of decision making and the major criteria used to accept or reject a permit application. The Internet-accessible USA National Park Service Research Permit and Reporting System webpage describes the review procedures in full detail (http://science.nature.nps.gov/permits/index.html). The procedures were made standardized and Internet accessible in January 2001.

park resources, such as historic sites".[44] Fourth, the permits stipulate that research results derived from collected specimens must be used for scientific and educational purposes only and may not be used commercially unless the permittee has entered into a Cooperative Research and Development Agreement (CRADA) or other approved benefit-sharing agreement with the NPS.[45]

In addition to the regulations and specified permit terms and conditions, NPS policy concerning access to national park resources is further articulated by the NPS Director. The NPS Management Policies is the basic Service-wide policy document of the National Park Service, and is the highest of three levels of guidance documents in the NPS Directives System. Interim updates or amendments may be accomplished through Director's Orders (the second level of the NPS Directives System), which also serve as a vehicle to clarify or supplement NPS Management Policies to meet the needs of NPS managers. The most detailed and comprehensive guidance on implementing Service-wide policy is usually in the form of handbooks or reference manuals issued by associate directors (the third level of the NPS Directives System).

Instructions, guidance, and directives for regional or otherwise limited application supplementary to and in conformance with Service-wide policies may be issued by regional directors or associate directors with formal delegations of authority. Superintendents may issue, within formal delegations of authority, park-specific instructions, procedures, directives, and other supplementary guidance (such as permit terms and conditions), provided the guidance does not conflict with Service-wide policy.

Chapter 4 of the 2001 NPS Management Policies ("Natural Resource Management") provides that NPS "will preserve the natural resources, processes, systems, and values of units of the national park system in an unimpaired condition" pursuant to the NPS Organic Act, the National Parks Omnibus Management Act of 1998, the National Environmental Policy Act (NEPA), and other laws, and summarizes NPS policies relating to studies and collections,[46] independent studies,[47] and collections associated with development of commercial products.[48] In addition, Chapter 8 ("Use of the Parks") of the 2001 NPS Management Policies provides that "[s]tudies, research, and collection activities by non-NPS personnel involving natural and cultural resources will be encouraged and facilitated when they otherwise comport with NPS policies", and that "[s]cientific activities that involve field work or specimen collection… require a permit issued by the superintendent that prescribes appropriate conditions for protecting park resources, visitors, and operations".[49]

While it is illegal to collect any biological material directly from a USA National Park without a proper permit, acquisition of samples from culture collections[50] has sometimes been attractive to researchers because they are assured of obtaining "pure cultures" (albeit not directly from a national park). Culture collections also can provide an *ex situ* source for biological material that in some

cases can help minimize the demands for *in situ* sampling at the parks.

Historically, culture collections have distributed biological materials collected from Yellowstone without coordination with the park or the NPS. This situation has effectively allowed researchers from industry as well as academia to circumvent NPS research specimen collection regulations. It has also effectively removed the parks from any benefit-sharing opportunities. For example, the Cetus Corporation (developer of the Nobel Prize–winning multi-million-dollar PCR technology) acquired the now legendary sample of Yellowstone's *T. aquaticus* from ATCC and not directly from the park.

In the past, Yellowstone and other national parks have not been positioned to monitor or benefit from third-party use of their natural resources acquired indirectly. NPS is evaluating steps to require culture collections to regulate distribution of any biological materials collected from national parks to ensure that all potential recipients understand that their use of such samples must be in accord with the policies that govern use of samples collected directly from a national park. There also are opportunities for national parks to develop more substantive joint research activities with culture collections concerning discovery, identification, and *ex situ* conservation of biological resources that could be of benefit.

Yellowstone-Diversa Agreement and Benefit Sharing

Despite the phenomenal success resulting from the chain of useful scientific discoveries that flowed directly back to the initial discovery by Brock of *T. aquaticus* in Yellowstone's Mushroom Spring, Yellowstone never was positioned to share any of the benefits that resulted from the isolation of the *Taq* polymerase and its successful use and development in PCR technology. Nonetheless, the discovery of *T. aquaticus* at Yellowstone, the identification and isolation of the *Taq* polymerase, and the successful use of *Taq* in the development of PCR technology is one of the classic examples of the contemporary utility of bioprospecting—the search for potentially useful biological compounds in nature.

Several observers noted the parallels between Yellowstone's situation and the use of biological samples acquired from rainforests and other tropical habitats around the world by many research firms. Not surprisingly, however, the large economic gains resulting from the successful research activities involving samples of *T. aquaticus* first acquired from Yellowstone prompted some alarming headlines such as "Industries Exploit First Park".[51] The most astute observers also noted that some of these places (such as Costa Rica) already were beginning to take steps to capture and reinvest some research benefits in ways that would yield future conservation dividends.

As public awareness and interest in the issue grew, Yellowstone began to evaluate different ways by which it might respond. Yellowstone staff convened a series of public meetings attended by National Park Service staff, academic and industry researchers, conservation interests, and journalists. As a result of this ongoing evaluation of the issue by Yellowstone staff, some opportunities for initiating a pilot bioprospecting benefit-sharing project began to emerge. In addition, the Director of the National Park Service also asked Yellowstone in July 1996 to begin to take some concrete steps that would position the park to share in the benefits of research activities in a way that would not chill research and that might serve as an example for other parks facing the same issue. As with so many other resource-related issues since its founding, Yellowstone was presented with an historic conservation opportunity.

In response to the NPS Director's request, Yellowstone evaluated use of the Department of the Interior's established guidelines for negotiation of CRADAS to address the benefit-sharing issue. A CRADA is defined by the Federal Technology Transfer Act (FTTA) of 1986 as "any agreement between one or more Federal laboratories and one or more non-Federal parties under which the Government, through its laboratories, provides personnel, services, facilities, equipment or other resources with or without reimbursement (but not funds to non-Federal parties) and the non-Federal parties provide funds, personnel, services, facilities, equipment, or other resources toward the conduct of specified research or development efforts which are consistent with the mission of the laboratory".[52] By entering into a CRADA, Federal and non-Federal partners can optimize their mix of resources to undertake cooperative research activities equitably and efficiently.

For CRADA purposes, the statute defines the term Federal "laboratory" to mean "a facility or group of facilities owned, leased, or otherwise used by a Federal agency, a substantial purpose of which is the performance of research, development, or engineering by employees of the Federal Government". The statute also gives Federal agencies broad discretion relating to laboratory determinations. The Senate Report that accompanied Congressional approval of the Federal Technology Transfer Act of 1986 also explains that "this is a broad definition which is intended to include the widest possible range of research institutions operated by the Federal Government".[53] It also states:

> To improve technology transfer, the Federal laboratories need clear authority to do cooperative research, and they need to be able to exercise that authority at the laboratory level. Agencies need to delegate to their laboratory directors the authority to manage and promote the results of their research. A requirement to go to agency headquarters for approval of industry collaborative arrangements and patent licensing agreements can effectively prevent them. Lengthy headquarters approval delays can cause businesses to lose interest in developing new technologies.[54]

The Department of the Interior's CRADA policy was outlined in May 1996 in the handbook entitled Technology Transfer: Marketing Our Products and Technologies (A Training Handbook for the US Department of the Interior). While the research specimen permits that are issued under 36 CFR 2.5 govern access to Yellowstone's biological resources for research purposes, CRADAS provide one type of framework that can be used to structure a benefit-sharing arrangement.[55] Significantly, the 1986 Senate Report suggests that the USA Congress believed when it enacted the CRADA statute that prospective and unknown future benefits associated with research activities (which are particularly characteristic of bioprospecting activities) are matters to be negotiated by the parties themselves:

> Often, collaboration between a laboratory and some other organization can be expected to lead to future inventions. All parties should be clear on who will have what rights to future inventions when the work begins. This amendment [codified at 15 USC § 3710a(b)(3)] allows Federal laboratories to assign rights in future inventions to the cooperating, outside parties. It is anticipated that agencies will normally retain for the Government a paid license to use or have future inventions used in the Government's behalf.[56]

On 17 August 1997, Yellowstone announced that it had reached agreement on a bioprospecting benefit-sharing arrangement with Diversa Corporation, an enzyme discovery firm headquartered in San Diego, California. The agreement was reviewed by the NPS Director and finalized in May 1998 (Box 1). This first ever bioprospecting benefit-sharing agreement involving a national park in the USA positioned Yellowstone to share in future economic and scientific benefits that might result from Diversa's research involving microorganisms collected at Yellowstone's hot springs and other thermal features. The agreement grandfathered in all of the biological material that Diversa scientists had collected at Yellowstone pursuant to permits before the benefit-sharing agreement was negotiated, as well as derivatives and other results that might flow from Diversa research involving the material.

In addition, the YNP-Diversa CRADA provided a package of revenue-sharing mechanisms that included a combined up-front payment ("creditable minimum annual royalty") to the park of $100,000 USD over five years, additional annual earned royalties based on a percentage of revenues generated by Diversa from Yellowstone-related research results, and supplemental in-kind contributions of laboratory equipment, scientific training, and other research and conservation related activities. While the term of the CRADA was for an initial five-year period, the agreement also provided that the benefit-sharing obligations survived termination (very important since development of valuable discoveries can sometimes take many years to achieve).

The royalty rates and related payment information contained in the YNP-Diversa agreement relate specifically to Diversa's commercial and pricing interests in products that may be derived from research results involving biological samples acquired from the park. The rates were the result of negotiations involving confidential business proprietary information obtained from Diversa, which advised Yellowstone that disclosure of this information would harm the company's commercial interests inasmuch as it relates to cost issues that are relevant to Diversa's pricing policies. Diversa also advised Yellowstone that it does not release this information to the public because of its pricing sensitivity. In light of this, the specific royalty rates were treated as confidential information under Exemption 4 of the Federal Freedom of Information Act.[57] Yellowstone did disclose, however, that the rates ranged from between 0.5 and 10% of net revenues[58] earned by Diversa on research results involving biological samples

acquired from the park.

The agreement did not expand the scope of authorized research specimen sampling activities at Yellowstone. The fundamental rules of access were not changed;[59] but the agreement did provide for the sharing of benefits resulting from Diversa's Yellowstone-related research activities—and that was something new.[60]

The YNP-Diversa CRADA was challenged in federal court in early 1998. After review, the federal judiciary upheld the CRADA as consistent with the National Park Service Organic Act, the Yellowstone National Park Organic Act, the Federal Technology Transfer Act of 1986, NPS regulations, and the "public trust doctrine".[61] The court

---

Box 1. Cooperative Research and Development Agreement for a Project between Yellowstone National Park and Diversa Corporation (Text presented as it was actually executed by the parties, the referenced appendices are not provided here.)

GENERAL PROVISIONS

This Cooperative Research and Development Agreement ("CRADA") is entered into by and between Diversa Corporation ("Collaborator"), a corporation organized under the laws of Delaware and maintaining its principal corporate office headquarters at 10665 Sorrento Valley Road, San Diego, California, 92121, and Yellowstone National Park (YNP) of the National Park Service (NPS), US Department of the Interior.

WHEREAS, NPS and Collaborator wish to engage in cooperative activities to promote the conservation, protection, perpetuation, and management of biological diversity while undertaking scientific research and investigating potentially useful applications and processes that might be derived from research on certain biological materials existing in YNP; and

WHEREAS, it is the intention of NPS to improve the conservation, management, protection, and perpetuation of park resources to the fullest extent possible consistent with their mandate to conserve the scenery, natural and historic objects, and wildlife, so as to leave them unimpaired for future generations; and

WHEREAS, it is the intention of NPS to cooperate in activities that benefit scientific research within the areas administered by them; and

WHEREAS, NPS coordinates research activities, facilitates the exchange of research-related information pertaining to the natural resources found at YNP, and promotes the opportunity to conduct symposiums and develop publications about such research, which will be supported by the cooperative research activities authorized by this CRADA; and

WHEREAS, Collaborator is dedicated to the discovery and development of new bioactive materials for chemical synthesis, diagnostics, industrial and pharmaceutical uses, and agrees to cooperate with NPS to undertake beneficial scientific research relating to certain biological materials existing in YNP, to share information and data relating to such research, and to protect and monitor those materials and other resources in YNP; and

WHEREAS, Collaborator agrees to apply the highest professional and scientific standards in its research and development

activities, and to pursue the discovery and development of new bioactive materials that advance humanitarian goals and the public welfare; and

WHEREAS, Collaborator agrees that efforts by the NPS to protect the physical, hydrological, and ecological integrity of YNP's thermal features, hot springs, and geysers, all of which contain globally unique microbial ecosystems, contributes significantly to the research and development of useful discoveries; and

WHEREAS, Collaborator further agrees that the aforesaid protection of YNP's microbial resources requires sophisticated interdisciplinary scientific work by YNP staff and dedicated effort by NPS management, including working with neighboring jurisdictions to ensure protection of the thermal features, hot springs, and geysers; and

WHEREAS, NPS agrees that Collaborator has incurred and will continue to incur significant time, effort and expense in research and development and management of technology which will facilitate the research and development of useful discoveries from samples received from YNP under this CRADA; and

WHEREAS, NPS further agrees that the aforementioned research, development and management of technology has required highly sophisticated, interdisciplinary work by Collaborator's staff and management; and

WHEREAS, NPS further agrees and recognizes that Collaborator has a capability to discover useful products from samples obtained from YNP under this CRADA utilizing Collaborator's proprietary technologies; and

WHEREAS, it is recognized that YNP derives national dignity and recognition of superb environmental quality through its inclusion in the National Park System preserved and managed for the benefit and inspiration of all the people of the United States, and the superlative natural microbial resources found in YNP may be considered invaluable and priceless in nature; and

WHEREAS, the aforesaid protection occurs at considerable annual expense to the taxpayers of the United States.

Now, therefore, in consideration of the promises contained in this agreement, the parties agree as follows:

also noted that Section 205 of the National Parks Omnibus Management Act of 1998, which was enacted after initial negotiation of the YNP-Diversa CRADA, specifically authorizes "negotiations with the research community and private industry for equitable, efficient benefits-sharing arrangements" involving NPS units.

Specifically, the court's analysis concluded that NPS units (such as Yellowstone) that satisfy the definition of a Federal "laboratory" as provided in the FTTA are eligible to negotiate CRADAS with qualified researchers. However, the court also ruled that NPS is required to complete an analysis under NEPA before the YNP-Diversa CRADA can be implemented.[62] Therefore, the CRADA was suspended

pending a showing of NEPA compliance. Thereafter, the court dismissed the plaintiffs' case challenging the YNP-Diversa CRADA with prejudice.[63]

Plaintiffs appealed the court's decision upholding the YNP-Diversa CRADA under the National Park Service Organic Act, the Yellowstone National Park Organic Act, the Federal Technology Transfer Act of 1986, and NPS regulations in the USA Court of Appeals for the District of Columbia Circuit. Following preparation and filing of NPS' brief in support of the district court's ruling upholding the YNP-Diversa CRADA, the plaintiffs asked the Federal appeals court to dismiss their appeal. The appeal was dismissed on 22 December 2000.

Box 1. Continued

ARTICLE 1. LEGAL AUTHORITY

1.1. This agreement is authorized under the National Park Service Organic Act, as amended, 16 USC §§ 1-4; and the Federal Technology Transfer Act, as amended, 15 USC §§ 3701-3715.

1.2. Payments accepted and retained by YNP from Collaborator are authorized under 15 USC § 3710a(b)(3).

ARTICLE 2. DEFINITIONS

2.1. The term "**Background Intellectual Property**" (BIP) refers to a patent or patent application covering an Invention or discovery of either party, or a copyrighted work, a mask work, trade secret, or trademark developed with separate funds outside of the CRADA by one of the parties or with others. BIP is not considered as a Subject Invention.

2.2. The term "**Collaborator's Assigned Employees**" means those employees of the Collaborator who are present at YNP for a continuous period of more than two weeks.

2.3. The term "**Cooperative Research and Development Agreement**" (CRADA) means this document and all attachments describing research activities jointly undertaken by NPS and the Collaborator.

2.4. The term "**created**" in relation to any copyrightable software work means when the work is fixed in any tangible medium of expression for the first time, as provided for at 17 USC § 101.

2.5. The term "**Generated Information**" means information produced in the performance of the CRADA.

2.6. The term "**Industrial Products**" means any product designed, developed or used in any process associated with manufacturing, agriculture, chemical products, commerce or industry.

2.7. The term "**Intellectual Property**" means patents, trademarks, copyrights, trade secrets, mask works, and other forms of comparable property protectable by federal, state, or foreign laws.

2.8. The term "**Invention**" means any invention or discovery that is or may be patentable or otherwise protected under Title 35 of the United States Code, or any novel variety of plant which is or may be protectable under the Plant Variety Protection Act (7 USC § 2321 *et seq.*).

2.9. The term "**made**" in relation to any Invention means

the conception or first actual reduction to practice of such Invention.

2.10. The term "**Native Enzymes**" means any catalytic proteins, not in a recombinant form, produced by living cells that mediate or promote chemical processes in living cells that originated from YNP.

2.11. The term "**Natural Products**" means any naturally occurring Research Specimen located in or taken from YNP.

2.12. The term "**Net Sales**" means the total gross receipts for sales by Collaborator, its licensees or sublicensees of Product(s) and copyrighted works created using the results of research under this CRADA, and from otherwise making Product(s) available to others without sale, whether invoiced or not, less returns and allowances actually granted, packing costs, insurance costs, freight out, taxes and excise duties imposed on the transaction (if separately invoiced), and the wholesaler and cash discounts in amounts customary in the trade. No deductions shall be made for commissions paid to individuals, whether they be with independent sales agencies or regularly employed by Collaborator, its licensee or sublicensees, or for the cost of collections.

2.13. The term "**Pharmaceutical Products**" means "drug" as defined by the Federal Food, Drug and Cosmetic Act at 21 USC § 321(g).

2.14. The term "**Product**" means any Subject Invention and any commercially valuable or otherwise useful material, compound or useful combination of compounds, protein, or metabolite [which is encoded by a nucleotide sequence recovered, obtained, derived, resulting, or otherwise isolated from scientific research conducted] on a Research Specimen acquired from YNP, or any derivative or analog of such material, compound, protein, metabolite or other isolate, or any discovery which is or may be patentable or otherwise protected under Title 35 of the United States Code, or any novel variety of plant which is or may be protectable under the Plant Variety Protection Act (7 USC § 2321 *et seq.*) and developed from Research Specimens acquired from YNP.

2.15. The term "**Proprietary Information**" means trade secrets or commercial or financial information that is privileged or confidential within the meaning of 5 USC § 552(b)(4), obtained in the conduct of research or as a result

In early 2002 while the CRADA was suspended, Diversa publicly announced that it had developed a new product from research specimens originally acquired from Yellowstone. The product development is significant because it represents one of the world's only examples where a company has brought a new product to market after it negotiated a benefit-sharing agreement with the provider of the original biological resources. Diversa has pledged payment of all royalties due provided that the agreement suspension is cleared. Also, it should be noted that Yellowstone has not spent any of the initial $100,000 USD. The funds are being held in escrow and will be kept until

completion of the environmental impact study conducted in compliance with the court's decision.

As a result of the cooperative research activities initiated under the CRADA, Diversa also contributed important genetic identification services to Yellowstone in connection with the park's management of its recently reintroduced wolf population. This research work was considered by Yellowstone to be one of the most valuable "in-kind" benefits derived by the park from the YNP-Diversa benefit-sharing CRADA, even though it was not directly related to Diversa's research on Yellowstone hot spring organisms. The genetic pedigree information developed and donated

---

Box 1. Continued

of activities under the terms of this CRADA from a non-Federal party participating in this CRADA, as provided at 15 USC § 3710a(b)(A).

2.16. The term "**Protected CRADA Information**" means Generated Information that is marked as being Protected CRADA Information by a party to this agreement and that would have been Proprietary Information had it been obtained from a non-Federal entity.

2.17. The term **"Research Reagent Products or Diagnostics"** means any product manufactured specifically and primarily for use in research tests, or applications in research laboratories or development centers. This term does not include items used for evaluation by a customer to make a prospective use decision.

2.18. The term "**Research Specimens**" means those items Collaborator has authority to collect under the collection permit or permits issued by YNP to the Collaborator.

2.19. The term "**Subject Data**" means all recorded information first produced in the performance of this CRADA.

2.20. The term "**Subject Invention**" means any Invention of the Collaborator or NPS conceived or first actually reduced to practice in the performance of work under this CRADA.

ARTICLE 3. STATEMENT OF WORK

3.1. Cooperative research performed under this CRADA shall be performed in accordance with the attached Statement of Work, which is incorporated by reference into this agreement. The parties may modify the initial Statement of Work by mutual agreement and incorporate it herein by amendment as set out in paragraph 15.9.

ARTICLE 4. REPORTS

4.1. *Research Reports.* As required by the collection permits that YNP issued to Collaborator, Collaborator will prepare and provide to NPS a written report concerning the research activities authorized by the collection permits, which shall include, but not be limited to, such information as the Superintendent of YNP may require, including, but not limited to, all information required under this CRADA. NPS shall have the right to use such reports for any Governmental purpose including but not limited to the conservation of natural resources at YNP. In the event Collaborator asserts that particular information delivered to NPS is proprietary, Collaborator agrees to provide to NPS a nonconfidential nonproprietary summary of such

information for public disclosure.

4.2. *Payment Reports.* Concurrently with each payment, or at such other time as payments are due, Collaborator shall submit a written report to NPS setting forth (a) the period for which the payment is made, (b) the amount, description, and aggregate Net Sales of the Product(s) sold or otherwise disposed of, upon which a payment is payable for such completed calendar year as provided under this CRADA, (c) the total gross income realized by Collaborator from the sale, licensing, or otherwise making Product(s) available to itself and others without sale, during such completed calendar year, and (d) the resulting calculation pursuant to this section 3 of the amount of all payments due thereon. If no payments are due NPS for any report period, the report shall so state.

4.3. *Copyright Reports.* Concurrently with each payment of royalties on copyrighted materials as required by Appendix B, or at such other time as payments are due, the Collaborator shall submit a written report setting forth the period for which the payment is made, the amount and a description of the copyrighted works upon which a royalty is payable, the net sales or other income received therefrom by the Collaborator, and the amount of royalties due thereon. If no royalties are due NPS for any report period, the report shall so state.

4.4. *Records.* Collaborator agrees to keep records showing the sales or other dispositions of all works upon which payments are due under the provisions of this CRADA in sufficient detail to enable NPS to determine the payments payable hereunder by Collaborator. Collaborator agrees to retain the records for a minimum period of five (5) years from the date a subject payment is due. Collaborator further agrees to permit an auditor selected by NPS to examine its books and records from time-to-time during its ordinary business hours and not more often than once a year to the extent necessary to verify the reports provided for in this Article. NPS will bear the initial expense of the audit. If the audit indicates that NPS was underpaid royalties by at least ten percent (10%) for any calendar year, or five-thousand dollars (US$5,000.00), whichever is greater, collaborator will reimburse NPS for the expense of the audit, together with an amount equal to the additional royalties to which NPS is entitled.

ARTICLE 5. FINANCIAL OBLIGATION

5.1. Collaborator hereby agrees to make the payments and other contributions set forth in Appendix B. Unless

---

to the park by Diversa enables park biologists to monitor and assess the genetic health of Yellowstone's growing wolf population, as well as to precisely identify any wolves that are found killed. The information also will enable park biologists to detect when wolves from other areas, such as Idaho or northwest Montana, migrate into Yellowstone.

The park has observed that corporations, universities, and others increasingly recognize the need to satisfy public benefit-sharing expectations. For example, with improved data relating to microbial distributions throughout various thermal systems at the park (which will be an ongoing scientific "benefit" that Yellowstone may obtain through

negotiated arrangements with the research community), Yellowstone can strengthen its protection of these resources by directing scientists to less studied pools known to hold desired organisms. Many firms also have told the park that their willingness to negotiate benefit-sharing arrangements that are favorable to Yellowstone is contingent on the contributions being used for resource conservation purposes, a very important underlying incentive.

Yellowstone also has observed that the likelihood of generating economic value from research results cannot be determined from a look at institutional affiliations only. This is because many academic researchers have close

---

Box 1. Continued

otherwise specified, Collaborator agrees to make all payments to NPS in US Dollars, net of all non-US taxes (if any), by check or bank draft drawn on a United States bank and made payable to "Yellowstone National Park." The parties estimate Collaborator's total contribution at a minimum of US$100,000, in funds (parties acknowledge that the payment for 1997 has been made) plus royalties, and in-kind services and resources valued at US$375,000. The method and scheduling of payment for current and subsequent years is included in Appendix B.

5.2. The contribution of YNP shall be in the form of resource protection, labor, expertise, equipment, facilities, information, computer software, and other forms of laboratory support, subject to available funding.

5.3. The Collaborator will make all payments to YNP in accordance with provisions of Appendix B. All payments by the Collaborator shall be mailed to the following address:

Yellowstone National Park
Office of the Superintendent
Attention: Yellowstone Center for Resources
PO Box 168
Yellowstone National Park, Wyoming 82190

5.4. Overpayments by the Collaborator shall be offset against payments due the following year.

5.5. If the audit described in paragraph 4.4, above, indicates that payments are overdue to NPS, an interest charge will be assessed on the overdue amounts for each 30-day period, or portion thereof, that payment is delayed beyond the periods described in Appendix B. The percent of interest charged will be based on the current value of funds to the United States Treasury as published quarterly in the Treasury Fiscal Requirements Manual.

ARTICLE 6. RECOGNITION OF CONTRIBUTION FROM YELLOWSTONE NATIONAL PARK

6.1. Collaborator recognizes that the priceless nature of the research specimens at YNP, and the efforts and expertise that NPS has invested in the preservation, conservation, and protection of the research specimens will contribute significantly to the discovery of Subject Inventions and development of products from the YNP research specimens, and, as a result, agrees that the US Government has a compensable interest in any Subject Inventions and products developed from YNP research specimens.

ARTICLE 7. PATENT RIGHTS

7.1. *Reporting.* The parties agree to disclose to each other every Subject Invention, which may be patentable or otherwise protectable, within sixty (60) days of the time that an inventing party reports such Invention to the person(s) responsible for patent matters in the inventing organization. These disclosures should be in sufficient enough detail to enable a reviewer to make and use the invention under 35 USC § 112. The disclosure shall also identify any statutory bars, *i.e.*, printed publications describing the Subject Invention or public use or sale of the Subject Invention in the United States. The parties further agree to disclose to each other any subsequent statutory bar that occurs for a Subject Invention disclosed but for which a patent application has not been filed. All such disclosures shall be marked as "CONFIDENTIAL" under 35 USC § 205.

7.2. *Collaborator Employee Inventions.* The Collaborator may retain title to any Subject Invention made solely by its employees. The Collaborator agrees to file patent applications on such Subject Invention at its own expense and in a timely fashion. The Collaborator agrees to grant to the US Government a nonexclusive, nontransferable, irrevocable, paid-up license in the patents covering Subject Inventions developed by Collaborator's employees to practice the invention or have the invention practiced, throughout the world by or on behalf of the US Government. Such nonexclusive license shall be evidenced by a confirmatory license agreement prepared by the Collaborator in a form satisfactory to NPS.

7.3. *NPS Employee Inventions.* NPS, on behalf of the US Government, shall have the initial option to retain title to each Subject Invention made by its employees under this CRADA. If a Subject Invention is made jointly by personnel of both parties under this CRADA, it and all patent applications and patents issued thereon shall be jointly owned by the parties, subject to the obligations contained in Articles 7.4 and 7.6 herein. NPS may release the rights provided for by this paragraph to employee inventors or to the Collaborator subject to a license in NPS.

7.4. *Filing of Patent Applications.* The party having the right to retain title and file patent applications on a specific Subject Invention may elect not to file patent applications thereon provided that it so advises the other party within ninety (90) days from the date it reports the Subject Invention to the

---

research ties with biotech and other industrial firms, while corporate researchers are not necessarily engaged in product-specific research. What seems increasingly clear, however, is that "value" can attach to research results at any stage in the research process without regard to who is conducting the research. Here, too, a negotiated benefit-sharing agreement can satisfy a park's needs, the public's expectations, and the incentives required to enhance scientific research in national parks consistent with the National Parks Omnibus Management Act of 1998.

Conclusion

Although the USA has not ratified the CBD, the access and benefit-sharing initiative pioneered by NPS is consistent with the CBD's main aims. The USA Congress enacted national legislation governing access to national parks a century ago with the aim of conserving and managing the resources to leave them unimpaired for "future genera-tions", and the law continues to be refined as circumstances require.

The NPS permit system, which is the pragmatic mechanism used to regulate individual access to national park resources for research purposes, implements the concept of PIC through the detailed permit application and approval

---

Box 1. Continued

other party. Thereafter, the other party may elect to file patent applications on the Subject Invention and the party initially reporting such Subject Invention agrees to assign its right, title, and interest in such Subject Invention to the other party and cooperate with such party in the preparation and filing of patent applications thereon. The assignment of the entire right, title, and interest to the party pursuant to this paragraph shall be subject to the retention by the party assigning title of a nonexclusive, irrevocable, paid-up license to practice, or have practiced, the Subject Invention throughout the world. In the event that none of the parties to this CRADA elect to file a patent application on a Subject Invention, either or both (if a joint invention) may, at their sole discretion and subject to reasonable conditions, release the right to file to the inventor(s) with a license in each party of the same scope as set forth in the immediate preceding sentence.

7.5. *Patent Expenses.* All of the expenses attendant to the filing of patent applications as specified in paragraph 7.4 above, shall be borne by the party filing the patent application. Any post-filing and post-patent fees also shall be borne by the same party. Each party shall provide the other party with copies of the patent applications it files on any Subject Invention at the time the application is filed at the US Patent & Trademark Office or patent office of another country. Each party also will provide the other party with the power to inspect and make copies of all documents retained in the official patent application files by the applicable patent office.

7.6. *License Provisions.*

7.6.1. If requested, NPS agrees to provide an exclusive license for a pre-negotiated field of use in any Subject Invention made in whole or in part by a NPS employee for reasonable compensation. The Collaborator's right to negotiate a license(s) begins at the time that a Subject Invention disclosure is filed and ceases six months after the termination of this CRADA for all Subject Inventions. The grant of an exclusive license to Collaborator shall be subject to a nonexclusive, nontransferable, irrevocable, paid-up license from Collaborator to NPS to practice the invention or have the invention practiced throughout the world by or on behalf of the US Government.

7.6.2. Collaborator, at any time, may license or sublicense in whole or in part, any rights and interests granted to Collaborator from NPS under the terms and conditions of this CRADA. Collaborator may exercise such right without obtaining additional authorization from NPS, but Collaborator expressly agrees that in so licensing or sub-licensing, it will specifically reserve to NPS all rights and privileges provided in this agreement for NPS, including the provisions of Appendix B. In the event of a license or sublicense, Collaborator will notify NPS of each license and sublicense to enable NPS to call for the reports provided for in this agreement.

7.7. *Enforcement of jointly owned Patents.* Collaborator must advise NPS of any events that cause Collaborator to suspect that a third party is or may be infringing on jointly owned patents resulting from research conducted under this CRADA (hereafter CRADA patents). Collaborator must institute and diligently prosecute proper legal proceedings at Collaborator's own expense in the event of infringement of CRADA patents. Should Collaborator fail to institute such proceedings within 90 days from receipt of written request from NPS to institute such proceedings, NPS may take the following actions:

- Institute a suit in its own name as subrogee of Collaborator's rights to enforce the patent; or
- Institute a suit against Collaborator for damages resulting from Collaborator's failure to terminate or abate the infringement.

In the event of institution of a suit for infringement by NPS pursuant hereto, it is understood that Collaborator may participate and be represented by its own counsel; however, any recovery damages shall be equitably apportioned, less the US government litigation costs. Either party may make reasonable settlements with respect to any infringements. Collaborator agrees to join in any legal proceedings brought by NPS if joinder is required by law.

7.8. *Commercialization.* The Collaborator agrees to inform NPS when any Subject Invention is commercialized by providing written notice to NPS.

ARTICLE 8. COPYRIGHTS

8.1. The Collaborator shall have the option to own the copyright in all software (including modifications and enhancement thereto), documentation, or other works created in whole or in part by the Collaborator under this CRADA, which is subject to being copyrighted under Title 17, United States process now instituted throughout the NPS. The emphasis on "cooperation" and "mutually agreed [that is, negotiated] terms" found throughout Article 15 of the CBD is further manifested in the NPS approach towards benefit sharing. However, whereas the CBD refers to "sharing in a fair and equitable way the results of research," the National Parks Omnibus Management Act of 1998 adds the qualifier "efficient" in reference to benefit-sharing negotiations.

It is clear that the public and Congress expect firms that profit from research involving national park resources to share the benefits resulting from their research with the park units like Yellowstone for resource conservation purposes. By linking the scientific and economic incentives associated with research activities and new incentives

for conserving biological diversity, Yellowstone aimed to strengthen research in ways that also might contribute significantly to the park's sustainable resource conservation efforts.

Through the development of its pilot bioprospecting project, Yellowstone has helped to create for national parks the opportunity to evaluate how negotiated benefit-sharing arrangements might strengthen their resource conservation mission while also stimulating research incentives in ways that could return scientific and economic dividends to the parks. Without discouraging research opportunities for the broad-based scientific community, the Yellowstone experience suggests that parks can be positioned to share in the full range of benefits of research results for resource

---

Box 1. Continued

Code. The Collaborator shall mark any such works with a copyright notice showing the Collaborator as the author or co-author and shall in its reasonable discretion determine whether to file applications for registration of copyright.

8.2. The Collaborator agrees to grant to the US Government, solely for its purposes, a nonexclusive, irrevocable, paid-up, worldwide license (hereinafter referred to as Government Purpose License) in all copyrighted software or other copyrighted works developed under this CRADA. The Government Purpose License ("GPL") conveys to the US Government the right to use, duplicate, or disclose the copyrighted software or other works in whole or in part, and in any manner, for Government purposes only, and to have or permit others to do so for Government purposes only. Government purposes include competitive procurement, but do not include the right to have or permit others to use the copyrighted software or other works for commercial purposes.

8.3. The Collaborator will clearly mark all copyrighted software or other works subject to the GPL with its name and the words "GOVERNMENT PURPOSE LICENSE."

8.4. The Collaborator shall furnish to NPS, at no cost to NPS, at least one copy of each software, documentation or other work developed in whole or in part by the Collaborator under this CRADA, subject to the terms and conditions of the GPL granted to NPS under paragraph 8.2.

ARTICLE 9. COPYRIGHT ROYALTIES

9.1. Appendix B covers the obligations of the Collaborator to compensate NPS from royalties produced from the sale or use of copyrighted materials. As provided in Appendix B, the Collaborator shall pay to NPS royalties over the life of the copyright from the licensing, assignment, sale, lease, and rental (hereinafter "disposition") of any copyrighted work created under this CRADA.

ARTICLE 10. DATA AND PUBLICATION

10.1. *Release Restrictions.* NPS shall have the right to use all Subject Data for any Governmental purpose, but shall not release such Subject Data publicly except:

(i) NPS, when reporting on the results of sponsored research, may publish Subject Data, subject to the provisions of paragraph 10.4 below; and

(ii) NPS may release such Subject Data where such release

is required pursuant to a request under the Freedom of Information Act, as amended (5 USC § 552 *et seq.*); provided, however, that such data shall not be released to the public if a patent application is to be filed (35 USC § 205) until the party having the right to file the patent application has had a reasonable time to file.

10.2.1. *Proprietary Information.* The Collaborator shall place a proprietary notice on all information it delivers to NPS under this CRADA that the Collaborator asserts is proprietary. NPS agrees that it will use any information designated as proprietary that the Collaborator furnishes to NPS under this CRADA, only for the purpose of carrying out this CRADA. NPS agrees not to disclose, copy, reproduce, or otherwise make available in any form whatsoever information designated as proprietary to any other person, firm, corporation, partnership, association, or other entity without the consent of the Collaborator, except as such information may be subject to disclosure under the Freedom of Information Act, as amended (5 USC § 552, *et seq.*). NPS agrees to use its best efforts to protect information designated as proprietary from unauthorized disclosure. The Collaborator agrees that NPS is not liable for the disclosure of information designated as proprietary that, after notice to and consultation with the Collaborator, NPS determines may not lawfully be withheld or that a court of competent jurisdiction requires disclosure.

10.2.2. *Background Intellectual Property.* Both parties agree to identify in advance and during the course of the CRADA Background Intellectual Property (BIP) that has value for the joint research but which was developed with separate funds outside the CRADA. BIP does not qualify as a Subject Invention and is not subject to a government use license.

10.3. Protected CRADA Information.

10.3.1. Each party may designate as Protected CRADA Information, as defined in Article 2, any Generated Information produced by its employees, and with the agreement of the other party, mark any Generated Information produced by the other party's employees. All such designated Protected CRADA Information shall be appropriately marked.

10.3.2. For a period of five (5) years from the date the Protected CRADA Information is produced, the parties agree conservation purposes consistent with their mission, while also contributing to the ongoing advancement of science and related beneficial research as mandated by the National Parks Omnibus Management Act of 1998.[64]

In accordance with the Federal court's order of 24 March 1999,[65] NPS is undertaking an environmental analysis under NEPA of the potential environmental impacts of various methods of implementing the provisions of law that authorize benefit-sharing agreements while ensuring the integrity of USA national park resources. Specifically, the analysis concerns the potential environmental impacts

of "negotiations with the research community and private industry for equitable, efficient benefits-sharing arrangements" as provided by the National Parks Omnibus Management Act of 1998. The study, which is expected to be completed sometime in 2004, is believed to be the first comprehensive analysis ever undertaken by any nation concerning the potential environmental impacts of bioprospecting benefit-sharing agreements in protected areas, and should provide a rich source of information for others interested in the pragmatic implications of genetic resource management in the 21st century.

Box 1. Continued

not to further disclose such Protected CRADA Information except:

(i) as necessary to perform this CRADA; and

(ii) as mutually agreed by the parties in writing in advance.

10.3.3. The obligation of 10.3.2 above shall end sooner for any Protected CRADA Information which shall become publicly known without fault of either party, shall come into a party's possession without breach by that party of the obligations of 10.3.2 above, or shall be independently developed by a party's employees who did not have access to the Protected CRADA Information, or as required by the Freedom of Information Act, as amended (5 USC § 552, *et seq.*).

10.4. Publication.

10.4.1. NPS may submit for publication the results of the research work associated with this project. Depending on the extent of contribution made, employees of the Collaborator may be cited as co-authors. In no event, however, shall NPS use the name of Collaborator or any of its trademarks and tradenames in any publications without its prior written consent.

10.4.2. NPS and the Collaborator agree to confer and consult at least thirty (30) days prior to either party's submission for publication of Subject Data to assure that no Proprietary Information or Protected CRADA Information is released and that patent rights are not jeopardized. The party receiving the document for review has thirty (30) days from receipt to object in writing detailing the objections to the proposed submissions.

ARTICLE 11. RIGHTS IN GENERATED INFORMATION

11.1. The parties understand that the Government shall have unlimited rights in all Generated Information or information provided to the parties under this CRADA which is not marked as being copyrighted (subject to Article 8) or as Proprietary Information (subject to paragraph 10.2.1) or as Protected CRADA Information (subject to paragraph 10.3).

ARTICLE 12. TERMINATION

12.1. The Collaborator and NPS each have the right to terminate this CRADA upon thirty (30) days notice in writing to the other party. In the event of termination by YNP, YNP shall repay the collaborator any prorated portion of payments previously made to YNP pursuant to Article 5.1 of the CRADA in excess of actual costs incurred by YNP in pursuing this project. A report

on results to date of termination will be prepared by YNP and the cost of the report will be deducted from any amounts due to Collaborators from YNP.

12.2. In-kind payments received by NPS under paragraph 5 of Appendix B may be retained in support of the project.

12.3. A report on results to date of termination will be prepared by Collaborator and the cost of the report will be deducted from any amounts due to NPS.

12.4. Termination of this CRADA by either party for any reason shall not affect the rights and obligations of the parties accrued prior to the effective date of termination of this CRADA. No termination or expiration of this CRADA, however effectuated, shall release the parties hereto from their rights, duties, and obligations under Articles 7, 8, 9, 10, 11, and 14, and payments due under Appendix B.

ARTICLE 13. DISPUTES

13.1. *Settlement.* Any dispute arising under this CRADA which is not disposed of by agreement of the parties shall be submitted jointly to the signatories of this CRADA. A joint decision of the signatories or their designees shall be the disposition of such dispute.

13.2. If the signatories are unable to jointly resolve a dispute within a reasonable period of time after submission of the dispute for resolution, the matter shall be submitted to the Director of the NPS, or his designee, for resolution.

13.3. *Continuation of Work.* Pending the resolution of any dispute or claim pursuant to this Article, the parties agree that they will diligently pursue performance of all obligations in accordance with the direction of the NPS signatory.

ARTICLE 14. LIABILITY

14.1. *Property.* The US Government shall not be responsible for damages to any property of the Collaborator provided to YNP pursuant to this CRADA.

14.2. *Collaborator's Employees.*

14.2.1. During any temporary assignment at YNP facilities that may result from this CRADA, the Collaborator's Assigned Employees (as defined in paragraph 2.2 of this CRADA) shall pursue their activities on the work schedule mutually agreed upon between them, the Collaborator, and NPS. The Collaborator's Assigned Employees must agree to comply with Federal Government security and conduct regulations that apply to YNP employees. The Collaborator's Assigned Employees shall conform to the requirements of the Office of Government Ethics "Standards of Ethical

Acknowledgements

The author wishes to express his appreciation to Mansir Petrie and Thom Minner at the World Foundation for Environment and Development for their research and editorial support and contributions for this chapter and to John Varley at Yellowstone National Park for his time and willingness to share important insights on the challenges facing national park and other conservation area management in the 21st century.

References

BROCK T.D. 1997. The value of basic research: Discovery of *Thermus aquaticus* and other extreme thermophiles. *Genetics* **146**:1207–1210.

BROCK T.D. 1998. Early days in Yellowstone microbiology. *ASM News* **64**(3):137.

BROCK T.D. and H. FREEZE. 1969. *Thermus aquaticus* gen. n. and sp. n., a non-sporulating extreme thermophile. *Journal of Bacteriology* **98**:289–97.

KEMPNER E. 1963. Upper temperature limit of life. *Science* **142**:1318–1319.

MARRS B. and M. MADIGAN. 1997. Extremophiles. *Scientific American* April: 82–87.

Box 1. Continued

Conduct for Employees of the Executive Branch" (5 C.F.R. Parts 2635 and 2636) and Security Regulations, hereby made part of this CRADA, to the extent that these regulations prohibit private business activity or interest incompatible with the best interests of the US Department of the Interior.

14.2.2. The Collaborator's Assigned Employees shall comply with regulations that apply to YNP employees with regard to disclosure of proprietary or procurement-sensitive information, refusal from any activities which may present a conflict of interest, including procurement or other actions in which the Collaborator may have an interest. The Collaborator's Assigned Employees may not represent the Collaborator or work for the Collaborator in competing for award from any other Federal agency during the term of the CRADA (*see* Article 16) or extension thereto.

14.2.3. The Collaborator's Assigned Employees are permanently prohibited from representing or performing activities for the Collaborator on any matters before NPS on which the Collaborator's employees worked at YNP while assigned to this project.

14.2.4. The Collaborator's employees are prohibited from acting as Government employees, including making decisions on behalf of the Government or performing inherently Governmental functions while working at YNP.

14.3. *No Warranty.* Except as provided in Title 28, United States Code, Section 1498, the United States shall not be liable for the use or manufacture of any Invention made under this CRADA nor for the infringement of any patent or copyright during the performance of this CRADA. NPS makes no express or implied warranty as to any matter whatsoever, including the conditions of the research or any Invention or product, whether tangible or intangible, made or developed under this CRADA, or the ownership, merchantability, or fitness for a particular purpose of the research or any Invention or product. These provisions shall survive termination of the CRADA.

14.4. Indemnification.

14.4.1. Collaborator's Employees. The Collaborator agrees to indemnify and hold harmless the US Government for any loss, claim, damage, or liability of any kind involving an employee of the Collaborator arising in connection with this CRADA, except to the extent that such loss, claim, damage or liability arises from the negligence of NPS or its employees acting within the scope of their employment. NPS shall be solely responsible for the payment of all claims for the loss of property, personal injury or death, or otherwise arising out of any negligent act or omission of its employees in connection with the performance of work under this CRADA as provided under the Federal Tort Claims Act. 28 USC § 2672.

14.4.2. Technical Developments and Products. The Collaborator holds the US Government harmless and indemnifies the Government for all liabilities, demands, damages, expenses, and losses arising out of the use by the Collaborator, or any party acting on its behalf or under its authorization, of NPS's research and technical developments or out of any use, sale, or other disposition by the Collaborator, or others acting on its behalf or with its authorization, of products made by Collaborator using the NPS's technical developments. In respect to this Article, the Government shall not be considered an assignee or licensee of the Collaborator. This provision shall survive termination of this CRADA.

14.4.3. Collaborator agrees to maintain insurance in amounts reasonably customary in the industry and to provide proof of liability insurance to NPS upon request.

14.5. *Force Majeur.* Neither party shall be liable for any unforeseeable event beyond its reasonable control not caused by the fault or negligence of such party, which causes such party to be unable to perform its obligations under this CRADA (and which it has been unable to overcome by the exercise of due diligence), including but not limited to flood, drought, earthquake, storm, fire, pestilence, lightening, and other natural catastrophes, epidemic, war, riot, civil disturbance or disobedience, strikes, labor dispute, or failure, threat of failure or sabotage of YNP facilities, or any order or injunction made by a court or public agency. In the event of the occurrence of such a *force majeur* event, the party unable to perform shall promptly notify the other party. It shall further use its best efforts to resume performance as quickly as possible and shall suspend performance only

Endnotes

[1] Information about culture collections around the world as well as specialized discussions about access and benefit sharing as it pertains to genetic resources acquired by and from culture collections may be obtained from the World Federation for Culture Collections (http://wdcm.nig.ac.jp/wfcc).

[2] There are no comprehensive directories of such information for the USA. The nation's size and complexity alone would require constant updating of obsolete information (such as office addresses, telephone numbers, and persons-in-charge). Nonetheless, relevant information is widely available throughout the USA (although legal and technical issues almost certainly require the assistance of a lawyer or other specialist in the field).

[3] Information about the voluntary guidelines (including the text) may be obtained directly from the CBD Secretariat (http://www.biodiv.org).

[4] A section-by-section analysis is under preparation separately. For more information, contact the World Foundation for Environment and Development in Washington DC.

[5] See, e.g., USA Department of the Interior (National Park Service), *Natural Resource Year in Review* (1999), at page 25.

[6] 16 USC 1 (2001).

[7] See 2001 NPS Management Policies, Section 1.4.3.

[8] The term "plants and animals" as used by NPS refers to the commonly recognized kingdoms of living things and includes such groups as flowering plants, ferns, mosses, lichens, algae, fungi, bacteria, mammals, birds, reptiles, amphibians, fishes, insects, worms, crustaceans, as well as all microorganisms.

[9] Yellowstone National Park Organic Act, 16 USC 21 (2001).

[10] Permit (dated 20 August 1898), signed by James B. Erwin, Capt.,

---

Box 1. Continued

for such period of time as is necessary as result of the *force majeur* event.

ARTICLE 15. MISCELLANEOUS TERMS AND CONDITIONS

15.1. *Successors.* Subject to the limitations stated in the *General Provisions*, this CRADA shall be a binding obligation to the successors and permitted assignees of all the right, title and interest of each party hereto. Any such successor or assignee of a party's interest shall expressly assume in writing the performance of all the terms and conditions of this CRADA to be performed by said party. Any such assignment shall not relieve the assignor of any of its obligations under this CRADA.

15.2. *Severability.* The provisions of this CRADA are severable and in the event any of provisions of this CRADA are determined to be invalid or unenforceable by a court of competent jurisdiction, such invalidity or unenforceability shall not in any way affect the validity or enforceability of the remaining provisions hereof, except that for so long as the Collaborator is receiving financial benefit from the use of a product, the Collaborator agrees to provide royalty payments as provided in Exhibit B.

15.3. *Waiver.* Neither party may waive or release any of its rights or interests in this CRADA except in writing. Failure by either party to assert any rights or interests arising from any breach or default of this CRADA shall not be regarded as a waiver of any existing or future rights, interests, or claims.

15.4. *Enforcement.* Collaborator and NPS specifically acknowledge the right to pursue all legal and equitable remedies necessary to cure any breach of their obligations under this CRADA that are not satisfactorily resolved under this CRADA.

15.5. *No Benefits.* No member of, or delegate to the United States Congress, or resident commissioner, shall be admitted to any share or part of this CRADA, nor to any benefit that may arise therefrom; but this provision shall not be construed to extend to this CRADA if made with a corporation for its general benefit.

15.6. *Governing Law.* The construction validity, performance and effect of this CRADA for all purposes shall be governed by applicable Federal laws.

15.7. *Entire Agreement.* This CRADA, consisting of the Statement of Work, Appendix A (collection permits issued by NPS to Collaborator), and Appendix B, constitutes the entire agreement between the parties concerning the subject matter hereto and supersedes any prior understanding or written or oral agreement relative to said matter.

15.8. *Headings.* Titles and headings of the Sections and Subsections of this CRADA are for the convenience of references only and do not form a part of this CRADA and shall in no way affect the interpretation thereof.

15.9. *Amendments.* If either party desires a modification in this CRADA, the parties shall, upon reasonable notice of the proposed modification by the party desiring the change, confer in good faith to determine the desirability of such modification. Such modification shall not be effective until a written amendment is signed by all parties hereto by their representatives duly authorized to execute such amendment.

15.10. *Assignment.* Neither this CRADA nor any rights or obligations of any party hereunder shall be assigned or otherwise transferred by either party without the prior written consent of the other party, except that the Collaborator may assign, subject to the provisions of 15.1, this CRADA to the successors or assigns a substantial portion of the Collaborator's business interests to which this CRADA directly pertains.

15.11. *Notices.* All notices pertaining to or required by this CRADA shall be in writing and shall be directed to the signatory(s).

15.12. *Independent Contractors.* The relationship of the parties to this CRADA is that of independent contractors and not as agents of each other or as joint venturers or partners. NPS shall maintain sole and exclusive control over its personnel and operations.

15.13. *Use of Name or Endorsements.*

15.13.1. The Collaborator shall not use the name of YNP, NPS or the Department of the Interior on any product or service which is directly or indirectly related to either this CRADA or any patent license or assignment agreement which implements this CRADA without the prior approval of NPS. The Collaborator shall not publicize, or otherwise circulate, promotional material (such as advertisements, sales

4th Cavalry, Acting Superintendent, Yellowstone National Park (copy on file at Yellowstone National Park).

[11] In 1980, the USA Supreme Court ruled that a live, human-made microorganism is patentable subject matter under the patent laws of the USA. *See Diamond v. Chakrabarty*, 447 US 303 (1980).

[12] It should be noted that the patent rights awarded in connection with *Taq* and the PCR process have been the subject of much dispute in the USA and abroad. The issues associated with who owns what rights to which inventions under what laws are very significant to the issues of principal concern to this chapter (the facts and circumstances surrounding access and use of genetic resources).

[13] Testimony of D. Allan Bromley, Director, Office of Science and Technology Policy, before the Committee on Science, Space, and Technology, USA House of Representatives, 20 February 1991.

It should be noted that Dr. Brock was affiliated with Indiana University (not Wisconsin) when *T. aquaticus* was first discovered in 1966 (not 1968).

[14] *See, e.g.,* "Yellowstone's Geysers Spout Valuable Micro-Organisms", *The Wall Street Journal*, 11 Aug. 1997, at B1.

[15] *See, e.g.,* "Industries Exploit First Park", *The Billings Gazette*, 6 Dec. 1994 ("Gazette Opinion").

[16] 447 US 303 (1980), at 305.

[17] Act of 21 Feb. 1793, Section 1, 1 Stat. 319.

[18] 447 US 303(1980), at 308, *quoting* 5 Writings of Thomas Jefferson 75–76 (Washington ed. 1871).

[19] *Id.,* at 310.

[20] *Id.*

Box 1. Continued

brochures, press releases, speeches, still or motion pictures or video, articles, manuscripts or other publications) which states or implies Governmental, Departmental, Bureau, or US Government employee endorsement of a product, service or position which the Collaborator represents. No release of information relating to this CRADA may state or imply that the Government approves of the Collaborator's work product, or considers the Collaborator's work product to be superior to other products or services.

15.13.2. The Collaborator must obtain prior US Government approval from NPS for any public information releases that refer to the Department of the Interior, any bureau or employee (by name or title), or this CRADA. The specific text, layout, photographs, etc. of the proposed release must be submitted with the request for approval.

15.13.3 By entering into this CRADA, NPS does not directly or indirectly endorse any product or service provided or to be provided by the Collaborator, its successors, assignees, or licensees.

15.14. *Compliance with Law.* The operations of the Collaborator will be conducted in all material respects in accordance with all applicable laws, ratified treaties, international agreements and conventions, regulations, guidelines and other requirements of all governmental bodies having jurisdiction over the Collaborator. The Collaborator shall have all material licenses (including a radioactivity license), permits, orders or approvals from governmental bodies required for the conduct of its business. All such licenses, permits, approvals or other requirements shall be in full force and there shall exist no violations or breaches of any such domestic licenses, permits, approvals or other requirements. Collaborator shall be in compliance in all material respects with all limitations, restrictions, conditions, standards, prohibitions, requirements, obligations, schedules and timetables contained in any applicable law or in any plan, order, decree, judgment, notice or demand letter issued, entered, promulgated or approved thereunder.

ARTICLE 16. DURATION OF AGREEMENT AND EFFECTIVE DATE.

16.1. *Effective Date.* This CRADA shall enter into force as of the date of the last signature of the parties as shown on the signature page, and will terminate five years from the effective date. In no case will this CRADA extend beyond the ending

date specified herein, unless it is revised in accordance with paragraph 15.9 of this CRADA.

16.2. *Review Period.* Notwithstanding paragraph 16.2 above, the NPS Director shall have the opportunity to disapprove or require the modification of this CRADA for a 30-day period beginning on the date the agreement is presented to the Director by the Superintendent of YNP, unless the agreement is signed by the Director.

SIGNATURE PAGE
SIGNATURES

In Witness Whereof, the parties have executed this CRADA on the dates set forth below. This CRADA may be signed in counterparts, each of which will be deemed to be an original. All such counterparts shall together constitute a single, executed instrument when all parties have so signed. Any communication or notice to be given shall be forwarded to the respective addresses listed below.

For NPS:

_____   _____
Robert Stanton   Date
Director
National Park Service

For YNP:

_____   _____
Michael Finley   Date
Superintendent
Yellowstone National Park

Mailing Address for Notices:
Office of the Superintendent
Yellowstone National Park
P.O. Box 168
Yellowstone National Park, Wyoming 82190

For COLLABORATOR:

_____   _____
Terrance J. Bruggeman   Date
Chairman, President & Chief Executive Officer
Diversa Corporation
Mailing Address for Notices:
Diversa Corporation
10665 Sorrento Valley Road
San Diego, California 92121

21 *Id.*, at 313.

22 The patent laws create enforceable monopoly rights in patented inventions. If there is demand for the patented invention in the market, the monopoly rights created and guaranteed by the patent law can generate significant economic power for the patent holder that typically translates into significant revenue or other earnings.

23 447 US 303 (1980), at 309, quoting *Funk Brothers Seed Co. v. Kalo Inoculant Co.*, 333 US 127 (1948), at 130.

24 USA Patent and Trademark Office (USPTO), Chapter 2100 Patentability—Section 2105 Patentable Subject Matter—Living Subject Matter (available at http://www.uspto.gov/web/offices/pac/ mpep/documents/0875.htm#sect2105).

25 *Id.*

26 USPTO, Patents Granted by Class by Year (dated 31 Dec. 1998).

27 *Id.*

28 *Id.*

29 *JEM Ag Supply dba Farm Advantage v. Pioneer Hi-Bred Int'l*, 534 US 124 (2001).

30 This distinction also has been recognized and upheld by the federal judiciary specifically in the national park context. *See Edmonds Institute, et al. v. Babbitt, et al.*, 93 F. Supp. 2d 63 (DDC 2000) (Memorandum Opinion and Order dismissing plaintiffs' claims with prejudice) ("This interpretation accords with the fact that patent rights derive from human ingenuity brought to bear on scientific specimens, not the specimens themselves.").

31 National Parks Omnibus Management Act of 1998, 16 USC 5935 (2001).

32 *See* 48 Fed. Reg. 30252 (30 June 1983). In August 1999, the National Park Service published new proposals relating to administering the scientific research and collecting permits authorized under 36 CFR 2.5 (2002). *See* 64 Fed. Reg. 46211 (24 Aug. 1999). The revised standardized guidelines became effective in 2001 (http: //science.nature.nps.gov/permits/index.html).

33 36 CFR 1.6(a) (2002).

34 48 Fed. Reg. 30252, 30254 (30 June 1983).

35 36 CFR 1.4 (2002).

36 36 CFR 1.6(e) (2002).

37 36 CFR 2.5(b) (2002).

38 The revised standardized "Application Procedures and Requirements for Scientific Research and Collecting Permits" guidelines became effective in 2001 and are published and made available through the internet. *See* http://science.nature.nps.gov/ permits/index.html. Research permit applications can be prepared and filed electronically throughout the entire USA NPS system.

39 *Id.*

40 *Id.*

41 *See Edmonds Institute, et al. v. Babbitt, et al.*, 93 F. Supp. 2d 63 (DDC 2000) (Memorandum Opinion and Order dismissing plaintiffs' claims with prejudice) ("The record discloses that defendants [Department of the Interior / National Park Service] have provided a thoughtful and rational approach to research conducted on Park resources.... Thus, in accord with these fundamental principles, the Park Service has interpreted its regulations only to allow researchers to study, not sell, Park resources.... [T]he court finds that defendants reasonably construed Park regulations....").

42 *See* "General Permit Conditions" at http://science.nature.nps.gov/ permits/index/html.

43 *See* "General Permit Conditions" at Section 6 ("Collection of specimens (including materials)"), available at http:// science.nature.nps.gov/permits/index.html.

44 *Id.*

45 *See id.* It should be noted that an analysis of the environmental impacts of implementing this provision is being conducted by NPS pursuant to NEPA.

46 2001 NPS Management Policies, Chapter 4: Natural Resource Management, at Section 4.2 ("Studies and Collections").

47 *Id.*, at Section 4.2.2 ("Independent Studies").

48 *Id.*, at Section 4.2.4 ("Collection Associated with the Development of Commercial Products").

49 2001 NPS Management Policies, Chapter 8: Use of the Parks, at Section 8.10 ("Natural and Cultural Studies Research and Collection Activities").

50 "Culture collections" are institutions that acquire, preserve, and distribute biological samples and related information, technology, and intellectual property to research scientists in academia as well as industry. There are an estimated 500 culture collections located in approximately 50 countries around the world. The largest is considered to be the American Type Culture Collection (ATCC), which is headquartered in facilities on the campus of George Mason University near Manassas, Virginia, not far from Washington, DC. ATCC currently holds approximately 40 different microbial samples originally collected from Yellowstone, plus several other biological samples acquired from other national parks in the USA and abroad.

51 "Gazette Opinion", *The Billings Gazette*, 6 Dec. 1994.

52 15 USC 3710a(d) (2001).

53 S. Rep. No.283, 99th Cong., 2d Sess. (1986), at page 11. The federal judiciary has upheld the designation of Yellowstone National Park as a "federal laboratory" under the FTTA. *See Edmonds Institute, et al. v. Babbitt, et al.*, 93 F. Supp. 2d 63 (DDC 2000) (Memorandum Opinion and Order dismissing plaintiffs' claims with prejudice) ("[T]he court finds that defendants [Department of the Interior / National Park Service] have provided a reasoned basis for concluding that the broad, statutorily-assigned definition encompasses Yellowstone's extensive research facilities.").

54 S. Rep. No.283, 99th Cong., 2d Sess. (1986), at page 4.

55 *See Edmonds Institute, et al. v. Babbitt, et al.*, 93 F. Supp. 2d 63 (DDC 2000) (Memorandum Opinion and Order dismissing plaintiffs' claims with prejudice) ("[T]he court finds that defendants [Department of the Interior / National Park Service] reasonably construed Park regulations and concluded that the CRADA was consistent with their requirements.").

56 S. Rep. No.283, 99th Cong., 2d Sess. (1986), at page 11.

57 In March 2002, a federal court in Washington ruled that royalty rates negotiated in CRADAS and research-related licensing agreements by the National Institutes of Health with private sector firms are subject to confidential treatment under Exemption 4 of the Freedom of Information Act. *See Public Citizen Health Research Group v. National Institutes of Health* (opinion by Judge Colleen Kollar-Kotelly dated 12 March 2002).

58 The term "net" was defined in the YNP-Diversa CRADA to mean "total gross receipts for sales by Collaborator [Diversa], its licensees or sublicensees of Product(s) and copyrighted works created using the results of research under this CRADA, and from otherwise making Product(s) available to others without sale, whether invoiced or not, less returns and allowances actually granted, packing costs, insurance costs, freight out, taxes and excise duties imposed on the transaction (if separately invoiced), and the wholesaler and cash discounts in amounts customary in the trade. No deductions shall be made for commissions paid to individuals, whether they be with independent sales agencies or regularly employed by Collaborator, its licensee or sublicensees, or for the costs of collections."

59 *See Edmonds Institute, et al. v. Babbitt, et al.*, 93 F. Supp. 2d 63 (DDC 2000) (Memorandum Opinion and Order dismissing plaintiffs' claims with prejudice ("[C]ontrary to plaintiffs' assertion, neither the CRADA nor its Scope of Work authorizes Diversa to take any natural materials from Yellowstone. Rather, the CRADA outlines the rights and responsibilities of Yellowstone and Diversa with re-

spect to information and inventions developed <u>after</u> the conclusion of research specimen collection and analysis." (Emphasis supplied by the court.)).

[60] *Id.*, ("If the court were to find that the CRADA was improper under the relevant statutes, Diversa could still collect specimens under a research permit, as it has since 1994. The only—albeit critical—difference would be that Yellowstone could not share in any of the potential benefits from Diversa's research. Instead, the positive gains from the research would go exclusively to Diversa.").

[61] *See Edmonds Institute, et al. v. Babbitt, et al.,* 93 F. Supp. 2d 63 (DDC 2000).

[62] *See Edmonds Institute, et al. v. Babbitt, et al.,* 42 F. Supp. 2d 1 (DDC 1999).

[63] *See Edmonds Institute, et al. v. Babbitt, et al.,* 93 F. Supp. 2d 63, at 72 (DDC 2000).

[64] The federal judiciary has ruled that the YNP-Diversa CRADA was consistent with the park's conservation mission, as well as with Congressional intent expressed in the National Parks Omnibus Management Act of 1998. *See Edmonds Institute, et al. v. Babbitt, et al.,* 93 F. Supp. 2d 63 (DDC 2000) (Memorandum Opinion and Order dismissing plaintiffs' claims with prejudice ("[T]he court finds that defendants [Department of the Interior / National Park Service] properly determined that the CRADA was consistent with the governing statutes because it would produce direct, concrete benefits to the Park's conservation efforts by affording greater scientific understanding of Yellowstone's wildlife, as well as monetary support for Park programs and 15...[T]he far-reaching terms of the Parks Management Act reinforce the conclusion that the Yellowstone-Diversa CRADA is proper.").

[65] *See Edmonds Institute, et al. v. Babbitt, et al.,* 42 F. Supp. 2d 1 (DDC 1999) (Memorandum Opinion and Order suspending the YNP-Diversa CRADA pending a showing of NEPA compliance (dated March 24, 1999)). Since entry of the 24 March 1999 Order, the Court dismissed plaintiffs' case with prejudice.

9

Australia: Draft Regulations on Access and Benefit Sharing

Sally Petherbridge

Australia's status as a megadiverse nation (one of seventeen in the world) is well known. Australia has the planet's second highest number of reptile species, is fifth in flowering plant species, and tenth in amphibian species. The Australian continent and its islands have an estimated 52% of the world's marsupials. More significant, however, is the high percentage of organisms that occur only in Australia. Seven families of mammals and twelve of flowering plants are endemic, giving Australia far more endemic families than any other country. At the species level, the mean percentage of endemism for terrestrial vertebrates and flowering plants is 81%. Australia's marine biological diversity, like that of the land, is notable for its high proportion of endemic species. In the south of the continent, about 80 to 90% of the species in most marine groups are considered to be endemic. On the basis of such statistics about biodiversity, Australia's National Report to the Fourth Conference of the Parties to the Convention on Biological Diversity concluded:

> *...whilst the potential of Australia's biodiversity as a source of food and useful pharmaceutical, medicinal and industrial products has scarcely been realized, attention is now being given to development of novel Australian bio-resources and bio-techniques* (ENVIRONMENT AUSTRALIA 1998).

Growing awareness of the potential value of Australia's biodiversity for such uses (as well as the importance of ensuring that Australia benefits in economic terms from such uses, while ensuring that they are ecologically sustainable) has resulted in the development of a draft regulatory scheme for access to, and benefit sharing from, such resources. The proposed scheme, has been the subject of extensive consultations with stakeholders and interested parties. The regulations are expected to be enacted in 2005.

Draft Access and Benefit-Sharing Regulations

On 7 September 2001, Senator Robert Hill, Australia's then-Minister for the Environment and Heritage, released the draft Environment Protection and Biodiversity Conservation Amendment Regulations of 2001 for a period of public comment ending on 5 October 2001.[1] These regulations will be made under section 301 of the Environment Protection and Biodiversity Conservation Act of 1999 (EPBCA) which came into effect on 16 July 2000. Section 301, which is headed "Control of access to biological resources," states that "the regulations may provide for the control of access to biological resources in Commonwealth areas" and, further, that the regulations may contain provisions about the equitable sharing of the benefits arising from the use of these resources; the facilitation of access; the right to deny access; the granting of access; and the terms and conditions of such access.[2]

The objects of the EPBCA are, among other things:

- To provide for the protection of the environment, especially those aspects of the environment that are matters of national environmental significance;

- To promote ecologically sustainable development through the conservation and ecologically sustainable use of natural resources; and
- To promote the conservation of biodiversity.[3]

The inclusion of section 301 in the EPBCA reflects, therefore, not only the importance of facilitating access to biological resources, but also the importance of ensuring that access is ecologically sustainable.

The access and benefit-sharing scheme in the draft regulations essentially reflects the scheme recommended by the report of the Inquiry into Access to Biological Resources in Commonwealth Areas (Inquiry) (VOUMARD 2000). The Inquiry recommended regulations which would require a party seeking access to biological resources in Commonwealth areas to apply for an access permit from the Minister for the Environment and Heritage. As the regulatory agency under the scheme, the Department of the Environment and Heritage would assess the application, in consultation with any other relevant Australian government agency, and make a recommendation to the Minister to grant or refuse the permit.

While the assessment process for the permit was underway, the applicant would be required to negotiate with the holder (or owner) of the resources a benefit-sharing contract which covered the commercial and other aspects of the agreement (in particular, matters such as up front payments for samples, royalties, and protection of indigenous knowledge). The Inquiry proposed that the contract be based on a model contract which the Inquiry report outlined and recommended be developed and agreed upon by governments, industry, indigenous organizations, and other stakeholders.

The Inquiry recommended that the regulations provide that the Minister may issue the access permit on being satisfied, among other things, that environmental assessment (if required) has been undertaken and the process completed; submissions from interested persons and bodies have been taken into account; and there is a benefit-sharing contract between the parties which addresses the following major issues: prior informed consent; mutually agreed terms; adequate benefit-sharing arrangements, including protection for and valuing of indigenous knowledge; and the use of benefits for biodiversity conservation in the area from which the resource was obtained. The benefit-sharing contract would only have effect if the Minister issued an access permit (VOUMARD 2000). The Inquiry and its report are discussed in more detail below.

Proposed Coverage of the Regulations

Australia has a federal system of government, comprising the national government, six State governments, and two self-governing Territories. The regulations will apply to "Commonwealth areas" which, expressed simply, are lands owned or leased by the Australian government and

marine areas over which the Australian government has sovereignty.[4] Therefore, the regulations will not apply to the States and Territories which have, in varying degrees, their own legislation and/or policies governing access to biological resources. Proposals for a "nationally consistent" system of access to biological resources are discussed further below.

The Inquiry was unable to obtain a comprehensive list of "Commonwealth areas" but was assisted in identifying major areas which either have been or are likely to be of interest to bioprospectors through submissions from Australian government agencies with responsibility for land and/or marine management. "Areas" thereby identified included three terrestrial national parks, Australia's Antarctic Territory, the Great Barrier Reef Marine Park, Commonwealth land in Norfolk Island, lands managed by government agencies such as the Department of Defense, and the Commonwealth's marine area[5].

Structure and Purpose of the Regulations

The draft regulations provide for a new Part (Part 8A) to be inserted into the existing regulations under the EPBCA and for amendments to Part 17 of these regulations (Part 17 covers all permits that may be issued under the EPBCA). While this structure has the advantage of avoiding repetition of elements that are common to all permits under the Act, it may also have the undesirable effect of making the access scheme more difficult to comprehend, as it is not set out in a self-contained Part under the regulations.

The purpose of the regulations is "to provide for the control of access to biological resources in Commonwealth areas" by: promoting the conservation of resources in those areas, including their ecologically sustainable use; ensuring the equitable sharing of benefits arising from their use by providing for benefit-sharing agreements between persons seeking access and access providers; recognizing the special knowledge held by indigenous people about biological resources; establishing an access regime designed to provide certainty, and minimize cost, for people seeking access; and seeking to ensure that the social and economic benefits arising from their use accrue to Australia.[6]

The regulations define "access to biological resources" as "the taking of biological resources of native species for: conservation, commercial application or industrial application of, or research on, any genetic resources, or biochemical compounds, comprising or contained in the biological resources." Examples of what this might involve, quoted from the Explanatory Memorandum of the EPBCA, are included: "Collecting living material, analyzing and sampling stored material, exporting material for purposes including taxonomic research, conservation, research and potential commercial product development."[7] In addition, the regulations provide that "a person is taken to have access to biological resources if there is a reasonable prospect that [the resources] will be subject to conservation, commercial application, industrial application or research."[8]

The meaning of access to biological resources is further clarified by reference to activities which it does not cover. These include:

- The taking of biological resources by indigenous people other than for a purpose mentioned in subregulation (1) or in the exercise of their native title rights and interests (addresses concerns that access might limit indigenous people's existing uses of these resources);

- Access to human remains (responds to concerns expressed by indigenous people that indigenous remains not be accessible and implements a recommendation to this effect in VOUMARD (2000));

- Taking public resources, other than for a purpose mentioned in subregulation (1) (makes clear that normal commercial and other uses of biological resources such as fishing or plant production are not regulated under these regulations. "Taking public resources" includes: fishing for commerce or recreation, game or charter fishing, or collecting broodstock for aquaculture; harvesting wildflowers; taking wild animals for plants or food; collecting peat or firewood; taking essential oils from wild plants; and collecting seeds for propagation);[9] and

- Access specified in a declaration under regulation 8A.04.

Regulation 8A.04 provides exemptions for specified biological resources. Under this regulation, the Minister may declare that the permit provisions do not apply to biological resources:

- If they are held in a collection by a Australian government department or agency, and if there are reasonable grounds to believe that access to the biological resources is administered consistently with the purpose of the regulations;

- If there are reasonable grounds to believe that access to the resources is controlled by another national, self-governing Territory, or State law, consistent with the purpose of the regulations (avoids duplication of any access arrangements applying in a Commonwealth area);

- If an international agreement to which Australia is a party, such as the FAO International Undertaking

on Plant Genetic Resources (1983), applies. This provision allows a declaration to be sought with respect to biological resources covered by the International Treaty on Plant Genetic Resources for Food and Agriculture (ITPGRFA), if Australia decided to become a party to this agreement.[10]

Ex Situ Collections

With respect to *ex situ* resources, the Inquiry identified collections held by Australian government agencies such as the Australian National Botanic Gardens, the Commonwealth Scientific and Industrial Research Organization (CSIRO), and the Australian Institute of Marine Science (AIMS). Although these collections are under Australian government jurisdiction by virtue of the legislation governing these bodies, as well as by the definition of Commonwealth areas in the EPBCA, the ownership status of particular collections (or parts of them) is less clear. This was an issue of particular concern to CSIRO which expressed concern that, without clear legal title, its rights to deal with its collections might be challenged (VOUMARD 2000). CSIRO houses several major national collections which include the Australian National Herbarium, the Tree Seed Center, and insect, wildlife and marine collections.

With respect to this issue, the Inquiry received legal advice that:

> It is not possible to make any definitive, general statement as to the ownership of all ex situ collections of biological resources. Each collection would have to be considered on its own merits having regard to a range of factors, including the ownership, if any, of the material when it was in situ and the circumstances under which the material passed into the possession of the ex situ holder, including the terms and conditions of any relevant agreement, or any relevant legislation (VOUMARD 2000).

In recognition of these difficulties, the Voumard report recommended that the Minister for the Environment and Heritage ask his department to discuss with holders of such collections, the value of a combined request for legal advice on ownership issues and that, subject to the advice obtained, the Minister consider any recommendation for legislative amendment to resolve outstanding issues by the holders of the collections (VOUMARD 2000). To date, however, the holders of these collections have not pursued the issue.

The Main Characteristics of the Draft Regulations on Access and Benefit Sharing

The draft regulations set out provisions with respect to the information required for access permits and the content of benefit-sharing agreements, as well as detailed provisions covering the way in which permit applications and benefit-sharing agreements are to be assessed and environmental assessment, if required, is to be carried out. Unfortunately, parts of the latter are somewhat difficult to read, requiring

cross-referencing between different provisions, but this was unavoidable from a drafting point of view. However, by indicating the administrative procedures which will be followed, including timeframes to promote expeditious decision-making, and the information and factors which must be taken account of in decision-making, the draft regulations do have the merit of promoting the transparency and accountability of the decision-making process. Fortunately, the regulations are written in Plain English with little or no legal jargon, although they do encompass some complex areas of the law such as ownership/sovereignty[11] and native title law. It should be noted that, although the regulations refer to the Minister of the Environment and Heritage as the decision-maker, the EPBCA enables the Minister to delegate his or her "powers or functions" to an officer or employee of the department. An identical provision applies to the Secretary of the Department of the Environment and Heritage.[12] Detailed administrative arrangements for the handling of access applications can be expected to be developed once the regulations are enacted.

Access Permits

A person may have access to biological resources only in accordance with a permit in force under Part 17 of the regulations under the EPBCA[13] This provision includes an explanatory note that the Minister may issue a permit only if the applicant has given the Minister a copy of each benefit-sharing agreement. Proposed amendments to Part 17 set out the information which will be required of persons seeking access to biological resources in Commonwealth areas. This includes: the name of the Australian government department or agency which administers the area in which access is proposed; if the provider is not the Australian government, the name of the provider; the resources to which access is sought; where the resources are; the amount of the resources that will be collected; the use the applicant intends to make of them; details of any other person for whose benefit access is sought or who proposes to use the samples; how the access is to be undertaken, including details of the vehicles and equipment to be used; the nature and extent of the likely environmental impacts of the access; whether the applicant thinks that further access to the resources will be sought; details of any other application by the applicant for a permit under this Part; and information about the progress of any negotiations with the access provider about sharing the benefits arising from their use.[14]

Benefit-Sharing Agreements

An applicant for a permit must enter into a benefit-sharing agreement with each access provider for the resources. An explanatory note states that there may be more than one access provider for biological resources; for example, if a Commonwealth area is subject to native title, the Australian government and the native title holders are both access providers.[15] If the access provider is the Australian government, the Secretary to the Australian government department that has administrative authority for the Commonwealth area may, on behalf of the Australian government, enter into the benefit-sharing agreement.[16] The agreement takes effect only if a permit is issued.[17] The benefit-sharing agreement must provide for reason-

able benefit-sharing arrangements, including protection for, recognition of and valuing of any indigenous knowledge given by the access provider.[18] If the access provider is the owner of indigenous people's land or a native title holder for the area, the access provider must have given informed consent to the agreement.[19]

Detailed requirements for ensuring informed consent by the access provider follow. In assessing whether informed consent was given, the Minister must consider the following matters:

- Whether the applicant gave the provider adequate information about the application and the requirements of the regulations and engaged in reasonable negotiations with the provider about the agreement;

- Whether the provider was given adequate time to consider the application, including time to consult with relevant people, and, if the provider is the owner of indigenous people's land, to consult with the traditional owners and to negotiate the agreement;

- Whether the provider is the owner of indigenous people's land and represented by a land council and, if so, the views of the land council about the matters in paragraphs a) and b);

- If access is sought to the resources of an area for which native title exists, the views of any representative Aboriginal and Torres Strait Islander body within the meaning of the Native Title Act of 1993 for the area about the matters in paragraphs a) and b); and

- Whether the access provider has received independent legal advice about the regulation.[20]

Assessment of Benefit-Sharing Agreements

The regulations then set out the procedures which must be followed once the Secretary has received the benefit-sharing agreement(s) and the permit application. The Secretary must give a report to the Minister within 30 days of their receipt. The Minister may extend this time if needed for consulting any persons who may have information relevant to the application or the agreement.[21] In assessing the agreement, the Minister may consult with any Australian government department or agency that may have relevant information; must take into account the provisions of the model benefit-sharing agreement, if any, and any variations from it; and must consider whether, under the regulations requiring consultation with the owners of land leased by the Commonwealth, reasonable benefit-sharing arrangements and informed consent have been complied with.[22]

Environmental Assessment

Detailed requirements for environmental assessment are also included. There are three ways in which this may occur: on the basis of the permit application; through "Environmental assessment by public notice", the requirements for which are set out in the regulations; or through the environmental assessment provisions set out in the EPBCA itself. The regulations provide that environmental assessment by public notice may apply to an application for a permit under the regulations if the proposed access is not a controlled action[23]. Assessment of an application by public notice is required if there are reasonable grounds for the Minister to believe that the proposed access is likely to have environmental impacts that are likely to be more than negligible.[24] This is not defined nor are there any guidelines to assist the Minister's decision. However, it would appear to encompass activities which pose a lesser threat to the environment than activities requiring environmental assessment under the EPBCA. In the latter case (a "controlled action"), an action will require approval from the Minister if it has, will have, or is likely to have "a significant impact on a matter of national environmental significance". The matters of national environmental significance are: World Heritage properties; Ramsar wetlands of international importance; listed threatened species and communities; migratory species protected under international agreements; nuclear actions; the Commonwealth marine environment; and national heritage. The *Administrative guidelines on significance* assist in determining whether an action should be referred to the Minister for a decision on whether an approval is required (ENVIRONMENT AUSTRALIA 2000).

If the Minister decides, however, that environmental assessment by public notice is required, the draft regulations set out in detail the consultation procedures and timeframes which apply. Within 20 days after receiving the application, the Minister must inform the applicant and the applicant must then give the Minister a summary of the likely environmental impacts of the proposed access (there is no timeframe for this activity). Within 10 days of receiving the summary, the Minister must invite anyone (by public notice) and each person registered under Regulation 8A.14 to comment on the likely impacts, and within 5 days after the end of the period given in the invitation for comments, the Minister must give the applicant a copy of the comments received. Finally, the applicant must give the Minister a response to these comments (again, there is no timeframe for this activity but, presumably, it is in the applicant's interests to respond expeditiously).[25]

Requirements for the consultation register are then set out. At intervals of not more than 12 months, the Minister must publish a notice inviting applications from persons who want to be registered, to be told of applications for access permits where environmental assessment by public notice is required.[26] The Minister is also required to keep a register of information about permits. The register must be available for public inspection; however, information is not be included in it if the Minister believes the information is culturally sensitive or, if disclosed, could damage a person's commercial interests, result in a risk to the environment, or harm the national interest.[27]

Assessment of Permits

Proposed amendments to Part 17 of the regulations set out the requirements for the assessment of permits. If the proposed access is a "controlled action", the Minister must decide whether to issue a permit within 10 days after approval of the action. If the access proposed is not a "controlled action", the Minister must decide whether to issue a permit within 30 days of receiving the Secretary's report and any comments and responses from the environmental assessment by public notice process. In making this decision, the Minister must take into account these documents, the views of any owner of land leased to the Australian government, the views of any Australian government department or agency consulted by the Minister, the assessment of the benefit-sharing agreement, and any other matters that the Minister thinks are relevant.[28] The Minister may seek more information from any person who may have information relevant to the application if he or she believes there is not sufficient information to make a decision.[29]

Several circumstances are then set out which must be present for the Minister to issue a permit. These are that the applicant has entered into a benefit-sharing agreement with each access provider; the applicant has given the Minister a copy of each benefit-sharing agreement; the Minister believes, on reasonable grounds, that some of the benefits will, if practicable, be used for biodiversity conservation in the area from where the resources were taken; the proposed access is consistent with any relevant plan for a Commonwealth reserve[30], and the proposed access will, taking into account the precautionary principle, be ecologically sustainable and consistent with the conservation of Australia's biological diversity. In addition for access in Kakadu, Uluṟu-Kata Tjuṯa, or Booderee National Parks, the proposed access must be consistent with any relevant lease.[31]

Requirements Arising from Native Title Rights

Following consultations with, and legal advice from, the Native Title Division of the Australian government's Attorney General's Department, several provisions were included in the draft regulations to protect the rights of native title holders under the Native Title Act of 1993. These include clarification that access to biological resources does not include the taking of resources by indigenous people in the exercise of their native title rights and interests.[32] The definition of "access provider" recognizes that native title holders for the area may be access providers[33] and that there may be more than one access provider for an area. For example, if a Commonwealth area is subject to native title, the Australian government and native title holders are both access providers.[34] The regulations also state that an agreement may be both a benefit-sharing agreement and an indigenous land-use agreement under the Native Title Act.[35] Further amendments require the Secretary/head of the Australian government department or agency that has entered into a benefit-sharing agreement with the applicant to advise the Minister whether he or she thinks that issuing the permit would be an invalid future act under the Native Title Act.[36] The Minister may issue a permit only if satisfied that it would not be an invalid future act.[37] One basis for being satisfied is that there is an indigenous land use agreement under the Native Title Act for the area in which native titleholders have consented to the issue of the permit.[38]

Review/Appeals Processes

The Inquiry report recommended that the parties to the contract be able to seek merits review of the Minister's decision not to grant an access permit (VOUMARD 2000). It was decided during the drafting phase, however, that merits review would not be available. Nevertheless, procedural review is available through the courts under the 1997 Administrative Decisions (Judicial Review) Act. Possible grounds include the following: a breach of natural justice occurred in connection with the making of the decision;

procedures required by law in connection with the making of the decision were not observed; the making of the decision was an improper exercise of the power conferred by the enactment under which it was made; the decision was induced or affected by fraud; and there was no evidence or other material to justify the making of the decision. An "improper exercise of power" includes taking an irrelevant consideration into account; failing to take a relevant consideration into account; exercising a discretionary power in accordance with a rule or policy without regard to the merits of a particular case; an exercise of power that is so unreasonable that no reasonable person would have so exercised the power; and exercising power in such a way that the result is uncertain.[39]

Enforcement of the Regulations

Enforcement of the access regulations will be the responsibility of the Department of the Environment and Heritage which manages compliance with the EPBCA. Fifty penalty units are set for contravening the regulation (8A.05) which requires a permit for access to biological resources.[40]

The Process Leading to the Development of the Access Legislation

The Inquiry

Senator the Hon. Robert Hill, then-Minister for the Environment and Heritage, announced an inquiry into access to biological resources in Commonwealth areas on 22 June 1999. This reflected the government's 1998 election commitment to introduce regulations to regulate access to genetic resources in Commonwealth areas (VOUMARD 2000).[41] Following the receipt of advice from his department as to how the process might be conducted, the Minister formally initiated the Inquiry on 22 December 1999.

The Inquiry's terms of reference stated that the Inquiry was to advise on a scheme that could be implemented through regulations under section 301 of the EPBCA to "provide for the control of access to biological resources in Commonwealth areas". The terms of reference stated that the scheme should take into account the following:

- Australia's obligations under the Convention on Biological Diversity (CBD), including the obligation to encourage the equitable sharing of benefits arising from the utilization of biological resources. The scheme should particularly focus on the equitable sharing of benefits arising from the utilization of traditional knowledge, innovations, and practices (article 8(j)).

- The objectives of the National Strategy for the Conservation of Australia's Biodiversity, such as:
  - Ensuring that the collection of biological resources for research and development purposes does not adversely affect the viability or conser-

vation status of any species or population;
  - Ensuring that the social and economic benefits of the use of biological resources derived from Australia's biological diversity accrue to Australia.

The terms of reference stated further that the scheme "should operate in a manner that promotes certainty for industry". Finally, consistent with the objective of the EPBCA, the scheme should:

- Promote a cooperative approach to the protection and management of the environment involving governments, the community, land-holders, and indigenous peoples.
- Recognize the role of indigenous people in the conservation and ecologically sustainable use of Australia's biodiversity.
- Promote the use of indigenous peoples' knowledge of biodiversity with the involvement of, and in cooperation with, the owners of that knowledge.

The Inquiry was conducted by a solicitor from South Australia, John Voumard. The reference group established to assist him comprised an environmental law specialist, an industry representative, an indigenous representative, an intellectual property specialist, and a representative from the scientific community.[42] The reference group met on four occasions, in January, April, June, and July 2000.

In announcing the Inquiry, Senator Hill invited submissions by 3 March 2000. The Inquiry was advertised in the national press and the major newspaper of each State, the Australian Capital Territory, and the Northern Territory during January 2000. The Inquiry secretariat also sent out approximately 600 notices inviting submissions, mainly to biotechnology organizations (based on a mailing list provided by Biotechnology Australia), as well as to indigenous land councils in the Northern Territory, Western Australia, and Queensland, environment groups, and overseas biotechnology companies. The Inquiry received 80 submissions (VOUMARD 2000), although, as a result of the tight deadline for submissions (seven weeks from public advertising), several submissions were not received until May. In addition to receiving submissions, the Inquiry held two public hearings, one in Canberra on 30 May 2000 and the other in Brisbane on 1 June 2000. In some cases evidence was presented by telephone (from Melbourne and from north Queensland). Extensive consultations were also held, most significantly with the traditional owners of the three national parks[43] and their representatives. The Inquiry was required to report to the Minister by 30 June 2000. The Chair sought a short extension, submitting the Inquiry Report on 4 August 2001.

Studies Prior to the Inquiry

Although the Inquiry was undoubtedly the most significant step in the development of access and benefit-sharing regulations, it was preceded by several studies which, while inconclusive in policy/legislative terms, were useful in identifying many of the major issues involved in access issues and developing general principles to guide further work (Table 1). The Inquiry report drew on and acknowledged the work of its predecessors.[44]

Australia signed the CBD on 5 June 1992. In February 1993, the Australian and New Zealand Environment and Conservation Council (ANZECC), a consultative group of Australian government, State, and Territory environment ministers, produced a report to First Ministers[45] on the Implementation of and Implications of Ratification of the Convention on Biological Diversity (ANZECC 1993).

In discussing Article 15 of the CBD, Access to Genetic Resources, ANZECC (1993) noted:

> ...the control of access to genetic resources is an issue of national importance requiring urgent attention... the introduction of procedures governing access... would enable Australia to take full advantage of the opportunities provided by this article and also to protect our interests.

Two further reports followed in quick succession. In March 1994 ANZECC released a paper on Access to Australia's Genetic Resources in which it noted:

> Currently, under existing legislation and guidelines it is possible to export a large range and volume of genetic resources for use in overseas research and development without appropriate returns to Australia (ANZECC 1994).

Also in March, the Office of the Chief Scientist in the Department of the Prime Minister and Cabinet released

Access to Australia's Biological Resources—A Discussion Paper (DPMC 1994). In May 1994, following advice from ANZECC, First Ministers established the Commonwealth State Working Group (CSWG).

The CSWG completed its discussion paper in October 1996. The paper was subsequently released and eight submissions received by April 1998. An important part of this public consultation process was the Roundtable Discussion on Access to Australia's Genetic Resources held in Canberra on 14 March 1994. Although the CSWG paper was the most detailed discussion of issues and principles to date, subsequent work on access issues was hampered by the lack of specific direction in its recommendations, both in relation to the form access systems might take and the bureaucratic/political processes required to take the work forward.

Australian government agencies with an interest in access issues and a working group, comprising the Departments of Environment and Heritage and Agriculture, Fisheries, and Forestry, and representatives of State and Territory Governments, continued to meet, but without a clear focus or political and bureaucratic support, little progress was made. This situation changed, however, in mid-

Table 1. Key steps in the development of the draft regulations on access and benefit sharing

Date	Steps
September 1992	Australia signs the Convention on Biological Diversity.
December 1992	Australia ratifies the Convention on Biological Diversity.
October 1996	The Commonwealth State Working Group Paper is released.
May 1999	Biotechnology Australia is established.
June 1999	The Minister for the Environment and Heritage announces an inquiry into access to biological resources in Commonwealth areas.
December 1999	The Minister formally initiates the Inquiry (VOUMARD 2000).
August 2000	The Inquiry Chair submits the Inquiry report to the Minister.
September 2000	The Minister publicly releases the Inquiry report.
August 2001	The Bailey report (*Bioprospecting: Discoveries changing the future*) is released.
September 2001	The Minister releases the draft regulations on access and benefit sharing for public comment.
December 2001	Responsibility for the development of a nationally consistent approach to the utilization of genetic and biochemical resources is given to the Natural Resource Management Ministerial Council .
Octoer 2002	Final comments on the draft regulations are received.

1999, with the establishment of Biotechnology Australia and the announcement of the Inquiry. Biotechnology Australia was established in the Department of Industry, Science, and Resources in May 1999, but comprised five departments: Industry, Science, and Resources; Environment and Heritage; Agriculture, Fisheries, and Forestry; Health and Aged Care; and Education, Training, and Youth Affairs. It was overseen by a Council comprising the Ministers responsible for these departments and a Committee of the Secretaries (executive heads) of these departments. The Inquiry was one of the major activities under Biotechnology Australia's Access Work Program and was funded through this Program.

Australia's National Biotechnology Strategy, released in July 2000, included as an objective, the "development of measures to enhance access to biological resources" and, among strategies to meet that objective, the need to address issues of access to biological resources in Commonwealth areas through regulations under the EPBCA; matters involving indigenous people and their ownership of biological resources; and work with the States and Territories to achieve nationally consistent regimes on access (COMMONWEALTH OF AUSTRALIA 2000).

The Inquiry (and its subsequent implementation) also drew extensively on international developments. The Inquiry examined existing and proposed access schemes in other countries, a summary of developments in Costa Rica, the Philippines, the United States, and Brazil being included in the report (VOUMARD 2000). A member of its reference group, Elizabeth Evans-Illidge, attended the first meeting of the Panel of Experts on Access and Benefit-Sharing in Costa Rica in October 1999. The Access Taskforce (the Inquiry secretariat) also participated in several other international meetings on access and related issues, by contributing to the Australian Government briefs for them and, in some cases, through its attendance.[46]

Consultations Following the Release of the Inquiry Report and of the Draft Access Regulations

When Senator Hill publicly released the Inquiry report (7 September 2000), he wrote to the Biotechnology Australia Ministers inviting their comments on it. From this date until the draft regulations were released a year later, the Department of the Environment and Heritage held extensive consultations with Biotechnology Australia departments, other agencies within their Ministers' portfolios (for example, CSIRO and Intellectual Property Australia (IPA)[47] in the Industry, Science and Resources portfolio), other interested Australian government departments such as the Department of Foreign Affairs and Trade, and officials of some State and Territory Government departments. Consultations were conducted through a series of meetings between the Access Taskforce and interested agencies, followed by analysis of written comments on the scheme proposed in the Inquiry report. Comments

were also received in response to presentations by Access Taskforce members at the International Marine Biology Conference (Townsville, September 2000) and the annual symposium of the Natural Products Group of the Royal Australian Chemical Institute at the University of New South Wales (Sydney, October 2000). Copies of the report were sent to everyone who had made a submission to the Inquiry, as well as to others who had expressed an interest in its work (this included a Chinese government delegation comprising representatives of national and provincial environment agencies which had met with the Department of the Environment and Heritage and several other organizations involved in access issues during a visit to Australia in August 2000).

Key Australian government agencies were invited to comment, not only on the report, but also on the drafting instructions for the proposed regulations. On 23 July 2001 the Minister sent drafting instructions to his counterparts for comment by early August 2001. Comments on the drafting instructions were reflected in the draft regulations which were released for public comment on 7 September 2001. The Access Taskforce then held further consultations with government, industry, indigenous, and environment stakeholders. There were thirty-eight submissions on the draft regulations, the final one being received in May 2002.

Towards a Nationally Consistent System

For several years before the Inquiry was established, there had been attempts to address the issue of establishing a nationally consistent system of access arrangements for the Australian, State, and Territory governments. The terms of reference for the CSWG (1996) paper had required it to "investigate and report on action required to develop a national approach to access to Australia's biological resources". The CSWG observed that a "national approach", understood as a common system of regulations and permits across Australia controlling access to all biological resources wherever they may occur and whoever owns them, was a position which would be "extremely difficult to achieve, both administratively and politically". It concluded, therefore, that it would be more appropriate to focus on a "nationally *consistent* approach" (my emphasis) which "seeks agreement to broad principles while allowing jurisdictions the freedom to apply those principles in ways which meet their needs and which take into account their existing legislative/regulatory frameworks" (CSWG 1996). The CSWG paper then addressed the benefits of a nationally consistent approach and set out "principles for" and "desirable features" of a nationally consistent access management scheme (CSWG 1996).

Although the terms of reference of the Inquiry did not include consideration of a nationally consistent approach, State and Territory Governments were invited to make submissions and the Inquiry Chair and/or secretariat held meetings with State Government agencies. The Inquiry report reflected the views of the governments of Queensland, South Australia, Victoria, Western Australia, the Australian Capital Territory, and Norfolk Island, concluding that "most States and Territories support a nationally consistent approach" and noting that "some support" had been expressed for the Commonwealth State Working Group, "although this is tempered by concern about a continuing lack of progress" (VOUMARD 2000). The report made three significant recommendations: first, that the Environment Minister endorse the CSWG principles; second, that further consultations be held with State and Territory Governments to address the broader issue of a nationally consistent approach across jurisdictions; and, third, that the Minister review the function of the CSWG and consider steps necessary to increase the involvement of key stakeholders and ensure that any future work done by that body was undertaken with defined outcomes and within agreed timeframes (VOUMARD 2000). In the meantime, as noted above, the National Biotechnology Strategy, released in July 2000, supported the Inquiry report's recommendations by adopting as one of its objectives "the development of measures to enhance access to Australian biological resources" and included as a strategy to achieve this objective: "Work with the States and Territories to achieve nationally consistent regimes on access" (COMMONWEALTH OF AUSTRALIA 2000).

The next significant support for a nationally consistent system (as well as the draft access regulations) came from the report of the House of Representatives Standing Committee on Primary Industries and Regional Services (BAILEY 2001). The terms of reference of the Bailey Report, referred to the Committee by the Minister for Agriculture, Fisheries and Forestry on 4 October 2000, were to

> ...inquire into and report on the following areas, with particular emphasis on the opportunities in rural and regional Australia: the contribution towards the development of high technology knowledge industries based on bioprospecting, bioprocessing and related biotechnologies; impediments to growth of these new industries; the capacity to maximize benefit through intellectual property rights and other mechanisms to support development of these industries in Australia; and the impacts on and benefits to the environment (BAILEY 2001).

The Committee received 39 submissions from organizations such as the Department of the Environment and Heritage and several others, both public and private, which had also made submissions to the Voumard Inquiry.

In discussing a nationally consistent access regime, the Bailey Report observed that the Committee "was told repeatedly of the need to establish a nationally consistent access regime for Australia's biological resources" (BAILEY 2001). It quoted from CSIRO's submission that, as a result of "significant variations in both policy objectives and administrative systems between all jurisdictions", there is a "real risk of intentional bioprospectors 'shopping'

between various jurisdictions to suit their own needs", and it noted the South Australian government's reference to the "frustratingly long time taken to establish policy and the jurisdictional and legislative framework" (BAILEY 2001). The Bailey Report also noted the Inquiry's work on this issue and commented that the "wide-ranging consultative process" planned for the draft regulations was a "useful approach to facilitating the development of nationally consistent arrangements" (BAILEY 2001). Finally, quoting Cerylid Biosciences that "what would be helpful would be to make it easier to know who are the bodies that you need to talk to", the Committee concluded that it was "important to have a single point of information about the arrangements for applying for access permits anywhere in Australia". It added that it was also "important that the permit system be streamlined, for example, with a single permit application acceptable to all jurisdictions and agencies" (BAILEY 2001).

Two recommendations followed: first, that the Department of the Environment and Heritage, "in consultation with state and territory agencies: develop an electronic gateway to information about access arrangements in all jurisdictions and take a lead in coordinating the development of a simplified, streamlined system of applying for permits" and second, that the departments of the Environment and Heritage and Agriculture, Fisheries, and Forestry "give a high priority to finishing the regulations on access to biological resources and the sharing of benefits from them and working with state and territory governments to establish nationally consistent arrangements" (BAILEY 2001).

At the initiative of the South Australian, Queensland, and Australian governments, a conference of Commonwealth, State, and Territory government representatives, was held to discuss work towards a nationally consistent system. The Bio-Access Forum met in Adelaide, South Australia, on 8 November 2001. On 17 December 2001, responsibility for the establishment of a nationally consistent approach to the utilization of genetic and biochemical resources was given to the Land, Water, and Biodiversity Committee established under the aegis of Australia's Natural Resource Management Ministerial Council (NRMMC). The NRMMC, which comprises Australian, State, and Territory government Environment and Agriculture Ministers, was established in June 2001 to promote the sustainable use of Australia's natural resources, replacing ANZECC, which had been responsible for the CSWG (1996) paper discussed above. Thus the Land, Water, and Biodiversity Committee effectively took over responsibility for work commenced, but not completed, by ANZECC on the development of a nationally consistent system of access. Responsibility for this task rested with a joint Australian government/State task group chaired by a senior official of the Australian government Department of the Environment and Heritage. The task group aimed to conclude development of a nationally consistent approach for adoption by the NRMMC at its next meeting in October 2002.

The benefit of this approach was that it placed the management of Australia's extensive genetic resources into the mainstream of significant attempts by Australian governments, particularly since the establishment of the Natural Heritage Trust in 1996, to address the management of the country's natural resources in an integrated manner which acknowledges the seriousness of the threats facing Australia's land, water resources, and biodiversity.

On 11 October 2002 the NRMMC agreed to a set of fourteen principles to underpin the development or review of legislative, administrative, or policy frameworks for a nationally consistent approach in each jurisdiction (NRMMC 2002). In the announcement released by the NRMMC several days later, the Council Chair and Federal Minister for Agriculture, Fisheries, and Forestry, the Hon. Warren Truss, MP, said, "It is our responsibility to ensure that [access to and use of resources] are undertaken in an ecologically sustainable way and that the community shares in the benefits that come from making resources available. Importantly, this approach provides greater certainty to industry and encourages continued investment in biodiscovery research and development. This is a world's first for Australia and it marks us as a desirable location for biodiscovery investment over coming years."

The Government of Queensland was the first state government to release draft legislation for public comment. The release of the exposure draft of the Biodiscovery Bill 2003[48] in mid-2003 for comment by 1 August 2003 followed the release of the Queensland Biodiscovery Policy Discussion Paper in 2002 (QUEENSLAND GOVERNMENT 2002). The Bill is expected to be enacted in 2004. The main purposes of the Bill are to facilitate access by biodiscovery entities to minimal quantities of Queensland's native biological resources for biodiscovery; encourage the development in Queensland of value-added biodiscovery; and ensure that Queensland, for the benefit of all persons in the State, obtains a fair and equitable share in the benefits of the biodiscovery. These purposes are achieved by providing for a regulatory framework for taking and using native biological resources in a sustainable way for biodiscovery; a contractual framework for benefit-sharing agreements; a compliance code and collection protocols; and monitoring and enforcement of compliance with the Bill.

The Bill requires that applications for a collection authority be made to the chief executive of the Queensland Environment Protection Agency (EPA). The collection authority allows the holder to enter and take minimal quantities of stated native biological material for biodiscovery in State land or waters; on private land (with the written consent of the owner); on native title land where there is exclusive possession, if a registered indigenous land use agreement allows the authority to be issued; and from collections held by the Queensland Department of Primary Industries, the Queensland Museum, and the Queensland Herbarium with the organization's written consent.

The Bill also provides that the Queensland Information and Innovation Economy (IIE) Minister may enter into a benefit-sharing agreement with a biodiscovery entity under which the State gives the entity the right to use native biological material or intellectual property derived from that material for biodiscovery if the material was taken from State land or waters under a collection authority or was sourced from that material, and the entity agrees to pay amounts, including royalties, and provide other benefits of biodiscovery.

The EPA chief executive may establish a compliance code for taking native biological material under a collection authority. The code may provide for: minimum standards for taking the material to ensure the sustainability of the State's native biological resources; measures for minimizing the impact of taking the material; and regulating activities (for example, the use of vehicles) in land or waters from where the material is taken. The EPA chief executive may also establish collection protocols for taking particular native biological material under a collection authority; taking native biological material from a particular area; or using a particular collection technique for taking native biological material.

Other issues covered by the Bill include the requirement to keep a register of collection authorities; provision for the IIE Minister to publish a model benefit-sharing agreement; penalties for offenses such as taking material without a collection authority; provision for review of decisions; and definitions of terms such as "minimal quantity". A criticism that has been made of the Bill is that it only requires a benefit-sharing agreement when collections are made in State land or waters. Benefit sharing is not compulsory where collections are made from native title (exclusive possession) or private land.

In December 2002 the Government of Western Australia released a consultation paper, A Biodiversity Conservation Act for Western Australia. The paper stated that the new Act would include a licensing regime for terrestrial bioprospecting activities that will ensure that: biological resources are used in an ecologically sustainable manner and biodiversity is protected; benefits arising from the exploitation of Western Australia's biological resources are shared with the Western Australian community; and Aboriginal people's native title and intellectual property rights are recognized and protected (GOVERNMENT OF WESTERN AUSTRALIA 2002). The paper sought comments by 5 March 2003.

In November 2003, the Department of Conservation and Land Management released a table summarizing comments received on the discussion paper[49] The Department summarized submissions on the issue of bioprospecting as follows:

Many submissions expressed the view that further community consultation is required on the issue of Bioprospecting ...the Act should provide the power for the Minister to make regulations about this matter, and the Government engage the community on how Bioprospecting should be dealt with. A number of submissions commented that provisions and funds for

Bioprospecting under the Act should only be granted for the development and research of Western Australia's native biota. Furthermore, it should be clearly identified on licence agreements that a percentage of wealth generated from Bioprospecting should be used for the protection, management and restoration of WA's biodiversity. Several submissions expressed

general support for the recognition and preservation of indigenous peoples' native title and intellectual property rights. It was suggested that a framework and mechanisms for negotiating benefit-sharing agreements between the State, corporations, academic institutions and indigenous people should be undertaken as part of the development of the Act.

Difficulties and Successes Experienced During the Design of the Draft Regulations

Compared to the lack of concrete progress during the period from 1993 until 1999, progress from the establishment of Biotechnology Australia and the Inquiry in mid-1999 until the release of the draft regulations in September 2001 was creditable. The Inquiry generated many responses, which, in light of the relatively short public consultation period, were reasonably comprehensive, generally relevant to its terms of reference and compared well in terms of quantity and quality to the submissions received by the later House of Representatives committee on Primary industries and Regional Services. The Inquiry also benefited considerably from the varied knowledge and experience of its Chair and reference group members. The Inquiry report (VOUMARD 2000) was well received by key stakeholders and other interested parties, but in some quarters there was a lack of understanding, reflecting, perhaps, that the report was long and the issues it attempted to cover in a fairly short period were many and complex.

Indeed, the Inquiry and subsequent consultations identified many issues which had only been referred to briefly in previous work, for example, environmental issues associated with bioprospecting; indigenous knowledge and intellectual property issues; and the need to harmonize a new access regime with existing schemes (which were either based on other legislation or informal administrative arrangements) at the Australian government level. Other issues had not been not raised at all, for example, native title rights to biological resources. Where the short inquiry period prevented adequate consultations about issues, the Inquiry report recommended, in general, that further research/consultations be undertaken (VOUMARD 2000). This was particularly the case in relation to the harmonization of existing Australian government access arrangements.[50] The proposal for accreditation (although the regulations do not use this term) of access schemes, reflected in the regulation which permits exemptions for specified biological resources, also evolved during consultations following the release of the Voumard report between the Department of the Environment and Heritage and various Australian and State government agencies.[51]

Ownership of Biological Resources

VOUMARD (2000) observed that "...debate about methods of regulating access to biological resources has been complicated by a lack of understanding about who owns the resources in question." As we saw above, the question of

ownership in relation to *ex situ* collections posed some difficulties for the holders of such collections and the Inquiry sought legal advice on this issue. The following advice was part of a longer legal advice, which became Chapter 4 of VOUMARD (2000):

The advice explains the legal status of the elements of the terrestrial and marine biota affected by differing forms of land tenures and sovereignty in Commonwealth areas. The effect of the advice is that in all Commonwealth areas, it is possible to determine either a legal owner of biological resources or a holder of the sovereign authority to control access and derive benefits from the biological resources.

It should be noted, since the question occasionally arose, that ownership under the common law is of particular biological resources, that is, of the physical specimens themselves, not of the particular plants which they represent or the species or genus to which they belong. As a result, the Australian government 's ability, for example, to sell samples of plants to a bioprospector for biodiscovery purposes would not prevent it (or any other owner of the same plants) from selling other samples of the same plants to another person (unless it had agreed with the first bioprospector not to do this).[52] However, the essential point is that neither a holder nor a buyer can claim ownership under the common law in the sense of exclusive rights to a particular plant or to the species or genus to which it belongs. The Inquiry report commented on the need for stakeholders to understand the law regarding ownership of biological resources and stated explicitly that it did not propose to make any recommendations "that would affect the existing ownership arrangements" [53] (VOUMARD 2000).

The Bailey report also considered the ownership issue, commenting that the advice provided in the Inquiry report should be widely available: "It is important that the perception of uncertainty and complexity is dispelled as far as possible as both are deterrents to making agreements about bioprospecting, and investing in it and the industries derived from it" (BAILEY 2001). The Bailey report observed further that "the lack of clarity about ownership applies to areas under state and territory jurisdiction" and that "legislative details vary from state to state", recommending accordingly, that "Biotechnology Australia and the Attorney-General's Department, in conjunction with the state and territory governments, ensure that information about the ownership of biological resources is compiled, and made publicly available as a single, easily accessible source" (BAILEY 2001).

One issue that could, perhaps, benefit from clarification is that raised by the submission from the Center of Indigenous History and the Arts to the inquiry into Indigenous Cultural and Indigenous Property Rights and quoted in JANKE (1998)[54] to the effect that amendments to Western Australian legislation could effectively deprive indigenous people of their potential intellectual property rights and existing use rights (see further, below, under "Indigenous Issues"). Similar comments were made by David Epworth, manager of the Caring for Country Unit of the Balkanu Aboriginal Development Corporation on Cape York with respect to the collecting arrangements between the Queensland Herbarium and AstraZeneca: "[The Herbarium is] actively accelerating their collection program in order to exclude Aboriginal people. In that process they're advantaging pharmaceutical companies at the expense of Aboriginal people." In response, however, the manager of the Herbarium, Gordon Guymer, said that the Herbarium had done extensive vegetation mapping on Cape York, but as far as he knew they had not been collecting on any Aboriginal land. He said that if they were going to do that they would certainly get in contact with the relevant people.[55] In any case, the impact of legislation, policies and agreements on indigenous interests may also be an issue for a nationally consistent scheme to address.

The legal advice also commented briefly on the ownership of intellectual property rights. Since this has been an important issue in debates over access and benefit sharing, particularly for indigenous people, the advice is quoted here in full:

> Prime facie, the intellectual property rights in any processes or products (i.e., patent rights) derived from ex situ collections of biological resources held by Commonwealth agencies will belong to the person responsible for developing [them] (the inventor). [Patents Act 1990 (Cth), s 15 (1) (a)]. This is regardless of the ownership of any resources from which [they] are derived, or where those resources may be held. However, it would be open to a Commonwealth agency to permit access only on the condition that intellectual property rights in any products derived from these resources are vested in a certain way, e.g., jointly with the inventor, the Commonwealth, and a representative of the traditional owners (VOUMARD 2000).

Finally, it should be noted, since this is a controversial and complex issue at the international level, that several submissions raised the issue that Australia's patent laws should not allow patenting of living organisms, whether modified or not.[56] As this issue was outside the Inquiry's terms of reference, however, the Inquiry declined to address it (VOUMARD 2000).

Benefit Sharing

The AIMS submission to the inquiry explained that the lack of benefit-sharing arrangements had resulted in lost opportunities through stalled projects, sometimes after biodiscovery leads had been identified. The reluctance of some marine resources-controlling agencies to grant permits was "over concerns that adequate benefit sharing will not take place, should commercialization of a discovery occur... some agencies have attempted to ... require some downstream benefit negotiations in the event of a commercial discovery. In other cases, access has been delayed, restricted, or denied." The Inquiry supported AIMS' recommendation that benefit sharing be negotiated at the outset of a project, rather than after a lead had been identified, and reflected this in the proposed scheme (VOUMARD 2000). Anecdotal evidence presented to the Access Taskforce in consultations following the completion of the Inquiry suggested that some agencies welcomed the establishment of benefit-sharing mechanisms, particularly where public moneys were being used to support research which could result (and in one case, was known to have resulted) in discoveries with commercial potential.

The Bailey report also addressed this issue: "One of the factors that has complicated and slowed the granting of access to biological resources has been uncertainty on the part of those granting access permits about the benefits that should be required from bioprospectors, should commercial discoveries result" (BAILEY 2001).

Overblown expectations of benefits has also caused some agencies to delay the issue of permits. AIMS reported to the Committee that in some cases delays had amounted to many years (BAILEY 2001). The Committee noted that experience was now being gained in development of benefit-sharing contracts and that the Department of the Environment and Heritage was developing a model benefit-sharing contract. Citing the Inquiry report, the Committee explained the purposes of the model contract: to promote parties' understanding of the issues; to facilitate negotiations and agreement between them; and to provide certainty for industry by ensuring that agreements are based on prior informed consent, mutually agreed terms, and adequate benefit-sharing arrangements, which will in turn provide an agreed set of standards against which industry's performance can be judged (BAILEY 2001).

Another issue which arose in the context of benefit sharing was the need to ensure that both the access scheme and the model contract are sufficiently flexible to allow benefits to be negotiated appropriate to both commercial and noncommercial situations. The Inquiry report related that many submissions, particularly those from research organizations, commented on the importance of access to biological research and of ensuring that an access system does not inhibit research. The Inquiry decided that, in view of the fact that in many cases research will have unforeseen commercial implications or possibilities, this should be considered, as far as possible, at the outset of negotiations and reflected in the contract. It recommended that "...terms in the proposed model contract anticipate that most contracts will be for commercial purposes but that in some cases, terms which reflect noncommercially motivated research purposes may need to be drafted, and benefit sharing negotiated accordingly" (VOUMARD 2000). The Bailey report reflected these concerns in its recommendation that "when finalizing benefit-sharing arrangements, the Australian government ensure that commercial activity is not discouraged by the benefits bioprospectors are required to provide" (BAILEY 2001).

Indigenous Issues

The terms of reference of CSWG (1996) discussed above included the obligation to take into account "the interests of Aboriginal and Torres Strait Islander peoples in the use and ownership of traditional knowledge, innovations, and practices and biological resources on Aboriginal lands". However, CSWG (1996) discussed the issue only briefly, concluding that it was not within its terms of reference to resolve this complex matter, and suggesting that "it was more appropriately dealt with in other fora, because wider policy issues concerning the treatment of indigenous peoples are involved, particularly in the context of reconciliation and social justice".

The issue of the appropriation of indigenous biodiversity knowledge was raised in the report of the inquiry into Australian Indigenous Cultural and Intellectual Property Rights. which found that a major concern of indigenous people was that "...their cultural knowledge of plants, animals and the environment is being used by scientists, medical researchers, nutritionists and pharmaceutical companies for commercial gain, often without their informed consent and without any benefits flowing back to them" (JANKE 1998). Janke related the story of the smokebush, a plant which grows in certain coastal areas of Western Australia and which has traditionally been used by indigenous people of the region for healing. In the 1960s, the Western Australian government granted the USA National Cancer Institute (NCI) a license to collect plants for screening purposes. In the late 1980s scientists at the NCI found that the smokebush contained the active compound conocurvone, which tests showed could destroy the AIDS virus in low concentrations. This "discovery" was subsequently patented. The NCI awarded AMRAD Discovery Technologies (known today as Cerylid Biosciences[57]) an exclusive worldwide license to develop the patent. Under amendments to Western Australian environmental legislation, the Western Australian Minister of the Environment has the power to grant exclusive rights to Western Australian flora and fauna species for research purposes. In the early 1990s, the Western Australia Government also awarded AMRAD the rights to the smokebush species, to develop an anti-AIDS drug. AMRAD paid $1.5 million AUD to secure access to smokebush and related species. If conocurvone is successfully commercialized, the Western Australia Government will recoup royalties of $100 million AUD per year by 2002 (see section "Examples of Access and Benefit-Sharing Agreements in Existing Bioprospecting Projects" for additional details about the smokebush agreement currently implemented by Cerylid).

Intellectual property rights issues for indigenous peoples were put forward by a submission from the Center of Indigenous History and the Arts (University of Western Australia) that was quoted by Janke as follows:

"The current legislation disregards the potential intellectual property rights that indigenous peoples in Western Australia have in flora on their lands. Furthermore, multinational drug companies could be sold exclusive rights to entire species of flora, preventing anyone from using those species for any other purpose without the consent of the companies. Indigenous peoples in WA now face the possibility of being prevented from using any of the flora which is the subject of an exclusive agreement. It is therefore vital that any reform of the intellectual and cultural property laws include provisions for the recognition of Indigenous peoples as the native title owners of all the biological resources of the flora and fauna that are on their lands" (JANKE 1998).

Among the rights which indigenous people want in relation to their cultural and intellectual property, Janke listed: "Control [of] disclosure, dissemination, reproduction, and recording of Indigenous knowledge, ideas, and innovations concerning medicinal plants, biodiversity, and environmental management" (JANKE 1998).

The launch of Janke's report, Our Culture, Our Future (JANKE 1998), in September 1999 coincided nicely with the announcement of the Inquiry (VOUMARD 2000) three months earlier. The terms of reference of the Inquiry stated that "The scheme should particularly focus on the equitable sharing of benefits arising from the utilization of traditional knowledge, innovations and practices" (VOUMARD 2000).

The issue was very critical for the Inquiry because three of the Commonwealth areas under s525 of the EPBCA are owned by indigenous people: Kakadu and Uluru-Kata Tjuta in the Northern Territory and Booderee on the south coast of New South Wales. As national parks, they are significant tourist destinations and could be expected to be of interest to bioprospectors. They are leased to the Director of National Parks and administered by the Department of the Environment and Heritage. The EPBCA provides for joint management, by the Director and a Board of Management, of Commonwealth reserves that consist of, or include, indigenous people's land. A majority of Board members must be indigenous people nominated by the traditional Aboriginal owners if the reserve is wholly or mostly on indigenous people's land.[58] The Boards, in conjunction with the Director, are required to prepare management plans for each of the parks.[59]

The Inquiry report quoted sections from the management plans for Kakadu and Uluru-Kata Tjuta on the rights and roles of the traditional owners in managing biological resources. The Kakadu plan includes sections indicating the importance of continuing traditional use and management of native plants and animals; the need for the Board's approval of applications for commercial activities in the park; plans to develop a strategy for research in the park; and provisions regarding the collection of specimens in the park. The Uluṟu-Kata Tjuṯa plan specifically refers to bioprospecting and states that the owners have important cultural and intellectual property rights that must be respected (Voumard 2000).

In light of these issues, the Inquiry consulted with the park owners and their representatives (in the case of Kakadu, the Northern Land Council, and in the case of Uluṟu-Kata Tjuṯa, the Central Land Council), making two visits to each of the Northern Territory parks and one to Booderee. The Inquiry carefully considered submissions from the owners of Kakadu (prepared in conjunction with the Northern Land Council) and the Central Land Council, reflecting both in some detail in the report, as well as suggestions for a scheme under s 301 of the EPBCA from other interested individuals and organizations. In addition, the Inquiry reflected its awareness of the importance of continuing consultations, recommending, among other things, that the Department of the Environment and Heritage "ensure that traditional owners and their representatives are further consulted on, and given adequate opportunities to contribute to, development of regulations under s 301 of the EPBCA" (Voumard 2000).

Many submissions expressed concern about the use of indigenous knowledge without consultation, prior informed consent, or benefit sharing. These views went beyond the issue of protecting the rights of the traditional owners of the parks in the context of the s 301 regulations (which could be achieved through the access and benefit-sharing arrangements recommended by the Inquiry) and were, in that respect, beyond the Inquiry's terms of reference. Nevertheless, in the knowledge that these are significant and sensitive issues for indigenous people, the Inquiry report summarized them, concluding that "in view of the complexity of these issues, their extension beyond Commonwealth "areas" under the EPBCA, and the fact that discussion about them is relatively recent in the Australian context, the Inquiry believes that further research, consultations with stakeholders, and community education are desirable". Voumard (2000) made four recommendations:

- The Department of the Environment and Heritage should monitor international research and debate by the World Intellectual Property Organization (WIPO), the World Trade Organization (WTO), and other fora on protection of indigenous knowledge, as well as debate and research on the issue in Australia.

- In the event that stronger measures to protect indigenous knowledge are introduced internationally or in Australia, the Department should consider the adequacy of the regulations in protecting indigenous intellectual property rights.

- The issue of protecting indigenous knowledge should be considered further in (but not necessarily limited to) discussions towards developing a nationally consistent system.

- IP AUSTRALIA should consider amending patent law to require proof of source and, where appropriate, prior informed consent, as a prerequisite for granting a patent.[60]

The Department of the Environment and Heritage has continued its involvement in these issues, through its participation in the Australian delegation to the second meeting of the WIPO Intergovernmental Committee on Intellectual Property and Genetic Resources, Traditional Knowledge and Folklore, held in Geneva in December 2001 and its contributions to briefs for meetings of the Committee. The Department has also funded several projects on indigenous knowledge including one by the Nepabunna Community in South Australia, and one by the Kuku Yalanji People Community and the Balkanu Cape York Development Corporation in Far North Queensland, and organized a workshop on indigenous knowledge in Canberra in February 2002, to consider the further implementation of Article 8(j) of the CBD.[61]

The Bailey Committee also addressed the issue of indigenous rights, commenting that "There are two elements to Indigenous involvement in bioprospecting: one is the result of indigenous ownership of the land and the other comes from knowledge of the uses to which native plants and animals can be put" (Bailey 2001). With respect to ownership, the Committee noted that in some parts of Australia significant areas are owned by Aboriginal groups (42% of the Northern Territory and 27% of South Australia) and referred to the recommendations of the Inquiry report regarding prior informed consent, mutually agreed terms, and adequate benefit sharing that protects and values traditional knowledge, as well as to recommendations that decisions by indigenous communities to deny access to bioprospectors should not be reviewable; and that advice be provided to indigenous communities on how to get the best deals possible with bioprospectors (Bailey 2001).

With respect to traditional knowledge, the Committee stated that "There has been some criticism and dispute in the past about the unacknowledged use of traditional knowledge in Australia," and included the example of the Western Australian smokebush (Bailey 2001). The Committee then cited, as an example of continuing criticism, the submission of the Royal Society of Western Australia relating to the contract between the Western Australia government and a company, BioProspect, which the Society claimed appeared not to allow for the recognition of indigenous knowledge. The Committee commented, however, that a national trust fund, such as that BioProspect proposed in its submission, would address this problem, adding that BioProspect does not rely on traditional knowledge to guide its bioprospecting, but prefers to use high throughput screening which is more effective in discovering bioactive materials than using traditional knowledge (BAILEY 2001).

The Inquiry report also commented that the Inquiry's informal discussions with industry suggest that indigenous knowledge is not widely used as a source of information about the potential uses of plants. VOUMARD (2000) stated that:

> One explanation offered for this was that, in the absence of clear and fair rules, companies were generally reluctant to pursue the application of indigenous knowledge to biodiscovery. Companies were concerned that irrespective of the good faith agreements they might make with indigenous groups, they might be vulnerable to criticism about the adequacy of the agreement unless there were independent standards against which they could be judged. The Inquiry also heard comments that, increasingly, the focus of biodiscovery is on microorganisms which industry believes did not play a role in indigenous culture."

Indeed, it is not clear from accounts of the smokebush issue whether indigenous knowledge was actually used to identify the potential healing properties of the plant or whether this was only revealed through screening.

With respect to intellectual property issues, the Bailey Committee acknowledged that Australia's intellectual property regime does not currently protect traditional knowledge, noted some of the difficulties in doing this, and commented that: "What may therefore be needed is a new category of rights that protects traditional knowledge from unauthorized use, recognizes its origin, and provides just compensation. Sui generis methods of intellectual property protection, such as those used for plant varieties, have been recommended in this context"(BAILEY 2001). The Committee noted recent developments (particularly the work of WIPO's Intergovernmental Committee on Intellectual Property) and concluded (without making a specific recommendation) that it "...supports IPA's work in promoting the use of existing intellectual property protection among Australia's indigenous people and assisting WIPO's efforts to provide a more comprehensive system for protecting traditional knowledge" (BAILEY 2001).

In October 2002, the Australian Senate considered amendments to the Plant Breeder's Rights Act 1994, including proposed amendments by Senator John Cherry, a member of the Australian Democrats, a minority Opposition party in the Senate. Addressing the Senate on 21 October 2002, Senator Cherry explained the purpose of the amendments as being to "...reduce the chances of biopiracy from Indigenous land and increase the capacity of the Indigenous community to object when biopiracy is occurring".[62]

However, the amendments did not have Government support. The Parliamentary Secretary to the Minister for Agriculture, Fisheries, and Forestry, Senator Judith Troeth, explained that "The amendments ... are not the subject matter of the bill. In addition, they are not particularly

well considered. They fail to recognize that the ...Act represents world's best practice through its basic principles, that the scope of the Act is limited, that it coexists with other legislation and that the exercise of [plant breeders'] rights is regulated by such legislation."[63] The issue does remain a live one, however, particularly in Queensland, as evidenced by a radio program in which various people, including the Executive Director of the Balkanu Cape York Development Corporation, Gerhardt Pearson, continued to express concern about the lack of opportunities for indigenous people to gain from benefit-sharing agreements and the lack of recognition by the government of the rights of indigenous people to biological resources and traditional knowledge.[64] Their concerns have not, it appears, been allayed by the QUEENSLAND GOVERNMENT (2002), which stated that the Government would ensure that the development of biodiscovery policy in Queensland "engages local indigenous communities, relevant community organizations, and Native Title Representative Bodies to identify methods to address and respect traditional knowledge of Queensland biological resources where such knowledge is used for biodiscovery". It should be noted that Principle 7 of the Nationally Consistent Approach is that legislative, administrative, or policy frameworks in Australian jurisdictions shall "Recognize the need to ensure the use of traditional knowledge is undertaken with the cooperation and approval of the holders of that knowledge and on mutually agreed terms" (NRMMC 2002).

This may be a narrower principle than that which indigenous people appear to be asserting. The fact that the debate continues, however, suggests that there may be a need for a more rigorous attempt to identify and clarify the issues and to develop acceptable solutions.

Exclusivity

Another issue which the Committee noted as being of particular concern in submissions to its inquiry was the question of exclusivity. We have seen, above, concerns quoted in JANKE (1998) about the impact of exclusive rights on the intellectual property rights of indigenous people and on access for other purposes, including traditional uses. The Inquiry report did not address this issue in detail, but did note similar concerns expressed by the Queensland Government and by indigenous people (VOUMARD 2000). It noted that the parties to the contract are free to negotiate "exclusivity" terms in whatever manner they wish and that a range of terms is possible. The Inquiry decided that it was not necessary to make any recommendations on this matter, as the proposed scheme would require the Minister, in deciding whether to grant or refuse a permit, to consider the fairness of "exclusivity" clauses in the contract, among other issues, against the indicia of proper informed consent, mutually agreed terms, and adequate benefit sharing. The report did suggest, however, that terms of a more "exclusive" nature which benefit the bioprospector should be reflected in the nature and/or amount of benefits payable to the resource provider (VOUMARD 2000).

Concerns which the Bailey report discussed included ensuring that arrangements made with commercial operators do not restrict noncommercial activities and do allow reasonable access to other commercial operators. The Committee noted the concerns of some operators, both commercial and noncommercial, that this type of restriction might (or indeed does) occur, and commented that "...care must be taken when setting the permit conditions and making benefit arrangements to ensure that reasonable opportunities are available to all wishing to access a particular area" (BAILEY 2001).

The Committee recommended that when granting access, the Australian Government ensure access for noncommercial activities and, with commercial activities, ensure a balance between open competitive access and restricting access by granting exclusive use. Exclusivity should be restricted by permit conditions such as duration, area or species collected, and uses to be explored (BAILEY 2001).

Criticism of the Proposed Scheme

The Bailey report is a useful source of evidence of criticisms which were made of the proposed access scheme, some of which were variously made in response to the Inquiry report, the drafting instructions for the regulations, and the draft regulations themselves. In particular, the Committee discussed criticisms of the proposed scheme by the Department of Agriculture, Fisheries and Forestry (DAFF). DAFF expressed the following concerns: first, that the proposed regime might alter existing property rights and interfere with intellectual property rights (or at least give that appearance); second, that it might jeopardize Australia's ability to access genetic material from overseas for crop improvement; and, third, that it was too onerous (BAILEY 2001).

With respect to the second point, DAFF claimed that "...while such international developments [the revision of the FAO International Undertaking on Plant Genetic Resources] do not preclude the application of an access and benefit-sharing system in Australia, the need to reconcile any domestic system with such international developments is highly important to avoid having two systems of access and benefit-sharing operating in Australia" (BAILEY 2001). Furthermore, DAFF related that Australia is a "significant net beneficiary" from the current and likely future multilateral system for the exchange of plant genetic resources, and further stated that: "If Australia were to charge for access to public biological material we would not be surprised if other countries were to do the same to us" (BAILEY 2001).

With respect to its third point, DAFF listed the following as "elements of the Voumard recommendations that if adopted could prove onerous and a disincentive to commercial bioprospecting": every interested person registered under s 266A of the EPBCA must be invited to make written submissions about whether a permit should be issued (on environmental grounds) and that these should be taken into account by the Minister in making his decision; the "precautionary principle" must be applied, "where appropriate"; any variations to the model contract must be "acceptable"; a maximum of three years would be set for the validity of an access permit; and the permit may be transferred only with the approval of the Minister (BAILEY 2001).

The key elements of the scheme which DAFF preferred were: a model material transfer agreement (MTA) for access to *in situ* material (and ex situ material in some cases) under Australian government ownership and control; inclusion in the MTA of a flexible benefit-sharing agreement contingent on the material being commercialized (for example, a percentage of the gross profits over the last five years of commercialization); exemptions for benefit sharing considered if the recipient company or institution is prepared to make the developed material publicly available for further research; access to, and benefit sharing of, biological resources on freehold property subject to private negotiation (although the model MTA for Commonwealth areas may serve as a model for the private sector); and encouragement extended to States and Territories to adopt the Australian government approach as a basis to achieve a nationally consistent framework (BAILEY 2001). DAFF also stressed the need for a detailed regulatory impact statement examining the practical impact of any regulations on government, business, and other users (BAILEY 2001). The Bailey report noted some of the responses of the Department of the Environment and Heritage to DAFF's points. In hearings before the Committee, the Department disputed that the scheme of the Inquiry report would replace the common law with new property rights or interfere with intellectual property protection. The Department also stressed that the proposed benefit-sharing arrangements would allow for considerable flexibility in what should be included in contracts (BAILEY 2001).

The Committee also noted that, with respect to the need to accommodate existing international obligations such as the International Undertaking on Plant Genetic Resources, the Inquiry report had recommended that material which is the subject of such agreements be excluded from the regulations. DAFF, however, took the view that this approach would introduce complexity because it would establish "multiple systems covering different biological material" (BAILEY 2001).

The Committee did not discuss these issues further but, in relation to them, recommended that in finalizing the regulations, the Australian government should ensure that the regulations did not create new property rights; should obtain a detailed regulatory impact statement[65]; and should examine fully the implications of the regulations for Australia's access to overseas plant genetic material (BAILEY 2001).

Bioprospecting Initiatives

There is already a history of bioprospecting companies negotiating with government agencies and other institutions for access to biological resources and agreeing to provide benefits. Some major examples of these agreements are outlined below.[66] It would seem unlikely that major bioprospectors would have any difficulties in operating within the terms of the Australian government regulations, in light of their experience in dealing with legislative and/or contractual requirements in other jurisdictions.

Under the draft regulations, the cost of a permit is notional and the same for all applicants (national or international, research or commercial): $50 AUD for access and no payment for a transfer of the permit or variation or revocation of a permit condition.[67] This fee would not even cover administration costs. Benefits, of course, are to be negotiated on a case-by-case basis.

Examples of Access and Benefit-Sharing Agreements in Existing Bioprospecting Projects

AstraZeneca R&D Griffith University

AstraZeneca R&D Griffith University has contracts with the Queensland Museum and the Queensland Herbarium under which the Museum and the Herbarium collect specimens for AstraZeneca's R&D facility located at Griffith University in Brisbane, Queensland. Key terms of these contracts include: payments to the collectors for the samples and a percentage of proceeds from commercial exploitation of compounds obtained from them; agreement by the collectors to keep confidential certain matters relating to samples and supply, while ensuring that essential taxonomic information is placed in a public collection; and the University's exclusive right to the collectors' services (VOUMARD 2000).

Australian Institute of Marine Science

The Australian government established AIMS in 1972 to generate the knowledge needed for the sustainable use and protection of the marine environment through scientific and technological research. For over a decade AIMS' activities have included bioprospecting research. The centerpiece of this research is the marine biodiversity collection which includes material from more than 10,000 marine macro-organisms and 7,500 marine microorganisms collected from over 1,500 sites around Australia (VOUMARD 2000). AIMS has had contracts with organizations such as the NCI and Cerylid.

AIMS' contract with the Queensland government (signed in July 2000) is the only Australian benefit-sharing arrangement whose text has been made public (see Box 1). The context in which it was negotiated was the Queensland government's interest in promoting the biotechnology industry in that state. The contract includes agreement regarding the payment of royalties (if a lead

emerges and AIMS derives net royalty income, AIMS shall pay 1.5% of the net royalty income to the state), but other benefits focus on research and biotechnology development opportunities, particularly in Queensland.[68]

Cerylid

Cerylid has entered into plant collecting contracts with a wide range of collectors: the Royal Botanic Gardens in Melbourne, Victoria, and the Victorian Department of Conservation and Natural Resources; the Parks and Wildlife Commission of the Northern Territory; the Arnhem Land Aboriginal Land Trust and the Northern Land Council; the Tiwi Aboriginal Land Trust; the Tasmanian Herbarium through the Trustees of the Tasmanian Museum; the Government of the State of Sarawak (Malaysia); the Kelam People of the Kaironk Valley in Papua New Guinea, through the Australian National University; and the Tillegerry Habitat Association, New South Wales. Agreements relating to microorganisms have been made with the Antarctic Cooperative Research Center; the Department of Ecology and Biodiversity at the University of Hong Kong; the Australian Tropical Mycology Research Center; Flinders University, South Australia; and Biotech International Limited. Agreements relating to microorganisms and macroorganisms were made with the Australian Institute of Marine Science (VOUMARD 2000).

Cerylid observes the following principles in its plant collecting arrangements: agreements are enacted with relevant government and indigenous authorities; agreements provide for sample/species collection; samples are collected by local botanical authorities; voucher specimens are maintained by local herbaria; agreements are long term and exclusive to the company; intellectual property rights are owned by or assigned to the company; and benefits, either commercial (payments for samples, royalties) or noncommercial (such as training), are provided to the custodians (VOUMARD 2000). Issues relating to the smoke-bush project and agreement were presented earlier in the section "Indigenous Issues." Additional details about the agreement are presented by TEN KATE and LAIRD (1999) as follows: In 1981 a USA botanist collected around 1,200 plant specimens in Western Australia which were then sent to the USA National Institutes of Health for screening. In the late 1980s, a species of smokebush showed promising activity in anti-cancer screens. The Institute obtained a patent on the active compound of the smokebush. At the same time, research by scientists in Western Australia also revealed the potential anti-HIV activity of the smokebush. To ensure that the development and production of any potential drug be based and coordinated in Western Australia, the Department of Conservation and Land Management (CALM) entered into an agreement with the company under which it was granted access to the smokebush and permission to develop it commercially. The company agreed to provide to CALM $370,000 USD, a share in royalties, and the right of first refusal to conduct any research on the active compound. The company also provided $320,000 USD for further research by a consortium of Western Australian scientists, in collaboration with the NCI, on some eight smokebush patents lodged by CALM. Benefit sharing took two forms: research funding (covering joint research and technology acquisition) and a share in royalties. The scientists received $150,000 USD to cover research conducted prior to the agreement that had led to several Western Australia patents on conocurvone. Over the year following the agreement, they received an additional $500,000 USD for further research. Government and university laboratories of consortium members were equipped with various technologies. CALM used the remaining funds to establish the Western Australia Biotic Extract Library, a library of biotic extracts for drug discovery.

BioProspect

BioProspect, a listed Australian company, was established in 1998 in Western Australia. The company negotiates access to biological resources for the purpose of drug discovery, screens plant extracts for a range of therapeutic activities in their laboratory in Perth, Western Australia, and supplies drug discovery companies with samples for further testing. In late 1999, Western Australia's then Environment Minister announced the "commencement of the largest scientific research for new medicines derived from Western Australian flora yet undertaken in Australia". Under this agreement, CALM would collect plant samples from Crown (government-owned) land for BioProspect under a license agreement. The company would pay a fee for each sample provided, as well as a percentage of all revenue earned from other companies seeking access to the

---

Box 1. Summary of the Biotechnology Benefit-Sharing Agreement between AIMS and the State of Queensland (QLD)

Recitals

- AIMS' marine research activities include biodiscovery (or bioprospecting) research whose goals include to discover biologically active molecules that can be developed as useful products by and with industry collaborators.
- AIMS' research has the potential to deliver benefits (both monetary and non-monetary) to QLD.
- When AIMS receives benefits, it seeks to equitably share those benefits with the resource owners.
- QLD is interested in facilitating ecologically sustainable access to and use of its biological resources for biodiscovery purposes; utilizing its biodiversity to facilitate incremental capacity building and value adding in the State's biotechnology industries; and capturing an equitable share of the benefits derived from the use of QLD's resources for biodiscovery purposes.

Purpose and scope of the agreement

- The purpose of the agreement is to set the framework within which AIMS and QLD fairly share in the benefits of biodiscovery research using QLD samples.
- QLD samples are samples obtained from coastal areas determined by the Seas and Submerged Lands Act of 1973 and the Coastal Water (State Titles) Act of 1990.

Duration

- The agreement commences on the date of the agreement and continues until terminated by one or both parties pursuant to the terms of the agreement.

Review

- The agreement is subject to review by both parties after it has been in operation for one year and every two years hereafter, at which time amendments can be negotiated by the parties.
- After 5 years, the operations of AIMS biodiscovery research will be independently reviewed (QLD to choose reviewer, cover costs, and keep information commercial in confidence; AIMS will have access to all information).

Access Arrangements

- AIMS has exclusive right to access QLD samples for its research (this does not extend to the species that are represented by the QLD samples).
- AIMS may collect new QLD samples for the purpose of biodiscovery research, subject to any requirements to obtain permission from the appropriate QLD government agency.
- AIMS has the exclusive right to supply biodiscovery research samples that are QLD samples to third parties for biodiscovery research in which AIMS is a collaborator (third parties may include industrial and/or commercial collaborators in Australia or overseas).
- If AIMS provides QLD samples to third parties, AIMS must ensure that under the third party agreement it is acknowledged that the State is the owner of the resource from which the QLD samples were derived.
- Under a biotechnology benefit-sharing arrangement with QLD, AIMS has the right to access and conduct scientific research on the samples.
- Before attempting to negotiate collaborative agreements with third parties outside Australia, AIMS must use all reasonable endeavors to satisfy the following criteria:
  - Similar collaborative opportunities are not available on reasonable terms, first, in QLD and second, elsewhere in Australia.
  - The option of transferring the technology from overseas, first, to QLD and second elsewhere in Australia, to eliminate the need to send QLD samples overseas is not possible on reasonable terms.
  - The quantity of material sent overseas is restricted to the minimum required for pre-agreed work and the overseas collaborator is required to return any unused material.
  - Data accompanying the material sent overseas will be limited to data reasonably required by the overseas collaborator to achieve the agreed objectives of the collaboration.

samples, and a royalty on the sale of the products derived from the samples. Funds received would be used to boost flora conservation and research. The agreement would not prevent others from applying for permits to collect plants, including those wanting to pick wildflowers commercially, academics wanting to further their research, and Aboriginal people wanting to use plants for medicinal purposes. The company planned to invest about \$40 million AUD over the next five years to equip its screening facilities and to employ scientific and administrative staff.[69]

BioProspect has identified the following as key elements of its contracts: access is on the basis of sustainable access; primary ownership of all intellectual property derived from a biological resource remains in the hands of the state (Western Australia); the state receives royalties from any commercial activity resulting or derived from its biological resources; and whenever possible, the infrastructure and human resources of the state are used to collect, process, and add value to the primary biological resource (VOUMARD 2000).

Biodiversity Conservation, Sustainable Use, and Benefit-Sharing Strategies

As required by its terms of reference, the Inquiry report addressed environmental issues at some length. Many submissions to the Inquiry emphasized the need for environmental assessment to be undertaken before bioprospecting activities could be approved, although only a few presented specific evidence about the possible adverse environmental impacts of bioprospecting (VOUMARD 2000). However, reflecting the current lack of knowledge about much of Australia's biodiversity (marine invertebrate fauna were cited as a specific example), submissions advocated the

need for a "precautionary" approach (VOUMARD 2000).

Possible environmental impacts of bioprospecting were considered by both the Queensland government and AIMS which, as related above, have entered into a major bioprospecting contract (Box 1). The Queensland government's submission said that:

> ...most primary biodiscovery collections involve relatively small samples sizes of less than 100 grams per species and, provided the target species are readily available with a sustainable population in the target area,

---

Box 1. Continued

- AIMS agrees to use reasonable endeavors to ensure any commercial arrangement with a third party complies with the following criteria:
  - Opportunities for intellectual property development are maximized, first, in QLD and second, elsewhere in Australia.
  - Opportunities are captured, first, for QLD and second, for elsewhere in Australia, for re-supply of material for a nominated sample; for full taxonomic consignment for the nominated sample; and for assessment of options for large scale long term supply of material for the nominated sample.
  - An appropriate QLD collaborator, first, or Australian collaborator, second, will share in any patent rights/ terms to leads whose discovery and/or development has involved an overseas party.
  - The share of monetary benefits to be paid to AIMS or another Australian collaborator will be stipulated and fair and commensurate with their input to the process.
  - Development of any leads will recognize QLD's or other parts of Australia's rights as the place of origin.

Benefits
- AIMS will provide an annual report, summarizing its biodiscovery research using QLD samples.
- AIMS will provide appropriate QLD resource management agencies with detailed collection data for new QLD samples.
- Where practical, or where stipulated in a permit or permission, a preserved voucher specimen shall be lodged

with the QLD Museum with collection data and any other information that may contribute to furthering the State's scientific knowledge.
- AIMS shall use its best endeavors to collaborate with the QLD Museum regarding the coordination and lodgment of preserved voucher specimens.
- AIMS shall use its best endeavors to collaborate with appropriate QLD government agencies to maximize the taxonomic and biosystematic research benefits derived from these collections.
- AIMS shall use its best endeavors to collaborate with non-AIMS scientists based in QLD in all aspects of its biodiscovery research relating to QLD samples.
- AIMS shall use reasonable endeavors to inform the appropriate QLD government agencies of any opportunities for biotechnology industry capacity building, value adding, or joint venture investments to allow those opportunities to be captured for the benefit of the State.
- If a lead emerges and AIMS derives net royalty income, AIMS shall pay 1.5 % of the net royalty income to the state (if non-AIMS QLD-based scientists also make intellectual inputs to the discovery of such a lead, AIMS may negotiate a distribution of part of the remaining net royalty income to those scientists and/or their organizations).
  - This clause continues to apply despite the possible termination of the agreement.

Intellectual property – confidential information
- Information provided by AIMS to QLD regarding its research will be AIMS' intellectual property and in some cases AIMS will require the State to hold such information "commercial in confidence."

---

are not considered threatened or endangered and proper collection methods are used, the environmental impact may be minimal. Secondary collections of a specific species, conducted after a lead has been identified, may first require an environmental impact and species distribution analysis to determine the viability and ecological sustainability of the proposed second or any subsequent collection (VOUMARD 2000).

AIMS went further, proposing increasingly stringent requirements depending on the nature of collection (VOUMARD 2000). For primary collections, allowable collection methods and procedures were desirable, which would ensure minimal environmental impact and avoidance of rare species. For medium-scale secondary collection, there should be a requirement for a separate permit as the re-collection would be targeted on a particular organism, noting the option of species-specific environmental assessment. For large-scale collections, there should be full-scale environmental assessment and mandatory concurrent investigation of alternatives such as synthesis or culture for long-term and large-scale supply.

In general, industry submissions did not make detailed comments about environmental issues, but support for conservation and sustainable use was implicit in many comments regarding the need to ensure continuing access to biological resources. To take one example, BioProspect stated that its corporate mission statement was based on the CBD. Key elements which the company insists be included in its contracts are as follows (VOUMARD 2000): access is strictly on the basis of sustainable access and contingent on agreement to collect only the minimal quantity required to satisfy screening for biological activity; all collections are "vouchered" and identified by qualified taxonomists, with voucher specimen libraries maintained by the state, for example, in herbaria or museums; no extract collections of endangered or protected species are ever collected from the wild (collections of protected species only occur if material is sustainably available from cultivated or farmed collections); and any requirement for further material is from cultivated or farmed collections or, in rare circumstances, from proven sustainable collections from natural resources.

The Inquiry report's recommendations for environmental assessment were generally reflected in the resulting draft regulations. However, the major difference between the approach of the report and that of the regulations was the addition in the regulations of the scheme for environment assessment by public notice. In effect, this allows a shorter, less complex approach to environmental assessment in situations where environmental impacts are likely to be more than negligible. This criterion, while not defined in the regulations, would appear to require environmental assessment of a proposed bioprospecting activity which does not reach the EPBCA's threshold for assessment of an action "that has, will have, or is likely to have a significant impact on certain aspects of the environment".[70]

The Inquiry report also recommended that in decid-

ing whether or not to issue an access permit, the Minister consider the precautionary principle and noted that this would require an amendment to section 391 of the EPBCA (VOUMARD 2000). Section 391 of the Act requires the Minister to take account of the precautionary principle in relation to making specified decisions set out in a table under the Act. The Act explains the principle as follows: "lack of full scientific certainty should not be used as a reason for postponing a measure to prevent degradation of the environment where there are threats of serious or irreversible environmental damage". This recommendation was reflected in the draft regulation which requires the Minister to take account of various matters before making a decision to grant a permit, one of which is that "the proposed access will, taking into account the precautionary principle, be ecologically sustainable and consistent with the conservation of Australia's biological diversity".[71] In considering whether this paragraph is satisfied, the Minister "must consider whether the proposed access may adversely affect: a) the conservation status of any species or population, or b) any ecosystem or ecological community".[72]

The Inquiry also considered and made recommendations relating to proposals that would promote further conservation-oriented research. This was in response, for example, to comments by the Queensland government that bioprospecting had significantly enhanced the discovery and documentation of Australia's biodiversity, yet this outcome had not always been a mandatory permitting requirement. A frequently cited example is the results of the agreements between AstraZeneca R&D Griffith University and the Queensland Museum and the Queensland Herbarium. The submission from Professor Quinn, the Director of AstraZeneca R&D Griffith University and the industry representative on the Inquiry's reference group, revealed that collaboration with the Herbarium to date had resulted in the discovery of 37 new plant species; new populations of threatened species in remote areas, providing the genetic material which can be used to propagate the species; records of weed encroachment in native forests which are useful for forest management; and the creation of new distribution records in the Herbarium. Collaboration with the Museum had resulted in the discovery of approximately 1,500 new species and provision of infrastructure to define accurately the distribution of marine sponges in Queensland and adjacent waters; this provided data which will eventually produce taxonomic expertise in these areas and is of great value in further understanding of marine biota (VOUMARD 2000).

To maximize potential scientific outcomes, the Queensland government's submission recommended that there be a strict requirement that representative samples of all taxa obtained from biodiscovery be lodged with a State or Australian government museum accredited by the Convention on International Trade in Endangered Species of Wild Fauna and Flora (CITES) together with collection data and any other information that may contribute to the scientific knowledge of Australian biodiversity (VOUMARD 2000). The Inquiry recommended that the regulations require the parties to the contract (in practice, this would usually be the collecting body) to lodge voucher specimens and information about the collection with a CITES-approved authority in Australia which has facilities for preservation (and further dissemination, when appropriate) of this material (VOUMARD 2000). This recommendation has not been reflected in the draft regulations.

Finally, the Inquiry report recommended that the regulations and the model contract include a requirement that at least some of the benefits under the contract (whether of a monetary or nonmonetary nature) should promote biodiversity conservation in the area covered by the agreement (VOUMARD 2000). This recommendation evolved from suggestions in some submissions, such as that by the Australian Conservation Foundation, that "…perhaps an identified percentage of the monetary benefits gained from the access [could be] placed into an environmental fund, managed by independent trustees, for conservation purposes" (VOUMARD 2000). BioProspect also supported a model where royalty income derived from bioprospecting would reside in a fund and be distributed to protect biodiversity and reward the use of indigenous knowledge for the sustainable development of the biota (VOUMARD 2000).

The Inquiry decided that, given the difficulty of predicting the nature and size of benefits under future contracts and the fact that potential providers of resources had not been consulted on such a proposal (which could affect their share of benefits), a preferable approach was to attempt to ensure that at least some benefits under the contract were used to promote biodiversity in the area covered by the contract (VOUMARD 2000). Such terms are not unknown: for example, CALM used $380,000 USD from its agreement with AMRAD for the conservation of rare and endangered flora and fauna and $190,000 USD for other conservation activities (TEN KATE and LAIRD 1999).

The draft regulations reflect this recommendation by including, among the circumstances the Minister has to consider in deciding whether to grant a permit, that "the Minister believes, on reasonable grounds, that some of the benefits of access will, if practicable, be used for biodiversity conservation in the area from where the relevant biological resources were taken".[73] A regulation along these lines could also be drafted to address the Inquiry's recommendation regarding the lodging of voucher specimens.

The terms of reference of the Bailey report also required it to inquire into and report on "the impacts on and benefits to the environment" of bioprospecting (BAILEY 2001). The Committee acknowledged that bioprospecting can harm the environment, for example, through over collecting (a particular danger in relation to rare and endangered species); the introduction of exotic species and pathogens to habitats visited by collectors; and/or the use of inappropriate collection methods that result in collateral damage to habitats or biota other than those being targeted (BAILEY 2001). The Committee also commented that much bioprospecting involves the collection of only small quantities of material and noted the potential for synthesizing active chemicals found in material, making further collections unnecessary (BAILEY 2001).

The Committee commented that existing legislation in many parts of Australia already addresses negative environmental impacts and is being used or could be used to control bioprospecting, referring to the Victorian approach and to the EPBCA (BAILEY 2001). The Committee also referred to "positive impacts" of bioprospecting, citing, for example, the outcomes of the research referred to above (BAILEY 2001). The Committee mentioned suggestions that voucher specimens and associated information be lodged with museums and herbaria and comments about the potential value of royalties and other payments as a source of revenue for conservation purposes. However, it also acknowledged the view of the Department of the Environment and Heritage that information collected in the course of bioprospecting may make a greater contribution to conservation than any monetary returns (BAILEY 2001).

The Committee concluded its discussion of the environmental issues involved in bioprospecting with the observation that the conservation of biodiversity is fundamental to biodiscovery and to building industries based on these discoveries. Although its terms of reference did not include a requirement to assess the adequacy with which biological resources are being conserved, the report noted evidence regarding the lack of resources for conservation and the lack of protection for some biodiversity and stated its belief that it is essential that state, territory, and Australian government conservation programs comprehensively cover Australia's biodiversity and are adequately funded to maintain it. The Committee recommended that the Department of the Environment and Heritage give a "high priority to continuing its work with state and territory governments to develop a nationally consistent approach to establishing conservation areas that comprehensively cover all species and ecosystems" (BAILEY 2001).

The Department of Agriculture, Fisheries, and Forestry has, in consultation with other interested government agencies (particularly the Department of the Environment and Heritage), prepared a response to the recommendations of the Bailey Committee. The response was submitted to the Committee in September 2002.

The Convention on Biological Diversity (CBD), the Agreement on Trade-Related Aspects of Intellectual Property Rights (TRIPS), and the International Treaty on Plant Genetic Resources for Food and Agriculture (ITPGRFA)

There have been few, if any, sustained and rigorous critiques of Australia's international positions on the relationship among the CBD, TRIPS, and the negotiations which led to the ITPGRFA. This probably reflects the complexity of the issues, as well as the lack of opportunities and resources available to interested parties to develop and express their concerns. Several issues relating to these agreements, particularly with respect to intellectual property and traditional knowledge, remain controversial at the intentional level. The following is a summary of Australia's positions on these agreements.

The CBD and TRIPS

One of the principles of TRIPS is that national laws should provide patent protection to inventions, without discrimination as to the field of technology concerned (Article 27.1).[74] In response to concerns about the patenting of plants and animals, members of the WTO agreed to an optional exception to this principle which provides that members may exclude from patentability "plants and animals and other microorganisms, and essentially biological processes for the production of plants and animals other than non-biological and micro-biological processes" (Article 27.3(b)). Australia, in common with many of its key trading partners, including the United States, Japan, the European Union, and New Zealand, allows for the patenting of plants, microorganisms, and related biological materials, provided that these meet the usual standards of proof for patentability.[75]

Since 1999 a review of this Article has been underway in the TRIPS Council. The Australian government submitted its views in a communication to the TRIPS Council in September 2001.[76] Australia's view is that the review is relatively narrow; that is, it is concerned with the effectiveness of the optional exclusion to patentability. Australia acknowledges, nevertheless, the importance of broader issues related to the provision, such as access to genetic resources and protection of traditional knowledge, and supports the work of WIPO's Intergovernmental Committee on Intellectual Property and Genetic Resources, Traditional Knowledge and Folklore on these issues.

Australia considers that these broader issues would be more appropriately approached under the Article 71.1 review of the implementation of the TRIPS Agreement. One of these issues is the relationship between the Agreement and the CBD (particularly Article 8(j) on the role of indigenous communities in preserving biodiversity, and Article 15 on access to genetic resources). It is Australia's view that these agreements are not in conflict; indeed, if properly managed, the national implementation of the obligations under the two agreements could result in a regime that substantially addresses these concerns. Australia's communication notes that WTO members had proposed the following amendments to Article 27.3(b) to provide additional conditions for patentability: a) the identification of the source of the genetic material; b) the identification of related traditional knowledge used to obtain that material; c) evidence of fair and equitable benefit sharing; and d) evidence of prior informed consent from the government of the traditional community for the exploitation of the subject-matter of the patent.

The communication expresses two reservations about these proposals. The first is that Australia feels that more analysis needs to be undertaken into the most effective way of ensuring that access to material that is subsequently the subject of a patent application was sourced in compliance with the provisions of the CBD. Rather than an amendment to the TRIPS Agreement, more efforts should be made to examine the potential for compatible implementation of both conventions at the level of national legislation and policy-making. It should be noted that the draft access regulations do not impose on the patent system requirements of this nature, which, even if they were to occur, would be more appropriately placed in patent legislation than in environment legislation. They do, however, include provisions requiring prior informed consent fair and equitable benefit sharing, and adequate valuing of indigenous knowledge in the benefit-sharing contract. As noted above, the Inquiry report recommended that IPA consider amending patent law to require proof of source and, where appropriate, prior informed consent, as a prerequisite for granting a patent (VOUMARD 2000). Australia's second reservation relates to the most appropriate location in the Agreement for any amendments: it is suggested that Article 29, which stipulates conditions to be fulfilled by patent applications, may be more suitable than Article 27.

In summary, Australia's position is that a specific amendment to TRIPS should only be considered when a complete survey of the situation has been made (within that context) Australia would support the examination of options for disclosing information about the source of biological material into the patent application process. Following this process, consideration could be given to whether this necessitates an amendment to TRIPS. With respect to possible initiatives at the national and local level to address the problems of protection of biodiversity and indigenous knowledge, Australia's communication outlines the draft access and benefit-sharing regulations, the Bailey report, the report by JANKE (1998) and, with respect to artistic/cultural expression (as distinct from ecological knowledge), eight case studies where the existing intellectual property system has been used to protect traditional knowledge[77].

The International Treaty on Plant Genetic Resources for Food and Agriculture

Australia voted for adoption of the ITPGRFA at the 31st session of the Conference of the UN Food and Agriculture Organization in Rome on 3 November 2001, signed the ITPGRFA on 10 June 2002, and is expected to ratify it. In the course of the long and somewhat tortuous negotiations on the ITPGRFA, Australia was subjected to criticism from some civil organizations, particularly the Rural Advancement Foundation International (RAFI) (now the Action Group on Erosion Technology and Concentration (ETC Group)), for its approach to certain issues in the negotiations, particularly intellectual property issues. In voting for the ITPGRFA, Australia issued a statement[78] to "emphasize certain aspects of [its] position and to avoid any misunderstanding on the possible future implementation of [the] treaty." Australia expressed its belief "in the global need for an effective and workable system of exchange for plant genetic resource for food and agriculture" and its commitment to ensuring "that a workable system, based on the provisions of [the] text, is achieved in practice." Australia emphasized four issues "considered necessary" for the implementation of the ITPGRFA:

- Article 12 3(d) and Article 2 are ambiguous with regard to the scope and application of intellectual property rights by participating countries. Australia considers that 12.3(d) and associated Articles do not impinge on national intellectual property rights laws and polices. Australia will insist on respect in this ITPGRFA for the intellectual property laws of member countries. To do otherwise would undermine this agreement.

- The ITPGRFA cannot and does not change the existing rights and obligations of the contracting parties under other international agreements.

- It will be essential that the material transfer agreements which underpin this ITPGRFA are commercially realistic in order to facilitate and encourage exchange and development of plant genetic resources for food and agriculture for the benefit of all parties.

- It is desirable that the list of crops under the multilateral system be assessed and extended. Exclusion of some important crops has the potential to distort the system of exchange with negative implications for the objectives of the ITPGRFA.[79]

Conclusions

The development of Australia's draft regulations on access and benefit sharing has been a long, complex, and in some respects, controversial process, but it is now close to completion. Initially, progress was assisted by the existence of adequate funds for staff and administrative costs through Biotechnology Australia and support at the political level. However, resource constraints subsequently slowed progress during Australian financial years 2003–03 and 2003–04. This was remedied in mid-2004 with renewed funding from Biotechnology Australia for the next four years. Some amendments to the draft regulations can be expected, based on submissions on them (the relationship between native title legislation and the draft regulations has proved to be particularly complex); the draft model benefit-sharing agreements remain to be completed; and administrative arrangements for handling permit applications and their associated benefit-sharing agreements are being finalized.

With respect to possible lessons for parties and other stakeholders involved in the development and implementation of access and benefit-sharing schemes in the future, it is suggested that providers of biological resources have realistic expectations about potential benefits from agreements and consider focusing on negotiating up-front and in-kind benefits, rather than focusing on potential monetary benefits (this should not, however, exclude agreement over fair and reasonable royalties). Providers should also exercise some caution about the users with which they deal, preferring those which have a good track record as bioprospectors. It is, of course, too early to assess the impact of the regulations, as well that of a nationally consistent system, on access to, and benefit sharing from, biological resources, but there would probably be some value in conducting a review of the system, from the perspective of all parties and stakeholders, two to three years after its establishment.

Acknowledgements

I would like to thank Jacqueline Gellatly, my predecessor on access and benefit-sharing issues, for her dedication to promoting this difficult issue, and Geoff Burton, Director, Access Taskforce (now Genetic Resources Management), for his comments on this chapter. Unless otherwise indicated, the views expressed are mine, not those of the Australian government.

References

ANZECC. 1993. Implementation of and implications of ratification of the Convention on Biological Diversity. Report to First Ministers from the Australian and New Zealand Environment and Conservation Council (ANZECC) in consultation with relevant Ministerial Councils. Canberra, Australia.

ANZECC. 1994. Access to Australia's genetic resources. Round table discussion of the Australian and New Zealand Environment and Conservation Council (ANZECC), 14 March 1994. Canberra, Australia.

BAILEY F. 2001. *Bioprospecting: Discoveries changing the future.* House of Representatives Standing Committee on Primary Industries and Regional Services. Canberra, Australia.

COMMONWEALTH OF AUSTRALIA. 2000. *Australian biotechnology: A national strategy.* Commonwealth Biotechnology Ministerial Council, Australia. URL: http://www.biotechnology.gov.au/library/content_library/BA_Biotech_strategy.pdf.

CSWG. 1996. Managing access to Australia's biological resources: Developing a nationally consistent approach. A discussion paper prepared by the Commonwealth-State Working Group (CSWG) on Access to Australia's Biological Resources. Canberra, Australia. URL: http://www.deh.gov.au/biodiversity/science/access/cswg/index.html.

DEST. 1996. *The national strategy for the conservation of Australia's biological diversity.* Department of the Environment, Sport and Territories (DEST), Australia. URL: http://www.deh.gov.au/biodiversity/publications/strategy/index.html.

DPMC 1994. *Access to Australia's biological resources: A discussion paper.* A paper prepared for the Coordination Committee on Science and Technology. Department of the Prime Minister and Cabinet (DPMC), Office of the Chief Scientist. Australian Government Publishing Service, Canberra, Australia.

ENVIRONMENT AUSTRALIA. 1998. *Australia's national report to the Fourth Conference of the Parties to the Convention on Biological Diversity.* Department of the Environment and Heritage, Australia. URL: http://www.deh.gov.au/biodiversity/publications/national-report/index.html

ENVIRONMENT AUSTRALIA. 2000. *EPBC ACT—Administrative guidelines on significance.* Department of the Environment and Heritage, Australia. URL: http://www.deh.gov.au/epbc/assessmentsapprovals/guidelines/administrative/index.html.

ENVIRONMENT AUSTRALIA. 2001. *National objectives and targets for biodiversity conservation, 2001–2005.* Department of the Environment and Heritage, Australia. URL: http://www.deh.gov.au/biodiversity/publications/objectives/.

GOVERNMENT OF WESTERN AUSTRALIA. 2002. *A Biodiversity Conservation Act for Western Australia, Consultation Paper.* Department of Conservation and Land Management, Western Australia. URL: http://www.calm.wa.gov.au/biocon_act_consult.pdf.

JANKE T. 1998. *Our culture: Our future—Report on Australian indigenous cultural and intellectual property rights.* Australian Institute of Aboriginal and Torres Strait Islander Studies and the Aboriginal and Torres Strait Islander Commission. Canberra, Australia.

NRMMC. 2002. Australia's genetic and biochemical resources—A nationally consistent approach. Resolution 3.23. Annex A. p 100–108 *in* National Resource Management Ministerial Council, Record and Resolutions, Third Meeting, Sydney, 11 October 2002. Australian Government. URL: http://www.mincos.gov.au/pdf/nrmmc_res_03.pdf.

QUEENSLAND GOVERNMENT. 2002. *Queensland Biodiscovery Policy Discussion Paper.* Department of State Development and Innovation, Queensland, Australia.

TEN KATE K. and S. LAIRD. 1999. *The commercial use of biodiversity: Access to genetic resources and benefit-sharing.* Earthscan, London, UK.

VOUMARD J. 2000. *Access to biological resources in Commonwealth areas.* Commonwealth of Australia. Canberra, Australia. URL: http://www.deh.gov.au/biodiversity/science/access/inquiry/pubs/abrca.pdf

Endnotes

[1] Senator the Hon. Robert Hill, "Bioprospecting Regulations Released for Public Comment," 7 September 2001. The Department of Environment and Heritage's homepage on Access to Genetic Resources is at the following address: http://www.ea.gov.au/biodiversity/science/access/index.html.

[2] s 301(1) and (2)(a) - (d).

[3] s 3(1)(a), (b) and (c).

[4] 'Commonwealth areas' are defined at s 525 of the EPBCA.

[5] 'Commonwealth marine area is defined at s 24 of the EPBCA. For an explanation of the legal and constitutional framework of Australia's marine areas (which, as a result of agreements arising from Australia's federal structure, are somewhat complex), see VOUMARD, 2000: 285-287 (Appendix 12).

[6] Regulation 8A.0l.

[7] Regulation 8A.02(1).

[8] Regulation 8A.02(2).

[9] Regulation 8A.02 (3) (d) and (4).

[10] Regulation 8A. 04 (1) (a}-(c).

[11] Regulation 8A.03 – "Meaning of access provider."

[12] s 515(1) and (2). The Secretary is the head of the Department of the Environment and Heritage which administers the EPBCA.

[13] Regulation 8A.05.

[14] Regulation 17.02(2) (g) (i)-(xii).

[15] Regulation 8A.06 (1).

[16] Regulation 8A.06(2).

[17] Regulation 8A.10.

[18] Regulation 8A.08.

[19] Regulation 8A.09(1).

[20] Regulation 8A.09(2) (a) - (e).

[21] Regulation 8A.1l(l) and (2). Each reference to "days" is to "business days" which are defined under s 528 of the EPBCA.

[22] Regulation 8A.12. Regulation 8A.06(4) provides that the Minister may publish in the Gazette a model benefit-sharing agreement as a guide for applicants. At the time of writing several model benefit-sharing agreements were being drafted.

[23] s67 of the EPBCA explains a controlled action as follows: "An action that a person proposes to take is a *controlled action* if the taking of the action by the person without approval under Part 9 [Approval of actions] for the purposes of a provision of Part 3 [Requirements for environmental approvals - Requirements relating to matters of national environmental significance] would be prohibited by the provision. The provision is a *controlling provision* for the action." In other words, controlled actions are subject to assessment and approval in accordance with the Act.

[24] Regulation 8A.13(2).

[25] Regulation 8A.13(3)(a) – (d).

[26] Regulation 8A.14.

[27] Regulation 8A.15.

[28] Regulation 17.03A (l)(a), (b), (c) and (d).

[29] Regulation 17.03A(2)(a).

[30] s343 of the EPBCA explains that the Governor-General (Australia's head of state) can proclaim Commonwealth reserves over areas of land or sea that the Commonwealth owns; or that the Commonwealth or the Director of National Parks leases; or that are in a Commonwealth marine area; or outside Australia that the Commonwealth has international obligations to protect. Examples of reserves (to give some idea of their diversity) are Christmas Island National Park and Conservancy; Norfolk Island National Park and Botanic Garden; the Australian National Botanic Gardens; Royal Australian Navy Weapons Range (Beecroft Peninsula); Great Australian Bight Marine Park (Commonwealth Waters); and Macquarie Island Marine Park.

[31] Regulation 17.03A(3).

[32] Regulation 8A.02(3) (a) (ii).

[33] Regulation 8A.03(1)(j).

[34] Regulation 8A.06(1).

[35] Regulation 8A.06(3).

[36] Regulation 17.03B(2).

[37] Regulation 17.03B(3).

[38] Regulation 17.03B(4).

[39] s 5(1) and (2).

[40] Regulation 8A. 05. Under the Crimes Act 1914, Section 4AA(1) (http://scaletext.law.gov.au/html/pasteact/0/28/0/PA000880.htm), a penalty unit is currently set at $110 AUD. At the rate of exchange at the time of writing, this would be approximately $80 USD.

[41] The government's 2001 election policy re-stated this commitment as follows: "The Coalition government has published draft regulations under the EPBCA dealing with the management of bio-prospecting in Commonwealth areas. The Commonwealth will take into account public comments and introduce final regulations governing bio-prospecting activities in Commonwealth areas."

[42] The reference group members were, respectively, Katherine Wells (formerly of the Environmental Defenders Office, Sydney), Professor Ron Quinn (Director, AstraZeneca R&D, Griffith University, Brisbane, Queensland), Henrietta Marrie, formerly Fourmile (Associate Professor, Centre for Indigenous History and the Arts, University of Western Australia; during the course of the Inquiry, Marrie took up a position with the Secretariat of the Convention on Biological Diversity, Montreal), Sandy McDonald (Partner, McDonald and Associates, Adelaide, South Australia),

and Elizabeth Evans-Illidge, research scientist, the Australian Institute of Marine Science (Townsville, Queensland).

[43] The three parks (and their representatives) are as follows: Kakadu (Northern Land Council) and Uluru-Kata Tjuta (Central Land Council) in the Northern Territory and Booderee on the south coast of New South Wales.

[44] This work was summarized in Chapter 3 (VOUMARD 2000).

[45] The expression "First Ministers" refers to the Australian Prime Minister and to the heads of State and Territory Governments.

[46] These meetings included the Ad hoc Open-ended Working Group on the Implementation of Article 8(j), the Fifth and Sixth Conferences of the Parties (COP 5 and COP 6) to the CBD (Nairobi, May 2000 and The Hague, April, 2002), the second meeting of the Panel of Experts (Montreal, March 2001), the Working Group on Access and Benefit -Sharing (Bonn, October 20001), the WIPO Intergovernmental Committee on Intellectual Property and Genetic Resources, Traditional Knowledge and Folklore, a WIPO regional workshop (Brisbane, June 2001), and meetings associated with the revision of the FAO International Undertaking on Plant Genetic Resources and TRIPS.

[47] IPA is the agency responsible for patents, designs and trademarks.

[48] See http://www.sd.qld.gov.au/innovation/biotechnology/downloads/biodiscovery_fs.pdf.

[49] See http://www.naturebase.net/biocon_act_pubsubs_summary.pdf and http://www.naturebase.net/biocon_act_pubsubs.pdf.

[50] See Chapter 8 of VOUMARD (2000).

[51] Regulation 8A. 04(1) (a) and (b).

[52] This raises issues of "exclusivity" which are discussed further below.

[53] The legal advice commented that: "The Commonwealth has not legislated to vest property in itself in the biological resources in [Commonwealth-owned land]."

[54] The report was researched and written by Terry Janke, at the time a solicitor and principal consultant of Michael Frankel & Company, under contract with the Australian Institute of Aboriginal and Torres Strait Islander Studies, and funded by the Aboriginal and Torres Strait Islander Commission.

[55] The full text of these interviews which were a part of a radio documentary about bioprospecting can be found at http://www.abc.net.au/rn/talks/bbing/stories/s303991.htm (Background Briefing: Bioprospecting in Queensland: Oceans of Opportunity, Forests of Concern, 27 May 2001).

[56] See, for example, the submission from the GeneEthics Network in association with the Gunggalidda Association, Doomadgee Aboriginal Community, Queensland, and evidence presented (by telephone) to the Inquiry hearing on 30 May 2000.

[57] Cerylid Biosciences, an Australian biotechnology company, located in Melbourne, Victoria was formerly known as ExGenix and before that as AMRAD Discovery Technologies. See http://www.cerylid.com.au/.

[58] s 374 EPBCA.

[59] s 376 EPBCA.

[60] IP Australia has not specifically taken up this invitation; however, interested agencies, including IP Australia, are currently closely monitoring the work of the WIPO Intergovernmental Committee on Intellectual Property and Genetic Resources, Traditional Knowledge and Folklore, which is examining a range of options for the protection of traditional knowledge through intellectual property systems.

[61] The review of *The national strategy for the conservation of Australia's biological diversity* (DEST 1996) identified as "not achieved" Objective 1.8: "Recognize and ensure the continuity of the contribution of the ethnobiological knowledge of Australia's

indigenous peoples to the conservation of Australia's biological diversity." The *National objectives and targets for biodiversity conservation 2001–2005* (ENVIRONMENT AUSTRALIA 2001) identified the maintenance and recording of ethnobiological knowledge as a key action to mitigate threats [to biodiversity] with the objective: "Ensure indigenous communities have access to resources to enable them to preserve their ethnobiological knowledge about biodiversity conservation." The government's 2001 election policy states that it will: "Work with traditional Aboriginal owners to record indigenous knowledge and use it to inform better land management procedures" and "in co-operation with indigenous people, work with state and territory governments to establish mechanisms to facilitate the inter- generational transfer of indigenous knowledge and identify high priority regions for research."

[62] http://parlinfoweb.aph.gov.au/piweb/repository/chamber/hansards/linked/2037-2.pdf.

[63] Id.

[64] http://www.abc.net.au/rn/talks/bbing/stories/s701553.htm. (Background Briefing: Plundering the Plants, 13 October 2002).

[65] Government regulators in all Australian government departments, agencies, statutory authorities, and boards are required to prepare Regulation Impact Statements (RISs). For further information about these requirements, see http://www.opc.gov.au/.

[66] It should be noted that there does not exist a great deal of publicly available information about these contracts. What is provided here is based on companies' submissions to the Voumard and/or Bailey Inquiries and on their websites.

[67] Paragraph 17.01(aa). At the current rate of exchange, the cost of a

permit would be about $36.50 USD.

[68] AIMS provided the Voumard Inquiry with a copy of the contract (See http://www.aims.gov.au/pages/about/corporate/bsa-aims-qldgov.html). A summary of the contract is presented in Box 1.

[69] This information is based on information on BioProspect's website which has been removed since the website was redesigned. See also http://www.bioprospect.com.

[70] S I I EPBCA.

[71] Regulation 17.03A(3)(f).

[72] Regulation 17.03A (4) (a) and (b).

[73] Regulation 17.03A(3) (c).

[74] See http://www.wto.org/english/tratop_e/trips_e/intel2_e.htm for additional information about TRIPS.

[75] For further information about the law relating to the patenting of plants, microorganisms, and related biological materials, see IP Australia's website at http://www.ipaustralia.gov.au/.

[76] See the website of the Department of Foreign Affairs and Trade at http://www.dfat.gov.au/ip/biotech.html.

[77] The case studies are at http://www.wipo.int/tk/en/studies/cultural/minding-culture/studies/finalstudy.pdf.

[78] Australian Statement on the ITPGRFA, Explanation of Vote, Rome, 3 November 2001.

[79] Australian Statement on the ITPGRFA, Explanation of Vote, Rome, 3 November 2001.

10

Chile: Early Attempts to Develop Access and Benefit-Sharing Regulations

Luis Flores-Mimiça and Dominique Hervé-Espejo

Since the entry into force of the Convention on Biological Diversity (CBD), many countries have begun to develop national biodiversity strategies and access regulations pursuant to the requirements in its Articles 6 and 15, specifically to regulate the access to genetic resources within their national jurisdiction. Their experience is very valuable for those countries that are just about to initiate the process. As a part of a comparative study of the policies and laws in charge of regulating the access and the exchange of genetic resources among Pacific Rim Countries, the main objective of this document is to review and analyze the situation of Chile on this matter.

As will be explained in this document, Chile does not have any kind of specific framework for regulating access and benefit-sharing issues, nor is it engaged in a serious process for developing such laws or policies. In 1994, shortly after Chile's ratification of the CBD, there was a brief initiative to regulate this matter, prompted by the political impact that some bioprospecting projects had on the environmental authorities of the time. In the long run, there were no significant results from this initiative. This failure was due, in considerable part, to the complexity of the subject and the many difficulties that the development and implementation of such an initiative has, but overall it was the result of a lack of political will among legislative and higher-ranked administrative authorities to consider this a matter of importance for the country.

Given the total lack of policies and legislation on the matter, in order to make an adequate analysis of the current situation in Chile in relation to the actual exchange, handling, and utilization of genetic resources and its eventual regulation by State authorities, throughout this paper the main related principles, rules, and concepts of the CBD will be used as a reference and as a means of confronting Chilean reality. With that perspective, the paper will present an overview of the actual institutional management of genetic resources in Chile, analyzing the questions of property, access, intellectual property rights, and bioprospecting agreements, concluding with some remarks about the process of developing a regulatory framework on access and benefit sharing.

Analysis of the Legal, Institutional, and Political Situation of Genetic Resources in Chile

The international legal framework of access and benefit sharing established by the CBD can give countries the opportunity to make substantial profits from the sustainable utilization of their own genetic resources, through a fair and equitable sharing of the benefits arising out of the use of such resources. Nevertheless, national governments must know how to take advantage of this opportunity, establishing some type of legislation to regulate the access and benefit sharing of their own genetic resources and, equally important, developing political awareness, institutional strategies, procedures, and capacities to implement these provisions.

The regulatory system created by the CBD should also be seen as a very useful mechanism of negotiation for those countries that are providers of genetic resources, although it has to be adapted to local circumstances and to national interests and priorities in order to achieve its goals. The manner in which countries approach this matter and finally enact a legal regime of access to their genetic resources will necessarily reflect the status of their economic, environmental, and technological development, as well as their legal, institutional, economic, and cultural situation. There is no ideal model to be followed, because each country has its own reality and is placed in a very singular position.

Thus, there are many alternatives by which the mechanism of access and benefit sharing formulated by the CBD can be set into practice in the particular scope of national legislation. However, according to the regulatory experience that already exists, from a formal point of view it would be possible to identify three basic ways to deal with the subject (CONAMA 1995):

- The Legal Approach, through measures that involve the development, implementation, and enforcement of legal, administrative, and policy provisions and frameworks. National governments are able to exert their authority through a variety of alternatives: taking advantage of general laws on environment; using framework laws; developing specific laws to regulate access and distribution of benefits or regulating genetic resources as a singular component of legislation of broader range; and adapting or modifying existing laws and regulations, etc.

- The Contractual Approach, by means of private arrangements or agreements directly made between the suppliers of genetic resources and those interested in using them. These private arrangements or contracts are essentially legally enforceable agreements between two or more parties, consisting of exchanges of negotiated promises or actions, set under the rules of national or international private law, generally made between stakeholders considering mutual benefits on access and distribution. There are multiple contractual alternatives for the exchange of genetic resources, from simple contracts to letters of understanding, licensing agreements, and many others. In the case of the exchange of biological samples, such agreements are usually known as Material Transfer Agreements (MTAS). These MTAS were the first formula through which the question of access to genetic resources and benefit sharing was ever approached.

- The Voluntary Approach, by means of codes of conduct or voluntary guidelines, generally elaborated as the result of a consensus among stakeholders or developed by someone with such authority. These regulatory instruments are not legally enforceable and their fulfillment and utility depend on the good will of those who are parties to the matter.

These different approaches can have advantages and

disadvantages that will, of course, be determined by the particular circumstances of each country. They differ from each other in a series of formal aspects that are applicable to many different situations. However, all these formal approaches can coexist without problems within the same internal legal framework. For example, a law that regulates access to genetic resources (the legal approach) can clearly establish that certain matters should be directly negotiated between the stakeholders, according to the rules of the private law (the contractual approach) but considering the guidelines designed by the competent authority (the voluntary approach).

So far, in all those countries in which the system of access and benefit sharing established by CBD has not yet been implemented, private agreements have been the main mechanism to regulate access to genetic resources and the way benefits are shared (the contractual approach). Such is the current situation in Chile, where political authorities have not yet been able to begin a serious legislative process for the implementation and enforcement of the rules and principles of the CBD, and the administrative authorities do not have a legal framework nor any specific provision to enable them to regulate the exchange and utilization of genetic resources.

The Political and Legislative Management of Genetic Resources

First of all, it is very important to point out that in Chile there are many endemic species (as many in flora and fauna as in microorganisms) that are broadly distributed in the national territory. A considerable number of these species have not yet been properly studied and remains almost unknown (UNIVERSIDAD DE CHILE 2000). In addition, in Chile there exists a considerable scientific and technological capacity to carry out projects of research and development in the area of biotechnology, which adds important value to Chilean genetic resources. This scientific and technological capacity is mainly placed within the scope of universities and the public sector (GIL and IRARRÁZABAL 1997).[1] All of these factors have made Chile a very attractive place for bioprospecting projects.

In spite of the above-mentioned, in Chile there has not been a parallel institutional and legislative development, with specific policies and laws established to regulate access to national genetic resources. Unfortunately, the complexity of the subject and the lack of political will have determined the complete absence of any kind of regulation. Chile does not have an official policy or a national strategy to confront any of the multiple subject areas of the utilization of genetic resources. Even though the CBD is a national law, the government and the political authorities have not yet given much significance either to this matter or to other important aspects of biological diversity. The situation is such that after more than nine years Chile has just completed its National Biodiversity Strategy and has initiated (mid-2004) its National Biodiverity Action Plan for the conservation and sustainable use of its biological diversity, nor has it fulfilled many of the obligations acquired when it ratified the CBD.

Since the date in which the CBD finally entered into force in Chile[2], the National Commission of the Environment (CONAMA) and the Ministry of Agriculture (through its different departments and offices) have been the two governmental institutions mainly responsible for the implementation of the different provisions of the CBD. Even though CONAMA has the general institutional task of coordinating the action of all the public entities with environmental responsibilities, in Chile the administrative authority that specifically manages the several components of national biological diversity is dispersed among a variety of institutions; in addition, these components are more often handled under the ideological conception of "natural resources" rather than of biodiversity. Furthermore, among the regulations related to the subject there are many cases of overlapping principles and provisions, which cause considerable confusion and, in the particular circumstance of genetic resources, an almost total lack of institutional definitions.

In fact, though it could be said that the corresponding articles of the CBD constitute the only legislation for access and benefit sharing that there is in Chile, it is a useless regulation, because it has not yet been properly implemented in the internal legal framework. This means that even though the basic rules exist, they are neither applicable nor enforceable. This situation has occurred because there are no authorities with specific responsibilities on this particular matter nor there is a mechanism to allow the rules and principles of the CBD to operate at the national level. So far, the only effective rules that regulate the exchange and the utilization of genetic resources in Chile are private arrangements, made under civil law, between stakeholders, upon whom the principles and provisions of the CBD can not be legally imposed, because of the lack of competent authorities and of an adequate national regulation.

Indeed, the implementation of an international legal instrument within a national legal regime cannot be made by the direct incorporation of its rules to the national legislation through a simple administrative or legislative act. Implementation should be a much more complex process. In fact, the success of such a process is essentially determined by the feasibility of the international rules to actually operate in an efficient and effective way at the internal level. On the other hand, the way in which the national implementation of international treaties takes place is widely determined by the degree of evolution of the internal legal and institutional framework. To carry out an effective and efficient process of implementation the internal legislative regime would, at a minimum, have to:

- Define and determine certain principles, objectives, priorities, and goals in relation to the matter.

- Impose certain obligations upon the authorities and the citizens of the country in relation to the provisions of the international treaty at issue.

- Prevent possible conflicts between the regulations in force and the provisions of the international treaty and, if necessary, create a mechanism to solve such legal conflicts.

- Establish an institutional structure to fulfill the previously determined objectives and goals, unless an existing structure is already sufficient.

Finally, for a national legislative regime to be really suitable for implementation, besides the fulfillment of the minimum conditions previously indicated, a serious and detailed assessment of the national legislation already in force should be made, and a national plan, capable of covering general and specific aspects of the matter, should be elaborated (with the purpose of fulfilling the particular principles and objectives of the international treaty at issue).[3]

So far, in relation to the CBD, and specifically in the area of genetic resources, none of the above has been done in a systematic and considered way by competent Chilean authorities.

What then has been the local evolution on the subject of genetic resources? As mentioned before, shortly after Chile's ratification of the CBD, there was a significant effort to start a process for developing a national legislation on access and benefit sharing. This initiative was mainly conducted by the Department of Natural Resources of CONAMA, which tried to coordinate the different national authorities that could eventually have some relation to the subject. After some internal debate, a working group was created with the participation of officials of CONAMA, the different departments and offices of the Ministry of Agriculture (Agricultural Studies and Policies Office (ODEPA), the Agriculture and Livestock Service (SAG), the National Institute for Agriculture Research (INIA), and the National Forestry Corporation (CONAF)), and the Ministries of National Goods and Foreign Affairs.

Besides taking the first steps to initiate the national debate on access and benefit sharing, one of the main efforts of the governmental working group on genetic resources was to try to identify the bioprospecting projects that were currently going on in Chile and interviewing those in charge of such projects. In fact, the presence of international institutions that, directly or through national universities, were carrying out such initiatives in Chile was one of the factors that provoked the interest of environmental authorities, making them aware of the need to implement the provisions of the CBD on access and benefit sharing of genetic resources in Chile.

In 1995, a couple of public seminars were conducted by the environmental authorities in order to generate national awareness on the subject. In the same year, an administrative agreement between the Ministry of Agriculture and INIA was signed, with the purpose of creating a National Program for Plant Genetic Resources. In 1996, after an internal institutional workshop organized by CONAMA and the Ministry of Agriculture, a National Commission on

Genetic Resources was informally created. The formation of this commission never had a supporting legal provision and its constitution was based only on an agreement among public officials. The work of this commission never gave any significant results. In less than a year, after two or three meetings, it vanished.

Throughout 1996 and 1997, a couple of consultants were hired by CONAMA in order to analyze the national legislative situation and propose ways of developing a national regulation for genetic resources. After some internal debate, it was concluded that the only way to initiate legislation capable of enabling the governmental authorities to manage the exchange and utilization of genetic resources in Chile was by confronting the question of ownership of genetic resources, through some legislative changes in the property regime.

This conclusion turned out to be the main obstacle for continuing with the regulating efforts of the time. This occurred because in the Chilean Constitution the property regime gives very strong protection to private property, and in order to make any kind of change to such a regime, it would be necessary to have a special quorum in the National Congress (CONAMA 1997). Some efforts were made by the relevant administrative authorities to explain to congressmen the importance of this subject and of its regulation, in order to take the first steps in the process of developing a national access and benefit-sharing framework. Unfortunately, the issue was not really understood and the political authorities of the country never considered it important.

By the end of 1997, most of the officials who were originally actively involved in this process had left their positions in the public sector, and the current political and administrative authorities were not worried about bioprospecting projects going on in Chile anymore. So, the process started to lose the momentum it had previously had.

Since 1998, CONAMA had not been directly involved in any significant activity related to this subject until the end of 2001, when the issue was considered again by the Department of Natural Resources.[4] At the Ministry of Agriculture, efforts on the subject continue, on a much smaller scale; they are mainly carried out by ODEPA, but the political importance originally assigned to this matter by the Ministry has been lost. Nevertheless, the Ministry is the only authority that has been permanently working on this issue by studying a way to solve the legislative obstacles related to ownership of genetic resources and by developing a ministerial policy regarding the protection and economical valuation of national genetic resources (AGÜERO 2000). In late 2003, the Ministry completed a first draft of a legislative proposal regarding access to and sharing of benefits derived from agricultural genetic resources, but it was discarded after being criticized by some sectors. However, since efforts to develop a better proposal continues, it is important to discuss some of its main elements which are:

- Its scope of application is limited to agricultural genetic resources.
- It is a stand-alone and brief piece of legislation which only establishes the basic framework of the access system and the obligation to inform the Ministry of any bioprospecting project.

A future proposal will therefore need further elaboration and the enactment of administrative regulations to determine, for example: a) the authority that would sign the agreements in the name of the Ministry; b) the kind and contents of the access agreements; c) the information required; d) the way in which benefits will be shared, and; e) the way in which traditional knowledge will be protected. This proposal is currently being discussed inside the government, but there is no public discussion nor information about when it will be sent to the National Congress.

It can be argued that the original initiative to start a process of developing a national regulation for access and benefit sharing in Chile was aborted at a very early stage. It was never based on a real national policy for biodiversity, and its beginning was essentially determined by circumstantial facts, such as governmental concern about bioprospecting projects going on in Chile at the time and the need to fulfill the obligations acquired by Chile when ratifying the CBD. The current initiative promoted by the Ministry of Agriculture lacks the support of a national policy for biodiversity which would allow the discussion and adoption of a regulation on this matter based on a serious commitment of the government and a broad acceptance by the different stakeholders.

Finally, concerning the FAO International Treaty on Plant Genetic Resources, in March 2002 the Ministry of Agriculture started a process of consultation and analysis within the public sector, in order to determine the consequences and benefits that signature and ratification may have for Chile. After a few months of discussions Chile signed the FAO Treaty on 4 November 2002.

The Ownership of Genetic Resources

The CBD makes no reference to ownership of land or genetic resources, dealing only with access to genetic resources and sovereign rights over natural resources. Questions of ownership and tenure inevitably have an important bearing on the practicalities of bioprospecting and are an important element of national legislation and policy that governments can use to "determine access" to resources, yet they are often overlooked by policy-makers. Users of genetic resources must be sure that the supplier has the authority to collect and provide such resources, or the CBD requirements would not be fulfilled. Such authority may rest not only with the government but also with those who have private rights or tenure over the land or resources. Because of this, at a certain point, governmental authorities may have to clarify the relationship between the ownership, tenure, and access regimes.

The international recognition of sovereign rights over genetic resources within national territory constitutes the foundation and the theoretical framework over which each State has the responsibility to specify its own legal regime, in order to establish concrete and specific rights, over concrete and specific resources. This international recognition only means that the State, by virtue of its sovereignty, has the legitimate right to "define and determine" the type and the modalities of property that are recognized, according to the principles and rules of its internal legal framework and in harmony with the international commitments that it has acquired. As with the legal framework for access, the different possibilities through which the sovereign power of a State can determine the property regime for genetic resources are multiple and diverse.

In order to enact and implement a particular legislation, one of the first tasks is to define the object that will be regulated and the ownership of the rights attributable to this object, particularly property rights. The determination of a specific property regime requires a clear identification of the goods to which it refers and of the rules and principles according to which it will be structured. In the case of genetic resources, this subject is new, extremely complex, and, in most countries, has still not been seriously confronted.

Today, private property prevails in the majority of the legal systems of the world. However, there are certain resources that are considered of such value for national interests that its ownership is left in the hands of the State. Other resources, however, are placed under the regime of private property and will belong to individuals or to the State, according to the rules and principles of the applicable legislation. Thus, nations usually retain certain goods under their control as public property (for example, in some countries mining resources are State-owned) and, in addition, they may maintain ownership of some goods as private property. Public property can be declared with respect to individualized and quantified goods, or with respect to an undetermined amount of resources belonging to a certain category. Such is the case, for example, in the public property established over waters or oil reserves.

Considering all that has been already said, it must be held in mind that both the definition and the implementation of a property regime (public or private) or other types of rights, in relation to genetic resources, are limited by the intrinsic nature of such resources. For any property regime on such resources to be effective, the subject to which it refers and the type of rights that are going to be granted must be defined in a suitable way. In the first place, it is necessary to establish a distinction between rights on the physical entities (the physical property or plant-animal) and the eventual rights on the genetic information contained in such entities (intangible property). The real value of genetic resources lies in the second element, and the legal questions that arise in relation to it are particularly complex.

In order to know how Chile interprets the legal definition of genetic resources, it is necessary to identify the legal provisions that, directly or indirectly, regulate the subject. The only definition of genetic resources that exists in the Chilean legal regime is in Article 2 of the CBD, which, in the absence of any other legal provision, determines the conceptual framework of the regulated object. With regard to attributing ownership or tenure to genetic resources, it is necessary, in the first place, to identify and analyze the general provisions of the property regime in the national legal framework and then to check if they are applicable to the objects that are legally conceptualized as genetic resources. If there is not such an express provision by extension the applicable provisions will be those that regulate the property of the biological resources which contain the genetic resources (CONAMA 1995).[5]

The Political Constitution of the Republic lacks all explicit reference to biological diversity or some of its elements; neither does it refer to it through other concepts, such as flora and fauna or plants and animals. It only alludes indirectly to these realities, when imposing on the State the constitutional duty of "maintaining for the preservation of nature", when determining that by law it will be possible to establish specific restrictions on the exercise of certain rights or liberties in order to "protect the environment" (Article 19, Number 8); and when indicating that a fundamental concept of the social function of property is "the conservation of the environmental patrimony" (Article 19, Number 24). In addition, the Constitution establishes "the freedom to acquire the ownership of all types of goods", with the single exception of "those that nature has made common to all men or should belong to the Nation and that the legislation has thus declared" (Article 19, Number 23). This provision, besides being a constitutional guarantee, establishes the freedom to acquire all types of goods as the general rule of the Chilean legal property regime. Under this provision, the possibility of acquiring property of any type of biological resource is totally granted (in conformity with the provisions of the Civil Law on goods and acquisition of ownership), unless a Law of Higher Quorum, when it is demanded by the national interest, establishes special requirements or limitations to the acquisition of the ownership of such goods.

The Constitution sets forth general rules for structuring the national property regime, but it is the law's responsibility to specify the particular regime of property applicable to specific goods and to establish the ways to acquire ownership. Therefore, it is necessary to review the pertinent provisions of the Civil Law.

The few references in the Civil Code to biological resources are made according to obsolete conceptual categories that have nothing to do with biological diversity. In relation to those biological resources that can be included in the concept of fauna, the Civil Code establishes that domestic animals are linked to the land they serve and that wild fauna such as fish, birds, and others are considered freely acquirable goods, in the condition of *res nullius*.[6] In relation to those biological resources that can be included in the concept of flora, the Civil Code considers that they follow the ownership of the land in which they are located. Given the fact that under the Chilean property regime there are no lands without an owner, the different biological resources associated with flora will be the property of the individual owners of the respective land or, in their absence, of the State of Chile. In relation to microorganisms (fundamental raw material of the biotechnological industry), national legislation has not established any type of provision for regulating their ownership regime.

This is the general legal framework that regulates the property of biological resources in Chile. There are other laws and regulations that deal with questions relative to the "handling" of biological resources, but they do not alter or modify the general regime of property established by the provisions described before.[7]

Evidently, in Chile's legal framework on property there is no particular and differentiated regime to regulate the question of ownership of genetic resources. Genetic resources constitute a new legal object, still not recognized by the legislature, and their ownership is not specifically regulated by any particular regime. Therefore, we can assume that, considering the nature of genetic material and the legal principle indicating that the accessory follows the principal or main thing, in Chile genetic resources are placed under the property regime applicable to biological resources, such as animals and plants.

The Regime of Access to Genetic and Biological Resources

The ratification of the CBD brings with it obligations that can be difficult to implement and that require profound changes in the internal legal framework. Article 15 of the CBD defines the obligations and rights of the Member Parties with respect to access to genetic resources and their subsequent use. These obligations and rights are based on the following principles and fundamental rules:

- National sovereignty over genetic resources and, as a consequence, the full authority of national jurisdiction to regulate access to such resources;

- Access to resources subject to the prior informed consent of the supplying nations; and

- Access to resources subject to mutually agreed terms and conditions that will define, in a concrete and specific way, the manner in which the sharing of the benefits will be carried out.

Two issues are basic for the development and implementation of a system of access in Chile:

- Determining the competent authority or authorities in charge of access to domestic genetic resources (competent national authority), and, secondly,

- Identifying the provisions regulating the way in which the access procedure should be carried out.

In addition, an analysis of the provisions charged with attributing competencies and establishing rules for access will allow the identification of interests and objectives of an eventual national policy regarding the matter in question.

As noted before, under current legislation Chile does not have a regulation directly establishing the competent authority regarding access to genetic resources. Indeed, genetic resources are not treated as such by any law, apart from the mandates established by the CBD. Nevertheless, taking into account the legal framework applicable to biological resources, there are several public institutions that could potentially serve as the competent authority regarding certain aspects related to access. These are: the Ministry of Agriculture (through INIA, CONAF, SAG, and ODEPA); the Ministry of Economy (through the Fishing Undersecretariat, the National Fishing Board (SERNAPESCA); and the Forestry Institute); the Ministry of National Goods; the National Commission on Scientific and Technological Research; CONAMA; and the National Corporation on Indigenous Development (CONADI).

Chile does not have any authorities with a specific and exclusive competency in genetic resources; nor does it have any particular regulation concerning access to such resources. In practice, as is the case of property, the only mechanism that might come near to fulfilling such a role are the legal provisions charged with regulating access to biological resources.

Access to biological resources found in fauna
Chile's legal structures generally define the components of fauna as *res nullius*, that is, as a good that does not belong to anyone. This legal situation allows the state to establish, via the corresponding mechanisms, certain restrictions to the access to these biological resources. In order to review the mechanisms we will distinguish between nonwild fauna, wild fauna, and hydrobiological species.

Access to faunal biological resources not included in the wild fauna category only requires the authorization of the owner of the land and specimen. In contrast access to biological resources found in wild fauna species, where such access necessarily requires the species' capture or hunt, will always need, in accordance with the Hunting Law, a hunting permit or license.[8]. This permit or license is also required for owners of estates where hunted animals are found. Since the law states that ownership of biological resources is not granted through the use of wild fauna species nor of its products, by-products, or parts if this is carried out by transgressing the regulations of the law or its jurisdiction, the permit or license may be particularly relevant. Hunting permission is granted by SAG.[9] A hunting permit allows the bearer to hunt big or small game as indicated. Granting permission is subject to passing an exam and payment of a fee.

However, there are certain cases in which hunting or capture is prohibited or restricted. This potentially controversial situation also implies the prohibition or restriction of access to the corresponding genetic resources. The following is a brief description of such cases:

- Hunting or capturing is prohibited in areas which constitute protected zones or other special zones.[10] Regardless of the latter, SAG may give authorization for scientific aims, such as controlling the activities of animals that cause serious damage to the ecosystem, establishing reproduction or breeding centers, or allowing the sustainable use of a resource.

- Hunting or capturing species in danger of extinction or vulnerable, rare and scarcely known species is prohibited, as is hunting or capturing species regarded as beneficial to forestry, fishing, and agricultural sciences, or to the maintenance of the equilibrium of natural ecosystems, or species with reduced population densities. Regardless of the latter, SAG may authorize such hunting or capture when the authorized party proves that hunting or capturing of specimens is necessary for research, for the creation of reproduction or breeding centers, for the sustainable use of a resource, or for controlling the activities of animals that cause serious damage to the ecosystem. In any case, the corresponding authorization should indicate the prevalence of the species, the maximum number and type of specimens whose hunting or capture is being authorized, and any other conditions under which the extraction will take place.

- For species not included in the above cases, the law establishes hunting and capturing seasons and areas, as well as the number of specimens that may be hunted or captured per day, season, or age group. The only exceptions to these restrictions are certain species of wild fauna which are considered harmful and which may thus be hunted or captured at any time of year, throughout Chilean territory and regardless of quantity or specimens. However, a hunting permission or license is still required for these species.

- On the other hand, the international trade and transportation of wild fauna species must be carried out according to the provisions established by the Convention on International Trade of Endangered Species (CITES). This international treaty aims to regulate the trade and transportation of wild animals and plants considered to be in danger or threat of extinction. This regulation not only encompasses live flora and fauna species but also includes all their derivatives and by-products (stuffed animals, furs, bones, tissue samples, pharmaceutical products, etc.). Although this Convention refers only to the protection of species and not to genetic diversities, its provisions constitute, in practice, an eventual requirement to be met in the case of international trading of a genetic resource contained in any one of the species included in the treaty.

Regarding the regulation of access to biological resources found in hydrobiological species, we should essentially consider the rules established by the General Fishing and Aquaculture Law which regulate the procedure of access to these resources in reference to fishing for extraction and research.

Extractive fishing activity may be industrial or traditional. Regarding the former, the law establishes a general mechanism and a special mechanism of access to resources that apply to Chilean Territorial Sea and Exclusive Economic Zone, with the exception of areas reserved exclusively for traditional fishing. The general mechanism of access to industrial extractive fishing means that persons interested in carrying out industrial fishing must request a fishing permit for each vessel. This permit is granted for an unlimited period of time according to the species and zones outlined. On the other hand, there are special access mechanisms applicable in the case of resources which are currently being fully exploited and in which fishing systems are in recovery or just starting. For every fishing unit declared to be in any one of those states, a management plan must be developed which must outline, among other elements, the means of conservation and access mechanisms which apply in the particular case.

For traditional fishing the access mechanism is that of freedom to fish. However, in order to carry out their activity, traditional fishermen and their vessels must previously register with the registry coordinated by SERNAPESCA. In any case, with the aim of protecting hydrobiological resources, granting permits may be temporarily suspended (by traditional fishermen category or by fishing company) when one or more species becomes fully exploited.

Regarding research fishing, the law determines whether the species and areas are subject to a general or special access mechanism. In either case, the Fishing Undersecretariat is responsible for authorizing the capture of corresponding hydrobiological species according to the approved research project. In the case of special mechanisms, global quotas, if they exist, must be obeyed.

Certain mandates also exist that allow restrictions on access to hydrobiological species with the aim of protecting and preserving the species. These mandates refer to the establishment of prohibition periods (biological, extractive, or extraordinary); to the temporary or permanent prohibition of capture of hydrobiological resources protected by international treaties in force in Chile; to the establishment of marine parks and reserves; and to the fixing of annual quotas of capture by species in a defined area.

Lastly, regarding the regulation of access to biological resources found in fauna in general, the restrictions on the capture of determined species set out by international treaties signed by Chile must also be considered. Among these we highlight the following: the International Agreement for the Regulation of Whaling (1979), the Convention for the Conservation of Antarctic Seals (1980), the Convention on Wetlands which is of international importance specially regarding the habitat of waterfowl, the Convention on the

Conservation of Migratory Species of Wild Animals (1981), and the Convention for the Conservation and Management of the Vicuña (1980), all in force in Chile.

By virtue of the above mentioned regulations we may conclude that access to biological resources found in fauna is quite exhaustively regulated in Chile. The only exceptions are land invertebrates which have not been included in the mentioned provisions.

Access to biological resources found in flora

Flora, in general, is considered by Chile's legal structure as a property that is defined by the fact that it is rooted to the ground; it thus belongs to the owner of the land in which it is found.[11] This legal situation prevents the state from establishing, in general terms, restrictions upon these biological resources. Regardless of this, Chile's legislation has a variety of laws and policies that regulate, particularly for certain cases, access to the biological resources found in Chilean flora.

In the first place, it is relevant to refer to the mandates directly related to the collection of plant material. The Forestry Law constitutes the first legal framework that regulates this aspect. The following are prohibited by Article 5:

- Cutting down of native trees and shrubs located less than 400 meters from fresh waters that spring from the hills and less than 200 meters from water banks from the point at which the fresh water arises until it reaches level ground;

- Cutting down or destruction of woods located within a 200 meter radius of water supplies that originate in plain terrains that are not watered; and

- Cutting down or exploitation of native trees and shrubs located on land that slopes over 45%.

Regardless of the latter, cutting down in such sectors may be possible when duly justified and with previous approval of an operating plan in conformity with Decree Law No. 701, 1974.

This mandate allows restriction of access to the biological resources contained in Chilean tree and shrub species, especially in specific in cases which Chile's legislature considers the species in need of protection. Nevertheless, this is not an absolute prohibition since CONAF[12] can expressly authorize this collection on "justified grounds".

On the other hand, the Decree Law No. 701 on Forestry Promotion also indirectly regulates the cutting of forests and plant material, by establishing incentives for the substitution of forest plantations. Another law, Decree Law No. 3557, (The Agricultural Protection Law), establishes certain mandates in relation to exportation of plant products, requiring a sanitary certificate issued by SAG[13], thus restricting the international transference of plant material. Finally, regarding the commerce and international transportation of wild flora species, the mandates that can be applied are those agreed upon by CITES, which has been discussed above with regard to wild fauna.

With such few mandates in mind, it can be concluded that Chile's legal framework does not expressly regulate access to plant material. Indeed, there is a huge imbalance in the regulation of access between floral and faunal biological resources (IRIARTE 1997). Regarding this, the current legislation on the matter of protected areas is of great relevance, as are the requirements that define the access to these areas, because both are indirectly applicable to the plant material found in them. This legislation is composed of the following legal texts: the Supreme Decree No. 531, 1967, approved by the Convention for the Protection of the Flora, the Fauna and the Natural Scenic Beauties of the Countries of America (Washington 1940 Convention); Law No. 17.288, the National Monuments Law; Decree Law No. 1939, on Purchase, Administration, and Disposition of State Goods; Supreme Decree No. 4363 the Forestry Law; Law No. 18.368, that establishes Protected Areas for Tourism; Law No. 18.362, that creates a National System of Wild Areas Protected by the State[14]; and the Environmental Framework Law No. 19.300. According to these laws, the following main categories of protected wild areas exist:

National Park: A generally extensive zone, where diverse environments that are unique or that are representative of the country's natural ecological diversity are found. These are not significantly altered by human action, are capable of self-perpetuation, and their flora, fauna, and geological formations are of special interest for scientific, educational, or recreational reasons. The objectives of this category are the preservation of our natural environments with the cultural and scenic characteristics that are associated with them; the continuity of evolutionary processes, and, whenever compatible to the aforementioned, research, educational, and recreational activities. The national parks constitute fiscal property, although some parks are partially owned by private organizations. This category of protected areas is constituted by Supreme Mandate of the Ministries of Agriculture and National Goods. CONAF authorizes the operating plans of the activities that are carried out inside each protected zone.

Forest (or National) Reserve: An area whose natural resources need particularly careful conservation and use because of its susceptibility to degradation or its relevance to the community's well being. The aim of this category is the conservation of soil and water of threatened species of wild fauna and flora, the maintenance or improvement of water production, and the development and application of efficient technologies of advantage to flora and fauna. A regulated intervention is allowed in these areas and it is therefore possible to give concessions and approve operating plans in them. Nevertheless, in practice handling plans for forest exploitation are only granted to fiscal entities. They are constituted by Supreme Mandate of the Ministry of Agriculture and their administration is also a responsibility of CONAF.

National Monument: A generally reduced area, characterized by the presence of native species of flora and fauna or by the existence of geological sites that are relevant from a scenic, cultural, educational, or research point of view. The aim of this category is the preservation of natural environmental samples and associated scenic and cultural characteristics and, whenever compatible, research, educational, or recreational activities. National Monuments have the same characteristics as national parks but are smaller areas or defined objects (e.g., the *Araucaria* and *Alerce* trees). They are also constituted by Supreme Mandate of the Ministry of Agriculture and CONAF is responsible for their administration.

Natural Sanctuary: Land or sea areas whose natural resources are so relevant that they offer special possibilities for scientific research. These areas are created by Supreme Mandate of the Ministry of Education (Council of National Monuments) and in practice they are nearly all privately owned lands. These areas allow forest exploitation under approval of an operating plan. In conformity with the National Monuments Law, all activities carried out in a Sanctuary need approval from the Council of National Monuments.

Protected Areas for Tourism: Areas comprised of private land of great scenic and tourist value in which CONAF regulates the cutting of trees and undertakes measures to protect natural resources. These areas are created by Supreme Mandate of the Ministry of Agriculture.

Furthermore, according to Law No. 19.300, all works, programs, or activities to be carried out must be submitted to the Environmental Impact Assessment System, coordinated by CONAMA. This applies to national parks, national reserves, natural monuments, virgin area reserves, natural sanctuaries, marine parks, marine reserves, or any other areas under official protection, when the respective legislation so permits. Thus to be able to carry out any activity in a protected area, including access to the biological resources found in it, an authorization from the appropriate authority and the corresponding environmental qualification is required.

Finally, it is also important to mention the mandates established by Indigenous Law No. 19.253, in which article No. 34 refers to indigenous participation. It declares that state administrative services and organizations that deal with territorial matters must take into account the opinion of the indigenous organizations acknowledged by this law when considering topics related to indigenous issues. Likewise, Article 35 states that the administration of protected wild areas that are in the indigenous development zones must include the participation of its communities. CONAF or SAG and CONADI will decide the manner and depth of participation on the rights of use of the area that correspond to the indigenous communities.

In conclusion, the current procedures in Chile regarding access to biological resources do not meet the main objective of the CBD with respect to the regulation of access to genetic resources: that is, the fair and equitable sharing of the benefits resulting from its use. Indeed, the procedures that we have taken into consideration regarding biological resources have specific objectives that are different from those established by the CBD's system of access to genetic resources.

The National Program for the Protection of Plant Genetic Resources

In Chilean institutional practice, INIA is the only public sector institution that has actively dealt with the issue of conservation and utilization of genetic resources (specifically plant genetic resources). This has been done through a Program on Plant Genetic Resources, with the general objective of looking after the preservation and distribution of both Chilean and foreign germplasm, and of trying to increase its availability for future generations (CUBILLOS and LEÓN 1995).

With the aim of obtaining official support for this Program of Development and Protection of the Country's Plant Genetic Resources, INIA and the Ministry of Agriculture signed an agreement on 2 August 1995. According to the agreement, the general objective of this program is to safeguard the preservation and interchange of germplasm of wild plant species and those improved and obtained by the State. Its specific objectives are the following:

- Avoid loss and promote better use of Chile's plant genetic material.
- Support and coordinate work on genetic resources carried out in Chile and other countries promoting national and international collaboration.
- Generate, with the use of Chile's plant genetic resources, new crops or variants, to be incorporated into the national production.
- Establish and operate germplasm banks.
- Propose to the Ministry policies for the handling and interchange of germplasm.

The actions carried out by the program are the following:

- Exploration and collection[15]: The agreement establishes that INIA must verify that all explorations or collections of plant genetic resources that are state property must be carried out according to the following requirements:
  - A request for exploration or collection must be made with tentative plans for the field mission, including the types of materials to be collected, their species and quantities, and the subsequent evaluation, storage, and use. Also, required is a description of the distribution of the germplasm that will be carried out and the information that those in charge of collection must present once the mission has finished.
  - The exploration or collection must be carried out with the participation of national equivalents designated by INIA and paid for by the collectors.

- The Ministry of Agriculture can forbid the collection of certain species and establish areas where collection cannot be carried out. Likewise, it can establish the types, origin, and quantities that must be deposited in Chile.
- Priority is given to requests of exploration or collection by the classification of species, as follows: native-grown species; native species of a potential interest; naturalized foreign species; species long introduced but that have not been collected or that have a low representation in the country's collections; ancestral species of cultivated species; and wild species related to cultivated species.

- Documentation, characterization, and evaluation of the resource[16]: Adequate information on the collected resources must be obtained (botanical descriptors and physiological, genetic, agronomic, industrial, and biochemical characteristics) in co-ordination with specialized personnel evaluating and characterizing the germplasm.

- Conservation[17]: INIA must use germplasm banks as its genetic resource conservation system with a basic collection and, when appropriate, an active collection, of each stored species.

- Information and distribution of genetic resources[18]: INIA will publish periodically updated catalogues of the genetic material stored in their banks. This material will be grouped in three distribution categories: free, restricted, and prohibited distribution. This classification is based on the desire to maintain a policy of reciprocity between research organizations and as well as the need to keep material that clearly represents a competitive advantage in the context of international commerce. Until now, INIA has not classified any genetic resource in the prohibited distribution category.

- National guardian of plant genetic resources[19]: INIA acts as National Guardian[20] of Chile's plant genetic resources, with the responsibility to define and determine priorities regarding the existing species in Chile that are considered as genetic resources; verify compliance with the general regulations established by the Ministry of Agriculture regarding the conditions under which the explorations and collections of Chile's genetic resources will be carried out; conserve in the germplasm Bank System samples of genetic resources entrusted by the state or left in custody by private entities; define the conditions that must be complied with when depositing in the germplasm Bank System; carry out follow-up and monitoring of the deposited samples; multiply and regenerate the deposited samples; document and report the existence of genetic resources conserved in the system; distribute and use the genetic resources that are entrusted by the state under the established regulations; and certify compliance with the regulations established by the Program for export of genetic material.

- Introduction of germplasm into Chile[21]: All internment of germplasm for INIA must be backed by a sanitary plant certificate issued by the organization officially in charge of plant sanitation in the country of origin, and the germplasm must be submitted to quarantine post-entry measures required by SAG.

In compliance with this Program, in past years INIA has subscribed to different bioprospecting agreements under a contractual approach, trying to follow the rules of the CBD. Nevertheless, being only a research entity, INIA does not have any institutional authority over national plant genetic resources nor has it any regulatory authority at all. So it cannot be said that these agreements are part of public policy or regulation on the matter.

Intellectual Property Rights and Genetic Resources

The intellectual property protection system currently in force in Chile has two different formulas that apply to inventions related to biological resources. These are patents, regulated by Law No. 19.039, 1991, and breeders' rights, regulated by Law No. 19.342, 1994. Both formulas have different scopes and structures. The breeders' rights system only applies to plant varieties, which are expressly excluded from the patent system.

Regarding the awarding of a patent and the consequent protection given to biotechnological innovations (products or procedures), the current legislation expressly excludes only the patenting of plant varieties and animal species.[22] Therefore, according to the tenor of Article 35 of the Regulation of Law No. 19.039 "inventions related to bio-technological procedures and products that either consist of life material or contain it" can be patented. This allows the patenting of inventions carried out on genetic material, but the patent must refer to an invention, not a discovery, and the requirements stipulated by Law No. 19.039 and its regulation must be complied with.

Given that inventions based on plant varieties and associated biological material (mainly seeds) are not covered by patent protection, they may be subject to protection via the breeders' rights mechanisms, as stipulated in the International Union for the Protection of New Varieties of Plants (UPOV) treaty and Law No. 19.342. Thus, plant varieties can be subject only to breeders' rights, but inventions based on biological material of plant origin (that are not included in the concept of variety) may be protected either by the breeders' rights system (indirectly, since the protection includes the variety of which it forms a part) or by the patent system (directly, on any innovation).

Regarding animals, there is no special legislation in Chile that contemplates a specific protection system, as with plant varieties. Nevertheless, material of animal origin can be protected by means of the patent system, as long as the stipulations and requisites of Law No. 19.039 and its regulation are complied with.

In the case of microorganisms, cellular composites, and other biological classifications, apart from those indicated by Article 35 of the regulation of Law No. 19.039, there is no provision that, directly or indirectly, refers to their inclusion or exclusion from the patent system. Given the fact that patentability is the general rule of the system and considering the reference to Article 35, it can be concluded that the aforementioned materials may be the object of patent protection, if and when the respective inventions comply with the requisites stipulated by Law No. 19.039 and its regulation.

Since the legislation that regulates patents has a general rule of broad patentability, alongside the mandates of Article 35, the possibility to patent all kinds of inventions based on diverse biological resources exists. Nevertheless, it is important to note that this is only a possibility and does not imply a systematic patenting of forms of life. Although the possibility exists, the system enacted in the respective legislation was not elaborated with such cases in mind, and, for now, does not have the necessary structure and institutionalization to handle the complexity surrounding the attribution of intellectual property rights over different life forms. It is the responsibility of the qualified institution (Department of Industrial Property of the Ministry of Economy) to determine the extent of the protection granted to the patent system of Law No. 19.039.

Beyond the possibility of patenting inventions carried out on live material, it is fundamental to define a national policy on the subject of intellectual property and its scope. A harmonious regulation can be established, with clear and efficient rules, founded on objectives relevant to national interests. Given the tremendous complexity of its implications, the possibility of attributing or not attributing intellectual property rights to biotechnological inventions must comply with such a national policy and not only manifest the interests of some sectors. In its current state, the legislation is unsystematic and vague in many of its mandates and concepts. This leaves the door open for a variety of interpretations and applications.

With this reality in mind, we will refer briefly to the current process of modification of the Chilean intellectual property legislation. It began in 1999 with the presentation of a Bill by the Executive Power in the National Congress[23]. that seeks to adapt the Chilean legislation to the international obligations it undertook by subscription to the Marrakech Agreement. (Indeed, by virtue of the ratification of the Marrakech Agreement, Chile acquired the obligation to adapt its internal legislation in matters of intellectual property. The deadline originally established was 1 March 2000. Today, Chile, like many other developing countries, has not complied with this stipulation).

Nevertheless, as we have already mentioned, during 1999 a Bill introducing modifications to Law No. 19.039, Related to the Regulations Applicable to Industrial

Privileges and Protection of the Rights of Industrial Property, was submitted for consideration in the Chilean Chamber of Deputies. The aim of the Bill is "the execution of obligations that, in matters of industrial property, were adopted by the Chilean State within the framework of the Marrakech Agreement, modifying Law No. 19.039 in conformity with the stipulations established in that international legislative body". Likewise, this Bill introduces some modifications to current laws that are destined to complete and comply with the Paris Agreement (in force in Chile since 1991).

Regarding the modifications proposed for the patents system, the main changes are related to the period of protection of the rights conferred by the patent (it increases from 15 to 20 years) and the procedural aspects for the granting of this right. Specifically, in relation to the patentability of different forms of life, the Bill reproduces, nearly identically, Article 27.3.b of the Agreement on Trade-Related Aspects of Intellectual Property Rights. Thus Article 37 of Law No. 19.039 would indicate the following:

The following will not be considered as an invention and will remain excluded from the patent protection of this legislation: b) Plants and animals, excluding microorganisms, and essential biological procedures for the production of plants or animals, that are not biological or microbiological procedures. The plant varieties will benefit from protection whenever they can stay within the boundaries of the mandates of Law No. 19.342 on breeders' rights of new plant varieties.

To illustrate some aspects of this incipient discussion in Chile on this matter, we will refer to the most relevant suggestions that have been formulated during the discussion of this proposal in Congress (CAMARA DE DIPUTADOS 2001). For example, a request has been made to add a new letter f) to Article 37 that establishes that the following would also be excluded from patent protection:

All or part of living beings as they are found in nature, the natural biological processes, the biological material found in nature or that which may be isolated, including the genome or germplasm of any natural living being.

This suggestion was proposed with the aim of preventing the possibility of patenting any kind of genome (plants as well) and not only human genomes.

Regarding biotechnology, the relevant suggestions are those formulated in relation to the current Article 32 of Law No. 19.039 that states:

An invention can be patented when it is new, has an inventive level, and is susceptible to industrial application.

The Bill in process does not incorporate modifications to this article; nevertheless, there have been proposals in the parliamentary discussion offering suggestions that would modify it. For example, one proposal would substitute the following for the text of this article:

Patents can be obtained for all inventions, be they prod-

ucts or procedures, in all fields of technology, with the condition that they be new, have an inventive level, and are susceptible to industrial application. Regardless of Article 37 of this Law, patents can be obtained and the rights of the patents can be used without discriminatory aspects such as the place of invention, the field of technology, or the fact that the products are imported or produced in the country.

There has also been a proposal to add a second paragraph to Article 32, as follows:

The principle of non-discrimination in technical fields will be recognized by safeguarding and respecting our national biological and genetic patrimony, as well as the traditional knowledge of indigenous or local communities. As a consequence, the concession of patents for inventions developed on the basis of material obtained from that patrimony or knowledge would be subject to the acquisition of the material in conformance with the relevant international and national Regulations.

It is also important to mention the paragraph formulated by Article 38 of Law No. 19.039 which currently states that:

Patents are not awarded to inventions that infringe upon the law; public order; state security; ethics and good customs; nor to any inventions presented by whomsoever is not the legitimate owner.

As with Article 32, the original bill did not modify this article. However, the Chamber of Deputies formulated the following paragraph, which aims to replace the text of Article 38 with the following:

Patents cannot be awarded to inventions whose commercial exploitation needs to be prevented in order to protect public order, state security; ethics and good customs; the health or life of persons or animals, or to preserve plant material or the environment, whenever such an exclusion is not carried out due to the existence of a legal or administrative clause that prohibits or regulates said exploitation.

The Chamber of Deputies' Permanent Economic Commission, which is in charge of studying the Bill in question, has approved all the above-mentioned paragraphs.

We must say, that in Chile, almost all biotechnological development is carried out by universities and a few government agencies (mainly INIA and SAG), with the fundamental aim of preserving resources and developing scientific research. Chile does not have a significant biotechnological industry, nor does it have a particularly developed economic activity in this area. Therefore, most of the pressure for a better adaptation of national intellectual property legislation to the patenting of biotechnological developments originates from abroad. To date, this pressure has not been significant.

Bioprospecting Projects in Chile

There is currently neither a regulatory framework nor a clear policy regarding this issue. Thus, regarding the activity of access to genetic resources (bioprospecting projects) the approach taken is predominantly contractual and is defined by the particular interests of the contracting parties and controlled by the regulations of private law (national or international). It does not include the concrete participation of the country's environmental authorities. Practically all cases of bioprospecting have been carried out via Chilean universities and with the supposed aim of developing research (ODEPA 1999). Since Chile does not possess a developed biotechnological industry and no Chilean stakeholder have shown an interest in developing the sector, most of the bioprospecting projects have their origins abroad, be it in the private or public sectors.

Given the fact that no entry control system exists, nor is there an obligation to register, no precise information is available regarding the exact number of bioprospecting expeditions that have been carried out or are currently being carried out in Chile. Nevertheless, these expeditions can be categorized into two clear groups: specific expeditions, carried out on a small scale and in relation to certain very special species (these probably constitute the majority but are less often registered), and large scale bioprospecting programs, which consist of the systematic analysis of samples in considerably large terrains carried out over significant periods of time. Among the latter the

most important have been: the project carried out by the International Cooperative Biodiversity Groups (ICBGs), under the guidance of the University of Arizona with the collaboration of the Chilean Catholic University[24]; the program developed by the British Technology Group and the University of Chile, with the participation of the University of Southampton Agrochemical Unit, the Institute of Arable Crops Research, and the Royal Botanical Garden, and the program carried out by INIA in conjunction with the Japan International Cooperation Agency (JICA)[25]. To a great degree, these three projects, at the time of their development, motivated the authorities responsible for environmental matters to politically approach the issue of genetic resources and their regulation. This led them to promote the development of a kind of regulatory instrument and policy to deal with the situations generated by these types of projects.

As mentioned above, these projects have had a predominantly contractual basis, with a minimum or total lack of involvement of the environmental authorities, local communities, nongovernmental organizations (NGOs), and indigenous groups. The majority of these projects have adopted the CBD's general principles and rules in order to define their frameworks. Nevertheless, in practice, their development has generated a great deal of distrust, while the willingness of the parties involved to comply with these principles and rules has been questioned by various sectors. The main criticism, apart from the lack of real participation, is related to the absence of clarity and certainty regarding the benefits owed to Chile or to its citizens in exchange for access to genetic resources.

This lack of participation and transparency is not necessarily nor exclusively due to the unwillingness of those involved in the projects. Rather, it is due to the fact that the Chilean authorities responsible for environmental matters have been incapable of offering clear guidelines regarding the procedures to follow, the organizations to be consulted, the principles and rules to be respected, etc. This is mainly due to the absence of a framework that regulates genetic resources in Chile. Because of the absence of public sector regulations, private law has been applied, in all legitimacy, and the private interests of contracting parties have prevailed.

Regarding organizations linked to the public sector, it is important to highlight the work of INIA in the contracting and development of bioprospecting projects. In compliance with its programs, INIA has subscribed to various contracts of access to genetic resources in Chile. Below we describe the fundamental aspects of two such contracts. It is important to emphasize that in both cases the parties recognize the sovereign rights of states over their own biological resources while making a commitment to comply with the contents and the spirit of CITES, CBD, and the national laws and regulations related to biodiversity, including access to plant genetic resources and their transfer.

- Contract of Access to and Participation in the Benefits, signed by INIA and the Trustee of the Royal Botanical Garden, Kew, United Kingdom (4 July 2001). Via this contract, INIA expressly awards its previously informed consent to the "Ex Situ Conservation of Endemic, Vulnerable, and Endangered Species from the Desert and Mediterranean Zones in Chile" project which is to be carried out by both institutions, according to the project summary attached in Appendix 1 of this contract. The main clauses of the contract refer to the following aspects: terms of transfer of collected material to the Royal Botanical Garden, Kew (Transfer Notification in Appendix 2 of the contract); a pledge of noncommercialization of transferred genetic resources, unless expressly agreed upon by the involved parties; a just and equitable distribution of the benefits; regulation of transfer of collected material to third parties (stipulated in an Appendix 3); a pledge to treat confidential information in a confidential manner; and duration of the contract and conflict resolution.

- Contract of Access to germplasm, signed by INIA and the C.M. Rick Tomato Genetics Resource Center (TGRC), of the University of California, Davis (5 October 2001). Via this contract, INIA expressly grants its previously informed consent to the TGRC to collect germplasm (seeds) samples from species and from places expressly indicated in the contract. The fundamental contents of the contract are as follows: the restriction of collection of material so as not to put the respective population in danger of extinction; TGRC pledge not to claim property rights over the germplasm collected; equitable distribution of collected material between the involved parties; regulation of transfer of collected material to third parties; pledge to share information generated among parties involved; TGRC pledges to assist INIA in increasing its technical capacities and genetic resource research; and conflict resolution.

The differences between these contracts lie in the clauses that do not refer to the essence of the agreement (for example, duration of the contract, conflict resolution mechanisms, and future technical cooperation pledge). The essential elements are practically the same, consisting of: previously informed consent, declaration of equitable distribution of benefits, and regulation of the transfer of material collected to third parties. As these contracts are just starting to be implemented there is yet no information about their results.

Conclusions

As has been explained throughout this paper, to date Chile has not yet developed a structural framework for the general implementation of the CBD, which would be a necessary base for specific formulation of an access and benefit distribution regime on the basis of objectives, goals, and priorities previously determined. However, the current National Biodiversity Strategy and the future National Biodiversity Action Plan are steps in the right direction. We have yet to see the results of the process leading to a National Biodiversity Action Plan, but it is certainly an approach that considers the integral and systematic implementaion of the CBD.

This process is being coordinated by CONAMA in its role as the authority in charge of proposing environmental policies to the government and as a national focal point for the CBD. Regarding a strategy for the formulation of the access and benefit-sharing regime, CONAMA and the other institutions with some competence on the subject will have to consider the different formal systems by which the matter can be treated through a legal, contractual or voluntary approach. In addition, it will be necessary to decide whether to structure regulation through an integral formula (framework) or a flexible one (amendments to the existing legislation), of immediate or gradual development. The characteristics and the effectiveness of the legislative and institutional framework that regulates access to the genetic resources of each country will have a close relation to the process through which this framework is developed and implemented.

Once established, in order to operate efficiently the legislative framework must, at least, fit within the national strategy for the conservation and the sustainable use of biological diversity and be endorsed by institutional procedures with sufficient capacities for implementation.

The effective formulation of a legal regime of access to genetic resources requires the participation of a high number of interest groups and experts. Governmental entities of different sectors must participate in the process as well as representatives of the scientific community and the private sector (for example, pharmaceutical and agricultural companies), local and indigenous groups, and NGOs. The collective experience and the technical knowledge of all the sectors will not only benefit the legislative process, but also will help to identify any type of potential opposition to the legislation.

When formulating the regulatory framework it is also important to have an integrated approach, so that the subject is not treated in an isolated manner. The regulatory framework at issue would have to be integrated within a broader set of policies and governmental activities. The discussion on how to regulate genetic resources would have to be carried out through a process of national planning, as required by Article 6 of the CBD. A similar process offers the opportunity to gain important knowledge on the state and distribution of the biological diversity of the country, which is important to determine the more attractive geographic zones for the exploration of genetic resources and, in addition, to establish if the resources at issue are shared with other countries. Such a process also allows the establishment of wider objectives and national policies, while facilitating the evaluation of the existing institutions, laws, and policies. Since the regulation of access to the genetic resources is a new area of legislation, few countries have the necessary institutions and resources for its implementation. To develop this capacity requires a long-term process and, for that reason, it is vital to begin it as soon as possible. However, considering the elements mentioned before, it is clear that there are tensions between the urgent need to take measures and the complexity of the process. Evidently the CBD is a superstructure difficult to implement for developing countries, and Chile is a clear example of this difficulty. Throughout recent years there has been only erratic consideration of the subject, and it has never been considered a question of importance for the national interests, which is demonstrated by a clear lack of serious actions on the part of the political authorities.

The subject is so difficult and complex that it is necessary to surpass the way in which these subjects are traditionally approached. The issue can be seen and treated from an ideal perspective or a practical perspective. The latter is able to diagnose and to recognize all the present difficulties and obstacles at stake to obtain the desired objectives and goals. We consider it advisable to follow a pragmatic approach to the subject in Chile, and to develop a process in a reasonable time frame with predetermined objectives, priorities, and goals.

References

AGÜERO T. 2000. Recursos genéticos terrestres nativos de Chile: Una propuesta para su conservación y uso sustentable. *Temporada Agrícola* **15**:124–139.

CAMARA DE DIPUTADOS. 2001. Informe de la Comisión Permanente de Economía de la Cámara de Diputados, sobre el Proyecto de Ley de Propiedad Intelectual. Chile.

CONAMA 1995. Estudio de diagnóstico sobre la propiedad y el acceso a los recursos genéticos. Comisión Nacional del Medio Ambiente (CONAMA), Chile, unpublished manuscript.

CONAMA 1997. Informe sobre recursos genéticos y el ordenamiento constitucional Chileno. Comisión Nacional del Medio Ambiente (CONAMA), Chile.

CONAMA 2002. Propuesta de registro nacional de contratos de acceso a los recursos genéticos. Comisión Nacional del Medio Ambiente (CONAMA), Chile.

CUBILLOS A. and P. LEÓN. 1995. Informe de la República de Chile para la FAO. Chile.

GIL. L. and C. IRARRÁZABAL. 1997. Estado actual de la biotecnología en Chile. p. 1–6 *in* Proceedings of workshop *Biotecnología en Chile: Oportunidades de Innovación Tecnológica.* CAMBIOTEC-Chile.

IRIARTE A. 1997. Regulaciones al acceso a los recursos biológicos en Chile: Un desequilibrio entre flora y fauna silvestre. p. 92–97 *in* B. TIMMERMAN and G. MONTENEGRO (eds.) *Noticiero de Biología. Organo Oficial de la Sociedad de Biología de Chile.* Taller Internacional: Aspectos ambientales, eticos, ideológicos y políticos en el debate sobre bioprospección y uso de recursos genéticos en Chile.

ODEPA. 1999. Investigación, uso y protección de los recursos genéticos endémicos y nativos de Chile. Oficina de Estudios y Políticas Agrarias (ODEPA), Ministerio de Agricultura, Chile.

UNIVERSIDAD DE CHILE. 2000. *Informe país: Estado del medio ambiente en Chile—1999.* Centro de Análisis de Políticas Públicas. Chile.

Endnotes

[1] In the case of the private sector there is no important development in this field.

[2] After the publication of Supreme Decree No. 1963, 1994, from the Ministry of Foreign Affairs, in the Official Journal, 6 May 1995.

[3] When set into practice, this national plan should be a significant element of the environmental policy of the country.

[4] Consultants were hired to make a comparative study of national access legislation. This study was merely for updating the information available in CONAMA and was finished in March 2002. It formulated some ideas for starting a new regulatory process in Chile, but its consequences and possible continuation are uncertain (CONAMA 2002).

[5] This statement is given on the basis of a legal rule established by the Chilean Civil Code: *"the accessory follows the principal or main thing"*. This rule states that the owner of a good is entitled to ownership of any of its products or other things which constitute a unity with the original or main good (articles 643 to 669, Civil Code).

[6] Those things that, being susceptible of appropriation, do not belong to anybody and which, therefore, any person can acquire the ownership of. Indeed, according to Chile's Civil Code, the ownership of things that do not belong to anybody is acquired via use. Hunting and fishing are a type of use through which ownership of wild animals is acquired (Articles 606 and 607).

[7] For example, Law No. 19.300 on General Bases of Environment; Law No. 18.362 that creates the National System of Protected Wild Areas of the State; Law No. 19.473 for hunting; Law No. 18.892, the General Law of Fishing and Aquaculture; Law No. 17.288 on National Monuments; Decree No. 3.557 on Agricultural Protection; and the Decree No. 1.939 on Acquisition, Administration and Disposition of Government properties. All these regulations will be mentioned in the following part of this paper.

[8] Alongside this permission, access will depend on the express authorization of the landowner.

[9] This Service is in charge of wild fauna, according to its organic law.

[10] The following are protected areas and other special zones: virgin area reserves, national parks, national reserves, natural monuments, nature sanctuaries, areas where hunting is prohibited, urban zones, railway tracks, airports, (in and from) public roads, places of scientific interest, and settlements of fertilizing wildfowl (Article 7 first paragraph of the Hunting Law).

[11] Article 569 of the Civil Code: "Plants are property if they adhere to the ground by their roots, unless they are in pots or boxes that can be moved from one place to another."

[12] CONAF is a private legal entity regulated by its own statutes, which must, among other functions, participate in the state management and development of forests made up of National Parks, Forest Reserves, and State Woods. That is, CONAF must safeguard the natural patrimony *in situ,* within the protected wild areas and all forests.

[13] Generally speaking, in compliance with its internal law, this Service must safeguard the conservation of agricultural flora. This means that it is not accountable for forest resources (under CONAF) and wild flora (which is not currently under the express charge of any institution, apart from the regulations that correspond to protected wild areas).

[14] This law is not yet in force since it is subordinate to the constitution of CONAF as a public institution, according to Law No. 18.348.

[15] Third clause of the agreement.

[16] Fourth Clause of the Agreement.

[17] Fifth Clause of the Agreement.

[18] Sixth Clause of the Agreement.

[19] Seventh Clause of the Agreement.

[20] In compliance with INIA Resolution N°369, 5 August 1999, the following functions are granted to the General Guardian of Plant Genetic Resources: the authority to plan, organize, co-ordinate, conduct studies of removal, collect plant genetic diversity, interchange germplasm, and assign a single serial and sequence number for each access agreement that enters the system; to participate in decision making related to quarantine, evaluation, characterization, classification, documentation, information diffusion activities, and adoption of the appropriate measures for conservation and sustainable use of plant genetic resources; and to act as consultant and member of the National Commission of Plant Genetic Resources.

[21] Eighth clause of the agreement.

[22] Article 37, Law No. 19.039: *The following are not considered inventions and are excluded from this law's patent protection:...b) plant material varieties and animal species.*

[23] Bill currently in process *(Bulletin No. 2416-03* Chamber of Deputies).

[24] This project lasting five years, started in 1993, under an agreement between the University of Arizona (UA) and the Catholic University (UC) with the purpose of preparing and supplying samples of biological material by the UC to UA. Regarding benefit-sharing the agreement establishes that any royalties on the sale of compounds isolated from extracts of plants collected in Chile will be distributed in the following way: 50% of all royalties to a fund for conservation and for the benefit of local people in the country of collection; 5% of all royalties to the collector of the plant that is the source of the commercialized compound; and 45% of all royalties to the institutions employing those named as inventors on patents covering the commercialized compound. This project was renewed in 1998 for another five years, and, according to the little information we were able to obtain, the main objective of this second phase was conservation rather than bioprospecting. The project ended in 2003.

[25] The Governments of Japan and Chile signed an agreement in 1989 to develop, during the following five years, a program for the "Conservation of Genetic Resources" that would be implemented by JICA and INIA.

11

Malaysia: Recent Initiatives to Develop Access and Benefit-Sharing Regulations

Mohamad Osman

Malaysia consists of two large landmasses over 500 km apart separated by the South China Sea. Peninsular Malaysia is a continuum of the Asian continent, a narrow landmass sandwiched by Thailand in the north and Singapore in the south, comprising eleven states, namely, Perlis, Kedah, Pulau Pinang, Perak, Kelantan, Terengganu, Pahang, Selangor, Negeri Sembilan, Melaka, and Johor, and two Federal Territories, namely, Kuala Lumpur and newly established Putrajaya. East Malaysia, comprising the states of Sabah, Sarawak, and the Federal Territory of Labuan, is situated on the island of Borneo and is bordered by Brunei and Kalimantan, Indonesia (Figure 1). The country occupies about 330,000 km² of land area, of which 40% is the Peninsula and 60% East Malaysia. Malaysia's population was 23.3 million in 2000 (date of the last Malaysian census). About 80% of the total population resides in Peninsular Malaysia, 9.9% in Sabah, and 9.4% in Sarawak.

Malaysia's territorial waters cover an area of 549,500 km². Its maritime area borders Indonesia, Singapore, Thailand, Brunei, and the Philippines. The principal water bodies are the Straits of Malacca and the South China Sea. The Straits of Malacca, one of the world's busiest shipping passages, is a narrow sea-lane between Peninsular Malaysia, the Indonesian island of Sumatra, and Singapore. The South China Sea is significant because of its continental shelf which is extremely rich in nutrients and able to support a remarkable diversity of species.

Malaysia has a hot and humid tropical climate marked by seasonal variations in rainfall. Generally, the climate is influenced by the northeast and southwest monsoons. The annual average rainfall in Peninsular Malaysia is approxi-

mately 2,540 mm, with most precipitation occurring during the southwest monsoon (September to December). East Malaysia receives most of its rainfall during the northeast monsoon (October to February). Sabah's average annual rainfall is 2,630 mm, while Sarawak's average is approximately 3,850 mm. There is, however, great variation in rainfall between locations. For example, northern Perlis on the average receives only half of Terengganu's annual rainfall, whereas parts of eastern Sarawak receive more than 5,500 mm of annual rainfall. Average annual temperature is 27°C with a diurnal range of 9°C. Relative humidity is high (85 to 95%), especially in the coastal areas.

Almost one-half of the total surface area of the Peninsula is granite of the Triassic Age. The central core is dominated by a series of parallel mountain ranges, which run northwest to southeast along the length of the Peninsula. Sabah is crisscrossed by a series of mountain ranges with the Crocker Range dominating its topography. Sarawak's topography shows a flat coastal plain followed by a narrow belt of many hills with a sharp rise of mountainous mass extending the full length of the state. Malaysia receives approximately 990 billion m³ of rainfall annually, of which 57% appears as surface run-off and 6.5% recharges the groundwater aquifers. Of this total, 360 billion m³ return to the atmosphere by evaporation and transpiration, leaving an estimated 566 billion m³ as theoretically available water resources. Only approximately 26% of the water resources are found in the Peninsula.

Of a total of 33.0 million ha of land, 7.15 million, 3.15 million, and 4.45 million ha are estimated to be suitable for agriculture in Peninsular Malaysia, Sabah, and Sarawak, respectively. The sector is dominated by plantation crops,

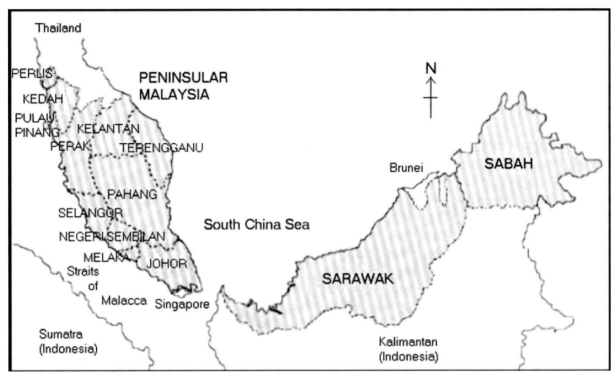

Figure 1. Map of Malaysia

of which rubber and oil palm occupied 14.8% and 12.1% respectively of the total land area in 1990, followed by cocoa. Of the food crops, rice is the most important, followed fruits and vegetables. Almost all the forests cleared for agricultural development were lowland forests with their large reservoir of genetic diversity of fauna and flora, because their high soil productivity was deemed ideal for agricultural production.

Sarawak agricultural land use constitutes almost a third of the total land area. The major user of agricultural land in Sarawak is shifting cultivation, or slash and burn farming, that accounted for 27.5% of the total land area in 1992. Shifting cultivation is the traditional way of life for the ethnic and native peoples. It is estimated that 5% of virgin forests are cleared annually for shifting cultivation. By contrast in Sabah, agricultural land use comprises only a small percentage of total land area (1.7% in 1992). In 1992, oil palm was the major land user at 4.6% of total land area and cocoa was the second major crop with 2.7% of the land area. Forest lands constituted approximately 6,042,082 ha (or 46% of Peninsular Malaysia's total land area) in 1992, of which 4,717,732 ha is designated as Permanent Forest Estates (PFES). The demand for land use, however, has led to the delisting of 698,781 ha of PFES in Peninsular Malaysia and 693,876 ha in East Malaysia from 1978 to 1994, largely for agricultural use.

As of 1993, Sarawak was still largely covered by forests (over 70% of the total land area was under PFES and other forests). PFES also include areas that have been developed for the production of forest products and logged-over areas replanted with forest species that have good timber

potential. Forests constitute the bulk of nonagricultural land in Sabah with 60.1% or 4.4 million ha in 1992, out of which 1.64 million ha were still undisturbed. This consists mainly of mangroves and swamps, lowland and hill dipterocarp, and montane forests. Deforestation of over 85% of the state's undisturbed lowland and highland dipterocarp forests during the last two decades has resulted in an overwhelming gross domestic product growth by the forestry sector in Sabah. Because of their differing histories, geographic locations and physical features, Peninsular Malaysia and East Malaysia are significantly different in their biological holdings. Both areas are inhabited by many endemic species, while even shared species have distinct genetic differences.

Malaysia is identified as one of the world's twelve megadiversity countries with extremely rich biological resources. Tropical forests, the most biologically diverse ecosystems on earth, cover much of the country. There are over 15,000 known species of flowering plants, 286 species of mammals, over 150,000 species of invertebrates, over 1,000 species of butterflies and 12,000 species of moth, and over 4,000 species of marine fishes in Malaysia's varied ecosystems, and the list goes on.

Therefore, Malaysia offers many opportunities to bioprospectors, and policy-makers have been working to develop regulations that promote and facilitate bioprospecting in the country. This chapter analyses current and future laws and policies that regulate access to these genetic resources, the process that is leading to the development of these laws, and bioprospecting initiatives that have been implemented in Malaysia.

Ownership of Genetic Resources and the Federal-State Jurisdictional Dichotomy

In Malaysia, the Constitution allocates to the thirteen states ownership of land and any minerals on or within it. More complex is the situation regarding inhabitants of the land. For example, Sabah and Sarawak have a different constitutional status vis-à-vis the Federal Government. Prior to joining the Federation, they signed a 20-point agreement with the Federation of Malaysia that guaranteed them special rights. Sabah and Sarawak are excluded from national plans for land use, local government, and development. As a result, the indigenous or local communities[1] in Sabah have been accorded certain special legal rights over land. In a way, we can think of such lands as lands that have been alienated to the indigenous communities. Legally, the indigenous communities do not "own" the minerals found in that land even though they are accorded certain special rights over the land. However, biological/genetic resources are not explicitly addressed in the law. It is, therefore, still uncertain whether the indigenous communities fully hold the "proprietary rights" or "access" to biological/genetic resources.

Sabah's land law, enacted under the Land Ordinance 1956, permits native customary rights over certain lands to indigenous peoples. The Sabah Land Law recognizes special classes of land rights, namely, native title to land and native reserves, which are applicable only to the native peoples. The situation is different in Peninsular Malaysia, where the indigenous communities are not accorded customary rights over land, even though the land may have been occupied and cultivated by them for long periods of time. In Peninsular Malaysia, indigenous communities occupy lands that have been reserved or designated for them by the States. As in Sabah and Sarawak, it is still uncertain whether the native people fully hold the proprietary rights or access to biological/genetic resources found on their lands.

It is also uncertain whether private landholders own the biological/genetic resources found on their land. This question remains open, but on the premise that private properties are considered as alienated lands, the relevant State may no longer hold the proprietary rights or access to biological/genetic resources found on such lands. However, it is clearly stated in law that the State holds the proprietary rights or access to minerals found on lands.

The constitutional situation in Malaysia prevents the legal implementation of a general and all-encompassing law governing all types of genetic resources and benefits. Indeed, it would be very difficult for a nationally administered policy or law to cover all of Malaysia's biodiversity. The Federal Government does not have the legal competency to do so. However, the Constitution does allow the Federal Government to take a coordinating role. For example, a federal law that ensures access to genetic resources is consistent on a nationwide basis. However, within the national boundaries, the concept of national sovereignty over such resources brings up several issues in need of resolution (OH 1996). The question of rights to access within the country presents a Federal-State jurisdictional dichotomy.

The Federal-State Jurisdictional Dichotomy

In Malaysia, the Federal-State jurisdictional dichotomy means that the jurisdiction over land and natural resources lies with the State governments and not the Federal Government. While it is the Federal Government that possesses the authority to enter into international agreements, such as the Convention on Biological Diversity (CBD), under the Ninth Schedule of the Federal Constitution, State governments govern land and natural resources. This division of responsibilities causes difficulties in implementing national policies and international commitments. The management of the environment and biological diversity in Malaysia is the joint responsibility of Federal, State, and local governments. The Federal Constitution divides legislative power between the Federal and State Governments into three lists: Federal, State, and Concurrent lists. Neither the environment nor biological diversity appears in the three constitutional lists as a matter for legislation, but are instead defined in their related subjects under all three lists.

The Federal Government has jurisdiction over commerce, trade, and industry, and is responsible for environmental protection and pollution prevention. The State Governments have control over land, water, agriculture, forestry, and local governments, and thus retain jurisdiction to protect, manage, and utilize natural resources. At the same time, both Federal and State Governments may exercise concurrent jurisdiction over issues such as the protection of wildlife and national parks, land rehabilitation, fishing and fisheries, and agriculture. The distinct division of Constitutional responsibility to the Federal and State Governments respectively has far-reaching implications for the management and use of natural resources and biological diversity, and undermines all efforts for a comprehensive and effective management of the environment.

An example of the dilemma this situation presents is in the management of Marine Parks. Legislative control over land and forests and the sea up to a limit of three km offshore is with the State governments. The Federal government has jurisdiction over the sea from three km to the Exclusive Economic Zone limits, 200 nautical miles offshore. It also has control over the fisheries and estuarine resources in Peninsular Malaysia, but shares concurrent responsibilities for the resources in Sabah and Sarawak. While the State Governments have jurisdiction over the land-based resources of islands, the Federal Government has jurisdiction over the marine resources of Marine Parks. This often results in the use of island resources that are in conflict with the objectives of marine park management systems. A conflict of interests between the Federal and State governments can be detrimental to efforts to protect and conserve marine biological diversity.

The implementation of an international convention that requires the management of a resource under state jurisdiction must be endorsed by the relevant State government. An example is the allocation of the 26,000 ha Tasek Bera site in the State of Pahang for designation as a site under the Ramsar Convention. The area continues to remain under Pahang State jurisdiction; however, it may be delisted as a Ramsar site if the State so wishes. It should be noted that the situation may be even more complex in Sabah and

Sarawak. The Federal Government has weaker jurisdiction over the East Malaysian states relative to the Peninsular Malaysian States. The States, Sabah and Sarawak in particular, will therefore have to develop clearly defined mechanisms at the state level and more refined Federal-State coordination for effective implementation of international commitments.

Another related issue is the right of indigenous and local communities to control access to biological diversity and to receive benefits generated therefrom. This question relates to the rights of indigenous and local communities to control access to their land and to the resources on those lands. Again, in terms of the Federal-State dichotomy with regard to special biodiversity rights, the implementation of any changes in the policy will present problems.

Implementation of the CBD in Malaysia

Malaysia was one among the first countries to sign the final text of the CBD at the Earth Summit in June 1992, and it ratified the treaty on 24 June 1994. Having ratified the CBD, Malaysia has incorporated it into its national policies and is planning more commitments under the treaty (Table 1). At the national level, Malaysia's efforts to implement the CBD are led by the Ministry of Science, Technology, and the Environment (MOSTE). To coordinate these efforts, a National Committee on Biological Diversity (NCBD) was established under MOSTE and chaired by the Secretary-General of MOSTE. Established under this National Committee is the National Technical Committee on Biological Diversity and its three task forces working on specific issues: the country study on biological diversity, the national policy on biological diversity, and access to genetic resources. A national Genetic Modification Advisory Committee (GMAC) was also established.

As a party to the CBD, Malaysia has the responsibility to conserve and utilize its biological diversity resources in a sustainable way. Based on a country study on biological diversity that resulted in the document entitled "Assessment of Biological Diversity in Malaysia" (MOSTE 1997), the first step taken by the country was to develop a national strategy on biological diversity[2] that would integrate conservation and sustainable use of biological resources into plans, programs, and policies for sectors such as agriculture, fisheries, and forestry, and for cross-sectoral matters such as land-use planning and decision making. This Assessment was commissioned as part of Malaysia's international commitment. As a consequence, the Government launched the National Policy on Biological Diversity on 16 April 1998. This national policy provides important guidelines to States and institutions in Malaysia to take affirmative actions to safeguard the country's biodiversity heritage. These guidelines are important to Malaysia, in particular to states like Sarawak and Sabah, because it contains within its boundary immense biodiversity, much of which is still

unknown and yet to be discovered and studied since tropical forests cover much of the country.

The national policy outlines the objectives and provides the direction for the nation to implement strategies and action plans to conserve Malaysia's biological diversity and to ensure that its components are utilized in a sustainable manner for the continued progress and socio-economic development of the country. Among the objectives are to optimize economic benefits from sustainable utilization of the components of biological diversity, to ensure long-term food security for the nation, to maintain and improve environmental stability for proper functioning of ecological systems, to ensure preservation of the unique biological heritage of the nation for the benefit of present and future generations, to enhance scientific and technological knowledge and the educational, social, cultural and aesthetic values of biological diversity, and to emphasize biosafety considerations in the development and application of biotechnology. It is the hope and the aspiration of the Government to transform Malaysia into a world center of excellence in conservation, research, and sustainable utilization of tropical biological diversity by the year 2020.

Both to safeguard and manage these rich biological resources in a sustainable manner as well as to support the National Policy on Biological Diversity and the CBD, Sarawak passed a State law in 1997 to establish the Sarawak Biodiversity Council and the Sarawak Biodiversity Center to manage the State's rich biodiversity in a prudent manner. Similar steps were taken by the State of Sabah which enacted the Sabah Biodiversity Ordinance in 2000 and subsequently established the Sabah Biodiversity Center. To strengthen further the governance of biological diversity in this country, the Government is now in the process of finalizing a number of major commitments, namely, the Access to Genetic Resources Bill, the Biosafety Bill, and the Plant Variety Protection Bill.

Current Measures that Regulate Access

Currently, there is no access regime in place at the national level with regard to access control and benefit sharing. Few specific measures currently exist in Malaysia to regulate access to biological resources, with the exceptions of the states of Sarawak and Sabah.

Some national- and state-level access controls are already in place for foreign researchers, but such mea-

Table 1. The CBD and Malaysia's actions and commitments, in chronological order

1992	Malaysia signed the CBD during the Earth Summit in Rio on 12 June.
1994	Malaysia ratified the treaty on 24 June, the 65th country to do so.
	Implementation of the CBD is coordinated by MOSTE.
	NCBD was established to carry out biological biodiversity planning and its implementation and subsequently created the following:
	National Technical Committee on Biological Diversity
	GMAC
	National Technical Committee on Biological Diversity established three Task Forces:
	Country Study on Biological Diversity
	National Policy on Biological Diversity
	Access to Genetic Resources
	GMAC established the Task Force on Biosafety.
1995	Country study on biological diversity was undertaken, from June 1995 to August 1996, by the World Wildlife Fund (WWF), Malaysian Nature Society (MNS), Universiti Putra Malaysia (UPM) and Institute of Strategic and International Studies (ISIS) of Malaysia (following the guidelines set forth in the United Nations Environment Program Guidelines for a Country Study on Biological Diversity).
1997	Country study on biological diversity entitled "Assessment of Biological Diversity in Malaysia" was published (MOSTE 1997).
	Sarawak passed a State law in December to establish the Sarawak Biodiversity Council and the Sarawak Biodiversity Center.
1998	National Policy on Biological Diversity was approved by Government in October, and officially launched on 16 April 1998.[3]
2000	Sabah passed a State law in November to establish the Sabah Biodiversity Council and the Sabah Biodiversity Center.
2001	National Biodiversity and Biotechnology Council held its inaugural meeting in December
	National Biotechnology Directorate under MOSTE established the Task Force on National Policy on Biotechnology in December.
2004	MOSTE is handling two draft legislative initiatives, namely the Biosafety Bill and the Access to Genetic Resources Bill.
	The Ministry of Agriculture handled the Plant Variety Protection Bill, passed by Parliament.

sures predate the CBD. For example, at the national level, a minimum procedure has already been put in place to control access to genetic resources by foreign nationals. The Economic Planning Unit (EPU), located within the Prime Minister's Department, administers the scheme. Foreign researchers intending to conduct research in the country need to obtain permission from the Government of Malaysia to do so. The permission granted by EPU is really not a permit, so a foreign researcher has to further obtain the relevant license/permit from Sabah or Sarawak. The permission is required even in areas where the federal government has no jurisdiction (i.e., the States). EPU does this to ensure that all collection activities by foreign researchers are properly and centrally monitored. These records, upon request, will assist the States in carrying out their own monitoring on such collection activities. Malaysians do not need to apply for permission from EPU; however, they do have to apply for relevant permits at the state level. Foreign bioprospectors also need to obtain the necessary visa for conducting any research.

In Peninsular Malaysia, one is required to have a permit or license to prospect in the forest. Under the Forestry Act of 1984, two types of licenses can be issued. One type is for major forest products like timber, poles, fuel wood, charcoal, and manau and sega rattans. A minor license can also be issued for forest products other than those mentioned above. Under section 4 of the same Act, the State Forestry director is empowered by the State authority to control the removal of plants or resources from the forest. In general, all licenses will correspond to a boundary demarcated on the ground. Licenses are usually issued for a term of three to 12 months and can be renewed from time to time. However, a license cannot be transferred and will be terminated upon the death of the license holder or dissolution of the body granted the license. Applicants will have to pay charges, which may consist of royalties, premiums, development fees, or administrative fees and these vary from State to State.

Malaysian researchers will have to apply for a Use Permit under section 34 of the Act to carry out research activities in a permanent forest reserve. For this, they have to first submit a research proposal which the Forestry Department will study. Once approval is granted, certain conditions, normally parallel with State interests, will be attached. In certain cases, there can be a joint expedition with department staff.

In the State of Sabah, the "Guidelines for Plant Specimen/Botanical Collecting" apply specifically to collecting from areas under the Forestry Department's jurisdiction or where special requirements necessitate Forestry Department approval. With the enactment of the Sabah Biodiversity Enactment 2000 and the subsequent establishment of the Sabah Biodiversity Council, any collector who intends to obtain biological resources from the State will now need to apply in writing to the Sabah

Biodiversity Council for an access license. In such cases, permission from the Sabah Director of Forestry is required prior to collecting. Collectors are required to lodge a good duplicate of any collection with the Forestry Department within 30 days. When the field work is finished, collectors must submit a field report listing plants collected and their numbers.

In April 1994, the state of Sarawak amended its Forests Ordinance to incorporate new controls on access to genetic resources. The new provisions require any persons wishing to remove or export trees (or any of their derivatives) to acquire prior authorization from the Director of Forests on the approval of the Minister of Forestry of Sarawak if they intend to conduct research into pharmaceutical or medicinal compounds. The legislation's coverage is limited to "trees". Thus, its main limitation is that it does not cover biological diversity other than trees found in forests or other habitats.

Currently, little information exists on the remaining eleven States' positions on the issue of access to genetic resources. Against the backdrop of the current political situation, it is remotely possible that some of the eleven States may enact their own access laws. However, with the setting up of the National Biodiversity and Biotechnology Council, which includes all Mentri Besar[4] and Chief Ministers, the States may adopt and implement the new "Access to Genetic Resources Bill". The inclusion of all Mentri Besar and Chief Ministers in the Council is significant, since natural resources, such as forests, are under State jurisdiction. In any case, so far, none of the Peninsular Malaysia states have adopted unilateral measures like Sarawak and Sabah, which now have their state laws in place through the enactment of the Sarawak Biodiversity Center Ordinance in December 1997, the Sarawak Biodiversity (Access, Collection and Research) Regulations in December 1998, and the Sabah Biodiversity Enactment in November 2000, respectively. The proactive positions of the States of Sarawak and Sabah are underscored by the fact that some of Malaysia's richest biodiversity is found in these two states, upon which their indigenous communities still depend for their livelihood and survival.

As for nonspecific measures, there is a fairly extensive framework of legislation for biological diversity conservation, which may relate indirectly to access to genetic resources. This framework can be broadly categorized into three types:

- Legislation directly related to the protection and conservation of biological diversity with emphasis on the flora and fauna of the country. However, protection of plants is currently not provided for in national legislation. The National Forestry Act of 1984 and the forest enactments of Sabah and Sarawak are intended to regulate and control the harvesting of timber and other forest products, but these are inadequate to cover the many species of wild plants found in the country. This omission

has become all the more significant in light of the renewed interest in natural and pharmaceutical products derived from plant samples. An exception to this general legislative omission is the Sarawak State legislation called the Wildlife Protection Ordinance 1990, Protected Plants Listing.

- Legislation related to the management and use of natural resources and natural habitats. There are a number of statutes that provide for the management of natural habitats and other critical areas such as water catchment areas and rivers. Existing legislation which relates to the establishment and management of protected areas includes the National Parks Act of 1980 in the Peninsula, the Sabah Parks Enactment of 1984, and the Sarawak National Parks and Reserves Ordinance of 1956. Such legislation also provides for the protection and conservation of biological diversity found within the boundaries of the parks.

- Legislation which has indirect impact on biological diversity. An example is the Land Acquisition Act of 1960 or the Town and Country Planning Act of 1976, in the sense that the acquisition of land or development in a particular area may threaten the biological diversity and the natural habitats which house such biological diversity.

The Sarawak Research Permit System

In 1994, the State of Sarawak proposed the idea of setting up a specific-purpose biodiversity center to enable Sarawak to protect more of its own biodiversity. The idea was thoroughly debated over the next few years. The debate culminated in late 1997 with the enactment of the Sarawak Biodiversity Center Ordinance 1997. This ordinance provided for the establishment of the Sarawak Biodiversity Council in February 1998 and the birth of the Sarawak Biodiversity Center (SBC) in July of the same year. Consequently, SBC will become the focal point for biodiversity inventory, monitoring research, education, utilization, management, and conservation.

Apart from being a focal point for biodiversity information and related activities in Sarawak, SBC is also charged with the responsibility of regulating the access to, collection of, and research on Sarawak's biological resources. To this end, in 1998 SBC put in place a Research Permit System (RPS) which also ensures the conservation of the State's biodiversity, its sustainable use, and fair and equitable benefit sharing from its use, in line with the three basic objectives of the CBD. As the RPS does not differentiate between commercial and noncommercial purposes, all scientists seeking access to genetic resources in Sarawak, whether local or foreign, have to go through this system to apply to the relevant permits.

The RPS provides for four types of permits: Research Permit, Export Permit, Sales Permit for Protected Species, and Ethnobiological Permit (Figure 2). The term "biological resources" as defined by the Ordinance includes any extracts, whether in liquid or solid form, tissues, by-product or derivative, or synthesized form thereof. In relation to biological resources, the term "derivative" includes their genetic and genomic form or material. The term "ethnobiology" means the knowledge or information pertaining to the uses by the native peoples of the State of biological resources for medicinal, food, health, or other purposes,

including the classification, indigenous nomenclature, conservation techniques, and general sociological importance of such biological resources to them.

Before any permit may be granted for research on biological resources or for ethnobiological research, a research agreement must be entered into between the Government and the person or institution intending to carry out such research. A research agreement shall include, but

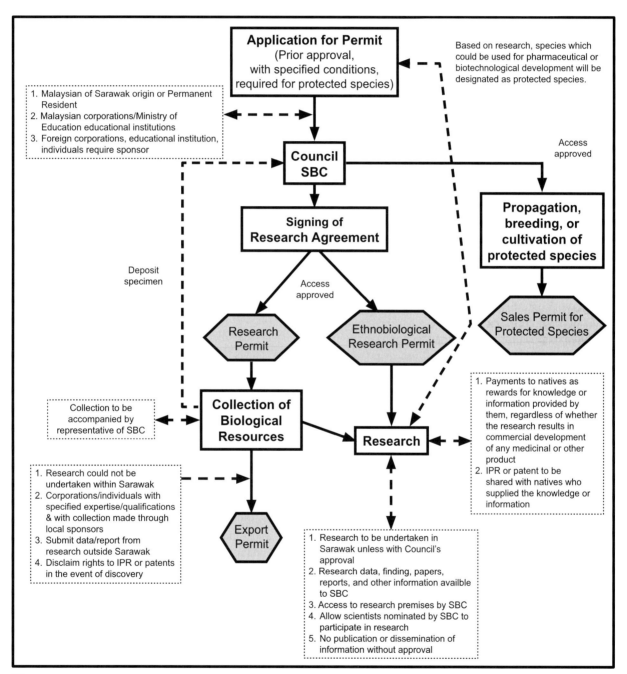

Figure 2. The research permit system as stipulated by the Sarawak Biodiversity Center (SBC). Four types of permits are provided (shaded hexagons). The solid lines designate the steps from application to receipt of permit and the undertaking which it allows. The dashed lines indicate information feedback pathways. The dotted boxes provide specific requirements or information needed at several steps. The unbounded text provides commentary on specific steps and results of the processes.

is not limited to the following:

- The place or institution in Sarawak or outside Sarawak where research is to be carried out;

- Access by the Council to any reports, data, studies, or results of the research undertaken;

- Rights of the Government to patents and intellectual property or over any discovery resulting from the research undertaken, and where appropriate, the sharing of such rights with other parties in accordance with the research agreement;

- The rights of the Government to license any patent or intellectual property and the entitlement to benefits derived therefrom;

- Confidentiality over any reports, data, studies, or results from such research;

- The transfer of technology, skills, and knowledge derived from such research, including the training of scientists from the State, and their participation in such research;

- Ownership of data and results accruing from research; and

- Other terms and conditions as may be mutually agreed upon.

For ethnobiological research, the permit holder may be required to make payments to native peoples as rewards for the knowledge or information provided by them in connection with the research. The payment may be made regardless of whether the research results in the commercial development of any medicinal or other products. Where such research leads to the development of any pharmaceutical or medicinal compound or any health or nutritional product, the patent or intellectual property right to such compound or product shall be shared with the native people.

The Sabah Access License

In 2000, Sabah passed the Sabah Biodiversity Enactment 2000 and established the Sabah Biodiversity Council. As stipulated by the Enactment, any collector who intends to obtain biological resources shall apply in writing to the Sabah Biodiversity Council for an access license. The application shall be in respect of access to biological resources found on: a) State lands; b) any reserves, indigenous peoples' customary lands, or any other sites over which indigenous and local communities exercise community-based or customary rights; or c) any other areas,

including rivers, tributaries, waterways or areas covered by water, marine parks, or territorial waters of the State, as well as any *ex situ* collections maintained by the State. There will be no export for research purposes of any biological resources without a license issued by the Council. With the establishment of the Sabah Biodiversity Center in 2001, it began taking on procedures for granting access permits in the State (Figure 3).

National Level:
The Access to Genetic Resources Bill

At the national level, the National Task Force on Access to Genetic Resources was established by the National Technical Committee on Biological Diversity with the specific mandate of addressing the issue of access to genetic resources (Box 1). In drafting the country's future access law and policy through a broad consultative process, the Task Force was represented by agencies with responsibility for the management of biodiversity in the country. In general, the Task Force opted for developing the Access to Genetic Resources Bill with wide consultative public input and with access requirements that are simple and clear, by taking into consideration the following:

- Promotion of local scientific research and development, i.e., to reduce unnecessary potential constraints on local research and development;

- Promotion of bioprospecting, in particular by private sector and multinational firms;

- Provision of ample opportunities for participation by all stakeholders;

- Securing and maximizing practical and enforceable sharing of benefits from the uses of biological resources and associated traditional knowledge and traditions, with emphasis on conservation of biological resources and associated knowledge, financial benefits, research collaboration, and technology transfer;

- Ensuring the practicality of prior informed consent (PIC) procedures and benefit-sharing arrangements with local communities;

- Ensuring that the emerging access regime is not overly bureaucratic; and

- Ensuring adequate government administrative and technical capacities to implement the laws and the access procedures with the relevant degree of centralization/decentralization.

Analysis of the Process that Led to the Development of the Access to Genetic Resources Bill

The process leading to the development of the Access to Genetic Resources Bill is summarized in Table 2. The process really took off in 1994, two years after the Rio Summit, when the NCBD was formed and began strategic

planning on biological diversity in Malaysia. The National Technical Committee on Biological Diversity then established the Task Force on Access to Genetic Resources (Box 1). To assist the Task Force, the AG played a pivotal role in the revision of the law on access to genetic resources. The process was intensified and culminated in the organization of the National Workshop on Access and Benefit Sharing of Genetic Resources in 1997 (Box 2).

The Task Force finally recommended, after a reversal of an earlier stance and in-depth deliberations, enactment of a national (Federal) framework legislation that would be known later as the "Access to Genetic Resources Bill" applicable to the whole of Malaysia. Earlier, based on the recommendation of the AG that no new legislation was required to address the issue of bioprospecting, access, and benefit sharing, the approach was to consider amending three statutes, namely the National Forestry Act of 1984, the Protection of Wildlife Act of 1972, and the Fisheries Act of 1985, by inserting new provisions relating to the establishment of a licensing system within the existing legislative provisions. The license (or access license as it is referred to in the amendments) was meant to be a form of access control. However, the approach of amending each piece of legislation was too fragmented to ensure a consistent approach. In addition, the process did not identify a single agency with the responsibility of administering the licensing system. Instead, it imposed responsibility on many agencies, depending on the responsible

authority for each piece of legislation amended. Neither did the process provide for a monitoring mechanism. Benefit sharing was addressed only in terms of technology transfer and the collection of fees and payment of royalties. The distribution of benefits for the purposes of conservation and local community development was not adequately considered. The amendments addressed the issue of access and benefit sharing (ABS) at one level, but no clear linkages were drawn from the amendments to the objectives of conserving biological diversity and equitable benefit sharing. Furthermore, in light of the vital contributions made by local and indigenous communities, the protection of indigenous knowledge and innovations becomes particularly relevant and needs to be addressed. Therefore, it was imperative that national legislation be enacted that would guarantee consistency in approach to key issues, for the purpose of fulfilling obligations under the CBD, despite the fact that the Federal-State dichotomy issues at hand would still need to be resolved.

At one point in the process leading to the development of the access law, the Task Force worked on the provision to establish a National Biodiversity Council responsible for matters relating to access to genetic resources and also to the biosafety of genetically modified organisms (GMOs).

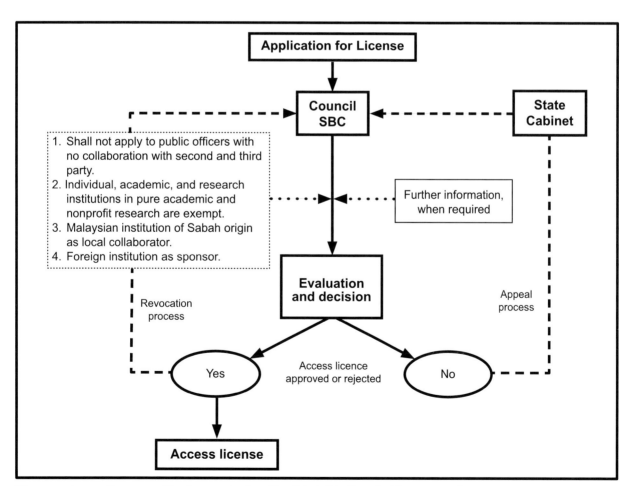

Figure 3. Access license application as stipulated by Sabah Biodiversity Enactment of 2000.

This meant that that there would be three separate bills to be considered together, namely, one bill for access to genetic resources, one bill for biosafety, and the third bill for establishing the institutional structure that would be responsible for administering and implementing the other two bills (Table 2). This approach, which would have created a colossal legal predicament, was proposed by the Task Force to MOSTE. It has now been decided that this approach will no longer be pursued, and two of the bills (i.e., access and biosafety), each with its own institutional infrastructure, will now be tabled separately.

Five years after its establishment, the Task Force officially completed its task when it adopted the final text of the Access to Genetic Resources Bill in October 1999. The whole process from the final draft to the passing of the Bill into law would be handled by MOSTE, in close collaboration with the AG and was expected to be com-pleted in not less than one year. In the meantime, the Bill was scheduled to go through the national consultative process in the years 2000 and 2001, then to the Cabinet for approval, and finally to the Parliament for the Bill to be passed into law. Be that as it may, the process has progressed at a relatively slower pace particularly with regard to national consultation. MOSTE is currently giving priority to passing the Biosafety Bill into law in 2004. Therefore, the process of completion and adoption by the government of the Access to Genetic Resources Bill will now extend beyond 2004. The responses from the different States, in particular Sarawak and Sabah, are crucial for the completion and adoption of the access law.

It should be noted that while the above process was taking place at the Federal level, the states of Sarawak and Sabah had their own processes underway, and these culminated in the enactment of the Sarawak Biodiversity

---

Box 1. Task Force on Access to Genetic Resources

Pursuant to the decision of the National Committee on Biological Diversity, the Task Force was set up to review or revise the relevant Malaysian laws to meet Malaysia's CBD obligations. One of the important areas identified by the Task Force for urgent revision relates to access to genetic resources as addressed under Article 15 of CBD to ensure that Malaysia's interest under the Article is fully protected.

The Task Force membership included representatives from the Attorney General's Chambers; MOSTE; Forest Department; Department of Agriculture; Wildlife Department; Fisheries Department; Veterinary Department; research institutions; universities; representatives from the states of Pahang, Perak, and Sarawak; and representatives from NGOs such as the Third World Network. With regard to biotechnology, a representative from the National Biotechnology Directorate under MOSTE and a number of researchers from several research institutions and universities also sat in as members of the Task Force.

There was no direct representation from the indigenous and local communities in the Task Force; however, their interests were represented by the relevant ministries and agencies. SBC was especially very helpful, since it is directly involved with various indigenous and local communities in Sarawak, and since the end of 1998, it has been administering and implementing the Sarawak Biodiversity (Access, Collection and Research) Regulations of 1998.

In the course of undertaking its task, the Task Force had consultations with all the states in Peninsular Malaysia and Sabah and Sarawak, taking into consideration different and *ad hoc* concerns pertaining to various issues relating to the CBD in general, and issues on access to genetic resources in particular. With MOSTE providing administration, the Task Force held a series of meetings from 1994 through 1999. In 1999, the Task Force sent the draft Bill to all States and requested their comments in writing. In 2000, MOSTE organized a consultative workshop on access and benefit sharing to explain the draft Bill to various ministries and agencies with responsibilities for the management of biodiversity in the country, including representatives from private sector, industries, and NGOs, and to obtain feedback from them. A national consultative process was also initiated in early 2001 and all States and relevant stakeholders had been asked for their responses and for feedback on the final draft.

The work of the Task Force can be summarized as occurring in two phases:

Phase One: Amendment of Existing Sectoral Legislation and Enactment of a Separate Legislation to Address the Gaps or Loopholes Applicable to Peninsular Malaysia.
The Task Force started its review with a focus on legal mechanisms already available within Malaysia's legal framework. It further restricted its review to laws applicable only to Peninsular Malaysia, since the relevant laws in Sabah and Sarawak are separate from the relevant laws in Peninsular Malaysia. Based on the framework of existing laws, the review would address, on a component by component basis, the following: forests, fisheries, wild animals, domestic animals, agrobiodiversity, and microorganisms. Subsequently, it was considered whether, based on the results of the review, the necessary legal requirements relating to access to genetic resources could be incorporated separately but uniformly into relevant existing laws, e.g., the National Forestry Act of 1984 or the Protection of Wildlife Act of 1972. These revised laws would then provide strict legal mechanisms for protection of genetic resources found in Malaysia and should legally reflect the various requirements under Article 15 of the CBD: access to genetic resources based on PIC, mutually agreed terms, participation in research and development by parties providing the genetic resources, and equitable sharing of benefits arising from commercial use and utilization of genetic resources and the results of research and development on them.

Having undertaken this initial review exercise, the Task Force came to several conclusions presented in the following paragraphs along with the current implementation status of each of them:

- Based on the relevant existing laws, the Task Force found that the requirements under Article 15 could be incorporated into existing laws for only some components of

Center Ordinance of 1997 and the Sabah Biodiversity Enactment of 2000.

Identification and Analysis of the Main Difficulties and Successes Experienced during the Design of the Access to Genetic Resources Bill

Many issues and questions experienced during the design of the Access to Genetic Resources Bill still remain unresolved. Therefore, considerable efforts are still needed before the access Bill is adopted by all States and passed into law. These were the main difficulties:

- Determining the authority (Federal-State dichotomy) to legislate on matters relevant to biological diversity;

- Promoting uniformity of the laws of the States;
- Intersections with other areas of law;
- Ensuring that access legislation meets all objectives of the CBD and is consistent with national priorities;
- Establishing the institutional structure for the implementation of the law (including the idea of an umbrella institution to be responsible for both access to genetic resources and biosafety, which turned out to be unworkable.
- Obtaining model laws to serve as templates or as sources of useful rules and principles to guide the development of access regime;
- Establishing/designating appropriate competent authorities with a clear mandate to determine matters related to access and benefit sharing, e.g., inter-

---

Box 1. Continued

biodiversity: the Animal Ordinance of 1953 for domestic animals; the Protection of Wildlife Act of 1972 for wild animals; the National Forestry Act of 1984 for forests; and the Fisheries Act of 1985 for fisheries. In other words, the only components of Malaysia's biodiversity that could be addressed under the present legal framework for the purposes of CBD Article 15 were these four. While a national (Federal) framework law applicable to the whole of Malaysia was also being considered, the Task Force took cognizance of the gaps or loopholes in these laws that would need to be addressed.

- With respect to agrobiodiversity, the Task Force found that existing relevant laws were inappropriate for the purposes of incorporating CBD Article 15 requirements, especially after taking into account, with respect to plant varieties, the various on-going international developments (i.e., TRIPS, the revision of the International Union for the Protection of New Varieties of Plants agreement, and the revision of the International Undertaking on Plant Genetic Resources). Therefore, the Task Force felt that this matter would be best addressed in a new and separate law so as to be consistent with these developments and to ensure that the new law would address the totality of issues relating to plant varieties. So, the draft Plant Variety Protection Bill was proposed.

- With regard to microorganisms, the Task Force found that existing legislation relating to plants and animals could not be readily extended to implement the requirements under CBD Article 15. This is because of the different nature of microorganisms, as opposed to plants and animals *per se*, and the finding that microorganisms have never been legislated upon in any manner in Malaysia. The Task Force felt therefore that it would best to embody the Article 15 requirements regarding access to microorganisms in a separate law. Therefore, the issue of microorganisms would be addressed by the national Access to Genetic Resources Bill.

- In order to formulate strict legal mechanisms for access

to genetic resources found in Malaysia, the Task Force was of the view that this should be approached on two levels: First, a mandatory statutory requirement should be imposed on persons gaining access to genetic resources in Malaysia to obtain a prescribed form of license under the law, whether or not such access relates to collection, use, export, or research of the genetic resources in question. Second, a separate contractual mechanism (as opposed to the statutory offenses mechanism) should be imposed whereby any persons intending to gain access to genetic resources in Malaysia must enter into an agreement with the Government of Malaysia regulating activities with respect to the collection, use, export, or research of the genetic resources. Both mechanisms were incorporated in the draft Access to Genetic Resources Bill. Any collector seeking an access activity is required to apply for an access license and also to enter into a separate contractual agreement. In this manner, apart from being able to impose sanctions as provided for in the governing statute, sanctions in the form of breach of contract can also be imposed.

- Further, the Task Force was of the view that although these mechanisms must be incorporated separately into the various laws, sufficient uniformity in its format to ensure basic principles and requirements (such as PIC, equitable sharing of benefits arising from commercial use and utilization, and results of research and development of genetic resources, and participation of parties in research and development) should be embodied. With respect to ensuring sufficient uniformity for the above mechanisms when incorporating them into the various laws, this would be addressed by the draft Access to Genetic Resources Bill.

- Consistent with the Task Force's approach to impose strict legal requirements to protect genetic resources, the Task Force took note of EPU's efforts to formulate a new set of guidelines relative to research and was of the view that the imposition of these guidelines would be insufficient for the purposes of CBD Article 15 because they were not agency composition, monitoring and enforcement of compliance;

- Establishing competent authorities/negotiating partners to take account of the interests of the holders of indigenous/traditional knowledge;

- Determining the nature of biological resources to be covered under the scope of the application, e.g., derivatives of biological resources and their associated intangible components; culture collections; migratory species; and resources collected before the CBD came into force and stored in *ex situ* collections;

- Adequate participation of the holders of indigenous/ traditional knowledge or their representative organizations in the development of appropriate terms of access, such as determining the PIC process and

benefit sharing to an access agreement;

- Determining the nature of traditional knowledge and innovations to be covered under the scope of the application as mandated by Article 8(j) and related provisions;

- Ensuring access regulations that will not hinder basic noncommercial research, e.g., education and taxonomy; and

- Promoting fairness and equity to a wide range of relevant stakeholders in developing the access measures.

The main successes included:

- A comprehensive Bill was designed to regulate access to genetic resources rather than simplifying or amending existing sectoral laws (i.e., if the CBD is to have any practical impact, it needs to be

---

Box 1. Continued

legally binding. Currently, there is little information on the proposal or on progress by EPU to formulate a new set of guidelines relative to research. However, pending the conclusion of revision and amendment of laws, EPU's Guidelines on Research should be adopted immediately as a temporary measure for the protection of genetic resources found in Malaysia. The EPU's Guidelines on Research are still in force as a continuing measure of protection of genetic resources found in Malaysia.

- The Task Force's general conclusion was that both the revision and amendment of existing laws with respect to wild animals, domestic animals, forests, and fisheries, and the setting up of new laws with respect to agrobiodiversity and microorganisms in the manner suggested above, would fully address Malaysia's concerns regarding access to genetic resources in the context of Article 15. The setting up of new laws with respect to agrobiodiversity and microorganisms to address the gaps or loopholes arising from the existing sectoral laws became unnecessary since the Access to Genetic Resources Bill was proposed.

- The Task Force further noted that Sabah and Sarawak have separate laws on forests and animals, and in the case of Sarawak, its laws have already been updated to meet the CBD's Article 15 requirements. The Task Force welcomed this effort by the State of Sarawak, but noted that where the relevant laws in these States had not been updated, it would be useful for these States to continue participating in the Task Force so as to achieve consistency and uniformity, where possible. However, it should be noted that with the enactment of the Sarawak Biodiversity Center Ordinance of 1997 and the Sabah Biodiversity Enactment of 2000, many relevant laws on forests and animals have already been updated to meet the CBD's Article 15 requirements.

- The Task Force also noted that implementing the revision of laws was to be done in accordance with the respective legislative authorities of the Federal and State Governments, as appropriate, as specified in the Federal Constitution. The Task Force was of the opinion that the

revision of laws should not require any amendments to the Federal Constitution, and this was to be done in accordance with the respective legislative authorities of the Federal and State Governments, as appropriate, as stipulated under Article 76 of the Ninth Schedule.

Phase Two: Enactment of a National (Federal) Framework Legislation Applicable to the Whole of Malaysia

The preliminary findings of the Task Force (*Phase One*) were presented to the National Committee on Biological Diversity before the launch of the National Policy on Biological Diversity in 1998. Important objectives of the policy are the optimization of economic benefits through the sustainable utilization of biological diversity and the identification of biodiversity prospecting activities as a priority.

The National Committee sought to appraise the adequacy of the measures which would be undertaken to implement the policy objectives on access and benefit sharing as stated in the National Policy on Biological Diversity. First, the National Committee was of the opinion that there was an absence of an integrative approach across sectors due to the limited scope of various enactments in relation to the overall objectives of biological diversity conservation. Second, the areas of jurisdiction of Federal and State governments as defined in the Constitution would lead to nonuniform implementation between States. Consequently, the National Committee decided that Malaysia's interests under CBD Article 15 would be fully realized and protected only if a national (Federal) framework legislation applicable to the whole of Malaysia were to be legislated.

With the new guidance provided for by the policy change intervention, the Task Force continued to progress on the draft access law, and to incorporate the legislative provisions to promote and enforce these objectives on a nationwide basis. The draft Access to Genetic Resources Bill was finally adopted by the Task Force in October 1999 and subsequently presented to MOSTE for further deliberations and actions.

translated into national law and then enforced).

- A system of cooperation between the Competent Authorities[6] of the Federal and State Governments was proposed to ensure uniformity in the administration of the law.

- Biotechnology and biodiversity prospecting, having considerable potential to add value to specific biological/genetic resources, have been given priority and will increasingly become strategic factors in the near future.

- A distinction was made between academic research and commercial bioprospectors.

- A system of mandatory licenses for access and access agreements between parties, containing minimum terms concerning the provision of information and samples, technology cooperation, and benefit sharing, was developed.

- A system of community intellectual rights was proposed for the purpose of: a) recognition of ownership rights of communities over their knowledge and innovations, b) protection of the communities' knowledge and innovations, and c) ensuring that an equitable share of benefits arising from use of such knowledge is channeled back to the communities. (This system was discussed but due to its controversial nature it was not taken on board in the Access to Genetic Resources Bill. However, the discussion of the system can be considered as one of the successes of the process.)

- The elements of a community intellectual rights system were determined, such as: a) identification of recognized community intellectual rights, including setting up a system of collection and registration of traditional knowledge and innovations, b) criteria, mechanisms, and procedures for

Table 2. Process leading to the development of the Access to Genetic Resources Bill

- NCBD, established in 1994, in turn established the National Technical Committee on Biological Diversity and GMAC.

- The National Technical Committee on Biological Diversity established in 1994 the Task Force on Country Study on Biological Diversity, the Task Force on National Policy on Biological Diversity, and the Task Force on Access to Genetic Resources.

- A Country Study on Biological Diversity was undertaken by ISIS, MNS, WWF Malaysia, and UPM, June 1995–July 1996. A Task Force, jointly coordinated by Universiti Kebangsaan Malaysia (UKM) and Forest Research Institute Malaysia (FRIM), which reported to the National Technical Committee on Biological Diversity, was responsible for overseeing the preparation of the document entitled "Assessment of Biological Diversity in Malaysia" (MOSTE 1997).

- The Task Force on Access to Genetic Resources held meetings from 1994 through 1999.

- The meeting 'Guidelines to facilitate access to biological resources and the equitable sharing of benefits in the South East Asian Region' was organized by UNESCO and the Malaysian Natural Products Society and held 6–9 April 1996.

- National Workshop on Access and Benefit Sharing of Genetic Resources, 4–6 August 1997, produced an assessment of national needs and opportunities with regard to access and benefit sharing initiatives, adopted the direction of amending existing sectoral legislation, and discussed the model agreement for biodiversity prospecting and reviewed the provisions of the draft *Agreement for Research, Collection and Utilization of Biological/ Genetic Resources for Environmentally Sound Uses* (drafted by AG).

- "Assessment of Biological Diversity in Malaysia" was published in 1997.

- The Sarawak Biodiversity Center Ordinance was adopted December 1997.

- The National Wetland Policy (currently still in the draft-

ing process) was expected to be ready in 1997.

- South and Southeast Asia Regional Workshop on Access to Genetic Resources and Traditional Knowledge was held in Chennai, India, 22–25 February 1998, with Malaysian participation.

- National Policy on Biological Diversity was launched on 16 April 1998.

- Sarawak Biodiversity Center was established, July 1998.

- Sarawak Biodiversity (Access, Collection and Research) Regulations were enacted in December 1998.

- A meeting on the ASEAN Framework Agreement on Access to Genetic Resources was organized by the Department of Environment and Natural Resources of the Philippines and the World Resources Institute (WRI), USA, 3–6 December 1998; Malaysia could not participate.[5]

- Consultation took place with all States on ABS issues throughout 1999.

- NCBD rendered a decision in 1999 with a new direction: To enact a national (Federal) framework legislation applicable to the whole of Malaysia.

- Final text of Access to Genetic Resources Bill was adopted in October 1999.

- First Meeting of Panel of Experts on ABS took place in Costa Rica, October 1999 with Malaysian participation.

- The International Conference "Biodiversity 2000", took place in Kuching, Malaysia, 1–3 November 2000.

- The Sabah Biodiversity Enactment occurred in November 2000.

- Consultation with ministries/agencies responsible for the management of biodiversity, and industries on ABS, Malaysian Center for Remote Sensing, Kuala Lumpur, 21 December 2000

- Second Meeting of Panel of Experts on ABS, Montreal, March 2001 (Malaysia participated)

- The Sabah Biodiversity Center was established in 2001.

- Ad Hoc Open-Ended Working Group on ABS met in Bonn, Germany, October 2001 with Malaysian participation.

implementing the system, c) identification of technical institutions, and d) registration of indigenous and local community organizations.

- Types of benefits[7] were specified to include: a) voucher specimens, b) support for conservation and related activities, c) participation/collaboration of nationals in research, d) sharing of research and development results, e) effective access and transfer of technology, f) capacity building of institutions

and indigenous and local communities, and g) financial benefits of various forms (e.g., collection fees, payments of agreed sums at various stages, and royalties).

Issues that were Controversial during the Discussions

Ownership of Genetic Resources:

- Access to biological resources found on public

Box 2. National Workshop on Access and Benefit Sharing of Genetic Resources: International Imperatives and National Needs (MOHAMAD 1997)

This workshop was organized in August 1997 by the Genetics Society of Malaysia and UKM, on behalf of the National Committee on Biological Diversity and the Task Force on Access to Genetic Resources in collaboration with the WRI. The objectives of the workshop were to: 1) formulate national responses to CBD articles 15, 16 and 19; 2) review existing national legislation with respect to access and benefit-sharing; and 3) review current initiatives in neighboring countries and other regions of the world while assessing the existing international situation on genetic resources utilization.

The workshop participants included representatives from government agencies, universities, and NGOs. Representatives from the WRI, the World Conservation Union (IUCN) Environmental Law Center, and the Royal Botanic Gardens, Kew, also attended the workshop as resource persons. The workshop was an awareness-raising consultative process involving the various stakeholders at the national level. Recommendations for developing the legal and institutional framework for access and benefit sharing in Malaysia were discussed and three issues were identified as targets.

Assessment of needs and opportunities
The workshop agreed that there was a need for a comprehensive assessment of the current situation in the country with regard to access and benefit-sharing initiatives. The objective of such a measure would be to assess the needs, opportunities, resources, and capacities in the country. The assessment could comprise surveys and consultations to 1) identify needs and priorities; 2) assess industry demand; 3) identify market opportunities; and 4) document biodiversity prospecting activities. An assessment would also create awareness on issues relating to biodiversity prospecting, access, and benefit-sharing. The assessment's findings would then form the basis upon which a national strategy for biodiversity prospecting could be formulated.

Access and benefit-sharing legislation
The primary concern about legislation relating to access and benefit sharing was the Federal-State system in Malaysia. The constitutional dichotomy raises the issue of legislative

authority over genetic resources. The workshop agreed that the constitutional issues should be examined further to explore the possibility for new legislation. In this context, the workshop identified a number of options that could be considered:

- Enacting a national (Federal) framework law applicable to Peninsular Malaysia;
- Enacting a national (Federal) framework law applicable to the whole of Malaysia;
- Amending existing sectoral legislation and enacting a separate law to address the gaps or loopholes; and
- Enacting model state legislation for the individual states to adopt.

The workshop also discussed the elements which should be included in legislation for access and benefit sharing, such as a definition of genetic/biological resources, the problem of administrative authority, enforcement issues, and constitutional issues.

A model agreement for biodiversity prospecting
The workshop agreed that a model agreement would be an important element within the framework for regulating biodiversity prospecting activities. It would ensure minimum standards and facilitate benefit-sharing arrangements. Legislation might be able to provide minimum standards, but a further set of standards could be incorporated into biodiversity prospecting agreements. As for benefit sharing, while the general character of benefits can be specified in legislation, specific agreements can spell out a detailed list of benefits and other operational aspects. It was also agreed that while a model agreement would provide a useful basis for negotiations, it should not be looked upon as a rigid prescription but rather as a checklist of items for consideration. With these points in mind, the workshop reviewed the provisions of the draft *Access Agreement for Research, Collection and Utilization of Biological/Genetic Resources for Environmentally Sound Uses* (drafted by the AG). A list of provisions to be reconsidered was compiled to forward to the AG for further action. The draft is apparently still under consideration by the AG.

lands belonging to Federal/State governments;

- Access to biological resources found on lands where ownership rights are communal or customary;
- Access to traditional knowledge and innovations; and
- Pre-CBD *ex situ* collections.

Indigenous Knowledge and Innovations:

- Establishment of a system of community intellectual rights and
- Elements of community intellectual rights.

Intellectual Property Rights:

- Exclusive or monopoly ownership rights exercised over biological/genetic resources and traditional knowledge/innovations.
- Exclusion of intellectual property rights, such as patents over:
    - Plants, animals, microorganisms, or parts thereof;
    - Cells, genes, or copies of genes,
    - Biological and microbiological processes for production of plants and animals; and
    - Traditional knowledge and innovations.

The above are the three major issues that are being addressed by the Access to Genetic Resources Bill. There are many questions surrounding them, especially the last two issues. These important questions still remain unresolved, not only at the national (inter-ministerial) level, but also at the international level. The need for quick action should form part of the national implementation process of the CBD; however, such action must be balanced by the need for a well-thought-out policy which meets the objectives of conservation, development, and equity. Lately, because of these reasons, there was even a proposal to reduce the scope of the present Access to Genetic Resources Bill. In other words, quick action might be achieved by concentrating only on access licensing and benefit sharing.

Access to Genetic Resources Bill (The Future Access Law)

Based on federal law, if the Access to Genetic Resources Bill is adopted and implemented at the federal level, then all the Sarawak access regulations, the Sabah guidelines, and other state laws will have to be modified accordingly. However, the expeditious passage of such modifications will largely be determined by the political will at the State level. The Access to Genetic Resources Bill will also have to consider the interests of Sarawak and Sabah regarding access to their genetic resources; however, at the same time it is important that the Bill is in line with the spirit and provisions of the CBD.

Main Parts of the Bill

The components consist of Preamble, Preliminary (title, application, commencement, savings, and interpretation/meaning of terms), Objectives, Scope, License for access, Access application, Evaluation of application, Decision-making procedure, Conditions for approval (terms of access license, endorsement of access agreement, assignment, and terms of access agreement), Disclosure of information to the public, Review of decision, Monitoring and enforcement (authorities, powers of entry and investigation), Costs, Appeals, Offenses, Institutional structure (competent authority), Traditional knowledge (ownership, proof of ownership, co-ownership, system of protection of traditional knowledge, system of records of traditional knowledge, technical institutions, registration of indigenous and local community organizations), Prior informed consent, Fair and equitable sharing of benefits/agreements (types of benefits, mechanisms for sharing of benefits arising from traditional knowledge), Intellectual property rights (nonpatentability, limitations, certificate of origin, PIC, and compulsory licenses), Exemptions/Nonapplicability (public officers and researchers), Relation to other Acts, Regulations, and Transitional provisions. Thus far, the issue of funding for the implementation of the access Bill has not been discussed.

Interpretation/Meaning of Terms

The term "access" will include all activities relating to prospecting, collection, commercial utilization, and research and development of biological resources or the associated relevant community knowledge and innovations. Terms such as biological resources, genetic resources, genetic material, *in situ* conditions will be as defined in Article 2 of the CBD. The term "biological resources" will include genetic resources, organisms or parts thereof, populations, or any other biotic component of ecosystems with actual or potential use or value for humanity. Biological resources in *ex situ* collections will include those resources and their components that are conserved outside their natural habitats such as in herbariums, research institutions, universities, botanical gardens, and any other similar conservation centers, while biological resources in *in situ* conditions will include those resources that exist within ecosystems and natural habitats, and in the case of domesticated or cultivated species, in the surroundings where they have developed their distinctive properties. The term "genetic resources" means genetic material of actual or potential value, and the term "genetic material" means any material of plant, animal, microbial or other origin containing functional units of heredity.

The term "community knowledge and innovations" will include the knowledge, innovations, and practices of indigenous and local communities associated with any biological resource or any part thereof with regard to its use, properties, values, and processes in various forms, whether written, spoken, narrative or anecdotal.

Scope

The draft law stipulates that access to genetic resources must be limited to the clear biological and geographical boundaries as defined by the Government. It is intended to regulate the access of biological resources found on public lands, communal or customary lands, and alienated or private lands, as follows:

- Public lands, which either belong to the State or Federal governments or come under their jurisdiction (e.g., forest, wildlife reserves, parks, and marine parks);
- Communal or customary lands, where the indigenous and local communities have the ownership rights which are collective or communal or based on custom (e.g., native customary lands and aboriginal reserves); and
- Alienated or private lands, which are lands held under individual title or by another legal proprietor.

The law will also regulate access to community knowledge and innovations associated with the biological resources. It also preserves the rights of indigenous and local communities to continue with their traditional customary practices of use, exchange, and marketing of biological resources. As an exemption, the draft law prohibits access to human genetic resources.

It is therefore apparent that the scope, as described above, is intended to cover biological resources and associated community knowledge and innovations as defined, with the exclusion of human genetic resources. This will impinge on many industries, i.e., the draft law will regulate access to genetic resources pertaining to agriculture, botanical medicine, biotechnology, and pharmaceutical products. As will be discussed later, the Sarawak Biodiversity (Access, Collection and Research) Regulations of 1998, for example, includes in its scope any compound, chemical or curative agent, molecule or product which has pharmaceutical, medicinal, biotechnological, scientific, commercial, or economic value, properties, or potential.

Two contentious issues invariably appear when we deal with the scope of the application of the draft law on access to genetic resources. The first is the issue of *ex situ* collections obtained pre-CBD, i.e., all exotic genetic materials (for example, rubber, oil palm, and cocoa) obtained through various collection missions and exchange programs before 29 December 1993. Malaysia is of the opinion that such materials should not be covered in the scope and thus be subjected to benefit sharing. Any reference to pre-CBD years should be outside the scope and context of the CBD as well. The second is the issue of benefits arising from the use of biological resources including derivatives and products. Malaysia is of the opinion that such benefits should be included in the scope of the draft law, since derivatives and products of the biological resources will offer value-added options for benefit sharing. However, this issue continues to remain unclear and contentious

at the international level. For example, when developing the Bonn Guidelines on Access to Genetic Resources and Fair and Equitable Sharing of the Benefits Arising out of their Utilization which was adopted in 2001 by the Ad Hoc Open-ended Working Group on Access and Benefit Sharing, one of the obstacles to progress, which remains unresolved, is the question of the kind of genetic resources and their benefits to be covered in the scope of the Guidelines.

***Ex Situ* Collections.** As previously discussed, the draft legislation to regulate access does not include in its scope *ex situ* botanical collections and seed banks that had already been available pre-CBD (See Box 3 for examples). *Ex situ* collections that were procured from other parties after 29 December 1993 are addressed by the proposed law and are included within its scope. However, it remains unclear how the various issues surrounding the pre-CBD *ex situ* collections could be expeditiously resolved, at both national and international levels.

In Malaysia, *ex situ* conservation activities of various plant genetic resources are carried out in aboreta, seed genebanks, field genebanks, and in vitro genebanks or under cryopreservation. Based on a survey in 1988, it was estimated that 38,255 accessions of plant genetic material were in *ex situ* collections of various institutions in Malaysia, inclusive of both indigenous and introduced plant species. The most established and common form of *ex situ* genetic resource collections in Malaysia is through the establishment of plants in arboreta. These can be found in arboreta of many research institutions. In Peninsular Malaysia, the major arboreta are found in FRIM, Rimba Ilmu in Universiti Malaya, Medicinal Plant Garden at UPM, Orchid Collection in the Malaysian Agricultural Research and Development Institute (MARDI) and in Penang Botanical Garden. In Sabah, *ex situ* collections include the Kinabalu Park, Sepilok Aboretum, Tenom Orchid Center, and several Agriculture Research Centers. In Sarawak, the Botanic Garden in Semonggok is the main center. With the exception of the aboreta in FRIM, most of the other forest genetic collections are small in size.

Commercial Versus Academic Access. Malaysia is of the opinion that if there were no discrimination or distinction between academic research and commercial exploitation, research would be stifled, since researchers would be required to undergo the same stringent process as commercial bioprospectors.[8] From current experience faced by researchers in two States, namely, Sabah and Sarawak, where the State law does not differentiate between the two categories of applicants, nondiscrimination has proven to be a hindrance to research activities. We are in favor of the principle based on the "Free For All Malaysians"[9] feature (i.e., free access to our own biological resources).

The restriction on access to genetic resources should be discriminatory so as to facilitate enforcement. Therefore, it is proposed[10] that reference to and approval of the competent authority is required in three circumstances[11], namely:

- When there is commercial exploitation;
- When R&D is done in collaboration with foreigners; and
- When the biological resources are to leave the country.

Access Procedure

All scientists, whether they are foreigners or Malaysians, would have to follow this access procedure in order to obtain access to genetic resources for commercial purposes. But international bioprospectors will have additional conditions for approval of the application. For example, the access application will require that a foreign biopros-

pector name a local collaborator (a Malaysian institution) that will collaborate in collection, research, development, and other activities in relation to the biological/genetic resource concerned. A foreign bioprospector is also required to name the foreign institution that will act as a sponsor organization and will be responsible for the actions of the collector (to whom the access license has been granted). Both national and international bioprospectors are required to sign an access agreement with the competent authority and the relevant resource provider. However, where appropriate, the competent authority may decide that the restrictions relating to access to resources shall not apply to Malaysian researchers conducting noncommercial and basic research.

The procedure for foreign scientists who want to obtain access for noncommercial purposes is still not clear at this

---

Box 3. Important Malaysian *ex situ* genetic resource collections

Cocoa

For cocoa, prior to the setting up of the Malaysian Cocoa Board (MCB) in 1989, various government agencies and plantations were involved in maintaining cocoa genetic materials. At present, there are over 800 clones held in various organizations in Malaysia. Since 1991, MCB has undertaken efforts to collect and to establish all available cocoa genetic materials, including imported and locally selected clones, in its regional research stations. With regard to fruits, various research bodies in the country have collected and maintained indigenous living collections of fruit genetic resources. Overall, the *ex situ* collections total more than 200 species with over 4,700 accessions (MOHAMAD et al. 1997). The various institutions that provide for *in situ* conservation of fruits include FRIM in Kepong, Forest Research Center in Sepilok, Sabah and Sabah's Department of Agriculture (SDOA).

Oil palm

The genetic base upon which oil palm breeding populations had been established in Malaysia is extremely narrow, as it originated from the four seedlings planted in the Botanic Garden in Bogor in 1884. Efforts to broaden the genetic base received a boost in 1973 when MARDI and the Nigerian Institute for Agriculture Research collaborated in large-scale prospecting in Nigeria, followed by many subsequent collecting and prospecting missions. The present field genebank collection in the Malaysian Palm Oil Board Research Center in Kluang totals more than 1,000 accessions of the oil palm species *Elaeis guineensis* and *E. oleifera* from various parts of Africa and tropical Central and South America.

Orchid

The *ex situ* orchid species collection is maintained in MARDI, Serdang. The collection of indigenous species began in 1976, and there are still active collection trips, especially to unexploited areas such as the Belum Forest. A small orchid species collection is also maintained in MARDI, Cameron Highlands. More than 400 species of lowland wild orchids are also being maintained by SDOA in the Tenom Orchid Center. Apart from collecting, the Center is also helping in conservation activities of orchid species through collection and culture of seeds or

seedlings of endangered species and reintroducing them into wild habitats. For example, *Paphiopedilum rothschildianum* was reintroduced in the Kinabalu Park in 1987.

Rice

At the national level, the total rice germplasm collection stands at more than 10,000 accessions including several local wild rice species (ABDULLAH et al. 1991). All these rice accessions are conserved *ex situ* in MARDI's Genebank at the Rice Research Center in Seberang Perai. About one half of this collection comprises indigenous varieties which had been collected from remote areas nationwide. Some rice germplasm was also collected and conserved in Sarawak at the Agricultural Research Center in Semonggok, which maintains 1,169 rice accessions. The SDOA maintains over 1,000 collections of three rice species.

Rubber

Rubber also has a narrow genetic base, as most of the present plantings are derived from a small collection of 22 seedlings brought from Brazil around 1876. This situation is further exacerbated by the planting of a few selected, high yielding clones. To prevent the possibility of a genetic calamity in the near future, the Rubber Research Institute of Malaysia (now known as the Malaysia Rubber Board) embarked on an on-going enhancement program by introducing materials from the centers of diversity. These comprised the 1951–1952 importation, the 1966 importation, and the 1981 prospecting mission. The 1981 prospecting mission carried out by the International Rubber Research and Development Board (IRRDB) resulted in a collection totaling 64,736 seeds and 1,522 m budwood from 194 presumably high yielding ortet[15] trees. In compliance with the International Code of Plant Collection, 50% were retained in Brazil while the balance was distributed to Malaysia (35%) and Ivory Coast (15%) for conservation, evaluation, utilization, and redistribution to other IRRDB countries. In 1995, Malaysia carried out another major prospecting mission in Brazil and successfully collected 24,030 seeds from eight *Hevea* species, of which only 15,128 seeds germinated and 12,988 plants were established.

point. The economic costs of applying for access are not expected to be prohibitive to the bioprospectors. However, such costs have not yet been ascertained. The country is fully aware of the fact that some neighboring countries in the region have similar biodiversity, and this fact is taken into consideration on such matters. Again, comparative analysis on such costs has not been done. The proposed access procedure is envisaged to comprise the following steps (Figure 4).

Application

Applications for an access license[12] shall be submitted to the competent authority[13] in writing, together with a prescribed application fee. There shall be no access to biological resources or community knowledge and innovation without an access license granted by the competent authority.[14] Upon conviction, any collector found guilty of an offense shall be liable for a prescribed fine.

Information required in the application includes:

- The collector's identity (including the identity of a foreign institution or organization that will act as a sponsor, responsible for the actions of the collector with regard to access activity);

- Details of collector's proposed access activity, namely:
    - Types of material to be collected or knowledge or innovation to be accessed;
    - Sites of access activity or where the resource is located;
    - Quantity and intended use of the resource, including intention to commercialize;
    - Time when the access activity is to be carried out; and
    - Environmental and socioeconomic impact assessment.

- PIC by the resource provider;

- Benefit-sharing arrangements (what benefits shall be derived: payments, royalties, beneficiaries, etc.); and

- The identity of the local collaborator or sponsor[16] (a Malaysian institution).

Upon receiving the application, the competent authority may make the information therein available to the

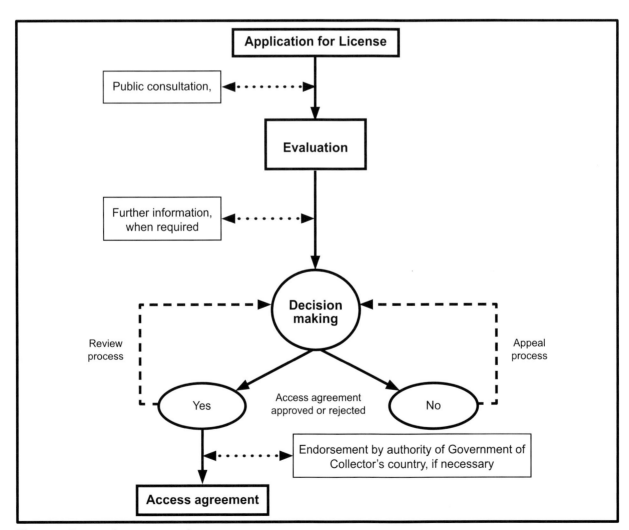

Figure 4. Proposed access procedure

public, and if necessary, provide for public consultation. Where the resource provider(s) is the indigenous and local community, the competent authority shall ensure that the concerned indigenous and local community who may be affected by the application are informed and consulted, and their PIC is obtained.

Evaluation of Application

Factors which the competent authority shall take into account in evaluating an application include:

- The activity should contribute to, and not undermine, the conservation and sustainable use of biological resources.
- Impact assessments on biological resources, the environment, and ecology are provided.
- Impact assessments on communities and their knowledge, innovations, and practices (Article 8(j) of CBD) are provided.
- PIC has been obtained in writing from the resource owner in accordance with the prescribed procedure.
- The benefit-sharing arrangement is fair and equitable.

When determining what is fair and equitable benefit sharing, the competent authority may take into account the factors such as: endemism or rarity of the biological resource; the conservation status of the biological resource; its existing, potential, intrinsic, and commercial value; its intended use; and whether traditional knowledge is involved.

Decision-Making Procedure

In making a decision on the application, the competent authority may, if necessary, request further information with regard to the application, and shall notify the collector in writing of its decision. The decision made by the competent authority can be either approved with or without conditions or rejected. A decision can be appealed and the appeal process begun at any time within three months of the date of receipt of the decision.

Conditions for Approval

Approval of an application may be contingent on an agreement in writing (an access agreement), an indemnity or guarantee, on obligations during collection or access activity (quantities or species of material to be collected), obligations after collection or access activity (deposit of specimens, records, report of activities), and other conditions.

Review of Decision

Any approval given may be revoked or subject to further conditions upon review of such approval. Grounds for such review include when new information or review of existing information establishes risks or adverse impacts on the environment, biological resources, or communities or when serious impacts or unanticipated effects on biological resources, environment, communities, and ecology occur.

Monitoring and Enforcement

Existing monitoring and enforcement authorities shall be responsible for monitoring and enforcement of this law, within their respective sectors or jurisdictions, and include the following:

- Monitoring of collection or access activity, reporting requirements, and procedures; and
- Powers of arrests, entry, search and seizure with respect to offenses under the law.

Institutional Structure

Two options[17] have been proposed with regard to the institutional structure under which the draft Bill might be implemented (Table 3). Option 1. The federal government is to designate a Federal authority as the competent authority. This means that the Federal authority shall receive, process, and grant all applications for a) access to biological resources and b) access to community knowledge and innovations. There will be a national body (the National Biodiversity Council, modeled on the Environmental Quality Council) to be set up to formulate policy and make recommendations to the competent authority on implementation of the law.

Option 2: State governments are to designate State competent authority to receive, process, and grant access applications for access to lands within the State territories. The federal government is to designate Federal competent authority to receive, process, and grant access applications for: a) access to lands within Federal territories, and b) access to community knowledge and innovations. There will be national body (e.g. the National Biodiversity Council which is modeled on the National Land Council) to be set up to advise the State and Federal competent authorities on implementation of the law. There will also be a Federal body (new or designated) which will be the national coordinating and clearinghouse mechanism, and which will receive and channel to appropriate competent authorities all applications for access licenses.

The relevant sectoral authorities will administer and implement the proposed law or policy. These include the national and State Departments of Agriculture, the national Veterinary Services Department, the national Fisheries Department, the national Department of Wildlife and National Parks, the State forest departments, and the various State ministries in Sarawak and Sabah.

Therefore, responsibility to enforce the law or policy rests with both national and State administrations. A coordinating body or national focal point is needed. No body exists presently to ensure consistency in decision making, to monitor implementation, to assess progress, and to act as a national focal point while providing recommendations on how the law or policy could be improved in the future.

Novel Provisions of the Future Law or Policy

There is a provision which allows exemptions or nonapplicability of the law if access to genetic resources is undertaken by any of the following:

- The general public for their own utilization;
- Public officers in the course of carrying out their public duties;
- Malaysian researchers affiliated with local institutions conducting noncommercial *bona fide* research;
- Indigenous and local communities, to continue with their traditional and customary practices relating to the keeping, use, exchange, sharing, marketing, or sale of biological resources by and among such communities; and
- Farmers to replant on their own land, exchange, or sell for further propagation, seeds and other

Table 3. Examples of the relevant sectoral authorities that will administer and implement the Access to Genetic Resources Bill

Federal Ministry of Agriculture
1. Department of Agriculture
   Enforcement of Pesticides Act of 1974 and Plant Quarantine Act of 1976.
2. Department of Fisheries (DOF)
   Administration and enforcement of Fisheries Act of 1985 and Exclusive Economic Zone Act of 1984 for the proper management and conservation of inshore and deep sea resources. The DOF also develops, administers and manages the waters of the 38 designated Marine Parks in Malaysia.
3. Veterinary Services Department
   The Animal Quarantine Station manages the import and export of wildlife.

Federal Ministry of Primary Industries
1. Federal Forest Department
   Responsible for administration and management of all forest resources and is guided by the National Forest Policy. States are empowered to formulate independent forest policies, and the Department provides advice and technical assistance to them.

Federal Ministry of Science, Technology and the Environment
1. Department of Environment
   Administers and enforces the Environmental Quality Act of 1974. It also assesses development projects subject to the environmental impact assessment order with respect to their impact on the environment.
2. Department of Wildlife and National Parks
   Manages wildlife reserves and national parks, and administers and enforces the Convention on International Trade in Endangered Species of Wild Fauna and Flora, and Wildlife Enactment of 1972.

State Ministry of Sarawak
1. Sarawak Biodiversity Center
   Ensures conservation of State's biodiversity, identifies new natural and biotechnological products (bioprospecting) that can bring socio-economic benefits, and facilitates and authorizes access to Sarawak's biological resources.

State Ministry of Sabah
1. Sabah Biodiversity Center
   Ensures conservation of the State's biodiversity, and facilitates and authorizes access to Sabah's biological resources.

propagating materials, that are grown on their own land.

Another provision proposes the establishment of a common trust fund where knowledge and innovation cannot be attributed to a particular community. Any access activity seeking to use traditional knowledge for commercial utilization shall pay to the fund a sum, to be determined, representing a percentage of the gross sales of any product or process utilizing or incorporating the traditional knowledge. The competent authority and the indigenous or local community shall then be jointly responsible for the equitable distribution of the monies solely for the benefit of the concerned indigenous or local community. The payment made to the said fund will be administered by the competent authority for use in promoting the welfare of the indigenous and local communities and for the conservation and sustainable use of the biological resources.

Provisions not Included in the Bill
The following three items were discussed earlier, but are still considered contentious, both at national and international levels and thus were not included in the Bill.

- When a patent has been granted over a product or process as a result of access activities in Malaysia, the establishment of a provision to regulate the inventions, including granting compulsory licenses on the grounds of public interest or necessity to compensate for the high costs or insufficient supply of the said product or process;

- The establishment of a proposed system of international cooperation with the relevant authorities of other countries to incorporate a provision that patents should not be granted without the prior consent of the country of origin, to prevent biopiracy or the misappropriation of traditional/traditional knowledge through patenting abroad of a product, process, or knowledge by persons or institutions of other countries; and

- The establishment of a system of community intellectual rights for the purpose of the recognition of ownership rights of communities over their knowledge and innovations, the protection of the communities' knowledge and innovations, and for ensuring that an equitable share of benefits arising from use of such knowledge is channeled back to the communities, including setting up a system of collection and registration of traditional knowledge and innovations, establishing technical institutions, and registering indigenous and local community organizations.

Bioprospecting Projects

Bioprospecting is defined as the search for new bioactive compounds from biological resources as diversified as plants, soil microbes, marine sponges, and insects. In general, bioprospecting involves the collection (access) of a diverse range of biological resources or organisms, the preparation of crude abstracts for multiple biological screening, and the isolation of chemicals, enzymes, secondary metabolites, genetic materials, and others that may provide leads for the development of new commercial products in the pharmaceutical, food, and agricultural industries. In bioprospecting, ethnobotanical information can serve as an important lead in drug discovery and other specific uses. Biotechnology is also increasingly being used to capitalize on various biological and genetic resources.

Currently, there are only a mere handful of bioprospecting projects that are going on in the country, virtually all of which are of a noncommercial nature. An exception is the involvement of the Government of Sarawak in a joint venture in bioprospecting collaboration, which will be described in more detail later. One of the most active aspects of these projects is the search for potentially valuable medicinal products or for potentially useful compounds for modern drug development from tropical plants carried out by research institutions and universities (Table 4). Many researchers, however, still consider such projects to be at the infancy stage, as well as expensive, technologically difficult, and better left to be carried out by affluent developed countries or multinational companies (AZIZOL and LEAN 1997). More recently, a few medicinal plants have been accorded research priorities by the National Biotechnology Directorate, for example, tongkat Ali (*Eurycoma longifolia*, Simarubaceae), hempedu bumi (*Andrographis paniculata*, Acanthaceae), kacip fatimah (*Labisia pumila*, Myrsinaceae), and pegaga (*Centella asiatica*, Apiaceae). The first three have even been aggressively promoted in commercial products.

Pharmaceutical products are also being developed from various marine organisms. Sponges, corals, tunicates, and algae are among the organisms which produce compounds that have been shown to have antibiotic, antitumor, antiviral, or anti-inflammatory activities. For example, UKM tested 51 samples of marine sponges on human tumor cell lines in cytotoxic tests and found 20 samples to be toxic to the tumors, while sea cucumbers were screened at Universiti Sains Malaysia for bioactive compounds (OTHMAN and LOFTI 1995).

More recently, preliminary screening for novel drugs has also been carried out on bacteria, myxobacteria, and fungi collected from rich lowland dipterocarp rainforests and mangrove forests. Excellent targets for such screens are components of the signal transduction pathway and cell cycle in the pursuit of effective treatment and the understanding of diseases such as cancer and Alzheimer's disease (HO et al. 2000).

During the past few years, several foreign and multinational companies were interested in applying for access to biological resources, despite the fact that the Government was in the midst of working on the law or policy to be adopted. For example, a Japanese company wanted access to soil samples for microbes and a multinational company wanted access to forest species for pharmaceuticals. In fact, a model agreement intended to ensure minimum standards and to facilitate benefit-sharing arrangements in biodiversity prospecting activities was developed in response to access interest from a foreign company. This model agreement became the basis of the draft "Access Agreement for Research, Collection and Utilization of Biological/Genetic Resources for Environmentally Sound Uses". Many prospective bioprospectors have some idea about what is in the offing for the proposed national legislation, and many are becoming fully aware of the State laws of Sarawak and Sabah. Most bioprospectors hope that Malaysia does not enact very restrictive national access legislation and regulations.

In any case, it should be noted that, at present, no Malaysian personnel are specialists in the negotiation of bioprospecting agreements. Negotiation is very critical, since during negotiation with a technology partner, rights and commercialization benefits are ascertained at the beginning of the relationship. The amount of rights and benefits available to the biological resource owner is quite dependent on negotiating skills as well as on the investment contributed. There is a need for capacity building for such personnel in the near future to assist government agencies, research institutions, and others who are involved in biodiversity prospecting arrangements. It is particularly important to be aware of the required "minimum" standards or terms where there is no existing legislation or policy on such matters. It should also be noted that bioprospecting arrangements are going to reflect commercial realities and common best practices, and we need personnel with the ability to negotiate mutually agreeable and satisfying terms. In order to prepare for increasing numbers of agreements to be negotiated by government agencies in the future, more attention should be devoted to developing the business and negotiating skills of those involved in prospecting agreements, since the quality of the agreements is essential in ensuring a practical contribution to an access regime. As previously mentioned, several companies were interested in bioprospecting attempts but these did not materialize into agreements for many reasons. One such reason could be due to the lack of negotiating skills, both at the Federal and State levels.

An Example of Commercial Bioprospecting and International Collaboration in Sarawak

In 1986, the USA National Institutes of Health, through the Natural Products Branch of the National Cancer Institute

Table 4. Examples of research on medicinal plants in Malaysia (adapted from MOHAMAD et al. 1995)

Common name	Species/Genus/Family	Use/Potential use/Study
Forest Research Institute Malaysia		
—a	*Leuconotis* spp.	Medicinal properties
Mambu	*Azadirachta indica*	"
Pokok minyak kayu putih	*Melaleuca cajuputi*	"
Kandis	*Dipterocarpus* spp.	"
Cempaka hutan	*Aromadendron* spp.	"
Edible medicinal plants (ulam):		Antioxidant activity (VIMALA et al. 1998)
Selom, Pegaga,	*Oenanthe javanica, Centella asiatica,*	
Terung kecil, Kesom,	*Solanum ferox, Polygonum minus,*	
Kadok, Ulam raja,	*Piper sarmentosum, Cosmos caudatus,*	
Cemumar, Beluntas	*Micromelum pubescens, Pluchea indica*	
Universiti Kebangsaan Malaysia		
Lada hitam	*Piper nigrum*	Phytochemical and pharmacological studies
Pinang	*Areca catechu*	"
Pokok minyak kayu putih	*Melaleuca cajuputi*	Survey of essential oils
Putarwali	*Tinospora crispa*	Studies on tissue culture techniques
—	*Alstonia angustifolia, Crotalaria* spp., *Mitragyna speciosa*	Cytotoxic effects (IKRAM et al. 1993)
—	*Goniothalamus* spp.	Antiproliferative effect (ZAUYAH et al. 1993)
Betik (flower), Putat,	*Carica papaya, Barringtonia macrostachya,*	Antitumor promoting activity (LIM et al. 1998)
Ubi keling/Kemili,	*Coleus tuberosus,*	
Pelam epal (skin),	*Mangifera indica,*	
Serai kayu	*Eugenia polyantha*	
Universiti Malaya		
Mempisang	Annonaceae	Widely used as medicines by local natives
Gambir	*Uncaria* spp.	Antihypertensive properties
Bintangor	*Calophyllum* spp.	Diverse bio-activities
—	*Trema orientalis*	Analgesic and anesthetic effects (HASHIM et al. 1993)
Universiti Malaysia Sarawak		
Oran, Pelai,	*Ageratum conyzoides, Alstonia scholaris,*	Antibacterial properties
Pedada, Rugin,	*Brucea javanica, Cassia alata,*	(FASIHUDDIN and GHAZALLY 1998)
Sengkayap, Engkara-bai,	*Eurycoma longifolia, Pasychotria viridiflora,*	
Kelapahit, Akar kelait	*Quassia indica, Unicaria longiflora*	
Universiti Putra Malaysia		
Zingiber	Zingiberaceae	Studies on medicinal properties
Jarum emas	*Striga asiatica*	"
Gelenggang	*Cassia alata*	"
Kenarah	*Goniothalamus* spp.	"
Bratawali/Putarwali	*Tinospora crispa*	"
Universiti Sains Malaysia		
Pokok kapal terbang	*Eupatorium odoratum*	As an analgesic
Gajah beranak or Selayak hitam	*Goniothalamus macrophyllus*	As an abortifacient and antifertility agent
Tongkat Ali	*Eurycoma longifolia*	For antimalaria action
Api-api	*Avicennia* spp.	Pharmacological studies
—, Selayak hitam, Pokok German	*Cerbera odollam, Goniothalamus macrophyllus, Eupatorium odoratum*	Toxicity screening (SAM et al. 1988)
—	*Malpighiaceae coccigera*	Antilithotrophic, antiasthmatic and as relief for yellow fever (UBAIDILLAH et al. 1988)
Universiti Teknologi Malaysia		
Kunyit	*Curcuma* spp.	Studies on medicinal roots
Medang	*Alseodaphne perakensis*	Studies on chemical structures and activities
Petai	*Parkia speciosa*	Study on hypoglycemic activity

aThe symbol '—' indicates that no common name was available for the species.

(NCI), commenced a program to acquire plant extracts derived from different parts of the world and to screen such extracts for anticancer and anti-HIV activities. One of the source countries selected by the NCI was Malaysia, and subsequently a collection mission was conducted in Sarawak in 1986 (JENTA et al. 2001). This led to the isolation of calanolide A from cuttings of the plant bintangor (*Calophyllum lanigerum*, Guttifereae), and the discovery in 1988 that this naturally occurring compound was active against HIV. Shortly thereafter, in 1992, calanolide B was discovered from samples of *C. teysmannii* through a re-collection mission. The original purpose of the re-collection mission was to obtain more quantities of calanolide A, since only small quantities of the compound were isolated in the first collection mission. Calanolide B was also found to be active against HIV, but unlike calanolide A, it was present in greater abundance from its natural source.

Following the NCI's confirmation of the therapeutic properties of the calanolides, efforts were directed towards obtaining sufficient quantities of the compounds for pre-clinical evaluation. In 1993, NCI awarded MediChem Research an R&D grant to develop a synthetic route to calanolide A. MediChem scientists were successful and their efforts were duly recognized by NCI in 1995. Subsequently, NCI awarded MediChem an exclusive license to their patents, which included the preparation and use of the calanolides. Under the terms of the license, MediChem was obliged to negotiate an agreement with the Sarawak Government

Negotiations began in 1995 between the State Government of Sarawak and MediChem Research, culminating in a Joint Venture Agreement between the two parties in 1996. This fulfilled the NCI's obligations, as specified in their "Letter of Collection" with the Sarawak Forestry Department in 1994. In 1996, the joint venture company, owned equally by the two partners and formally known as Sarawak MediChem Pharmaceuticals, Inc., commenced operation with the primary function to advance the development of calanolide A as an anti-HIV agent. Secondly, Sarawak MediChem's function was to spearhead the development of other promising calanolide-based therapeutics. In 1999, MediChem's original share in the company was wholly transferred to Advanced Life Sciences, Inc. Through co-ownership, the Sarawak Government and NCI will receive royalties on any future sales of a calanolide drug, apart from the benefit from the transfer of technology and training. There continues to be direct involvement of scientists from Sarawak in the management of the company and in the company's pre-clinical and clinical drug development programs. Under Sarawak's 1997 Biodiversity Center Ordinance and 1998 Access, Collection & Research Regulations, there is a framework for discovery and partnering in future drug development initiatives based on materials derived from the rainforests of Sarawak.

Intellectual Property Rights and the Agreement on Trade-Related Aspects of Intellectual Property Rights (TRIPS)

By virtue of the CBD, we have sovereign rights over our natural resources but not automatic rights over products or derivatives developed from these resources. These rights belong to the party who owns the intellectual property rights (IPRs) to the products or derivatives. And more often than not, such a party is the one with the technology to derive commercial value from the biological resources. In this regard, it is the owner of the biological resources who is responsible for coming up with an intellectual property framework (laws and procedures) under the CBD.

Intellectual property includes patents, copyrights, trademarks and designs. IPRs, especially patents, are said to help those in control of the resources to obtain economic benefits from them, and this in turn would be an incentive to conserve rather than destroy the forest. According to section 11 of the Patents Act of 1983, patents are granted to a novel invention which is commercialized. An inventive step must also be involved in developing the product. Plants, animals and biological processes to obtain new varieties or strains are not patentable by virtue of section 13(1) of the Act unless, they are human-made living microorganisms or microbiological processes.

The Access to Genetic Resources Bill includes a "non-patentability" provision which means that no patents shall

be recognized with respect to a) plants, animals, and naturally occurring microorganisms, including parts thereof and b) essentially biological processes and naturally occurring microbiological processes. No application for patents with respect to inventions involving biological resources shall be granted without the prior approval of the competent authority so as to ensure that the patent protection thereof shall be supportive of, and not run counter to, the objectives of the Bill.

The provisions on patentability have to be read in conjunction with the provisions of the Malaysian Patent Act of 1983[18] (Act 291) on the requirements of patentability. It is noted that amendments to the Patents Law are being considered, in order to comply with TRIPS, specifically with regard to the patenting of life requirements of Article 27.3(b) of TRIPS. To satisfy the requirements of TRIPS, a draft Protection of New Plant Varieties Bill was developed. It is essentially a *sui generis* system for the protection of plant genetic resources. The Bill was supposed to be have been tabled in the Parliament as early as 2000, but only became law in 2004 (Protection of New Plant Varieties Act 2004, Act 634, Laws of Malaysia).

There are no other intellectual property right instruments that protect inventions derived from genetic resources and traditional knowledge. However, it has been determined that the provisions of the Patents Act of 1983 are "insufficient" to protect Malaysia's interest under Article 16 of the CBD. The scope of what can be patentable is not very clear as to whether genes are patentable. Moreover, there is no specific provision in this Act that could relate to the protection of traditional knowledge related to genetic resources[19]. Given the development in the international arena especially relating to genetic resources, it is necessary to review the Patent Act of 1983 to harmonize the provisions of this Act with Malaysia's international obligations under the CBD and TRIPS and with the Protection of New Plant Varieties Act of 2004 (Malaysia's response to Article 27.3(b) of TRIPS)

The Impact of IPRs on Biodiversity and Traditional Knowledge

It has been argued that IPRs could encourage access and benefit sharing, if applications for such rights require identification of the source of genetic material used in the development of subject matter protected by IPRs and proof of PIC of the competent authority of the provider country, if the genetic resource was acquired after the entry into force of the CBD and does not fall within the scope of a possible multilateral system for plant genetic resources for food and agriculture.

Article 16 (5) of the CBD recognizes that patents and other IPRs may have influence on its implementation. In this regard, subject to national legislation and international law, the contracting parties to the CBD shall cooperate to ensure that such rights are supportive and do not run counter to the CBD's objectives. This can be done by harmonizing the different approaches of the CBD and TRIPS, as the former recognizes the sovereign rights of States over their genetic resources, and the latter treats intellectual property as a private right.

The objectives of the CBD, particularly for ensuring the fair and equitable sharing of benefits arising out of the utilization of genetic resources, could be achieved if the application procedures for the IPRs require that the applicant submit evidence of PIC. However, obtaining the PIC of competent national authorities and holders of traditional knowledge may prove to be difficult, especially if the material is obtained from a research institution lacking knowledge of the origin of the material, or if it is a plant genetic resource for food and agriculture covered by a possible multilateral system for access and benefit sharing on certain plant genetic resources for food and agriculture.

The traditional forms of IPRs are inadequate to protect indigenous knowledge, because they are based on protection of individual intellectual property rights, whereas traditional knowledge is collective. Such knowledge, developed over a period of time and codified in texts or retained in oral traditions over generations, may not be able to satisfy all the conditions required, such as the novelty and innovative steps required for the granting of patent protection to traditional knowledge. For the protection of traditional knowledge, innovations, and practices in relation to the use of genetic resources, the following forms of mechanisms could be considered: documentation of traditional knowledge, a registration and innovations patent system for traditional knowledge, a sui generis system for protecting traditional knowledge.

The FAO International Undertaking and the International Treaty on Genetic Resources for Food and Agriculture

The International Undertaking has had a strong influence on the national policy and the proposed access bill, in particular with regard to *ex situ* collections procured pre-CBD. However, issues surrounding the *ex situ* collections still remain largely unresolved. Malaysia is really in a unique position, because the country is considered to be important both as a donor as well as a recipient country.

After a long negotiation process, the International Undertaking became the International Treaty on Plant Genetic Resources for Food and Agriculture (ITPGRFA, adopted 3 November 2001). The treaty establishes a multilateral system of access and benefit sharing for plant genetic resources, for an agreed list of crops (ITPGRFA Annex I) established on the basis of interdependence and food security. Malaysia is not a signatory of the treaty and, at this point in time, it is still too early to assess the impact of the treaty on the Access to Genetic Resources Bill and the State laws. However, Malaysia now has a strong interest in and a commitment to become a member country in the very near future. The provisions of the treaty should be taken into account in the draft access Bill, particularly with respect to existing *ex situ* collections; for example, rice is included in the Annex I of the treaty.

Early Lessons and Recommendations that can be Identified from the Process Leading to the Development of the Draft Access Bill

Early lessons learned include:

- Setting up an ad hoc committee/task force for national planning for access to genetic resources is imperative for developing a comprehensive legislation.
- The involvement of AG, ministries, and agencies with responsibilities for the management of biodiversity in the country, and NGOs in the *ad hoc* committee/task force is crucial to the process.
- The involvement of the indigenous and local communities at the early stage of the process would be desirable in outlining an enforceable access determination process, in particular with regard to PIC and equitable sharing of benefits.
- The involvement of the State's representatives and the private sector and industries as early as possible would also make the process more efficacious.
- A national workshop on access to genetic resources was an effective means to assess the needs, opportunities, resources and capacities in the country.
- The contributions from resource persons in the national workshop, (e.g., from the WRI, the IUCN Environmental Law Center, and the Royal Botanic Gardens, Kew), were particularly useful in formulating a national strategy for biodiversity prospecting.
- For certain biological resources, experience and expertise was lacking; for example, microorganisms had never been legislated upon in any manner in Malaysia.
- Sustained awareness-raising endeavors involving various stakeholders with regard to assessment/inventory of biological diversity and biodiversity prospecting in the country could contribute effectively to the process.
- The enactment of their own state laws in Sarawak and Sabah reflected the gravity of the Federal-State jurisdictional dichotomy.
- The enactment of their own State laws in Sarawak and Sabah also highlighted the paramount importance of both their biological diversity and their indigenous and local communities.
- In formulating strict legal mechanisms for access to genetic resources in Malaysia, we should consider the imposition of a) a mandatory statutory requirement to obtain a license and b) a separate access agreement.
- In order to promote *bona fide* local research and development, there is a need for discrimination or distinction between academic research and commercial bioprospectors.
- A model access agreement would provide a useful

basis for negotiations and also serve as a checklist of items for consideration.

- The national consultative process should be initiated as early as possible and be given adequate time for the benefit of all relevant stakeholders.
- Amending existing laws and enacting a comprehensive new law is usually a very complex and long-term process, since we need to deal with wide-ranging issues from the appropriate administrative authority to enforcement to constitutional issues.
- The important objectives of the National Policy on Biological Diversity to optimize economic benefits through the integrated conservation/sustainable use of biological diversity and to give priority to biodiversity prospecting activities need to be promoted.
- Political intervention may be necessary to speed up the process.
- Pending the passing of the draft access Bill, EPU's Guidelines on Research should continue to be adopted as a temporary measure of protection of genetic resources found in Malaysia.

Some specific recommendations with respect to the national implementation process include (OH 1997):

- Increase awareness of the issues related to biodiversity prospecting and access and benefit sharing at the Federal and State levels.
- Initiate a strategic planning process to define the national strategic goals in terms of biodiversity prospecting, including a national consultation process with key players and stakeholders.
- Assess the role of legislation in the context of strategic goals and examine the feasibility of a framework legislation to ensure a nationally consistent approach to the legal aspects of biodiversity prospecting.
- Evaluate the legal protection of local and indigenous knowledge and livelihoods and consider the use of existing legal provisions to afford such protection.
- Build and develop the required institutional capacity to address biodiversity prospecting issues, including further defining the role of the national focal point for biodiversity prospecting issues.
- Evaluate existing rural development and other community programs for replication as benefit-sharing mechanisms.
- Develop model agreements in consultation with relevant experts and build capacity in business and negotiating skills.
- Consider appropriate funds or funding sources to carry out the above recommendations.

Conclusions

At present, there is no legislation specific to access to genetic resources in Malaysia at the national level, but two States (Sabah and Sarawak) have regulations that facilitate access to their genetic resources. However, Malaysia supports an effective regulatory framework for access to genetic resources and the commercial utilization of such resources, so as to ensure that the economic benefits accruing therefrom are channeled towards conservation of biodiversity and to the indigenous and local communities from whom knowledge of genetic resources are derived. It would appear that opportunities exist for reaping benefits from the commercialization of biodiversity use. Based on this premise, Malaysia is currently undertaking relevant policy review to ensure that the proper measures are adopted to prevent negative impacts on biodiversity and to ensure fair and equitable sharing of benefits, among other goals. This pragmatic approach has been followed through by the drafting of the Access to Genetic Resources Bill, an effort that was initiated as early as 1994.

The Access to Genetic Resources Bill is being drafted as a comprehensive national legislation that will form part of the national implementation process of the CBD. In line with Malaysia's commitments, the National Policy on Biological Diversity is based on many salient principles, one of which is the recognition of the role of local communities in the conservation, management, and utilization of biological diversity, as well as their rightful share of the benefits accruing therefrom. In addition, the action plan lists the undertaking of activities in biodiversity prospecting as a priority.

The eventual relationship between the federal EPU permission and the new law is not clear. When the appropriate competent authority(s) is set up under the new law to grant an access license, it may be able to carry out the EPU's function. Thus the permission from EPU may no longer be necessary. Applications for access licenses/permits may be made directly to the competent authority(s); however, such required information may be kept, managed, and made available by the designated competent authority.

References

ABDULLAH M.Z., D.A. VAUGHAN, and MOHAMAD O. 1991. Wild relatives of rice in Malaysia: Their characteristics, distribution, ecology and potential in rice breeding. MARDI Report No. 145. Available from Malaysian Agricultural Research and Development Institute (MARDI), Serdang, Malaysia.

AZIZOL A.K. and T.N. LEAN. 1997. Bioprospecting in Malaysia: FRIM's perspectives. Paper presented at National Workshop on Access and Benefit Sharing of Genetic Resources (ABS), Awana, Malaysia.

FASIHUDDIN A. and I. GHAZALLY. 1998. Medicinal plants used by Iban Community in Sarawak. p. 121–128 in Z. ZURIATI, Y. NIK IDRIS, M. S. IKRAM, and D. LAILY (eds.) Interdisciplinary approaches in natural product sciences. Proc. 14th Ann. Seminar Natural Products Research Malaysia, Bangi, Malaysia.

HASHIM Y., M. Sri NURESTRI, and M. SHAHIMI. 1993. An investigation into the analgesic and anaesthetic effects of the plant Trema orientalis. p. 61–69 in M. S. IKRAM, Z. ZURIATI, and H. HARUN (eds.) Bioassay guided isolation of natural products. Proc. 10th Annual Seminar and UNESCO Reg. Workshop on Bioassay Guided Isolation of Natural Products, Bangi, Malaysia.

HO C.C., N.S. LAI, L.Y.C. VOON, S. DAIM, H.Y. CHEAH, and C.W. LO. 2000. Microbial biodiversity in Malaysia and the screening for novel drugs. p. 77 in T.K. CHUA and E.Y.E. LEE (eds.) Biodiversity 2000 Kuching. Proc. International Conference on Prudent Biodiversity Management and Sustainable Development, Sarawak Biodiversity Center, Kuching, Malaysia.

IKRAM M.S., Y. NIK IDRIS, S. MOHD. WAHID, Z. ZURIATI, M. RAHMAH, and Z. SITI HAJAR. 1993. Cytotoxic effect of some Malaysian medicinal plants. p. 43–46 in M.S.

IKRAM, Z. ZURIATI, and H. HARUN (eds.) Bioassay guided isolation of natural products. Proc. 10th Annual Seminar and UNESCO Regional Workshop on Bioassay Guided Isolation of Natural Products, Bangi, Malaysia.

JENTA T.R., Z.Q. XU, and M.T. FLAVIN. 2001. Bioprospecting and international collaborations—the case of the calanolides. p. 78–82 in T.K. CHUA and E.Y.E. LEE (eds.) Biodiversity 2000 Kuching. Proc. International Conference on Prudent Biodiversity Management and Sustainable Development, Sarawak Biodiversity Center, Kuching, Malaysia.

LIM Y.M., A. ABDUL MANAF, A.W. NORHAMOM, M.S. KAMARUDDIN, A. FAUJAN, and L. NORDIN. 1998. Anti-tumor promoting activities and antioxidant effect of Malaysian traditional vegetables "ulam". p. 245–249 in Z. ZURIATI, Y. NIK IDRIS, M. S. IKRAM, and D. LAILY (eds.) Interdisciplinary approaches in natural product sciences. Proc. 14th Annual Seminar on Natural Products Research in Malaysia, 21–22 October 1998, Bangi, Malaysia.

MOHAMAD O. 1997. Access and benefit sharing of genetic resources: International imperatives and national needs. Bull. of the Genetics Society of Malaysia 3:9–11.

MOHAMAD O., P. MANSOR, and M. AMINUDDIN. 1995. Potential crops from the wild. p. 107–145 in A.H. ZAKRI (ed.) Prospects in biodiversity prospecting. Genetics Society of Malaysia/Universiti Kebangsaan Malaysia, Kuala Lumpur, Malaysia.

MOHAMAD O., A. RUKAYAH, I. SALMA, and O. KAMARIAH. 1997. Indigenous fruits of Malaysia and their potential. The Malayan Forester 60:84–106.

MOSTE 1997. Assessment of biological diversity in Malaysia. Ministry of Science, Technology and the Environment, Malaysia. 186 p.

OH C. 1996. Access, benefit-sharing and intellectual property rights—Developing a Malaysian perspective. WWF Malaysia Briefing Paper, June 1996. WWF Malaysia, Kuala Lumpur, Malaysia.

OH C. 1997. A preliminary assessment of access and benefit sharing measures in Malaysia. WWF Malaysia Discussion Paper, WWF Malaysia, Kuala Lumpur, Malaysia.

OTHMAN R. and W.M. LOFTI. 1995. The status of marine biodiversity in Malaysia. p. 77–93 *in* A.H. ZAKRI (ed.) *Prospects in biodiversity prospecting*. Genetics Society of Malaysia/Universiti Kebangsaan Malaysia, Kuala Lumpur, Malaysia.

SAM T.W., A.S. NG, P.B. CHEAH, and K.S. ONG. 1988. Toxicity screening with the brine shrimp (*Artemia salina*) of plant extracts. p. 50–57 *in* M.S. IKRAM and D. LAILY (eds.) *Systematic identification of natural products*. Proc. UNESCO Sub-Regional Seminar/ Workshop on Systematic Identification of Natural Products, Bangi, Malaysia.

URAIDILLAH M., I. ZILARI, and I. NORHATATI, and 3. ISMAIL. 1988. Theophylline from *Malphigia coccigera L.* p. 112–113 *in* M.S. IKRAM and D. LAILY (eds.) *Systematic identification of natural products*. Proc. UNESCO Sub-Regional Seminar/Workshop on Systematic Identification of Natural Products, Bangi, Malaysia.

VIMALA S., A. MOHD, ILLHAM and A. ABDULL RASHIH. 1998. Antioxidant activity in Malaysian ulam. p. 69–74 *in* Z. ZURIATI, Y. NIK IDRIS, M. S. IKRAM, and D. LAILY (eds.) *Interdisciplinary Approaches in Natural Product Sciences*. Proc. 14th Ann. Seminar Natural Products Research Malaysia, Bangi, Malaysia.

ZAUYAH Y., J. STANSLAS, and L.P. AZIMAHTOL HAWARIAH. 1993. Antiproliferative effect of Goniothalamin on three different human breast cancer cell lines. p. 55–59 *in* M.S. IKRAM, Z. ZURIATI, and H. HARUN (eds.) *Bioassay guided isolation of natural products*. Proc. 10th Ann. Seminar and UNESCO Regional Workshop on Bioassay Guided Isolation of Natural Products, Bangi, Malaysia.

Endnotes

[1] Indigenous or local community means any group of individuals who have one or more of the following characteristics or that falls within any of the following definitions: a group of individuals who occupy or occupied a particular territory for many generations, and whose cultural and economic traditions are integrally connected to their occupation and customary uses of those territories; an aborigine or aboriginal community as defined in the Aboriginal Peoples Act 1954; and the natives of Sabah and Sarawak as defined by Article 161(6) and (7) of the Federal Constitution.

[2] The National Policy on Biological Diversity aims to provide the direction for Malaysia to implement 15 strategies through various action plans until the year 2020. There are no specific time periods indicated for the strategies; neither are the implementing institutions or agencies identified. However, the Government's goals have been further enhanced by the setting up of the National Biodiversity and Biotechnology Council chaired by Hon. Deputy Prime Minister in December 2001.

[3] http://www.arbec.com.my/NBP.pdf

[4] This is the Malay term for Chief Minister of a State. As handed down in history, Malaysia, in brief, comprises two "types" of States: a) Federated Malay States and b) Unfederated Malay States. The former States are those which had never been ruled directly by the British (e.g., Kedah, Kelantan), while the latter have had direct British administration/intervention (Penang, Malacca, Sabah, and Sarawak). Thus, the former have Menteri Besars while the latter have Chief Ministers. Both have equal powers.

[5] In 1998, there was an initiative to develop the ASEAN Framework Agreement on Access to Genetic Resources but it has seen little progress. Thus far, this initiative has provided little or no bearing on our efforts to develop a national law or policy on access to genetic resources. The question of whether something similar to that of the Andean Community regional legislation was appropriate for ASEAN had been raised in many discussions, perhaps leading to what is now the proposal for the ASEAN Framework Agreement on Access to Genetic Resources. There was already a model that ASEAN could have looked at for this purpose. However, what was really seen as more important was the harmonization of national laws and policies, since many countries share similar biological diversity. The priorities accorded to the matter (i.e., access to genetic resources) by countries were also a factor, since the matter of GMOs was seen as more urgent. Therefore, a regional harmonization for GMO's regulation took precedence. The 21st Meeting of the ASEAN Ministers for Agriculture and Forestry held on 28–29 October 1999 in Bandar Seri Begawan, Brunei Darussalam, endorsed the ASEAN Guidelines on Risk Assessment of Agriculture-Related Genetically Modified Organisms.

[6] In order to ensure uniformity in the administration of the law, it is important to have close cooperation between the competent authorities of the Federal and State Governments.

[7] These benefits are listed by the "Access to Genetic Resources Bill."

[8] The Access to Genetic Resources Bill states that the competent authority may formulate guidelines for the exemption of researchers from local academic and research institutions involved in the conduct of noncommercial research from the provisions of the Bill, provided always that such exemption is without prejudice to the right of the competent authority to withdraw the exemption where appropriate.

[9] This is intended for Malaysians who want to apply for access for noncommercial purposes.

[10] This (the Ministry's) position has emerged as a result of reviewing several draft laws from other countries, such as India, and is likely to be the position supported by the Government.

[11] This (the Ministry's) position came into focus after the final text of the draft Access to Genetic Resources Bill, and therefore, the position and the three circumstances are not stated in the Bill. No distinction is made in the access procedure to differentiate between the three different circumstances.

[12] The application for an access license shall include, among other things, PIC in writing and certified by the resource provider. The competent authority shall establish an appropriate process for securing PIC of the resource provider that may be affected by the application. The process shall be prescribed by the competent authority, after consultation with relevant parties, in order to ensure and verify that PIC is properly obtained. The consultation procedure shall include, but is not limited to, the following measures: a) participation of representatives of the indigenous and local communities and b) wide and effective dissemination of all the relevant information to the concerned communities and other interested parties on the proposed access activity. At this point in time, such an appropriate procedure has yet to be established.

[13] The competent authority has not yet been determined. The draft Bill provides for the two options previously mentioned.

[14] The scope of the draft legislation covers biological resources, found both in *in situ* conditions and *ex situ* collections, on public lands, communal or customary lands, and alienated or private lands. In the case of access to biological resources, where the land comes under the Federal jurisdiction, the competent federal authority shall negotiate on the benefits. Where the land comes under the State jurisdiction, the competent authority shall negotiate on the benefits. As for communal or customary lands, and alienated or private lands, the competent State authority may take into account relevant factors as may be appropriate (such as the status of endemism or rarity of the biological resource, conservation status, existing and potential value and use, and whether traditional knowledge is involved), including the resource provider, in determining the nature and combination of benefits in accordance with the merits of each case. In the case of access to traditional knowledge, the competent authority may take into account relevant factors (such as whether the knowledge is in common use by large sections of the population, whether the knowledge can be attributed to a particular indigenous or local community, the number of communities involved in the conservation and use, and the uniqueness of the traditional knowledge).

[15] This is a term used by plant breeders to describe plants which are selected from seedlings, usually not out of planned hybridization, and these plants are later cloned for further breeding use.

[16] Foreign scientists who want to apply for access to genetic resources are required to have a local collaborator or sponsor. A similar requirement has already been put in place by the Sarawak Biodiversity Center Ordinance of 1997 and Sabah Biodiversity Enactment of 2000.

[17] The two options were proposed by the Task Force on Access to Genetic Resources after consultative discussions.

[18] In drafting the Access to Genetic Resources Bill, there was always active participation and strong input by the representative of the Ministry of Consumer Affairs with respect to the need to review the Patent Act of 1983 vis-à-vis the access bill.

[19] Personal communication with Rozina Ayob of the Ministry of Science, Technology and the Environment, Malaysia on 22–26 October 2001.

$$12$$

Legal Issues Regarding the International Regime: Objectives, Options, and Outlook

Tomme Rosanne Young

The years 2002–2004 have seen some of the most dynamic action in the realm of access and benefit sharing (ABS)[1] under the Convention on Biological Diversity (CBD) since the convention was adopted in 1992.[2] Key decisions within this time frame include:

- CBD-Conference of the Parties (COP) Decision VI-24[3] (March 2002), at which the voluntary Bonn Guidelines on Access to Genetic Resources and Fair and Equitable Sharing of the Benefits Arising out of their Utilization (hereafter Bonn Guidelines) were adopted in a decision that clearly requires the Parties to keep this document under review and also to undertake additional work regarding key definitions and concepts relating to ABS more generally;

- Plan of Implementation of the World Summit on Sustainable Development (WSSD)[4] (September, 2002), which called on all countries to "negotiate within the framework of the CBD, bearing in mind the Bonn Guidelines, an international regime to promote and safeguard the fair and equitable sharing of benefits arising out of the utilization of genetic resources";

- The CBD meeting on the Multi-Year Programme of

Work (MYPOW) for the Convention[5] (March 2003) which integrated an adapted version of a provision of the WSSD Plan of Implementation, calling for the parties to consider the process, nature, scope, elements, and modalities of an international regime and provide advice on how it may wish to address this issue; and

- CBD COP Decision VII/19,[6] which sets the Terms of Reference for the process of negotiating that regime.

The ABS issue, however, has long suffered from critical limitations inhibiting national implementation. Key issues of interpretation of the CBD and of the application of existing legal and institutional systems to new concepts have proven to be a significant stumbling block to the creation of a functional ABS system.

Hence it is not enough simply to make the decision to go forward with new negotiations. It is essential that underlying legal concepts be clarified, and practical implementation measures identified, so that the negotiators and policy makers can base their work on a clear understanding of what is possible and what it will cost in money, manpower, and other trade-offs to bring an effective ABS system to life.

Opening Comment: The International Regime

One of the first points that must be made in any discussion of the negotiation of an international regime on access and benefit sharing is that a regime[7] already exists. Although its coverage is extremely "patchy" in many ways, the regime includes a variety of international laws, policies,

guidelines, and other instruments, as well as both regional and national implementation measures. Internationally, the most commonly mentioned documents and institutions, in addition to the CBD, that comprise the international regime are the International Treaty on Plant Genetic Resources for

Food and Agriculture (ITPGRFA),[8] the World Intellectual Property Organization (WIPO) system, and the Bonn Guidelines. However, the Seventh Conference of the Parties to the CBD (COP-7) has identified at least 18 other international instruments that must be evaluated to determine how they fit into the regime.

At the regional level, the best publicized components of the regime have been Decision 391 of the Andean Community of Nations on access and benefit-sharing processes and procedures (ANDEAN COMMUNITY 1996), the European Union's Directive 98/44 on disclosure of origin of biological sources of natural material in biotechnological inventions,[9] and the Organization of African Unity's adoption of the the African Model Law for the Protection of the Rights of Local Communities, Farmers, and Breeders, and for the Regulation of Access to Biological Resources.

On the national level, eighteen countries have so far adopted access and benefit-sharing legislation or other instruments that directly address some or all of the ABS-related commitments under the CBD (CABRERA 2004). A number of other countries have asserted that their existing national legislation adequately addresses ABS matters, although initial evaluation suggests that many of these claims should be more clearly examined.[10]

In addition, contractual agreements for access and benefit sharing must also be considered to be part of the regime. This is not only because these instruments are adopted and interpreted under national ABS systems,[11] but also because they are often directly negotiated by at least one government.[12] As such, their interpretation (in practice and through the courts) is a critical input into the regime.

This leads to a basic question: What exactly is meant by the phrase 'negotiate an international regime on [access and] benefit sharing'? Although the final decisions about what and how will be negotiated will not be made for some time, a few observations (based on facts and research set forth in the rest of the paper) are warranted. First, the international regime itself cannot be negotiated in its entirety. Even if the CBD's entire existing provisions regarding access were completely renegotiated, this action would still not impact the following:

- Other international instruments;
- National implementing instruments;
- Existing contracts; and
- The legal interpretations developed from applying and interpreting existing contracts and other instruments.

Contrary to many statements, the current choice is not between 'negotiating an entirely new regime' and 'negotiating a parts or interpretations of the regime', because any negotiation will involve only part of the regime. The regime is and will be a combination of established and new instruments, concepts, and principles. The only

question is "what kind of instrument will be added to this mix—interpretation, protocol, annex, guideline, or COP Decision?" From a legal perspective, however, the type of instrument that is developed is perhaps less important than its particular characteristics. In this connection, this paper should start by considering the frequent discussions about whether it should be binding or voluntary. This question blends two concepts—binding versus nonbinding and voluntary versus mandatory.

Binding and Nonbinding Provisions

In international law, binding refers to a commitment by a country to take a particular action. Often, binding commitments are expressed in language that 'softens' their impact ("endeavor to regulate", rather than "regulate") or that recognizes priority among commitments ("subject to available resources"). It should be noted that these softeners do not affect the binding nature of the commitment. The countries continue to be obligated to make a 'good faith' (e.g., nontoken) effort to comply, and will be in violation otherwise. Nonbinding international instruments may be adopted as guidelines and declarations, but the governments involved specifically state that they are not committing to take these actions.

At the national level, binding refers to whether a commitment has legal effect. A promise to pay money, for example, may be binding (if it is a part of a contract in which another party has made commitments or taken action), or nonbinding (if it is simply an indication of intent or a statement made to convince a beggar or borrower to "go away and try again tomorrow").

Voluntary and Mandatory

By contrast, the concepts of voluntary and mandatory refer to a different kind of legal question—the contrast between what one may do and what one must do. Laws are typically seen to fit into three categories—enabling laws (telling the regulated public[13] what they are permitted to do—these express voluntary options), mandatory laws (telling the regulated public what they must do), and prohibitory laws (telling the regulated public what they cannot do).

Within particular areas of law, there are also voluntary (enabling), mandatory, and prohibitory components. In the area of private contracts, for example, the law specifies that only certain kinds of contracts are legally enforceable—those in which:

- Both parties are informed of all relevant information (i.e., no party intentionally or inadvertently lied or concealed facts relevant to the contract);
- Both parties are reasonably interpreting the contract terms and agree on what those terms mean; and
- Both parties have given or are committed to giving consideration (payment of money, performance or abstention from some action, giving of tangible or intangible items or rights, etc.).

These three elements are mandatory in all contracts, that is, the law will not enforce a purported contract without them. However, there are many voluntary elements of contract law. Initially, it must be an absolutely voluntary choice to enter a contract or not. The law will not enforce a contract if either party was forced to enter into the contract against his will. The terms of the contract are negotiated by the parties—thus the selection of terms is voluntary. In some cases, however, the law will identify 'standard terms'—it may say, for example, that in payment-for-services contracts, payment will be owing after the services are provided, *unless otherwise provided in the contract.* This is a voluntary provision. The parties may adopt another payment option, however, if they don't specify the order of payment, the law will assume the order is services first, money second. There are also many prohibitory elements of contract law. For example, in most countries, a contract provision that sets excessive interest (usury) or that forces a party to take action against his will (extortion) may not be enforced.

Mandatory, Binding, Voluntary, and Nonbinding Components of the Regime

The most important point relating to both of these concepts (binding/nonbinding and voluntary/mandatory) is that they do not affect the application of the ultimate laws. The same is true where a country decides to adopt a law recommended in a nonbinding international instrument. In either case, where a country meets its binding obligation to adopt a law, that law applies to all members of the regulated public according to the terms of the law (if the law says that it is mandatory, it is mandatory.) The law's effect is not altered by the fact that the country was not internally obligated to adopt it.

Similarly, where legislation creates a set of voluntary contractual provisions, the parties have a choice about whether to adopt those provisions or not. However, once the parties have exercised that option and included some of these provisions in a binding contract, then they are enforceable obligations, no different from other terms of the contract. As further discussed below, nearly all of the ABS-related provisions in the CBD are legally binding on the countries that are part of the CBD. Similarly, the statement that the provisions of the Bonn Guidelines are voluntary—only means that the parties have a choice between these provisions and other approaches, in their efforts to implement the binding provisions of the CBD.

The Current Situation: ABS and the Bonn Guidelines

As a basis for substantive analysis, this section summarizes the ABS issue, its role in the CBD, and the issues, concerns, and processes that led to the adoption of the Bonn Guidelines. This summary is not designed to be a complete description, but instead to provide an idea of what the international regime will seek to create and foster.

ABS in the CBD

Most commentators begin by noting that ABS is the heart of the third primary objective of the CBD, which calls for "fair and equitable sharing of the benefits arising out of the utilization of genetic resources".[14] However, within the CBD, ABS is more than just an aspiration. Although this fact is often overlooked in discussions, the CBD contains 10 separate, non-optional obligations[15] relating to ABS. These 10 obligations, in the order they appear in the CBD, are:

- "create conditions to facilitate access to genetic resources for environmentally sound uses by other Contracting Parties and not to impose restrictions that run counter to the objectives of this Convention" (Art. 15.2).

- "develop and carry out scientific research based on genetic resources provided by other Contracting Parties with the full participation of, and where possible in, such Contracting Parties" (Art. 15.6).

- "take legislative, administrative, or policy measures,

- …with the aim of sharing in a fair and equitable way the benefits arising from the commercial and other utilization of genetic resources with the Contracting Party providing such resources" (Art. 15.7).

- "take legislative, administrative, or policy measures, …with the aim of sharing in a fair and equitable way … the results of research, development arising from the commercial and other utilization of genetic resources with the Contracting Party providing such resources" (Art. 15.7).

- "take legislative, administrative, or policy measures, …with the aim that …developing countries, which provide genetic resources, are provided access to and transfer of technology which makes use of those resources, …including technology protected by patents and other intellectual property rights…" (Art. 16.3).

- "facilitate the exchange of information, from all publicly available sources, …taking into account the special needs of developing countries.… Such exchange of information shall …where feasible, include repatriation of information" (Arts. 17.1 and 2).

- "take legislative, administrative, or policy measures, …to provide for the effective participation in biotechnological research activities by those

Contracting Parties, especially developing countries, which provide the genetic resources for such research, and where feasible in such Contracting Parties" (Art. 19.1).

- "take all practicable measures to promote and advance priority access on a fair and equitable basis by Contracting Parties, especially developing countries, to the results and benefits arising from biotechnologies based upon genetic resources provided by those Contracting Parties" (Art. 19.2).

- "provide, in accordance with its capabilities, financial support and incentives in respect of those national activities which are intended to achieve the objectives of this Convention…" (Art. 20.1).

- "developed country Parties …provide, and developing country Parties avail themselves of, financial resources related to the implementation of this Convention through bilateral, regional, and other multilateral channels" (Art. 20.3).

The existence of these commitments underscores three basic understandings that will be critical to the rest of this paper, and to the entire discussion of the international regime: First, the above commitments are not optional. Each party is *required* to endeavor to take these actions. As noted above, the 'endeavor' language may soften these requirements for those who try but cannot achieve them, but it does not make the commitments less obligatory. Parties are required to try to take the relevant actions, and will only be considered to meet these commitments if either a) the requirement is fulfilled or b) the country made a serious and significant attempt, but was not able to fulfill it (due to external preventing factors). These requirements will not be excused by a lack of political will, for example. Countries having acceded to the CBD are *required* to take action. A country will have violated the CBD unless it has made every reasonable effort to adopt measures, or to take other required actions, irrespective of whether or not it has been successful.

Second, these commitments are not directly binding on individuals, corporations, NGOs, other entities, or even sub-national (state and provincial) governmental structures. They bind only *the Contracting Parties to the CBD*—that is, the 188 *national governments,*[17] which must adopt the relevant measures directly. The only way that any person, business, NGO, or other entity can become subject to the requirements set out in the Convention will be through national law adopted by each Contracting Party.[18] And then, the individuals or entities are subject to the relevant national law, and not directly to the Convention or any processes under the Convention.

Third, these provisions do not address purely domestic ABS situations (i.e., those in which a country's genetic resources are sampled, studied, and utilized by entities and activities within the national jurisdiction of that country.) The access requirement, for example, is specifically limited to the facilitation of "access to genetic resources for envi-

ronmentally sound uses *by other Contracting Parties…*".[19] Parties are clearly allowed to adopt domestic ABS frameworks, of course, (and in fact, the adoption of comprehensive frameworks for all genetic resource issues may be necessary to make the international system effective) but the Convention specifically does not cover them.

Hence, it is essential (and mandatory) that all Contracting Parties must adopt the various kinds of measures and take the other actions described above. In this connection, it is also useful to note that ABS is only one of the genetic-resource-related issues addressed in the CBD. As further discussed below, it is possible that the provisions on ABS should be viewed in conjunction with the provisions addressing agriculture, biosafety, and Genetically Modified Organisms (GMOs), and with subsequent work on these issues, including the Cartagena Biosafety Protocol that came into force on 11 September 2003 and the national legislation and policy frameworks on biosafety and GMOs that have been developed and are being developed around the world.

The Bonn Guidelines

The Bonn Guidelines were adopted in 2002, by the Sixth Conference of Parties to the CBD (COP-6). Although an important first step toward enabling the creation of a network of national law systems addressing ABS issues, the Guidelines cannot be seen as a positive development if they are perceived to represent a final decision or guidance. In fact, the Bonn Guidelines represent ideas expressed by the parties, but in many cases, those ideas either have never been tried in practice or their use has not been made public and scrutinized from all perspectives. Hence, these ideas are designed as starting points for national framework development processes and national ABS negotiations, rather than as "tried-and-true" recipes for implementation.

The Guidelines recognize this fact specifically—calling themselves "evolutionary" in nature. At their adoption, the Parties clearly agreed that "the Guidelines are intended to be reviewed and accordingly revised and improved as experience is gained in access and benefit sharing". In this first iteration, these Guidelines rely rather substantially on information regarding the views of businesses working with genetic resources. As such, they appear to answer an unasked question—"Why are there only a few ABS agreements?" (see Chapter 3). Most do not address developing country concerns or conservation/sustainable use issues. This approach has resulted in a rather strong focus on streamlining national processes and providing forms and lists that will streamline the negotiation and documentation of ABS agreements and other relevant instruments. Since their adoption, the Bonn Guidelines have been relatively controversial. Some parties and participants have been very strong in promoting national legislative development, but saying that development should be "based on the Bonn Guidelines". Other parties have noted that many critical components of necessary national legislation are not discussed in the Bonn Guidelines—suggesting that "national legislation based on the Bonn Guidelines" would be fatally flawed. These arguments may be resolved by recalling that, according to the terms of the Guidelines themselves, they are voluntary and understanding that the term voluntary:

- Applies only to the Parties (national governments or countries) adopting legislation—they have the option to follow recommendations of the Guidelines or not as they choose.

- Does not mean that compliance is optional, when these terms are included in an agreement or a law. If national law states that they are mandatory, or if the contract by which the corporation/entity obtains access rights so provides, then the corporation must comply or it will be in breach of contract.

Framework Approaches at International and National Levels

The creation of an international regime involves both international instruments and also the implementation and adoption of national legislation based on these international decisions and commitments. It is useful to examine briefly the components of an international regime and how they work together.

At the international level, 'policy-style' instruments exist which focus on obtaining general agreement among sovereign governments to address key issues. Many of these are also 'framework' instruments.[20] The CBD is such an instrument. It is different from other international conventions, in that its object is promoting concerted national implementation in a programmatic way (providing the economies and strengths of collaborative action), and with the assistance of so-called "framework tools"[21]

developed under the framework system. Another type of international instrument is regulatory in style. It contains specific requirements, under which each country is obliged to take clearly identified action. Examples of this kind of instrument include the Cartagena Biosafety Protocol, the Convention on International Trade in Endangered Species (CITES), and the Montreal Protocol on Substances that Deplete the Ozone Layer[22]. Where the framework system is working well, these regulatory-style conventions may be able to utilize the framework tools, and thus be relieved of the necessity of separately developing tools and instruments that are relevant to all instruments within the framework. A third international element is the development of guidelines and soft law. For example, as noted above the Bonn Guidelines are not obligatory on any Party, but are offered only on the chance that they may assist the Parties and others in implementing international objectives.

At the national level, a similar structure exists. National policy provides overarching guidance and coordination among national laws, with guidance on national objectives and compliance with regard to and implementation of international conventions and obligations. This policy provides an idea of the outcomes and objectives toward which legislation should be directed. National laws and regulations focus more specifically on the actions to be taken to achieve national policy mandates and outcomes, in order to, *inter alia*, fulfill international commitments. Yet another level of implementation is found in the form of both hard and soft rules, as well as contracts and other action by the private sector, NGOs, and others. In optimal situations, this national level pyramid begins to be developed early in the international process. Together these processes (in all relevant forums) constitute the international regime.

Why Revise/Reconsider the International Regime?

At this point, it may perhaps not be obvious why the "negotiation of an International Regime" was proposed by the WSSD. In simplest terms, the answer is that, even 12 years after the CBD was adopted, and despite significant interest and commitment (particularly by developing countries), the world's governments have not been able to create a functional ABS system. Based on initial detailed research into existing national and regional legislation on ABS and initial inquiries into a few available ABS agreements, it is clear that there has been a notable lack of progress in fulfilling the ABS-related obligations under the CBD (CABRERA 2004) (see Chapters 1, 2, and 3).

Fewer than 20 countries and regional organizations have adopted specific national ABS legislation (CABRERA 2004), and in most cases there are doubts about whether the legislation has been effective or even fully implemented (PERIA 2000). The basic theory of this paper is that the failure to progress on the implementation of an effective ABS system is tied to incorrect concepts and assumptions,

supplemented by the lack of a shared understanding and clarification of key concepts. The country whose overall ABS regime is generally considered the most successful (Costa Rica),[23] for example, is rather emphatically not replicable.[24]

A great many articles and opinions have been published and circulated about the reasons behind this lack of progress in the development of a functional legislative/administrative system through which ABS arrangements can become recognized contractual/property interests and can develop their potential as components of the "biodiversity triad". Many of these were stated in the preamble of the Bonn Guidelines and in documents submitted to the COP-6. In general, these sources focus on the fact that corporations' representatives in ABS and Bonn Guideline negotiations strongly indicated a general corporate unwillingness to pay the transaction cost associated with negotiating ABS arrangements under existing national legislation (often described as overly complex and demanding).[25] Hence, relying on this industry perspective, many commentators (and the Bonn Guidelines) suggest solutions proposed by these sources focus on simplifying national legislation, minimizing national legislative requirements, streamlining governmental processes, and harmonizing the countries' various approaches to domestic requirements, such as public participation[26] (TEN KATE and LAIRD 1999, SWIDERSKA 2001).

Research under the IUCN ABS Project[27] suggests that this may not be the case. Based on examination of specific content of some national legislative and policy frameworks, and comparing them to general information about ABS activities within the country, it appears that legislative choices have not had a particular impact on the country's success in attracting ABS arrangements (EKHASSA 2003, CHISHAKWE and YOUNG 2004, WYNBERG et al. 2004). Those that have attempted to streamline, or adopt specific provisions about PIC, for example, have not seen a more positive industrial reaction than others. It may be that several deeper underlying reasons explain why the system is not fully functional, even in those countries which have adopted the required legal measures. These arise out of two key legal assumptions (about ownership and about the ability of existing contract law to address genetic resource issues) which were made by the negotiators of the CBD, but which were not actually legally correct—then or now.[28]

Assumptions about Ownership

The negotiators made a primary assumption about ownership—that "the ownership of genetic resources will be determined under national law" (GLOWKA 1998). While providing a relatively easy solution at the time for the negotiators (enabling them completely to avoid addressing ownership in the Convention), the legal basis for this statement had not been fully analyzed at the time. In fact, as further discussed below, then and now, no clear legal concept exists under any country's national law to delineate what a genetic resource is, what it means to own one, what it means to use one, or how any of these concepts can be applied.

Existing law relating to ownership generally focus on two kinds of subject matter:

- Physical tangible property (land,[29] plants, animals, equipment, furniture, cars, etc.) The right to own an interest in physical property derives from the right to dispose of it—originally seated in one person or entity; and

- Intangible property (intellectual property, financial rights, licenses of the use of trademarks, processes, etc.). The one quality that these various kinds of intellectual property share is that they are created by a single individual or entity (they are human-created ideas, processes, designs, etc.). Rights to own such property derive from that original creation. Intellectual property that has been independently or collaboratively created by a variety of people

(who are not contractually related) usually cannot be effectively protected through this system.

As further discussed below, genetic resources do not appear to fit in either category. They do not appear to be tangible, given that they are based on DNA and RNA (substances which, under generally promulgated theories of life, are thought to be the *information* from which any life form can be synthesized). The use of genetic resources, the ownership implications that arise from the fact that the same species exist in many countries, and the overall nature of the concept are not yet clearly understood and agreed upon, even by experts.

Assumptions about Contract Law

The second overarching assumption is reflected in the frequent statement that ABS would generally be addressed by contracts and governed under national contract law (TEN KATE and LAIRD 1999). This statement is based on the expectation that existing contract law could govern the creation, execution, implementation, and oversight of ABS agreements, as well as address compliance or noncompliance under those agreements.

As discussed in more detail below, this statement also appears to have been based on some slightly flawed assumptions. Primarily, it assumed that contracts can be created and implemented even when there is no legal concept or understanding regarding the subject matter of the contract. In fact, however, contracts can exist only where law and shared understanding embody a unified perception of the contract, including physical subject matter, the activities that are permitted or required (or forbidden) under the contract, and the conditions and terms that govern the obligations of the individuals or entities that are bound by the contract.

Expectations about National Law

There was a general expectation that all parties would adopt legislation or take other action implementing the 10 ABS-related commitments listed above. As noted above, to date this expectation remains unfulfilled in more than 90% of the Parties. To some extent, this lack of progress creates a "chicken-egg" situation, in which countries are reluctant to attempt to develop new legislation without the positive stimulus of a successful example, while at the same time no national law is able to operate a system focused on international trade in genetic resources, when the other countries involved have not adopted coordinating frameworks.

The Parties to the CBD have always very strongly emphasized that "implementation of the Convention will be through national law".[30] In most instances, this focus has not significantly impeded implementation, because the concepts addressed (*in-situ* and *ex-situ* conservation and sustainable use of natural resources) already existed, were clearly subject to national sovereignty, and were governed under national law. The CBD's provisions were designed to enable this global net of national controls and programs to function efficiently together—to achieve economies of scale through international cooperation and collaborative development of programs of work.

In other contexts, however, the national implementation approach is less efficacious. Some of these issues include the problems of invasive species (frequently caused by importation and other activities of global trade and transit), migratory species (which frequently cross international boundaries),[31] and particularly ABS.

The ABS-related provisions of the CBD are rather specifically directed at transboundary agreements—i.e., situations in which a user from one country seeks access to genetic resources from another country. Domestic access to and use of genetic resources is not regulated, nor are the domestic issues regarding how benefits are distributed, once the user has complied with the requirement to share them with the source country.[32] Despite this purely international scope, however, the CBD assumes that its ABS requirements (like all other parts of the CBD) will be satisfied through the development of national laws, policies, and institutions.

In combination, the transnational nature of ABS transactions and the preference for national implementation strongly suggests that governance of these transactions

must be rigorously overseen by both the law of the source country and the law of the user country. To date, however, fewer than 10% of the CBD Parties have adopted legislation addressing their primary ABS obligations, and these are all developing countries that generally perceive themselves to be source countries (potential beneficiaries). During the negotiation of the Bonn Guidelines, for example, some of the most controversial discussion centered around the fact that the draft guidelines attempted to govern/guide the actions of "source countries" and "users". It was noted that developed country negotiators intended the latter term to refer only to corporations or other entities directly acquiring the assets, rather than the countries that are Party to the Convention.[33]

The current call to reconsider the international regime on ABS seems to arise out of the lack of progress to date, as well as the lack of clarity on some terms and mutual understandings which would, if present, enable that progress. These issues can generally be thought of in three categories:

- Concepts that require clarification;
- Assumptions that need to be reconsidered; and
- Critical issues and areas that have not yet been addressed.

Concepts Insufficiently Clarified

The CBD's provisions of ABS do not address a number of issues that are needed to form the basis of an integrated or collaborative international regime. In general, a policy instrument such as the CBD is seen as setting out the overarching objective. National and subnational governments then develop legislation whose task is to find or create a concrete method of achieving all or part of those objectives. This is the primary task of legislation—to look at both the objectives that the policy makers seek to achieve, and the available tools, and, on the basis of this analysis, to determine what action is possible and adopt a concrete system for requiring, facilitating, or controlling that action.

In the years immediately following the CBD's entry into force, it was hoped that national implementing legislation would take on this task, clarifying these points. If many countries did this, there would eventually be one or more recognized approaches which could be unified into a generally international understanding, which in turn might then be reflected in a document like the Bonn Guidelines. Unfortunately, however, national legislation to date has almost uniformly adopted the policy-style language of the CBD, rather than adopting practical systems for applying that language (CABRERA 2004). This means that a number of large gaps and inconsistencies still exist that the regime discussions will have to address.

Law and Consistency

A critical basis for the call for clarification is the fact that the international system must, necessarily, be legally governed and enforced consistently across borders. At present, although ABS agreements are negotiated under the law of the source country, there is often no basis for source country enforcement in cases of later violation. Typically, by the time any violation of the source country's ABS law is known, the user may be completely removed from the source country. Unless the violator or some valuable assets of the violator remain in the source country, the only way to compel the user's compliance will be to take action in another country—one in which user is present or has assets. This is true even if the contract specifies that it is "governed under the law of the source country".

It may be (financially or otherwise) difficult or impossible for the source country to obtain access to the courts in a developed country. Even if a legal action is undertaken, the contract will be interpreted by a judge or arbitrator in a country of the user, who cannot be a good judge of the intentions and practices of the source country. Without international consistency, based on clearly agreed international concepts, another country's courts will probably interpret the source country's contracts quite differently from what the source country expects.

Concerns about clarity seem to be one of the primary drivers motivating detailed processes and complex institutions in national and regional ABS legislation. Governments, when entering into transactions for the use of patrimonial property or assets subject to sovereign control, are bound by high standards and duties to protect the interests of the people. Individual officials who breach this responsibility of care may be subject to large fines and other penalties, and may lose their careers due to a lack of trust. It is no wonder, then, that they insist on a high level of procedural protection, detailed contracts, and other complex requirements, when they are undertaking such transactions as to kinds of property and use rights that are not clearly understood. The call from industry to simplify legislation and procedures may have the impact of diminishing protection of national patrimony, increasing the risk of inappropriate or even corrupt transactions, or, in the alternative, increasing possible exposure of officials to claims that they have violated their fiduciary obligations.

Explanatory Guidance on Terms and Concepts

One of the most frequently recognized needs relating to ABS is the need for clear, shared understanding of key terms and concepts. This primarily definitional process, however, is integrally connected to the conceptual development process. Agreement about the outcomes and mandates that will be embodied in the international ABS regime must develop first, and definitions be concretized based on the substance of this agreement, as a means of rendering it clearly. In a number of instances, potentially useful concepts have been sketched by the CBD, and seem to need only to be more concretely clarified. The following discussion briefly identifies several such concepts.

Access and Benefit Sharing as Distinct Concepts

In general, the CBD seems to draw a distinction between access (the processes of obtaining samples, generally including screening) and benefit sharing (the later sharing of profits and other benefits that the user of those resources obtains through their commercialization). This issue was discussed in the mid-1990s, in the context of the revision of the International Undertaking on Plant Genetic Resources (now superseded by the ITPGRFA). Looking at the question of access to and use of genetic resources for food and agriculture, this concept was noted repeatedly: "'free access' does not mean 'free of charge'".[34]

This point was particularly relevant in this context, because the ITPGRFA does not necessarily contemplate any direct payment of benefits. ITPGRFA sets up a multilateral system to facilitate exchanges of germplasm from a large list of important food and forage species. In essence, the parties agree that they receive a benefit from mutual sharing of "plant genetic resources for food and agriculture", for purposes of plant variety development and improvement—an activity that virtually all developing countries are directly undertaking. This sharing of resources is agreed to be "benefit sharing" for ABS purposes, without the need for specific ABS contracts. However, this is a collective benefit, but the burden of providing access (letting strangers collect samples on their land) may fall on a single farmer or community. This person or community must be compensated for access in addition to sharing in the collective benefit.

Distinguishing Between Countries of Origin and Source Countries

The CBD identifies two categories of countries providing access and receiving a share of benefits, based on their relationships to the genetic resources that they provide. The "country of origin" of a species is defined as the country which possesses in it conditions where genetic resources exist within ecosystems and natural habitats, and, in the case of domesticated or cultivated species, in the surroundings where they have developed their distinctive properties.[35] Rather clearly, where a species, subspecies, or variety[36] is widely distributed, it may have more than one country-of-origin. This is also true for species which migrate across national boundaries and for traditional varieties that have been historically and prehistorically developed, traded, and carried over large areas. Although the CBD notes that countries-of-origin "should" receive certain types of voluntary capacity-building,[37] none of the CBD's mandatory commitments relating to benefit sharing are directed at countries-of-origin.

By contrast, the "country providing genetic resources" (generally referred to as source country) refers to the country supplying the particular specimens of genetic resources[38] in a particular transaction. With the development and proliferation of botanical gardens, zoos, herbaria, and more generalized international trade and transportation of plants and animals over the past century-and-a-half, many species (even those of highly localized origin) may have dozens of potential source countries. However, the ABS obligations in the CBD are specifically directed at one source country (the one in which samples are collected), rather than any country-of-origin.

Hence, the source-country definition, and its relation to the equity concept that is the *raison d'être* of ABS implementation, poses one of the most difficult challenges in the CBD. In 150 years of international species movement, there has been little or no tracking. Even today, most botanical gardens do not keep records of transactions by which third parties obtain samples from their collections, and downstream sharing by private users of specimens is almost completely untracked. Scientifically, it is increasingly possible (provided funding and equipment are available) to identify the species of an extracted DNA sample from genetic analysis of that sample (without direct observation of any part of the physical specimen.) However, it remains virtually impossible to credibly determine the source location from which a particular specimen or its genetic material was collected.

The Concept of Potential Value

As discussed below, the definition of genetic resources in the CBD is tied to the whether the resource has "actual or potential value". At present, it is not clear whether the quoted language would exclude any species' or specimen's genetic resources from the coverage of the CBD. (In the world of genes, it is not yet clear whether there are some species whose genes are more valuable and useful than others,) Recently, significant work in the field has been focused on microbial biodiversity (often found in brackish waters), and various weed species that were formerly thought to be valueless.

The Basis for the Term Equitable

In general, ABS is perceived to be the 'third pillar' of the CBD and the only direct statement of the commitment to equity within the CBD. The legal meaning of the term equity, however, has not been well explained. Equity is a legal concept that embodies many kinds of fairness. For purposes of developing the international regime, it is important to understand many aspects of equity, but especially those that are expressly applied to ABS in the terms of the CBD.

At its most basic, the CBD requires Parties to ensure that conservation and sustainable use is also equitable. The CBD, however, does not simply impose a general duty of equity—presumably because this duty that already exists in both national and international law. Rather, in the ABS provisions, it identifies a particular area of equity-related concern and obligation—the use of genetic resources. This focus on genetic resources arose because there was a lack of general legal principles addressing these resources. Throughout distant and recent history, where there is a legal vacuum and limited capacity on an issue relating to the exploitation of resources, many (especially developing) countries have been legally and equitably disadvantaged when other countries obtained and used those resources. In the 1980s and 1990s, as information became known about many new and very profitable uses of genetic resources, there was a fear that a similar pattern of inequitable exploitation was developing (GLOWKA 1997).

As to this type of inequity, the CBD invokes a specific component of the larger concept of equity sometimes called "unjust enrichment". Equity law provides that unjust enrichment should lead to fair compensation. In other words, it is not fair for one person or entity to obtain benefits through the uncompensated exploitation of the resources belonging to another.[39] The CBD makes this clear—stating the obligation of "equitable sharing of the benefits *arising out of the utilization* of genetic resources". The term "benefits ...of utilization" is a clear reference to the benefits received by the users. This seems to be separate from the CBD's more general equity provisions, where it calls upon the parties to endeavor to work in the country of origin of the genetic resources, and undertake other actions that benefit local people, for example.[40] Such benefits seem to be in addition to, and not a substitute for, a "share of the benefits arising from utilization"—i.e. profits, intellectual property rights, and other value. Other parts of the convention suggest that countries have broader equitable obligations, however the obligation of equitable benefit sharing is specifically the obligation of the user *to share the benefits that it receives*.

The Relationship of ABS to Other International Legal Frameworks

A third area in which further clarification may be needed is the manner in which the ABS system interacts with other legal systems and frameworks, both domestic and international. Here also, although the CBD includes some important provisions on this issue, many open issues remain. It is not possible to incorporate the discussion of this issue into this paper, in part due to limitations in time and length, but more particularly because the full range of legal analysis into these issues is still ongoing. One example may be useful to illustrate this issue—marine biodiversity. The CBD addresses the conservation of oceans beyond the coastal and exclusive economic zones through four primary provisions. First, the Parties specifically take on "the responsibility to ensure that activities within their jurisdiction or control do not cause damage to the environment of other States or of areas beyond the limits of national jurisdiction".[41] This undertaking is enhanced by jurisdictional provisions noting that "the provisions of this Convention apply ... within the area of its national jurisdiction or beyond the limits of national jurisdiction".[42] Most important, the parties are to engage in appropriate cooperation "directly or, where appropriate, through competent international organizations, in respect of areas beyond national jurisdiction..., for the conservation and sustainable use of biological diversity".[43] Finally, the parties are specifically mandated to "implement the CBD with respect to the marine environment consistently with the rights and obligations of States under the law of the sea".

Unfortunately, the 1982 United Nations Convention on the Law of the Sea (UNCLOS),[44] which is recognized to be a comprehensive unified framework for international governance of oceans was negotiated for nearly 20 years, beginning well before the commencement of the CBD negotiations, being formally adopted nine years before the CBD, but entering into force two years after the CBD. All of this occurred, at a time when a) the legal concept of 'genetic resources' as some type of ownable property right did not yet exist; b) it was generally assumed that there was little or no life in the oceans below 200 m depth; and c) it was believed that marine mammals were the primary targets of high-seas conservation, because pelagic fish and other commercially harvested high-seas species were thought to be so plentiful that even drastically increased harvest levels would still be sustainable.

Since that time, however, many kinds of marine species of remarkable scientific value and other potential have been found on the deep seabed, well below 200 m, and in fish and other marine organisms in the water column beyond national jurisdiction (BŁAZKIEWICZ 2004, PATTON 2004). The sustainability of commercially harvested pelagic fish species is being called into serious question. UNCLOS is unclear about whether and how it governs ABS issues and the rights to marine genetic resources (CBD Secretariat and

UN DOALOS 2003). Within the world's oceans there are both areas within national jurisdiction and control (territorial seas, exclusive economic zones, continental shelves, etc.) and so-called international waters that are outside of any country's jurisdiction. However, it does contain a mechanism (the International Seabed Authority) and other mandates which may be useful for international sharing of the benefits from genetic resources of the seabed. It is possible that this mechanism may not only be used for sharing the benefits from seabed genetic resources, but may also be a useful example of how benefits may be shared nationally and internationally. Similar issues may apply in integrating ABS with frameworks relating to Antarctica, international trade, migratory species, intellectual property, and others.

Relationship of ABS to Other Obligations of the Parties

ABS issues, although firmly entrenched concepts in international law, are only one part of a much broader set of issues—genetic resources. These issues are addressed by a number of international instruments, which create or address specific obligations of their Parties, including especially the Cartagena Protocol on Biosafety in conjunction with the CBD's other provisions on biosafety issues (issues relating to genetically modified organisms), the ITPGRFA (issues related to the sharing of agricultural varieties of important crops for food security), and the WIPO instruments and the Agreement on Trade-Related Aspects of Intellectual Property Rights (TRIPS) (issues related to the creation of intellectual property rights in innovations using genetic resources.) All of these instruments and others are very similar to ABS in the sense that they address outcomes in many of the same fields of endeavor, seek to promote a similar type of systematic development, and involve at least some aspects of genetic resources.

A recurring theme that arose in nearly every aspect of the first year of the IUCN ABS Project has been the need to address these issues in a synergistic way, particularly at the national level. There is a well-recognized value in expanding the issue of consistency beyond the confines of ABS, to include all legal issues relating to genetic resources—in essence, to consider the need for an integrated framework that encompasses not only ABS, but also biosafety, genetic resources for food and agriculture, and genetics-based research. To a large extent, the separation among these issues is artificial. The separation was originally designed to simplify the CBD negotiations. However, there is no clear reason for maintaining these distinctions permanently, if the merger of the issues will be of assistance.

Certainly the linkage between the issues should be more clearly recognized legally. For example, the primary subject of the Cartagena Protocol is GMOs. All (or at least a significant number) of GMOs are products of the use of "genetic resources" as defined in the CBD—i.e., they have been developed utilizing at least some of this genetic material. In essence, where the ABS discussion focuses on the needs and desires of source-countries/countries-of-origin (to be compensated as providers of genetic resources), the Cartagena Protocol focuses on the needs and desires of the users (to be able to introduce and market GMOs around the world).

As further discussed below, it may be appropriate to consider reuniting these issues at the national level, through the development of a single National Framework on Genetic Resources and their Use. This approach would enable a unified compliance with this range of international agreements, and avoid inconsistency, overlap, or unregulated gaps in the system. A unified approach to implementing these issues might be of real assistance. Perhaps more important, as discussed below, this re-linkage might tie two market components together in a way that enables better development of incentives and other financial tools.

Assumptions Insufficiently Considered

The negotiators of the CBD made a number of assumptions about legal issues and how genetic resources issues will operate. These assumptions underlie a significant part of the current conception of ABS at the international political level. They have not generally been borne out in practice. As such, they are probably the most immediate (and difficult) hurdles that must be surmounted in the regime negotiations.

This paper will briefly examine three of the primary assumptions that were promulgated during the negotiations of the CBD and explain how they prevent, impact, or restrict the implementation of ABS concepts—a) the nature of genetic resources, b) reliance on existing national contract law to provide the framework for ABS, and c) valuation of genetic resources. Although these are discussed as separate issues, they are interconnected to such an extent that it

appears that they can only be addressed collectively.

Genetic Resources As Property under National Contract Law

In the years of the negotiations (the 1980s), there was only a very rudimentary understanding of genetic research, even among biologists and specialists in scientific research and development (the primary technical advisors to the negotiators of the CBD).[45] As a consequence, there were strong concerns during the negotiations regarding coverage. It was feared that definitions and primary provisions relating to genetic resources would be either:

- Too restrictive (which might mean that some users would still be able to benefit inequitably from the use of omitted types of resources) or

- Too broad (which might mean that the system would apply to uses that are already operating in a fair and equitable manner).

In the end, the negotiation of the CBD appears to have sidestepped the primary coverage questions relating to ABS—i.e., decided not to answer the questions "What are 'genetic resources' and how are they (legally) different from 'biological resources'?" Clearly, however, the resolution of these issues will color the nature and content of the entire regime negotiations.

The failure to address this definitional problem left the field open to the multitude of commentators who promoted the assumption that genetic resources were simply a new type of property that is similar (under the law) to all other types of property—that national legal frameworks governing ownership of property and commercial transactions would also directly govern ABS-related activities (in the same way that the first inventors and marketers of radios were able to use the markets and rules applicable to furniture, to market their inventions[46]). The basic problem regarding the nature of genetic resources is exemplified by the relevant definitions within the CBD ("biological resources", "genetic material", and "genetic resources") as well as by two concepts that are completely omitted from the CBD—the *use* of genetic resources and their *ownership*.[47]

Recognizing/Defining Genetic Resources

The most important single concept relating to ABS is probably the definitional or conceptual understanding of what a genetic resource actually is, and how it is distinguished from other resources. The CBD's provisions, and many statements of the Parties thereafter, have made it clear that ABS and requirements apply only to genetic resources, so that a clear understanding of their nature is essential to application of these provisions.[48] Unfortunately, the relevant definitions in the CBD itself (Article 2) do not provide a basis for this understanding:

> *"Genetic resources" means genetic material of actual or potential value.*
>
> *"Genetic material" means any material of plant, animal, microbial, or other origin containing functional units of heredity.*
>
> *"Biological resources" includes genetic resources, organisms, or parts thereof, populations, or any other biotic component of ecosystems with actual or potential use or value for humanity.*

On their face, it is difficult to see a distinction among these definitions. It is generally assumed that the phrase 'functional units of heredity' refers to DNA and RNA. Currently, DNA and RNA are thought to be the biological components that determine the nature and heritable properties of every life form—and to be present in every cell of all organic (and no nonorganic) matter. Hence, all biological resources (including "parts thereof") contain functional units of heredity.

However, the very fact that there are separate definitions of the two, and that the CBD uses them in very different contexts, suggests that the negotiators intended the meaning of genetic resources to be different from that of biological resources. Lacking a clear definition, good legal practice suggests that the difference must be determined by examining the usage of the terms within the CBD and in subsequent decisions and practices.[49] In general, the CBD's provisions discussing genetic resources are entirely directed to the use of those resources. They seem especially focused on transactions that do not involve bulk purchase of organic matter as for normal bulk uses. The assumption seems to be that a genetic resource can be synthesized or propagated based on a single sample, so that there is little long-term need for additional samples.

Even the access requirement (Article 15.2) focuses on use. It speaks directly to the need to "facilitate access to genetic resources *for environmentally sound uses...*". Nearly all of the other ABS provisions described above address either the use of the genetic resources, information developed or discerned from accessing them, or various particular benefits from those uses.[50] Taken together with the literature of the period in which these issues were being negotiated (late 1980s), it appears that the general assumption was that the DNA pattern of each species, (or more particularly, each subspecies or variety) was the resource. It may also have been assumed that DNA was a separate physical substance that could be separately controlled. But it was generally recognized as an informational resource—one that could be synthesized or used in the process of synthesizing so-called artificial DNA or creating GMOs. At a minimum, the clear expectation was that ABS would focus on the special issues surrounding the use of functional units of heredity.

By contrast, the provisions addressing biological resources are focused very directly on activities and impacts on species and ecosystems, and on positive measures within each country to preserve biodiversity both *in situ* and *ex situ*. It appears, then, that the distinction between genetic resources and the rest of biological resources is the manner in which they are used. Genetic material and genetic resources, as used in the CBD, refer to either:

- The genetic code or unique genetically defined characteristics of species (a type of information) or
- The use of samples: i.e., particular analysis and utilization of their DNA, genes, and other genetic components (a right of use).

A genetic resource would thus be, not a type of material, but an intangible property—a type of information or use. The buyer of a blue flower buys the biological resource when he intends to use the flower as a decoration on his table. He buys a genetic resource if he intends to use the DNA to create a new strain of blue carrot. For the latter activity, he would need an ABS arrangement or license. This kind of distinction between biological resources and genetic resources seems clearly to be what the Convention envisions, but it needs to be stated in legislation and other instruments, so that it can be applied in implementation and enforcement of the ABS process.

At the same time, the above clarification is at the heart of many difficulties encountered in attempting to implement ABS obligations and objectives. The same material, specimen or sample would be treated differently in the ABS system, depending on how it will be used. ABS measures and controls in provider-based contractual ABS arrangements would be legally effective, then, only where the governments and providers have the ability to know, oversee, and control the uses that are made of the resources. However, in the case of ABS, the provider government's involvement occurs at the 'front end'—the ABS process requires negotiation of contracts and other actions before any use has been made. *By the time the resource is used, the samples are usually outside of the jurisdiction of the agencies that conducted the negotiation and signed the contracts.* Most source countries cannot know how the resource is being used, and cannot enforce permits and contracts against a bioprospector who violates his restrictions or commitments after he has left the source country.

Use of Genetic Resources

A second question that is rather clearly still not understood is what it means to *use* genetic resources. During the negotiations of the CBD, overwhelming attention focused on genetic laboratory processes—the sampling of species and direct commercial use of their DNA for the laboratory-based creation of new biochemical compounds, GMOs, and the artificial propagation or synthesis of substances having biochemical properties.[51] It was sometimes difficult for agricultural organizations to ensure that the negotiators remembered other kinds of variety development that might also be a part of the ABS concept. This leads, however, to an interesting question. Exactly what activities are considered to be use of genetic resources? If we think of this as *utilization of a species' 'functional units of heredity'*, then:

- The most common use of any species' functional units of heredity is by ordinary reproduction of that species—including by planting seeds that have been purchased or saved or breeding animals held in captivity. This is the basis for claims of inclusion of conventional plant breeding (hybridization and selection) as uses of genetic resources.

- The theory of genetics that is generally based on the DNA discoveries made by Watson-Crick and others holds that a species' biochemical properties are determined by its DNA. On this basis, some commentators have suggested that bulk use of biological resources (as ingredients in commercial products, herbal medicines, components in other medicinal products, cosmetics, spices, tea, etc.) constitutes a utilization of genetic resources.

In virtually all countries, however, the ownership of or other legal dominion over a plant or animal usually carries with it the right to ordinary methods of propagation or breeding of that plant or animal, or at a minimum, some clear rules regarding any limitations on that right. One of the main factors in determining the value of a horse or cow, for example, is by whether it is capable of reproduction. Similarly, the rights to bulk cultivation and/or collection and sale of wild and domesticated plants (and animals) is a well-accepted component of the ownership of seeds and seed sources.[52] An ABS regime that casts its nets too widely may include these traditional uses—thus creating either a disruption of existing markets or an inconsistency in the ABS system.

The international regime, as well as national legislation, must clarify what activities constitute utilization of genetic resources for which access and benefit-sharing arrangements will be required. One of the critical challenges will be to define this concept in a way that is broad enough to enable oversight of new or special uses and ensure that middlemen and agents cannot circumvent ABS requirements, while ensuring that the legislation does not create difficulties of enforcement application. In this connection, it seems important to ensure that the ordinary sale of bulk goods is not included. A farmer's sale of his crop of cotton, maize, bananas, etc. should not be subject to restrictions under benefit-sharing concepts. At the same time, it should be clear that a purchase of beans from a farmer's market does not confer on the purchaser a right to commercially utilize the genetic material from those beans without complying with ABS requirements.

Practical Implementation: Owning and Tracking Genetic Resources

As a practical matter, ownership and resource tracking issues are probably the greatest hindrances to progress on ABS.

Owning Genetic Resources. Virtually any definition of genetic resources and the use of genetic resources will still be incomplete without a unification of the issue of ownership of those resources. The difficulties in this respect arise out of three sources:

- Genetic resources are often not country specific. If the same species, subspecies, or variety is present in two countries, then under the CBD, both countries have sovereign rights to its genetic resources (that is either genetic information or the right to make use of that information). The genetic resource is the same for both of them.

- Negotiation of ABS arrangements occurs between the user and the specific country in which the species samples are collected (which will provide the genetic material to be studied and utilized.) It does not even involve notice to other countries of origin. When the benefit-sharing element of the arrangement comes into play, the benefits are shared only with the source country (or in some cases, only with the particular community or property owner from which the specimens were taken)

- However, if the user applies for the relevant intellectual property right or other legal protection for innovations based on or using this genetic material, he will obtain a patent or other right that is valid against all the world.

Although obtaining the rights from and providing benefits to only one person or community or country, the user's IPR application can essentially prevent other countries from engaging in a similar use of the same species, despite equal sovereignty over the species within their borders. The genetic resource is localized for payment (minimizing the cost to the user) and globalized for protection (maximizing the protection and potential value to user.) The benefits to source countries and their people are essentially caught in a squeeze.

The inherent inconsistency can be illustrated by a simple story: Suppose that five people cowrite a song. They all agree that any of the five may, if he chooses, sell the song to anyone (multiple ownership.) Then one of the five sells the exclusive rights to the song for a large sum, and does not share his profits with the others. The buyer then copyrights the song, based on his exclusive rights. At this point, the buyer can claim that he is the only owner with a continuing right to sell the song. He is protected against any other claim, including from the other four original co-writers. None of the others can ever sell the song again. Realistically, if the international regime is to function as a legally consistent and rational process, it must find a way to rationalize these ownership issues. On the surface this would suggest that it must either:

- Recognize single ownership through the entire process (in which case the buyer could not patent the resource against countries that do not share in benefits); or
- Consider the genetic resource to be an international resource from the beginning (in which case benefits from genetic resources should compensate all countries which possess that resource).

Both of these options, although satisfying the needs for equity and consistency, would be difficult or impossible to apply in practice. However, the need for consistency is not simply a matter of aesthetics. In order for a legal regime to operate it must not only contain clear, enforceable statements, but also be organized into a rational, consistent framework. Without rational consistency, every time an issue arises that is not directly discussed in the legislation, new legislation will be required. If the system is consistent, judges and administrators (and enforcement officers) will have a basis for determining how each new question fits within the overall system, and need not continually return to Parliament for guidance. Accordingly, it is critical to reconsider the questions of ownership. All of the various aspects of access, benefit sharing, patenting (and/or using) innovations based on genetic resources must fit into a single unified property framework.[53]

Tracking Genetic Resources. Two other practical elements that must be addressed in this connection are downstream transactions and the concept of a research exception. A number of institutions (particularly botanical gardens, universities, and other research organizations) have strongly asserted that exceptions should be generally created under which they can gain access to genetic resources more easily, and not be bound by stringent controls on subsequent sharing of the genetic resources and information concerning it. These assertions are based on the public and scientific nature of these institutions—their research is undertaken to increase knowledge and is thus different from commercial research and development.

This position strongly supports the view that genetic resources are actually rights of use. It also illustrates the related point—that the use of genetic resources cannot be known at the time of the transaction and can change over time.

The promotion of research is a vital activity. It remains true, however, that even where resources are being taken solely for research, their use can change in the future. As a result, any simply expressed research exception will probably serve as a major loophole in the international regime. Already, botanical gardens have indicated that they do not track lateral transfers of genetic resources to other gardens and collectors and do not intend to do so. A system has been proposed that will seek to ensure that this lack of tracking does not invalidate the ABS system, but it is still not adopted by internationally active associations of botanical gardens.[54]

Other research institutions have even less willingness to support a genetic material tracking system. Noting that noncommercial researchers are the primary current mechanism by which key developing country research needs are addressed,[55] they point out that even transaction and time costs that would be acceptable to commercial entities may be impossible within the tight budgets of noncommercial research.

Mechanisms for tracking traffic in genetic resources and monitoring downstream transactions seem to be essential to the oversight of any direct use-based system of benefit sharing. Discussions of some of these mechanisms are already underway, even though the configuration of the ABS system is still not clear (RUIZ 2003).[56] Many commentators, however, suggest that due to the difficulties involved, such tracking should not even be attempted (PIRES DE CARVALHO 2000). Instead, they suggest relying on new provisions of patent law that would require disclosure of origin when any patent is sought for an invention that utilizes genetic material. This mechanism may be partially effective. It cannot be thought of as the entire solution, however. For example, it would omit many significant types of commercial utilization of genetic resources,[57] and for enforcement it would require a kind of technological oversight that is currently unavailable and unlikely to be generally accessible by developing countries in the near future.[58]

National Contract Law as a Basis for ABS Arrangements

The assumption that ABS issues can be addressed through national contract law seems valid on the surface.[59] However, the complete novelty of the legal concept of genetic resources as a specific type of property or property right actually means that there is no existing legal basis through which ABS arrangements can be regulated.

At its simplest, this can be explained in terms of the most basic contract principle—mutual agreement (sometimes called the "meeting of the minds"). If the persons entering into a contract do not share identical understandings about what the contract covers and requires, then it is not a contract. Thus, if X promises to pay for Y's trip to Rome, in exchange for certain performance by Y, it may seem that they have a contract. However, if X is referring to Rome, Italy and Y is referring to Rome, New York, then there has been no mutual agreement. Due to lack of specificity and mutual understanding, the contract is invalid (see Box 1 for an analysis of contract components).

In many cases, national law clarifies common areas of contractual misunderstanding. For example, there are numerous laws governing contracts for the sale of intellectual property rights. Often these provide that, if the contract is silent about an issue, then the definition or explanation in the law will govern the contract; but if the contract clearly addressed the issue in another way, the contractual provision will control.

The underlying need for both legal and individual understanding is clearest when considering situations in which one party fails to perform or otherwise violates the contract. The lack of shared understanding about what the contract covers would make it almost impossible for a court to mediate or adjudicate such a dispute. If it is not clear what a genetic resource is, then it is almost certainly also not clear whether an individual or entity has a right to dispose of it or indeed whether the contract disposes of it. If the right of the party giving access to genetic resources was challenged (by either party or by some other individual), a court could not confidently decide the issue if it does not know what genetic resources are. This is also true of a claim that someone using genetic resources was exceeding his rights, for example.

Valuation of Genetic Resources: Markets

One of the most insidious continuing assumptions relating to ABS is the assumption that the value of the genetic resources can be determined by negotiation of each ABS arrangement on a case-by-case basis. Within this assumption lurks the most serious insufficiency of the ABS system—the lack of any kind of market oversight or regulation. One of the most important and unaddressed aspects of the ABS issue is the fact that it seeks to create a *market* in a completely new kind of property. While the concept of a market is virtually universal and dates back to very ancient times, in today's world even the simplest retail markets are subject to legal oversight and controls in most countries.

Many companies and users suggest that regulation will prevent or impede the formation of ABS arrangements. In practice, however, the opposite may well be true. If a clear, consistent market system were in place and subject to appropriate oversight and control mechanisms, parties on

---

Box 1. Analysis of contract components

The need for supporting legislation and a body of legally recognized facts and issues may be illustrated by the following nonsense example[60]: A simple contract is entered into as follows: **"YOUNG grants CARRIZOSA an EXCLUSIVE RIGHT to DO-SI-DO with the ÜBERMEISTERIN, IN RETURN FOR a TOT of RATATOUILLE".** Before this contract can be enforced, several questions must be answered. First are factual questions, including:

- *Who or what are Young and Carrizosa?* Different rules and standards may apply if they are individuals rather than if they are corporations or other entities.
- *What are "do-si-do" and "übermeisterin"?* It may not be common knowledge that do-si-do is a series of steps in (American) Square Dancing, and übermeisterin is a German official (a female lord mayor, sometimes called the lady mayor.)
- *What is a "tot" and what is "ratatouille"?* A tot is an obsolete liquid measure and ratatouille is a French dish—a very delicious vegetable stew.

Thereafter, the parties or the court must consider legal questions, including:

- Does Young have a legal right to determine who may dance with the übermeisterin? If so, how broad or restrictive is that right?
- May Young legally alienate that right to others?
- Is Carrizosa a kind of person or entity that can legally receive that right?
- Are there any restrictions on transactions involving rights to do-si-do with government officials or transfers of ratatouille? (That is, are such transactions legal? And, if so, must licenses be obtained or taxes paid?)
- Is this contract equitable? (That is, is a tot of ratatouille an appropriate level of payment? And, if not, were the negotiations fair? Is public policy satisfied or should government intervene in the contract or adjust its terms?)
- Can the performance of the contract be verified, monitored, and enforced?

The answers to all of these questions can be evaluated, and their impact on the contract and its enforceability assessed, only if there are clear supporting laws and understandings applicable and relevant to the type of property, the type of use (activity), and the type of entities that are involved in the contract.

both sides would have greater assurance that their interests would not be injured by entering into an ABS arrangement. In fact, the Andean Pact Decision 391, which is perhaps the most complex and difficult ABS law adopted to date, may well have become so complex in an effort to ensure that the parties' interests would be protected in this new and unregulated market.

Until the national and international ABS systems contain generally accepted legal underpinnings, they cannot operate in a more streamlined, flexible manner while still adequately protecting the parties to ABS arrangements. As a consequence, national ABS laws and contracts will have to contain highly protective provisions, despite their impact on the users' transaction costs. The primary tools needed to create markets and market confidence are oversight and transparency. Given the international/transboundary nature of many ABS transactions, it appears that these tools must operate or coordinate at the international level. This basic point can be illustrated very simply by comparing the amount and nature of existing instruments and commitments on ABS at the international level with the similar information regarding another new international market in development—the trade in carbon credits under the UN Framework Convention on Climate Change (FCCC) (ORLANDO et al. 2002).

The FCCC, adopted at the same time as the CBD, has regulated and negotiated at great length endeavoring to define these credits and to set up a consistent enforceable leakproof system by which they can be created, marketed, traded, and regulated. This has been a long and difficult process, even though there exists an example that is used at the national level. (For purposes of implementation there is a strong similarity between carbon credits and various kinds of "transferable development rights" that have been in use in many developing countries for decades.) When contrasted with genetic resources, for which there is no parallel or template in national or international law, the FCCC's provisions and approach are very instructive.[61]

Oversight Tools: The Need for International Cooperation

On examination, the primary gap in the international regime relates to collaborative action—a need that is much more essential than any additional agreement on commitments[62] or terms (YOUNG 2004). Cooperation, and a consistent legal framework for that cooperation, is essential to enable mutual action to enforce ABS arrangements involving private entities, academic institutions, etc.

Other important services, such as mechanisms for oversight of the users and uses of genetic resources, interchange of patenting and other relevant information, and monitoring of post-removal compliance with ABS arrangements might also create economies of scale if shared among similarly situated countries. It would be financially very costly and, in some cases, practically much less effective, to address these needs at the national level, when a single solution would be both cheaper and more effective. It is

important to note that those mechanisms are not voluntary enhancements of the ABS concept, but basic necessities of the system. Virtually all formal retail markets, even those dealing in tangible commodities, must be bolstered by a range of legal mechanisms and institutions to protect consumers from illegal practices and to ensure that markets are protected from informal acquisition of products without compensating the seller. ABS, like all of these markets, presents opportunities for intentional deception and unintentional misunderstanding on both sides that must be controlled.

Market Transparency: Information, Registration, and Fairness

The lack of market information and the connected need for some protections of the participants in ABS arrangements have greatly restricted ABS development. Without this information, government officials in provider countries cannot be certain that they are properly protecting and representing national interests and the interests of persons and entities under their jurisdiction. Nearly all government officials are charged with a fiduciary duty when entering into contracts relating to national or patrimonial assets or otherwise acting on behalf of the state or its citizens. Governments typically adopt detailed procurement and contracting policies and laws that call on officials to document that they have received proper compensation in such transactions.

A government official who does not have credible market information telling him that the price and terms being offered are fair and reasonable will be open to the claim that he has failed to meet that obligation. The lack of transparent market information may mean that he cannot easily satisfy these requirements and would be unprotected against later claims. In markets dealing in intangible goods (stocks, intellectual property, or futures), principles of good governance require greater market oversight, at the national or international levels, to protect parties against abuse.[63] This is also true of markets that are controlled or limited by one side of the transaction (trade in gold and other limited commodities controlled by a small number of buyers or sellers).

The entire realm of access and benefit sharing is basically a market in a new intangible commodity—genetic resources. However, most ABS contracts require that the terms of the arrangement (or at least the value given) must be kept confidential, as a condition of the contract.[64] Information regarding these matters is essential to the parties' (especially the provider countries') ability to enter confidently into these arrangements, however. This lack of knowledge creates a risk and a fear of entering into a bad deal and thereby failing in their obligation to protect national interests and the public.[65] This fear, in turn leads to more cautious and complex negotiation and approval processes, more detailed legislation, more internal ratification and verification processes, etc., which lead commercial entities to refuse to participate in ABS arrangements until the process can be streamlined.

The CBD Parties have clearly recognized the importance of market data in achieving the equity requirements of the convention and of general international commercial law. In COP-6, for example, they called for, *inter alia,* "information regarding… (b) The market for genetic resources; (c) Non-monetary benefits; [and] …(h) 'intermediaries,'" among their short list of the information that is "a critical aspect of providing the necessary parity of bargaining power … in access and benefit-sharing arrangements".[66]

A variety of market tools could be adapted to the ABS context, as part of the development of an international regime, including a) the registration of transactions (including or excluding pricing information or the manner of calculating benefit-shares); b) certification (including certificates of origin or legal provenance) of genetic resources, as a prerequisite of use or further transfer; c) oversight institutions and mechanisms (annual reporting and permit requirements); and d) the creation and empowerment of oversight bodies, institutions, or frameworks. Contractual protection mechanisms and institutions can also play a key role in ensuring that markets are fair where one party to a financial arrangement has fewer financial resources or less technical or legal sophistication. These measures are also necessary to protect the environment and third parties (people and entities that are not included in the Agreement, but may be injured by it) against possible system-based abuses. In an international system, it may be that some of these processes will have to be integrated or harmonized across national boundaries. The possibility of an international ombudsman has been suggested in this context.[67]

In a few cases, specific mechanisms are already under discussion, even before the CBD's international regime negotiations begin. Many Parties, for example, are seeking to promote international agreement on specific approaches and procedures, including the issues of genetic tracking (using certificates of origin or legal provenance, disclosure of origin and source in patent applications, etc.) (PIRES DE CARVALHO 2000). To some extent, this agreement may be premature—it is usually necessary first to come to critical decisions about the coverage of a system and the nature of its requirements, before deciding how to implement those requirements and adopting specific tools. If such measures are used, it will be necessary to integrate them firmly into legally mandated processes relating to international transport of genetic material, IPRs, and controls on marketing and commercialization, so that the user will have a strong incentive to comply with these mechanisms.

Expectations Insufficiently Realized

Finally and briefly, it is important to mention again that the CBD already obligates all Parties to adopt and implement measures that will create and support the ABS regime, but that as of this writing, only 18 have done so. The ABS component of the CBD is an international framework that was intended to be implemented through national law. With only 9.6% of Party governments having met this obligation, it should be unsurprising that the system is not functional, despite the fact that 12 years have elapsed since it was adopted. General implementation is about more than just ABS. It is an important tool of the achievement of all three CBD objectives. The WSSD has recognized that it is also a component of broader international objectives such as equalizing participation of developing and developed countries (with regard to both access and benefits), maximizing capacity and understanding, and empowering and mandating sustainable development as a part of a larger contractual reality.

ABS-related expectations have another face, however—national expectations of the reasons for developing a national ABS system and of participating in work on the international regime. Investigations and workshops have demonstrated that most developing countries that attempt to develop ABS legislation have been preoccupied by possible profits. However, not all countries share this approach. In the late 1990s, a brief effort was undertaken to promote the creation of national ABS strategies (TEN KATE and WELLS 2000). Although this attempt was not ultimately successful,[68] its results were somewhat surprising. During the discussion of the ABS Strategy idea, many quipped that the national ABS strategy would consist of a single phrase: "make lots of money from our genetic resources". In a few situations, however, particularly countries with low endemism, large indigenous populations, and populations living in traditionally mobile lifestyles, the primary genetic resource strategy was identified to be the preservation of genetic resources and the traditional practices associated with them (EKHASSA 2003). Concerns that urbanization and modernization will eliminate these important resources and knowledge still transferred by oral traditions have proven a much stronger motivation than the as-yet-unproven expectation of financial and other direct benefits. This is particularly true in arid and tundra countries, in which the volume of species and varieties may be relatively small, but the number of highly localized endemics quite high. In these countries, it is not generally expected that income from ABS arrangements would ever be sufficient to cover the cost of employment of an ABS focal point. However, there are strong interests in protecting genetic resources and associated traditional knowledge, both as a part of the country's natural heritage, and as key resources (WYNBERG et al. 2004). In other countries (including developed countries), it has been reported that the primary motivation underlying their draft access legislation is tracking and the desire to be aware of (and have control over) the kinds of research being undertaken and the nature of the products that will result.[69] These nonfinancial interests have nowhere been addressed in the international regime, guidance, or model laws developed to date.

Conclusions and Recommendations

At present, the international ABS regime, although existing, is not functional. Usually, where legislation is rather sketchy in its direct provisions, it may be "fleshed out" by implementation (laws, regulations, practices, and interpretation.) This often happens with international obligations, which become more concrete and implementable when countries adopt legislation to implement them. Unfortunately, that process has not happened in the decade since the CBD's ABS obligations entered into force. However, in order for a regime to be implemented through commercial mechanisms (contracts and property ownership systems), it must be complete and consistent—capable of being enforced by the courts and implemented through legal processes. Moreover, this system must be legally consistent internationally. It will be nearly impossible to operate an ABS system if the basic definition of genetic resources is markedly different from country to country, for example.

Serious attention must therefore be given to clarifying the concepts left vague in the international policy negotiations that resulted in the CBD. Key definitions that define the nature and coverage of ABS, including the terminology genetic resources and use of genetic resources, must be developed and applied. Once the exact nature of genetic resources has been clarified, then basic inconsistencies in their legal ownership must be addressed. Beyond these most basic hurdles, the ABS system's most serious deficiency is its failure to address key financial components of the creation of a new market in a new kind of commodity. It will be essential to develop legal mechanisms to define that market and provide mechanisms and institutions for oversight and transparency of the market and the use rights obtained through it.

Hard Realities: Negotiation of an International Regime

It is necessary at this point to return to the fact that the CBD is beginning a process which it is calling "negotiation of an international regime on access and benefit sharing". While the exact nature of the work that will be done under this description is not yet agreed, it is clear that international work is intended to make some clear progress in creating an effective system. In selecting among options, at each stage of these negotiations, it might be useful to keep several facts in mind. First is the duration of negotiations. Negotiation of the Cartagena Protocol on Biosafety took more than eight years (those issues were intensively negotiated even before the CBD was adopted) (KOESTER 2000). Another key recent negotiation—the Fish Stocks Agreement under UNCLOS—took somewhere between four and 12 years,[70] and the Kyoto Protocol to the UN Framework Convention on Climate Change is taking even longer.[71] Moreover, negotiation is a mechanism of

compromise, so it is important to realize that the ultimate regime is unlikely to live up to the expectations of those who are most assertive in pressing for the creation of a new instrument. One needs only look at the CBD's provisions relating to biosafety, and compare them to the Cartagena protocol as finally adopted, to see that there is a dramatic difference between pre-negotiation expectations and the actual result.

Another factor, however, is the unique quality of environmental negotiations, as compared with other international negotiations. As a general matter, international instruments are negotiated as a way of harmonizing or standardizing activities, conditions, or requirements across borders. Negotiations start from a base of national understanding both of how the issues are handled at the national level and of the nature of particular international problems or needs. By contrast, international environmental negotiations in particular, have increasingly sought to address new issues as potential problems before they can cause expected harm or to address concerns about harm in advance, so that those concerns will not cause commercial disruption or have other negative social impacts. Thus, despite complete disagreement at the highest expert levels regarding the nature of risks (scientific/biological, economic, and social) inherent in the introduction and consumption of GMOs, for example, the Cartagena protocol was negotiated and adopted with impetus from two mandates—the desire to utilize and market these new innovations and the concern that uncontrolled introductions might have serious consequences to biodiversity, health, and other factors of human livelihoods.

Negotiation of the CBD identified the use and development of genetic resources as an activity that might have major impact on conservation in the future. At that time, however, understanding of what it might mean in practice was quite limited. The result was an attempt to address the issue through provisions that were designed to be somewhat open-ended, but to clearly evince the primary objectives and basic commitments of the parties. Fifteen years later, the system has still not been operational, so that even the new negotiations will not have the advantage of experience with functional market systems. Accordingly, the current negotiation of the international regime on genetic resources will have to go forward without the benefit of direct experience in any country. This lack of experience also suggests another potential complexity of these negotiations—the final result will be relatively inflexible and extremely difficult to change. International agreements tend to be long lived, and the process of amending them often takes additional decades following the adoption of the amendment, while the existing parties decide whether to ratify or not. During that interim period, both old and new versions remain in force, with increasingly complex legal rules for their application.

Recommendations: Working 'Outside the Box'

One of the most common problems encountered in international policy forums under the CBD is that of repetition. Many very important issues seem to arise again and again in COP meetings and other high level sessions, each time leading to a decision that varies little from past meetings and decisions. ABS is one example of this phenomenon. Some part of this repetitive approach can be explained by lack of financial resources and capacity in developing countries—problems not easily solved. It is possible, however, that by now these oft-repeated statements are only easy solutions that fail to consider the efforts of the past 12 years. In its initial year, the ABS Project has discerned, and partially investigated, a number of possible avenues for new approaches. Two in particular may form part of the pathway to an effective ABS regime.

Integration and Consistency: Re-linking ABS to Other Genetic Resource Issues (GMOs and Agriculture)

One recommendation to the negotiations is to consider re-linking the suite of genetic resource issues—considering them collectively in the negotiation.[72] There are several reasons to think such a merger might be useful, but the most important is the possibility of developing useful incentives. The complete lack of national ABS policies in developed countries (which would normally be very capable of creating and adopting such measures) suggests that there is little incentive for developed countries to comply with their ABS obligations to develop "legislative, administrative, or policy measures", as described above. In essence, by severing biosafety issues from ABS (and other genetic resource issues), the negotiators separated two sides of the market:

- ABS is primarily directed at the source countries' issues and desires.

- Biosafety and GMOs, although not the only use made of genetic resources, are certainly of particular importance to user countries.

Eliminating this unnecessary distinction would emphasize the tie between the primarily-source-country concerns over access and development and the primarily user-country concerns regarding the open acceptance of products of ABS research, including new varieties and especially GMOs. Even the most difficult definition and coverage issues might be more easily resolved if the full range of genetic matters were included in a single framework. At least, negotiators would know that a decision to delete something from ABS coverage would not remove it entirely from the CBD's governance.

In particular, this re-linking would provide a framework on which strong incentives could be credibly created and applied. Rather than the weaker incentive of doing equity, for example, user countries and institutions might have a stronger incentive of improving the market position or

status of their GMO products within developing countries that are signatories of the CBD. This would also create reciprocal business motivations for source countries in the development of their biosafety frameworks. In addition, it might give source countries confidence to streamline the procedures for developing ABS arrangements. Where the contents of those agreements and procedures are not the only bases on which countries may protect their rights and where an international framework exists, governmental negotiators will be able to develop simpler procedures for documenting their decisions and confirming that the interests of the country and its people are adequately protected.

Partners and Partnership

Another potential new entry into ABS is the creation of new kinds of collaboration among the Parties. To date, ABS issues have been negotiated in CBD Ad Hoc Working Groups and other committees-of-the-whole, in which countries which are primarily users and those which are primarily sources have been called upon to develop consensus together on many issues. This approach ignores the basic premise of ABS work to date—that ABS is primarily governed by contract.

From a business perspective, it is essential that each side of a contractual negotiation should separately develop its positions based on the particular facts of the individual contract, and thereafter negotiate for the best ultimate result on the basis of this position. Hence, it would not be appropriate to pre-negotiate the terms of any agreement by consensus of both sides of such future negotiations. Countries that view themselves as primarily suppliers of genetic materials (either of specific types, e.g., tropical plants, or more generally) may find it more useful to develop collaborative and consensus positions among themselves, which could then be used in the international regime negotiations or in the negotiation of ABS arrangements themselves. The Group of Like-Minded Megadiverse Countries may serve as the first example of this kind of collaboration within the international negotiating forums.[73] Other such groupings, whether regional or based on shared species or situations, may also be possible.

With regard to negotiation of ABS arrangements themselves, the concept of collective action has thus far received little attention. Some commentators, however, have developed some valuable insights into the development of conglomerates of developing countries for purposes of increasing their access to and influence in ABS markets (VOGEL 2000). This issue may be very important to the future of the international regime.

Seller-Oriented Valuation

One final fact has begun to become obvious in the first year of the IUCN ABS Project—the value of genetic resources has, up to now, been primarily determined by the users. There is virtually no objective way of valuing these resources in the absence of clear definitions and market information (and little basis for valuation even then). The primary suggested methods of valuation to date relate to the value of the user's end-product (TEN KATE and LAIRD 1999). Typically, this value is determined based on prior or similar products, to which some factor (volumetric calculation or extrapolation of the value of the component that genetic resource are replacing) is applied. Often, the amount is just a flat fee—a small percentage of product net profits (which is determined by the price set for the product). In rare cases, the users have attempted to assign a commercial value to particular species' or varieties' genetic material, but again the basis of that valuation is difficult to justify.[74]

There are some apparent flaws in this approach to valuation, however. First, the ABS provisions are not focused on the value of the resource as used, but on an equitable share of the benefits. In this case, the objective of equity appears to be the compensation of countries for their historic contribution—that is, for their actions (conservation and responsible land stewardship) or omissions to act (the fact that they did not develop lands, but left them in a natural state). These contributions resulted in the protection and continued existence of entire ecosystems, not only the individual species.

Even apart from the question of equity-based valuation, the user orientation of current valuation fails to take account of some serious ABS-related issues. Especially,

it is noted that the cost to countries of their participation in an ABS system (institutional development, legislative development, personnel commitment, and especially the costs of oversight and monitoring) may be significant, even if some or all parties develop collaborative mechanisms. It is, therefore possible that the value of genetic resources may be better determined by consideration of the source country's perspective.

This can be illustrated by one final hypothetical example—suppose Product x is currently being manufactured using chicken eggs as a primary ingredient. It is then discovered that Product x is much improved if caviar is substituted for chicken eggs, creating a new product (Product x⁰.) In paying for the ingredients, it is not appropriate to value the caviar according to the former cost of eggs. Instead, the cost of Product x⁰ is greater than that of Product x, reflecting the increased ingredient cost, including the costs of obtaining permits to acquire and import caviar[75], and any national conditions imposed on the harvesting of caviar, to ensure that such harvests are sustainable and use environmentally sound methods.

The most valuable contribution anyone can make to these negotiations will be a willingness to think outside the box. The negotiations must dig deeper into existing assumptions about ABS, its operations, and potential, as well as its limitations.

Acknowledgements

This chapter reflects the expert opinion of the author only and does not reflect the view and positions of IUCN. Much of the analysis of this chapter is supported by the initial work of the IUCN ABS Project (of which the author is project manager), a three-year project of the IUCN Environmental Law Center, financed by the German Ministry for Development Cooperation (BMZ). The objective of the ABS Project is to provide concrete research delving into the ABS issue, the manner in which it has been addressed up to now, the reasons for its apparent failure to meet expectations, and solutions based on expert advice and analysis for critical legal impediments to compliance. The Project gives particular attention to researching unproven assumptions and frequently restated conditions, "facts", and objectives that have not been formally studied and confirmed. Interested readers are invited to find out more about the Project from its website at http://www.iucn.org/themes/law/abs01.html or from the project manager at tyoung@iucn.org.

References

ANDEAN COMMUNITY. 1996. Decision 391: Common regime on access to genetic resources. http://www.comunidadandina.org/ingles/treaties/dec/d391e.htm.

CABRERA J. 2004. *A comparative analysis on the legislation and practices on access to genetic resources and benefit sharing (ABS): Critical aspects for implementation and interpretation.* IUCN/BMZ, Bonn, Germany.

CBD Secretariat and UN DOALOS 2003. Conservation and sustainable use of deep seabed genetic resources beyond national jurisdiction: Study of the relationship between the Convention on Biological Diversity and the United Nations Convention on the Law of the Sea. UNEP/CBD/SBSTTA/8/9/Add.3/Rev.1. URL: http://www.biodiv.org/doc/meetings/sbstta/sbstta-08/official/sbstta-08-09-add3-rev1-en.pdf.

BŁAZKIEWICZ B. 2004. Raising the floor: Legal issues regarding the biological richness of the area (an initial inquiry). p. 21 *in As knowledge evolves: Applying the Marine Governance Regime to recent genetic resource discoveries.* IUCN/BMZ, Bonn, Germany.

BROWNLIE L. 1979. *Principles of public international law.* Oxford Press, 3rd Edition, London, UK and New York, USA.

CHISHAKWE N. and T. YOUNG. 2004. *Access to genetic resources, and sharing the benefits: International and sub-regional Issues.* IUCN/BMZ, Bonn, Germany.

EKHASSA B. 2003. La plantation des acacias. Abstract of presentation at the 1st Inter-Regional Session of the Global Biodiversity Forum: Integrating Biodiversity Conservation and Livelihood Security. Havana, Cuba.

GLOWKA L. 1997. The next rosy periwinkle won't be free: Emerging legal frameworks to implement Article 15.

Environmental Policy and Law **27**:441–458.

GLOWKA L. 1998. A guide to designing legal frameworks to determine access to genetic resources. Environmental Policy and Law Paper No. 34. Environmental Law Center, IUCN, Gland, Switzerland, Cambridge, UK and Bonn, Germany.

KOESTER V., 2000. Excellence in the art of the possible. IUCN Environmental Law Newsletter, vol. 2000/1, Bonn, Germany.

MACKENSIE R., F. BURHENNE-GUILMIN, A.G.M. LA VIÑA, and J.D. WERKSMAN. 2003. An explanatory guide to the Cartagena Protocol on Biosafety. IUCN Environmental Policy and Law Paper No. 46, FIELD. Bonn, Germany.

ORLANDO B., D. BALDOCK, S. CANJER, J. MACKENSEN, S. MAGINNIS, M.S. MANGUIAT, S. RIETBERGEN, C. ROBLEDO, N. SCHNEIDER. 2002. Carbon, forests and people: Towards the integrated management of carbon sequestration, the environment and sustainable livelihoods. IUCN Occasional Paper, Gland, Switzerland.

PATTON S. 2004. The ecological significance of seamounts: Threats and conservation. p. 1 *in As knowledge evolves: Applying the Marine Governance Regime to recent genetic resource discoveries.* IUCN/BMZ, Bonn, Germany

PERIA E. 2000. The ASEAN framework agreement on access to genetic resources: An access instrument or impediment? 15th Global Biodiversity Forum: Sharing the Benefits from Biodiversity. Unpublished manuscript. Nairobi, Kenya.

PIRES DE CARVALHO N. 2000. Requiring disclosure of the origin of genetic resources and prior informed consent in patent applications without infringing the TRIPS agreement: The problem and the solution. *Washington University Journal of Law and Policy* **2**:371–401.

RUIZ M. (ed.) 2003. Regional workshop on the synergies between the Convention on Biological Diversity and CITES regarding access to genetic resources and distribution of benefits: The role of the certificates of origin. IUCN/BMZ, Bonn, Germany.

SCHLOSSER E. 2002. *Fast food nation.* Perennial, New York, NY USA.

SWIDERSKA K. 2001. *Stakeholder participation in policy on access to genetic resources, traditional knowledge and benefit-sharing: Case studies and recommendations.* Biodiversity and Livelihoods Issues, vol. 4. International Institute for Environment and Development, London, UK. URL: http://www.iied.org/docs/blg/synthesis_final.pdf.

TEN KATE K. and S.A. LAIRD. 1999. *The commercial use of biodiversity: Access to genetic resources and benefit-sharing.* Earthscan. London, UK.

TEN KATE K. and A. WELLS. 2000. *Preparing a national strategy on access to genetic resources and benefit sharing: A pilot study.* Royal Botanic Gardens Kew, UK. URL: http://www.undp.org/bpsp/thematic_links/docs/ABS_Manual_RBGK.pdf.

TOBIN, B. and K. SWIDERSKA. 2001 *Speaking in tongues: Indigenous participation in the development of a* sui generis *regime to protect traditional knowledge in Peru.* Participation in Access and Benefit-Sharing Policy Case Study No 2. Biodiversity and Livelihoods Group, International Institute for Environment and Development, London, UK. URL: http://www.iied.org/docs/blg/perustudy.pdf.

VOGEL J. 2000. Conclusion: An economic justification for the cartel and a special protocol for the Convention on Biological Diversity. p. 101–114 *in* J. Vogel (ed.) *The biodiversity cartel: Transformation of traditional knowledge into trade secrets.* CARE, Proyecto SUBIR. Quito, Ecuador.

WYNBERG R., L. HAIDAR, W. NASSER, and A. GARANE. 2004. *Biodiversity access and benefit-sharing in arid countries and those with low diversity and high endemism.* IUCN/BMZ, Bonn, Germany.

YOUNG T. 2004. *Instruments in the existing international regime on ABS: A coverage analysis.* IUCN/BMZ, Bonn Germany (forthcoming).

Endnotes

[1] Primarily for purposes of length, this paper does not address the issues of "traditional knowledge" as expressed in the Convention on Biological Diversity and elsewhere, except in the sense that some kinds of "genetic-resource-related traditional knowledge" will be subject to the same legal development and analysis that is being slowly developed and molded into a body of law on genetic resources. It is the development of the latter body of law that this paper addresses. Traditional knowledge issues are very differently expressed in the CBD (see, e.g., Articles 8(j) and 10(c) of the Convention) which creates a mandate that is from a legal perspective both very different and very much broader than the ABS systemic mandate that is discussed in this paper. It is hoped that the creation of a functional and effective regime on ABS will provide a key component that will help in the development of the much more inclusive issues of traditional knowledge and the biodiversity-related rights of indigenous, mobile and rural peoples.

[2] Convention on Biological Diversity (entry into force December 1993). The nature and implementation of ABS has been an important and somewhat controversial topic from the earliest negotiations leading to the Convention. It has appeared in some form in every international negotiating committee (INC) and Conference of the Parties (COP) since the Convention was adopted. *See, e.g.,*

Decisions I/9, II/11, III/15, IV/8, V/26, VI/24 and VI/19 (decisions focused on ABS. The issue arises in other decisions as well.) It is integrally related to other controversial issues and negotiations, including especially the Cartagena Protocol on Biosafety (Montréal, 2000, entry into force, 11 Sept. 2003.) Reports of CBD COP and INC meetings as well as the INC and COP-MOP meetings of the Cartagena Protocol are all available on-line at the CBD Secretariat website at http://www.biodiv.org.

[3] CBD Resolution VI-24. UN Document UNEP/CBD/COP/6/L-24, available on the CBD website (see note 2).

[4] In this connection, it should be noted that the WSSD was an international forum with no direct legal mandate. As such, its outputs are aspirational rather than mandatory or even "good faith" commitments. They are less binding than either Conventions or COP resolutions.

[5] UNEP/CBD/COP/7/5 later generally adopted by the CBD Conference of Parties through decision VII/31 (UN Document UNEP/CBD/COP/7/L.31.), available on the CBD website (see note 2).

[6] UN Document UNEP/CBD/COP/7/L.19, available on the CBD website (see note 2).

[7]In this paper, the word "regime" is used to mean the "totality of norms, rules, standards, and procedures as expressed in international and national law instruments and other formal documents relevant to the subject" (in this case ABS).

[8]An explanatory guide to the ITPGRFA, written by Gerald Moore and Witold Tymowsky is currently in the final editing process, with English publication under the auspices of the ABS Project expected by the close of 2004. For more information, and electronic copies when available, see the IUCN ABS Project website (URL: http://www.iucn.org/themes/law/abs01.htm).

[9]Recital 27 of this directive provides that the patent application should, where appropriate, include information on the geographical origin of biological material if known. Although this is entirely voluntary, as it is without prejudice to the processing of patent applications or the validity of rights arising from granted patents, it remains one of the few developed-country laws that address any ABS issues directly.

[10]The CBD's ABS commitments, as discussed below, are quite specific, and relate to kinds of property that have not been recognized in law prior to 1992. Accordingly, the claims that national contract and commercial law, without additional amendment, is sufficient to satisfy the Parties' ABS commitments suggests a need for further inquiry. This work is in process under the auspices of the ABS Project (IUCN/BMZ), with a final publication expected in 2006.

[11]Judicial interpretation of private instruments with relevant legal effectiveness are also a key component of any legal regime.

[12]Most ABS contracts are between a government entity in the source country and a private entity or academic institution. Even where such agreements may, by law, be directly negotiated with the owner of the property from which the samples are to be taken, government oversight or approval of the agreement may be required (TOBIN and SWIDERSKA 2001).

[13]In this paper, the term "regulated public" simply refers to the group whose activities or status is covered by the law.

[14]CBD Article 1. The quoted material is enhanced by the next phrase in Article 1: "including by appropriate access to genetic resources and by appropriate transfer of relevant technologies, taking into account all rights over those resources and to technologies, and by appropriate funding".

[15]In addition to the 10 binding commitments in text, the parties are subject to one nonmandatory provision that is particularly relevant to ABS—the commitment to "consider strengthening existing financial institutions to provide financial resources for the conservation and sustainable use of biological diversity" (Art. 21.4).

[16]All section references are to the CBD unless otherwise noted.

[17]As of this writing, there are 188 parties to the CBD, and one other country signed the Convention in 1993, but has never ratified it. (Information from ECOLEX, a continuously updated IUCN/FAO/UNEP environmental law database, now available online at http://www.ecolex.org.)

[18]Some countries have enacted legislation that says that any international agreement that the government ratifies or accedes to becomes the law of the land. These provisions would be very difficult to apply in practice, since international treaties do not specify rights, duties, or potential liabilities of individuals and the civil society. However, this "blanket legislation" is still national legislation, and is the vehicle by which those requirements become binding on persons and entities within such countries.

[19]CBD Article 15.2 (emphasis added.)

[20]There are some "framework" instruments that are not "policy-style". In particular, the United Nations Convention on the Law of the Sea provides regulatory levels of detail on a great many issues, but still provides a comprehensive framework under which other instruments can be developed.

[21]CBD framework tools include the Ecosystem Approach and the Sustainable Use principles. Others, including ones on technology transfer, incentives, and liability, are being discussed.

[22]CITES entered into force in 1975 and the Montreal Protocol on Substances that Deplete the Ozone Layer came into force in 1989. The Protocol was also amended in 1990 and 1992.

[23]This general perception is a function of the prominence of the first major ABS arrangement (the InBio-Merck Contract detailed in Reid, W., et al (1993) *Biodiversity prospecting: Using biodiversity for sustainable development.* World Resource International), coupled with its frequent description of its overall program (national institutional arrangements and InBio—a public-private entity) as having more than 35 existing contracts on which users are reporting, with the post-script that other private arrangements are not included.

[24]The excellent Costa Rican system (including a comprehensive legislative and institutional structure), for example, has been developed with very substantial levels of donor assistance over more than a decade. Presentation of Rodrigo Gámez, Instituto Nacional de Biodiversidad (INBio), 4th Norway/UN Conference on Biodiversity (Trondheim, 2003). More than 10 years after its inception, however, the amount of income received from this system is far overshadowed by this ongoing external assistance. Among the primary payments received from user entities under access contracts to date have been in-kind donations of equipment for INBio's operations. To date, post-access "benefit-sharing" provisions have not been applicable, as none of the pharmaceutical companies has "hit" on a compound triggering such payments. This strongly suggests that the Costa Rican example is not replicable. It is probably not reasonable to expect this level of support to be generally provided to the more-than-80 developing countries, and to countries in economic transition. Moreover, it is not clear that there is sufficient level of demand to ensure that 80 or more comprehensive programs of this type would be as operationally successful as the government-owned genetic-resource research and collection institution (INBio) has become.

[25]Although a very small number of corporate entities remain involved in ABS negotiations, this number has diminished (and continues to do so) over the past decade. In many instances, after an agreement is partly negotiated, additional legislative/institutional restrictions or requirements are discovered which add to previous transaction costs throwing the total above a corporation's declared willingness to pay.

[26]As noted above, the CBD's provisions focus solely on governmental processes. And the requirements of Prior Informed Consent (PIC) and Mutually Agreed Terms (MAT) as written in the Convention refer only to getting informed consent from, and negotiating terms with, the national government. Hence it is a matter of national domestic governance whether and how the source country's governmental system delegates its rights to information and responsibilities regarding consent and terms. These matters are outside the purview of the Convention.

[27]See Acknowledgements.

[28]This is not a failing of the negotiations, but a "growing pain" of the international law process. In the past, international law (other than peace treaties and trade agreements, both of which are essentially contracts between sovereign governments) was created where many countries had adopted principles on a particular subject, and it appeared valuable to develop a single mutually agreed consensus-based statement about them. The CBD is part of an evolution away from this. Given that biodiversity will be irretrievably lost if not protected immediately, the CBD seeks to address issues and problems that are generally recognized to be coming, but not yet present. The speed of ideas and development is such that, where possible, such problems must be governed before they are actually seen on the ground. Unfortunately, however, this means that conventions like the CBD must take action before there is direct experience on the particular issue at the national level. Specialists participating in such negotiations are rarely experts in all of the

subject areas that may be impacted. In the case of the CBD, it appears that the experts involved were experts in law relating to conservation, but that no experts in contract law or (real and intellectual) property rights participated in or advised the negotiations.

[29] As noted below, ownership of land (and many other kinds of physical property) is really an intangible concept, but is undisputedly linked to a particular physical area, and thus, essentially, tangible.

[30] See CBD Articles 3, 4, and 5. In furtherance of this approach all CBD COP decisions adopting workplans or specifying action focus on either recommending action at the national level or providing tools for such action. Even provisions relating to regional cooperation meet with resistance in COP discussions from parties who note that the CBD is implemented by national action.

[31] The Convention on Migratory Species (Bonn, 1979, entry into force in 1983) which predates the CBD, is now working under a joint program of work to ensure the integration of international protections of migratory species with national implementation of CBD objectives and programs of work. See Decision VI-20 (http://www.biodiv.org).

[32] This point is interesting in itself. Nearly all other aspects of the CBD specifically address both purely domestic activities (within national boundaries, jurisdiction, and sovereignty) and those that cross national borders, whether physically or in other ways. See, e.g., Article 8 (ex-situ conservation) which includes specific discussions of many matters of national jurisdiction, including land and water matters (which are typically among the most protected concepts in national sovereign jurisdiction) and indigenous peoples. Even as to the discussions of "alien species which threaten ecosystems" (article 8(h)), it has been noted that unless speaking of human beings, the term "alien" does not refer to nationality. Hence, this paragraph refers to "species not normally found in a particular ecosystem" (whether domestic or foreign) rather than "species brought in from other countries". The specific avoidance by ABS provisions of any mention of domestic ABS governance is very noticeable in this context.

[33] In the final version, the Bonn Guidelines speak of the responsibility of user countries, as well as users.

[34] FAO Conference Resolutions 4/89 and 3/91 (http://www.fao.org/).

[35] CBD Article 2, definitions of "country of origin" and "in-situ conditions".

[36] In many cases, genetic resources vary widely at taxonomic levels below the basic "species" level. Particular varieties (subspecies that have been bred to consistently possess particular qualities, such as color, size, texture/flavor (for foods), durability, time to maturity, and other characteristics) are often more important for genetic research or utilization.

[37] These references are found only in the 11th clause of the preamble and Arts. 9(a) and (b) (ex situ conservation) of the CBD (http://www.biodiv.org).

[38] "[G]enetic resources collected from in-situ sources, including populations of both wild and domesticated species, or taken from ex-situ sources, which may or may not have originated in that country." CBD Art. 2 (http://www.biodiv.org).

[39] Another relevant component of "unjust enrichment" is the fact that a country may have made a historical contribution to the asset that is being exploited, which should in fairness be compensated. In the case of genetic resources, this contribution may have been the improvement of traditional plant (or animal) varieties, or a long history of nonexploitative behavior, which resulted in the continued existence of an ecosystem or species that has died out in industrialized or overexploitive countries.

[40] Requirements about undertaking activities in countries of origin (Article 9); and protecting traditional and indigenous rights (Articles 8(j) and 10(c)), for example. The ABS Project will be undertaking additional research on the general equity requirements of the CBD, and how they relate to the ABS regime, with publication

expected in 2005.

[41] CBD, Article 3.

[42] CBD, Article 4.2.

[43] CBD, Article 5.

[44] Entered into force in 1994.

[45] A similar statement about our lack of complex understanding of the issue will undoubtedly be made by those who analyse the outcomes of the coming negotiation of the international ABS regime.

[46] Even in this example, of course, there was eventually a need for new laws to address minimum standards of safety and quality and to ensure that frequency markings were uniform on all radios tuned to particular bands.

[47] The CBD Parties have noted a number of other definitional issues on which they believe clarification is needed, including those relating to "access to genetic resources", "benefit sharing", "commercialization", "derivatives", "provider", "user", "stakeholder", "ex situ collection", "voluntary nature", and possibly "arbitrary restrictions". See Decision VII/19, UN Document UNEP/CBD/COP/7/L.19. While a number of interesting issues exist with regard to this terminology, this paper will not examine any of these issues. Further work on them will be done through the IUCN ABS Project, however.

[48] Article 15 and relevant parts of Articles 16 and 17 of the CBD specify that they are applicable to genetic resources, where the rest of the operative provisions of the convention are specifically applicable to biological resources. COP decisions on ABS have been carefully limited to genetic resources.

[49] It is notable that, in international law, "legislative history" is usually not considered to be a reliable guide to interpretation (BROWNLIE 1979). Relatively few international forums include verbatim transcription of debates leading to new instruments or decisions. Even where some portion of the deliberations are memorialised in nonverbatim reports (e.g., "report of the meeting" or "report of the session"), those reports usually only encompass the plenary discussions and/or discussions from within formal working groups. However, as to matters of controversy, it is common to create other informal groupings including "contact groups" and "friends of the chair". In some cases, these meetings are only available to specified delegates. These deliberations although never reported frequently return to the meeting with a new text that is simply presented and reported as the agreement of the Contact Group. Finally, where a wide-ranging discussion has taken place (in working groups, contact groups, FOC groupings, and elsewhere), the Chair may sometimes develop a new "chair's text" again, with no reporting of the discussions, thought processes, and other inputs.

[50] CBD Articles 15.2, 6, and 7; 16.3; 17.1 and 2; 19.1 and 2; 20.1 and 3; and 21.4.

[51] The science of molecular genetics, and the practical issues of its use in commercial application, were incompletely understood in the negotiations. It is recognized that genetic modification technology is only one of the many ways in which biological material is used as a template for the development of commercial products or other value. The questions of how "genetic resource" concepts apply to these nongenetic uses are highly complex and not resolved. The paragraph to which this footnote is appended describes what was considered in the negotiations, and not what is actually happening in practice—then or now. The ABS Project is in the process of developing further legal and advisory documents addressing these issues.

[52] The ownership of plants is often delimited by geographical boundaries, this kind of right is known in various countries by various names, including "easement", "profit a prendre", and other terms. Many of these terms are used in different countries to represent different kinds of rights.

[53] Although difficult, this challenge does not appear impossible. Note that the current system for protecting and marketing software also

required the creation of a new and consistent approach. Other current challenges of this type include the digital downloading of recorded music and the posting and use of online-but-proprietary information.

54 "Principles on access to genetic resources and benefit-sharing for participating institutions" have been developed and independently adopted by 28 botanical gardens worldwide. The principles are available online at http://www.rbgkew.org.uk/conservation/principles.html.

55 University researchers, for example, are among the primary sources of progress toward new amoebacidal compounds and medicines—work that is critical for developing countries where amoeba-related illnesses may account for more deaths than AIDS or cancer. (M. Merchant, pers. comm. May, 2004)

56 Following on the initial work of RUIZ et al. (2003), the IUCN ABS Project is commissioning a study of the mechanisms for tracking gene flows at national and international levels. Publication is expected in 2005.

57 Many products are not patented, for example. And in a number of cases, a genetic material or biochemical compound are integral parts of the process of creation of a product, but do not appear in the product itself.

58 Patent officials do not currently posses the ability, expertise, and equipment to evaluate the whether it will be necessary to enquire into the genetic/biochemical source of any component of a product or invention being developed. Within industry, the technology to determine the species/variety that is the source of a particular molecular structure is improving rapidly. It is highly unlikely, however, that the equipment necessary for this work will become available to developing countries at a price that they can afford, or that they will have the capacity individually to watchdog the relevant industries to test their products in cases of possible violation. Leif Christiansen, Diversa, presentation at International Workshop "Accessing genetic resources and sharing the benefits: Lessons from implementing the Convention on Biological Diversity", 29-31 October 2003, University of California, Davis. See http://www.grcp.ucdavis.edu/projects/ABSdex.htm.

59 Except perhaps to lawyers who practice in the area of commercial transactions.

60 The author hopes that this hypothetical example will be useful in helping the reader to focus on the particular conceptual issue addressed and not be confused by other facts not relevant to the point.

61 It may be that the primary lesson to be learned, however, is that "these things take time". Although significantly more has been accomplished in legal terms toward that regime, the FCCC's "mechanisms" for creating and operating the market in carbon credits are still not in force or operational.

62 As noted above, the commitments of the Parties are already binding and mandatory.

63 In this connection, it should be noted that such abuse is not the fault of the commercial or industrial entities. Rather, it is an outgrowth of the basic nature of such entities. They are created to engage in commerce and to earn profits. They are not created for charitable purposes or the conservation of the environment. In many countries, they are specifically required to demonstrate that

they put their shareholders' interests first—that is, that they do not allow other nonprimary objectives to interfere with their primary responsibility to make money for their shareholders. As a result, it is not reasonable or possible simply to expect corporate, commercial, or industrial entities to take actions voluntarily that would either empower the parties with which they are negotiating or otherwise diminish the entity's profits from a particular transaction. This is the basic justification for official governance.

64 In many commercial situations, it is common to keep the contents (or at least key financial matters) of particular contracts confidential. These confidentiality clauses often state that the contract will cease, if the confidentiality requirement is breached.

65 These fears are not unfounded. For a useful case study of the dangers to bulk commodity providers who are convinced to operate through unregulated commerce, where the market is controlled by a small group of buyers, see SCHLOSSER (2002).

66 CBD COP-6 Resolution V/26.

67 See, e.g., IUCN World Conservation Congress Resolution 2.41 "International Ombudsman for the Environment" (Amman, 2000).

68 By and large, opposition to this approach related to the goal of eliminating multiple planning and strategy development processes. One of the primary advances of the CBD (and the United Nations Conference on Environment and Development where the CBD was adopted) was its recognition of the value of integrated planning, both as a way of minimizing the costs of multiple internationally mandated planning processes and as a way of improving the manner in which those processes function. A separate ABS strategy seemed to roll back both of these hard-won advances.

68 While legislation is being negotiated, the source of these comments has asked that his name and national government affiliation should not be disclosed. When the legislation is adopted (expected in 2005 or 2006), its unique and important characteristics will be well publicized, and their relationship to this footnote will be clear.

70 Estimates of how long this process took depend on whether prior unsuccessful rounds of negotiations are included.

71 The Kyoto Protocol to the FCCC was adopted 16 March 1998, but has still not entered into force.

72 In this connection, it is important to keep in mind that the Cartagena Protocol addresses only a few particular issues relating to the transboundary movement and introduction of GMOs. The larger issues of biosafety and national policy responses are, as yet, not covered (MACKENSIE et al. 2003).

73 The GLMMC was formed in February, 2002, with the Cancun Declaration. It consists of about a dozen countries that are home to more than 70% of the world's biodiversity. In addition to CBD meetings, it has now exerted its influence in CITES COPs, the WSSD, WTO, WIPO, and other meetings.

74 Economic valuation of biological diversity is a debate that has been ongoing for many years and remains active. At present, no agreed mechanism for valuing species within ecosystems has been found. Once that is agreed, however, it will still be necessary to engage in further economic discussion regarding how a species' "genetic resources" can be valued.

75 An Appendix II species under CITES (http://cites.org/).

13

Conclusions, Lessons, and Recommendations

Santiago Carrizosa

Eleven years have passed since the Convention on Biological Diversity (CBD) came into force and only 22% of the 41 countries analyzed in this study have developed some sort of access and benefit-sharing (ABS) policy or law and all of these countries are still perfecting those regulations (see Chapter 1). Furthermore, ABS laws and policies of these countries have approved only 22 bioprospecting projects between 1991 and July 2004 (see Chapter 3). This record of policy development and implementation does not necessarily show that countries have been inefficient, but rather cautious and inexperienced. Before the CBD was signed, most, if not all, of these countries had a permit system to regulate the extraction and management of biological resources. The transition from these permit systems to more comprehensive ABS frameworks has run into obstacles that include finding the economic means to develop such frameworks, consolidating the technical expertise, and obtaining the much-needed consensus about new and controversial issues raised by the CBD.

In any case, implementing these ABS laws and bioprospecting agreements have provided valuable lessons (see Chapter 3) about the limitations, ambiguities, and implications of these policies that operate in complex scenarios where the providers and users of genetic resources range from holders of traditional knowledge such as indigenous communities to high-end users that include biotechnology companies. Today, the challenge is to figure out a participatory strategy to develop, implement, monitor, evaluate, and enforce ABS policies for genetic, biological, and biochemical resources and the information associated with these resources. The diverse social, economic, ethical, and political implications of these policies demand the participation of a wide variety of stakeholders that include agriculture research centers, environmental NGOs, indigenous and farmer communities, government agencies, biotechnology firms, and universities.

National ABS laws and policies presented in this report are one of the main elements of the future international regime on ABS. The analysis of these frameworks (see Chapters 1 and 3) illustrates many of the gaps and limitations that will challenge policymakers during the negotiations process of the international regime. In addition, it will be imperative for policymakers to revisit key ABS concepts and assumptions (see Chapter 12) in order to bring clarity to the process.

Complex Issues

ABS and IPR policies address the question of how to pursue the public good through cures for diseases, highly productive crops, scientific opportunities, and biodiversity conservation, among others (REID et al. 1993, SWANSON 1995, ROSENTHAL et al 1999, TEN KATE and LAIRD 1999), but these policies also result in opportunity costs, ambigui- ties, and uncertainties for various socioeconomic groups (GREAVES 1994, BRUSH and STABINSKY 1996, SHIVA 1997, MOONEY 2000). More than any other natural resource policy, ABS policies have been the target of misconceptions, politics, and negative publicity. Biopiracy claims, poorly defined ownership rights over genetic resources, the patenting of life, the protection of traditional knowledge, and equity issues have thwarted access initiatives and have also contributed to the cancellation of bioprospecting projects in countries such as Mexico (see Chapters 3 and 6). Bioprospecting projects also remain the focus of fierce and intensive criticism by advocate groups that have great influence among indigenous organizations, government actors, and environmental groups worldwide (see Chapters 6 and 8).

The fact that most of these policies and projects will indulge or deprive specific stakeholders tends to mobilize them to shape the policies in their interests. Taking into account the importance of this debate, Chapter 1 presented a comparative analysis of eight key issues (i.e., ownership, scope, access procedure, prior informed consent (PIC), benefit sharing and compensation mechanisms, intellectual property rights (IPRs) and the protection of traditional knowledge, *in situ* biodiversity conservation and sustainable use, and monitoring and enforcement). In spite of the novel and experimental nature of most of these issues, it is possible to distill the following set of conclusions and recommendations for improving ABS regimes, to help countries to develop more effective approaches, and to alert policymakers about the challenges they will face while negotiating the international regime on ABS.

Conclusions

- The scope of most ABS policies is very broad and comprehensive. This has impaired the effective and efficient implementation of these policies. The scope covers nonhuman genetic (DNA and RNA), biological (specimens and parts of specimens), and biochemical (molecules, combination of molecules, and extracts) resources found in *in situ* and *ex situ* conditions.

- Since the main implication of Article 15(3) of the CBD is that *ex situ* genetic resources collected before the CBD entered into force are not covered by it, pre-CBD *ex situ* collections should not be covered by the scope of ABS policies. However, in practice, most ABS policies cover these collections. In any case, access to pre- or post-CBD *ex situ* collections has not been clearly defined by the ABS polices presented in this report. Ownership of these collections is still controversial. The scope of most ABS policies also applies to traditional knowledge associated with these resources, but it excludes traditional uses of these resources by indigenous and local communities in accordance with their traditional practices.

- Under the CBD, bilateral agreements have formalized the negotiation of benefits derived from the use of genetic, biological, or biochemical resources. Some national ABS laws and policies have defined criteria for the minimum benefits (Costa Rica, Philippines, Peru, and Samoa) that they expect to receive. Policymakers must be reminded that bioprospecting is not a gold mine. Since royalty rates are usually below 5%, contracts have been criticized as being inequitable benefit-sharing mechanisms. However, depending on the industry, it can generate significant monetary and nonmonetary incentives for local capacity building and technological development as demonstrated by the Costa Rican experience (see Chapter 5).

- Traditional and *sui generis* IPR laws and policies, registers of traditional knowledge, PIC requirements, certificates of origin or legal provenance, and benefit-sharing agreements are some of the mechanisms used by most countries to protect scientific and the traditional knowledge at different levels.

- Patenting of life is a very controversial issue debated at national and international forums. It is interesting to note that in some countries, such as Costa Rica, ABS policies initially excluded genes, microorganisms, plants, and animals from patenting, however, the exclusions have been repealed years later by amendments to national patent laws. Furthermore, many countries argue that the Agreement on Trade Related Aspects of Intellectual Property Rights (TRIPS) must be revised to prohibit the patenting of plants, animals, and microorganisms. This position has support among several developing countries (e.g., the African Group) and many grassroots, indigenous, and some environmental groups.

- Almost all ABS policies address the need to promote the conservation of biological diversity and impose some ecological restrictions and impact mitigation requirements on bioprospecting. According to the Costa Rican experience, which has the longest record of implementation of bioprospecting projects in the world, bioprospecting has not been a significant source of funding for biodiversity conservation when compared to other sources of funding (see Chapter 5).

- Monitoring bioprospecting activities and the rightful use of samples collected for commercial and noncommercial purposes is a difficult, expensive, and resource consuming task. No Pacific Rim country has in place either a national or an international monitoring system. Once samples leave the country it is very difficult to follow their use and the exchange of information about them. Some countries such as Nicaragua might require bioprospectors to pay for monitoring and evaluation procedures and other countries such as the Philippines and Peru might require purchasing a compliance or ecological bond.

- Some national ABS and IPR policies propose using a certificate of origin or legal provenance to track the patenting of genetic resources acquired illegally. This measure, however, has limitations.

For example, patent clerks lack the expertise and equipment required to identify genetic resources or biochemicals used for the creation of inventions, unless the patent applicant discloses this information. A certificate or origin or legal provenance has also been proposed as a key element of the international regime on ABS.

- Should States be directly involved in the negotiation of benefit-sharing agreements? Or should this negotiation be left to the direct providers of genetic resources and traditional knowledge? The issue of State intervention is a complex and controversial question in most countries. While some commentators demand that the State needs to be directly involved in the negotiation of benefit-sharing agreements (see Chapter 6), others claim that this practice results in bureaucratic hurdles (see Chapter 4) that lead to inefficiencies and high transaction costs (see Chapter 3).

- The complex nature of ABS policies and empirical data suggest that these policies are likely to be revised, refined, and altered over time. The complexity of ABS issues helps explain why policymakers and other stakeholders do not anticipate the problems that almost inevitably arise once policies are enacted.

Recommendations

- Defining clear ownership rights over genetic, biological, and biochemical resources is a condition to facilitate the development of legitimate ABS policies. While ownership rights over *in situ* genetic, biological, and biochemical resources is relatively clear in many countries reviewed in this report, these rights still need to be clarified for resources found in *ex situ* conditions. Some countries such as Malaysia also need to clarify ownership of genetic resources found in indigenous land (see Chapters 2 and 11).

- Obtaining access has been a long, confusing, and frustrating process for many bioprospecting actors that have commercial and noncommercial goals. In some countries there is confusion about who regulates access to *in situ* and *ex situ* genetic resources. Source countries must define an office or focal point to process all access applications.

- The broad and comprehensive scope of ABS policies has caused confusion among users and providers of genetic resources about the type of activities that must be regulated. Countries may follow two courses of action. First, if they decide to adopt a comprehensive scope it is important to clarify the range and type of activities that are covered by the scope of the policy. Second, countries may want to define a less ambitious and more concrete scope (see Chapters 4 and 9) that is likely to facilitate

access and thus minimize financial and human resources for both users and providers of genetic resources. The scope of the international regime on ABS will also have to be clearly defined and must acknowledge and be consistent with national ABS policies. Furthermore, the scope of the international regime must be clear about its limitations and the type of activities (see Chapter 12) that constitute utilization of genetic, biochemical, and biological resources.

- ABS policies of some countries such as the Philippines have defined specific access procedures for bioprospectors that have noncommercial purposes. Some policies also facilitate access to national bioprospectors. However, all policies have the same access procedure for the biotechnology, pharmaceutical, seed, agrochemical, ornamental, botanical medicine, and food industries that use genetic, biological, and biochemical resources. This creates confusion and high transaction costs among access applicants. Unlike a modern pharmaceutical company, a small domestic industry that extracts aromatic oils may not have the economic resources to go through a complex and expensive access procedure. Therefore, it may be appropriate to define criteria that facilitate access to low-tech and small commercial users of genetic, biological, and biochemical resources. Such a differentiated access procedure would also mean that countries would need less human and financial resources to facilitate access. In most ABS policies access procedures for resources found in *ex situ* conditions remain a gray area due to ownership issues. In all cases, however, such access must be for environmentally sound uses as mandated by Article 15(2) of the CBD.

- PIC should be obtained from both national authorities and the providers of genetic resources and traditional knowledge. According to ABS laws and policies reviewed in this report, PIC from the government can be obtained through collecting permits or access agreements and PIC from the providers of genetic resources or traditional knowledge can be obtained through agreements or certificates that are usually the result of a consultation process. In any case, PIC procedures must be clearly outlined in a way that reduces time and transaction costs for bioprospectors and these procedures must also be simplified for noncommercial bioprospectors. Bioprospectors should be aware about the main cultural, economic, and social characteristics of the providers of genetic resources. They should be able to explain complex and controversial aspects of the research and research implications such as IPRS.

- ABS policies of some countries, such as Costa Rica, Philippines, Peru, and Samoa, set minimum benefit-sharing standards that must be followed by all bioprospectors. However, given the broad diversity of domestic and international commercial bioprospecting initiatives that seek access, even applying a minimum standard across the board to all of these initiatives might not be realistic or fair. If countries choose to develop such standards, they should define a range of them to be applied in a differentiated manner and depending upon the commercial nature of the bioprospecting activity.

- Ensuring the effective protection of traditional knowledge and preventing the illegal appropriation of genetic resources must occur at two levels: a) TRIPS must require patent applicants to disclose the origin of samples, traditional knowledge, and ABS agreements used for the development of products that they wish to protect and b) countries must include similar requirements in national ABS and IPRS policies. More than half of the 41 countries examined in this report comply or are in the process

of complying with TRIPS requirements.

- Some countries, such as Chile, have chosen to develop national biodiversity strategies and action plans (designed to implement the CBD as a whole) before they complete ABS policies. These plans and strategies may provide not only a national legal and political context for the development and implementation of ABS policies, but may also raise awareness about key issues and build local capacity and community-based processes that will facilitate future debates about ABS issues.

- Developing a regional ABS policy or strategy may clarify access rules for bioprospectors and also prevent them from negotiating the best deal among countries that share common ecosystems and species. This was one of the original goals of Decision 391, but national differences in the adoption and implementation processes of the law have interfered with this purpose.

Complex Stakeholders

Defining the scope of access policies, identifying strategies to protect traditional knowledge, and ensuring that benefits provide for conservation of biological diversity are just a few of the most challenging tasks faced by policymakers (see Chapter 1). The great variety of agendas, perspectives, and opinions regarding these issues pose quite a challenge for anyone seeking endorsement of ABS policies by all stakeholders. Our research identified a wide range of these perspectives from key national and international stakeholders. For example, a common perception among some indigenous and farmers groups and advocate NGOs from countries such as Colombia, Costa Rica, Mexico, the Philippines, and Australia is that bioprospecting is a new form of colonialism. Many are against commercializing traditional knowledge and any form of bioprospecting. To them traditional knowledge should not be considered anyone's property, nor should it be used to divide neighboring communities that bid for the best deal offered by bioprospectors. Instead, such knowledge should strengthen relationships and responsibilities among and within indigenous communities. Some also question the efficacy and appropriateness of a contractual approach to protect indigenous interests and knowledge and to ensure the equitable sharing of benefits. Other groups, however, support the need to develop national ABS policies to fill current gaps of national laws and protect the interests of indigenous communities (see Chapters 4, 5, 6, 7, and 9).

Some scientific and biotechnology groups from countries such as Costa Rica and Australia advocate ABS policies that facilitate bioprospecting activities in their countries. They support flexible policies. Policies that do not restrict research, but that encourage ethical behavior, fair benefit sharing, and the growth of the local biotechnology industry. Many emphasize that the lack of such a policy results in the loss of opportunities from bioprospecting and benefits

to society. A few express concern that a bioprospecting policy can encourage access to foreign multinationals and the potential loss of benefits and opportunities for local scientists. Many, however, support partnerships and collaborative research with foreign organizations as long as this brings opportunities to local researchers. While some argue that ABS policies should differentiate between commercial and noncommercial research, others believe that making this distinction is difficult task (see Chapters 5 and 9).

Some environmental groups from countries such as Colombia, Mexico, and Australia advocate for a bioprospecting policy that addresses not only commercial and market-related goals but also environmental protection objectives. They are usually concerned about equity issues and a few use the term "biopiracy" to describe unfair and inequitable bioprospecting contracts. Biopiracy is also associated with the stealing of genetic resources, the inadequate consultation of local communities, and the use of intellectual property rights to obtain monopolies over genetic resources and traditional knowledge. Some argue that it may be more valuable to preserve traditional knowledge rather than commercialize it. Others emphasize that society at large should benefit from bioprospecting by promoting biodiversity conservation, economic growth, and human health. Some are concerned about environmental impacts of bioprospecting activities (see Chapters 4, 6, and 9).

On the other hand, some policymakers from countries such as Colombia and Mexico are burdened by pressure from local stakeholders and international commitments to implement the mandate of the CBD and the FAO International Treaty on Plant Genetic Resources for Food and Agriculture (ITPGRFA). They usually support commercially oriented ABS policies that attract technology, foreign investment, and opportunities for local scientists and industries. Others are concerned about a political backlash from indigenous and environmental groups caused by decisions to grant access to genetic resources under illegitimate ABS policies or inequitable benefit-sharing agreements (see Chapters 4 and 6). Bringing together this variety of perspectives, concerns, and agendas is the challenge faced by policymakers to ensure legitimate ABS policies as indicated by policy processes carried out in countries that include Colombia, Costa Rica, Philippines, Malaysia, and Australia (see Chapter 2).

Complex Policymaking and Implementation Scenarios

How do policymakers deal with the complexity of ABS issues? Motivations are as complicated and multiple as are the policy objectives. Some policymakers usually complain about the complexity of the issues and users they face. The inability to face this complexity may be responsible for the failure to uphold appropriate standards of equity, respect for traditional knowledge, and biodiversity conservation. The opposite danger is that the recognition of complexity sometimes stimulates an overreaction that puts too much authority in the hands of technicians mistakenly thought to be the experts on complexity (ASCHER and HEALY 1990).

In any case, few things are more difficult for policymakers to do than to pursue the development of ABS objectives in complex policymaking and implementation scenarios. The demands of interest groups, self-interest of specialized government and nongovernmental organizations, the complexity of the interactions within the system, and the possibility for unexpected and perverse side effects are ingredients certainly present in any policymaking and implementation processes, as exemplified by the experiences in countries such as Colombia, Australia, Malaysia and the Philippines (see Chapter 2). Furthermore, these factors are compounded in other countries examined in this report. These countries have had to face social and economic crisis (Solomon Islands), severe shortages of trained personnel (Samoa, Cook Islands, Nicaragua), limited fiscal and technical capacity (Vietnam), fragile political relationships (Cook Islands), and weak institutions (Laos) (see Chapter 2). In addition to these and other economic, political, or social conflicts, these and many other countries have had to address ABS policymaking and implementation processes in the context of different forms and levels of centralized and decentralized government structures that influence and determine opportunities for success or failure.

Centralization vs. Decentralization: Finding the Conditions for Participatory Scenarios

In most if not all of the countries examined in this report, ABS policymaking and implementation was often regarded as synonymous with centralized top-down initiatives and decision-making was usually monopolized by national governmental organizations (see Chapters 2 and 3). This is the heritage of both government regimes (where the source of all power is usually found in the capital of the nation) and the top-down nature of the CBD and its Conference of the Parties (where the rules of implementation of the CBD are defined by a minority that not always represent the diverse interests of each country). Centralization of authority has been used in all societies as a way to improve both information flows and the ability to design and implement policies. Centralization can also refer to concentration of power in the hands of: a) a central national government rather than states, provinces, or municipalities; b) ministries or departments rather than semi-autonomous authorities or corporations; c) local authorities rather than local communities; and d) local community elites rather than the broad spectrum of community members (ASCHER and HEALY 1990). A major and well-known problem of centralization is that technical expertise becomes increasingly scarce as one moves from the center to the periphery of a society and this is certainly the case in most of the countries examined in this report (see Chapter 2). This issue is compounded by the fact that ABS concepts are particularly complex and complexity implies the need for good information. The uneven quality of information among stakeholders influences the focus of attention.

Centralized expertise also fails to understand and respond to specific local conditions. In other words, the least powerful members of society may be exploited by local elites, they are literally invisible to centralized planners, and national elites always find ways of dominating policymaking (see Chapter 4). These least powerful members of society, particularly in developing countries, include unionized workers, bureaucracies, and farmer and indigenous communities. Another circumstance is that centralized agencies usually deal with local notables partly because the local elite simply is more articulate and informed than the mass of the population.

Decentralization by itself, however, does not translate automatically into local people's participation in the policymaking and implementation process of ABS. Decentralization also requires incentives such as strong local capacity and effective participation channels. Village cooperatives, labor unions, peasant organizations, and NGOs have become increasingly important channels for the activism of indigenous, peasant, and university-educated people. These participatory scenarios facilitate the articulation of a valid counterpoint to centralized governmental input that enriches the debate and contributes to more balanced ABS policies (see Chapter 2). Besides, common sense dictates that locally originated proposals can be aggregated and shaped to ensure that they are compatible with top-down policymaking approaches such as the CBD requirements.

In addition, in every participatory process, it is important to be aware of the subtleties of different stakeholders that are likely to determine the outcome of the development and implementation process of ABS laws and policies. These include:

- Public authorities are not always responsive to public opinion, especially when government organizations assume they have sufficient technical capacity and expertise as illustrated by the development process of Decision 391 (see Chapters 2 and 4).

- Government and nongovernment organizations are not passive recipients of public opinion but consciously try to shape, modify, organize, and even control it. This is common among all organizations but mainly among well-funded and strong organizations.

- On most ABS issues most policymakers and other stakeholders do not have an opinion in the sense of having thought about the issue or having a consistent body of information about it. Instead most people are prepared to take a party line or position rather than invest time and effort analyzing a specific issue as exemplified by the development process of the Law of Biodiversity of Costa Rica (see Chapter 2).

Nevertheless, as the Costa Rican and Australian experiences indicate, chances of developing and implementing effective ABS policies are likely to increase in a decentralized context where the common denominator is strong local capacity and participatory mechanisms coupled with strong local government and nongovernment organizations (see Chapters 5 and 9). Evidently, the central government has to be part of the development process of ABS policies or laws from beginning to end. However, the Costa Rican record of implementation of bioprospecting projects shows that successful implementation of ABS laws and policies will be facilitated when agreement and negotiation of projects take place between a minimum number of parties that share a common mission and with minimum intervention of bureaucracy and centralized government agencies. In contrast, as demonstrated by the Colombian experience an extensive and centralized bureaucratic process results in delays in the negotiation of projects that damage the morale and trust of implementers and recipients, thereby hampering successful implementation of ABS policy (see Chapters 3, 4, and 5).

Building Local Capacity

Policy estimation (see Chapter 2) and implementation (see Chapter 3) involve and demand technical expertise in IPR issues, biodiversity conservation, business, commerce, economics, negotiation, biotechnology, national and international law, social, and cultural issues just to name a few. The interdisciplinary nature of these issues was limited if not absent in most countries addressed by our study (see Chapter 2). These issues demand the involvement of a great variety of stakeholders in development processes of ABS polices. Building a solid national capacity to develop and implement these policies is a requirement in all the countries analyzed in this report. It is important not only to understand the social and economic aspects of the process, but also to learn about the latest technological developments (e.g., combinatorial chemistry or bioinformatics) and the main markets (e.g., pharmaceuticals, seed, agrochemicals, or medicinal botany) that benefit from the use of biological diversity. Countries must be aware of the latest scientific developments that fuel these markets (see Chapter 5). This knowledge will contribute to improve the negotiation stance of less industrialized countries. Most countries also lack negotiators. It is clear that legal and technical expertise of any multinational is quite superior compared to the understaffed and overworked negotiators of many of the countries analyzed in this report.

Future Scenarios

Successful ABS policies are usually a reflection of the policy process followed for their development. Ideally, such a process must include the participation of all sectors of society. ABS issues have presented new conceptual, political, and operational challenges to stakeholders. The essential role of policy experts and facilitators in explaining the multiple dimensions and implications of ABS policies is certainly needed in all the countries that are attempting to develop and implement the CBD. To actually work once established, the ABS policy must have the broad support of all relevant sectors of government and society; fit within the country's larger strategy for conserving and sustainably using biological diversity; and be supported by decentralized government and nongovernment processes and capabilities sufficient to implement it (MUGABE et al. 1997). Building local capacity to improve policy initiation and estimation is a priority for most of the countries reviewed in this study.

A hopeful scenario for the next ten years might find that at the celebration of the 20th anniversary of the CBD, countries will have found the necessary conditions to facilitate the access to genetic resources and the equitable sharing of benefits derived from them. Bioprospecting will be a significant source of income for local communities that in turn will be able to invest a percentage in the conservation of the habitats from which samples were collected. ABS policies will no longer be perceived as a barrier for academic and scientific noncommercial research. The concept of biopiracy will no longer be associated with inequitable benefit-sharing agreements and large multinationals. Instead these firms will be part of a voluntary international network of "biomonitors". These biomonitors, assuming they have the right incentives, will be the recipients and users of genetic resources and biochemical compounds, they will ensure that these samples include basic information about their source country, fair benefit-sharing agreements, and whether traditional knowledge was used for the collection of samples. This information will be reported to an international clearinghouse mechanism that will report to the source country of genetic resources and traditional knowledge. Unfortunately, this optimistic and naïve account of events is quite unlikely.

Instead, in the next ten years countries and bioprospectors will probably continue to experience many of the policy development and implementation obstacles, limitations, and problems described in this report (see Chapters 2 and 3). Many will have completed their ABS policies, but most will still be fine-tuning key provisions. Some countries will still be looking for financial assistance and technical expertise to complete ABS policies. It is hoped that most ownership rights of *in situ* and *ex situ* genetic resources will have been clarified. Under the FAO ITPGRFA, germplasm exchanged by participants in the multilateral system will not be entitled to any IPR protection, but some will argue that isolated genes should be given such protection. Patented and marketed products derived from the germplasm (exchanged under the rules of the multilateral system) will have to pay a sum of money to an international fund of the FAO. The size, terms, and fairness of such a payment will certainly be a key issue of debate. Patented products that are not commercialized will not have to share economic benefits but new products derived from them that are patented and commercialized will have to contribute financially. Monitoring and enforcing this

chain of improvements and obligations will certainly be a logistical nightmare.

The International Regime on ABS (see Chapter 12 and Appendix 1) will most likely include a mix of voluntary and mandatory components that will continue to rely on contracts as a primary mechanism for ABS. Given biopiracy concerns, a key discussion in the negotiation will probably revolve around the need for an international monitoring mechanism or certification system for samples and bioprospecting projects. TRIPS may have to be amended to include requirements to disclose the source of samples, traditional knowledge, and nonconfidential terms of benefit-sharing agreements when products and processes are patented.

The 2001 Bonn Guidelines on ABS adopted by the Sixth Conference of the Parties of the CBD will continue guiding countries embarked on the development of ABS frameworks. However, governments and bioprospecting groups will continue facing controversial issues such as the patenting of life, access to traditional knowledge, and the perception that all benefit-sharing agreements are not equitable. These issues will continue to control the development and implementation of national ABS frameworks. Developing and implementing national ABS laws and policies will continue to be a slow process in which multiple sectors of society with different interests, agendas, views, and backgrounds must and will continue playing a role.

References

ASCHER W. and R. HEALY. 1990. *Natural resource policymaking in developing countries.* Duke University Press, NC USA.

BRUSH S.B. and D. STABINSKY (eds.) 1996. *Valuing local knowledge: Indigenous people and intellectual property rights.* Island Press. USA.

GREAVES T. (ed.) 1994. *Intellectual property rights for indigenous peoples: A source book.* Society for Applied Anthropology, Oklahoma City, OK USA.

MOONEY P.R. 2000. Why we call it biopiracy. p. 37–44. *in* H. SVARSTAD and S.S. DHILLION (eds.) *Responding to bioprospecting: From biodiversity in the south to medicines in the north.* Spartacus Forlag. Oslo, Norway.

MUGABE J., C.V. BARBER, H. GUDRUN, L. GLOWKA, and A. LA VIÑA (eds.) 1997. *Access to genetic resources: Strategies for sharing benefits.* ACTS Press, WRI, ELC-IUCN, Nairobi, Kenya.

REID W.V., S.A. LAIRD, R. GÁMEZ, A. SITTENFELD, D.H. JANZEN, M.G. GOLLIN, and C. JUMA. 1993. A new lease on life. p. 1–52 *in* W.V. REID, S.A. LAIRD, C.A. MEYER, R. GÁMEZ, A. SITTENFELD, D.H. JANZEN, M.G. GOLLIN,

and C. JUMA (eds.) *Biodiversity prospecting: Using genetic resources for sustainable development.* World Resources Institute, USA.

ROSENTHAL J.P., D. BECK, A. BHAT, J. BISWAS, L. BRADY, K. BRIDBOARD, S. COLLINS, G. CRAGG, J. EDWARDS, A. FAIRFIELD, M. GOTTLIEB, L.A. GSCHWIND, Y. HALLOCK, R. HAWKS, R. HEGYELI, G. JOHNSON, G.T. KEUSCH, E.E. LYONS, R. MILLER, J. RODMAN, J. ROSKOSKI, and D. SIEGEL-CAUSEY. 1999. Combining high risk science with ambitious social and economic goals. *Pharmaceutical Biology* 37:6–21.

SHIVA V. 1997. *Biopiracy: The plunder of nature and knowledge.* South End Press, Boston, MA USA.

SWANSON T. (ed.) 1995. *Intellectual property rights and biodiversity conservation: An interdisciplinary analysis of the values of medicinal plants.* Cambridge University Press, Cambridge UK.

TEN KATE T.K. and S.A. LAIRD. 1999. *The commercial use of biodiversity: Access to genetic resources and benefit-sharing.* Earthscan. London, UK.

A1

Appendix 1: Conclusions from an International Workshop

"Accessing Genetic Resources and Sharing the Benefits: Lessons from Implementing the Convention on Biological Diversity"

Held at the University of California, Davis USA on 29–31 October 2003. Workshop participants discussed preliminary results of the findings presented in this report. Information about the status of ABS laws and policies and bioprospecting projects in the Pacific Rim countries that signed the CBD was updated until July 2004. The workshop also provided an opportunity to define the main elements and gaps of the existing international system of ABS governance, the main elements of the future international regime on ABS , and measures that might be taken by the international community to enhance effective international governance. Forty-five experts on ABS issues from seventeen Pacific Rim countries, multilateral organizations involved in CBD implementation, NGOs with CBD expertise, collections-based organizations, industry, and academia participated[1].

Background

In 1992, the *Convention on Biological Diversity* (CBD) provided a mandate for countries to develop national genetic resources access and benefit-sharing (ABS) policies. In the last ten years, however, countries have encountered multiple obstacles in developing such policies. Further motivation for developing national ABS policies was provided by the *2001 Bonn Guidelines on Access to Genetic Resources and Fair and Equitable Sharing of the Benefits Arising out of their Utilization.* In addition, the *Plan of Implementation* that came out of the *2002 Johannesburg World Summit on Sustainable Development* recommended (a) promotion of the wide implementation of and contin-

ued work on the Bonn Guidelines on ABS as an input for countries developing ABS policies and (b) the negotiation of the development of an international regime to promote the fair and equitable sharing of benefits derived from the use of genetic resources. Only a limited number of countries have developed and implemented ABS policies and there has been a slowing of the flow of genetic resources and reciprocal benefits between countries.

These are the main conclusions reached during the workshop:

Main elements of the existing international system of ABS governance

- Hard law elements (CBD, TRIPS, International Treaty on Plant Genetic Resources for Food and Agriculture, international phytosanitary laws, regional and national ABS, IPR, and traditional knowledge laws and policies).

- Soft law elements (Bonn Guidelines, national biodiversity strategies and action plans, and regional policies, such as Organization of African Unity ABS Model Law).

- Codes of Conduct: Professional societies (such as the International Society for Ethnobiology), institutional groups (such as botanical gardens), and private sector companies have adopted codes of conduct or ethics that provide guidelines about the collection of samples and traditional knowledge and benefit-sharing criteria.

Gaps in the existing international system of ABS governance

- Many countries are struggling to develop national ABS laws and policies. Lack of technical expertise, budgetary constraints, weak government structures and political support, local social conflict, and conflict over ownership of genetic resources are some of the factors that have prevented the development of these laws and policies. In the Pacific Rim region 41 countries have signed the CBD. Only 22% of these countries have developed a national ABS law or policy, 63% of these countries are in the process of developing these laws and policies, and 15% are not engaged in any systematic process leading to the development of these ABS frameworks (last update July 2004).

- Implementation of ABS policies and laws has been relatively poor all over the world. In the Pacific Rim region, national ABS laws in Costa Rica, Mexico, the Philippines, Samoa, and the United States (not a CBD member) have been invoked to facilitate access to a total of 22 bioprospecting projects between 1991 and July 2004 (other projects have been implemented under bilateral ABS agreements). Issues identified with the slow implementation of national laws include PIC conflicts, lengthy and overly complex application procedures, ambiguities in the scope of ABS frameworks, inadequate biodiversity conservation incentives, and variation in the expertise on these issues among the individuals assigned the responsibility for carrying out the development of ABS policies from nation to nation.

- There is a gap between expectations of what bioprospecting might deliver and the reality of what it can deliver. For some persons, the issue is that as yet there are no clear guidelines on what amounts to equitable benefit sharing; there is an excessive focus on monetary benefits; and technology transfer is neither well defined and understood nor well linked to genetic resources access and utilization; For others, however, the issue is an excessive focus on nonmonetary benefits and technology transfer thereby obfuscating the crux of the problem: unrealistically low royalty rates that are entertained in negotiations only because of rent-seeking behavior by authorities in the source country.

- There is a wide perception that the CBD has not led to any significant increase in technology transfer, one of the pillars of the CBD's ABS provisions.

- Knowledge of the processes of science and discovery in biotechnology, of intellectual property, and of market-established agreement (or contract) terms is fragmentary.

- There is an absence of compliance and verification mechanisms to monitor and enforce the CBD's ABS provisions, however, it is widely accepted that the courts should be only a final recourse.

- There is a shortage of information gathering, exchange, and dissemination mechanisms, and a need to enhance the capacity and scope of the CBD clearinghouse role.

Main elements of the future international regime on ABS

- An international regime will continue to include elements of both soft and hard law, and may involve implementation of the CBD, strengthening of the Bonn guidelines, and development of provider and user measures and international arbitration systems.

Measures that might be taken by the international community to enhance effective international governance

- User measures such as disclosure of origin, voluntary certification schemes, and adoption of incentives and other measures to secure technology transfer and import/export and transport regulations might promote compliance with ABS policies and help to ensure the equitable sharing of benefits and an increase in transfer of technology.

- Components of national ABS policies designed to attract researchers (including both academic and corporate bioprospectors) to study biodiversity could be an effective means to counter the global trend of declining bioprospecting efforts and increase opportunities for benefit-sharing, advancement of science, and furthering our understanding of biodiversity.

- Development of an internationally recognized system to document the flow of genetic resources, including where appropriate a means to provide evidence of PIC, has an important part to play in consolidation of an effective system of international ABS governance. The use of the terms certificates of origin, source, and provenance have different political and practical implications. Studies to clarify these concepts would be useful.

- The transfer of samples to third parties should not be carried out except to the extent authorized by the countries of origin or the authorized *ex situ* collection that provided the sample.

- Transfer of technology is one of the principal forms of nonmonetary benefit sharing provided for in the CBD and is a crucial component of ABS. It would be useful if the CBD could initiate gathering of information and analysis of these questions: Where do genetic resource-related technologies occur and where have they been transferred?; What is the extent of recipient capacity to use and further develop such technologies?; Where has transfer been sustainable and where not?; and What are the reasons for success or failure in transfer of technologies?

- It is important to explore the possibility of developing guidelines for technology transfer in the context of articles 16 and 19 of the CBD. One approach meriting consideration would be to have the CBD include within its program of work the development of guidelines on technology transfer.

- An ombudsman or complaints authority associated with the CDD, as well as at regional and national levels, offers an interesting possibility for development of alternative dispute resolution mechanisms. An ombudsman office at the level of CBD may be linked to a linked series of regional structures for monitoring compliance with the CBD and Bonn Guidelines in ABS agreements.

Endnotes

[1] A roster of workshop particpants is available at URL: http://www.grcp.ucdavis.edu/projects/ABSdex.htm.

A2

Appendix 2. Biographical Sketches of Authors and Editors

Paz J. Benavidez II

Paz J. Benavidez II, a lawyer specializing in environment and natural resources issues, received her B.S. of Laws from the University of the Philippines in 1995. Atty. Benavidez is a legal research consultant of the Committee on Ecology, House of Representatives, Republic of the Philippines. She was a legal counsel of the Department of Environment and Natural Resources (DENR) for two years focusing mainly on access to biological and genetic resources and protected area management. Atty. Benavidez actively participated in the formulation of the implementing rules and regulations of Philippine Executive Order No. 247 and served as one of the legal counsels of the Technical Secretariat of the Inter-agency Committee on Biological and Genetic Resources (IACBGR). She was also involved in the development of a manual on the implementation of Philippine executive order on bioprospecting, the drafting of the model Academic/Commercial research agreements and the Code of Conduct for Academic Collectors of Biological and Genetic Resources. She was part of the multi-sectoral group that reviewed the said Philippine executive order in 1998.

Stephen B. Brush

Stephen Brush is Professor of Human and Community Development at the University of California, Davis. His research focuses on the human ecology of traditional agricultural systems. He has conducted long-term research in Peru, Mexico, and Turkey on farmer knowledge systems, selection, use, and on-farm conservation of crop genetic resources. He has published extensively on the ecology and conservation of crop genetic resources in cradle areas of domestication as well as on farmers' rights. Brush served as Program Director for Anthropology at the National Science Foundation and Senior Scientist at the International Plant Genetic Resources Institute. His current research concerns the relationship between cultural diversity and maize diversity in the Maya highlands of Mexico and the sustainable development of minor tubers in the Cusco area of the Peruvian Andes. His book, *Farmers' Bounty: Locating Crop Diversity in the Contemporary World* (Yale) appeared in 2004.

Jorge Cabrera-Medaglia

Jorge Cabrera-Medaglia, a lawyer specialized in environmental, agrarian, and economic law, is currently a legal adviser to the National Biodiversity Institute of Costa Rica. His responsibilities at INBio include the negotiation of bioprospecting contracts and material transfer agreements and IPR policies of the Institution. Mr. Cabrera-Medaglia was member of the National Biodiversity Commission from 1995 to 1998 and a member of the commission that drafted the biodiversity law. He has also been a government delegate at many CBD-related meeting including several Conferences of the Parties. He was also chairman of the CBD ad hoc group on access and benefit sharing. He has participated as a consultant in the preparation of draft laws and regulations on ABS in El Salvador, Nicaragua, and Bhutan, and regionally in Central America. He has authored several books and articles.

Santiago Carrizosa

Santiago Carrizosa is a research ecologist with the Genetic Resources Conservation Program (GRCP) at the University of California (USA). Dr. Carrizosa holds a B.S. in Biology from the Universidad de los Andes (Colombia) and received an M.S. and PH.D. in Renewable Natural Resources from the University of Arizona (USA). Dr. Carrizosa's research interests are on the relationships among the Convention on Biological Diversity, national laws and policies that regulate access to genetic resources, and the exchange of genetic resources between countries. His interests extend to the impact of these international and national laws on local biodiversity conservation and sustainable use initiatives. Dr. Carrizosa has written extensively on a wide variety of issues that include biodiversity conservation and sustainable use strategies in Colombia, financial incentives for forest plantations, bioprospecting models in Chile and Argentina, and biodiversity monitoring and evaluation indicators. In 2000, he also published a book titled "Bioprospecting and access to genetic resources" that, among other issues, analyses the pros and cons of the Andean Pact Decision 391 and examines bioprospecting models implemented in the region.

Francisco Chapela

Francisco Chapela is the head of the project "Indigenous and Community Biodiversity Conservation in Mexico". Mr. Chapela holds a degree in Agricultural Engineering from the Universidad Autónoma Metropolitana–Xochimilco (Mexico) and an M.S. in Forest Management from the Colegio de Postgraduados and Instituto Tecnológico Agropecuario de Oaxaca. Mr. Chapela specializes in forest management, land use planning, and analysis of natural resource use policies. He presided over the Estudios Rurales y Asesoría Campesina from 1998 to 2000 and is an independent consultant on environment, indigenous, and rural communities. In 2000, Mr. Chapela was the Mexican contact for the Forest Stewardship Council, A.C. He has coordinated and written various publications on community-based management of biodiversity.

José Carlos Fernández-Ugalde

José Carlos Fernández-Ugalde is the head of the Environmental Economics area of the National Institute of Ecology. Mr. Fernández-Ugalde holds B.S. and M.S. degrees in Economics from the Instituto Tecnológico Autónomo de México and Cambridge University respectively. His research interests include trade, structural adjustment and environment, economic valuation of urban reforestation, and economic analysis of environmental policies. Mr. Fernández-Ugalde worked at the World Conservation Monitoring Centre analyzing the impact of commercial uses and regulatory measures on biodiversity conservation. He headed the Department of Ecological Land Planning and Natural Areas at El Colegio de la Frontera Sur (1997–2000) where he started working on bioprospecting, traditional knowledge, and intellectual property through a project for the Maya communities of the Chiapas highlands. In 2000 he was the National Coordinator of Environmental Policy for PRONATURA, A.C., his work included the design and analysis of incentive mechanisms for biodiversity conservation on private lands. Mr. Fernández-Ugalde was the Mexican representative to the Panel of Experts on Access to Genetic Resources and Benefit Sharing of the Convention on Biological Diversity..

Paola Ferreira-Miani

Paola Ferreira-Miani, a biodiversity researcher and consultant for Latin America, received a B.S. in Biology at the Universidad de los Andes (Colombia) and an M.S. in technology and Policy at the Massachusetts Institute of Technology (USA). Mrs. Ferreira's main interest is the development of renewable natural resource policies, including biodiversity in developing countries. She led the development of Colombia's National Biodiversity Strategy and Action Plan, as well as the country's Forest Policy in 1996. Her recent work has been on access to genetic resources, focusing on identifying strategies of value addition in the country of collection of the resources. Her latest publication "Protección al Conocimiento Tradicional. Elementos Conceptuales para una Propuesta de Reglamentación. El Caso de Colombia" (Co-author), relates to the protection of traditional knowledge in Colombia.

Luis Flores-Mimiça

Luis Flores-Mimiça is a legal advisor for the London-based NGO Consumers International. Mr. Flores-Mimiça holds a law degree from the Universidad Católica de Chile and received his M.S. in environmental law and sustainable development from the same university. Mr. Flores-Mimiça has been a consultant for the National Commission for the Environment of Chile on access and benefit sharing issues, including the implementation of the Convention on Biological Diversity.

Dominique Hervé-Espejo

Dominique Hervé-Espejo, a lawyer and researcher at the Environmental Law Center from the University of Chile, received her Master of Laws (LL.M) in Environmental Law from University College London in 1998. Her research interests are the relationship between international and national environmental law, mainly in the area of biodiversity and biotechnology. Regarding access to genetic resources in Chile, she has worked for the National Commission of the Environment analyzing and providing legal assistance in the development of a national regulatory framework. Ms. Hervé-Espejo has published several articles in Chile on the issue of biodiversity and biosafety.

Jorge Larson-Guerra

A biologist from Universidad Nacional Autónoma de México, since 1992 Mr. Larson-Guerra has collaborated with the National Commission for the Knowledge and Use of Biodiversity (CONABIO) in activities related to biodiversity policy. He was technical coordinator of the Mexican Delegation to the negotiations of the Cartagena Protocol on the Transboundary Movement of Living Modified Organisms, 1998–1999. He was also fellow of the Leadership Fund of the MacArthur Foundation with the project "Intellectual property and biological resources in rural Mexico", 1998–2000. In 2000 and 2002 Mr. Larson-Guerra was also a Member of the Mexican Delegations to the Intersessional Meeting of the Ad-Hoc Working Group on Article 8j and related topics in the Convention on Biological Diversity. Currently, he is the coordinator of the Collective Biological Resources Program at CONABIO.

Christian Lopéz-Silva

Christian Lopéz-Silva is a lawyer specialized in biotechnological law. He holds an M.S. in biotechnological law and he is currently pursuing doctoral research in the Sheffield Institute of Biotechnological Law and Ethics, in the United Kingdom. Mr. Lopéz-Silva has worked in the environmental sector as legal adviser for the Mexican government in the regulation of biotechnology. He worked for the Ministry of Environment and the National Commission for the Knowledge and Use of Biodiversity, which involved collaborating with the Interministerial Commission on Biosafety and Genetically Modified Organisms. Mr. Lopéz-Silva has advised in the negotiation of scientific and bioprospecting agreements and has been involved in the analysis of regulation on access and benefit sharing, traditional knowledge, intellectual property rights and biosafety.

Patrick McGuire

A geneticist, with Ph.D. from the University of California, Davis (1980), he serves as director of the University of California's Genetic Resources Conservation Program (GRCP), a statewide program in the Division of Agriculture and Natural Resources. His research focus has been plant cytogenetics, crop improvement, and genetic resource conservation. The mission of GRCP is with California's biological diversity and its conservation in the broadest sense: onsite and offsite conservation of the native flora and fauna, collections of germplasm amassed for agricultural, medicinal, and industrial uses, and collections of genetic stocks, tissues, cells, and DNA developed for teaching and research purposes. With GRCP, he has organized and supported training in genetic and genomic resources conservation, organized symposia and conferences, and coordinated and edited several publications: symposia and conference

proceedings, reports from task forces, and descriptions of major collections.

Mohamad Osman

Mohamad Osman is an associate professor with the School of Environmental and Natural Resources Sciences in the Faculty of Science and Technology at the Universiti Kebangsaan Malaysia (UKM), and holds a B.S. in Agricultural Genetics and M.S. in Genetics from the University of California, Davis in 1977, and Ph.D. in Plant Breeding and Genetics from the University of Wisconsin, Madison in 1984. He was involved in agricultural research for 18 years with the Malaysian Agricultural Research Development Institute (MARDI), and had served for a long time as a rice breeder and in various other positions at MARDI before joining UKM in 1995. Dr. Mohamad's research interests are on the applications of DNA molecular markers and the use of induced mutations in crop improvement and breeding research. Currently, his research focus is on rice and roselle improvement. Over the years, he has developed a strong interest on genetic resources, biodiversity and their intellectual property, biosafety, legal and other related issues, and was actively involved in many national committees including Task Force on National Policy on Biological Diversity, Task Force on Access to Genetic Resources, Task Force on Biosafety and Drafting Committee on National Policy on Biotechnology. Dr. Mohamad has published several articles on access to genetic resources and has represented Malaysia in international meetings and forums.

Sally Petherbridge

Sally Petherbridge received her LL.M. in environmental law from the Australian National University, Canberra, in 2002. From 1999 to 2002 she worked in the Access Taskforce and Biodiversity Policy Section in Australia's Department of the Environment and Heritage. She was closely involved in policy issues relating to access to genetic resources, traditional knowledge and intellectual property, in particular, the Voumard Inquiry into Access to Biological Resources in Commonwealth Areas and the subsequent development of draft regulations on access and benefit sharing. She presented papers on developments in Australia at the second meeting of the Panel of Experts on Access to Genetic Resources (Montreal, March 2001) and at a WIPO regional workshop (Brisbane, June 2001). She also attended the second meeting of the WIPO Intergovernmental Committee on Intellectual Property and Genetic Resources, Traditional Knowledge and Folklore (Geneva, December 2001) and the sixth Conference of the Parties (COP 6) to the Convention on Biological Diversity (The Hague, April 2002). Access and benefit sharing and traditional knowledge were two of the major items on the COP 6 agenda.

Manuel Ruiz

Manuel Ruiz, is Director of the International Affairs and Biodiversity Program of the Peruvian Society for Environmental Law, based in Lima, Peru. Mr. Ruiz holds an M.S. degree in Intellectual Property and Competition Law. He has been working on biodiversity- related issues since 1992 and has been actively involved in developing national and regional policies and laws related to genetic resources, biosafety, and protection of traditional knowledge. He has been advisor to the Peruvian Government and consultant on these issues to FAO, ICTSD, IUCN, WRI, IPGRI, Andean Community, and other international organizations. Mr. Ruiz has written multiple books and articles on the implementation of Decision 391, the protection of traditional knowledge, and practical aspects related to the implementation of the FAO International Treaty on Plant Genetic Resources for Food and Agriculture.

Preston T. Scott

Preston T. Scott is a founder and currently serves as Executive Director of the World Foundation for Environment and Development (WFED), which is an independent nonprofit organization based in Washington, DC. WFED was established in 1992 to promote international cooperation and conflict resolution initiatives in the field of environment and development. Mr. Scott is a graduate of the college and law school of the University of Virginia (having received degrees in law, and with honors in history, government, and political theory) and is a member of the bars of the District of Columbia and Virginia. While at the University of Virginia School of Law, Mr. Scott served as Executive Editor of the *Virginia Journal of International Law*. After entering law practice in 1980, he developed environmental audit and compliance programs under various air, water, hazardous waste, and toxic substances laws. His work subsequently focused on international technology transfers, embracing issues relating to environmental law, intellectual property rights, finance, and trade as a partner with the Palo Alto, California law firm of Fenwick & West, where he served as counsel to many different national parties in various international disputes involving matters of substantive policy formulation as well as procedural issues relating to institutional arrangements and public participation. Mr. Scott's recent work has focused on specialized institutional arrangements relevant to biodiversity conservation initiatives, with emphasis on access and benefit-sharing issues involving national parks and other protected areas.

Jorge Soberón-Mainero

Jorge Soberón-Mainero has served as Executive Secretary of the Mexican National Commission for the Knowledge and Use of Biodiversity since 1992. He holds B.S. and M.S. degrees in biology from the Universidad Nacional Autónoma de México and a Ph.D. in Biology from Imperial College, London University. Dr. Soberón-Mainero was a member of the Subsidiary Technical Advisory Panel of the Global Environment Facility (1995–1998) and participated in the Scientific Advisory Council of the UNEP-World Conservation Monitoring Centre. Dr. Soberón-Mainero has been a researcher at Universidad Nacional Autónoma de México and his interests include population and conservation biology and mathematical modelling, topics in which he has published more than forty papers and chapters in books. He has been member or president of the Mexican Delegation to most Conferences of the Parties of the Convention on Biological Diversity.

Tomme R. Young

Tomme Young is a graduate of Hastings College of the Law (1981), and the University of Southern California (1978). Ms. Young is Senior Legal Officer at the IUCN Environmental Law Center in Bonn, Germany. Throughout her 19 years as a lawyer, she has developed a specialized expertise in many areas of environmental law and policy. Internationally, Ms. Young has served as a special advisor on environmental and sustainable development issues to foreign governments, under the auspices of several UN agencies. She has advised the governments of 16 countries in Europe, Africa, Asia, Oceania, and the Americas, on legislative drafting and negotiations and regulatory development. In the field of international agreements and ABS, Ms. Young has focused particularly on the legal and legislative issues of practical implementation, most recently through designing and managing *The ABS Project*, a three-year project aiming at providing tools and support to direct implementation of the ABS objectives at international, regional, and local levels. Prior to this project, she has written extensively on a number of key legal and institutional issues relating to the creation, operations, and activities under the CBD, UNCLOS, CITES, Ramsar, the World Heritage Convention, and UNFCC, as well as regional instruments and institutions. Her work focuses on increasing effectiveness, analyzing obstacles, and implementing sustainable use through legal, legislative, administrative and policy measures. Ms. Young's other international publications include legislative reports and analyses addressing national and regional legislative status and particular environmental issues in the fields of forest, conservation, environmental protection, pollution prevention, coastal and marine management, IPR issues, liability, and compliance.

A3

Appendix 3.
Contact Information of Primary Contributors

Part 1. Persons consulted for specific country information (case study authors and survey respondents) grouped first by status of country with respect to ABS policies and then by country

A. Countries with ABS policies

1. Colombia
Paola Ferreira
Consultant
85 G Prospect St.
Ridgefield, CT 06877 USA
ferreirap@aol.com

2. Costa Rica
Jorge Cabrera-Medaglia
Consultant
Apdo. 1487-1002
San José, Costa Rica
jorgecmedaglia@hotmail.com

3. Ecuador
Luis Suarez
Director Ecociencia
Fundación Ecuatoriana de Estudios Ecológicos
San Cristóbal N44-495 y Seymour
Quito, Ecuador
Biodiversidad@ecociencia.org

Joseph Henry Vogel
Associate Profesor
(formerly Professor of Economics at FLACSO, Ecuador)
Department of Economics, University of Puerto Rico
Rios Piedras
PR 00931, San Juan, Puerto Rico
josephvogel@usa.net, josephvogel@hotmail.com

4. Mexico
Francisco Chapela
Estudios Rurales y Asesoría Campesina
Priv. Elvira 120, Fracc. Villa San Luis 68020
Oaxaca, México
era@mesoamerica.org.mx
http://www.mesoamerica.org.mx/era/

José Carlos Fernández-Ugalde
Dirección de Economía Ambiental
Instituto Nacional de Ecología
5to nivel, Av. Revolución 1425, Tlacopac San Angel 01040
México, D.F. México
cfernan@ine.gob.mx, jc_fernan@hotmail.com
http://www.ine..gob.mx/

Jorge Larson-Guerra
Cordinador del Proyecto Recursos Biologicos Colectivos
Comisión nacional para el conocimiento y uso de la biodiversidad (CONABIO)
Avenida Liga Periférico - Insurgentes Sur No. 4903,
Col. Parques del Pedregal, Delegación Tlalpan
14010 México, D.F. México
jlarson@xolo.conabio.gob.mx
http://www.conabio.gob.mx/

Christian López-Silva
Consultant
Avenida Liga Periférico - Insurgentes Sur No. 4903,
Col. Parques del Pedregal, Delegación Tlalpan
14010 México, D.F. México
christian_adicional@yahoo.com

4. Mexico continued

Jorge Soberón
Secretario Ejecutivo
Comisión nacional para el conocimiento y uso de la
biodiversidad (CONABIO)
Avenida Liga Periférico - Insurgentes Sur No. 4903,
Col. Parques del Pedregal, Delegación Tlalpan
14010 México, D.F. México
jsoberon@xolo.conabio.gob.mx
http://www.conabio.gob.mx/

5. Philippines

Paz J. Benavides II
Consultant
408 Sterten Place Condominium, 116 Maginhawa Street,
Teachers' Village
Quezon City 1100 Philippines
pjbcaps@broline.com

6. Peru

Manuel Ruiz
Sociedad Peruana de Derecho Ambiental
Prolongación Arenales 437
Lima 27, Peru
mruiz@spda.org.pe
http://www.spda.org.pe/

7. Samoa

Vainuupo Jungblut
Principal Environment Officer
Department of Lands and Environment, Private Bag
Apia, Samoa
Vainuupo.Jungblut@mnre.gov.ws

Clark Peteru
Environmental Legal Advisor
South Pacific Regional Environment Programme
PO Box 240
Apia, Samoa
clarkp@sprep.org.ws, peteru@samoa.ws

Cedric Schuster
Director
Pacific Environment Consultants Ltd
PO Box 3702
Apia, Samoa
cmlschuster@yahoo.co.nz, cschuster@conservation.ws

8. Thailand

Jade Donavanik
Consultant
Thailand Biodiversity Center
15th Floor Gypsum Metropolitan Tower,
539/2 Sri-Ayudhya Rd.
Bangkok, 10400 Thailand
jade@biotec.or.th

Chaweewan Hutacharern
Head of Entomology and Microbiology Group
Dept. of National Parks, Wildlife, and Plant Conservation
61 Paholyothin Road, Chatuchak
Bangkok 10900 Thailand
chahut@forest.go.th

9. United States of America (USA)

Preston Scott
Executive Director
World Foundation for Environment and Development (WFED)
1816 Jefferson Place, NW
Washington, DC 20036-2505 USA
PTScott@aol.com
http://wfed.org/

B. Countries working towards the development of ABS policies

1. Australia

Sally Petherbridge
Environment Australia
3 Myall St
O'Connor ACT 2602 Australia
Sally.Petherbridge@ea.gov.au
http://environment.gov.au/

2. Cambodia

Men Sarom
Director Plant Breeding
Cambodian Agricultural Research and Development Institute
(CARDI)
P.O. Box 01
Phnom Penh, Cambodia
msarom@bigpond.com.kh

3. Canada

Kelly Banister
Assistant Professor
School of Environmental Studies, University of Victoria
University House 4, Box 3060
Victoria, BC, V8W 3R4 Canada
kel@uvic.ca
http://web.uvic.ca/~scishops

4. Chile

Luis Florez-Mimiça
Consultant
El Vergel 2647, Departamento 302, Providencia
Santiago, Chile
lucasarbol@yahoo.com.ar

Dominique Hervé-Espejo
Professor
Facultad de Derecho
Universidad Diego Portales
República 105
Santiago, Chile
Dominique.herve@prof.udp.cl

5. China

Dayuan Xue
Director of Nature Conservation and Biodiversity Division,
Nanjing Institute of Environmental Science, State
Environmental Protection Administration (SEPA)
8 jiang-wang-miao St., P.O.Box 4202
Nanjing 210042 P.R. China
duedayuan@hotmail.com
http://www.nies.org

6. Cook Islands
Ben Ponia
Aquaculture adviser
SPC-Secretariat of the Pacific Community
B.P. D5 - 98848 Noumea Cedex
New Caledonia, Cook Islands
Benp@spc.int
http://www.spc.int/

7. El Salvador
Jorge Ernesto Quezada Díaz
Gerente de Recursos Biológicos
Ministerio de Medio Ambiente y Recursos Naturales
Alameda Roosevelt y 55 avenida norte Torre El Salvador
(IPSFA), 4 nivel
San Salvador, El Salvador
quezada@marn.gob.sv
http://www.marn.gob.sv

8. Fiji
Luke V. Qiritabu
Department of Environment
P. O. Box 2131, Government Buildings
Suva, Fiji
lqiritabu@govnet.gov.fj

Manasa Sovaki
Principal Environment Officer
Department of Environment
PO Box 2131, Government Buildings
Suva, Fiji
biodiversity@suva.is.com.fj, msovaki@yahoo.com

9. Guatemala
Yuri Giovanni Melini
Centro de Acción Legal-Ambiental and Social de Guatemala
(CALAS)
13 calle 8-61. zona 11,
Nivel 2 Apartamento «D» Colonia Mariscal
C.P. 01011 Ciudad de Guatemala, Guatemala
direccion@calasgt.org and yuri@melini.com
http://www.calas.org.gt/

10. Honduras
José Antonio Fuentes
Director General de Biodiversidad
Secretaría de Recursos Naturales y Ambiente (SERNA)
100 Mts. al Sur del Estadio Nacional
Tegucigalpa, M.D.C. Honduras
dibio@sdnhon.org.hn, ddibio@sdnhon.org.hn
http://www.serna.gob.hn/

Carlos Roberto Midence
Analista Ambiental
Secretaria de Recursos Naturales y Ambiente (SERNA)
100 Mts. al Sur del Estadio Nacional
Tegucigalpa, M.D.C. Honduras
carlosmidence@hotmail.com
http://www.serna.gob.hn/

11. Indonesia
B. Satyawan Wardhana
Head of Division for Biodiversity Conservation
Ministry of Environment
4th Floor, Building B, Ministry of Environment; D.I. Panjaitan
Kav 24
Jakarta 13410 Indonesia
iwan_wardhana@hotmail.com; chmcbdri@rad.net.id
http://www.menlh.go.id/

12. Japan
Junko Shimura
Principal Research Scientist
National Institute for Environmental Studies
16-2 Onogawa Tsukuba
Ibaraki 305-8506 Japan
junko@nies.go.jp
http://www.sp2000ao.nies.go.jp/

Seizo Sumida
Managing Director
Japan Bioindustry Association
Grande Bldg 8F, 26-9 Hatchobori 2-Chome, Chuo-ku
Tokyo 104-0032 Japan
sumida@jba.or.jp
http://www.jba.or.jp/

13. Malaysia
Mohamad bin Osman
School of Environmental and Natural Resource Sciences
Universiti Kebangsaan Malaysia
43600 UKM Bangi
Selangor, Malaysia
mbopar@pkrisc.cc.ukm.my

14. Marshall Islands
Raynard Gideon
Ministry of Foreign Affairs
P.O. Box 1349
Majuro, Marshall Islands 96960
mofaadm@ntamar.net

15. Micronesia
M. J. Mace
Former Assistant Attorney General
FSM Department of Justice
400 Magazine Street, Suite 401
New Orleans, LA 70130
mjmace02@yahoo.com

16. New Zealand
Doug Calhoun
Partner Law at A J Park
Huddart Parker Building, 1 Post Office Square,
PO Box 949
Wellington, New Zealand
doug.calhoun@ajpark.com, becky.white@ajpark.com
http://www.ajpark.com

17. Nicaragua
Javier Guillermo Hernández Munguía
Asesor legal
Ministerio del Ambiente y los Recursos Naturales
Km. 12 ½ Carretera Norte
Managua, Nicaragua
javihermun@hotmail.com
http://www.marena.gob.ni/

18. Niue
Tagaloa Cooper
Head Environment Officer
Environment Unit, Department of Community Affairs
PO Box 77
Niue
environment.ca@mail.gov.nu
http://www.gov.nu/appeal.htm

19. Panama
Marisol Dimas and **Adela Olivardia**
Departamento de Conservación de la Biodiversidad,
Autoridad Nacional Ambiental
Albrook, edificio 804
Panama City, Panama
biodiversidad@anam.gob.pa
http://www.anam.gob.pa/

20. Papua New Guinea
Rosa N. Kambuou
Principal Scientist
National Agricultural Research Institute
PO Box 1828
Port Moresby, National Capitol District, Papua New Guinea
dlplaloki@datec.com.pg
http://www.nari.org.pg/

21. Republic of Korea
Sang-Weon Bang
Research Fellow
Korea Environment Institute (KEI)
Bulkwang-Dong 613-2, Eunpyong-Gu (Zip:122-706)
Seoul, Republic of Korea
swbang@kei.re.kr
http://www.kei.re.kr

22. Russian Federation
Sergey M. Alexanian
N.I. Vavilov All-Russian Research Institute of Plant Industry
42-44 Bolshaya Morskaya St.
190000 St. Petersburg, Russian Federation
s.alexanian@vir.nw.ru
http://www.vir.nw.ru/

Vera Moshentseva
Senior Analyst
Department of Life and Earth Sciences
Ministry of Industry, Science and Technologies
of the Russian Federation
125009 Moscow, Tverskaya 11 Russian Federation
moshentseva@minstp.ru

23. Singapore
Lena Chan
Assistant Director (Nature Conservation)
National Parks Board, Singapore Botanic Gardens
1 Cluny Road, Singapore 259569
Lena_CHAN@nparks.gov.sg
http://www.nparks.gov.sg/parks/sbg/par-sbg.shtml

24. Solomon Islands
Moses Biliki
Director
Environment and Nature Conservation Division,
Ministry of Forests, Environment and Nature Conservation
P.O Box G24
Honiara, Solomon Islands
mbiliki@hotmail.com, komaridi@welkam.solomon.com.sb,
mosesb@solomon.com.sb

Carolina Lasen Diaz
Staff Lawyer
Foundation for International Environmental Law and
Development (FIELD)
52-53 Russell Square,
London WC1B 4HP UK
carolina.lasen@field.org.uk
http://www.field.org.uk

Cedric Schuster
Director
Pacific Environment Consultants Ltd
PO Box 3702
Apia, Samoa
cmlschuster@yahoo.co.nz, cschuster@conservation.ws

25. Vanuatu
Donna Kalfatak
NBSAP Project Coordinator
Environment Unit
Ministry of Agriculture, Livestock, Forestry, Fisheries and
Environment
Private Mail Bag 063
Port Vila, Vanuatu
environ@vanuatu.com.vu

26. Vietnam
Hoang Duong Tung
Deputy Chief, Networking and Database Management
Division, National Environment Agency (NEA) of Vietnam
67 Nguyen Du
Hanoi, Vietnam
htung@nea.gov.vn
http://www.nea.gov.vn/

C. Countries not involved in any process leading to the development of ABS policies

1. Kiribati

Tererei Abete-Reema
Environment and Conservation Division-ECD, MESD,
Ministry of Environment
P.O. Box 234, Bikenibeu
Tarawa, Kiribati
tererei.mesd2@tskl.net.ki

2. Laos

Sourioudong Sundara
Director General, Research Institute of Science, Science
Technology and Environment Agency, Prime Minister's Office
P.O. Box 2279
Vientiane, Laos
sourioudong@yahoo.uk, science@laotel.com

3. Nauru

Cedric Schuster
Director
Pacific Environment Consultants Ltd
PO Box 3702
Apia, Samoa
cmlschuster@yahoo.co.nz, cschuster@conservation.ws

4. Palau

Steven A. Daugherty
Assistant Attorney General
PO. Box 1365
Palau
StevenAD@palaunet.com

5. Tonga

Aminiasi Kefu
Senior Crown Counsel
The Solicitor General, Crown Law Department,
P.O. Box 85
Nuku'alofa, Tonga
aminiasi.kefu@tcc.to

6. Tuvalu

Cedric Schuster
Director
Pacific Environment Consultants Ltd
PO Box 3702
Apia, Samoa
cmlschuster@yahoo.co.nz, cschuster@conservation.ws

Part 2. Editors and authors of analysis chapters, alphabetically by surname.

Stephen B. Brush
Professor
Department of Human and Community Development
University of California
One Shields Avenue
Davis CA 95616-8602 USA
sbbrush@ucdavis.edu

Santiago Carrizosa
Research Ecologist
Genetic Resources Conservation Program
University of California
One Shields Avenue
Davis CA 95616-8602 USA
scarrizosa@ucdavis.edu.edu, scarrizosa@yahoo.com
http://www.grcp.ucdavis.edu/index.htm

Patrick E. McGuire
Director
Genetic Resources Conservation Program,
University of California
One Shields Avenue
Davis CA 95616-8602 USA
pemcguire@ucdavis.edu

Brian D. Wright
Professor
Department of Agricultural and Resource Economics,
University of California
207 Giannini Hall #3310
Berkeley, CA 94720-3310 USA
wright@are.berkeley.edu

Tomme Rosanne Young
Senior Legal Officer
IUCN Environmental Law Center
Godesberger Allee 108-112
53175 Bonn, Germany
tyoung@elc.iucn.org
http://www.iucn.org/themes/law/